THE GUARIJÍOS OF THE SIERRA MADRE

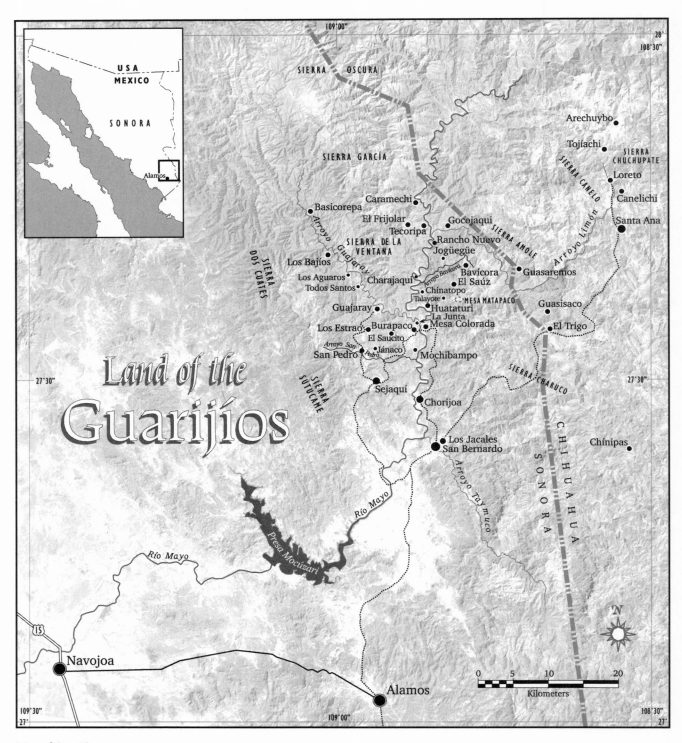

Map of Guarijío country.

THE
GUARIJIOS

OF THE SIERRA MADRE

Hidden People of Northwestern Mexico

DAVID YETMAN

Published in cooperation with the
University of Arizona Southwest Center

UNIVERSITY OF NEW MEXICO PRESS

ALBUQUERQUE

Library of Congress Cataloging-in-Publication Data

Yetman, David, 1941–
The Guarijíos of the Sierra Madre : hidden people of northwestern Mexico / David Yetman—1st ed.
p.   cm.
"Published in cooperation with the University of Arizona Southwest Center"
Includes bibliographical reference and index.
ISBN 0-8263-2234-4 (cloth : alk. paper)
1. Guarijío Indians—History. 2. Guarijío Indians—Social life and customs
3. Guarijío Indians—Ethnobotany. 4. Subsistence economy—Mexico—Sierra Madre.
5. Ethnobotany—Mexico—Sierra Madre. 6. Sierra Madre (Mexico)—Social life and customs.
I. University of Arizona. Southwest Center. II. Title.
F1221.G82 Y48 2002
305.897'45—dc21
2001008477

A UNIVERSITY OF ARIZONA SOUTHWEST CENTER BOOK
Joseph C. Wilder, Series Editor

DESIGN: MINA YAMASHITA

Contents

List of Figures

UNLESS OTHERWISE NOTED, ALL PHOTOGRAPHS
WERE TAKEN BY THE AUTHOR.

Acknowledgments

I proposed this project while working as a researcher at the Southwest Center of the University of Arizona. I received strong encouragement from the director, Joe Wilder, who also provided financial support. The project also received strong support from Agnese Haury, the National Geographic Society, Native & Nature, the Social and Behavioral Science Research Institute of the University of Arizona, and the Wallace Research Foundation, all of which provided funding and support. Without generous contributions by all, I could never have begun this project, the fulfillment of the wish of a nine-year-old child.

I wish also to acknowledge the assistance provided by Dr. Jesús Armando Haro of El Colegio de Sonora, who provided medical services to many Guarijíos and carried out a study of their medical needs. Armando is most knowledgeable about Guarijíos and shared his knowledge with me freely, helping me arrange some early trips into Guarijío country. The late Dr. Leobardo Quiroz of the Instituto Nacional Indigenista was also immensely helpful, providing me a place to stay in San Bernardo plus demographic information about Guarijíos unavailable elsewhere. Sr. Angel Flores of San Bernardo, a schoolteacher at Mesa Colorada, helped me arrange things and was generous with his time, helping me understand some Guarijío characteristics. Paul S. Martin read the manuscript and made important and tempering suggestions, especially about the flora of summertime in pine-oak forest near Loreto. Paul J. Underwood and Jeff Banister made some incisive points as well. Among my non-Guarijío companions along Guarijío *caminos* were David Burckhalter, Richard Felger, Rex Johnson, Mark Kaib, José Luis Palacios, and Doug Yetman. They patiently tolerated my idiosyncrasies and endless chats with Guarijíos. The Guarijíos who assisted me are acknowledged in the text.

Since Mexicans use metric measurement, I have chosen to use it in the text. One kilometer (km) equals .62 mile. One meter (m) equals 3.3 feet or 39.36 inches, just over a yard. One centimeter (cm) equals just over a third of an inch, the width of a pencil.

1
Predestined

One day when Naty took me to on a walk to
the river, I saw something jump behind the rocks.
It was very agile and disappeared quickly, so
I thought it had been a deer. Then I asked Naty:
"What was that?" "A Guarijío. They're Indians
who live here in the mountains," she answered.

—Buitimea Romero and Valdivia Dounce,
Como una huella pintada

When I was a child, lying in bed sick with asthma, I learned to forget my struggle to breathe by creating fantasies of faraway places. I had ample time to construct imaginary countries and landscapes, for I was not burdened by school. I often envied the active life other children had. I eagerly awaited the hour when my older brother and sister would arrive home from school with all manner of children's stories and grade school gossip. The rest of the day I was alone with my mother in the huge drafty parsonage. My father was a pastor in a tiny rural New Jersey community. He had numerous ministerial duties that kept him at the church or visiting the hospital and the homes and farms of parishioners during the day and tending to their spiritual (and often practical) needs. I had gone to school a few days in first grade, fewer in second, a month or so in third, and not at all in fourth. Much of my time at home I was alone with books. Around the family table at night, others related their day's activities. I could only spout what I had learned reading. I owe a huge debt to my family for their tolerance of my often endless recitation of autistic facts and figures.

It was in my ninth year that my parents bought me what was then a thick book called *Anthology of Children's Literature*. In it were geographical essays describing forays to the four corners of the earth. This tome was supplemented by third-hand copies of the *National Geographic Magazine* which thoughtful parishioners bestowed on our poor

family. I was mesmerized by the pictures and stories from impossibly distant lands and unfamiliar folk. Soon thereafter my father presented me with a thick world atlas. I wore it out within a year. For reasons I will never know, what stood out most in my geographical musing was Mexico. I resolved then that when I was older and no longer sick, I would visit Mexico, not so much the cities, but the mountains, the jungles, and the rivers. I wanted to be an explorer, to visit exotic peoples in distant places where only hardy wanderers ventured. Mexico became a magnet for me.

My first trip south of the border was in 1961 at the age of twenty. My family had moved to Arizona to keep me from dying of asthma, and I reaped the benefits of the warmer and (then) purer air. I ventured into southern Sonora by motor scooter. Seeing the colonial town of Alamos, with its exotic setting in tropical deciduous forest, I then and there resolved to know that countryside better. Although in the intervening years I have traveled from one end of Mexico to the other several times, I still found myself thinking of Alamos and the lands around it, mysterious mountains, rumors of Indians and jungle-like forests. Still, it was thirty years before I managed to mount a mini-expedition to a land that matched my childhood fantasies: the land of the Guarijíos. I had read bits and pieces about them, enough to know that they were a reclusive people in a reclusive land, that they lived in small settlements and tiny villages, and they had for many years been thought by anthropologists to be extinct until Howard Scott Gentry visited them in the 1930s.

And so it was with great anticipation that I ventured for the first time into Guarijío lands, backed by support from the Southwest Center of the University of Arizona and later by a grant from the National Geographic Society, those very folks who had piqued my interest as a skinny, bed-ridden, nearly dying child more than forty years earlier.

The following chapters detail my travels and conversations in Guarijío countries. All the people about whom I write spoke Spanish, though of varying degrees of passability, all a distinct advantage for me. At times these stories may seem a bit pedantic, but the details of Guarijío country and Guarijíos are what made them come alive for me. I have chosen to use the actual names of people I came to know. I have always explained to the Guarijíos that I was involved in writing about them, even though for many of them just what that meant was decidedly unclear. All the consultants, except for those in governmental positions, were compensated for their assistance. I explained that I was hiring them both to guide me and to teach me about the Guarijíos and their land, and most of all, about their plants. Most of them were aware that I was writing about them, for nearly all would remind me on occasion to write things down.

I have tried in these stories to portray the life of Guarijíos, the historical context in which their way of life is embedded, the economic foundations of their existence, and their relationship to the dominant Mexican and global cultures and economies. I have relied heavily on our mutual interest in plants. More simply, these chapters give a glimpse into what the Guarijíos are up to, as Clifford Geertz might say. And what they are up to often needs to be understood in the context of what non-Guarijíos are up to in their dealings with Guarijíos. It is difficult for an outsider to assess the internal dynamics of a social group as small and as dispersed as the Guarijíos. It is far easier to detail the interactions with the dominant society, for the distinction between Guarijío and non-Guarijío, while never sharp, is as discernible as for any other indigenous group in North America. In telling what Guarijíos have told me, in describing what (I think) I saw them do, and what others say and have said about them, I hope to increase our collective understanding of them. In describing what I learned about the plants they use, I hope to reveal details of their life that might otherwise go unnoticed.

Readers will detect herein a strong undercurrent of natural history of the Guarijío region and its influence on the Guarijíos. It is my unabashedly nondeterministic contention that Guarijíos are first and foremost people of their lands and that without an understanding of their land and what grows in and on it, we cannot begin to understand them. An awareness of the biology (particularly the plants) and geology of the Sierra Madre is a necessary step to awareness of the people who have settled there and survived from its productivity (and suffered from its lack of productivity). Later settlers who relied on *imported* alien technology (and alien agriculture) are less affected.

Readers will undoubtedly notice a paucity of commentary on Guarijío women. This is an accurate observation and is perhaps as it should be. Guarijío women are for the most part reluctant to speak Spanish, unwilling to speak to outsiders, and usually unable, for what I take to be strong cultural constraints, to venture far from their hearths. As a male outsider with only a limited Guarijío vocabulary, I could only gather incidental observations about Guarijío women. The task of describing the world of Guarijías must be relegated to the fortunate woman willing to endure the

rigors of life in the *monte* (the bush, forest) of the Sierra Madre and devote the many hours required to develop intimacy with half of this most remarkable race. We should all look forward to the day when such a document is published.

Readers who tire of my descriptions of plants may conveniently skip portions of chapters 7 and 14 and leave the plant list to more biologically oriented souls. However, chapter 14 contains a brief introduction to Guarijío plant use by way of their most important plants. I urge the reader to attend to at least one plant in that section! Richard Felger spent many days with me in the field, and together we traversed some fine country. His remarkable knowledge of plants and what the plants are up to made the plant list possible.

2
The Invitation to Jánaco

"Cipriano expected you yesterday," said Benjamín, the *campesino yori* (mestizo peasant), outside the ancient adobe ranch house at San Pedro as David and I greeted him, stepping down from the Carryall. Those were not the words I had hoped to hear. The man I was looking for, veteran of the Guarijíos' struggle for liberation from peonage and subject of an autobiography, had been waiting for me, had given up and gone home over the mountain.

Benjamín, sporting a week's growth of whitish beard, sat on a stool, wrapped in a worn, thickly padded jacket. He was alone, scrunching over a fire in the shade of a large *tempisque (Sideroxylon tepicense)* tree. Surrounding him were perhaps a dozen small scroungy dogs and a single cat that completed the circle around the glowing coals. Benjamín Valenzuela Gutiérrez lived at San Pedro with Cipriano's mother. Cipriano's father had died when Cipriano was eighteen. Benjamín had moved up here from the coast many years ago and lived an unhurried existence in the tiny settlement deep in the mountains of southern Sonora. He had a wide reputation as a character, but a very hard worker.

"I know," I said apologetically. "Yesterday we couldn't cross the Río Mayo at San Bernardo. The water was too deep and swift at Nahuibampo, so we had to go back to Alamos—that's thirty-five miles away, and Navojoa, another thirty-five, then north to Quiriego by the dirt road. It's a long way, about a five-hour detour. It was dark when we got to the bad hill, so we camped at Rancho El Chino last night. I didn't want to try to drive up the steep curve at night. The truck could have slid off the side."

"*Ni modo,*" he said. No problem. "Cipriano will be here soon. Sit down and enjoy yourself." I was happy to join him. I leaned over the bed of coals, and my body sucked in the warmth while the swirling glow captured my stare as only fire and color television can.

San Pedro consisted of one two-room house and a couple of outbuildings huddled on a tiny flat area, the only such buildable spot within miles. The roadway, competing for the same flat space, passed within twenty feet of the wall of the house. Great cliffs of ancient basement sediments capped by volcanic tuff and rhyolites nearly surrounded the homestead. Gravity-defying octopus agaves and rock figs sprouted from the broken vertical surfaces. The gentler slopes—still steep—were covered with a velvet mat of tropical deciduous forest. The narrow track of a road leading to San Pedro had been carved from a precipitous volcanic hillside. Below fell a deep box canyon so steep that ropes were needed to descend into it. That approach was a vehicular ascent into a Conradian heart of darkness. It was as if, aside from our Carryall, we had left the modern world behind.

The narrow valley bottom was still dark, but the first rays of blinding morning sunshine bathed the cliffs above San Pedro. The dew sparkled on the agaves that clung to the cliffs like enormous gray spiders. Exploring like this, and getting paid to boot, was one fine job.

I was here as a researcher from the University of Arizona to study what plants the Guarijíos used—all of them I could find. I was driving a Carryall that said in rather small lettering on the side "State of Arizona. For Official Use Only." I was officially using it.

I parked the vehicle off the narrow track of a road so that in the unlikely occurrence of the arrival of another vehicle (only a few vehicles came by each week) it would have room to pass. Much of the road up to San Pedro was so narrow that if vehicles met one of them would have to back up—usually for a considerable distance in order for the other to pass. That was the unwritten rule of the sierras: at an impasse, the ascending vehicle backs down.

Benjamín dragged an ancient stool of balsam-like *chilicote (Erythrina flabelliformis)* wood to the fireside. I shooed away a couple of barking dogs and sat down. David had already grabbed his camera and was shooting photos of the crew of scrofulous, tiny curs that rimmed the warmth.

"Do you like dogs?" I asked Benjamín, laughing.

"*A la madre sí, me gustan*" (You're damned right I do), he answered, stirring the glowing coals. "The government has ordered me to raise dogs. This one is Pati, that one is Compañero, this is Tejón," and he went around the circle naming them all. David and I looked at each other and broke out laughing again. This was a good ole' boy if ever there was one.

Just then the sun's rays streaked over the gray-green hills and dark volcanic cliffs, and the first few rays stuck an ancient *trinchera* (rock wall) near the house. It was early on a damp, January morning, so things would dry slowly. David and I yanked our tents and ground cloths from the truck. They were still sopping wet from the heavy dew of the night before. We

Benjamín Valenzuela and dogs, San Pedro. Photo by David Burckhalter.

plopped them out on the wall to dry. An ancient Barred Rock hen staggered by, and I almost stepped on her.

"Who is this?" I asked Benjamín, wondering why they would keep such a wretched creature in a place where a laying chicken is an asset. Talking about peoples' domestic animals is an effective icebreaker. It also makes for novel conversation. People's animals reflect their economy and their hearts. People are often more protective of their dogs than they are of their children. But a hen?

"Oh, she's an old hen. She's sixteen years old, blind and deaf. We keep her around because she's an old friend. She was already laying eggs when Andrea, that's Cipriano's daughter, was born and now Andrea's fourteen." He gestured inside the dark interior of the house where I saw soft and shadowy human movements but could make out no one. San Pedro didn't have electricity. It wouldn't be arriving for a long time.

The hen clumsily joined the circle of dogs near the fire. David gave a guttural laugh and photographed the venerable fowl.

While I sat among the intermingled fauna, David pulled out a coffeepot from his rucksack and asked Benjamín for some water to boil. We knew of the poverty among Guarijíos and brought our own coffee. It makes a great gift among mountain people who live far from grocery stores.

"Just use the stove. Angelita will give you some," he said. An older, heavy woman no more than five feet tall with strong Indian features appeared from a dark passage-way but said little. She was Cipriano's mother, a Mayo who grew up with Guarijíos. I had met her briefly when I had passed through San Pedro a year earlier. She took the pot from David silently and puttered off to the stove, which lay under a ramada in deep shadows behind the house. The stove was a thick adobe platform topped by a fire pit covered by a metal grill. Inside was a clay oven. A chair alongside permitted Doña Angelita to sit while she cooked. On chilly mornings it was the warmest place around. Before long the water boiled and David poured us coffee through a *talega* (cloth strainer). He liked his fresh brewed, not the powdered instant *Café Combate*. Benjamín casually accepted his, hardly breaking his conversation.

I found myself jumping up from the fire again and again looking down the road for a sign of Cipriano. Benjamín seemed to notice my anxiousness but appeared to write it off to gringo behavior. *"No te preocupes,* David. *Ahora viene"* (Don't worry, David, he will come soon).

Across the arroyo three horses and a couple of burros were quietly foraging on the green weeds of winter. A pig grunted in a pasture right below us, and goats were bah-hah-hahing in a tightly built coyote and mountain lion-proof stake corral twenty feet away. No enclosure was secure from the depredations of a jaguar, but the huge cats seldom came around. A turkey gobbled and scrapped with a rooster. I wondered just what work Benjamín did and asked him.

"*¿Yo?* Well, I take care of cows and cut wood, work on the road, build fence. There's plenty of work that I do." Just not today, I thought. *"En la mañana voy a bajar a Mesa Colorada,"* he added. The next morning he would ride down the narrow valley to Mesa Colorada, a tiny Guarijío town on the east bank of the Río Mayo, which he would have to cross.

"What's in Mesa Colorada?" I asked.

"Cigarettes. It's not far—three, four hours by horse. I'll be back by night. The horse finds the path in the night. No problem." Mesa Colorada was where I had met Cipriano and had an all-too-brief conversation with him.

"Gringos are all screwed up," he announced out of the blue. I didn't argue.

"Mexicans are worse," he added.

I left David and Benjamín drinking coffee, trading lies, and cracking jokes and climbed onto the trinchera that was now in full sun. David spoke fine Spanish and relished light-hearted, mildly obscene macho banter. I shook out the tents and rearranged them, worried about missing Cipriano Buitimea Romero after he had walked all the way from Jánaco the preceding day, the appointed time when we were to meet. We had arranged months ago for me to spend a few days with him at Jánaco. Driving here from Tucson had taken two full days, and the last few hours we crawled up a mean road that punished vehicles and passengers. Now it was nearly ten o'clock and another precious day was slipping away. I constantly peered down the narrow roadway as I arrange the camping gear. Then it was 10:15, then 10:30.

Some of the richest moments in my life had happened in recent years as I came to know some of Sonora's indigenous people and wandered with them through their lands. After a few years of roaming the bush with Mayos and North American botanical comrades, all of whom shared their learning with me, I had become reasonably knowledgeable in the trees and shrubs of the region. I could identify most of them fairly quickly. I was certainly not as capable of identifying them as indigenous experts, who commonly look casually at a tree and spout off its name, even though there are well over a hundred species. But I had resolved that I would get to know the plants of the Río Mayo in spite of my lack of professional credentials.

I am a philosopher by training. I backed into philosophy as an undergraduate when I discovered that of all disciplines, it presented me with the greatest challenge. I went on to garner a Ph.D. at the University of Arizona, teaching there and at Arizona State University along the way. Somehow, though, my childhood itchings for the wild pulled me away from academia. Even while I struggled with my doctoral dissertation, I spent hundreds of days with the Seris of Sonora's Gulf Coast. For a while I considered abandoning my academic career and taking up life among the Seris. But I was too traditional to do that. I completed my work, snatched my degree, and quit academia. I moved my family to the Chiricahua Mountains of Arizona and spent four years managing a youth camp.

That should have been enough of a wilderness plunge for me, but it wasn't. A friend urged me to run for political office. I followed his advice, was elected against frightening odds, and spent the next twelve years on the Pima County (Tucson) Board of Supervisors. During my three four-year terms I missed the monte terribly. I made frequent trips to Seri county. After my second re-election (I won by a comfortable margin) I knew it was time to get out of politics. Toward the end of my tenure I attended fewer public meetings and grew slack in my practice of reading memoranda from the bureaucrats around me. Instead, I wrote a book about my Seri experiences and found a publisher willing to take it on. I left office still goofily enamored of Mexico.

In the early 1990s I was commissioned to write a book about Sonora, which I had come to know rather well following my first adventure on motor scooter. It was an intervention that enabled me to get back into the monte. Soon afterwards, I joined the University of Arizona in a position that required me to carry out fieldwork in Mexico. Imagine! Being paid to do what I wanted most to do! I turned to southern Sonora with great delight and explored and talked my way through much of the region.

And so now I was here as part of my job. The best way to get to know Cipriano was to hike with him through the monte. That way I could learn what he knew about the great Río Mayo tropical forest, about the Guarijíos and what it was like to be one. If I were lucky he would invite me to visit him at Jánaco, his home. Only there could we relax and chat for a few hours, maybe even a couple of days. I hoped I hadn't blown my opportunity.

Finally, far down the canyon, a disembodied hat materialized, almost floating through the greenery with only a slight bob. Then Cipriano came into view, treading in his smooth stride up the narrow road, leading a burro. Guarijíos seem to glide rather than walk, holding their upper bodies on the vertical while their feet rise well from the ground. They have tripped over enough vines and stones that they early learn to step smartly and smoothly. Cipriano wore a worn long-sleeve shirt, khaki pants, and *huaraches de tres puntas* (three holed sandals) that were simple soles of tire held on the feet by strategically laced strips of rawhide. He waved and I waved back. From afar I made out his roundish cheeks, which bespeak the Mayo part of his background. The Guarijíos are typically thinner and narrower of cheek than the Mayos.

I walked down to greet him. He met me with a generous smile and the gentle touch of a Guarijío handshake, then a phantom embrace, a mutual brushing of fingertips on the inner arm. I apologized for not arriving yesterday, but he understood, he said. This year the Río Mayo was running high after the heavy *equipatas* (winter rains). He tied up the burro and we walked to the fire. I introduced him to David Burckhalter, Tucson photographer, who would be taking photos. Cipriano offered a perfunctory *"buenos días"* to Benjamín, his ersatz stepfather, who made no attempt to get up. Then he passed into the low passageway that separates the two rooms of the house. David and I had to stoop to enter, but Cipriano had no problem.

He greeted his mother and, I thought, nodded to his daughter Andrea, whom I had yet to meet. Later he told me she was his daughter by his second wife who had run off with another Guarijío when the girl was still young. His mother had raised her right there at San Pedro. Since we had arrived Andrea had remained well hidden, as Guarijío women are wont to do in the presence of strange men, especially *blancos* (whites); *especially* the almost unknown gringos.

I gave Cipriano some presents, clothing for him and his family and a heavy sack of food—beans, sardines, and *Maseca* (corn meal for tortillas). He looked over the clothing carefully, nodded, and put it in a bag.

Angelita, Cipriano's mother, by now had settled into a

Cipriano Buitimea armed for the hunt, San Pedro.
Photo by David Burckhalter.

comfortable position in a sunny spot at the rear of the ramada and was busily weaving a *guari* (basket) from palm leaves. I watched her for a while as her nimble, practiced fingers expertly wove the long split *cogollos* (branch shoots) of palm in and out in a complicated pattern. I asked if she also made hats. Guarijío hats are well known in the region.

"Of course I make hats. Very good ones," she answered with a half smile that told me my question was foolish and unnecessary. Noting that Cipriano didn't wear a Guarijío hat (his was a factory-made model), I requested her to make me one. "Of course. I'll start on it right away," she answered as though my request were a trivial matter. I paid her on the spot, but learned later that the hat would take a couple of weeks to make. I liked the idea, however, because it would forge stronger ties between San Pedro and me: I would have to return to pick up my hat.

"Shall we go off into the *monte,* David?" Cipriano asked, after we had shared some coffee and stories. I agreed heartily.

This wasn't the first time we had hiked together, but it was the first time I had explored around San Pedro. Cipriano understood that I wanted to learn about plants. He knew a lot. And he knew that I knew he knew a lot. I threw together a lunch and David did the same. We packed up the now-dry tents, and I parked the car under the shade of the tempisque where, Benjamín thought, it would be safer from *el gobierno* (the government) by which he meant the army or the federal police. From time to time they fly over in helicopters, he said. If they see something interesting they land. Then they turn up in brigades looking for drugs, guns, free food, or anything else that may interest them. Cipriano watched our preparatory movements with reserve, and, I thought, a bit of amusement.

He shouldered an ancient twenty-two caliber single-shot rifle, its barrel pointing toward the sky, but from time to time when he bent over it inclined disquietingly in my direction. "We may see a *venadito* (white-tailed deer), David," he remarked with utmost seriousness. I was not enthusiastic about chasing down the tiny white-tailed deer of the sierras, but if Cipriano managed to find some game I would root for him. At times venison is the only animal protein available to the Guarijíos. They ration it in homeopathic doses. So important is venison to them that when they eat venison soup, they are careful not to blow on it, lest they blow the scent of deer meat far into the monte and ruin their chances of hunting.

From San Pedro he led us up the arroyo between the cliffs of the narrowing valley into a deep box canyon, through which a gentle stream ran. We crisscrossed the creek while I craned my neck, taking in the forest canopy and the immense precipices above.

The middle and upper Río Mayo flows through a tortured, folded, and broken landscape. Throughout the region fissures formed as the volcanic rock cooled or as the whole country stretched and cracked while the underlying colliding plates grew tired of their collision course and shifted direction. As the land was torn apart, some of these fissures widened and became arroyos, the easiest way for water to escape from the higher mountains to the Río Mayo. Some, like this one, are a thousand feet deep in places. In summer the sun illuminates the bottom for a few hours. In the winter, sunlight lingers only for a few moments before it moves on to more important lands. Although during the two dry seasons (spring and fall) months go by with no rains, the *cajón* (canyon) bottoms remain humid throughout the year. It almost never freezes, so tropical trees take advantage of the humidity and grow as fast and tall as their genes will let them.

The trees in this dark narrow fissure were enormous. They were what I had hoped to see. I've developed an insatiable curiosity about trees, especially the big ones, and Cipriano knew it. Tracking the distribution of trees produces important ecological information about the evolution of the region's plants. It is also gratifying to find new northern record for a tree, especially a big one. Though I was no botanist, I had pretensions and had given into my passion for finding the big trees—the tall ones ranging from fifteen meters and up. Their charisma appeals to me.

I had asked Cipriano to show me *monte verde* (evergreen vegetation). He did so by bringing me here and helping me identify the giants. "That's a *bebelama,*" he pointed, craning his neck to see the top. "We eat the fruits. You can eat them raw, but they burn your mouth. They're best stewed in milk." I grew dizzy and nearly fell over backward looking at the leaf patterns against the sky. The tall trees' leaf patterns viewed against the light from above cast a characteristic signature. That was one way I learned to identify them. Bebelama *(Sideroxylon persimile).*

I staggered forward, writing as I walked. "Is that the one the Guarijíos call *joyarí?*" I asked him of another, nearly thirty meters tall, trunk a meter wide. He said it was, but there was some hesitation in his voice. Seeing another, he changed his mind.

"No, David, you see, we call them both *palo verde* in *castellano* (Spanish). But they are different." His voice echoed eerily in the narrow box canyon. He moved to another giant and patted the trunk, a meter in diameter. *"This* is the one I call *joyarí."* The great tree was so tall its closest leaves were twenty meters above my head. Sometimes the branches of tall trees in these canyons intertwine making it impossible to tell which leaves belong to which tree. There is just no way to get leaf samples from a crown nearly seventy feet above one's head. In this case I was lucky. I found a sapling growing from its parent. I pulled off a tiny branch. Alternate leaves. Joyarí *(Drypetes gentryi).* A tree in the Euphorbia family. That was a good one indeed. In Sonora it was found only in box canyons like this. And only in Guarijío country. It was named after Howard Scott Gentry. Cipriano didn't have to make the leaf test. He knew the tree by its Gestalt, its Zen, its totality.

"What do you call the other one?" I asked him. "I don't have a name for it." It did not much matter because he said he never used either one in his remedies. The ones he did use, he was unequivocal about—*tescalamas, torote prietos, berracos.* Later Benjamín identified it for us. *"Guasimilla,"* He said. An elm. No Guarijío name, no Guarijío significance.

Cipriano gave me a long talk on the virtues of *jahué,* the octopus agave called *amole* in Spanish. "David, if you peel these long leaves and pound the flesh inside, it begins to foam and you get a fine soap, the best there is. The soap you buy in powder won't clean your clothing as well. But even better, if you use it to wash your hair, you will never get *canas* (gray hairs)." We looked at each other and simultaneously realized we were onto a commodity of great value, for neither of us yet sported traces of gray. I told David, who did, and his eyes perked up as well. Imagine the commercial possibility! If we could just start young people on this shampoo, they would have to buy it for the rest of their lives. . . . We moved on.

Cipriano took us on through the dark, narrow box until the canyon widened. In a huge *chalate* (fig) tree he pointed out an *enjambre* (beehive) dripping with honey. He wanted that honey in the worst way, I could tell, because he circled below it, his eyes darting around searching for toeholds. But it was too far up for any of us old men to climb. He noted it and I knew full well he would be back with a younger fellow to climb up, smoke out the bees, and clean up the honey. The numerous cliffs of the region are dotted with inaccessible grottos brimming with honeycomb. Guarijíos are noted for their climbing ability, but stories abound of honey seekers falling to their death while attempting to obtain the sweet stuff. Cipriano's own father may have tumbled to his fate while attempting to clean out a wild beehive. He had disappeared when Cipriano was a teenager. Later someone found his bones scattered, but arranged in an attitude that suggested he had fallen to his death.

Cipriano watched the hive and the bees flying in and out for a while, then reluctantly turned his gaze away. Guarijíos love honey above anything, I've decided. They evaluate their hunts based on the honey and venison they bring back.

Guarijíos gather the figs from that chalate, he said. During the gathering season they have to fight off the birds, insects, and mammals that like the fruits just as much. Those sweet fruits, along with *etchos* (fruits of a large columnar cactus), *pitahayas* (organ pipe cactus fruits), and acorns from the *tojá* (encino oak) are the best suppliers of food, he thought. Close behind are the fruits of the *tempisque* (*Sideroxylon tepicense*), the *matácachi* cactus (*pitahaya barbón*), even preferable to the proclaimed pitahaya fruit because its

skin possesses no spines, *igualamas (Vitex mollis)* and a host of other fruit-bearing trees and plants.

From the canyon floor Cipriano led us up through the bush on a barely detectable path that wound steeply up the side, to a tiny terrace. On it was a nearly new hut of palm thatch and wattle and daub siding. Next to it was about an acre of cleared hillside. His brother Joaquín had built the neat little house two years ago and had already planted banana trees inside a primitive corral. He moves there when *las aguas* (the summer rainy season) begin, Cipriano said, to plant and tend his *mahuechi* (cleared hillside plot) and his garden. In times of promising summer rains he will plant corn and beans in the mahuechi and vegetables and watermelon in the garden. The hut and mahuechi are invisible from the canyon below and nearly inaccessible from above. It looked as though no one had been there for months. That is just how the Guarijíos like it, Cipriano said. The nearest neighbors were at San Pedro, a couple of kilometers away. It was about the right distance between neighbors.

"How are your cows?" I asked him as we climbed through the fence, remembering the hellish drought of the previous year. Cows were the basic source of income for the Guarijíos.

"Not doing very well," was the sad reply. "I [the *ejido,* commonly owned land] lost five cows and a burro to sickness."

For a herd of fewer than a hundred cows this was a terrible loss. "That's very, very bad," I said. "What was the illness?"

He shrugged. "Some people say it is rabies."

"Rabies?" I asked. "In winter? How can that be? Rabies is a disease of summer. And to kill five cows! Usually it kills only a cow or two a year in the whole state. Have any dogs or wild beasts caught the disease?"

"No," he said unhappily, "just the cows. That's what the veterinarian says."

That news filled me with foreboding. Maybe the so-called veterinarian was a quack. I would find out more about this.

It was quite warm by now and we basked in the sun outside the hut's ramada, built of tough beams of *mauto* and *amapa.* We sat on a bench and watched an inch-wide trail of *mochomos* (leaf-cutter ants) resembling a miniature pink conveyer belt. The workers hauled bits of rose-colored amapa flowers to their den somewhere nearby, while others scurried in the opposite direction, back up the tree to the very tips of the bare branches to pick up more food. On this particular day they spurned other greenery; only the pinkish floral parts decorated their path. Little by little they were deflowering the tree. They haul their burdens underground and chew them up as fodder for their private mushroom plantations.

Cipriano, though he had seen the mochomos lugging amapa flowers a hundred times before, was content to let me study the scurrying workers, wasting his time. He enjoyed the scene as well. In a day or two, the tree would be stripped of flowers. The ants would locate other amapas, or perhaps change crops. They can strip a garden in a matter of hours if they set their hearts to it. Fortunately for Guarijío farmers, the growing season for their crops is a time of great growth, and the mochomos have plenty of other tender plant parts to harvest.

The ants were utterly dedicated to their task. My presence to them seemed a matter of indifference. Their devotion to their work reminded me of the hard-working Ramón Hurtado, a Guarijío mask and instrument maker from San Bernardo, a few leagues to the southeast on the Río Mayo.[1] Did Cipriano know him?

"Ay, sí, lo conozco" (You bet I know him), he responded. "He's a relative of mine."

This gave me a chance. I had known Ramón for some time. He had converted to an evangelical Protestant sect nearly ten years ago and was a devout follower and preacher. Since that time he had refrained from drinking, smoking, and carousing and had dedicated himself to producing his artistic wares and studying the bible with his *hermanos de la fe* (brothers in the faith). In my experience the *evangelistas,* referred to derogatorily by many Mexicans as *aleluyas,* condemn fiestas, pageants, and dances. Others have told me, though, that Ramón, although he was no longer willing to speak Guarijío (the language was as pagan as the customs), still played music and sang at the fiestas, at least when his Guarijío spirit overcame his newly acquired religious proscriptions.

"Look, Cipriano," I said. "I know that you love fiestas, you play the violin, others dance the *pascola,* you have these . . ."

"Tuburadas," he filled in my sentence. "That's what we call them."

"Right," I nodded, "*tuburadas.* The *evangelistas* teach that fiestas and those things are a sin. How is it that Ramón can continue to participate?"

I knew by now that the Guarijíos' fiesta, the tuburada, was at least originally a fertility dance, preoccupied with corn and human reproduction. The sexual symbolism throughout the long ceremony was unmistakable. Surely the evangelicals' condemnation of worldly pleasures would cause them to denounce the festivals in the sternest terms.

Cipriano stared out over the canopy of greenery below us and smiled serenely. "You see, David, the tuburada is a three-day fiesta. and the *evangelistas* know why it is a three-day fiesta and so they don't mind. I will tell you why. Do you want me to tell you the story?"

He sat on a bench of soft chilicote wood and began. "This came from my grandfather, and he swore it was the correct story. I always try to tell it just the way my grandfather did.

"In the very, very beginning, a century ago or even more, there were only Tata Diós (Grandfather God) and his brother Satanás (Satan). In those times on the earth there was only water, everywhere they looked. No earth could be seen. Tata Diós and Satanás wondered what could be done with all that water. Then Tata Diós scraped his fingernails under his armpits and hurled the *mugre* (grime) from there into the water. Where the grime struck the water, there earth was formed and the grime caused the water to dry up.

"When the waters had parted, Tata Diós and Satanás called a raven and watched it. It landed on the newly formed earth, but went around doing evil things and causing mischief, so Tata Diós made it fly away. Next, Tata Diós called forth a *chuparoso* (hummingbird) and it came whirring by and fluttered all over the earth, but it could not find anywhere to land, so Tata Diós sent it away, too, back where it came from.

"Finally, Tata Diós called forth a *tortolita,* that is, a small dove, as we call it. It was able to land, and the mud stuck to its feet. Tata Diós saw it and said, where the mud sticks the hardest to the earth, there will be a fiesta. And where the tortolita landed the mud stuck and there they had the first fiesta of all, *los guarijíos.*

"In the first fiesta they used a *santa cruz* (holy cross) made of pure gold, but nowadays the crosses are made of wood. They could celebrate the santa cruz anywhere they wished. But Tata Diós ordered that the fiesta should last three days. Nowadays we just do it for one day and night, sometimes two. Now there isn't the respect there used to be. In the beginning we didn't even have musical instruments. The Mayos invented them and taught us how to play them. They are great musicians, the Mayos.

"Then Satanás said, 'Let's have a fiesta; I'll have mine and you have yours. Let's see who can have the better.'

"'Fine,' said Tata Diós. And he had the fiesta we call the *tuburada* while Satanás had a fiesta of dancing and drinking.

At the fiesta of Satanás people were dancing *bichi* (naked) and then started getting drunk and fighting and killing each other. They had a three-day *satanal*. But the *tuburada* was a better fiesta and it helped the people more, so Tata Diós won the contest. Satanás couldn't stand Tata Diós's choice, however, because it was too quiet, too sober and even a little sad, he said, and the women danced apart, all by themselves. They have their own dance. So he complained and nowadays most of the fiestas people have are more like Satan's fiesta.

"So, you see, David, that's why the *evangelistas* are permitted to participate in the tuburada. Because Tata Diós himself created it. We don't have drinking, at least not much at the *tuburadas.*"

Indeed, it did explain a lot. I realized, however, that I had listened to the story rather than write it down. "Cipriano," I said, "could we sit down at San Pedro and could you tell me the story once again so that I can write it down? I want to be sure that I get the details in order. It's an important story."

He paused for a moment and shook his head. "*Pues,* David, I don't think I should tell the story there at San Pedro. There is too much joking and saying bad things there. Maybe you should come to my home instead and I will tell you there."

I agreed about San Pedro. The atmosphere there was not one of cultural sensitivity. "Very well," I said, "I could come down tonight and David and I could camp at your place, if that's all right, or we could walk down and come back and sleep at San Pedro. You tell us which is best for you."

"No," he said, gently but firmly. "Not tonight. Tomorrow morning I'll come to San Pedro and bring a burro and we'll bring your things down to Jánaco. You can stay at my house for a few days."

And so it was. The following morning he appeared on foot, as always. Two young boys, perhaps eight and ten years old, had showed up earlier with a horse and a couple of other Guarijío men materialized as well. While David and I watched, the two boys gathered a pile of the bizarre, spike-covered, baseball-size fruits of the *josocura* (*Randia echinocarpa,* papache), a basic fruit in the lives of native peoples of the region, specially relished by boys. They ate their papaches and watched us in silence, scrutinizing our movements as though we were aliens of unknown inclinations. We had to wait an hour for the tents to dry, so heavy was the dew. Finally we were ready and Benjamín

and Cipriano, assisted by the two lads, loaded our trappings onto a horse, carefully balancing the load by adding things and taking away things from a gunnysack on each side. Then we set off.

Cipriano did not set off with us, however. The two boys walked ahead, leading the horse up the steep path in the opposite direction from yesterday, and David and I followed. "I will follow in a bit," Cipriano promised. We passed into the forest, older men being led by boys.

We walked through the low forest, called tropical deciduous forest by scientists because of its tropical origins and its tendency to lose its leaves in the dry season. This was not virgin forest. These lands had seen human activity for centuries. *Chírahui* trees of uniform height, about four meters, their old spines curling into boat-shaped thorns, revealed mahuechis farmed and abandoned long ago, hardly a hint left of the old cornfields. Ancient rock walls, the trincheras, made irregular, never ending patterns, demarking boundaries with a silent, forgotten language of property. Stumps had sprouted; others had rotted. Great *torotes* and *palo mulatos* showed by their scarred bark a history of harvest by native *curanderos* wringing their magic from nature to cure infirmities. Marks of the machete were everywhere, and the forest's quick growth camouflaged human predations.

We climbed a steep hill, crossed a wooded mesa, then dropped into a draw, and suddenly I realized that Cipriano was walking with us. He had materialized from a different path and melted into our midst. After a couple of kilometers we passed a small *represo* (dirt-dammed stock tank), built by the government, where a few cows were grazing. A hundred yards ahead he stopped us at a great overlook and gestured with a nod of his head. Far below on a partially cleared knoll was perched a palm-thatched hut. "That is Jánaco, my house," he said with a measure of pride.

"My God," murmured David. "Man, Dave, I've never seen anything more beautiful." Gauguin himself could hardly have selected a more idyllic sight. Far in the distance, to the northeast across the Río Mayo lay the misty, pine-covered ramparts of the blue Sierra Charuco. To the north jutted the more gentle peaks of the Sierra del Venado, yellow with old grass of the previous summer and dotted with oaks. Much farther below in the valley the uniformly green patches revealed where forest had been once been cleared for mahuechis. Otherwise, except for the hamlet below, there was no sign of human presence.

I complimented Cipriano on his choice of location.

"Yes," he said, "I love to live where I can see things. Jánaco was home to a *vaquero yori* (mestizo cowboy) many years ago. But three years ago, after we won the right to own our lands, I chose it. The *gobernador* (governor) of the Guarijíos gave me permission and so I built the house. From there I can see what is our land. We Guarijíos are people of the mountains and we like to live where we can see plenty of mountains."

It took another twenty minutes to work our way down the steep and rocky mountain trail and up the knoll to the house. Cipriano's wife, three daughters, and son stared at us uncertainly as we walked up. Their looks were not unfriendly, but tentative and shy. The two boys leading the horse unloaded our bundles. I paid them and they both climbed into the saddle, one in front of the other, and continued down the valley to their home, ten miles away at Mesa Colorada.

This was the culmination of a long-held dream. I had first met Cipriano a year earlier at a fiesta at La Junta, near Mesa Colorada. I had been sick, that night, though, and barely had an opportunity to speak with him. The all-too-brief conversation convinced me that he could teach me much about plants and about the Guarijíos. A few months later he guided my brother and me along with some botanists up the Arroyo Guajaray as we searched for new plant sightings and recorded the Guarijío uses of native plants. Cipriano and I had ample opportunity to chat on that trip, and I realized I was just beginning to comprehend the complexities of Guarijío life. When he suggested that I visit him at Jánaco I let him know I was eager to do so, but still it was ten months before I was able to fulfill my promise. I had sent word through Dr. Leobardo Quiroz of San Bernardo who was in constant contact with the Guarijíos and a liaison between them and the Mexican government. In the meantime I spoke with Teresa Valdivia Dounce, the Mexico City anthropologist who produced *Como una huella pintada,* Cipriano's remarkable *testimonio* or autobiography. She urged me to visit him. Tere had worked among the Guarijíos and was now finishing her doctoral dissertation on Guarijío history. A literature search turns up little documented material on the Guarijíos. The most prominent is botanist Howard Scott Gentry's 1963 monograph, *The Warihío Indians of Sonora-Chihuahua: An Ethnographic Survey,* based on his notes from the late 1930s when he conducted intensive plant collections in the region. *Cycles of Conquest,* Edward Spicer's classic study of the native peoples of the Southwest United States and

Northern Mexico, makes only a single, passing reference to them. Even Sonoran historical and anthropological records have only sparse references to the Guarijíos. Anything I wanted to find out, I would have to gain first hand.

I greeted the family members, touching hands with all except for two-year-old Cruz, who shied away, shrinking from the strange-looking intruders deep into the safety of mother Dolores's arms. Melecio, ten, was not at all shy and walked around the yard whistling and busying himself with whatever chores seemed to be necessary while happily spying on us. Benita, fifteen, hung tentatively in the background, while Luz Elena, six, stared openly and unabashedly. I could not help admiring the house. The peak of the perfectly thatched roof stood a good ten feet high. I estimated the hut's size to be fourteen by eighteen feet. It had an opening in the front, but no door. I asked Cipriano to tell David and me how he had built it.

"The roof is of *palma* but it doesn't grow around here. I brought it—forty *cargas* (bundles, in this case) of it—four to a burro, from about twenty kilometers away. The walls I built of *otate* (a bamboo-like grass). Then I made the adobe mud and covered the *otate,* and so you see it. Not a drop of rain comes in through the roof."

"Isn't it hot in the summer months?"

"Oh, yes it is! It's so hot sometimes we come out under the *ramada* and sleep in the open. We even sleep *bichi* sometimes."

"Don't the bugs bother you?"

"Well a few, but they aren't bad here, not like they are down below, and we have a *mosquitera* (mosquito netting). We all climb under it." I was delighted for his sake that that most compassionate of civilized inventions was available to them. I love to share the outdoor life of the Guarijíos and other native peoples, but I'm skittish about ectoparasites. I shudder at the misery imposed on people of the monte who have no refuge from chiggers, mosquitoes, no-see-ums, and biting gnats.

Cipriano deserved any compliments I could muster, for it was a splendid house. Even so, I felt I dared not snoop by looking inside, for the inside of one's house is a private place, indeed, and the Guarijíos are the most private of people. After we had returned to Alamos, David asked me if I had peered inside the house, for he had not. His reaction had been the same. He was curious, but didn't dare peek and Cipriano never invited our inspection.

I thought a lot about that house, then and afterwards. Cipriano was proud of it. His family was impressed and

Cipriano Buitimea and his family, Jánaco. Photo by David Burckhalter.

delighted by its function of providing shade and shelter. David and I were taken by its beauty and the simplicity and fine quality of its construction. On an analytic level the house represents a deep structure, a physical object casting tentacles in all directions and on many levels. Cipriano had to have intimate knowledge of a variety of plants to build it, especially the batayaqui and palma, but also the mauto, *copalquín,* and *vara blanca* that went into its construction. He needed to know where he could acquire these plants and how to harvest and transport them. He had to know the properties of these plants and their parts, to know for instance that batayaqui, because its thin trunks are springy and resilient, weaves well into durable walls, and to know that a roof of palm will last twenty-five years but can go up in flame in an instant. Without that knowledge, his hundreds of hours of labor could be wasted.

He also needed to know the dirt—clay loam—which went into making the wattle and where he could find it. Not just any old dirt would do. A soil with insufficient clay would crumble. Too much clay would be hard to work and

would make a mess in the rain. Then there was the floor. Although I never saw it, I knew no one could sleep on that rocky soil. He had to bring in some fill, remove large and small rocks, level it off, and tamp the air and looseness out of it.

But walls, roof, and floor do not yet make a house. To be a proper house, the structure had to conform to the needs and aspirations of Cipriano's family. Cipriano had to internalize a design, including an orientation. It had to be the sort of house a good husband would provide a good wife, one that children would find protection and family security in. Even if they only slept inside in the cold months and spent the rest of their year out of doors, the house stood as a symbol.

Finally, the house, at least for Cipriano, was a statement of his nationalistic pride, one he wanted passersby, infrequent though they be, to see. Whether the viewer be Guarijío or yori, the house inspired notice and respect. He had succeeded.

Besides the house atop the knoll were a small eight-by-ten-foot ramada with a carelessly made roof of miscellaneous sticks and branches, intended to give partial shade. Behind it was a rustic table and behind that the cooking area, all protected by a ramada with a carefully built roof. Cipriano had built two stoves for Dolores, one, a massive adobe brick and clay structure with a fire pit over which was suspended the family *comal* (griddle) which in this case resembled more a wok than the traditional comal. It was simply a disk from a tractor-pulled cultivator culled from a junk pile in Navojoa, far down in the valley. With this Dolores and her fifteen-year-old daughter Benita toasted five or six large tortillas at a time. Behind the first oven was a second, smaller clay firepit on which continually boiled an olla of water with beans or rice (on those few occasions when they were available) or for hot coffee.

The living area, with a radius of perhaps forty feet, was surrounded by a circular fence of four strands of barbed wire to keep out marauding livestock, especially burros, whose appearance of sleepy guilelessness belies a thieving, marauding heart. Wire gates had been constructed in front and back, however, which could be opened or closed to let people or livestock in or out. The night before we were to leave, the family burro was brought inside the enclosure so that he would be easily found in the morning. Chickens, knowledgeable in the human ways of dropping crumbs, frequented the living and eating areas but were constantly driven away by Dolores and Benita who chased them with an effective "Whoosh, whoosh." A large *palo zorillo* tree outside the living area was furnished with a simple pole ladder. At dusk the chickens climbed the ladder and roosted in the ample branches and foliage of the tree as a protection against predators. Inside the compound several palo zorillos remained as a source of welcome shade in the searing heat of late spring, summer, and early fall. As Cipriano also reminded me, they bloom a dense blanket of soft yellow blossoms in April and May and bestow a natural beauty on the home. In summer they provide dense shade.

It was mid-afternoon by now and we sat languidly around the campfire area on ancient, hand-made chairs of local *guásima*. The fireplace was simply a bare spot on the ground near the kitchen. Cipriano reviewed the history of the creation of the Los Bajíos ejido, how the Guarijíos had been held in economic bondage by local ranchers, how guerrillas from Chihuahua had helped Guarijíos understand their plight, and how in the mid- and late 1970s he and other leaders had faced impossible odds, but with a small cadre of obdurate Guarijío had persisted and ultimately won the battle (see pp. 34–37 for more details). The opposition

was a sizeable group of small yori ranchers who were accustomed to using federal lands as their own. They had threatened Cipriano and his late co-leader in the *lucha* (struggle), José Zazueta. Four times the yoris had managed to have José imprisoned by the notoriously corrupt *judiciales* or state police. Many times he had been threatened and even beaten. Cipriano himself had been threatened. He resorted to carrying a pistol. He had escaped arrest and beating.

"Then we had the big day, up there in Hermosillo [the state capital]. We sat in the judge's office. There were thirty-two of them, *los pequeños propietarios* (small-time ranchers) and only four of us, José Zazueta, La Tere (Teresa Valdivia), our lawyer, and I. But the judge asked each of the *yori rancheros*: 'Do you have papers to prove you have title to the land,' and each one of them had to say, *'No, señor.'* All thirty-two of them! You should have seen them squirm! So the judge said, 'Very well, then it is not your land. It belongs to the Guarijíos.' And so we won!

"Then the government invited us to Mexico City, eight of us. We took a bus. It was very cold. They took us up in the mountains to where there was snow. I had never seen it before. Everybody told me, 'Cipriano, buy some shoes to protect your feet from the cold and the snow.' But I said, 'Why should I buy shoes just for one day? I'm a Guarijío and I wear *huaraches de tres puntas.*' So I walked through the snow in my *huaraches.*"

It appears that in the last decade the Guarijíos have been treated benignly by the Mexican government. Not only did their struggle for land succeed against mestizo small landowners, but the government has continued to provide comparatively generous subsidies to the tribe, as we shall see. Cipriano has no bad words for the government. The persecution endured by some Guarijíos during and after the guerrilla incidents of the 1970s had little effect on him. He downplays their significance, even though he recalls that a few guerrillas were shot on the Guajaray. The realization of the ejido during the administration of President López Portillo is an event so overwhelming, so transcendent, that all other historical events pale in comparison. The Guarijíos have also made peace with most of the mestizo ranchers and now have good relations with them.

I later learned that it was Guarijíos from Bavícora, twenty miles away, who sheltered the guerrillas. They and Guarijíos of Los Bajíos often differ in policy, in tactics, and in beliefs. One challenge in the struggle for lands was getting the two groups to work together.

"That's why we're happy, David. We have our land. Each Guarijío can have a *mahuechi* and a place to build a house and have a few burros and chickens. We used to have nothing. Now we're still poor, but we have our land. Now our children have schools and teachers. The Guarijíos are still *atrasados* (backwards). We're very timid. We hide in the forest and run away from people from the outside. We're not like the Mayos and Yaquis."

That gave me another opening. "Cipriano, I've noticed most of the place names around here are Mayo and not Guarijío. Why is that?" I named several mountains, settlements, and places. All had Mayo names, not Guarijío or Spanish.

We all stared dreamily across the distant lowlands, the valley of the Arroyo Guajaray and into the distant sierra. "I think it's because the Mayos and Yaquis were civilized long before us," he said. "They learned to read and write long ago and were able to leave their names on the mountains. We're still not very civilized. Look at me, I can't read and write." We both laughed at that, for indeed it seemed the most insignificant thing we could imagine.

"So where did the Guarijíos come from?" I asked.

He shook his head easily. "Maybe we were always here. My *abuelito* (grandfather) said the Guarijíos were here a long time, even in the last century. Up around Los Conejos [on the upper Arroyo Guajaray] there are some caves. We always find old Guarijío things in them, old pieces of guaris, and pieces of clothing, *ollas,* things like that, things that are just the way my *abuelito* and *abuelita* (grandmother) made them. So the Guarijíos have been here a long time."

"Some people say the Guarijíos are close to the *rarámuri* (Tarahumara). What do you think of that?"

He shook his head. "No. Some of our words are the same, but mostly that's true of the Guarijíos from up there," and he pointed to the north, "up in the mountains around Arechuybo. They use a lot of words different from ours. We get together sometimes and we have a hard time understanding each other because we use different words down here. And they speak with an accent. But I have heard stories about the Tarahumaras. My *abuelito* said they run all the time, up the mountains, just like *chivos* (goats). He said he saw one once carrying a whole *fanega* of corn [perhaps a hundred pounds] from a cord around his head. He was running straight up the mountain, without a path, anything! We're not like *that*. Tarahumaras are people of the pine forest. We are people of the *monte* (in this case the tropical deciduous forest)."

"And what does *Guarijío* mean?"

He did not understand, so I explained that for many indigenous groups the names used for them were given by outsiders. "Mayos call themselves *yoreme*, Yaquis, *yoeme*, Seris, *comcáac*. How about the Guarijíos?"

He thought for a while about this. "Well, I guess we just call ourselves Guarijíos. Sometimes we say *makurawe*, but usually we say Guarijío. Maybe it comes from all the *guaris* we made from *palma*. So some people say it means "people who make baskets." But we do not know. We're just the Guarijío. Sometimes we call ourselves *makurawe*."

It was a good answer.

Cipriano thought that the Guarijío language was close to the Mayo language. He and I had already noticed similarity between many plant names in Guarijío and the corresponding name in Mayo.[2] These probably are more an indicator of cultural influence than of deep linguistic relatedness. The Guarijío language was extensively studied and analyzed by linguist Wick Miller in the 1980s. Miller (1996) spent several years among the Guarijíos and came to know their language as well as any outsider. He demonstrated conclusively that Guarijío has close affinities with the language of the Tarahumaras, with considerable dialectical variations among Guarijío populations. He also theorized that Guarijío diverged from Tarahumara between five hundred and a thousand years ago (Miller 1983:188). Miller's brilliant work ended when he was killed in a pedestrian-auto accident in Hermosillo in the early 1990s. His death was a tragic loss to the Guarijíos and to the world. The Guarijíos remember him with fondness and respect.

Mayos, though, have had a great influence on Guarijíos. Intermarriage between the two groups was common. The Guarijíos of San Bernardo are acquainted with many Mayos from the Mayo Valley below. Mayo and Guarijío families live close to each other in the village of Chorijoa north of San Bernardo. Nahuibampo, Vado Cuate, and Macoyahui, all on the Río Mayo are Mayo villages within twenty kilometers of San Bernardo. Most teachers in Guarijío schools are Mayos.

By now the shadows were lengthening and Dolores (a Bavícora Guarijía) had moved the handmade table into position to serve us beans, potatoes, and tortillas. The four men, Cipriano, David, Melecio, and I sat at the table, while the women hovered in the background. Benita constantly replenished a guari with massive tortillas made from the Maseca I had brought. Cipriano offered us *chiltepines* (fiery hot tiny red chile peppers) and sprinkled fresh cilantro from the *aguaje* (spring) below. Only once in my stay did I catch the women sitting and eating. Usually they ate while standing, leaving the comforts of eating seated to the men.

Melecio, a rangy, small boy wearing a straw cowboy hat and a cowboy shirt too small for him seldom sat still for more than a few minutes, although he was intensely interested in the conversation. When his stepfather spoke, he lingered on every word. As the sun lowered Cipriano said something to him in Guarijío. Melecio dashed out of the compound and down the hill, whistling as he trotted away. I whistled his melody back at him, and he stopped and laughed gaily. He and I were going to hit it off well. Twenty minutes later there was a loud dragging sound, and the lad appeared, driving the burro with two long trunks of *brasil* wood lashed to its back. He loosened the logs that fell with a crash into the woodpile near the house. He snatched up an axe and with an adult's ease proceeded to chop the hard, dense wood into three-foot chunks. Brasil, whose heavily fluted trunks provide the preferred firewood of forest people in the region, gives a nearly smokeless, greenish flame.

The evening wood supply secured, Melecio returned to sit at the fire, but not for long. Soon Cipriano gestured with his head toward the galvanized tub that sat atop the built-in rough-hewn surface that constituted the kitchen counter. The water supply was low. Melecio sprang up and heaved two five-gallon plastic cylinders on a sling tied to the burro, one on each side, and led the reluctant beast through the back gate and down the hill behind the compound to the aguaje at the bottom, the empty drums bonging like tympani with each step. Benita followed close behind. They returned in another twenty minutes, the jugs full of water. These were too heavy for Melecio to hoist, for I doubt if he weighed more than fifty pounds. Instead, Benita, short but strong, hefted the jugs and dumped the contents into the tub that is the family water supply. She had climbed up the long hill balancing a five-gallon jerry can of water on her head.

It was hard work hauling the water, Cipriano acknowledged, but the aguaje was faithful. It had held sweet water throughout the five-year-long drought and even through the brutal famine of the previous year when cattle starved and water holes in Sonora and Chihuahua that had never before been known to fail had dried up. It was what made habitation possible at Jánaco. Without it, Jánaco would be just another nondescript, uninhabited hilltop. The flow was enough that one could even bathe in the runoff below the pool where the jugs were filled. The mountains of the Los Bajíos ejido are dotted with reliable water holes and streams.

The most valuable resource is the never-faltering arroyo of the Guajaray whose babbling flow varies only when swollen by heavy rains. (Guarijíos love to bathe several times a day in the crisp, deep pools of that great arroyo.)

The area around the aguaje was always green, even in the dry season, so much so that on occasion army helicopters had landed nearby, inspecting for marijuana and opium poppies. Now that the generous equipatas foretold a year of good rain, Cipriano harbored notions of putting in a few fruit trees below the spring to complement the bananas that were already nearly mature. The army patrols the area, Cipriano says, and will spray any suspected crops with a herbicide that kills everything. He was indignant about the fate of a friend who was unfortunate enough to have his mahuechi near someone else's field of *rama* (marijuana). The *ejército* came in a helicopter and sprayed everything around, killing off his corn and bean crop as well as the marihuana. On second thought, he figured that maybe the marihuana had survived.

He had spoken with some of the soldiers. "One of them told me that he doesn't understand why they are supposed to kill the marijuana. He uses it, and all the others do too, 'So why are we killing it?' he asked. I don't understand, either. But they say the United States wants us to kill it, so the government does."

Melecio's last task for the evening, which he did with a smile, was to bring from a box in the house a large double-handful of salt and sprinkle it on some rocks on the flats outside the fence. Within a few moments two horses and a mule appeared and energetically licked the rocks where he had sprinkled the salt. This is a common practice of the hill people of the region; salt, they say, makes the *bestias* (generic name for burros and mules and sometimes even horses) tame and accustomed to human presence. I approached one of the horses, a handsome chestnut mare and patted her on the neck. She showed no sign of fear, only a mild curiosity about this different-looking stranger.

I set up my tent outside the compound. Cipriano had urged us to sleep under the ramada and David agreed to, but, I pointed out, I was more like the Guarijíos, who like to live apart. The tent was a large high-tech Eureka with shock cords and a fly, looking like a space-age dome. Everyone in the family was most curious about it, especially wondering if it had a floor. I zipped open the door and they stuck their heads in, oohing and admiring its security. How was it during the day? I told them it was hotter than blazes, an oven worthy of cooking bread, but at night it protected me from the dew and biting insects, and in the rain I would be dry. Cipriano concurred in the wisdom of using a tent, but I thought his endorsement a little too polite. He really thought I was weird to use the tent, especially when I could sleep outside with open world all around me. I wondered as well when one of the horses approached the tent gingerly, then galloped away when someone threw a tiny rock at it.

Melecio brought out a *petate* (mat of woven palm) for David to sleep on, and one for himself, for he thought it would be jolly fun to sleep outdoors near the gringos, Cipriano said. David had a foam mattress pad, but Melecio and all the Guarijíos sleep on the ground protected only by the thin mat and covered with a cotton blanket. The one fleeting glimpse I got of the inside of the house revealed that all sleep on petates that are rolled up during the day. I surmise that the only article of furniture inside is a small chest where the few personal items they own are protected from dust and pests.

The sun had scarcely been down an hour when David and I started yawning. Cipriano noticed and suggested we should go to bed. "You will be like the Guarijío," he said smilingly. *"Somos gente de la madrugada"* (We are people of the dawn), he said. "We start to work very early. My *abuelito* said a man only needs to sleep three hours a night if he wants to live long. If he sleeps longer, he won't live to be old." I worried about that. I like seven hours. The life of rural folk requires a predawn awakening. Most, I think, sleep through the night. Most.

I fussed around in my tent for a while, getting comfortable and arranging the hundred gadgets and indispensable junk that filled my backpack. I listened to the horses stamping, chewing, and snorting and was relieved to hear Cipriano drive them off with a rock. "That will let you sleep better, David," he called to me from his palm house. I thanked him in a loud voice.

I slept fitfully, as I always do on the first night camping. The first few times I awoke I heard the voices of Cipriano and Dolores as they talked to each other far into the night. He did not appear to dominate the conversation as I thought he might, for her cheery voice and laughter carried well out into the valley.[3] Twice I got up to pee and saw the light of the fire they had built *inside* the hut. It burns all night, keeping them warm through the chill of the winter months. Then it dawned on me that I had never before stayed in the presence of people who had no radio or television. The absence of the blast of speakers was a blessing and a curiosity,

for my experience in the third world has been that even the poorest and most remote of native peoples managed to obtain transistor radios and usually use them nonstop. The absence of a radio, I decided, was Cipriano's deliberate choice, not a result of lack of opportunity, for many Guarijíos have them. Or perhaps it was just that the cost of batteries was more than his meager budget could spare.

I've found in Mexico that the most coveted nonessential possession is a battery-powered radio. Even in remote indigenous villages with no electricity, radios blare from before dawn until well after sundown, often deep into the night—except in hard times when batteries become too expensive. A pair of batteries cost nearly $2, more than half the daily wage of a laborer in that region. But Cipriano had none and seemed content that way.

I wouldn't dream of living without electricity, at least not for more than a few days—long enough so I could brag that I could rough it. My hometown of Tucson in the summertime is very hot. Without the evaporative cooler my house would be uninhabitable. I like to read by electric lamps at night. I like the preserving effect of refrigerators, the cool or cold liquids they provide me whenever I want them. I like the water pressure maintained in my neighborhood by powerful electric motors and pumps. I've come to rely on the computer for typing and as a source of information from the outside world. I could hardly get by now without my computer to write with and to consult the Internet. I curse telephones while relying on them for contacts and information. City traffic would be an anarchic suicide zone without stoplights and signals.

So electricity pampers my life. Why, then, do I find it so refreshing, so quaint, so well, honest, to find people who live without it? Perhaps it's intellectual hypocrisy. Perhaps, on the other hand, it's that I harbor deep Rousseauian convictions that civilization brings with it discontents, that electricity, more than any other technological advance, epitomizes contemporary civilization. Las Vegas—the most electrified of cities—represents the technological perversion of the human soul, an electrified empire where the lights must never go out and where everything natural, even great human creations, is copied. Then the originals are cast aside amid the improbable falsified cornucopia of amps, watts, and volts. My deepest intuitions intimate that people uncorrupted by electricity stand a greater chance of being purer, untainted by the dark forces of industry and mass society.

Blah, blah, blah. All this is patent romantic nonsense, of

course, but part of me believes it nevertheless. Another part of me scoffs at this fiction. One batch of corrective data my meanderings with indigenous people have taught me is that virtue cuts across civilizations and classes. I nurture a working-class bias but am under no illusion that working-class or peasant people are somehow morally purer than the more fortunate members of the ruling class. Rural dwellers have no more monopoly on goodness than do urban dwellers. Native people are not innately more spiritually whole than are transplants. I'm acquainted with a wealthy saint and also with a paupered sinner. I have been robbed several times by hayseeds, more often than by city slickers. Some Guarijíos are inclined to abuse their lands. Some wealthy landowners are inclined to treat theirs as good stewards.

All the same, the closeness to nature that a simple, ancient lifestyle reflects, has a certain bucolic freshness about it that I find downright exciting. Perhaps the attractiveness of Jánaco and Cipriano and his family was elicited by a genetically determined reaction within me, some atavistic response reflecting my DNA's origins in the wilds of Africa. There was something satisfying about being here at Jánaco with a family living as such families might have lived a hundred years or more ago, with only the nylon of my tent and my learned Europe-inspired pretenses separating me from nature.

I awoke at down to a chorus of roosters and burros and the sound of Cipriano's happy voice. I dressed quickly, but dragged a little, realizing I had come down with a cold that combined with asthma to give me an embarrassing cough. Cipriano was concerned. "You woke up sick," he said. "It sounds as though it's deep in your lungs."

I assured him it was not as bad as it sounded but worried that I might infect one of the Guarijíos with some pestilence of civilization. "What do you do for a cold?" I asked him. "I will tell you later," he said. "Before you go to bed tonight you need to take some tea of *gordolobo* and *torote prieto.*"

Lord, what a mornin' it was! The sun sparkled through the moist mountain air and backlit the heavy dew in the wet canyon bottoms. A million pinpoint rainbows glittered. Every shadowed crevice in the mountains exaggerated the distances, and we seemed to be poised on top of a new planet. The air was still and the silence profound. From far, far away I heard the bray of a burro, the sound echoing for miles off the lava cliffs. I marveled once more at Cipriano's choice of a home site. Then pheasant-like *chachalacas* began squabbling in the forest at the bottom of the hill and the

Cipriano Buitimea and the author, Jánaco.

reverie was broken.

Chachalacas are a game species that the Guarijíos eat from time to time, pronouncing the flavor to be most agreeable, better than chicken, they say. The meat of chicken is the standard of comparison for many meats for Guarijíos, just at it is for us. Chachalaca numbers are not as great as they once were. Sometimes, Cipriano said, the chachalacas descend on his yard and fight with the domestic chickens, invariably to the disadvantage of the latter. The Guarijíos also relish venison, usually downing a deer or two each season, but the drought seemed to have cut down on deer population as well. The *jabalí* (javelina) are also savored, cooked with *laurel* (bay leaves) gathered wild in the higher mountains.

We sat shivering around the fire, accompanied by the family dog and a cat. David and I got a good laugh from the scrawny cat, whose coat was covered with dark singe marks. "The silly cat sleeps near the hot coals to stay warm," Cipriano explained, "so it's always getting its fur burned. At night it sleeps in the ashes in the oven. Imagine that!" I could not.

Dolores served us tiny cups of coffee she had roasted in burned sugar. She nodded good morning and answered *"Bien, bien,"* when I asked her *"¿Cómo amaneciste?"* (How did you dawn this morning). That was the only Spanish I could coax from her. She appeared to understand my words, for she frequently laughed at our conversations, but whether because she spoke only haltingly, or was embarrassed to speak Spanish, in my presence she spoke only in Guarijío. The girls did the same. Melecio, however, was quite willing to speak in his accented Spanish. He had attended the *albergue* (boarding school) in Mesa Colorada, where the children learn Spanish. Right now, though, he was not attending school. Cipriano expressed frustration at the schooling problem. At the albergue the students must arrive on Monday morning and leave on Thursday afternoon. That means someone must accompany them and pick them up, a time-consuming and tiring activity. The school is about three hours away on foot, so traveling back and forth is a nuisance. The boy's labor is also most useful around the house. He cannot be learning the ways of the monte when he is living away at a boarding school. That spring, however, Cipriano said, the lad would return to school, for he must know how to read and write well to serve the Guarijíos and get by in the land of los blancos. All the struggles they had gone through in the seventies were aimed at two things: land for themselves and schools for their children.

Dolores, Cipriano told us, was from Bavícora, a hamlet on a tributary of the east bank of the Río Mayo, several leagues to the northeast of Mesa Colorada. From Jánaco, where we looked out to an open world, Cipriano pointed out its location, deep in a canyon under a great outcropping of white rock in the distant Sierra Charuco. In Bavícora, he says, the people speak a slightly different strain of the Guarijío language. There are also political differences between them and the Guarijíos of Guajaray that I think can be summed up as this: Bavícorans view Guajarayans as tainted with mestizo values (as does Cipriano). Guajarayans suspect that Bavícorans are foolish purists, ignorant rustics. Some day I would go to Bavícora and find out this—and many more things.

Dolores was Cipriano's third wife. His first, whom he had met far up to the northeast, had died after the birth of their second child, a son, who also died. The first child, now a young woman, lived at El Saucito, a few kilometers below Jánaco. Cipriano lived there until about 1990 when he chose to move to Jánaco. His second wife had left him for another Guarijío man, leaving his daughter Andrea to be raised by his mother. She still lives with doña Angelita at San Pedro.

Dolores was the best wife of all, he observed. She had two children by a previous marriage as well, and they had two children of their own, one of whom was born in the hospital in Alamos. Clearly Cipriano and Dolores had a strong relationship, for they laughed heartily together and talked over many things, none of which were intelligible to the outsider not conversant in the Guarijío language.

"How do Guarijíos marry?" I asked him. "And then, how do they divorce?" He found this to be an interesting question, for he gave a lengthy answer.

"For the Guarijío marriage isn't what it is for the *blancos*. They, the yoris, have big fiestas and things in churches with priests and then a civil ceremony besides. That's not the Guarijío way. Ours is much simpler. If a man wants to have a woman for a wife, he must first ask her father. The father must consider if the man is going to be good for his daughter. Will he bring her food and build her a good house? Will he be a good father to children? All of these things he has to consider.

"If her father agrees, then he asks his daughter, do you want to marry this man? Then the woman must think, 'Do I want this man to be my husband? Will he treat me well and bring me food and build a good house?' So, then, if she decides that, yes, she will marry, they can be married right there."

"Is there any kind of ceremony," I asked, "A fiesta or something involving someone religious?"

"No," he smiled. "We don't have that. We may have a little celebration with tortillas and a little other food, maybe some *venadito* or some chocolate. But that's all. Then they are married."

"Do they live with the family of the husband or of the wife?" I asked, careful to gather all the appropriate anthropological data.

"Wherever they want to live. Some live with the husband's family, some with the wife's family. But some go off to live in their own place. That's how the Guarijío are." He added, though, that he had been careful to see that all his children's names were entered in the civil registry to assure that their social rights would be protected. If parents fail to register children they may be denied enrollment in school and will face all manner of difficulties in later life, such as obtaining identification papers necessary for traveling on public transportation and health care through the social security system.[4]

For divorce, well, they just part, that's all, he said. Sometimes one of the partners runs off with someone else, but it does not happen very much.

By this time Dolores had served up plates of beans and potatoes. Just as we were sitting down, however, Melecio, who had disappeared a half hour earlier, came tramping and whistling into camp bearing a woven cloth bag stuffed with something. Dolores pulled out a mass of greens and poured water from the tub over them. Then she set the glistening pile on a metal plate and set them on the table in front of us. *"Guacharay,"* Cipriano explained. "They're

Melecio Buitimea on the trail to El Saucito. Photo by David Burckhalter.

also called *mostaza* (mustard greens) in Spanish." They were sparkling fresh, a gift of this years' generous equipatas. I took one and chewed it up. It was as fresh as watercress. Combined with the fresh mustard, the cilantro and chiltepines, the fresh tortillas and beans turned into a delectable breakfast.[5]

"Today I will take you to El Saucito for you to see other Guarijíos," Cipriano announced after we had finished eating. "Then we will return in the afternoon and talk some more. I love to talk!"

I fixed up my day pack and David his camera bag and we set off down the "camino" as locals refer to every pathway. Cipriano showed me a level spot two hundred yards below his house where he hoped to put in an orchard, piping in water from the aguaje. Orange, lime, grapefruit, banana and papaya, he wanted. Then his family could eat the fruits all year round. The lower Guarijío lands are frost-free, so freezing is no consideration. Temperatures below forty degrees are unusual. The previous morning my thermometer registered forty-one degrees, and everyone had pronounced it to be a very cold morning.

This year the hills were abnormally green, blessed by bountiful equipatas. "What will these hills look like in May

and June, in the dry season?" I asked him.

He raised his eyebrows. "Oh, there won't be a leaf left. No green at all except for the *etchos* and the *pitahayas,* the big cacti. The color disappears until *las aguas* arrive in late June or early July."

The pathway led down, along a chilly, dark arroyo moistened by a tiny stream, then up and over a steep ridge. Melecio ran ahead on the trail accompanied by the family cur, Toro. From time to time the lad would dash off the trail and up the hillside as though he were a dog chasing a rabbit. He would then meet us half a kilometer farther and resume as though nothing had happened. He whistled constantly and I whistled back to him. He showed inordinate interest in the plants Cipriano and I discussed, which were a great many. Frequently he would name the plants for me, anticipating my questions and beating his stepfather to the punch. At one point he reached into a clump of thick weeds and from the ground produced two pinkish, sharp-ridged fruits the size of plums. "*Chocalá,* David," he said, to my delight, for these were the fruits of the endemic *Jarilla chocola.* The plants are renowned in the region for the nutritious content of their tuberous root and for their sour fruits, but also for their strange behavior. After the plant sends up a shoot a half a yard into the air, it fruits, withers, then dies back, vanishing without a trace except for the pinkish fruits that fall to the ground and lie untouched by animal foragers.

"Do you eat these with limes?" I asked him.

"No, just as they are. They're quite sour. We eat them with other foods." Not bad for a ten-year old, I thought. My conclusion was buttressed when he pointed out a *tavachín,* gave me its Guarijío name, *tacapache,* and described some medical uses. Melecio watched with eyes sparkling as I jotted his comments in my field notes and asked him more questions.

Use of plant remedies is no theoretical matter. We passed several trees reported to be useful and noted the scarring on the trunks where for decades bark has been hacked off by machetes. Another tree, *corcho,* whose heartwood is said to be good medicine for heart problems, had been nearly cut in half as the medicinal inner wood was extracted. Cipriano nodded when I pointed out that the bark of the *nesco* tree was widely used to make a bath for curing mange in dogs. I said this specifically because his dog Toro was clearly suffering from the mange and could use a nesco bath. My subtle allusion did not take effect.

On the trail we twice met two Guarijíos, one on foot, the other on horseback. The latter is unusual, for Guarijíos often state their preference to walk rather than ride. In both instances they were young men on their way to San Pedro to find food, for there was none to be had in the hamlet below. I did not quite know how to take this, for there seemed to be adequate livestock. When I asked Cipriano he explained that due to the extended drought no one had any stores of food, and they relied on shipments of food from the government to San Pedro, primarily of Maseca (for tortillas) and rice. Beans were a luxury that they had only occasionally. The meat of the livestock would be sold for precious currency and could be eaten only under emergency conditions. This was not yet emergency status.

After a few kilometers the trail descended to a narrow valley and mahuechis appeared around us. Then we crossed a fence and were in a settlement of three houses. Two old men stood up and welcomed us, while two women scurried into the shelter of a small thatched house within a ramada. These were relatives of Cipriano's (all the Guarijíos I was to meet were relatives of one sort or another.) A younger man was putting on chaps for a trip into the monte. The chaps were simply wide bolts of home-cured leather that were strapped to the legs as protection against thorns, spines, poking branches, and broken limbs. At the far end of

the fenced compound a calf was running free. It was kept there to be fed, they said, because its mother had died while it was still nursing. It trotted around, following anyone who passed like a puppy, hoping for food or attention.

We were glad to sit in the shade after the hike here. Soon, however, I became uncomfortably aware that gnats were biting at my hands. I slapped a few away, but a couple that I mashed left bloodstains on my hands. "You have got bad *moscas* here, Cipriano," I informed him and the others.

They all laughed heartily. "Yes, they are a plague. The *equipatas* bring them out."

"Do they bother you?"

"Well, yes, but not as much as they bother you. They like the smell of new blood."

The others thought this was mighty funny. So paradise was not such a paradise.

"Do you have biting insects all the time?" I asked, half in jest.

"Many," was the reply. "We call these *mocúzari* or black flies. They bite us a little but they love outsiders. In May we have *motéquichi,* or what the castellanos call *bobitos.* They swarm in our ears and noses so badly that sometimes we have to cover our faces. Then in June we have *seguá,* called *jejenes* (no-see-ums, vicious biters). When the rains come we get *guajuóy* or mosquitoes, and *muri,* what blancos call *baiburines* (chiggers). They get under your belt and leave a long *roncha* (rash) of bites that itch terribly. Then we have plagues of ordinary *sa'ori* or houseflies as well. We have plenty of insects! The scorpions, spiders, and centipedes are a nuisance, but we hardly notice them."

Around El Saucito a network of trincheras remained, well built still, but in places in need of supplementation by fences. I asked Cipriano who had built the old, solid stone walls. "Nobody knows, David. Maybe it was the ancient Guarijíos, the same ones who left the stone *metates* and pieces of *ollas* everywhere. Those *trincheras* have been here forever."

He took us to another house, scarcely a hundred yards away. A young woman with a powerful, stolid face was holding a toddler to her breast. We sat under an enormous ramada, recently constructed, the posts and *vigas* of the freshly hewn logs of mauto, *palo colorado* and amapa. The young woman was Cipriano's oldest daughter Maximiana, twenty-three years old. She was married to a Guarijío named Lolo Macari who at the time was out punching cows. I remarked to Cipriano that from the looks of the ramada and the well-built house, he was an industrious fellow, indeed.

Cipriano nodded with satisfaction.

We had hardly sat when Maximiana sprang up and walked briskly into the house. There were a few squeals and oinks, and a small pig ran out, chased by a little boy of four or five, who hurled stones at the wretched creature. It stumbled as it scrambled up the hill. It ran clumsily, nearly sideways. What was wrong with it, I asked Cipriano.

"It had its spine broken when it was but a piglet," he said. "But they kept it and it eats fine, even if it doesn't walk beautifully." He laughed at the poetry of his pronouncement. Cipriano did not yet have a pig at Jánaco, but he had explained that he really did not like the taste of beef and was not too fond of pork, either. Wild meat was something else, however.[6]

At the end of the ramada hung a stretched cowhide that appeared to have been cured only recently. Guarijíos don't slaughter cows. They sell them. Where did the hide come from? I was about to ask about it when Cipriano told me in a low voice that someone was coming. Juan Enríquez of Burapaco, he said in a hushed tone. I frowned, knowing that the Enríquez family were known as big-time ranchers and had systematically intimidated and threatened the Guarijíos in the struggle for the establishment of the ejido. I heard the clanking of spurs and a tall Mexican about fifty years of age wearing worn cowboy clothes stepped under the ramada. He saluted Cipriano, shook hands and embraced in the Guarijío fashion, speaking a few words in Guarijío. Cipriano then introduced David and me. For some reason I took an instant liking to the chap and congratulated him on his ability to speak the language of the Guarijíos.

He sat on one of the handmade chairs and spoke in Spanish to David and Cipriano as well as me. He was frankly scared by the loss of more cattle. He had lost several more, and a horse as well. When I asked him what was killing them, he answered laconically, *"La rabia"* (rabies).

I sat up straight in my chair. What were the symptoms? Well, he said, the cows foam at the mouth, the cows fall, they act strange, and they die. The veterinarian from the Asociación Ganadera (Cattlemen's Association) pronounced the disease to be rabies, although no tests had yet proved it.

How in the world could it be rabies, I asked. That's a disease of hot weather. It's usually spread by rabid dogs, skunks, *cholugos* (coatimundis), and badgers.

"The government agents believe it's being spread by vampire bats," was the answer, and I immediately realized it could well be so. Mexico's all-out attempt to maximize cattle production had provided ideal habitat for the increasing vampire bat population. Vampires *(Desmodus rotundus)* nest in numerous locations and find the slow moving and numerous cattle much to their liking. They flit nearly silently through the air and land on the ground in the dark near resting cows. Then they literally walk on their modified wings to the sleeping or dormant animals, finding the blood vessels near the skin above the hoofs and around the ears irresistibly attractive. They anaesthetize the skin with their saliva as they bite, and the animal never realizes that its blood is feeding a bat. Even though they lap up the blood and don't suck it, they transmit rabies if they happen to be rabid, as a tiny percentage of them are.

"Don't you vaccinate against it?" I asked Juan.

"Yes, we do," he replied. "But it's hazardous work. They warn us not to prick ourselves with the needles or we could get a dose of live virus. Then we have to get just the right amount of vaccine in the cows. It has to be kept cold or the virus may grow. I'm scared to give the shots."

I explained how the laboratory test for rabies required the brain of the supposedly infected victim. Even more I explained the need for immunization of all the people of the region. Juan was quite well informed about the disease, realizing it spread through the saliva of mammals and could easily attack human victims. The government's involvement to that point had been disappointing, he said. There was talk about fumigating all the known caves of the region to get rid of the vampires, he said, but agreed when I pointed out that that would kill all the beneficial bats as well and leave most of the vampires unaffected, since they roost in trees and on cliffs as well as in caves. With all those plagues of biting insects the people of the monte needed all the help they could get from insect predators, and bats were the best at killing flying bugs. Juan was worried about all their cattle, their families, their future. Juan was not a wealthy man, Cipriano was quick to point out. He was a friend of the Guarijíos, a solid neighbor, a salt of the earth fellow. Furthermore, he was a respected curandero. He was also knowledgeable about plants of the region. Guarijíos and yoris alike came to him with all manner of infirmities and diseases. He was reported to have a high success rate. He never demanded money. He treated all people with respect. He didn't fit in with my image of a racist exploiter.

We talked about rabies for another half hour, then Juan set off on his horse to other settlements to talk with other Guarijíos about the problems wrought by rabies.

We took our time walking back to Jánaco. Melecio scampered back and forth, showing me trees and plants, explaining which make good fence and which make good firewood. I was preoccupied with the rabies scare, since it presented an aspect I had never encountered, a permanent reservoir of the virus, a year-round threat, making permanent immunization a necessity for all in the region, an economic burden the poor folk there could not possibly endure.

Halfway back it dawned on me that no one at El Saucito had been eating. That was remarkable, for ordinarily, at least, someone is eating something. If they had had anything they would have offered us some coffee or a tortilla. The shortage of food must have been real; the urgency of the task assigned to those two fellows we had met on the trail grew even greater. Without government largesse or at least until summer rains came once again to the Guarijío lands, the people would have a hard time obtaining enough food to eat. It would be another ten months before a crop of corn could be harvested.

At Jánaco the women were happy to have us back. Cipriano told them the latest news, which they absorbed greedily. The isolation of women must be overwhelming at times, I thought. Dolores from the top of the knoll had a picture window to an open world, but many days must go by when there is no one to talk to except her daughters.

We slapped at the black flies as we sat looking once again over the great valley and the mountains beyond. I pulled my binoculars from my pack and showed them to Cipriano, explaining how to focus. He laughed loudly when things came into view. "Everything is close, so close!" he exclaimed. He peered for a long while, closing in on places and objects long familiar from a distance, now available for closer inspection. After he had his fill he handed them to Melecio, who erupted into gales of delight. *"¡Que grande es todo!"* (How big everything is), he exclaimed. He kept the glasses to his eyes, then, unable to contain his excitement, showed Benita how to use them. One by one the children passed the binoculars around. Two-year-old Cruz was afraid to look and shied away into her mother's arms. When her turn came, Dolores wiped her hands on her apron, then clasped them in hesitation, then in anticipation. Cipriano urged her on. Timidly she put them to her eyes and I watched with delight as her face broke into immense happiness. She gave a smile of exhilaration and handed them back to Melecio as though the experience was more than she could comprehend.

I supposed that binoculars might prove useful to a cowman and suggested to Cipriano that I might bring him

a pair. He nodded, but then added, "What I need even more is a *cachimba* (headlamp)."

"A headlamp?" I repeated. "Very well, but what do you use it for?"

"Para venadear (For deer hunting). With the lamp I can find the deer's eyes at night when they are easy to shoot."

I agreed uneasily, hoping that the introduction of night hunting would not make undue inroads on an already diminishing deer population. A look at the vast expanses to the north suggested, however, that ample areas in which deer can run unmolested still remain in the Guarijío lands.

Cipriano then sent Melecio off down the hill to find the burro. Ten minutes later he was back, driving the patient beast into the compound and closing the gate behind him, but not before twirling a rope and lassoing the tolerant burro, to a hearty applause by David and me. "We want to make sure he is here in the morning so we can load him up," Cipriano informed me. Obviously he had done this a multitude of times before. I went over to the burro and patted it while Melecio tied it up. "What is the burro's name?" I asked. I could not imagine a boy having a burro without naming it. "Tonchi," he answered, smiling. What a fine name! Tonchi is the local name for the fruit of a milkweed vine. When young and tender it is edible by humans. The slightest scratch causes silvery milk to ooze from the scratch.

Dolores once again served us beans and tortillas as we watched the moon, nearly half by now, rising above the mountains. Before long it was dark and I suggested we all view the moon through the binoculars. Cipriano looked for a long time, followed by Melecio, whose voice once again rang out in delight, *"¡Ay, que grande es la luna!"* (Look how big the moon is!) Then the others looked as well. Benita looked for a long while without saying a word, then looked again when the others had finished. Melecio tracked an airliner's flight lights with great interest.

"Can you see the rabbit in the moon?" Cipriano asked me.

I laughed, saying that I had had trouble figuring out the Man in the Moon and the Old Lady Gathering Sticks, but now I would try to see the rabbit. He described and I found, or thought I found, the image of a rabbit.

"Do you know why there is a rabbit in the moon?" He asked.

"No, but I'd like you to tell me the story," I replied.

"Good, because I love to tell this story. In fact I have dozens of stories I like to tell. La Tere [Valdivia Dounce, Mexican anthropologist] has recorded some of them and says she wants to put them in a book!"

He proceeded to relate a long story about a rabbit that repeatedly tricked a coyote, each episode proving how foolish the coyote was, and how in the end the rabbit flew off into the heavens and appeared on the moon. At each episode Melecio broke into gales of laughter. I watched his face, illuminated by the moon and the flames of the campfire. He was a study in delight. He had heard this story many, many times, but never wearied of hearing of the clever exploits of the rabbit and the stupidity of the coyote. At the end, when the rabbit made a complete fool of the coyote, he nearly fell out of his chair laughing. Someday Melecio will be relating stories around a campfire himself, delighting his and other children with his anecdotes and clever lines. At least I hoped he would.

Cipriano had no stories to tell about famous or legendary Guarijíos. He apologized for the "backwardness" of his people, as he put it. Mayos and Yaquis have famous leaders, heroes, and villains, but Cipriano didn't mention any Guarijío who would qualify. Apart from his collaborator, the late José Zazueta, who, he relates, fearlessly pursued his mission to get land for the Guarijíos, he named no historical figures.[7] He said only that the tuburada was what makes the Guarijíos what they are. A hero, a legendary figure, a revolutionary, a fiery orator, a prophet, any of these could have galvanized the Guarijíos into action. None came forth until the most humble José Zazueta and Cipriano Buitimea emerged from anonymity to guide them toward fulfillment of their deepest desire, possession of their own lands, the Guarijíos' ancestral lands.

These were the lands they wanted. Those below in the valley were too flat and hot. Those above in the higher sierras were too cold. Where they lived, the lands were just right.

Dolores brought us some tea made of gordolobo, which Cipriano had promised me in the morning. He said it was the best remedy for colds. They always kept a supply of the dried flowers around.

"Do you cure people," I asked, knowing he did, for he had suggested I make a tea the previous night from the bark of the torote prieto and copalquín.

"Yes, I help when I can," he confessed. "Sometimes I help deliver babies. We don't have a *partera* (midwife) around, so I do what I can. When people are sick and the doctor isn't at La Junta or they can't go to San Bernardo or Alamos for *pastillas* (pills) I make remedies for them from the plants and animals around here."

"Do they pay you," I asked, unable to resist.

"Most of the Guarijíos are too poor to pay. They will give me some food, some tortillas, or a little venison, or maybe a *guari* or some honey they have found in a *panal* [hive of comb honey]. They always give me something when I cure them. Most of the time I am successful. But people here, the Guarijíos come to us from all around, even from Bavícora. We use whatever we can to help cure them, or to help bring babies into the world. That's why I'm always interested in finding new remedies. If I see a plant I don't know I like to taste or smell it. Maybe it will be a new remedy. (See the description of *Bursera simaruba*, p. 188)

He paused. "Sometimes, though, the people who come are very sick. Sometimes the children are so sick they look as though they will die. Then I wish we had a doctor."

So did I.

We talked for another hour. The chill of the night deepened. "You are leaving in the morning, is that right, David?" Cipriano asked.

I told him we needed to go, had schedules, other work that needed doing.

"I will miss talking to you. As you can see, even though I'm a Guarijío, I love talking to people, people who know things. I talk to my family and I love them, but somehow, well, the women, they don't understand things, they don't seem to know much about the things out there in the world. Do you understand? Even around here," and he gestured into the vast country around him, "I don't have *con quien platicar* (people to chat with)."

I told him I understood well how he felt. His conversations with me were something I valued deeply.

"We Guarijíos like the gringos to come," he told David and me. "The *blancos* come up here and they don't like to walk around with us. They would rather be on horses and go somewhere and come back the same day. They show disdain for us because we walk and don't ride. The gringos walk the *caminos* the way the Guarijíos do. "*A pie*, (on foot) I tell the *blancos*. That's why we welcome them."

This was gratifying. I thought of gringos who had proceeded me—Ted Faubert, Barney Burns (see Fontana, Faubert, and Burns 1977), and Wick Miller—and silently thanked them for the respect and sensitivity with which they treated the Guarijíos. They had made my work easier.

We talked on into the night. Melecio added wood to the fire from time to time, placing logs in the four corners of the fire so they could gradually be pushed toward the center. Fire somehow cuts across cultures and attacks the depths of the soul. No one can resist staring into a fire on a dark, chilly night. Even the appearance of fire warms the body. I discovered many years ago that fire also obscures and pulls us from nature by diverting our attention from night sounds and night visions. I learned that to appreciate the night I had to sit without fire and listen. I figured that by not consuming firewood I was helping nature and learning more. I forced my views on others who seemed to agree. And so I still spend my nights. But when Cipriano already had a fire, I loved every second of it. Our susceptibility to hypnotism by fire is a genetic disposition derived from our deepest primitive origins. Some day the human genome people will locate a gene specific to hypnotism by campfire. Heaven knows if we should delete or enhance the gene.

Presently Dolores materialized from the darkness, walking lightly and quickly up to the fire and murmured something to Cipriano. He looked up and gestured toward the back of the hut. A few minutes later Melecio appeared in the same way and added something in a low, excited voice. I thought I deciphered the word *yori*. What was going on, I asked, to cause all the excitement.

"Someone is coming," he said, matter-of-factly. "Maybe a yori."

I felt a twinge of uneasiness. Once before I had been tied up and robbed camping in the mountains not far away. This was surely a safe, isolated place, however, I told myself.

Perfectly safe.

Benita tiptoed in with another report. *Yori*. I heard the word again.

"Would the yoris be looking for David and me?" I asked, trying not to appear concerned.

"No," he said calmly, "no."

Now Melecio appeared, even more excited. He spoke aloud but in a barely audible voice. Cipriano nodded, and the lad evaporated from the fire area.

Next came Dolores a second time, her face shining. This time I heard the word *Guarijío*.

I had to find out. "Who's coming, Cipriano?"

"It's a Guarijío."

Two more furtive reports. Then, "It's some Guarijíos from Todos Santos [a tiny settlement, perhaps ten miles away on the Guajaray]. They are coming to visit. They're relatives, a fellow named Ricardo Ciriaco." I mentioned that I knew his father.

"How soon will they get here?" The first report had been fifteen minutes ago. No dog had barked.

Cipriano smiled. "Look behind you." No more than twenty feet away a family of four, barely visible in the half-moon light, stood motionless, accompanied by two burros.

They were speaking almost silently with Dolores.

"How did they get here without making any noise?" I asked Cipriano, astonished that the group could have arrived unnoticed by what I viewed as my experienced outdoorsman's ears.

"They are Guarijíos. We move very quietly."

Ricardo approached the fire and shook hands silently in the noiseless Guarijío way. He held a small boy of three who clung to him tightly, staring all the while at the alien gringo faces.

We chatted just enough for me to make Ricardo's acquaintance and convince him that I was not a mere newcomer. He was reserved, but friendly. Then it dawned on me that my presence was an impediment to the reunion of the two families. I retired to my tent and David to his petate.

I did not sleep long. Hoofbeats near my head awakened me. Many of them. I yanked open the zippered door and looked out. In the moonlight at least twenty horses were staring at me, milling around the flat. I put on my boots and thumped out of the tent. I gave a loud "Hyah," and hurled a couple of rocks at the dark figures. They stampeded away, down the hill and into the deep underbrush below. I congratulated myself, dusted off my hands, returned to the tent, and fell asleep.

No more than a half hour later I heard the sound again. This time there were even more horses. Again I exploded from the tent and drove them off. Again they returned. And so went the night. This time I had no help from Cipriano, who was asleep with his guests in the comfort of the fence and house. That was one of my longest nights.

In the morning Cipriano told me the ejido had more than twenty-five horses and a few mules plus many burros. The government was encouraging them to raise pack animals and horses, he said. He did not understand why. After all, he remarked, horses and mules eat much more forage than cows and are more destructive. They could not sell the animals for food and did not know what to do with them. Couldn't they just get rid of most of them? He shrugged. Something was happening here that he was not prepared to deal with. I figured it was a way the government had of making the Guarijíos into cowboys who would look after not only their own herds but also be a reservoir of cheap cowboy labor for nearby private ranches as well. The Guarijíos had been liberated from serfdom, only to become "free" laborers under the same conditions. But that was a cynical conclusion based only on my suspicions.

By nine o'clock we had breakfasted and packed. I collapsed the tent and stuffed it into its bag, much to the amusement and entertainment of the Guarijíos. The burros were loaded and we were prepared to leave. Ricardo's wife had still not appeared. The Guarijío modesty or reserve kept her hidden in the hut. Finally, as we were about to step off into the bush, I spied her standing next to Dolores at the stove. She stared at the ground when I greeted her. I bade all the women good bye. Dolores had an air of immense satisfaction on her face in the presence of other womenfolk in her home.

The long walk back to San Pedro gave me time for reflection. Ricardo had shown up in time to assist Cipriano in building some new fence to create more pastures so that stock could be rotated. That meant they intended to increase their stock numbers. The government provided them with barbed wire, but they had to provide their own posts. Melecio told me proudly of the fence posts they would cut—*chopo, cacachila,* mauto, and palo colorado.

Cipriano showed me two mahuechis along the pathway, one where he had planted a crop of *ajonjolí* (sesame seed) as a cash crop. The plants fared poorly in the drought and he received only about $25 for the entire harvest and all his work. In the other he hoped to plant corn and beans, if the summer rains came, that is. He demonstrated the work involved, cutting down the trees, clearing away the shrubs, pulling the weeds, burning off the slash, then breaking the soil with a heavy stick or pick and planting the seed. It was backbreaking work and he looked forward to it eagerly. He hoped to combine beans with the corn, but would have to purchase seed, for the failed crops and famine of recent years had left him with no seed at all.

Was there enough land for all? Oh, yes, he thought. The ejido of Los Bajíos contained six thousand hectares, about fifteen thousand acres. That should be ample for the seventy families of the ejido, he thought.

"When we were involved in the *lucha* we met with some Yaquis from down below," he said. "They respected us and assisted us and were generous. They said 'Come live with us; we have plenty of land. There is room here for the Guarijío.' But we are people of the *monte* and the *sierra,* not of the coast. We love the hills and the valleys and arroyos and love to live apart from others. Down there it is terribly hot and humid and people have to live close together. The *blancos* never leave them in peace. Here I can have my *mahuechi* and work it just as I please without worrying about other people."

And so it is, for now.

His only complaint is the failure of the government to provide a road to Los Bajíos. "They promised it would be built, but they never finished it. We have to carry all the materials for the school in by mules and burros. Ay! The work it takes. But that is the only big problem we have."

Now some of the *ejidatarios* want cars, he says. They want highways built into the monte so they can drive, just like the blancos. "I tell them, we have our land. We don't need cars. We'll spend all of our money on cars and it will be noisy here and all manner of outsiders will come here to bother us. Better to live like Guarijío than like yoris."

At San Pedro it took but a few minutes to unpack the burros and load our trappings into the truck. I paid Cipriano and bid the others good-bye. He wanted to know when I would come back, for he had other places to take me. I told him it would be soon, and that next time I would stay longer and we would walk farther, that I liked the Guarijío custom of walking the caminos. Then David and I were off and Cipriano, Ricardo, and Melecio disappeared into the heavy brush along the trail back to Jánaco and the waiting fences. As we drove from the Guarijío lands I wondered how many vampire bats were waiting to visit their plague on the poor people of the Upper Mayo.

I learned later that the sickness visiting the cattle was a pseudo-rabies, a virus that kills cows but does not infect people. That was a relief. The government, late in the game, I fear, provided low-cost vaccine and the herds were all vaccinated. The Guarijíos lost some twenty cows, a small fortune for people with next to nothing. But the government, I heard, will replace the lost cattle as well. They want the Guarijíos to become cattlemen. So far the Guarijíos are going along with the scheme.

According to a young Guarijío, in 1998 members of the Los Bajíos ejido were about to vote whether or not to divide the land among themselves and allocate individual parcels. In 1999 while Cipriano and his family were visiting elsewhere, his house was broken into by a cow and the walls were damaged considerably. Cipriano announced his intention to move from Jánaco to Los Estrao, where there is a school and vaccinations for children are made available at regular intervals. It is not a particularly pretty place.

3
Guarijíos

A HISTORICAL SKETCH

In 1994 Mexican anthropologist Teresa Valdivia Dounce published *Como una huella pintada* (*Like a Painted Footprint*) (Buitimea Romero and Valdivia Dounce 1994), a short autobiography of Cipriano Buitimea Romero. Tere wove the manuscript from dozens of hours of taped conversations with Cipriano. I read it a month after I had spent several days with him. His written words forced me to take a more measured perspective of the Guarijíos' relation to the "outer" world of the mestizos. The shy, retiring Guarijíos, it turned out, were successful revolutionaries.

I also thought back to when I heard Cipriano and Juan Enríquez talking about the rabies scare and the death of a small herd of cows from the epidemic. The tough reality of life in Guarijío lands tempered my westerner's idealization of what I had seen—or thought I had seen. Even with the bugs, the heat, the grueling work, and the uncertainties wrought by the drought, the Guarijíos' life had *seemed* idyllic. In fact, the reality of Guarijío life until recently included starvation, disease, and political repression. Even today the Guarijíos' existence as a people is tenuous as they struggle to survive in a part of the world that does not graciously yield to human needs and to preserve their ways in a world whose indifferent economics seek to annihilate them as a distinct culture.

So I accepted the fact that Guarijío life cannot realistically be understood in isolation. Guarijíos may live and move on the fringes of the global economy, but they cannot escape it. In my travels from the sophisticated cities to the underdeveloped countryside, it was easy to exalt their way of life as that of primitive folk in the state of nature. That is, of course, utter nonsense. To understand their place in the world I needed to find out how the Guarijíos came to be what they are today. History gets us to where we are. Here is what I have found, told with impossible brevity. I do not hesitate to speculate in this narrative. I hope that a more detailed history of the Guarijíos will soon be available.

Few outsiders have even heard of Guarijíos. In Alamos and Navojoa, the nearest urban areas of consequence, the

name is nearly unknown. I suspect that that is fine with the Guarijíos. Centuries before Hernán Cortés set foot on the Mexican mainland at Veracruz and began the European conquest of Mexico, they had already settled in the profound canyons and mountains of southern Sonora and adjacent southwestern Chihuahua. The lands they chose for a homeland are as tough and stingy as any in Mexico, a seemingly unending series of peaks, canyons, ramparts, and gorges. The valleys are narrow, the mesas few, and the soils young and thin. It is as if the topography dares humans to plant a crop. The unreliability of rain adds a snicker from the rain god when they do. That tortured terrain cannot sustain even a small urban population. Then, as now, they must have lived in isolated small settlements.

In the lower reaches of these lands grow dense and vast stands of tropical deciduous forest—its farthest northern reach in the Western Hemisphere. The lowland, river Guarijíos, *Guarijíos del río,* as we shall call them, know this complex plant community as well as any people in the world. Above the intricate and varied tropical habitat is a belt of twenty or so different oaks. Still higher grow forests of a dozen different pines interspersed with palms and orchids that join the oaks. These latter regimes are intimately known to the highland or mountain Guarijíos, the *Guarijíos de la sierra.*

The Guarijíos' territory is small—their ejidos[1] and adjoining lands (the majority owned by non-Indians) are only slightly larger than Rhode Island—surrounded by more developed regions and areas populated by more cosmopolitan folk. Yet within this "island," Guarijíos continue to subsist in some of the most isolated settlements in all of Mexico. Places like Basicorepa, Los Bajíos, Bavícora, Guasisaco, Jogüegüe, and Tojíachi have never been visited except on foot or beastback or by military helicopter.[2]

To outsiders Guarijíos, or Macurahui, as the river Guarijíos sometimes call themselves,[3] appear variously as a reclusive, taciturn, or suspicious people. Among themselves they are none of these, and if the above adjectives do apply to their intercourse with non-Guarijíos, it is with good reason. They have suffered greatly at the hands of the conquering Spaniards and the dominant Mexican culture after them. They have known centuries of famine, hunger, beatings, rapes, massacres, and early death. Several Guarijíos with whom I chatted found both amusing and insulting, for example, the claims that they were "discovered" in the mid-1970s. They have roamed, hunted, and cropped their lands for hundreds of years and have never felt discovered.

The Guarijíos were also referred to historically as Uarojíos, Varohíos, and Warihíos. They inhabit the lower and mid ranges of the Sierra Madre Occidental of southeastern Sonora and southwestern Chihuahua (Almada 1937; Gentry 1942, 1963; Hadley and Gentry 1995; Pérez de Ribas 1645; Sauer 1935). They speak a language closely related to that of their neighbors to the northeast, the Rarámuri (Tarahumaras) of the higher Chihuahuan sierras and in the great barrancas that drain them (Miller 1996). Nearly all Guarijíos live in the basin of the Río Mayo sandwiched between the Tarahumaras and the Mayos of the low foothills and coast of Sonora to the southwest. Their principal landmark is the Río Mayo that empties into the Gulf of California just south of Huatabampo, Sonora some eighty kilometers south of the Guarijíos' southern outpost at San Bernardo.[4] Chihuahuan Guarijíos live primarily within a fifty-kilometer radius of Loreto, Chihuahua in the *municipio* (county) of Uruáchic, while Sonoran Guarijíos are found within a fifty-kilometer radius of Mesa Colorada on the Río Mayo, in the municipio of Alamos. The two groups speak substantially different dialects and profess varying degrees of difficulty understanding each other. Hinton (1983:333) believed that by the 1970s the Guarijíos del río were losing their identity, while the Guarijíos de la sierra remained distinct. I shall describe below my reasons for thinking the situation is just the opposite.

When the conquering Spaniards arrived in northwest Mexico in the early seventeenth century, Guarijío lands extended considerably more to the east and south than they do now. Their territory was the broken, isolated mountain and canyon country of the western Sierra Madre now included in the state of Chihuahua, probably reaching to the east and south of Chínipas, perhaps extending into limited portions of Sinaloa.[5] They apparently preferred settlements of no more than a few families, as they do today, rather than the larger towns typical of the Cáhitas (extinct groups such as Ahomes, Tehuecos, and Zuaques, and the contemporary Mayos and Yaquis) to the south and west. Gentry (1942) suggested that prior to the twentieth century maize might not have been as central to the Guarijíos' diet as it was for other indigenous Mexican peoples. He suspected that Guarijíos subsisted on wild and gathered materials far more than either Tarahumaras or Cáhitas.

No record exists of the Guarijíos' pre-Columbian social organization, but brief accounts of early missionaries describe them as combining gathering and fishing with limited swidden or shifting agriculture. Guarijíos of the Arroyo Guajaray believe their ancestors lived in abundant and large caves, which are seen along certain reaches of the river. They point to remnants of baskets, palm mats, hides, embers, and rock paintings, as fragments left by generations of their ancestors. Their oral traditions speak of their forebears as having been cave dwellers as well as dwelling in huts near water sources. Their numbers may have been as many as seven thousand[6] (Sauer 1935:23) at the time of contact with Europeans, compared with the roughly eighteen hundred that survive.[7]

While the early Guarijíos probably lived in dispersed, small hamlets, they were bound by a common identity, linguistic and cultural, for they were known even then to the Spaniards as Varohíos or Uarojíos. The many settlements were isolated from each other by steep mountains and precipitous canyons. Sauer (1935:22) considered them "the most primitive" people in the region. They successfully organized against the Spaniards, however, and developed a reputation as a tough and mean people, so they must have had well-established communications among themselves. They early developed a reputation as secretive, solitary, and resistant to Christianity.

The earliest documented references to Guarijíos are from Pérez de Ribas (1645) and other Jesuits, who made only brief references to the "Varohíos" and their warlike ways in the early to middle seventeenth century.[8] Pérez de Ribas noted that Varohíos were the most numerous of the various indigenous groups who lived in the sierras. Almada (1937:37) reports (without citation) that Fr. Padre Pascual baptized "Uarojíos" in 1626 in a crudely constructed church on a branch of the Río Fuerte.[9] At that time the Guarijíos apparently practiced agriculture on small riverside plots, supplementing their crops with hunting and fishing in the Río Chínipas or Oteros. In addition to evangelizing the pagan natives, the Jesuit missionary activity was apparently intended to "pacify" the Guarijíos, in the process making the adjacent lands safe for extracting gold and silver that recently had been discovered (1937:38). In early 1632, Guarijíos allied themselves with the Guazapares (a neighboring but linguistically distinct group,) and revolted against Spanish dominance, murdering two Jesuit missionaries and a number of their flock, and despoiling their bodies. Thus the Guarijíos gained a reputation as being fierce, resistant to "reduction" around missions, and violent.[10] In reprisal the Spaniards sent a military expedition to avenge the Jesuits' death and teach the Guarijíos a lesson. In the encounter, eight hundred Guarijíos and Guazapares were killed, and a large number, especially women and children, were captured and shipped to missions in Sinaloa. The remainder fled to the wild canyon country where they hid from soldiers and missionaries for more than thirty years.[11] Almada notes the founding (at an unspecified date) by Jesuits of La Misión de Nuestra Señora de Uarojíos near the present-day Chihuahuan village of Guadalupe Victoria. It was sacked during the uprising of the Guazapares and Guarijíos of 1632 and still lay in ruins on a private ranch in the 1930s (1937:18).

From this point in the narrative, the uprising of 1632 until the twentieth century, I rely nearly exclusively on *Apuntes históricos de la región de Chínipas,* the account written in 1937 by Francisco Almada, the renowned Chihuahua historian.[12] In addition to the Jesuit archives and other materials from the Chihuahua State archives and the National General Archives in Mexico City, Almada made extensive use of archival materials from the Chihuahua town of Chínipas.[13] For 150 years, Guarijío missions were administered from Chínipas, hence the importance of the place.

In the absence of Spanish influence following the uprising of 1632, the Guarijíos reestablished their previous way of life in the sierras.[14] In 1652 Fr. Alonso Flores founded a mission at Baboyahui (in present-day Sonora, near where it borders with Sinaloa and Chihuahua). He considered this the gateway to the sierras and a base from which to launch the pacification of pagan and wild Guarijíos who were thought to frequent sierras north and west of the new mission. Flores died after only one year, and the mission folded.

After the death of Flores, the Guarijíos appear to have been free of evangelism until 1675 when two Jesuits, Frs. Pecoro and Prado founded the mission of Santa Inez at Chínipas. With the new mission as a base, they undertook the reduction of the people known as the Chínipas. This accomplished, they then traveled north into Guarijío country. Pecoro visited the Guarijío settlement formerly occupied by the mission of Guadalupe Victoria. He was received coldly by the Guarijíos and was warned that his life was in danger. Much to his surprise, however, the Guarijíos abruptly had a change of heart and invited him to establish a presence among them, and the Mission of Guadalupe Victoria was refounded. Shortly thereafter the padres also founded missions at Santa Ana and at Loreto, some thirty kilometers to the north, where many Guarijíos live today. Fr. Prado also founded a mission at Caramechi on the Río Mayo, the only location mentioned in extant Jesuit archives that pertains to the current Guarijíos del río. The mission activity extended to the east as well, and

several other Guarijío villages, now vanished, received ministrations from the padres (Almada 1937:60).

Pecoro and Prado reported that the Guarijíos of the region lived in *rancherías* (small settlements), dwelling in huts along the banks of streams where they fished and raised corn on adjoining fields. Their language was closely related to Tarahumara, with whom they appear to have intermarried, according to the Jesuits.[15] In 1678 the mission of Guadalupe Victoria was inspected by Padre Juan Ortiz de Zapata who made the following observations:

> Six leagues to the north [of Chínipas] and somewhat to the east is the pueblo of Our Lady of Guadalupe de Uarojíos . . . called Tajírachi by the natives. . . . It is situated on the banks of the Río Oteros, in the district of Chínipas or Gorojaqui, which is the Guarijío name for Santa Inez [Chínipas]. Guadalupe consists of 85 families and 290 persons. The natives are now as well behaved as those of Santa Inez, demonstrating the effect of their having embraced the true faith and the letter of the doctrines. The language in both pueblos is Guarijío and according to those who know, it is the same as Tarahumara, although it differs slightly, especially in its grammar.[16] (Almada 1937:64, translation mine)

Next Padre Juan described Loreto:

> Seventeen leagues to the north, slightly to the east of Santa Inez, is the pueblo of Our Lady of Loreto of the Uarojíos, the farthest village of the department of Guadalupe, which is only six leagues from Santa Inez, along an extremely rough and overgrown trail. This pueblo is situated along a stream in a small valley formed by lofty ranges. Fifty-seven families that number 269 persons of both sexes and all ages dwell therein. The natives, only recently converted, are in their customs, language, and behavior, similar to those of Santa Inez. The pueblo is called Sinoyeca in their language. They have borrowed a small shrine where the rites of the divine office can be celebrated, and they hope to found a larger church. In the vicinity of the village paganism remains entrenched, which the holy yoke of the Blessed Evangel endeavors to overcome. (Almada 1937:65, translation mine)

Fr. Juan also noted missions of Batopilillas and Gosogachi among the Guarijíos, settlements that remain inhabited to this day but are purely mestizo.

The Jesuits' goals were simple: stamp out the "primitive" beliefs and "savage" customs of the indigenous people, build churches, baptize as many natives as possible, teach them European agriculture (cattle raising, planting wheat, and growing fruit trees), and above all, obtain by faith or by force the natives' submission to the Spanish Crown. As Almada notes, the early Jesuits were the true *conquistadores* of the region (Almada 1937:71).

In 1696 Tarahumaras of the high sierras and canyons to the east of Guarijío country, rose in rebellion against Spanish rule. They had rebelled before, in 1648, 1650, 1652, and 1690 (Spicer 1962:33-36), but the latest uprising was especially violent. Tarahumaras had been forced to labor against their will in the recently opened silver mines in the sierras where working conditions were ghastly, the hours interminable, and the benefits none. The Jesuits, who purportedly protested the enslavement of Tarahumara miners, forced Tarahumaras into "reduced" missions and made them work for the missions without pay. Furthermore, the priests applied corporal punishment to all native peoples who failed to observe the required Catholic practices. The rebellion engulfed the Tarahumara region, inflaming the passions of most of the indigenous people of the sierras, including Guarijíos and Pimas, and threatened to spread well beyond the Tarahumara country.

By 1697 at least some Guarijíos had joined ranks with the rebels. The church at Batopilillas was sacked and burned (Almada 1937:81)[17] causing priests of other Guarijío settlements to fear for their lives. The exception was Loreto, whose missionised natives apparently remained loyal to their priest. They formed a bow-and-arrow militia to defend the Loreto mission from rebel attackers and their allies. They were never tested in battle, however, and appear to have disbanded quickly. Meanwhile, General Retana, the Spanish commander in charge of putting down the rebellion, ordered a squadron from Alamos to be stationed at Guadalupe Victoria to assure that the Guarijíos of that settlement did not rise up in sympathy with the Tarahumaras. There the Spanish troops were augmented by a reported force of several hundred Guarijíos and Chínipas recruited by the priests. This small army proceeded north and surprised the tiny battalion of rebels near Batopilillas. They took several rebel prisoners, while suffering minimal loss (84). Shortly thereafter, the Spanish commander ordered the execution of the captured Guarijíos and their captured allies in the plaza of Santa Ana. The Spanish squadron then made a surprise attack on Batopilillas, burning the villager's stores of corn. The attempt to take Batopilillas was repulsed, however, and a combined force of Tarahumaras and, apparently, Mountain Pimas and Guarijíos roundly defeated the Spanish forces and their allies, forcing them to retreat along the road to Loreto.[18] The Guarijío and Chínipas auxiliaries seem to have lost heart and fled to less hazardous locales. The Spanish discovered that by burning the crops, they had managed to alienate those natives (a majority) who up to that point had remained loyal to the Spaniards. The Spaniards, without indigenous backup, felt compelled to abandon Loreto, fearing it could not be defended. The priests were of little help, for they were occupied in healing their wounded Indian charges. Even General Retana's Spanish recruits wished to return to Alamos, having no desire to risk their all in what appeared to be a futile attempt to subdue the unsubduable (90). Spanish troops in full retreat arrived at Loreto only to find it abandoned. They feared an ambush by its former inhabitants, concluding wisely that the conversion of Guarijíos had been insufficient to overcome deeper and more historic loyalties and had not erased the memory of recent atrocities visited upon them by the Europeans.

Time was on the Spaniards' side, however. In 1698 Spanish forces crushed the rebellion at the cost of thousands of Tarahumara dead. Furthermore, the rebel Guarijíos had been too busy fighting to plant crops in 1697, and by the winter natives of the region were facing starvation. The well-supplied Spaniards offered them food if they would agree to locate in three villages—Guadalupe Victoria, Santa Ana, and Chínipas—where they would reside under the benevolent scrutiny and tutelage of priests and the Spanish armed forces. The Guarijíos agreed and took up residence near the mission. Even so, for the next two years the region was rife with rumors of new uprisings. Military leaders were on constant alert and colonists and missionaries alike walked the earth uneasily.

Sometime after 1700 a new mission was founded in Batopilillas, and the priest and army permitted former inhabitants who had been exiled to the three garrisoned villages to return home. Only three years later, however, whispers of rebellion once again spread throughout the region. The Spaniards viewed the rumors with alarm.

In late 1704, five (presumed) Guarijíos of Batopilillas were reported to Spanish authorities by the local priest for attempting to incite the region to rebellion. They were speedily arrested. The apprehending officers were under strict orders from the provincial authorities not to execute the offenders without express authorization from the provincial governor. A few months later three of the accused were transported to Chínipas, along with a chieftain of Loreto named Cosme. He had been arrested and was also being transferred to the lowlands to answer accusations that he practiced witchcraft (i.e., continued to practice Guarijíos pre-Columbian religion). Cosme, who had a long history of unruliness, was "accidentally" killed along the way, purportedly choking on the reins while falling from a horse, an early example of *la ley fuga* whereby prisoners were executed while supposedly trying to escape. Charges against the others were dismissed for lack of evidence. This entire incident demonstrates a remarkable change in Spanish administration, showing an increased awareness by the government that the continued assassination and harassment of indigenous people had resulted in unending rebellions and a general hatred of Spaniards and their institutions. On the other hand, the use of la ley fuga against Cosme illustrated a convenient means of executing unpopular prisoners when higher authorities might be lenient with the putative offender.

The trials of maintaining administrative authority from a distance over a wide, topographically disordered region fraught with uncooperative natives led the Spanish authorities to create a more local administrative department known as Baja Tarahumara. It included much of the western Sierra Madre of present-day Chihuahua and Sonora, such settlements as Chínipas, Batopilillas, and Santa Ana, but not Loreto, which had been abandoned.

In 1714 a new challenge to Jesuit/Spanish domination of the Guarijíos appeared. The mission priest from Batopilillas complained to military authorities in Chínipas that an apostate group of Guarijíos living in a remote settlement refused to acknowledge his authority. He requested military assistance to force compliance among his charges. The unruly bunch were Guarijíos who had taken up residence in the vicinity of Babarocos on the Río Mayo, a region of profound canyons and towering cliffs. They had rejected the restrictions of mission life and were living lives of pagan dissipation.[19] To add to the priests' frustration, the insubordinates settled in terrain so rough and inaccessible it was doubtful that they could easily be brought to submission even by military force. The missionaries complained that they repeatedly called on these apostates to submit to their rule, but the Guarijíos stubbornly refused, mocking the pleas of the priests (Almada 1937:111). Military authorities in vain

tried to lure them into joining the reduced populations at Chínipas, offering them food and protection in return for submission, but the Guarijíos ignored the entreaties and threats and continued happily in their independent and heathen ways.

The provincial governor called a council of war, hoping to devise a strategy for corralling the apostates and forcing them to missions at Parral (in Chihuahua) or Chínipas. He decided on direct military attack and organized a squadron of Pimas for this purpose. The terrain was impossibly rough for a straightforward military assault, however, and the Guarijíos fortified an inaccessible site on the cliffs far above the river. From on high they called out to the assembled forces of pacification that they could not possibly descend to meet the Spaniards and their allies congregated below. The terrain was frightfully steep, they lamented (sarcastically), and they feared the precipitous descent. They suggested, however, that if the Spaniards so desired, they could climb up to them and baptize their children. This taunting offer must have been accompanied by wry smiles on the Guarijíos' faces. The captain of the forces considered a siege, but looking around to assess his strength, found that his Pima allies had fled. The siege never even began. In his frustration, he laid waste to the cornfields in the narrow valley and returned to the comforts of Alamos having failed in his mission. Destroying native crops was for the Spaniards a standard measure of desperation and the simplest message they could leave. To the Guarijíos it must have seemed barbarism of which only Europeans were capable.

The Spaniards left the Babarocos Guarijíos alone for several years. In 1718 a new expedition sought once again to dislodge the free-living Guarijíos with the same lack of success. Following this failure, the provincial governor, realizing that military conquest was impractical, decided to take the gospel to the natives rather than force the natives to the mission. He authorized the creation of a new mission zone, and priests were soon assigned to Batopilillas and to Babarocos. The Guarijíos accepted them but only on the condition that the clerics arrive unaccompanied by military personnel. Priests arrived and the difficult task of evangelizing the free-spirited Guarijíos began.

Their results were unimpressive. For years the secular Spanish authorities decried the lack of progress in pacifying the indigenous people of the newly formed ecclesiastical jurisdiction. In 1751 one such authority groused that under the policy of nonconfrontation the natives of Babarocos had for many years lived dissolute, rowdy, and pagan lives (Almada 1937:113). The message was that the velvet glove approach would not work with such avowed heathens. The Guarijíos were not eager to be assimilated into the mores of eighteenth century Europeans.[20]

During this curious period, we see glimpses of the frustrations facing both the secular and ecclesiastical authorities, as well as the limitations of the Jesuits' mission strategy and the Crown's imperial designs. The unconverted Babarocos Guarijíos were hardly a military threat, for they showed no inclination toward rebellion or toward fomenting uprisings. Their numbers were small, no more than two hundred. They seem to have wanted only to be left alone. Yet their example could undo hard-won conversions at places like Loreto and Batopilillas, where constant murmurs of discontent worried the authorities. They knew that Babarocos had extended and ongoing communication with indigenous people throughout the sierras. If the Guarijíos of today can move quickly and unobtrusively through the much-reduced monte, those of the eighteenth century must have been even more capable of stealthy movements in the "natural" environment. The military expenditures required to force the apostates into submission, however, could hardly be justified by the limited chances of success.

So, for the regional governor, turning the matter over to missionaries constituted a frank concession to the impossibility of a military solution. It also established the first historic records regarding Guarijíos on the Río Mayo. Until the 1990s Caramechi, in present-day Sonora, was a Guarijío settlement. San Luis Babarocos, some twenty kilometers upstream at the junction Río Babanori and the Río Mayo, was home to Guarijíos well into the 1950s.

These few missions the Jesuits established among the Guarijíos generally failed, especially in the face of ongoing Guarijío resistance—both passive and active. By the time of the expulsion of the Jesuits in 1767, Babarocos, Batopilillas, Caramechi, Guadalupe Victoria, and Loreto had no resident priest—all were *visitas* of the *cabecera* (religious center) of Santa Ana. That can only mean that mission activity had declined in the region or had ceased altogether in some missions. Whether this was due to a general evangelical apathy, lassitude or hostility among Guarijíos, a shortage of priests, or a gradual depopulation of Guarijíos is currently impossible to determine. Disease took an enormous toll on indigenous people in the seventeenth century, so numbers may have fallen off so drastically that there were simply not enough potential converts or neophytes to justify a priest.[21] Certainly Guarijíos remained in the region, for Loreto to

this day retains a sizeable Guarijío population, suggesting it retained a strong Guarijío population through time. Portions of the Loreto church can be traced to the eighteenth century (Pablo Enríquez, personal communication, 1999).

Following the Jesuits' expulsion in 1767, the Bishop of Durango ordered an inventory of ecclesiastical property they had left behind.[22] The reports included a large herd of cattle (eighteen hundred head) at Santa Ana and smaller herds of cattle and smaller livestock at Batopilillas (Almada 1937:188). The Jesuits in Sonora had required two days' work from each parishioner (West 1993), and the same was undoubtedly true in the Baja Tarahumara, so it is safe to assume that Guarijíos had been delegated responsibility for caring for the herds. What the Jesuits planned to do with eighteen hundred cows makes for interesting speculation, but they were probably destined to be sold in the mines that were flourishing on the Río Fuerte at Batopilas and Tepago and farther east. The existence of such large cattle herds implies a well-organized force of overseers, primarily indigenous, to guard the herds, move them from pasture to pasture, see to their medical needs, castrate the baby bulls, and drive them to markets. Guarijíos probably became sophisticated cowboys over the years. The potential worth of the herds was considerable and must have raised the investigating Bishop's eyebrows.

The Bishop also ordered an inventory of the contents of the missions. In the report the chapel at Guadalupe Victoria is described as rundown and virtually devoid of religious artifacts. The mission at Santa Ana is described in some detail as an adobe building with a lengthy list of religious paraphernalia, suggesting that the mission had recently been active. The building had been turned over to the custody of an "Indian," undoubtedly a Guarijío (Almada 1937:192–95). The mission compound at Loreto included an adobe chapel with doors and windows and a modest collection of religious accouterments (197). The missions of Batopilillas, Babarocos, and Caramechi are not mentioned.

In 1768, only a year following the expulsion of the Jesuits, the Bishop assigned nine Franciscan monks to fill the Baja Tarahumara missions vacated by the Jesuits. Of the Guarijío missions, only Batopilillas is mentioned as receiving a priest (Fr. Francisco García), although Santa Ana was clearly more important and undoubtedly also had a priest assigned to it. The Bishop ordered a reorganization of the missions of the sierra, placing Guadalupe Victoria under the auspices of Chínipas, Loreto under the auspices of Santa Ana, and Babarocos under Batopilillas.

A Franciscan missionary by the name of Francisco García Figueroa in 1792 describes the three Guarijío settlements:

> The Santa Ana Mission is occupied by Lower Tarahumaras, about seven leagues distant from Chínipas as the crow flies, but fourteen by road. It is situated in a small valley formed by the sierras to the east. It has a small, permanent stream and includes a small visita and a mine. The visita is made up of Tarahumaras, and it is called Loreto. It is north of Santa Ana two leagues as the crow flies and six leagues by road. . . . To the north of Santa Ana is the Mission of Batopilillas, situated in a deep valley alongside a stream with abundant water that runs south to north at a distance from Santa Ana of eight leagues as the crow flies and sixteen leagues by road. It has a *pueblo de visita* called Babarocos, to the northeast at a distance of eight leagues as the crow flies and sixteen by a dangerous road that requires a day and a half to negotiate.[23] It lies in a short valley on the bank of a large and fast-moving river that flows from the northeast to the southwest [the Río Mayo]. (Almada 1937:205, translation mine)

Fr. Francisco makes no distinction between Tarahumaras and Guarijíos. This may simply be a reflection of his recent arrival, or it may suggest that the church no longer distinguished between the two ethnic groups, since their languages were similar. There is no reason to believe that Tarahumaras had replaced Guarijíos of the region. Guarijíos make strong distinctions between the two groups.

Following the arrival of Franciscans, archival references to Guarijíos decreased and then vanished. Nonindigenous settlers gradually populated the region, probably displacing indigenous people in missions, undoubtedly to the disadvantage of the latter. Almada notes that in 1780 a wealthy Spanish mineowner died in the village of Santa Ana. In his will he bequeathed funds for "100 masses in each of the missions of Santa Ana, Chínipas, [and seven others] . . . and 100 in the chapel of Batopilas"[24] (Almada 1937:222). The request indicates a probably strong degree of Hispanization of the missions, implying that the congregations consisted of Spaniards and, undoubtedly, mestizos in addition to Guarijíos. Of Guarijío population numbers, we have no record.

The departure of the Jesuits also had repercussions for the rights of Indians. Almada notes that in 1780 the Mayor of Batopilas issued a decree stating that "no Indian or person of mixed color, shall dare to raise a hand against any Spaniard or decent person [white person]; the penalty shall be fifty lashes and a month in jail" (Almada 1937:222). Indians were indentured to labor in the mines and were not allowed to leave without permission of the owner or boss and without paying a special fee.

In one of Almada's final references to what were undoubtedly Guarijíos, the Captain General of the Baja Tarahumara in 1794 initiated charges against an army lieutenant from Guadalupe Victoria. The charge read that the officer had sanctioned a state of affairs whereby "the Indians adored as gods an Indian named Manuel and an Indian named Lucía, and allowed the Indians to place their local [Indian] governor in stocks and whip him." Furthermore the pragmatic lieutenant had ordered this Lucía "to protect the village from the disease [smallpox] that was approaching from the sierras" (Almada 1937:231). This episode can only mean that the Guarijíos of Guadalupe Victoria were divided. One faction, apparently the majority, wished to return to practicing their primordial beliefs, while the other faction, loyal Christianized converts, tried to prevent the heresy. If the status in Guadalupe Victoria was at all representative of the region, we must assume that Christianity in the region had never taken powerful hold of the indigenous people. The hapless lieutenant must have been a pragmatic soul, preferring to allow the natives to carry on as they pleased rather than risk potentially violent controversy. And maybe he reasoned that Lucía might have been able to prevent smallpox from decimating their village in the way so many others had been devastated.

As gold and silver were discovered and exploited in the region in the later eighteenth and nineteenth centuries, resident Guarijíos were joined by other indigenous people who came to work in the mines. Mayos and Yaquis were especially given to mine work following the Muni rebellions in the mid-eighteenth century (Spicer 1980:125), then in greater numbers as the wars between settlers and Mayos and Yaquis increased in ferocity.[25] Tracing and estimating indigenous populations in the region thus becomes complicated by a diaspora of non-Guarijíos, and the general movement of Mayos, Opatas, and Yaquis well beyond the confines of their aboriginal territory (Spicer 1962). An example is the consternation expressed by regional authorities when they learned that a group of eighty Yaquis settled in Guadalupe Victoria in 1827, during the height of the Juan Banderas rebellion of the Sonoran indigenous groups.[26]

Investigation revealed that the authorities' fears were groundless, for the new residents were "gentle" Yaquis, who only wished to flee the violence in Sonora, and they were permitted to remain though for how long is not documented (271). At roughly the same time the flames of the Banderas rebellion reached the Guarijíos of Babarocos.[27] They expelled their missionary, and he was forced to relocate at the Pima mission of Moris (271). There is no further mention of Guarijío uprisings during the Banderas rebellion or thereafter.

The Franciscan missionary efforts in the Baja Tarahumara were plagued with lack of resources. The missionaries also were forced to contend with the proliferation of boom-and-bust mining activity in the region, which led to social chaos and the politics of Mexican Independence. The Franciscan presence declined drastically, and by 1836, only three missionaries remained to serve the entire region. In 1849 the missions were all secularized (Spicer 1962:318), ending the assignments of the Franciscans along with the continuity that might provide ongoing cultural and historical records.[28] After the secularization, no continuing missionary activity among the Guarijíos is documented. The missions established among the Guarijíos were only intermittently served, if at all, and the whereabouts of any mission archives that might shed light on the Guarijío culture are unknown. Further searching may some day turn up more information on this period, but in the meantime we are left in ignorance.

In the 1960s evangelical Protestants established missionary activity targeting Guarijíos in and around Arechuybo, Chihuahua. Linguists from the Summer Institute of Linguistics have labored since that time at translating the Bible into Guarijío. Guarijíos of both regions have been the object of intense proselytizing efforts by several fundamentalist Christian groups.

All the missions thus mentioned in the Jesuit and Franciscan archives pertain to Guarijíos de la sierra. Of the settlements inhabited by Guarijíos del río, only Caramechi is mentioned in the archives. Places like Bavícora, Conejos, Guajaray, and Mochibampo are absent from the historical record. Between the time of Almada's last references at the end of the eighteenth century and Howard Scott Gentry's classic study *The Warihío Indians of Sonora-Chihuahua: An Ethnographic Survey* (1963) no useful archival records have come to light.[29] Nearly a hundred years of Guarijío history are unrecorded or unknown, and nearly three hundred years of their life in the sierras is viewed only from the viewpoint

of the priests who strove to convert them. Only oral tradition remains to fill in the gap of some six generations. Almada (1937) noted briefly the contemporary existence of Guarijíos:

> Concerning the Uarojíos [Guarijíos], some traces remain, currently referred to as "Uarijíos". They are concentrated in the villages of . . . Santa Ana, Loreto and the ranches of Canelas, Guazaremos, and San Rafael in the municipio of Chínipas and in Babarocos, Jecopaco, Tojíachi, Arechuyvo, Caramechi[30] and other ranches of the municipio of Uruáchi which border the latter, their number being approximately one thousand of both sexes and all ages. (Almada 1937:17)

Almada makes no mention of river Guarijíos; nor did other scholars of his time whose work has come to light.

By the 1930s influential anthropologists generally assumed that Guarijíos had long since been assimilated into other cultures and had vanished as a distinct ethnic people (Hadley and Gentry 1995).[31] Two exceptions were Carl Sauer, the renowned geographer, and Sauer's colleague at the University of California, the anthropologist Alfred L. Kroeber. Kroeber studied the Guarijío language and classified it as Uto-Aztecan (Kroeber 1934). In the 1920s Sauer mapped the languages and distributions of the indigenous people of northwest Mexico and found references to Guarijíos in mission records and the manuscripts of missionary historians. In the early 1930s he visited the region and thought he had found Guarijíos there.[32] Howard Scott Gentry, a student at California, came under Sauer's influence. When Gentry expressed his interest in exploring the Río Mayo region, Sauer urged him to find out if any Guarijíos remained. Sauer had written that Guarijíos were "still a numerous people, little affected by outside influence and living in a most inaccessible and unexploited country" (Sauer 1934:33). He suggested any that remained in Sonora might be found near the small remote town of San Bernardo. Gentry found them there, and between 1933 and 1937 he spent much of his time among them, studying their way of life and especially their uses of plants.

Gentry was, above all, a naturalist in the tradition of Von Humboldt and Darwin. He was obsessed with exploring undescribed lands and collecting exotic biological specimens. While well studied in the natural sciences, he had only a couple of undergraduate courses in anthropology to prepare him for his ethnographic work. (He had needed to pass a proficiency exam in German to enter into the graduate program in anthropology at the University of California and failed the exam totally. So he never took up anthropology). So it was indeed remarkable that he would produce such a seminal ethnographic document. Gentry became intrigued by the Río Mayo, for its basin was an unknown land marked by blank space on current maps. He set out to explore it, hoping to fund his explorations by collecting insect specimens for museums in the United States.

Gentry arrived at San Bernardo in 1934. Previously he had set off ("quite blindly") for Guarijío country on foot from Ciudad Obregón. Much to the surprise of anthropologists (Sauer was a geographer), Gentry indeed found Guarijíos at San Bernardo and in the wild country to the north. Between 1934 and 1937 he spent much of his time among them, plodding up and down their trails with a mule and an assistant (Hadley and Gentry 1995). Employing Guarijíos as guides and informants, Gentry spent those years studying and collecting plants in the Guarijío portion of the Río Mayo basin. He was particularly intrigued by the extent to which the Guarijíos incorporated native plants into their lives. He took extensive notes of his findings. During that time he visited several Guarijío settlements on the Río Mayo, the Arroyo Guajaray, and the upper Arroyo Limón, including its tributary, the Arroyo Loreto. Undeterred by the hardships posed by drought, rocky terrain, heat, insect plagues, and by the threat of dysentery, malaria, and yellow fever, he traveled with Guarijío guides up and down the canyons, valleys, hills, mesas, and sierras of the Guarijío country, describing them as no one has done since. He visited Guarijío country again in the late 1940s. His 1963 study, which he published at the urging of anthropologist Edward Spicer, was based on his field notes of the 1930s.

Gentry spent his last years in Tucson, which is where I got to know him. I spent hours with him and his wife Marie, asking both of them to relate adventures among the Guarijíos. He told of their early visit to Conejos, now Los Bajíos, as they celebrated their honeymoon. A storm came up and their tent capsized. Their mestizo assistant, a fellow from San Bernardo, led Marie to a Guarijío hut where the accommodating folks put her up for the night on a new petate and new blanket. Gentry got soaked. Marie stayed dry and warm. Gentry shrugged it off; he was impervious to heat, bugs, and damp cold. Marie was not. She suffered in the steamy, buggy climate.

Gentry's monograph remains the most informative source of information on Guarijíos. The absence of documents pertaining to the Guarijíos before Gentry's time indicates the relative absence of interest in the region; it is also a tribute to its tortured topography and its remoteness from roads, all of which discouraged exploration. The fact that no extensive mineralization has been documented in the Guarijío region has also protected it from penetration by outsiders. Over the centuries, small mines were developed in the region, and large mines were exploited adjacent to the region, but large deposits have never been worked in Guarijío country, leaving most mining to prospectors. In the 1890s a mercury mine at Arechuyvo employed a number of Guarijíos, but it was a small operation (Gentry 1963:66). The Guarijíos' preference for living only in small settlements added to their elusive nature and also helps explain the lack of literature about them.

Little if any documented information on the Guarijíos has surfaced for the thirty years that followed Gentry's studies. Beals, Redfield, and Tax, distinguished anthropologists all, reported in 1943 that all Guarijíos lived in Sonora. They added, "This little-known group on the upper reaches of the Mayo River is potentially one of the most interesting northwest Mexican peoples. Virtually no record of the tribe exists in colonial or republican times. No missions ever existed in the area" (Beals et al. 1943:5–6).

Recent history of the Guarijíos is better known. The wave of Third World insurrections in the late 1960s and early 1970s propelled the Guarijíos into the public light.

In 1973 a tiny guerrilla group with revolutionary slogans calling themselves the Communist League of the 23rd of September descended into Guarijío territory from Chihuahua, fleeing a mopping up operation by the Mexican military.[33] They arrived at Bavícora in Guarijío country and offered the natives an appealing message: the Guarijíos, they pointed out, were being mercilessly exploited by mestizos who were becoming rich while the Guarijíos who were doing the rich peoples' work lived in starvation and misery. The guerrillas were convincing: they cultivated friendships, and the Guarijíos were apparently delighted to meet outsiders who did not abuse or attempt to convert them. They gave the guerrillas refuge and shared the little food they had. In return, the guerrillas provided literacy classes and organized discussions among the Guarijíos about their plight. They also used Bavícora as a quasi-military base. The guerrillas launched a couple of kidnappings of wealthy mestizos in and around San Bernardo, Sonora. The first operation succeeded. The guerrillas abducted an old patriarch, a popular, nonpolitical scion of San Bernardo, and wheedled a million-peso ransom for his return. The second kidnapping, of Agapito Enríquez, the patriarch of the family of Burapaco, began smoothly, but his sons grabbed their rifles and pursued the guerrillas into the hills. A confrontation resulted in a shootout in which a guerrilla and the father and a son were shot dead.[34] In retaliation, the guerrillas burned down the Burapaco homestead and company store with all its contents. The kidnappings and the shootout drew the attention of the government. The army was ordered into the area, and the members of the tiny band soon found themselves surrounded by a large contingent of Mexican soldiers near the settlement of Guajaray. They offered to surrender in return for a guarantee of safe conduct to the authorities, hoping to make a public statement. The soldiers agreed to the terms, then massacred the guerrillas anyway, and thus ended the guerrilla threat.[35]

The Mexican government saw a larger conspiracy in the saga, even though the rebels' numbers never exceeded seven or eight (Cipriano Buitimea Romero, personal communication 1995). Indeed, the revolutionaries had influenced the Guarijíos, who now had some embarrassing questions to ask the government. To fend off any uppity behavior by the Guarijíos, soldiers proceeded to exact revenge on them. Guarijíos, they claimed, had harbored the guerrillas and must be taught a lesson. From 1973 to 1976 San Bernardo became a virtual garrison. The guerrillas were dead and gone, but the government wished to take no chances. The guerrilla legacy had to be stamped out. Soldiers detained and tortured several Guarijíos, accusing them of sheltering and abetting the insurgents. They harassed many others, even those who had no idea who the guerrillas were or what they were up to. To be a Guarijío in those times was to be liable to instant arrest, torture, or beating. This treatment led the Guarijíos to conclude that the guerrillas had been correct all along, that the government protected the wealthy landlords and was something to be avoided. Understandably, the Guarijíos became even more reclusive, avoiding contact with blancos at any cost. Some of them retreated far into the rugged canyons of the Sierra Madre to hide from military or police patrols (Calderón Valdés 1985 V:320).

The brief revolutionary movement bequeathed a more positive lasting effect, however. The guerrillas raised the political consciousness of the Guarijíos of Bavícora. From that isolated hamlet a slowly coalescing movement of Guarijío nationalism emerged to claim their rights and demand title to their land. Some Guarijíos understood that they need not accept a destiny of starvation and backbreaking work. Their rights, they perceived, included the right not to be held in peonage by ranchers and to have land of their own. Why should they starve while producing food for the wealthy yoris?

In 1976 a Canadian named Edward Faubert appeared in Guarijío country. He had somehow accosted the governor of Sonora and demanded that he be given an important task to do as a volunteer. The astonished governor assigned him the job of compiling a collection of indigenous arts and crafts of Sonora. While Faubert found some fine handiworks made by Guarijíos, what interested him even more was the feudal system of land tenure he observed in the Guarijío region. A handful of mestizo ranchers held Guarijíos in peonage and worked them unconscionably long hours at starvation wages or niggardly sharecropping, with the full support of the local authorities and police. He also saw firsthand the Guarijíos' unspeakable poverty. Faubert raged with indignation and stormed into government offices—including the governor of the state, demanding an end to the virtual slavery. He got no response. He went back to Guarijío country and spent months documenting the extreme exploitation of the Guarijíos. He compiled his findings in a paper entitled "Un Caso Extremo de Marginación: Los Indígenas Guarijíos en Sonora." In it he named names—listed the ranchers who had enslaved the Guarijíos, where their ranches were located, the particulars of their oppressive activities, and how many Guarijíos each had enslaved. He noted that the marginalization (i.e., the poverty, the economic destitution of the Guarijíos) was so extreme that they had no real options but to accept the grim terms offered by the ranchers: accept their starvation wages or starve. Many did both. And the state police were ever available to back up the ranchers should any Guarijío show signs of complaining about the arrangement. The ranchers and the government viewed the Guarijíos as little more than beasts of burden, not as rational human beings. After a long campaign and repeatedly being dismissed by authorities, Faubert succeeded in drawing national attention to this deplorable situation (Aguilar Zeleny 1996; Faubert ca. 1977; Valdivia Dounce 1994). Despite the publicity, hard times continued for the Guarijíos. Mestizo ranchers and miners who had the ear (and the pocketbook) of the government, claimed ownership of the Guarijíos' primordial lands while the Guarijíos lived in abject, landless poverty. If they complained to the authorities, police responded with brutal reprisals. The Mexican government still viewed the Guarijíos as traitors who had abetted the guerrillas. The police, who were paid off by the landowners, viewed them as a nuisance to be eliminated.

When Faubert had no success in raising any interest locally, he gathered a small group of Guarijíos and journeyed with them to Mexico City to visit President Echeverría. They camped outside the presidential palace demanding that the President meet with them, but Echeverría declined to do so. Abandoning traditional politics, Faubert and the Guarijíos apparently aroused the interest of a television station that found his story intriguing and sent a crew to Sonora. They ventured into Guarijío country and captured the plight of the Guarijíos on film. The resulting exposé caused a minor sensation in Mexico.

Faubert's energetic hell raising through government circles created a national stir, and the consciousness-raising that lingered from the guerrilla days began to take root. In the late 1970s, in response to Faubert's revelations, a popular exposé, and the Guarijíos' own organizing, the Mexican government finally reversed its policies. President Echeverría announced the "discovery" of a new, previously unknown indigenous group, the Guarijíos (Aguilar Zeleny 1996:144). He instructed the Instituto Nacional Indigenista (INI) to provide services to them and lessen the tension between mestizos and Guarijíos. This presidential order produced considerable discomfort among INI officials, for up until that point, they had denied the Guarijíos' existence. Their records revealed no such indigenous group. However, the President's order was law, so, following the announced "discovery," INI established an administrative arm at San Bernardo. Their orders were to begin to provide services to the Guarijíos, but no one among them had any idea of the number of Guarijíos, what sort of people they were, what customs they followed, and what assistance they required from the INI. Indeed, the early INI proceedings suggest that the initial Guarijío program was a sham created for political publicity with no real intent to change anything or assist the Guarijíos in any way.

As a preliminary step, the government sent out census-takers to conduct surveys assessing the Guarijíos' living conditions. The results revealed what all knew, that the Guarijíos were living in deplorable circumstances, with high rates of diseases, anemia, and malnutrition and nearly total illiteracy. None of them owned the land they worked. All were forced to work as peon sharecroppers

for the *latifundistas* of the region.

The government's response to needs assessment was agonizingly slow. Eventually, though, the INI helped established schools and initiated basic nutritional programs. Mexican anthropologists (especially Teresa Valdivia Dounce) assisted Guarijíos in establishing title to their lands. By the early 1980s two Guarijío ejidos and one mixed Guarijío-Mestizo ejido had been established by presidential decree (Valdivia Dounce 1994), mostly at the expense of mestizo ranchers who, the government agreed, had occupied the Guarijíos' lands illegally.[36]

One of those who rose to become a Guarijío leader in the 1970s was Cipriano Buitimea Romero. He recalls the Guarijíos as a historically landless people who were born and lived miserable lives as virtual slaves, who held no hope of owning land, and who could dream for no better economic future than sharecropping, with the landholder determining what was the share. Cipriano describes how it was:

> We Guarijíos never missed a day of work, just like other poor people. . . . Poor folks like us live having to work, we have to work to survive. It's not right to say that just Guarijíos work, because all poor people have to labor. But white people, they aren't all poor; actually there aren't many poor whites, whites who are day laborers like us.[37] We Guarijíos, we were all equally poor, destitute. No one could say of one of us, "He's doing well, he has plenty to eat, he has money to spend." All of us were the same, backwards. . . .
>
> [We started by requesting just enough land near Los Bajíos for a school.] The richer mestizos were unwilling to give us any lands; they became violent when we started to ask for our own. "Let's not let them get any," they said, knowing that all the while the Guarijío tribe was making them rich because we were the only ones who worked on their lands. They themselves couldn't cut a post, nor string barbed wire, nor sow seed. They had no idea how to. They would always say "This year we will plant." It was a lie, because they never planted, it was we, the poor Indians who planted. It was our hands that became the hands of the rich, I do believe, because we made the yoris rich by our labor. . . .
>
> The *pequeños propietarios*[38] never allowed the Guarijíos who were living on their lands[39] a chance to plant for themselves. They only permitted

sharecropping, and we submitted to that because we knew it was the only way we could get food on the table. They would say, "Hey, boy, if you want food, get over here to my place and I'll give you some corn." But in the end we would work all day for five liters of corn and they would tell us that would have to last a week. Now, who can live on five liters of corn a week? And how much worse if you had three or five kids, and there were many who had kids. And sometimes after the Guarijíos did all the harvesting they would fail to pay them, and we would be stuck with credit worth nothing. Sometimes food would just run out and we'd have nothing to eat. We did all the work, weeding and planting and plowing, everything. We gathered in all the harvest and they would even take away our share of the crop. So often we wouldn't even get our measly five liters; it was the same for all of us, we kept planting until we couldn't take it any more, and thus we began our struggle for land. We wanted lands of our own so that we wouldn't have to work for the yoris any more. All of us in the tribe were worn out and were treated worse than animals; we worked from sunup to sundown. We were tired of that life; we were growing old too quickly from overwork. Many died from weariness, working when they really couldn't. We had almost no old men. (Buitimea Romero and Valdivia Dounce 1994:16–20)

Cipriano Buitimea scouting for honey.

Out of the long, victorious struggle came a sense of hope and fulfillment.

> Now we have schools, we have land and a place to plant. Things are good for us. We aren't nearly as backward as we were. Some of us are even cattlemen. We get some help from the bank and from INI. There is a dentist,[40] a livestock doctor. They work with the community. So, as I have been saying, it took a lot of work to make a little progress, you have to go out a lot, you have to learn things. It cost us a great deal of work to get what we have. But now we are content, because we have a place to plant our corn, for here in the sierras that is what we plant, nothing else. Corn, beans and sesame, nothing else, these are the three things we plant. Well, some plant a little *macuchi* tobacco, a little sugar cane, a few watermelons. But all that extra planting is just to add a little enjoyment during the rains. So little that it hardly lasts for two weeks. . . . But now we are comfortable, and no one bothers us. Even the *pequeños propietarios* have come around and accept our victory. (Buitimea Romero and Valdivia Dounce 1994:65–66)

Cipriano, who had worked for ten years as a day laborer in the fields of the Yaqui Valley, had some knowledge of ejido politics. He was no stranger to the brutalities of political repression. While working as an agricultural laborer near Ciudad Obregón, he had participated in political demonstrations of landless peasants demanding ejido lands. One such gathering was broken up by the police, who arrested and beat several of the demonstrators.

It was in 1976 that Cipriano called on what he had learned from his association with Faubert and his experience as a field laborer. He convened a group of Guarijíos at Los Bajíos to look into forming an ejido. He soon learned that José Zazueta had done the same in Mochibampo and that José Ruelas of Bavícora had done the same there. Thus was a small nucleus of Guarijío activists formed in the late 1970s.

These early organizing efforts centered on the apparently innocuous request that the government provide them with schools for their children and the landlords provide a little piece of land on which to build a school. The petition seemed harmless, but the landlords viewed it as a call to insurrection aimed directly at them. They correctly perceived that not far behind this mild supplication would come a demand for all the land now illegally held by the landlords. The Guarijíos were subversives. The landowners hired/bribed state police to teach the Guarijíos a lesson. Thus was José Zazueta arrested, beaten, and imprisoned on four occasions. The police let the Guarijíos know that the landowners meant business and any attempt at organizing would be met with violence. This was still the Echeverría *sexenio* (six-year term) in Mexican history, and this rural ruling class, local *caciques,* feared no retribution when their opponents in a land dispute were mere Indians.

Cipriano managed to avoid arrest and a beating. Given his diminutive size and peaceful demeanor, it is difficult to view him as threatening to anyone, and the Guarijíos to this day are given to avoiding physical confrontations with mestizos.[41] Nevertheless, he was warned by yoris to curtail his organizing, to mind his own business. In the face of numerous threats, he decided to arm himself:

> After a while someone from over there gave me a small pistol. It was .22 caliber. I don't know if it worked, because I never shot it, but it served me well because thenceforth the yoris respected me. I made them take note that I was carrying a pistol, thus—sticking out from my belt, and they stayed a little farther away and didn't come close. I was the only one who carried a .22, though. (Buitimea Romero and Valdivia Dounce 1994:35)

José Zazueta persevered through the beatings and death threats, leaving jail only to take up the Guarijíos cause as though nothing had happened. He organized groups in Los Bajíos, Mochibampo, Bavícora, and Burapaco.[42] Illiterate and speaking only broken Spanish, he called on Cipriano to present the Guarijíos' case to Mexicans because of the latter's ability to speak Spanish.

Their struggles were long and frustrating. For four years Cipriano and José sought out bureaucrats, politicians, and potential allies to help them gain title to their lands and get their school started. Official after official refused to speak to the Guarijíos or if they granted an audience of a few minutes, spoke to them scornfully and patronizingly. An official from the office of Agrarian Reform dismissed their quests for land. He observed that maps showed vast acreages in the Guarijío sierras that were national lands and unclaimed. Why didn't the Guarijíos just claim them? He was uninterested in the fact that those very lands had been illegally fenced, that they were already being ranched by mestizos, and that those same ranchers became violent if the unarmed Guarijíos dared to encroach in their illegally occupied lands.

During these times it seemed that their only other support came from other indigenous people, especially Yaquis and Mayos, who met with them on several occasions. To the Guarijíos' astonishment they found that other native peoples faced the same problems they had and had learned to deal with yoris effectively. The Guarijíos viewed the Yaquis and Mayos as highly sophisticated organizers who knew how to deal with their enemies and with the government. They listened to these experienced organizers.

After some initial fumbling following their establishment in San Bernardo, INI officials sent a bona fide field anthropologist to study the Guarijío situation.[43] The anointed investigator was a young native of Veracruz, Teresa Valdivia Dounce (La Tere), a recent graduate in anthropology. Tere arrived at San Bernardo from Mexico City in 1978 nearly fresh out of the university and began work under the most difficult of situations, which she describes in her extraordinary little book *Sierra de nadie* (1994).

Tere had a rude reception at San Bernardo when she arrived in June at the height of the spring drought when the Sonoran landscape is a pitiless brown-gray. A *chilanga* (resident of Mexico City) she found the heavy heat, dust, and soon the summer floods of Sonora oppressive. The amenities of cosmopolitan city life—libraries, museums, restaurants, theaters, vibrant taverns, sidewalk cafés, intelligent conversation—were all conspicuously absent. She found no housing in San Bernardo, a rustic pueblo at best. She had nowhere to sleep, nowhere to cook, no bathroom, no shower. She improvised, setting up a cot surrounded by netting behind the tiny INI office. Her male colleagues tried to creep into her cot with her. Villagers denounced her for walking and working alone. That a woman would undertake to work in the monte and work with primitive

Indians was simply unheard of. At the outset (and thereafter) she grappled with the machismo and sexism that pervaded INI as well as the systematic confinement of women in San Bernardo to domestic work. She was referred to universally as "La tropóloga" ("the tropologist") an indication that there was virtually no understanding among mestizos of her work or its significance. Her first boss offended and intimidated the Guarijíos, alienating them almost beyond redemption.

> In the first organized meeting I had with the Guarijíos all these accusations were expressed against José [the director of INI at San Bernardo], citing specific instances: he treated them like children, he yelled at them, he told them they had to quit being *Indians* (using the word in the same sense as "fools."); he ordered them to come down from the mountains to deal with him at his desk in San Bernardo; he was constantly drunk and he hung out at the saloon with *yoris* (Mestizos). (Valdivia Dounce 1994:23, translation mine)

She discovered that the same racist director had announced, when he learned that a female anthropologist would be joining him in San Bernardo, that "she was his."

Her first meeting with assembled Guarijíos quickly brought her anthropological idealism to earthly reality. They convened on a small ranch far north of San Bernardo, summoned at her request by Guarijío leaders the day before from as far away as forty kilometers. Her mission was to ascertain from them what the government might do to help them:

> The previous night several [Guarijío] men had departed to notify the Guarijíos [of the meeting] ranch by ranch, house by house, contacting even the most distant place they knew of. They returned in the morning with all the people gathered, after having traveled the whole night in order to begin at the earliest possible time. Then, exhibiting admirable discipline, they all took their places on the ground under a ramada and remained in silence awaiting the news that we [she and a Guarijío collaborator] were going to present. It was incredible to observe those lean faces, those bodies in which the skeletons were clearly outlined, and, even more, to realize, on smelling their breath, that the stench resulted from the absence of food in their stomach since two or four days before. (Valdivia Dounce 1994:36)

Following up this meeting, Teresa led a team in conducting a thorough census, interviewing or visiting every Guarijío in the region. The results were appalling:

> One hundred percent of the Guarijíos are without land; one hundred percent work as peons and as sharecroppers receiving a half or a third of the crop; one hundred percent do not own their homes; they pay rent for them; probably one hundred percent suffer from second or third degree anemia; ninety-five percent are monolingual Guarijío speakers; in general, their living conditions are unsanitary and marginal and they suffer from a complete lack of services. (Valdivia Dounce 1994:58)

Teresa discovered that José Zazueta, a Guarijío who had become her guide, was, unbeknownst to her, also quietly organizing the Guarijíos to lodge a claim against the small ranchers who, the Guarijíos believed, illegally occupied lands rightfully belonging to the Guarijíos. Zazueta incorporated into action what he had learned from the guerrillas and from Edward Faubert, whom he and other Guarijíos referred to as "Mundo."

As she gathered more information about the Guarijíos' plight, Teresa (or "Queresa" as the Guarijíos called her) expanded her investigation to include the status of the Guarijío lands. Accompanied by José Zazueta and Cipriano, she paid a visit to the state land registry in Hermosillo, a long day's bus ride from San Bernardo. At the registry, bureaucrats and corrupt politicians placed roadblocks in their path, refusing to see them, failing to come to their office, breaking appointments, and ultimately denying the existence of the records she sought. The little team persisted, and Tere determined that indeed, the lands claimed by the mestizo ranchers were mostly not theirs at all. They were federal lands and had never been legally claimed by the ranchers or anyone else. They were up for grabs, with the historic tenants having a prima facie claim.

She worked among the Guarijíos for a year or so, traveling on foot and on horseback up and down the endless sierras to the Guarijío country, crossing and recrossing flooded rivers and washes. She daily saw the Guarijíos' grinding poverty, their widespread malnutrition, and their landlessness, and their virtual enslavement. She realized that for them to establish a historic claim to their land and gain title to it, they would have to document their historic tenancy, would have to prove that they had occupied the land longer

Guarijío cultural center, Mesa Colorada.

than anyone else. She decided, against the express wishes of her superiors, to devote her spare time to working on the Guarijíos' land question. She discovered to her dismay that the only ethnographic description of the group was Howard Scott Gentry's 1963 monograph.

From San Bernardo to Phoenix is a two-day trip. Teresa journeyed there and found Gentry at the Phoenix Botanical Gardens completing his comprehensive monograph on agaves. She spent a memorable time with him discussing the Guarijíos. She was surprised and delighted to discover that such a distinguished fellow spoke perfectly good Spanish. As for more detailed information on the Guarijíos, Gentry pointed out that it had been forty years since he had spent time with them, and he had since gone on to study other subjects.[44] Furthermore, he lamented, he was a plant man, not an anthropologist. Still Tere gleaned valuable information from their conversation, coming to realize that the huge variety of plants in use by Guarijíos implied intimate familiarity with the land possible only after occupation of land over many generations, long

before yoris had settled in the region.[45] Gentry's testimony would be a powerful tool in establishing the Guarijíos' claim to their lands.

Tere returned to San Bernardo knowing that her studies of the Guarijíos would be the first since Gentry's. Once it became known that she was acting not as a mere researcher but also as an advocate for Guarijíos, she was routinely followed by government agents whenever she left Guarijío lands. Within the lands, she was often stalked by yoris. One day while she was walking alone in the sierras of Guarijío country, a rancher stuck a gun in her face and warned her if she didn't back off her work with Guarijíos he would kill her. She retorted that if he did he would have to deal with the government that had sent her. The rancher rode away.

That threat strengthened her resolve. She pored through legal documents scattered all over Sonora. She was able to demonstrate conclusively that Guarijíos had the legal right to their lands. All it would take would be a government decree. She also began carrying a dagger in her belt, a practice that impressed Guarijíos and yoris alike. Looking back on it she was able to laugh about it, about the intransigence of the ranchers, about the endearing naïveté of the Guarijíos, and about her lack of preparation for the huge struggle. At the time they presented nearly insurmountable obstacles and debilitating frustrations.

It was not to be an easy victory. Government agents warned her to quit meddling in affairs that were not hers. Her director forbade her to distribute copies of Mexico's law of agrarian reform among the Guarijíos. The state director of the land registry stonewalled her requests for access to the state archives. When he learned what she was researching, he secretly notified the yori ranchers that they should register their land claims. Her adversaries complained to her director at INI. He cancelled her project, depriving her of any basis for working among the Guarijíos. He cited vague charges of insubordination and exceeding her authority. Undaunted, she submitted to INI for publication an anthropological study of the Guarijíos, outlining the Indians' desperate needs and deplorable living conditions. The paper was rejected as inflammatory. She resubmitted it as a descriptive essay of Guarijío customs but included a section outlining the results of the government's neglect and the exploitation of the Guarijíos. The article was published, but the critical section was deleted.[46]

Finally she resigned, realizing that without a project she could have no influence in San Bernardo. She returned to Mexico City and succeeded there in publishing articles sharply critical of the government's inaction in assisting the Guarijíos and remedying the dreadful ongoing suffering they routinely experienced. As a result of her work and the dogged persistence of the Guarijíos themselves, the government finally created the Guarijío ejidos. They expropriated the illegally held lands from the yori ranchers (though all were compensated!), condemned other parcels, and from them created the Los Bajíos and Mesa Colorada (Burapaco) ejidos. Thus the government provided the Guarijíos with title to much, though by no means all, of their ancestral lands. In 1982 and 1983 President López Portillo signed the papers officially acknowledging the lands as belonging to Guarijíos. Shortly thereafter programs to benefit the Guarijíos were dramatically increased. Schools were established, teachers provided, immunizations were administered, and programs of food supplementation were undertaken. The government provided the ejidos with some eighty head of cattle as a starter herd. And thus began the modern history of the Guarijíos. The Guarijíos' lands are now more or less secure. Every Guarijío now has access to land, though it be located on a steep, rocky mountainside and without rain for nine months of the year. Every family has a mahuechi, and many have a few goats, chickens, and pigs. All families raise cows owned by the ejido and share in the sales proceeds.

José Zazueta died of pneumonia in the mid-1980s. I never met him. From Cipriano's and Teresa's descriptions, I was deprived of a great experience. He was surely the Martin Luther King of the Guarijíos. Today the small cultural center in Mesa Colorada bears his name on a large sign. Inside the rather dark room are shelves and small tables bearing artifacts used in the tuburada—masks, violin, harp, *ténaborim* (gravel-filled cocoons that are wrapped around the legs by dancers and give off a most agreeable swish), a *sonajo* of the type held by the cantador, and a few documents from the lucha (struggle for land). Its simplicity seems appropriate as a tribute to José. His memory is revered throughout the region.

4
The Last Tuburada at Los Bajíos

Perhaps it was not the last tuburada, but it was surely one of the last. The *huicastame* or *cantador*,[1] without which there can be no tuburada, was in his eighties. No one can say just how old he is because Guarijíos, at least the older ones, don't keep track of years. They have no need to. They just say he is very old, and when he dies, no one will be left to sing the *cantos*, the chanting ritual songs that are the backbone of the festival.

None of the younger men want to invest the time to be a cantador. They have more practical things to do, such as riding their mules or horses up and down the rugged hills and mountains, or running pick-up horse or mule races on the rare flat spots, hoping for the day when they can move to the big cities and live the fast life, maybe even own a pickup truck. Their fathers, in contrast, dislike riding horses, mules, and burros. They prefer to walk, live in isolation, hunt an occasional deer, and be surrounded by wild monte, the tropical deciduous forest. It is the Guarijío way. I'm with the fathers. But I also have another life and partake of the urban affluence when I choose. They don't and can't.

I came to Los Bajíos because Cipriano Buitimea had told me months ago at Jánaco that on *el día de San Isidro,* the fifteenth of May, a tuburada, the traditional Guarijío ceremonial, would be held at the remote Guarijío center, as it is every year. San Isidro is the patron saint of the farmer, the man of the soil. It seemed a fitting time to celebrate with a tuburada. Cipriano had made it clear that if I wanted to understand Guarijíos, I had to attend a tuburada. By all testimony, the tuburada at Los Bajíos, planned for weeks in advance, would amount to what Singer called a "cultural performance" (Singer 1955). The Guarijíos contend that it is the tuburada that differentiates them from other people.

I contacted the head administrator of the Guarijíos in San Bernardo for permission to attend, mentioning that I needed a guide and a burro. For weeks David Burckhalter and I had talked about the trip deep into the land of the Guarijíos. We knew it would be blazing hot, dry, dusty, and brown. But it was Cipriano's favorite time of year, and I had to go.

Getting to Los Bajíos was a tough business. We drove in a four-wheel drive pickup over dirt roads to San Bernardo, a couple of hours north of Alamos, then over gradually deteriorating roads into the deep mountains to the northwest where the road becomes little more than a rocky track, through San Pedro and over an interminable ridge to the Guarijío village of Guajaray. It adds up to five hours of pummeling beyond San Bernardo. From Guajaray we obtained a guide and a burro and trudged the seven miles up the Río Guajaray to the village of Los Bajíos.

Originally Cipriano had said he would accompany us. But that was in January and this was mid-May, the time of heat, the time of preparing the scorched land for planting. David and I stopped at the shady roadside house in the narrow, deep valley of San Pedro and took the two-mile ancient trail over the ridge that switchbacked down to Jánaco, to let Cipriano know we were ready to go. The country was a harsh gray-brown now in the intense spring drought, no longer green and silver-soft as it had been in January.

Cipriano was at his palm-thatched hut, looking tired and acting preoccupied. His shirt consisted mostly of tattered patches and his trousers were torn and soiled. His wife Dolores and his three daughters tittered excitedly at our arrival. He didn't. He sat on one of his rickety homemade chairs and looked off into the distant blue mountains. He barely acknowledged the food and clothing I had brought. He wouldn't be attending the tuburada, he said. He still hadn't begun to clear land around his house for his mahuechi. "*Mira*, David," he said to me in his winsome fashion. "Here it is the twelfth of May and my *mahuechi* still isn't cleared. Before long *las aguas* will be upon us and I will have no crop. I have to plant corn, beans, squash, and sugar cane now. And oh! This year I'll plant *sandía* [watermelon] as well. But if I go spending my time up in Los Bajíos I'll never get my planting done. A Guarijío without a *mahuechi* isn't very much."

I told him I understood. Indeed, he was living up to his reputation as an industrious fellow. Sometimes a Guarijío has to make the tough choice between his mahuechi and the tuburada. But there had to be something else wrong. I looked around. "Where is Melecio, your son?" I asked, knowing the boy was actually Cipriano's stepson. I had looked forward to seeing the little fellow who had so impressed me a few months earlier.

"He's not here. He went off to work down near Sejaqui or San Juan." He stared off into the forested ridge above his house. These were villages eight and ten miles away.

"He went off to *work*?" I protested. "But he's only eleven. What is he doing?"

"There's a *ganadero* (ranch owner) down there who's hiring fellows to *desmontar* (clear the land). He's going to plant buffelgrass, and the forest has to be cut down first."

I knew that was backbreaking work. And the results were devastating; thousands of acres of dry tropical forest leveled, the residue burned off, to make way for cows and a pasture of thick clumps of a seeded African grass. The rancher would in all probability be a *mafioso* (drug lord). Melecio was a child laborer in a scheme to launder money.

"What does he get paid?" I wanted to know.

"Fifteen pesos a day," Cipriano answered weakly.

"Fifteen pesos?" FIFTEEN PESOS?" I raised my voice with indignation. "Cipriano, that's not even three dollars a day. That's a crime!"

He nodded soberly, better controlled than I. "It's very little. Just like they used to pay the Guarijíos. We'd work all week for five liters of corn."

"When will he be back?" I asked, controlling my consternation. I was also disappointed because I had brought the lad a nice pocketknife and had spent more than a few minutes imagining the joy in his face when I gave it to him.

"*Sabe,*" (who knows?), he answered. "He's been gone a month now. He said something about coming back for the tuburada, but, no, well . . ." And his voice trailed off.

David and I trudged sadly up the now-barren hills and down the canyon to San Pedro. We would have to find another guide and would miss out on the pleasure of hearing Melecio's happy whistle and his gay laughter.

In Guajaray, a village strewn out on a barren, deforested mesa above the river, we had trouble finding a guide. Ignacio Ciriaco, known as "Nacho," a quiet, most knowledgeable Guarijío who had guided me up the river a year earlier, was in the middle of putting a new palm roof on his hut. He explained from the roof where he was working that he had gone to enormous trouble to gather the palm leaves, making six trips of two days each with a train of burros to gather the branches at the place up on Sierra El Cuate where the palms grew. His whole clan was involved in helping him put on the roof, and he couldn't just up and leave them with an unfinished roof. He could leave the following day, maybe, but, no not right then. I surely understood his problem.

Eliazar Valenzuela, a younger man, part Guarijío who had also guided me in the area couldn't go either. He wasn't even home, but his wife, María Rufina, a most handsome, strong woman, uncharacteristically outgoing for a Guarijía, said he was off in the monte cutting logs to make a house. He wouldn't be back till late. Besides, in another couple of days he would be going to Alamos to a meeting about the Guajaray school. Just the trip there would take a day, day and a half. No, he couldn't go to the tuburada, either.

I asked another fellow if he could guide us. No, he shook his head, he couldn't; he had *negocio* (business) to attend to. He had no time.

This was strange. After all, the tuburada at Los Bajíos was a pivotal event in the life of the Guarijíos of this region, marking off their annual cycle. I'd heard about it for months. It appeared no one in Guajaray was interested.

It wasn't until a year or so later that I learned that Guajaray and many of its folks are viewed with somewhat jaundiced eye by Guarijíos from Bavícora, Los Bajíos, and Mochibampo, the more traditional villages. Guajaray is only partially Guarijío, its residents said to be more mestizo-ized than other settlements. There are exceptions, of course, but what I was experiencing apparently was part of a pattern of mestizo behavior characteristic of Guajaray. Guajaray has its own tuburada, in June, and at least part of its residents thought its celebration was enough. No need to visit other villages.[2]

Finally I found a young fellow, a mere lad of nineteen named Chal. He was dressed more like a dandy cowboy than a Guarijío, wearing boots and a cowboy shirt, but seemed competent for the job. He also seemed delighted at the prospect of guiding a couple of gringos to the fiesta and getting paid to boot. First, though, he had to round up his burro. This took three hours, (burros run wild in that region and are diabolically skillful at hiding themselves when they know they will be asked to work) and by the time he arrived with the beast, who looked at us suspiciously, it was too late to depart that day. David and I camped by the river that night, not a terrible curse because the murmur of the water tumbling over the rocks was soothing and a deep pool just a hundred yards upstream would provide a bath in the morning.

As we waited we watched a young Guarijío break a handsome young mule in the sand by the river's side. (We had no choice but wait, for his arena was the very place where we would camp.) Mounted on a horse, a rarity for Guarijíos who traditionally prefer to walk rather than ride, he pulled the mule after him by a rope attached to the mule's head, skillfully anticipating the beast's kicks and bites. When the bewildered mule was catching its breath after a heated fit of kicking and bucking, the cowboy deftly looped a rope around the mule's nose and ran the rope through a cinch around the critter's waist. Then he tugged on the end of the rope, forcing the mule's nose close to its side, straining its neck so that it was unable to fight back. He alternatively patted and goaded the mule. It kicked once, but its off-balance posture caused it to fall to its side at which point the cowboy scolded it angrily, pummeled it, then soothingly reassured it. The breaking would take three or four days, he said, and after that the mule would be an excellent saddle beast or pack animal.

I mention this scene because it portrayed a sign of the times: Guarijíos were becoming cowboys and mule-breakers. Ten years earlier they probably owned no mules. Traditional Guarijíos prefer to walk. They use burros for transport and leave mules and horses to the yoris who always owned them. Guarijíos were too poor ever to own saddled beasts. The younger Guarijíos appear to covet animals to ride. They see the mestizo way as the fast, exciting life. The Guarijío way is backward and dull.

Finally, the fellow was through with the breaking session for the day. He put his hat back on and led the mule away. We were now alone on the river.

The Río Guajaray is the largest tributary of the Río Mayo, emptying into it from the northwest roughly fifteen air miles north of San Bernardo. It originates to the northwest in the oak and pine slopes of the vague jumble of mountains called the Sierra Oscura that form a hazy boundary between Sonora and Chihuahua. It would hardly earn designation as a stream when compared with watercourses in the temperate United States, but for an arid region like southern Sonora it is a river indeed. Its faithful flow never fluctuates much, for through wet and dry years it remains a reliable source of water and fish.

The incised and rocky canyon through which the Guajaray flows for thirty miles or so is of youthful volcanic origin and leaves no flat terraces for planting and irrigating. The Guarijíos subsist exclusively on dry farming the hillsides, carving out their mahuechis on slopes of nearly precipitous steepness. From these parcels claimed with back-breaking labor, they harvest corn, beans, squash, and, with luck, watermelon, for a couple of years. Then they leave the land to lie fallow for a decade and move on to another plot. Some of the mahuechis are so distant that it takes two or

three hours just to reach them. The slopes often or even usually exceed thirty percent, the angle at which talus forms. I have climbed up a mahuechi that must have approached a 100 percent slope (45° angle) and marveled that anyone could work such a field. At the time of our visit summer rains had more or less failed for three consecutive years, the last being almost without rain. This caused a calamity among the Guarijíos; some of whom were forced to eat their seed stock and now were dependent on commercial seed purchased from commercial farms down in the delta region.[3]

Chal said the walk to Los Bajíos would take three hours. There were nineteen crossings of the river, he warned. We'd get our feet wet on all but the first. It took us more like six hours. We lollygagged. We stopped to look at flowering trees. We visited in the hamlet of Todos Santos where five Guarijío families live. We rested briefly in the chill of the dark box canyon of La Cañada del Rincón de Ardillas (Squirrel Corner Canyon). We paused in the shade of willows along the river while lunching on tortillas wrapped around beans that Chal's mother had prepared. We rested again, this time in the cool shade of a giant igualama tree next to the river. It was impossible not to slow down to gaze upward at the thousand-foot cliffs that rimmed the river in places or peer into the temptingly cool fifteen-foot deep pools that dotted the river. I stopped to stand under a flowering amapa amarilla tree just to experience the ethereal glow produced by the sunlight filtering through the brilliant gold of the flowers. We were not in a hurry.

The trail, worn down by centuries of heavy use, seldom remained very long in the river bottom. It would head cross-country, up a steep hill and across an arid mesa to avoid a gooseneck or an oxbow in the river or to bypass rocky narrows. These shortcuts were less interesting than the river bottom, so we would gain a little time with each one. Chal was most patient with our lazy pace; he had been to Ciudad Obregón and there had heard stories of gringos. We had to move carefully, for the youthful canyon is carpeted with boulders, not sands and gravels, as are older canyons. In the current, these large rocks develop a mantle of moss as slick as a greased bowling ball. The Guarijíos, on the other hand, glided with practiced ease across the stream, picking their way nearly automatically among the familiar boulders. Chal avoided getting his nifty cowboy boots wet by hopping on the burro's haunches at each crossing and riding the patient beast across. The burro didn't seem to object, for Chal couldn't have weighed much more than 110 pounds.

I said the canyon was youthful, and it is, in geological

time, but still it is several million years old. Between 40 and 20 million years ago this region was racked by a seemingly unending series of cataclysmic volcanic explosions that deposited two kilometers of rock—volcanic mudflows, ash, ignimbrites, flows—on top of the existing mountains. The earth-shaking, climate-altering blasts simmered into silence for many millions of years. Then some twelve million years ago the continental mass on which the Guajaray lies began to stretch to the west, slowly extended like a prisoner on a rack. The Pacific Plate had changed direction, and the land west of the Sierra Madre was part of it. It pulled apart relentlessly like taffy; the stretching persisted for another 8 million years. Massive blocks of mountain and valley cracked and tore apart as the plate lumbered away and the terrain was drawn and quartered. As the very ground stretched, gigantic blocks broke off and dropped into the depths created by the stretching. Some of them teetered like immense ice cubes, seeking their center of gravity, showing tilted strata when they finally came to rest. The great cliffs over the Guajaray show the effects of the Basin and Range stretching and tearing, but they never tilted. Their foundations extend thousands of feet into the earth's crust. In some places it is possible to reconstruct the geological sequence where the mountains had been torn apart, the bottom dropped out, and the canyon resulted. It is as if a piece from a thousand-foot thick layered torte fell straight down, but remained upright and preserved the original layering. (For a more complete description, see pp. 97-99).

When you are hiking fast on round rocks, you dare not look up often, lest you fall and break something that you do not wish to have broken. Concentrating on our footing, we could not marvel as much as we would have liked at the sheer walls above us, walls carved not by the river but by nature's blasting and tearing. Only when we left the river in favor of a shortcut to Los Bajíos could we take in the immensity of the canyon. The trail for the last mile and a half was uphill and hot. Away from the cooling influence of the river, the thinned forest was parched and leafless, the landscape an unending dusty brown. The temperature was in the high nineties and the climb was steep. The powerful May sun burned down on us. In that desiccated, shimmering heat the world seemed to move. Though all of nature is stilled, and even the doves are driven to silence in the heavy heat, there is a sound of heat that seems quietly noisy. I stopped and listened several times. Above our footfalls and the clopping of the burro's hooves, I could not identify a single sound. Only occasionally did I notice a lizard rustle

or the hiss of a piece of wispy torote bark waving in the warm air currents. Yet the quiet air seemed full of sounds.

We finally rimmed out a half mile from Los Bajíos. The valley and village unfolded below, the view slightly distorted by the dancing currents of heated air.

Los Bajíos sits on a mesa in a short but wide valley, perhaps an ancient caldera with an open end above the river. Thirty or so palm-thatched huts grace the valley floor. Stark white buildings—four of them—of the albergue interrupt the otherwise bucolic view, for the appearance of the palm thatching is most agreeable, and the Guarijíos have perfected the aesthetics as well as the practicalities of that sort of construction. On top of a small bluff on the far side of the valley rising like a huge ostrich egg from the dark lavas of the landscape, stands a white water tank resting on a fifty-foot high steel tower. The glistening white tank has the word *Solidaridad* painted in large, colorful lettering on its side. That was the name of the public works organization created by former Mexican President Carlos Salinas de Gortari. He controlled the budget personally. It allowed him to fund public works projects directly and get credit for them. So the tank was a gift of the Salinas administration. Good idea.

The tank holds no water. Bad public relations. The pump, which runs on gasoline packed in on muleback, broke down after only a few months after it was installed in the late 1980s. It hasn't worked since. The tank and tower are enjoyed by local youths, however, who scale it for fun and for the commanding view of the village it yields and for the proof they can offer to young women that they will make daring and strong husbands.

Chal led us to the hut of the gobernador of the ejido, for Los Bajíos is the name of an ejido (communally owned tract of land) that includes several other settlements as well as the village. Rafael Méndez was a man in his early forties with a tired, though compassionate visage. He was referred to then as *gobernador,* a title bestowed by an early INI bureaucrat and forced on the unsuspecting Guarijíos who had no such expression in their lexicon. His demeanor was that of a man with great cares and utter dedication to his duties, the sort of man in whom I instantly felt trust and confidence. He eyed David and me with appropriate suspicion but not with malevolence. Indigenous people there are accustomed to being treated with condescension or arrogance by blancos so he did well to look at us doubtfully. We asked him for permission to attend and photograph the tuburada, assuring him that we would in no way interfere with the proceedings and that we would respect all the

Guarijío customs and ceremonies. He gave a silent nod, then quietly added that he would have to get permission first from the *fiesteros* (sponsors or organizers of the fiesta).

That proved to be no problem and in fifteen minutes he was back and led us to the dormitory of the boarding school. He was accompanied by Rafael Buitimea, a cousin of Cipriano's and a man of ample girth. The "Rafael Gordo," (the fat Rafael, as he is universally called) unlocked the padlock that sealed the dormitory and announced that we should sleep there. He then ceremoniously turned the key over to David.

The school boys' dormitory (there is a separate one for the girls) was a stuffy place more like a warehouse, crammed full of desks and benches stacked on end, stacks of worn, often coverless textbooks, musty piles of blankets, sheets, towels, and a maze of bunk beds, all of which had been packed in by mule train from Guajaray. Both the cement for the buildings and the reinforcing steel had also been brought in by burros and mules. The mere existence of those buildings is a testimony to the determination of the government to provide the children with an education and of the Guarijíos (who did all the work) to guarantee their children an educated future. One of the classrooms in an adjacent building had glass windows, a miracle in itself, for the tough trip up the river would break almost anything that could be broken. If the contents of a pack were not dented, cracked, or broken by the natural movement of the pack animals, the mules would see to it that by sheer ornery movement the appropriate destruction would take place. I've seen a fully laden brute roll over in the sand and squirm around as if trying to scratch his back.

The school had 76 students, Rafael Méndez explained. Each grade, one through six, has a separate teacher. The teachers are mostly Mayos, for complicated reasons, and they not only teach the children, they live among them as well, making for a remarkable camaraderie between teachers and pupils. According to a San Bernardo administrator, this closeness, this common *thrownness* to use an old existentialist term, results in a close bond that is most beneficial to the education of the children. At Mesa Colorada, accessible by motor vehicles, the teachers live apart, and the administrator reports, the children lack the enthusiasm, the group spirit, and the scholarship of those at Los Bajíos. Motor vehicles, he thought, undermined the group's sense of solidarity. I think he was right.

By most standards, the school is austere. Books are few, supplies lacking. The buildings are Spartan in design as well

as in function. The children are fed beans and tortillas with occasional soup and a rare taste of meat. The school lacks running water (as does the entire community, since the promised pump never delivers), and neither it nor the village of 150 people has electricity, nor will it for a long time. The school buildings are stuffy and visited by mosquitoes and flies. The walls are papered with posters stressing the necessity of sanitation and warning of potentially lethal diseases, especially childhood diarrhea. Children are exhorted to wash their hands, but without water this is not easy.

Nearly all the children live far away—some as far as five hours' walk. They arrive Monday morning and leave Friday afternoon. Their parents miss them, of course, both for themselves and the labor the children provide. At the school they do not learn the Guarijío language except from the rare teacher who speaks it. They learn to speak Spanish and learn also that Spanish is the language of commerce, learning, power, and success, while Guarijío is the language of backwardness. Nevertheless, the school is a well-functioning unit, and those teachers who walk to the school from Mesa Colorada, fourteen miles away over a grueling trail, have my undying respect.

I returned to the hut with Rafael Méndez and we chatted. He had a wife, he said, but she was in Ciudad Obregón a hundred miles away. He gave no further explanation. They had no children. Rafael lived alone and his hut showed it. It was in a sad state of disrepair. The palm roof had partially collapsed. His few possessions lay untidily around, a *tapeste* (a bed consisting of otate poles placed across two handmade benches); a faded cotton blanket; a dented, scorched metal cooking pot; a small chest with half-sprung hinges; and a couple of old hand-made chairs of dubious solidity. On a table sat a large olla (usually a clay pot but in this case a plastic bucket) from which he dipped water with a metal cup. The water came from the river a half mile and three hundred feet below the village. He hauled it up each day, a half hour job. In a separate room, perhaps eight feet square, was the kitchen where he kept a fire going to heat his tortillas and cook his beans. That was all he had besides the clothing he wore.

Rafael asked why I had come to Los Bajíos, and I explained that I was interested in the plants used by Guarijíos but even more I was interested in the Guarijíos themselves, how they lived and how they viewed the world. He seemed quite satisfied with this and told me he had traveled as well— to Tijuana, Hermosillo, Culiacán—a wide range of experience for a Guarijío. How had he come to be gobernador? Well, he sat on the edge of his tapeste and thought.

Unlike most of the residents of Los Bajíos, Rafael was born there. Prior to the creation of the ejido in 1982 the place had been known as Conejos (rabbits), or, more precisely, Tohuí, which means *conejos* (rabbits) in the Guarijío language. Howard Scott Gentry, in his seminal 1942 work *Río Mayo Plants*, mentioned Conejos as being a small Guarijío village that had been abandoned not long after his first visit in 1934. Rafael explained that the Guarijíos were not allowed to live there permanently because it was not officially their land until 1982. The land was claimed by ranchers who refused to allow the Guarijíos to build permanent residences, lest they establish a claim to the land. By the time the land finally became theirs, many Guarijíos had through economic necessity become dispersed over the lower Río Mayo Valley and as far away as Ciudad Obregón in the Yaqui Valley. When they were notified of the good news, they began trickling back into the region, settling in and around Los Bajíos. Because Rafael was one of the few who had been there the entire time, he was appointed chief and had held the position for some time.

That's the way he told the story, with disarming modesty. The truth was that he was a man whose integrity showed clearly and whose agenda included little more than being a conscientious leader and making life better for the Guarijíos. The others must have sensed that as well. He was a good guy, the sort of man anyone of discernment would want for a governor. I would certainly vote for him.

I needed a hat, I told him. Mine, a double-woven palm hat from Nácori Chico a hundred miles to the north, had begun to fall apart in the walk from Guajaray and only a fool will go anywhere in that sun-blasted region without adequate head covering. Besides, Los Bajíos was renowned throughout the region for its palm baskets and hats as good as those from Nácori. Where could I find a hat? I asked Rafael.

He smiled pleasantly and tolerantly. He didn't know if anyone had any right then. Most of the men wore hats they purchased at the store in Burapaco, down in the Mayo Valley (not as good as palm hats, he admitted). A couple of women might have some, though. Chal had come by during our conversation. Rafael suggested some places to him and Chal led us from house to house, without luck. Someone suggest a woman living in *la otra banda* (the other side of the dry arroyo), a neighborhood a long quarter-mile away from the nearest hut, across the arid mesa. Chal led us there across the sere, cracked soils of the floor of the valley, so flat it resembles a mesa. At the bottom of the deeply eroded arroyo that separates the two parts of the valley, a young woman, almost hidden in the defile, was filling a bucket from a muddy seephole. Chal called down to her in Spanish, asking if she made hats. She did not answer. He called again, in a somewhat louder voice, did she make hats?

"No." Was her curt answer.

"Is there anyone up here who makes hats," he asked, indicating the little group of huts just beyond the arroyo.

The woman did not look up from her work. "No," she said and hoisted the heavy bucket to her head.

Chal looked at us with a wry smile. He called over once again. "Isn't there some old woman or someone who weaves hats?"

"No." And the woman climbed up the hill, gracefully balancing on her head the bucket with more than forty pounds of water inside. She did not look in our direction.

A man had been standing semihidden behind an etcho cactus perhaps forty yards away on our side of the arroyo, watching us. Chal called to him. "Look, I'm from Guajaray, my father is Eliazar Valenzuela, and I'm trying to help these two American friends find a hat. Is there any here in *la otra banda* who makes them?"

The fellow nodded and looked off into space. He waited a few moments, then nodded again. He said in a quiet, barely audible voice, "*Sí,* there is a woman right there. She might have a couple of hats."

We clambered down the steep bank of the arroyo and scurried up the other side, then climbed the short, steep hill and passed through a gate in an ancient trinchera, the same gate through which the young woman with the bucket had just passed. We didn't need to ask which hut, for another man pointed to a hut in the doorway of which stood a very old woman. Chal asked her in Spanish (he spoke no Guarijío) if she had any hats. She produced two, one of which, with a little adjustment, fit me perfectly. These adjustments took a little longer than I had hoped, but the woman spoke only Guarijío and her son, who watched me through the doorway with studied interest, had to translate. I paid her and we left.

If one part of the Guarijío culture stands out it is the extreme separation of the sexes. Traditional Guarijío women stay apart from all men except those in her immediate family. Their shyness with outsiders is extraordinary. I have seen them literally run away as I approached their dwelling, a phenomenon Gentry noted sixty years earlier. Whether it is because many of them speak no Spanish or because they have a general fear of the violence inflicted upon them by

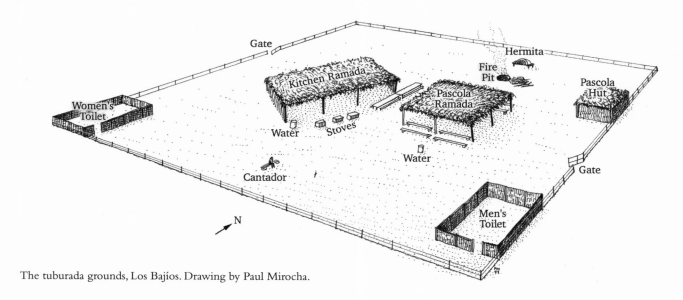

The tuburada grounds, Los Bajíos. Drawing by Paul Mirocha.

blancos in their recent history is difficult to say. As we shall see, this fear of outsiders in general and males in particular is reinforced at the tuburada.

Let me note here that some Guarijíos claim that each true Guarijío man is obligated to sponsor three tuburadas to show his thanks to God. Each woman is obliged to sponsor four fiestas, because Mamá Diós, God's wife, wants it that way. Some Guarijíos are fiesteros many more times than that. And the younger ones are often not fiesteros at all. It takes money, time, perseverance, endurance, and, above all pride in being a Guarijío to be a fiestero. The only reward is the enhanced prestige for sponsoring a successful and enjoyable tuburada.

A year earlier, the gobernador of Los Bajíos had appointed three men to be fiesteros for this tuburada. They were identified by the bright red new bandannas they wore. The fiesta in Los Bajíos is the social highlight of the year there. Tuburadas may be organized for a number of occasions, but they are not common (mercifully, as far as fiesteros are concerned), and the association with San Isidro, the patron saint of the farmer, is especially apt, for the Guarijíos live close to the soil. Some years there are almost no tuburadas anywhere due to the poverty of the people. The job of the fiesteros was to organize the fiesta and make sure everything came off as it should. Their responsibilities were many, the most important of which was planning for and acquiring the large amounts of food for the two full days of fiesta (most of it was provided by the government) and seeing that everyone was fed. In addition they journeyed to distant settlements to recruit the musicians and the *pajacola*

(pascolas, ritual dancers). They notified the huicastame (cantador), obtained fireworks, and, above all, they oversaw the preparation of the fiesta arena.

Getting the arena in shape for the tuburada required enormous work. The arena stood out as we descended from the overlook into Los Bajíos, the fresh green of the newly-cut branches covering the ramadas contrasting agreeably with the barren brown of the ground.

In the center of the small, flat valley, the town folk had fenced off an area roughly seventy yards square. This involved constructing a three-wire fence with newly cut fence posts every twenty feet or so, and two gates, one on the east and one on the west. The gates would admit people but prevented the ubiquitous livestock from wiping out all the hard work with their stamping, pawing, chewing, gnawing, urinating, defecating, and general wrecking tendencies. Pigs, dogs, and cats were undeterred by the wire. The entire community had pitched in to clear the arena, removing every weed, every rock (and there were many), and every clod of the rock-hard clay soil larger than a Ping-Pong ball. They had raked the arena with a passion until it was as clean and neat as possible, then had broken up the clay hardpan soil into marble-sized pieces, which prevented dust but was still easy to walk on.

Next they constructed three important *ramadas*. One was for the kitchen. This was perhaps thirty by twenty-five feet, the posts of freshly cut, enduring *tepeguaje* wood, the beams of stout mauto poles. On top of the beams they laid hundreds of freshly cut branches of guásima, which produced remarkably cool shade. Under the cooking ramada they constructed three large stoves, solid mounds of adobe, atop which fireplaces were installed for cooking tortillas on comales. Two smaller stoves were also made for holding the immense ollas (steel pots, in this case) for boiling the beans and the burro stew. The women's convenience was clearly in mind when these stoves were constructed, for they were designed so that the women could cook tortillas on the higher stoves without having to bend over, while they could lift the heavy cauldrons of water onto the lower stoves without breaking their backs. At the south end of the cooking ramada stout racks were built from posts covered with horizontal lengths of otate, one about four feet high, three feet wide, and four feet long, the other a foot lower and about the same size. On these were stored the piles of foodstuffs, both to keep them out of the dirt and to protect them from the dogs, chickens, and pigs who found in the fiesta area a bounty of consumables free for the scavenging. I was able to follow the progress of the fiesta by noting the decreasing size of the pantry stocks on the racks. From the beams of this cooking ramada lines of cord were strung to other ramadas and large thin slabs of more or less fresh burro meat and fat were suspended to jerk during the festivities. From these same lines brightly colored cloth flags were draped both as a decoration and to provide a visual warning of the presence of the cord which could nearly decapitate someone running by unawares. Great attention had been paid to the kitchen, for without it there would be no food. Without food there can be no tuburada.

The food (as well as the skyrockets) for the tuburada had been provided by the government through the Instituto Nacional Indigenista (INI). The previous day the voluminous supplies had been burroed in from Guajaray. The INI took the tuburadas seriously enough, understanding that food was essential to have the fiesta, and without the tuburada there would, before long, be no Guarijíos.

The second ramada was the pascola ramada or *ramadón,* built some thirty feet east of the cooking ramada. This was smaller, twenty by twenty-five feet, with a smooth surface for the relentlessly pounding feet of the pascolas. I should explain that the soil of the valley is high in collapsing clays. These soils expand during the rainy season, but when they dry out, large cracks appear in the soil. These fissures were constantly producing holes in the dancing surface. To prevent injuries to the feet and ankles of the dancers, the fiesteros always had a wheelbarrow of fine soil and a shovel available to fill in the holes as they appeared. Those fellows' feet take a terrific beating in the forty-plus hours of fiesta,

and a slight depression in the ground could cause an injury.

Two long benches were placed at either end inside the posts of the pascola ramada. These were for the musicians and the waiting pascolas, who danced in turn. Additional benches were located on the sides outside the posts. These were for spectators. The roof of this ramada was of the same construction as that of the kitchen ramada, except that the guásima was supported by a layer of otate. The double insulation kept the temperature remarkably cool under the boiling sun of the late spring in the tropical deciduous forest. At midday more than forty men could huddle in the shade of the ramada while the pascolas continued to dance.

Two large tables with benches were placed between the cooking ramada and the pascola ramada. Here the men would come to eat and be served by the fiesteros. The table surfaces were high relative to the benches, a perverse design, so the men frequently found the bowls at their chins. This merely facilitated drinking from the bowls as from a goblet and in no way impeded the flow of nourishment. The bowls in which the beans, bean stews, and stews were served, were of fired clay, manufactured in the town. Only the metal spoons and enameled coffee cups and the large pots for stew and beans were of nonlocal production.

A third structure was rather different from the others in that it was constructed with enclosed walls and a roof. This was the pascola hut, reserved for the pascolas and the musicians, butting up against the fence at the eastern end of the fiesta arena. The walls of this small building, perhaps eight feet square, were of willow freshly cut from the river and woven securely into place. Inside the musicians stored their instruments—violins and harps—and the pascolas their paraphernalia—their *cha'éhuari* (ténaborim), their *cascabeles* (belts with silver and brass pendant bells that produced a most agreeable jingle during the dance), and most important their *máscaras* (the grotesque masks). Only men were permitted in this hut, and those not involved in the dances were apparently also excluded, although they might look in, and urchins took great delight in sneaking in and examining the various artifacts inside. This practice was tolerated by the fiesteros. The pascolas would don their apparel in this enclosure and emerge ready to dance.

Also constructed were a men's toilet in the northeast corner and a women's toilet in the southeast corner. These were built of strong posts with a partition at the opening that permitted easy entry but maximum privacy. The walls were of handsomely woven fresh willow. The women's toilet was twice the size of the men's and because the prevailing wind blew from southwest to northeast, after two days a noticeable aroma began to emanate from it. As the festival progressed, blankets were hung from the sides, either to air out or to provide additional privacy.

A small table over which a shroud and muslin cover were placed had been built to the north of the pascola ramada. Chal informed me that this *ermita* (hermitage) would house *los santos* (the saints). During portions of the festival the pascolas would deposit their hats underneath the tabletop of the ermita, so a variety of hats were usually present. Immediately south of the cooking ramada two large rocks had been placed and poles of otate located across them, making a bench of sorts, on which the huicastame would sit. Twenty feet to the east was a three-foot high cross—the santa cruz—on which had been placed a rosary. Both were covered with a muslin shroud.

A large drum of water was located just to the south of the cooking ramada and another to the south of the pascola ramada. Inside these floated *jícaras* (gourds that had been split to form a drinking and pouring cup). Men drank only from their barrel, women from theirs. People were constantly drinking from the barrels, and the water was constantly replenished by the fiesteros who routinely staggered up the plain under a yoke bearing two large bucketfuls of the cool flow of the Arroyo Guajaray.

The only other feature of the fiesta arena was a fire pit located to the north of the pascola ramada. A fire burned here all night, providing warmth in the chill darkness. The fiesteros maintained a sizable pile of brasil wood at one side. Only men and boys were supposed to use the fire, someone told me, although I spied an occasional little girl soaking in the warmth as well. The women were expected to derive their warmth from the fires in the cooking ramada.

Just as David and I returned from purchasing the hat, at perhaps 6:00 P.M. in the afternoon, one of the fiesteros set off a series of *cohetes* (skyrockets) that exploded to the great delight of the gathered crowd. Almost immediately pascolas emerged from their hut and began to dance inside the pascola ramada. At this time only two musicians performed, a violinist and a harpist. The latter was a heavy, blind man with a distorted face. He had been borne with great care from Guajaray by mule. Throughout the fiesta he was attended to with gentle respect and concern by many of the participants.

Each pascola dancer carried on for only a few minutes then was relieved by another, three in all. They wore paper flowers in their hair but no masks, for, as it turned out, no masks were available. No one in the town produced masks, and none had yet arrived from Mesa Colorada, where carvers do produce masks. The fiesteros had left out only this one detail.

Each of the pascolas had danced for a few minutes each while the music continued. The violinist was a fine musician, the harpist still reacquainting himself with the harp, which appeared to be quite new. After a few turns, the lead pascola, a most serious older man named Chémali, herded everyone except for the blind harpist out of the pascola ramada to the ermita, the saints' table. A row of children—boys and girls—lined up and bowed reverently first to the pascolas, then to the santos' table. The pascolas in turn bowed to the children. A fiestero set off another cohete and the whole group, followed by a procession of a few men and a lot of boys and girls, set off in search of the santos. At this point I was unsure just what their santos were like. David and I joined the group that marched up the valley, parading from house to house. The violinist was now accompanied by a guitarist. They played a marching song, and the fiestero released a constant bombardment of fireworks. At the first hut, nearly at the western end of the valley, the pascolas emerged with nothing. They then proceeded to another hut, then another, and emerged from each holding a santo, which turned out to be any framed drawing or painting of a saint (among them San Isidro, Santo Niño de Atocha, St. Mary, and San Francisco) or even a famous person (in one case, a ballerina). At the last house they found several santos. The head pascola handed one to each child, then ordered all the children to kneel and hold one of the saints. Then he shooed everyone back to the fiesta arena still accompanied by guitar, violin and cohetes. Back at the ermita, once again the children kneeled, followed by the pascolas who bowed and crossed themselves in a ritualistic fashion. The head pascola then carefully mounted all the framed saints upon the saints' table, lit votive candles in front, and considered the fiesta begun.

The layout of the fiesta arena and these preliminary activities reveal rudiments of Catholicism but only rudiments. The santos on the table were primarily Catholic but not strongly so. The cross and rosary are of obvious Catholic origin but are not viewed clearly as such in the actual working of the tuburada. These elements have been incorporated from times in the distant past when Catholic missionaries were present or have been assimilated from other tribes, but the Guarijíos do not view themselves as strongly Catholic. No priest regularly visits them, and until 1998 there was no church in the Guarijío region.[4]

Pascolas and children with *santos,* Los Bajíos. Photo by David Burckhalter.

The remnants of Catholicism in the ceremonies were just that. Priests were not necessary for the ceremony and would be irrelevant to it.[5]

The men now gathered around the pascola ramada. Most of them, even younger boys, smoked cigarettes (including hand-rolled ones), and the air was thick with tobacco smoke. Those women of the village who were not already cooking, coalesced in the area of the cooking ramada. From all directions they came, carrying rolled-up petates under their arms, along with blankets and mesh bags. Children of all ages trundled alongside. There was no mixing of the sexes. Men did not speak to the women nor women to men. Neither approached the other's territory. From time to time young girls wandered over to the pascola ramada, but more than once I saw them shooed away by the fiesteros. These were decent, extremely hard working fellows who served their companions efficiently and with great politeness and whose personal sacrifice had to be great. They summoned men individually to the eating tables in shifts of ten or so, saying, in most polite Spanish or in Guarijío, "Would you like to eat?" serving each arrival a bowl of *guacabaqui,* a traditional stew of beans, squash, potatoes and meat (in this case, burro meat) accompanied by piles of corn tortillas, canned jalapeño chiles, and excellent coffee served in homeopathic doses. Women remained apart from the table, lingering in the immediate vicinity of the cooking ramada, their backs to the men, approaching the table only occasionally when necessity required that a young woman replenish a basket of tortillas or remove some dishes. The men acted as though the women were hidden from view, seldom if ever casting a glance in the direction of the feminine throng, though they were hardly twenty feet away from the tables.

It was now completely dark. The sole illumination was from the cooking fires, the campfire, and the votive candles on the ermita table. All those present watched and several commented as the full moon rose over the great Sierra San Joaquín that separates the Arroyo Guajaray from the Río Mayo. The soft light of the moon illuminated the many straw hats worn by the men, all, it seemed, of the same brand and shape. When the light was right, the reflection on the light-colored hats made the wearer's movements appear to be disembodied points of illumination. Even boys of five and six wore the hats, most of which were relatively new, apparently for the occasion. New shirts also appeared, mostly cowboy shirts. At an event that takes place only once each year, even for people of such meager means as the Guarijíos, a new shirt is a matter of intense personal pride. (The men crave cowboy-type apparel worn by Mexican boys and men, cowboys or not.)

Many women wore bright new dresses, skirts and blouses, as well as gaily colored scarves. Some held a nursing child in one arm and stirred and cooked with the other. The women were less visible, partly because they were working over bright cooking fires which obscured their features and because their heads were largely uncovered and their dark black hair reflected no moonlight. Several of them smoked fat hand-rolled cigarettes of cornhusk and native grown *tabaco rústico,* a practice apparently confined to fiestas or perhaps to tuburadas. When they sucked on their cigarettes, the glow appeared to be floating, a red firefly light that blinked and vanished. Around the cooking ramada, however, lay dozens of petates, sleeping mats woven in the village from the same palm used to make hats and baskets. On these and on sticker- and dust-resistant cotton blankets mothers laid their young children and, later on, themselves when they became sleepy as well they might, for they had been working hard all day preparing tortillas, cooking vats of beans and burro stew, and brewing strong coffee from freshly toasted beans for a couple of hundred people. As the evening wore on, this sleeping crowd took on the appearance of a ghostly massacre in the silver-plated moonlight. A handful of dogs and one cat mingled with the crowd, keeping close to their mistress, hoping for an errant crumb or morsel to fall to the ground.

It was as though an invisible line separated the women from the men. The western third of the fiesta arena belonged to the women, the eastern two-thirds to the men. Only the fiesteros and an occasional man or boy mingled with the women, and their mingling was only to ascertain that adequate food was being prepared and to fill the bowls, cups, and baskets of the hungry men. The fiesta was male-dominated and male-run. This seemed odd, for the tuburada is defined by the *tuburi,* the dance of women without which there is no tuburada. Pascola dancers are probably a tradition borrowed from Mayos. Tuburis are purely Guarijío.

When the moon was fully up and a lull in activity made it appear as though the fiesta would languish in apathy, the smell of burning *torote copal* (incense) wafted over the ramada. At the base of the cross, the huicastame, don Rufino, was burning marble-sized globes of fragrant torote copal of the *tecahuí (Bursera stenophylla)* in a large tin can filled with glowing coals, an olfactory signal that the tuburi would soon start. It was his decision when it would start, and he took his responsibility seriously. Shortly thereafter he seated himself on the otate bench and began to shake the *isahuira cuyabi* (sonajo, a pebble-filled gourd with a handle), summoning the young women to dance. This most pleasant sound continued for a good fifteen minutes. I watched the old man in the moonlight. He wore a light-colored cowl over his head, the mark of the cantador, a fellow told me. Presently he began to chant, and as if issuing from cracks in the earth, six or seven girls rose lightly from the ground nearby, hands joined, and floated toward the cross which they faced in a tight row, their backs to the cantador. He was silent for a moment, then began to chant steadily. In one motion the girls turned, all in the same direction. Tightly pressed together, they walked in a straight row toward him. Directly in front of him they halted and began to sway as one body to the rhythm of his cantos. At each extreme of the swaying, they stamped an outside foot, then swayed in the other direction and stamped that foot. This was the tuburi, the women's dance that forms the basis of the tuburada. I must add that while it was done with serious intent, the girls enjoyed it immensely, often giggling with glee when one got out of step or tripped in the effort. The oldest of the girls appeared to be fourteen or fifteen, the youngest no more than five or six.

The tuburi continued for perhaps an hour. The row of girls, illuminated only by the moonlight and occasionally flickering light from the cooking fires, swelled to about twelve. Some came and went, some went running to the toilet and running back to reclaim their place in the row. Finally the cantador said something and stopped singing. The girls dispersed and dissolved into the night.

As I returned to the pascola ramada, it dawned on me that I had been the only man watching the tuburi. None of the Guarijío men had watched or had even glanced in the direction of the tuburi, as far as I could determine. I surmised that this was not a show for men, but strictly a woman's affair and the men respectfully stayed away, just as the women refrained from snooping at the pascolas. Two different fiestas were taking place.

How different were the rules for men and women! The pascolas are invited to dance only if they have demonstrated

The *tuburi*, Los Bajíos. Photo by David Burckhalter.

Pascolas dancing the *canario*, Los Bajíos. Photo by David Burckhalter.

superior ability to dance, to beat out the rhythms of *sons* (folk songs) with their feet, and to follow memorized routines that may last for hours. Noninvited dancers (usually in a drunken state) are tactfully corralled and ushered from the ramada floor. They lack the skill and knowledge of the traditions necessary to be invited to be a pascola at the tuburada.

For the tuburi, on the other hand, there are no apparent requirements. All women appear to be invited to participate. Women of all ages come and go. Experience is not an issue. The women's dance is more a participatory than a spectator activity. So in the tuburada, most women dance, most men watch. It is as if for one night the confinement of women to home and chores is lifted and they join with their mothers, sisters, daughters, and friends to celebrate *their* fiesta.

The pascolas continued, taking occasional breaks of fifteen minutes, then resuming their rotation. The music was quite similar to that of the Mayos, from whom the Guarijíos acknowledge they learned about musical instruments. The violinist played the melody and variations, all of which were familiar to the pascolas who beat their bare feet to the cadence of the sons, and the lyrics also, someone said. The harpist provided both the bass notes and the rhythm. While the music was repetitious, it was not at all boring. After listening for several hours I realized I had not heard any piece of music repeated. The musicians played without expression as though they were expected to be pure background accompaniment and no competition for the stars of the show, the pascolas.

I slipped from the tuburada to sleep for a few hours. I had hoped for a quiet night in the dormitory, a quarter-mile from the fiesta arena, but it was not to be. The atmosphere was close in the stuffy, hot room, making sleep nearly impossible. From time to time more people came in, clicking cigarette lighters to show them the way, boys, mostly, but a couple of men as well, claiming a bunk, talking loudly, their boots stomping (boys like to wear boots, not the hua-raches of three points that their fathers wear) as they came in to catch a couple of hours of sleep and then return to the fiesta. Mosquitoes buzzed me, but it was too hot to cover myself with a blanket, so I lay listening to the myriad sounds, the still, sad music of humanity. Every hour or so a barrage of firecrackers and skyrockets exploded at the fiesta below, awakening all but the most profound sleepers.

At 5:00 A.M., following a night of little sleep, I arose and made my way to the fiesta arena. The pascolas were dancing still. Soon came the full light of day, however, and around 8:00 A.M. the fiesteros, looking weary but still good-natured and alert, summoned the first shift to the tables for the morning meal. The activity for the day was done. After the meal all except for the fiesteros and the cooking women gradually retired to their homes to relax and sleep. It was then that I realized that the crowd had swelled considerably during the night. Some folks had arrived from Guajaray, so the village was represented after all. Others had come from Mesa Colorada on the Río Mayo, some from Todos Santos, a few miles downstream, a few from Basicorepa, farther up the Guajaray, and a delegation from El Frijolar, a rancho of Guarijíos and mestizos in the higher mountains far to the north. Furthermore, pascola masks had arrived from Mesa Colorada, along with two more musicians (one a talented harpist) and two more pascolas as well. The tuburada would be in full swing tonight.

By mid-morning I was feeling hot and dusty. The dry tropical forest in the late spring when the soil is bone dry and all the leaves have fallen from the trees is a monotonous silvery brown color locally called *mojino.* The desiccated mojino aspect of the landscape only added to the parched appearance of the village as it shimmered across the rising hot air currents of the valley floor. By late morning my thermometer registered 101 degrees. A super-heated wind was blowing dust over everything. I admired the busy fiesteros and Guarijío women as they continued to work through the scorching day.

I thought of the river. It was close enough that it beckoned. I crossed the sun-baked landscape and visited Rafael Méndez briefly with one purpose in mind. After a brief conversation I asked him about swimming in the river. I had no bathing suit.

"Rafael," I asked hesitatingly, "I would like to go swimming. Is there a good *aguaje* down at the river?"

"Yes, David," he answered with a half-smile. "There's one that's very deep, but you must be careful because it is so deep you could easily drown."

I assured him that would not be my problem. "Well, I wonder if your customs permit people like me to swim, well, *bichi* or if it is necessary to wear clothing? I don't want to offend anyone after you have been so gracious in your hospitality."

Rafael laughed. "Well, David, you can wear clothing if you wish, but we Guarijío men swim with bare bottoms just as we were born. That's how we do it all the time!"

I bolted for the river. The path or camino followed the flat valley floor for a quarter mile then dropped abruptly, snaking down the face of a cliff, then working its way the rest of the way down along a ravine that over the centuries had been trod by countless feet, shod and bare. The way was treacherous, for many of the volcanic rocks were round and acted as excellent ball bearings conspiring with gravity to trip the careless passerby.

Where the ancient trail dropped off to the river below I heard human sounds and watched two horses emerge from the brush two hundred feet below me. I walked down the narrow trail as the horses began to work their way up. On them were mounted five Guarijíos, a man who appeared to be in his late twenties with a little boy mounted in front of him and a woman with downcast eyes with a nursing child mounted in front and boy slightly older behind her. A fourth child, a lad of no more than seven or eight years old, walked behind, accompanied by a dog. When I greeted them the fellow asked me if the *juez* (judge) were in the village. He had heard a rumor of the dignitary's presence and had made the trip, for he needed to register his children so that they could receive benefits, enroll in school, and some day vote or own property. He was from El Frijolar, high in the mountains, a ride of a day and a half to the north, many miles from the nearest government outpost. The previous night they had stayed at a ranch halfway to Los Bajíos. He looked most sad when I told him I doubted that the judge was there. It meant that he had made the three-day trip for naught, unless he wanted to go the additional day and a half to Quiriego. Los Bajíos, unlike other Sonoran Guarijío villages, is located under the legal jurisdiction of the Municipio of Quiriego, not of Alamos, so all legal proceedings must be done through that ancient capital to the west. The fellow spurred his horse and continued anxiously up the trail. The children stared at me in wonder. The woman averted her gaze and clutched the infant. The dog lifted a suspicious eyebrow then sauntered on behind them.

I reached the river bottom and followed a trail through the dense underbrush a hundred yards upstream where I found a pool that must have been ten feet deep. The water was a deep blue-green. Many fish traced their way through the water. These were not large, since these introduced *talapia* reach only eight or nine inches in length, unlike the large catfish and perch they have gradually replaced. I looked around, up the dark volcanic cliffs, covered with amoles and tescalamas (rock figs) and up and down the narrow, brushy canyon bottom, and saw not a soul in sight. I stripped off my clothes, trying not to be self-conscious, and dived into the cool water. I splashed and dove like a teenager. Upstream a group of Guarijío lads were doing the same. They wore trunks or cut-off Levi's.

Refreshed, I slipped my clothes back on and began to plod back up the trail. Ahead was a short Guarijío man staggering under the weight of two five-gallon buckets filled with water suspended from a yoke on his shoulders. I waited at a respectful distance, realizing that all the village water had to be hauled this way. Among their many responsibilities, the fiesteros needed to keep the barrels full for the nearly two hundred men and women, requiring multiple trips to the river. Carrying that eighty-pound load of sloshing liquid up those hills was a fatiguing chore, and it had to be repeated numerous times. After seeing all the labor that went into providing water to the village, I conserved all the water I could. I also wondered at the political cynicism symbolized by the lofty water tower that promised much and delivered nothing and how much easier the villagers' life would be made by a functioning gravity flow water supply. (One reason for the expansion of the village was the assurance of available water through the tinaco.)

That evening the pascolas, now five of them with two additional musicians seated at the opposite end, danced even more vigorously, their feet pounding to the rhythms of the sons and the cocoons and bells maintaining an almost constant beat. They danced in a row for a time, advancing and retreating in unison. Darkness fell and still they danced. The musicians, seated at opposite ends of the pascola ramada, took turns playing. In the vague, pre-light of the moon I realized that at the cantador's bench more than twenty young women and girls were now dancing the tuburi, the number diminished or augmented according to the whims of the dancing women. Still the men stayed well at a distance, not even casting a glance at the dancing women. At the pascola ramada the pascolas ceased their dance and began an odd ritual, rolling up corn husks into thick, ear-like sheaves, attaching them to stalks, and with the help of a heavy sharpened steel bar, plunging the point into the ground surrounding the ermita until about thirty of these pseudo-cornstalks stood upright. A quiet Guarijío named Remigio Ciriaco sat next to me on the bench. He explained that this was an important part of the tuburada, for in the morning the pascolas would "pick" these symbolic ears, signaling an end to the fiesta. We talked for a while, and he urged me in a most humble fashion to be at the pascola ramada at about 3:00 A.M. when the pascolas would begin to frolic, engaging in all manner of outrageous activities, culminating with the milking of a cow and the lassoing of a bull. I would like this very much, he assured me earnestly. This part of the tuburada was unpredictable and the bull injected a note of risk as well.

The night deepened. The moon came up, casting its eerie light on the busy fiesta. I wandered through the crowd of hats worn by men of all ages who were focused now on the pascolas. Two un-Guarijío-looking men, tall and well-built, wearing expensive cowboy clothing, approached me. I had noticed them earlier as they rode into the village on well-fed, handsome horses. They were from a nearby ranch called La Vinata (The Still), they said, and had brought some *bacanora,* a moonshine Sonoran liquor revered throughout Mexico. One of them offered the bottle and I tried it. Smooth as silk. The good stuff. I expressed my endorsement.

"Want to buy some?" he asked, pushing his face close to mine. His companion nodded. "I've got more than five liters on my horse. The best. Real *bacanora.*"

I thought for a minute. If he had brought just one bottle, he would pass it around and it would be gone quickly. Maybe I could knock down just a drop and fit right in with the fiesta. But more than a gallon, and for sale! This was deliberately aimed at the Guarijíos. Catch them at the height of the fiesta, give them a taste of good moonshine, let them buy the rest and get drunk. I wanted no part of it.

I walked away from the hustlers. I had been warned that bad things would begin to happen when booze appeared on the scene. I could feel it coming.

It was about midnight. I left the fiesta and returned to the now crowded and even stuffier dormitory. Young people came and went, including another delegation from Guajaray. I heard voices of youths, boys and girls, throughout the blackness. Mosquitoes buzzed me to add to the confused, trying night.

At three thirty I awoke from a brief sleep. From the direction of the fiesta arena came laughter and music. In the moonlight I made my way once again toward the fiesta arena, not wanting to miss the activity. On the pathway a Guarijío man I did not recognize in the dark passed going in the other direction. I greeted him and he me. "Are you going to the fiesta?" He asked me in soft Spanish. I said I was.

"It's dangerous there," he said simply. "*Mucho borracho* (a lot of drunkenness going on)."

"I know," I said, not wanting to be treated like a naïve outsider. Sounds of humans involved in fun were luring me to the fiesta. I took a step toward the arena, then stopped and turned to him, realizing that he was being most thoughtful and I was being an ass.

"Do you think I shouldn't go down there?"

He nodded several times in the Guarijío fashion. "*Mucho borracho.*" He repeated.

I had been warned a few days ago in San Bernardo that some fellows of questionable repute might be at the fiesta. The warning I had just received was enough. I thanked my guardian angel and walked back to the dormitory. He vanished into the night.

It grew light at 4:45 A.M. I hurried to the fiesta arena, regretful at the thought of missing a great spectacle. I wove my way through the throng, many of whom were staggering and slurring drunken words. Remigio still sat on the bench, appearing not to have moved. I resumed my seat next to him.

"Did you sleep?" he asked. I told him I had dozed a little.

"There's a lot of drinking here," he said, matter of factly.

I nodded and shook my head in sadness. I was close enough to him to tell that he had not been drinking himself.

I looked across the arena. The mestizos who had brought the bacanora were surrounded by a gang of drunken Guarijíos. One of them leaped up and jumped inside the pascola ramada, yelling in Spanish, demanding music in a loud voice. When none was forthcoming he danced a rapid jig, trying to imitate a pascola, but with exaggerated, aggressive motions, utterly unlike the subtle, gentle movements of the pascolas. He loudly sang a Mexican song all the while. The onlookers laughed (uneasily, I thought) and seemed relieved when he sprang from the ramada and went running back to the group of revelers. Soon he was back, still calling for music, trying to snatch a violin away from the musician, who remained seated and impassive. A fiestero hastened to rescue this violinist as well, trying politely to urge the young man away. Across from me sat the three boys from El Frijolar whom I had met on the trail the day before. They wore identical new shirts and hats. They stared gravely at the drunken activity. Twenty feet away the mestizos were still passing around bottles of bacanora, although many of the Guarijíos could barely stand. A young woman with a baby timidly approached the pascola ramada and watched from a distance. She was accosted by a drunken Guarijío who tried to embrace her and the baby. The child screamed in protest but the fellow persisted. The young woman retreated to the cooking ramada.

Just as I sat, Chémali, the leader of pascolas began shredding cornhusks into small pieces and dropping them carefully on the ground of the pascola ramada. Nacho, another pascola who was obviously inebriated, cupped a large basket in his hands and held it below his crotch for all to see. In the basket he held a small gourd with a curving, protuberant stem that clearly resembled a penis. The men and boys took great delight in this spectacle.

I asked Remigio what was happening. "This is the owl dance. The pascolas will pick up the 'eggs' (corn husks) and put them in the basket just the way an owl does."

As he spoke, Nacho kneeled as though he was going to vomit, but instead cradled the basket in front of him. The musicians began to play and the other pascolas danced around Nacho, picking up the pieces of cornhusks and placing them in the basket. Some of the pascolas pretended to copulate with Nacho the owl, provoking widespread guffaws from the audience of men and boys. Then Nacho rose and all five pascolas danced back and forth in a row, reaching a near frenzy.

The pascolas sat down shakily. Chémali, the lead pascola, appeared with a clay bowl of ashes from the fire pit and carefully sifted them between his fingers onto the ground, drawing a large X from one end of the ramada to the other. Remigio indicated this was to be the canary dance. Chémali directed the other pascolas to their positions. They held cowboy hats in each hand. They danced, following the legs of the X, passing each other clumsily, and acting confused. Nacho, drunk as he was, managed to help Chémali straighten them out and direct their motion in the complicated dance. Back and forth they went, hopping from the X formation into a row, turning abruptly in the opposite direction, then turning once again and back into the X, constantly under Chémali's strong guidance. Suddenly they stopped in front of the musicians at the east end of the ramada. They bowed in turn to each of the musicians and shook their hands. Shortly after this the fiesteros appeared and began to carry off the instruments to the pascola hut.

I turned and looked at Remigio with consternation. He nodded gravely. "The fiesta is over," he told me sadly.

"I thought they were going to pick the corn, milk the cow, and lasso the bull," I protested.

"They were supposed to, but the pascolas are too drunk to do it." Indeed, watching the pascolas (except for Chémali, who appeared sober and highly irritated) drooling and staggering, babbling nonsense to each other, I understood the futility of further ceremony.

Chémali mustered all his resources and gathered the pascolas around the saints' table. He called on the older violinist and summoned the girls and boys. They stood in perfect formation as he handed to each one of the santos from the table until all were distributed. Then he pointed in the direction of the houses and the procession set off in the reverse order in which they had picked up the saints two days ago. Some members of the procession experienced difficulty in negotiating the path to the houses. Chémali led with magnificent patience and dignity, however, and at the last house the children kneeled and returned the last of the saints. A fiestero sent up a skyrocket. The sound reverberated off the hills. A weary silence fell over the valley. It was over.

Chémali came walking in my direction. I grasped his hand and thanked him for the tuburada. He replied humbly, "Thank you, American friend, for coming to visit us

Sierra García and the end of the tuburada,
Los Bajíos. Photo by David Burckhalter.

and seeing our fiesta." He walked wearily back to the fiesta arena, which was now depleted of its former crowd. He was exhausted but, I thought, happy.

The sun was already hot as David and I packed our trappings and waited for Chal and the burro. The women were plodding up the hills away from the fiesta arena, their arms full of blankets and bundles. Their children walked alongside, each carrying something. A woman walked by preceded by a little girl hardly more than a year old. She toted a tiny bundle. David and I watched her toddle off into the distance to her palm-thatched hut, followed by the slow footsteps of her stolid mother.

Chal arrived and packed the burro. It had taken him nearly two hours to locate the rascal, and after all that he had been found hiding next to one of the huts only a hundred yards away. We set off just as a fight broke out near the ramadas. Two brothers had been arguing, then came to blows. Others rushed in to separate them. Both brothers were drunk. Chal knew them and shook his head sadly. The Mexican booze venders were mounted on their horses, faces red and swollen but seemingly happy, their purses undoubtedly heavier with proceeds from the sale of bacanora.

We climbed the steep hill out of the valley to the mesa above the village. At the fence gate the young man who had so boisterously and drunkenly danced the evening before was seated on the ground, two older men blocking his departure. His fine horse was tethered to a tree. He was cursing and lamenting in Spanish, "Why are you hiding me here? I want to go and have fun. Let me go." The men made no answer. As we passed they nodded politely, regretfully. When the young man saw us he abruptly changed his demeanor. "Come again to see us. Say hello to the people below." Then he returned to his blasphemies and wailing. Punishment, Guarijío style, was in progress. The judges were patiently carrying out their sentence.

We reached the ridge and plunged down the other side, leaving the view of Los Bajíos behind. A few Guarijíos passed us on the trail. Their faces betrayed no hint of emotion. Were they feeling a letdown after the excitement of the tuburada? Were they scandalized by the failure of the pascolas to end it properly? What was really going on? Had Guarijíos come from all over because it was a social event that interrupted what must be arduous solitude? Did they come because as Guarijíos they were drawn to the power of the tuburada? Was it an affirmation of their Guarijío-ness? Or is such an idea Anglo-European anthrobabble? Could it be that they came just for a good time? How would I ever find out the "real" meaning of the tuburada? Forget it, I told myself.[6]

I thought of Chémali's distressed face on being unable to finish the fiesta. What could I read into that? I thought back on Remigio's (I thought) sober countenance when the events he had promised did not take place. What did that mean?

Then it struck me that I had concluded wrongly about the end of the tuburada. I thought it had failed. It had not. I was interjecting my Waspish interpretation inside the Guarijíos' heads.

The tuburada had ended prematurely, I thought, because the participants were too drunk to continue. What did "prematurely" mean? That the festival ended without part of the rituals being completed. But from what I could see, the fiesta was still viewed as a successful tuburada by the Guarijíos. Chémali appeared to be irritated, but no one else shared his ire. Maybe he is a cranky sort of fellow. The women had gathered and danced the tuburi. They had nearly three days of happy chattering. They had brought their young children to be with other Guarijío children. They and their daughters had heard the chanting voice of the cantador. They had swayed to the rhythm, pounded the earth with their feet. That was the perfect tuburada.

From the fiesteros' viewpoint, they had done their task well. The guests had been fed. The ramadas had withstood three days of intense use. The water barrels had been kept full. The musicians had been honored, and the foreign guests had been treated politely. Boys had observed the gathering of the santos, the sanctification of the ermita, they had watched the pascolas, seen the owl and the canary dance, laughed when others laughed, remained serious when others remained serious. The magic of the tuburada had surely rubbed off on them.

What, then, of the drinking and drunkenness? I asked Cipriano later about that. He explained patiently that some drinking (and, I think, the altered consciousness associated with it) was always a part of the tuburada. People once drank *tepachi,* and to some extent still do, but the stronger bacanora often takes its place. The mestizos took advantage of the Guarijíos by selling bacanora, but the tuburada is still the celebration of Tata Dios's fondness for the Guarijíos, and a little drunkenness is part of a good celebration. Cipriano did not approve of the bacanora. But he wasn't about to condemn it, either.

No, the tuburada did not dissolve into chaotic drunkenness. It ended when the pascolas could no longer carry on. The degree of their inebriation may have been the result of a miscalculation of the strength of the brew, but they had no regrets, I now think. They had performed for Tata Diós. And that was the important thing.

We reached Guajaray in less than four hours, making only one stop. In the village, people stared as we plodded by. Nacho's palm roof was finished. Farther on a family was camped out under a ramada, a half-thatched hut behind them. A pile of newly cut logs lay next to Eliazar's house. The burro stood stoically while we untied our belongings from his back and dumped them in the truck. We sat down to rest at the small square table in the shade of the large ramada.

"Comida," (food) Chal ordered his mother. "Bring a chair," he snapped at his little six-year-old niece. "Coffee," he barked again at his mother. María Rufina protested mildly that we had gotten home so suddenly that she hadn't had time to fix the meal, but her son glared at her and she ceased. Soon we were served tortillas and beans and fine coffee. I was embarrassed by Chal's behavior but could think of no way to express the feeling. We thanked María Rufina and her daughters profusely, paid them, and were in the truck and off, leaving behind the remnants of the last tuburada in Los Bajíos.

In 1997 Chal was shot and killed in an argument with another young Guarijío of mixed ancestry. The incident took place during the tuburada of Guajaray. His uncle reported that both youths were drunk.

In 1998 don Rufino, the huicastame (cantador) of Los Bajíos, died of a stroke. The blind harpist, apparently a diabetic, also died.

5
Guarijíos

Guarijíos are a tiny indigenous group. Government sources estimate that roughly eighteen hundred Guarijíos remain in Guarijío lands (Leobardo Quiroz, personal communication 1995).[1] My surveys suggest this figure is somewhat high and a figure of twelve hundred is more realistic.[2] Whatever the accurate figure, Guarijíos constitute little more than one-tenth of one percent of Sonora's population. I suspect that fewer than one percent of Sonorans have ever heard of Guarijíos.

Many older Guarijíos are still functionally monolingual in the Guarijío language. This, however, is changing as children are taught Spanish as their primary language in the schools. For the majority of the grade-school-age children in the larger villages, Guarijío is now the second language. Often they do not speak it at all. Boarding schools (in Los Bajíos, Mesa Colorada, and Loreto) place children in a Spanish-speaking milieu for extended periods of time, where peer pressure, teacher influence, and the environment tend to reproduce Spanish speaking and discourage the children's use of the Guarijío language. Children learn that the language of social acceptance is Spanish. Parents, wanting the best for their children, do not demur.

Guarijíos' adherence to traditional ways has been reinforced by their topographical isolation. Most of the Guarijío country is still accessible only on foot or in the saddle. Among larger settlements only Guajaray (partially mestizo), Mesa Colorada, and Loreto (largely mestizo) are accessible by motor vehicle. The mountainous terrain harbors a vast network of caminos that connect all villages with all other villages. Along the Río Mayo the shortest trails involve numerous crossings of the river. Alternate routes are used during times of flooding. Some of these are extremely steep and circuitous, a necessity in the convoluted topography of the region. One well-known (unmarked) intersection deep in the forest is noteworthy: The eastern trail leads to El Saúz and Bavícora via Talayote. The western link drops down to the mestizo settlement of Tepara on the Río Mayo. The northern route leads to Charajaqui, Jogüegüe, and Gocojaqui (with connections to Bavícora!). The southern link connects to Mesa Colorada and Mochibampo via Huataturi.

Little-used routes tie Bavícora and Caramechi to the mountain sites inhabited by Guarijíos de la Sierra. An arduous pathway leads from Bavícora to Guasisaco. From there another arrives at Loreto, many hours away. At Loreto connections can be made to Tojíachi and Chiltepín and so on. A couple of Guarijíos are said to walk everywhere in the region. In addition, Cipriano Buitimea notes that many Guarijíos have their own trails that they use when they do not wish to meet up with other beings. For a few weeks just before las aguas, when no leaves remain on the trees and the forest resembles a wasteland of dried sticks, the crisscrossing network of trails is visible from afar. With the rains, the verdure nearly covers the evidence within a few days, and the traces of human passage visible from afar mostly disappear.

Guarijíos live a semisubsistence way of life, raising small crops of corn, beans, amaranth, and squash on hillside mahuechis for their own consumption. In the last decade recurring dry cycles in Chihuahua and Sonora have produced crop failures and forced Guarijíos to rely heavily on Mexican government food provisions. The period of September 1998–June 2000 was the driest on record. No measurable rain fell through most of the region from September 1998 through June 1999. The summer rains of 1999 were sparse, and no equipatas fell.

In spite of such dry cycles, most years Guarijíos are able to extract corn Hopi-like from soils that appear to be parched. In the lowlands, however, after mid-August 1999 there was no rain for six months. The cornstalks withered and the plants died. No one harvested corn.

Guarijíos supplement their cultivation with widespread gathering of native plant resources. This is not surprising, given their history of marginalization, exploitation, and extreme poverty and their confinement to the mountainous, agriculturally unproductive *serrano* region. Gentry (1963) documented the impressive diversity of their ethnobotanical practices in the 1930s. Most of these persist, as can be seen in the plant list (chapter 15). Nearly all Guarijíos supplement cultivated crops with foods gathered from the forest. Several older men who live a peripatetic life in the mountains, may subsist for days almost exclusively on gathered plant products. José Ruelas, a nomadic Guarijío, spent several days on the trail with me expounding at length on wild food resources. In all the households we visited, food and medicinal products of the monte were present. Nearly all huts are constructed entirely of local resources. In villages removed from roadways, the only materials from outside sources are often machetes and knives, clothing, metal cooking utensils, occasional tinned and packaged foods, and plastic or metal water containers.

Guarijíos, by their own proud admission, are loners. They prefer living in small groups of only a couple of families. Multiple families live in the larger villages, Mesa Colorada, Guajaray, Los Bajíos, and Loreto. Many Guarijíos live in these centers due to government programs, not because the Guarijíos prefer it that way (Mesa Colorada was a large cornfield before the INI established it as a Guarijío service center in the mid-1980s). Even in these new villages, the homes sprawl over a wide area. Where huts are built close together, it is a reflection of kinship rather than social desire.[3] The twenty or so homes of Bavícora sprawl for nearly a kilometer up and down Arroyo Bavícora, the bulk of them invisible from any other house. The Guarijíos of Loreto live in dispersed sites around the periphery of the village. Only in San Bernardo have Guarijíos given up their traditional Daniel Boonesque preference for living apart. They live atop a mesa in close proximity on land that is not their own. And, other Guarijíos say, they are a people apart. Still, even they clearly demark their lots with fences of closely spaced slats of pitahaya ribs through which it is nearly impossible to see. Fences give the illusion of apartness.

The Tuburada

Anthropological descriptions of the Guarijíos are scant. Gentry's is the most complete but distressingly brief. Without pretending to provide a comprehensive ethnology of the Guarijíos, I point out that their social cohesion is perpetuated by their language and the tuburada, their festival. Since it is the latter that Guarijíos believe distinguishes them from other indigenous people, I describe it in some detail (see chapter 3 for a field description).

Each village and many settlements sponsor a tuburada each year. Some festivals take place on a fixed date. Impromptu special occasions often call for a tuburada as well. For example, a tuburada was held at Jánaco in May 1993 to celebrate the return to Guarijío country of Teresa Valdivia Dounce. Another took place at La Junta around Christmas 1993 to celebrate the opening of a small clinic. Whether or not a tuburada takes place often depends as well on the availability of a sponsor to provide food for the guests and money for the musicians and pascolas. Tuburadas among the Guarijíos de la sierra have declined in number and now appear to be confined to Tojíachi. Loreto no longer observes one.

Guarijíos everywhere look forward to the tuburadas as their most important and exciting occasions of the year. This contrasts with mestizo culture in which Easter Week and Christmas, in that order, are the most important tunes. Neither of these is observed by traditional Guarijíos. In many areas a tuburada was (and some still are) held to celebrate the planting of corn and another to coincide with the corn harvest. In the sponsoring village or settlement the entire populace marshals its efforts to prepare for the fiesta, especially to clear, rake, and sweep the flat or field where the event is to be held. Festival officials (*alaguásim* or fiesteros) oversee all preparations. The villagers erect several ramadas, one for the kitchen, one for the pascola dancers, and others to provide shade for those attending the fiesta. In the lowlands ramada roofs are usually made of guásima branches, though other plants may be used as well. Guásima leaves remain attached to the branches for several days and also retain their green tint. In the highlands, willows are used for the same purpose. At San Bernardo *guachomó (Baccharis salicifolia)* was used. The village folk also sweep the entire area meticulously to remove any impediments to dancing. Usually, they also erect a fence along the perimeter of the fiesta area to keep out livestock, especially cows and, above all, burros, whose innocent appearance belies a treacherous heart. Dogs and pigs invade the hallowed grounds. These are often chased off, but they may also be tolerated.

Usually the fiestas last two days, sometimes only one. Older Guarijíos decry this brevity, maintaining that a proper tuburada lasts three days, the way Tata Diós intended it, they say. Several important features stand out in the festival. First, it is a gathering of folk of all ages from all parts of the region. Part of the excitement generated at the tuburada is the anticipation of seeing old friends and relatives, of wondering who will arrive at the fiesta. Women and children, after all, often do not leave their village for many months at a time except to attend tuburadas or school. In anticipation of guests arriving, children often act as sentinels at lookout points and report on travelers as they near the site. The greetings are reserved, quiet affairs. The Guarijío greeting is a soft, semiembrace, or an extended handshake in which the fingertips gently brush the inside of the other's arm.

A second integral part of the tuburada is the ritual and prolonged preparation of food. The menu for all meals consists of corn tortillas, beans, a watery meat-based stew (of burro, goat, coatimundi, or in unusually good times, beef) called guacavaqui,[4] and coffee (when available) from green coffee beans toasted with sugar in a skillet. The

Guarijías preparing the grounds for tuburada, Mesa Colorada.

kitchen ramada consists of several mounded adobe stoves atop which sit great ollas full of slowly boiling beans and stew. Other fires burn beneath comales, tractor discs used for heating tortillas.

For many hours the kitchen ramada is alive with the gentle sounds of the Guarijío language and the pat-pat-pat of female hands shaping tortillas. Men are generally excluded from the kitchen. When the food is ready the fiesta leaders graciously invite all in attendance to dine at the common table, a long series of raised planks, while other planks act as benches.[5]

At night many of the women smoke large cigarettes hand rolled from corn husks filled with dried, chopped *papante* (macuchi, tabaco rústico), a native tobacco. Normally, Guarijío women do not smoke. The Guarijío tobacco has a strong smell, rather like that of marijuana. I asked someone at the tuburada if they were smoking *mota* and he laughed, thinking I must be a dunce.

Guarijíos plant and raise their own papante from seed saved fastidiously each year. One January day I happened upon a freshly plowed plot perhaps a third of an acre in size on the very banks of the Río Mayo. Two men were planting carefully measured rows. I asked what they were planting, and they showed me the tobacco seed. The plot was vulnerable, I supposed, to flooding should a powerful equipata blow in. The moisture from the river kept the soil moist by capillary action, so they would not need to irrigate, and the risk was worth the potential benefit. They would harvest it later and have enough for most of Mesa Colorada. Smoking it is an indispensable part of the tuburada.

A third component of the fiesta is the opening, an elaborate ceremony in which the participants parade through the village or settlement to the accompaniment of skyrockets and firecrackers. The procession is headed by pascolas,[6] the central attraction of the tuburada. Pascolas wear a carved wooden mask with a grotesque expression festooned with a beard and hair. Wound around their ankles and calves pascolas wear long strands of ténaborim that swish when they are shaken. Around their waists they attach a wide leather belt from which dangle cascabeles or *coyoles*—

brass bells—or hooves of goat or deer.

The procession pauses at each Guarijío home to gather santos.[7] These are saints or revered household items and may be anything from images of Catholic saints to patently secular photographs of movie stars or cherished trinkets. The pascolas then display the santos collectively on a central plank table called the ermita. The pascolas watch over this shrine to assure that a host of illuminating candles is never extinguished through the long daytime and night of the tuburada. The pascolas and musicians reverently store their hats beneath the ermita table.

Fourth, the men establish their separate area, including a ramada, where they are entertained by ongoing pascola dances of a wide variety and considerable intricacy. The dancers don their masks and ténaborim and cinch up their coyole belts. As they walk they shake their waists to jingle the coyoles and wiggle their legs to make the ténaborim swish. They are accompanied by musicians, primarily harpists and violinists, who may have journeyed from afar.[8]

The tuburada proceeds according to a predetermined schedule of these dances, which continue all night, pausing only during the heat of the day, affording the participants a chance to sleep. Women do not enter the pascola ramada area. Sometimes, not often, women can be seen watching from a distance. Young girls may venture closer but are then shooed away by the fiesteros. The dances are grouped in phases throughout the tuburada, with the most important coming at the conclusion.

Finally, and most important, the women perform their own dance, the tuburi.[9] The huicastame (cantador, *cantaturi, nacantáturi*), an old man, sings cantos to lead the dancers. He can be seen after dusk, a solitary figure with a cloth draped over his head, seated apart from the other centers of activity. He is the only male participating in the tuburi.

The dance is the backbone of the tuburada. Indeed, Guarijíos stress that without the tuburi, there can be no tuburada. While the pascola dance is shared with (perhaps borrowed from) other indigenous groups of northwest Mexico and the musical instruments are of European origin, only the Guarijíos perform the tuburada, they say.[10]

The ritual is performed only after sunset and before sunrise. The ritual area is illuminated by a small bonfire, not far from the kitchen ramada where the women are gathered. The cantador's head is covered with a kerchief so that his upper face cannot be seen, or, perhaps, so that he cannot see the women. He sits on a seat of cane poles resting on twin rocks. He faces a cross (the santa cruz) sunk upright in

Pascola mask. Drawing by Paul Mirocha.

the ground some ten meters distant and covered with a cloth shroud. He may shake *bulis* (gourd rattles) as he sings, his high, old voice wailing eerily but melodically. Women of all ages (including little girls) line up in a tight row facing him. As he sings, they sway back and forth in unison, stamping their outer foot at each swaying to the beat of the music. Then they abruptly turn about and march to the cross. They then turn around and return in step to the cantador. This process is repeated until the cantador grows tired. The women return to the kitchen. The cantador rests for a while, then summons the women again and they repeat the ritual. And on and on it goes through the night.

Although the tuburi is a most serious ceremony, the women and girls take great delight in participating. If one makes a misstep, the others giggle and pull her back into rhythm. They leave and return at will without any appearance of competition, and they dance without any hint of self-consciousness. No men look on, none except for the cantador even approach the site of the tuburi.

The tuburada ends preferably following the dawn of the third day but more often the second. The pascolas complete the ritual dances and thank the musicians for their music. Then they reverse the gathering of the santos and people slowly file away from the fiesta grounds and return to their homes. The fiesta's end is usually followed by a time of good will among all Guarijíos who, they say, return to their fields and homes with renewed pride at being a Guarijío and a renewed sense of closeness to the earth, especially now that the land is theirs.[11]

Physical Appearance

While generalizations about ethnic physical differences are potentially misleading and can lead to unfortunate stereotypes, they can also be useful when viewed merely as rough guidelines and little more. Since Guarijíos, Mayos, Tarahumaras, Yaquis, and mestizos have been living in close proximity for centuries and intermarriage has been widespread, any attempt to establish a Guarijío "type" would be folly. The record of migrant Yaquis living in Guadalupe Victoria in the nineteenth century is a clear example (Almada 1937:271). There are Guarijíos of all shapes and sizes. Some are indistinguishable from mestizos, while others seem decidedly "Guarijío" in appearance.

Still, (and with the above caveat in mind) a number of things can be said of their appearance. Whether for nutritional or genetic reasons, both men and women tend to be shorter in stature than mestizos or Mayos, and the gender differences in size are less noticeable. While there are obese Guarijíos, most are lean, especially the men. A study carried out by El Colegio de Sonora in 1993–94 (Salazar and Salido 1996) found clearly detectable effects of malnutrition on growth.[12] Nearly half the children in the albergue of Mesa Colorada demonstrated reduced growth and signs of varying degrees of malnutrition. Another study of Guarijío children in boarding schools shows them to be small for their age, below average in weight for their age, and below average in weight for their size (Palacios et al. 1996). On a superficial and unscientific basis, I have repeatedly noticed the small size of Guarijío children, even those enrolled in the albergue where they might be expected to receive more nutritious meals. Teenage boys often do not exceed five feet in height.

Another superficial observation of mine is that the Guarijíos possess a distinctive gait that makes their upper bodies appear to float. They raise their feet high when walking and hold their upper torsos steady. This most agreeable motion is probably derived from their constant climbing and descending of their mountains, even by toddlers, which necessitates habitual lifting of the feet in anticipation of obstacles. Indeed, Guarijíos complain at

having to cross extensive plateaus and flatlands.[13]

Guarijío men and boys are inordinately fond of commercial straw hats, which they wear at every opportunity, beginning as little boys as soon as they are able to hold a hat on their heads. At the tuburadas the sight of a hundred or so light colored hats gliding through the dusky chiaroscuro of the ramadas is agreeable indeed.

Women, especially those from the more isolated villages, are often shy and retiring. They will go to great lengths to avoid contact with outsiders. This reticence may well stem from a history of abuse by outsiders as well as a cultural manifestation of separation from people of other ethnic backgrounds.

Guarijío women are almost never seen wearing pants. They prefer long, full skirts and colorful blouses, and they wear their hair long. Any typical Guarijío dress, however, has long since disappeared. So great has been the poverty of the Guarijíos that traditional dress was a luxury they could never afford.

Language

The Guarijío language is close to that of the Tarahumaras. Their linguistic similarities were noted by Jesuits (Almada 1937:64) and detailed by subsequent linguists (Kroeber 1934; Miller 1983, 1996). Some Guarijíos claim they can understand Tarahumaras (Donald Burgess, personal communication 1995). At times river Guarijíos even refer to sierra Guarijíos as Tarahumaras (Miller 1996).[14]

The language belongs to the Uto-Aztecan family of languages (Kroeber 1934). Miller (1983) distinguished, as do the Guarijíos themselves, between the language of the Guarijíos del río and that of the Guarijíos de la sierra. The variant spoken at Bavícora apparently represents a melding of the two. Bavícora is socially connected with the Guarijíos del río (many Guarijíos of Mesa Colorada and other settlements were born in Bavícora), but it is closer linguistically to the sierran dialect then the river dialect (Barreras 1996; Miller 1996).

Some of the notable characteristics of the language include the following: The letter *l* of the river Guarijío is not differentiated from their *r*. This has made it difficult for me unambiguously to phoneticize some plant names. In some cases I found the sound closer to the Spanish *l;* in others it had more affinity to the Spanish *r*. The same is true of the *b* and *w*, leading to the alternate spellings *tuburi* and *tuwuri*, *chichihuó* and *chichibó*. The river Guarijíos lack the consonants *d, f,* and *g.* The plural is usually formed by a

Through the fence, Mesa Colorada.

repetition of the initial syllable, rather than a change in the ending as is the case in Cáhita and Spanish.

Guarijíos and the Outside World

The creation of the Guarijío ejidos in the 1970s and 1980s brought with it new governmental programs in education, nutrition, medicine, and livestock grazing that have forced the Guarijíos into increasing contact with the non-Guarijío world.[15] The government provides stake-bed trucks for daily transportation between San Bernardo and Mesa Colorada and between San Bernardo and Alamos, a small city. From Alamos buses run every half hour to the larger city of Navojoa. Occasional transportation is also available between Guajaray and San Bernardo. In the highlands INI from time to time drives truckloads of Chihuahua Guarijíos from Loreto and Tojíachi to Ciudad Cuauhtémoc and Ciudad Chihuahua as well. The Guarijíos of Guasisaco and El Trigo de Russo, both in Chihuahua, have no apparent connection with INI or government programs.

The Mexican government has established self-governing units in the ejidos, ruled over by what they call *gobernadores tradicionales* (traditional governors), whose role is that of a cacique. The Guarijíos of the twentieth century had no tradition of a strong central governor (Gentry 1963), but the Mexican government required such a structure in order to coordinate policies and assistance. Apparently the term *gobernador* was the brainchild of an early INI social worker. At any rate, the governor is invested with considerable local authority. He is elected by the members of the ejido and is endowed with "traditional" powers. In working among the Guarijíos I have routinely reported to the gobernador and asked and received permission to carry on my studies. The gobernador is empowered to allocated parcels of land for houses and mahuechis, to settle disputes, and to rule on policy matters within the ejido. The gobernadores take their positions seriously and exercise their power conscientiously and occasionally with a hint of tyranny. Still, they must be maintained by popular support and are not inclined in general to abuse their considerable powers.

Mexican government officials have encouraged the

lowland Guarijíos, whose poverty was the most extreme, to develop a new source of income by raising calves for sale.[16] They donated a small herd—eighty cows, and for several years offered free barbed wire and veterinary services. The government has also encouraged the Guarijíos to clear pastures and sow buffelgrass, an exotic African grass, to increase forage and beef production. Gradually the number of cows on the ejidos has increased and fences and cleared pastures have proliferated. Most Guarijío men have become cattle raisers. For some reason, they are also raising many more burros, mules, and horses. Some are raising goats as well.

To sell the weaned calves (most of which are owned by the ejido), the Guarijíos may drive them to buyers in San Bernardo. Or, they may pay a trucker to transport them, or they may sell to itinerant buyers who roam the Guarijío lands purchasing cows and goats.

The Guarijíos de la sierra possess more fertile land and better marketable resources and are thus more capable of self-subsistence than their lowland counterparts. They, too, raise calves, but as ejidatarios of the Ejido Loreto where, due to the greater political acumen of the mestizo ejidatarios, they have better access to governmental assistance, subsidies, and credit. In 1998 a new sawmill was being installed at Loreto, the result of an initiative between the ejido and a private timber buyer.

Even with these better resources, however, the Guarijíos of Ejido Loreto are marginalized. Within the ejido they have little influence. They are not inclined to speak up in ejido meetings. Their opinions are not sought after. They do not feel they will benefit or will benefit only a little from the new sawmill. Some felt that the operation would not bode well for the ejido's extensive pine and oak forests on which they rely for fuel and lumber and use in a variety of ways. Their fields are located on the periphery of the valley, on steeper slopes and in washes subject to flooding. The Guarijíos of Loreto live a life apart from the rest of the village. At Canelichi they are sharecroppers.

A separate Guarijío colony called Los Jacales occupies the mesa north of the Arroyo Taymuco in San Bernardo. Their huts overlook the arroyo and the rest of San Bernardo. According to residents, they are hostile toward the INI and so have avoided government programs as much as possible. Their *jacales* (huts) are built on lands loaned to them by the Ejido San Bernardo. They operate their own school and vow that their children will grow up speaking the Guarijío language and respecting the tuburada. The men work

almost exclusively as day laborers on ranches in the area, where pay is shockingly low.

Apart from subsidies to various components of stock-raising, governmental programs for economic development have yet to reach the Guarijíos. In 1998 officials of the INI provided weaving workshops in Mesa Colorada for Guarijío women to encourage them to produce palm baskets for the commercial market. Several women have woven for decades, however, and the supply of the cogollos is finite and decreasing. In many cases the Guarijíos were forced to purchase cogollos from mestizo vendors.

Most Guarijío children now receive schooling. Those who live in tiny settlements attend albergues in the larger settlements, Los Bajíos, Loreto, Mesa Colorada, and San Bernardo (a mixed mestizo-Guarijío school). They attend these during the week and return home for the weekends. The children receive basic meals and school supplies without charge.

The albergues present parents with a dilemma. All wish for their children to read and write, but are uneasy about losing their children for the school week and to the influences of alien (usually Mayo) schoolteachers. For some families the labor of the children is economically important for survival. The trip to the albergue is burdensome (a walk of up to five hours). Furthermore, the children tend to lose their ability to speak Guarijío during these years of absentee schooling. This places the parents in a quandary: if the children speak Guarijío, the parents fear they will never gain the social standing they need to improve themselves in Mexican society; if the children lose their ability to speak Guarijío, they will no longer retain the values and traditions that make them Guarijíos. They become like yoris, incorporate the habits and customs the Guarijíos for so long found offensive (and which they still ridicule in some of their ceremonial dances).

My survey suggests that for the most part, children who attend the boarding schools are losing the Guarijío language and the Guarijío way. Many of their teachers frown upon children speaking Guarijío.[17] Those who remain in the smaller villages and settlements retain it.

Organized religion is not an active force among a majority of the Guarijíos del río. Until recently Mesa Colorada had no church. In 1998 a small Catholic church was completed in the village, but a priest visits only sporadically. Guarijíos who have not been converted to *evangelismo* are nominally Catholic. Most have house crosses in their homes, take part in the tuburada, and

Finally, they tend not to participate in tuburadas, which the pastors condemn as the work of the Devil. Without the tuburada as a social adhesive, the evangelistas tend to lose their identity as Guarijíos. To some extent, traditional Guarijíos view them as outcasts. For several years the gobernador of Mesa Colorada refused to allow the evangelistas to preach or practice in Mesa Colorada. One of their number charged that the reason was he enjoyed having fiestas where tepachi flows abundantly, a practice the evangelistas denounce loudly.

Since the government intervention in Guarijío affairs began in the 1970s, Guarijío parents are now more concerned that their children become officially registered with a Mexican judge. In Mexico a child must have registration papers to be enrolled in school and later in life cannot be enrolled in social security (for medical care), vote, or even travel on public transportation without a *credencial* (an identification card). This important document is not available to those whose names are not listed on a civil registry. Most parents, even those living in the most wildly remote settlements, now hope to have their children "legitimized" in the eyes of the government.

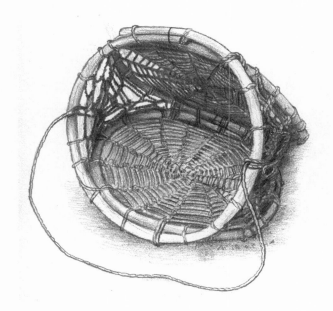

Angarilla. Drawing by Paul Mirocha.

recognize such institutions as baptism and the mass, even though they may not partake of them.

A vigorous fundamentalist, evangelical Protestant group has made some converts, but their fortunes wax and wane. The evangelizing sects originate in San Bernardo in the lowlands and Arechuybo in the highlands. Missionary activity is brisk in both areas. It was promoted in the highlands by North American missionaries. In the San Bernardo area proselytizing is carried out by Mexicans, primarily Mayo and Guarijío converts. The evangelistas, as they call themselves, offer a life of puritanical virtue. They emphasize abstinence—from drinking, smoking, dancing, non-marital sex, and general carousing—while stressing the brotherhood of all mankind [*sic*]. They emphasize the blurring of ethnic lines, treating all members as equal (although women are still urged to be subordinate to their husbands and may not serve in positions of authority).

Conversion to this fundamentalism often makes a significant difference in the lives of the converts. Primarily, they begin to deny their Guarijío-ness. They tend to speak Spanish, to condemn the tuburada, and to extol the virtues of hard work and individual responsibility. They view capitalistic Mexico as the economic ideal, the Guarijío way as backward. Secondarily, they no longer drink alcohol and they tend to monitor their families more closely. Since alcohol consumption by men has a long ritualistic significance (and a more recent destructive influence), their teetotaling tends to isolate them from mainstream Guarijíos.

6

The Last Cobijas *at Bavícora*

"Bavícora? Oh, that's a long way, David. *Un camino muy difícil* [a hard trail]. You must climb high over the mountains. You'll pass through oaks, pines. And it's very dry. No water along the way." I might have been deterred by the old Guarijío's words, but he pointed to an even older man who had arrived at Mesa Colorada from Bavícora the day before to attend a tuburada. If an old man could make it just to attend a party, I could certainly make it to study plants.

Bavícora is a very long way from Mesa Colorada, which is the farthest north settlement on the Mayo accessible by motor vehicle. I could only get to Bavícora by foot. Other people got there by horse or mule. Not me. Bavícora lies nestled far inside the real Sierra Madre Occidental, buried in a deep canyon amidst a series of mountain ranges that climb ever more loftily toward the north and east. I had gleaned enough information about the route to know even without maps that the journey required a good bit of climbing and descending. I had to go there, because it is a traditional village, because it takes a tough hike to get there, and because I could tell from topographical maps that both upstream and downstream were cajones that almost certainly harbored big trees and tropical plants. No one could claim to know Guarijío country who had not been to Bavícora.

I had asked an older Guarijío about going there as we sat in the ramada of a house in Mesa Colorada. When I told him I planned to go to Bavícora he had raised his eyebrows slightly, about as dramatic a motion as Guarijíos are prone to make.

Once before I had tried and failed. I had arrived in Mesa Colorada at the height of the spring drought in mid-May seeking a guide and burros to Bavícora. Mesa Colorada is a settlement of perhaps fifty families and a small Guarijío Cultural Center sponsored by the INI. The modest mud brick building houses a few tuburada artifacts, some photos, and some historic documents. Nothing fancy. Mesa Colorada might be called the capital of the Guarijío del río nation, for many government programs for the Guarijíos are run through Mesa Colorada.[1]

It is a most modest village, however, with only a single

Mesa Colorada.

unreliably open store selling the barest essentials. A storage barn, an albergue, a humble new church, and a scattering of small houses, that's about it. On that hot day it seemed all the men in Mesa Colorada were drunk, at least the first dozen or so I saw. Someone had put on a fiesta and a few men had mixed a batch of Maseca—corn flour—and a little fermenting agent (I was afraid to ask) to brew some tepachi, a corn beer of low alcohol content. To produce intoxication from the batch one must consume large quantities of tepachi, which the men, it seemed, had been more than willing to do. Even through their drunken state, they seemed perplexed that I would want to go to Bavícora. One of them measured me and leaned back uncertainly.

"Bavícora, eh? It's a long, hot trail. You must climb, very, very high. This time of year there is no water. It's seven, eight hours of walk. You'll need at least seven liters of water. You only have three. Don't go now! Come back when it is cooler. Seven, eight hours of walk. Bring more water. Seven, eight hours of walk. Seven, eight hours . . ."

I wasn't deterred by his discouraging words. First of all, he was intoxicated. And even though daytime temperatures were in excess of 100 degrees, I considered myself a rugged hiker, inured to hardship and unmoved by normal human inconveniences. I assumed he was associating me with yoris who don't go places on foot and are not accustomed to undertaking long treks. I was different, surely. I still wanted to go. After all, the Guarijíos walk the camino routinely. But to make the trip I had to have a guide and a burro. I made the fact well known.

An hour and a dozen inquiries later a guide came forward. This man would guide me to Bavícora, another fellow informed me in a tipsy voice. He would provide a burro as well. If I really wanted to go, that is. I would need seven liters of water, he reminded me.

I took in my prospective guide. He was young, perhaps in his late twenties, apparently sober. We shook hands gently. I introduced myself and asked his name. He looked at the ground and breathed a few inaudible syllables. "What was that?" I asked him as courteously as I knew how. He said the same thing in a louder voice but still not loud enough. Finally I got his name: José Miguel Rodríguez. Miguel, they called him. I asked him about the walk to Bavícora. He again uttered something unintelligible. I asked him again. He repeated. Twice. I asked him about water, burros, hiking time. Same inaudible response, same clipped answers. No information without excruciating repetitions. Finally, after ten minutes of trying to gain a good idea of what I was getting into, I decided that the gods were discouraging me from going to Bavícora. I thanked José Miguel, explained that I would wait for a better time of year and returned, heavy of heart, to San Bernardo, two hours to the south.

Leobardo Quiroz, the INI director there, laughed heartily. "Well, yes, Miguel doesn't talk much, but he would be a good guide. You probably wouldn't have enjoyed your walk to Bavícora, though. Hot and dry. Come and visit in the cooler weather."

Thank God I made that decision, for I would never have survived the hike in May. Even in mid-December it was quite hot and parched by drought. Here I was, back seven months later in Mesa Colorada with my nephew, Doug Yetman, to make the assault on Bavícora once again. I had written in advance requesting a guide and burros and harbored a faint hope that they would be ready.

But of course it was never that easy, and Guarijíos have more important things to do than to schedule their days around hypothetical gringos who may or may not show up. The guide who had been recommended by knowledgeable folk in San Bernardo, Ramón Rodríguez was his name, was out punching cows when I arrived at Mesa Colorada and would not be home until that night. I presented Ramón's wife with my offering, packages of Maseca, beans, sugar, and unroasted coffee beans. A younger man was hanging out there. Over coffee, seated with Doug and me around a tiny table, he thought about my request. No, he said, no one else could go that day, either. Lino Leyba, the Guarijío gobernador, the fellow who could best recommend a different guide, was in far away Alamos on business.[2] Doug and I would have to wait until Ramón arrived at his home late that afternoon. He would round up the burros, and we could leave the following day. In fact, the fellow assured me, he himself would stay there to make sure Ramón was informed.

I was feeling bleak about this situation, resigned to killing a day in Mesa Colorada, which wouldn't be that difficult (plenty of Guarijíos to chat with), but would eat into my time at Bavícora. Sensing my dismay, the young fellow consoled me. "Look," he said, "there's a tuburada tonight at Burapaco. You won't want to miss that." Not only that, he said, but a fellow in the next hut was leaving right that very moment for Huataturi, a hamlet a few kilometers up the Río Mayo and would guide us there if we wished. We could hike to Huataturi and return in time for the tuburada.

Much relieved, Doug and I stuffed our daypacks and we were off, led by Jesús Corpo, an appropriately named Guarijío, who lived in Huataturi. Jesús is a somewhat red-skinned, corpulent, and nervous fellow, but he was most eager to lead us anywhere. He even owned that he could lead us to Bavícora the following day if we wished. He knew the route and had relatives there. He was just finishing shelling corn from a pile of diminutive ears, part of this years' crop from his mahuechi.[3] He winnowed the nearly white grain a couple of times in the light breeze, then poured it into a bag. Lashing the opening firmly, he shouldered a fifty-pound sack of the corn, and we set off at a smart pace. We crossed fields abandoned to fallow, through young stands of chírahui, the leguminous tree that grows rapidly in abandoned mahuechis, and into the forest. Soon the trail led up a steep mountain to a pass called Masocoba ("deer head" in Mayo), then descended again to the Río Mayo, which we had to cross twice before arriving at the hamlet of Huataturi. The swift-running river was deep and crystal clear. Even where we forded, it was nearly knee deep. The day was hot and we were sweaty and we had to fight our way up another hill and through dense, thorny bushes at the river's edge. Jesús suggested we take a dip in the Mayo, even though it was a bit chilly for him. That sounded inviting, but first I wanted reassurances from him that swimming naked was the norm and would not be offensive to anyone. Jesús laughed when I said that some people found swimming naked to be rude. He said that during the hot months he and all Guarijíos with access to the river frequently swim ten times a day to cool off and keep clean.[4] Jejenes were also a problem in summer, he complained. Little can be done to avoid them, he said, for the cursed midges penetrate ordinary mosquito netting. A jump in the river is a temporary respite.

Huataturi, about five kilometers north of Mesa Colorada,

has three families living in four or five houses. They haul their water from the Mayo, fifty feet below them. Jesús reported that they had been somewhat hungry since the flood eleven weeks earlier, because the raging torrent, which washed down enormous trees, huge numbers of shrubs, and massive boulders, killed off most of the big fish, primarily *bagre* (catfish), which are a staple food for them. The fish population would reestablish itself, but only very slowly, he lamented. Still, we spied a fisherman here and there along the river, an indication that enough fish must remain to reward the persistent angler.

The people of Huataturi (a Mayo name meaning "good willow") live very close to the land; only their clothing and a few modest metal implements such as buckets and comales are signs of industrial society. Their homes have flat, dirt roofs, unlike those in some other villages that have A-frame houses with palm thatch roofs (the nearest palms are a day's walk away, Jesús reported). Palm-shaded ramadas abound, however, providing an abundance of shade and showing that local people know where the palms grow.

Jesús excused himself and hurried up to his hut, encouraging us to visit the other families. Doug and I waited outside the yard of the first hut until a woman called out *"Pasen, pasen,"* inviting us into the shady ramada area. Although the people of the hamlet are desperately poor, the atmosphere under their ramadas was pleasant indeed and a general air of happy isolation prevailed. Each hut exhibited a metate and *mano* for grinding corn by hand. They also used chairs made from guásima wood, which they immediately offered to us to sit in. One of the huts also had a hand grain mill mounted to a stout stump. They had broods of chickens and a couple of pigs. A rough ladder led to the roof of one of the huts where chickens could roost safe from predators.

Jesús has no family. He lives alone with his mother in the hut farthest from the river. She appears to be in her seventies. He did not invite Doug and me inside as the other families had done. From inside he brought out a guari, which he offered us for sale. It was a nicely woven piece made by his mother. She appeared in the doorway behind him. I bought the basket. After introducing her Jesús appeared anxious for us to leave, so we stayed only a few moments. She seemed rather pleased to make a sale but remained near the doorway of her hut, not even venturing out to offer the gentle Guarijío handshake.

The sources of cash for the people of Huataturi can only be sale of an occasional guari, whatever wages they may get for working as a *vaquero* or as a *jornalero* (day laborer) for nearby absentee landlord ranchers, and any excess corn they can sell. Jesús's poverty was dismaying; his clothes were in tatters; even his huaraches were worn. Still, he and the other families have the Rio Mayo below, a natural source of food and a blessing of water. Huataturi is built on a slightly tilted riverbank, a small inholding surrounded by private ranches, whose Mexican owners have historically been contemptuous of and hostile toward the Guarijíos. Each Huataturi family, however, now has access to ejido lands and a mahuechi, a source of comfort and pride to all.

Doug and I hurried back to Mesa Colorada, not wanting to miss any of the tuburada. In the late afternoon, after a simple but tasty meal of boiled beans and corn tortillas (cooked from the food I had brought), I crammed the carryall full with Guarijíos, and we set off for Burapaco, six kilometers away. The distance wasn't much, but it lay on the other (west) side of the Río Mayo, which we would have to cross. My passengers, primarily older men, assured me that crossing the river would be no problem in spite of the great flood of September 15, 1995 that had utterly altered the river channel, rendering it unrecognizable from the way I had known it before. The Mayo is Sonora's second largest river and nearly always sports a hefty current at Mesa Colorada, so much so that a boat is secured nearby for crossing when the current is high. Since the flood the previous September, Guarijíos had labored in the current to line the river bottom with slabs and mark the crossing with rock piers so that trucks could get in and out of Burapaco. Guarijíos and Mexicans alike need to market their cattle and without that crossing they have to unload cows from the trucks, herd them across the river, and find another truck on the east bank to take them to market in San Bernardo. The only other route is a mountainous track to the southwest that is impassable when it rains and not much better in dry weather. During the flood, Burapaco and all the residents of the area had been isolated for two weeks. The crossing at Mesa Colorada was a necessity for the local economy.

My passengers were in a festive mood, for the tuburada brings Guarijíos together from many isolated hamlets, where they renew old ties and themselves. Each village has at least one regularly scheduled tuburada each year (provided that food is available), so there are usually eight or nine major fiestas, plus several others that are organized to celebrate specific occasions, or, if someone has money to spend, just for the hell of it.

My riders assured me vigorously and proudly that the old Chevy Suburban I was driving would negotiate the Mayo crossing with no difficulty. It did. I hesitated, then plunged into the current. The water was running swiftly and perhaps two and a half feet deep. The vehicle lugged, then churned its way over the newly set slabs and lumbered up the far side, negotiated the steep hill, then bounced over the road to Burapaco, which means "white-tailed deer out there" in the Mayo, not the Guarijío language.

We waited there a couple of pleasant hours for the tuburada to begin. The ramadón was gaily decorated immediately adjacent to the Burapaco general store. Burapaco has no electricity besides a solar collector that powers feeble fluorescent lights, but the store is the best-equipped in the region, dispensing basic food supplies, blankets, a few items of clothing, medicine, and, above all, Mexican factory-produced hats. School children had cut designs into colored paper napkins and strung them from the beams of the ramadón with a most agreeable effect. The floor of the ramadón had been sprinkled with water and tamped to suppress the choking dust produced by the three months of no rain. The ground for a considerable distance had been meticulously swept. A few women cooked. Perhaps thirty men and a few boys loitered.

It was hard to know when the fiesta would begin. I took heart when a small group of Guarijíos built a modest campfire fifty feet away from the ramadón, warming the area for the cantador. A two-foot high wooden cross, the santa cruz, had been pushed into the ground about twenty feet away from where the cantador sat. This would be the location for the dancing of the tuburi. An occasional skyrocket was launched and exploded happily as additional people arrived in the eerily silent Guarijío fashion. As dusk enveloped the area, the cantador, a very old man, materialized and set up his cross and seat. Cipriano was the alaguasi. He greeted me and we chatted briefly, he assuring me that he had managed to harvest a decent corn and bean crop this year. Then he went about his duties, which included decorating the ermita in readiness for the santos. Daniel and Raúl Enríquez, Mexican ranchers, whose family has occupied Burapaco for generations, were also busy. Daniel operates the Burapaco store and was a partial sponsor of the tuburada.[5] Guarijíos are his best customers.

Quietly the organizers began serving food, donated by the Enríquez brothers. A Guarijío gently and politely invited each individual to the table, (a long series of planks placed against a wall) in shifts, where they sat on benches

Waiting for the tuburada.

and were served tortillas and steaming bowls of guacavaqui. They ate silently, facing the blank wall. I declined, knowing the guacavaqui was made with a meat base and I don't eat meat. Doug eagerly accepted, however. He came away with a grim face proclaiming the stew to be among the worst foods he had eaten, a simple soup of water, bone, and grease. Perhaps the Enríquez brothers were not as generous as they might have been. The people at the fiesta, however, seemed to relish it. They would feast on a diet of tortillas, the soup, and coffee for the duration of the tuburada.

Finally they had all eaten. Pascolas, fully masked, their ténaborim swishing, accompanied by musicians (harpists and violinists) emerged single file, like Hopis from a kiva, from a rear hut well hidden in the maze of small buildings that is Burapaco. Each carried a pole-like cane in the right hand. A procession of thirty people formed following the pascolas across the barren and dusty village square in the direction of one of the dirt-roofed, wattle-and-daub walled houses. Each Guarijío house has an earthen-roofed ramada that acts both as a porch and as a kitchen. The parade trooped under the ramada. One of the pascolas pounded on the closed plank door with his staff and demanded santos. Someone in the house opened the door and after a few moments ceremonially produced from the dark interior a stack of framed copies of paintings and photographs. To the accompaniment of violins and sonajos, the swish of ténaborim, and the pop of skyrockets, the group of pascolas carried the various santos across the open space to the ermita, stopping frequently to kneel, cross themselves, and pray, then proceeding with loud, happy whoops. They deposited the various photographs, statues, and framed posters on the table, then dropped to their knees for a while in front of the ermita, rose, and disappeared again into the well-hidden enclosure which is theirs alone.

During this interim Doug and I had the fortune to meet a local schoolteacher, Angel Flores, from San Bernardo. He was enjoying the spectacle as much as we were. Perhaps an hour later the pascolas emerged once again from their ramada, dancing a *canario* (canary dance) in an obscenely tight line, gyrating sexually explicit gestures into the dancer in front. They spoke loudly in Spanish (as opposed to their quiet Guarijío delivery). They performed an exuberant skit around the large harp, which one of the musicians played. The theme was a discussion of whether the harp was male or female and whether they could have sexual intercourse with it. Each pascola in turn probed the harp's resonating baffle hole with his pole. Then each in turn tried to mount the harp, making exaggerated gyrations of their hips, then falling away in a convulsive fit upon discovering that it was an instrument, not a female, as the others jeered and laughed. Then as a group they turned their backs to the harp and did a staccato-jig toward the far end of the ramadón, their ténaborim buzzing and swishing rhythmically. All of this was done with crude gestures and loud obscenities to the immense delight of the audience, which dissolved in laughter. Even women and young girls watched from the distant sidelines and were given over to helpless laughing.

Meanwhile in the shadows cast by the battery-powered fluorescent lamp that faintly illuminated the ramadón, the cantador began chanting and a few women materialized from the darkness to dance the Apollonian tuburi, gently rocking back and forth, turning, marching up to the santa cruz, then repeating the process over and over deep into the chill darkness of the December night. The contrast between the dance of the men and that of the women was every bit as great as their actual differences.

Why were the pascolas speaking in Spanish, using the foulest of a language given to colorful profanity? I interpreted their skit (and Angel later corroborated my interpretation) as ridiculing the behavior of yoris whom the Guarijíos view as crude, loud, and boasting. The delight of the onlookers, nearly all of whom were Guarijíos, indicated that they approved of the message as well as the action. Guarijíos have few opportunities to express their resentment at the mistreatment they have traditionally received (and, according to many, continue to receive) at the hands of the dominant mestizo culture, which intellectually celebrates Indian cultures but in practice denigrates them. This was the Guarijíos' chance to flaunt their defiance of yori culture and do it in a way that communicated to their community the depth of their contempt.

Doug and I retired midway through the night, thinking of our journey the following day. We pitched camp near Burapaco and were lulled to sleep by the periodic explosion of skyrockets and the distant thrumming of the music and the pascolas.

I assumed that the recrossing of the Mayo the next morning would be a repeat of the easy crossing of the day before. I had two little boys with shining faces in the back seat of the van, their first ride ever inside a vehicle. They had been walking home to Mesa Colorada when Doug and I passed them. They could scarcely believe their ears when we offered them a ride and sat with rapt enchantment as we bounced along the rough dirt track. I descended the steep bank to the Mayo with confidence. The carryall churned through the current and began to lumber up the opposite bank when the rear wheels began to slip and the vehicle slowly, agonizingly slid back into the current. I tried reverse, forward, reverse. No hope. We were quite definitively stuck in the loose gravels of the Río Mayo.

The two little boys looked at each other wonderingly, their expressions changed from utter joy to suspicion. I helped them out of the vehicle. They rolled up their pantlegs and stepped gingerly into the icy current, departing with stares of suspicion and resentment. Doug and I clambered onto the hood and jumped to the bank, looked at the stuck vehicle with despair, and with bleak hearts set off on foot to Mesa Colorada, a half mile away on top of the mesa.

Ramón had returned and was seated at his old table under the ramada, eating a breakfast of tortillas and beans. I greeted him and explained the problem. He looked around with a slight furrow to his brow. I knew this was going to be difficult the morning after an all-night fiesta when most men would be feeling the effects of the celebration. I held out little hope for the vehicle's rapid emergence from the depths of the Mayo. Ramón shrugged and swallowed his mouthful. Then he rose, put on his hat, and walked to a neighbor's hut. (The Guarijío dwellings in Mesa Colorada are set well apart from each other.) He returned alone, went to another house, and came away equally empty handed, his face unsmiling. A stranger in an alien land, I had nothing to offer. Ramón walked in another direction and came back with two men. He motioned to me to follow him and we returned to the path to the river. At the first hut he called out to a man hunkering by a smoldering fire. The fellow did not budge but merely turned his head vaguely and coughed out a laconic reply. Ramón shrugged and moved on, the tiny, hapless party following in his tracks.

Then, as though Ramón were playing a pipe, men emerged from the background, from out of huts, from behind bushes, rocks, and trees. Soon we were six, then eight, and finally, twelve, marching without words, our footsteps crunching in the cobbles over the wide expanse of barrens along the river's edge. With eleven men lifting and pushing, their trousers wet to their upper thighs, the carryall was out of the river in minutes, rearing and sliding up the soft slope. I carried seven of the men back in the vehicle. They were a happy lot, boisterous for Guarijíos, joking about the river and its mysterious ways. Maybe our day wasn't going to be so dismal after all.

Ramón informed me he couldn't go to Bavícora, however. He had *chamba,* the mysterious term that translates *work* but denotes any sort of excuse for not doing something. He would get us a guide and two burros, however, one of which would be his own, he assured me. Wait there at his house, he said, and he would be back. We did. I spent a couple of hours chatting with old Guarijío acquaintances, men recently arrived in Mesa Colorada from up and down the river and from Guajaray. We talked of news, of mahuechis, of no rain, of fish, of tuburadas, of Mayos, of cows. Presently I realized that two burros were waiting, packsaddles in place. They had arrived in full daylight without my noticing any arrival. Either I was getting less observant or the Guarijíos can move silently and invisibly in full sunlight. Beside one of the burros stood our guide, none other than José Miguel. Miguel, the mumbler.

I swore to myself. I was on the verge of protesting but thought better of it. A silent guide was better than no guide, and if we didn't leave now we would have to wait another day. I nodded to him, shook his hand, gently, as I had learned,

Saddling up for Bavícora.

reminded him of my name, helped load our bundles, and we set off. Ten-thirty in the morning for an eight-hour hike. The sun would set that December 12 at 5:35 P.M.

It was slow going, mostly because the lead burro seemed not to want to leave the certainty and security of Mesa Colorada. Before we had taken ten steps Miguel had begun barking at the burro, issuing a string of orders and threats that were to continue nearly unabated for the next nine hours, even when I could not determine any basis for the imprecations. This cold-eyed beast, which I named Alonso (burros are not usually given names), tried deviating from the path, from time to time only to be outflanked by Miguel who set him right smartly. We plodded north, over the same small mountain as yesterday, back to the Mayo, then up a serious mountain where the real hike began.

Mesa Colorada is surrounded on four sides by steep mountain ranges. To the north and east, where the highest ranges lie, the mountains exceed five thousand feet in elevation. This is not a great height by Rocky Mountain

On the trail to Bavícora. Note organ pipe cacti.

standards but considering that Mesa Colorada is only about six hundred feet above sea level, the overall increase in height is nearly as great as the amount the San Francisco Peaks tower over Flagstaff, Arizona. As we departed I looked at the slopes we would climb and felt a twinge of anxiety knowing that it would test our physical conditioning as no other hike I had ever done in Mexico. I tried to remind myself repeatedly that children and old people make the hike frequently, so I had nothing to worry about. Hah.

Mercifully for us, the burros' pace was slow. The second burro, Renaldo, I named him, was inclined to stop frequently to scarf a mouthful of leaves, especially *chicura* (canyon ragweed), on which burros flourish and which cows disdain. At first I scolded Renaldo roundly, trying to imitate Miguel. I swatted his scrofulous gray backside with a switch, making very little impression on him, but when I realized that after a few mouthfuls of herbage he would quickly catch up with the crafty Alonso, I quit railing on the impervious beast and let him hike at his own pace. Alonso, on the other hand, required constant urging and flicking with a switch that

Miguel carried. His pauses kept Doug and me from losing our breath completely. We climbed fifteen hundred feet in the next two miles, hardly stopping for a rest. Finally, drenched with sweat, we crowned out on top of Mesa Matapaco, where a natural grassland, one of the finest in all of northwest Mexico flourishes. After the nearly unending closeness of the tropical deciduous forest, the open, savanna-like mesa was a pleasant change. Trees are few on the mesa, but it is rich in the variety of grasses and small shrubs. And, because water sources are distant, cows have not denuded the grassland. From it, the mountainsides below and above could be seen spotted with mahuechis of varying stages. The Guarijíos plant for two years (sometimes three), then leave the fields *en barbecho* (fallow) for four or five, or, increasingly, less. During that time they tend to keep cows out of the pastures so that fertility can be restored to the soil during the fallow. The fallow time is less here than at Los Bajíos, for Bavícora and Mesa Matapaco are higher and more moist than the lower village.

We paused for lunch and great gulps of water at the

high saddle above the mesa, where we looked down on it. Miguel accepted a Powerbar and some cookies without expression. He was not winded at all and far less damp with sweat than we were. I thanked the mountains and heavens that I had not attempted the hike in the hot weather. This was cool December weather and I was dry, hot, and thirsty. I wouldn't have made it in fiery blasts of May. I can't imagine how the Guarijíos do it.

Not far away a herd of twenty or so cows gazed at us with suspicion. The climb up our trail had been over steep slopes including several cliffs with sharp precipices. There was room on the trail for only one person, and it was slippery to boot. How in the world did the Guarijíos deliver these cows to market? How could they have driven them down that narrow, switchbacking trail? I asked Miguel. He didn't understand. I asked again, how in heaven's name did the Guarijíos manage to drive these cows to Mesa Colorada and the market?

Ah, he understood. "Well," he said, "we can do it because we are Guarijíos."

I thought about his reply and decided it was correct and sufficient.

We were not finished climbing, however. For another hour and a half we gained altitude, passing through rich forest with fine specimens of *palo joso,* a tall leguminous tree of the tropical deciduous forest with a silvery, straight trunk and bean pods that persist for months, affording the tree an orangish crown in the dry season. Here also were large copal trees, *Burseras* of several species, spreading trees that betray their presence by the intensely aromatic gums they exude. Then we emerged once again into a broad area of grass and low shrubs, another concentration of mahuechis. Then back once again into the forest. Finally leaving the dense and crowded tropical deciduous forest, we emerged into a land of broad sky, the open oak forest, what Gentry called "the pleasant land of the oaks," where my altimeter read nearly three thousand feet. A few straggling long-needled pines *(Pinus oocarpa)* grew near the summit as well, apparently flourishing in the cooler air, intermingled with three species of oaks and a variety of other plants not known below. Miguel was able to identify some of them. He even stopped to pick a few acorns to eat. I knew these oaks, *cusis* and *encinos,* from other such hills, growing broad and shapely in soils of white, indurated ash, where no plant should grow.

For the next several hours we plodded up steep hills and down the other side, crossing narrow canyons, bone dry in the drought, then climbing the interminable succession of hills. We passed only one human habitation, the ranch called El Saúz, home to one Guarijío family. Still we plodded onward and upward once again, the burros needing less prodding once stripped of the notion that they would be returning soon to Mesa Colorada. The sun set, darkness fell, and still we tramped on along the ancient, unending path that wound up and down the canyons and mountains. Doug and I began to stumble and slide as darkness confused our perspective and dimmed our vision. Miguel walked on silently, effortlessly, unhurried. We crossed a pass, opened and closed a barbed wire gate, then headed down into a dark canyon. I extracted two flashlights from my pack and gave one to Doug. The darkness in the deep side canyon was nearly total; there was not a hint of moon, only a bright Venus, called *Sopori* by the Guarijíos (according to Miguel). It winked at us from time to time when the forest opened up. Even with our battery-powered lights, we tripped and slid over protruding roots and loose stones. Miguel strode without any illumination, never missing a step. His homemade huaraches were surely no more capable of gripping the terrain than my expensive lug-sole boots, but still he walked nearly soundlessly, never breaking his rhythm except to swat a burro or shoo it back onto the trail. For another hour we staggered on, reached a pass and another gate, and began descent into a valley where far in the distance I spied lights. The downhill trail was perilous, with sharp drops on both sides, a host of treacherous round stones littering the path, and nearly vertical drops. Doug and I struggled with the path, both by now bracing ourselves with hiking sticks, our feet aching, our muscles nearly cramping from exhaustion. We had been hiking for more than eight hours. Miguel proceeded well ahead of us, scampering down the steep trail behind the revitalized burros, hidden in the darkness, sprinting from time to time from the trail to bring an errant burro back to the true path.

Then after what seemed an eternity of forced marches, suddenly we were there. The trail ended at a palm-thatched adobe hut in a small yard with a ramada, which our lights illuminated. We waited as instructed by Miguel as he wandered through the compound, trying to find out who owned the place. He had said he had acquaintances in Bavícora, but he clearly did not know his way around here. We stood and sat for half an hour waiting, hungry, and thirsty. When he returned he said we could camp right there for the night, and we would find out more in the morning. We quickly untied our trappings, and Miguel led the burros off to pasture.

Before we had arrived at Bavícora I had instructed

Guarijío home, Bavícora. Hand-woven blanket is draped over railing at bottom left.

Miguel carefully. There were two important points for him to remember. One, we needed a small, flat place to pitch a tent. Two, we needed a family to whom we could give the bulky and heavy bags of food in return for their providing meals for us for a day and a half. I doubted that he had communicated the latter to whomever he had talked. But I didn't want to worry about that. Doug and I broke out our food and camping stove, cooked dinner, wolfed it down, pitched the tent, laid out our sleeping gear, and went to bed amid the usual crowing of roosters, barking of dogs, and braying of burros. I heard Miguel unrolling his blanket nearby. Doug was asleep instantly and I followed shortly. Before I slept, however, it dawned on me that to one side of our tent were four rolls of barbed wire. This was always an ominous sign. What could it be for?

Morning brought the grunt of pigs all around. I popped out of the tent, fearful that they would damage our duffel bags, but Doug had thought to place them atop the ramada, and the piglets found only minute crumbs from last night's dinner. We were located at the edge of a compound of five huts which had been built on laboriously constructed terraces perhaps a hundred feet above the arroyo below, of which only scummy green pools remained as reminders of the recent flood. Far downstream the deep canyon curved away to the northwest and the Río Mayo, perhaps five miles away, while upstream the canyon seemed to split in two and was lost in the ever higher mountains to the east. Great fig trees grew below along the river, along with other trees of the arroyos, *guamúchiles,* bebelamas, and igualamas. Children's' voices carried upward to our campsite. I turned around, and three little boys were staring at the tent and me unabashedly. They had probably never seen gringos before.

I looked around at the vegetation. Teresa Valdivia wrote that in the late 1970s Bavícora was lush compared with San Bernardo:

This community has a climate and vegetation totally distinct from the semidesert sierras [near San Bernardo]. Here there were ferns and palm trees in abundance, rivulets that ran nearby the houses, forming little waterways; the air was thicker and cool, and there were no goats or cows, only a few sheep and chickens. (Valdivia Dounce 1994:88)

Since Tere's visit, the Guarijíos had acquired cattle as part of the government development program. Now the land was heavily grazed. The vegetation for the most part appeared trampled, hardly distinguishable from the drier second growth around San Bernardo. I found none of the rivulets I had hoped to see.

Miguel slipped off quietly to somewhere or another, vanishing in the mysterious way of the Guarijíos. I chatted with the boys as Doug and I heated coffee and ate breakfast. We gave them some cookies, and I explained what I was doing there. I don't think they believed me or could comprehend just what the hell we were up to. Why would anyone come here to talk about plants? But it was interesting all the same.

While we were eating I noticed that the food bags were still plopped on top of the ramada. Miguel hadn't delivered them. I pulled the flour-laden sacks down and staggered through a small maze of huts to where a small family of Guarijíos was gathered on a hearth, seated happily around a fire. I introduced myself to a man in his late forties named Sebastián, assuming that Miguel had made our presence and desires known. "Well, here is the food," I announced. I deposited the heavy food bags with them and shook hands all around. They were friendly and, of course, curious. Sebastián could not recall the last time gringos had been to Bavícora, which made me feel most significant.

Sebastián produced chairs and we chatted for a few moments and I returned to arrange our trappings. Before long Sebastián appeared and announced that breakfast was ready. They had a small table with two chairs situated in a well-shaded breezeway between two huts. A woman in her early thirties was heating tortillas on a tractor disc (the universally used griddle in rural Mexico) over an open fire. We sat in the handmade guásima chairs at the handmade guásima table. She served us fried beans in an enameled plate, offered us each a metal spoon and freshly brewed, delicious coffee in china mugs. Soon a plate of tortillas appeared as well. We ate heartily, even though we had eaten only an hour earlier. On the table as well were a small bag of *chiltepines,* which one crushed over the beans, a few limes harvested from a nearby tree, and a bag of salt.

When we had finished, I asked Sebastián if they had any hats, for I noticed a woven palm hat. He disappeared inside a hut and emerged holding one, dusting it off. I examined it

and Doug tried it on. With a little adjustment it would fit well. I paid the woman (her name was Rosenda), then wondered where there was water to dampen the palm. Sebastián indicated a spigot at the edge of the clearing and, marvel of marvels, it delivered fresh water (from an aguaje above the village, I was to learn). I held the hat under the stream of water that ran from the spigot. When the hat was thoroughly wet I set it on Doug's head and shaped it as Sebastián looked on. Then I set it on top of a ramada to dry. I had learned this technique from other Guarijíos and fancied that the family viewed my manipulations with approval. It looked like a good beginning.

A younger man, perhaps thirty, appeared and we shook hands. His name was Lolores Rodríguez Rascón, thirty-one years old, he said, a relative of Ramón's. Ramón maintained a hut here in Bavícora as well as one in Mesa Colorada he said. Yes he would be glad to lead us up the Arroyo Bavícora and show us plants. I leaned on a wooden railing chatting with him. After a while, I noticed that draped over the railing were two heavy woolen blankets, obviously hand woven and also quite old. I looked at Lolores, excited. Are these Guarijío blankets? I asked. They were, he said. Who weaves them? I asked, excited by this. He indicated an old woman sitting by the fire.

"She wove them a long time ago. She doesn't weave any more. Nobody does."

"Nobody," I asked, dismayed, "not even someone from another village?"

"Nobody," he replied.

Doña Nechi Rodríguez appeared to be some seventy-five years old. No one knew exactly; the Guarijíos have never placed great emphasis on one's specific age. It only became important when they had to know when to enroll school children and if they were old enough to register for certain governmental requirements, such as voting and receiving social security. She puttered about the compound, maintaining the fire and shooing chickens away from the corn placed in a pan, intended to fatten a friendly young boar, which frequented the campsite. Lolores seemed indifferent to the disappearance of blankets. Why would there be more? He was patient with his answer: Because there were no *borregas* (ewes), hence no wool. You can't weave blankets without wool. And there are no wool-bearing sheep because the government has promoted the raising of calves for sale rather than the raising of ewes for *lana* (wool). The feedlot owners in Ciudad Obregón need calves to fatten much more than the Guarijíos need ewes to provide wool for their blankets.

So only two Guarijío blankets remained. I put a hand on each and stroked them, wondering at the shameless elimination of such a fine craft, smoother and finer in texture than those the Mayos are now producing. Later in the afternoon I decided to try to buy one of the blankets. Both were in bad shape, gaping holes in the middle, some unraveling at the ends, but they would be fine samples of Guarijío weaving for some museum. Doña Nechi is partially deaf. I told her in a loud voice that I had an interest in blankets and wondered if she would consider selling me one of hers. She gave a small, humble laugh, as if she could not fathom why anybody would want to buy an old blanket like that. She demonstrated the holes and the unraveling. She was not proud of these. Well, then, I still would be happy to buy one of them from her. No, she couldn't do that. They were her last blankets. She needed them for warmth in the cool winter nights of Bavícora. I could hardly argue. I suppose I could have traded my sleeping bag, but it would have worn out long before those blankets had reached the end of their use. I looked sadly at the marvelous old textiles and went to my camp to cook lunch.

There was a brief renaissance of blanket weaving in Bavícora in the 1970s when Ted Faubert and anthropologist Barney Burns supplied the women with carded wool. Once that source dried up, there could be no more weaving, for there was no wool locally available.

We set off up the arroyo, past the concrete-and-stone *pila* or reservoir that stores the hamlet's water supply, past the last hut where several women were weaving guaris and another was tending to a small, fenced garden. In the arroyo were intermittent pools shaded by gigantic figs—chalates, *tchunas,* and *nacapulis*—that gave deep, cool shade. The water was clean and fresh, too cool to swim in. Lolores said that in the heat of summer these pools have running water and people come to swim. When the rains come the canyon is full of short waterfalls and deep pools, a delightful relief from the sweltering, insect-ridden discomfort of the Río Mayo summer. At one point a rocky dry waterfall was so steep that someone had constructed a makeshift ladder to gain access to the next level. Overhead was an enormous palo verde *(Drypetes gentryi)* a tree limited to moist, deep canyons of the Sierra Madre. It was a joyarí, Lolores confirmed.

We wandered about a mile up the canyon, clambering over rocks, ambling ever so slowly so that I could examine the great trees and shrubs. I hoped to find something

different, some exotic tree, but saw nothing new, nothing that I hadn't seen with Cipriano. No one recognized my description of *Bursera simaruba,* the gumbo limbo of the Caribbean that I had found with Cipriano near San Pedro and I hoped to find here. So we talked about wildlife instead. The people ate game when they could, Lolores said. Jabalí and cholugo, an occasional deer, and chachalaca, a pheasant-like bird. This latter was curious, for I was quite surprised to see one in the company of a group of hens pecking and scratching back at Lolores' hut.

"How did you ever tame a *chachalaca?*" I asked him, laughing.

He gave a modest smile. "Well, we find the *chachalaca's* nest and steal a couple of eggs from it. Then we slip them under a *culeca* (broody hen), and she never seems to notice the difference. Pretty soon we have *chachalaca* chicks. The chicks that hatch grow up tame, thinking they are chickens. When they get fat we eat them because they won't lay eggs in ground nests like chickens."

That was a new one on me. Chachalacas are known as tasty game, but the Guarijíos' semidomestication seemed to me an ingenious adaptation to a game source. Other animals were seen, but not eaten: the *león* (mountain lion), less frequently the *onza,* a large cat whose existence is assumed by most serranos but which constantly eludes biologists, and very rarely, a *tigre* or jaguar. Bears have not been seen in that country in modern times, and wolves exist only in stories told by older folk. Wild game in general is scarce due mostly to overhunting. I found this hard to accept, looking at the great mountain ranges in all directions but forced myself to remember that people are everywhere in those mountains, Guarijíos and mestizos alike. No matter how remote I thought I was, someone was never far away. Many a time I have fancied myself alone in the vast wilderness of the Sierra Madre only to stumble from the forest into a mahuechi and find someone working the soil or weeding a crop.

I asked about snakes. Lolores knew of the venomous *co'ópoli* (pichicuate, Mexican moccasin, *Agkistrodon bilineatus)* but said they are extremely rare. Rattlesnakes are unknown in the forest of that region, even though they are common in the coastal valleys and the deserts to the north. *Coralillos,* coral snakes *(Micruroides euryxanthus, Micrurus diastema)* are more common, and they are extremely venomous. The smaller species *(Micruroides)* is no threat, for they are easily seen and not inclined to bite, but the *Micrurus* has no such reservations. More common were the *nahuí (corua,* boa

José Miguel Rodríguez *(above)* and Lolores Rodríguez *(below)*. Photo by Doug Yetman.

of rocks above. I could hardly detect any movement from the great snake, for though it was darting through the rocks, its back is uniformly black and the moving scales reveal no pattern of movement. It simply flowed through its terrain. I wouldn't have tried to catch it (babatucos give off foul-smelling excrement when they are caught), but I'd hoped to see it up close. My Guarijío friend smiled indulgently at my clumsy stalking of the snake, relieved, I suspect, that I had failed. An acquaintance of mine once caught one, and the serpent shat upon him profusely. He struggled to clean the vile mess off his skin and clothing, but the foul odor remained. He was banished to the back of the pickup truck and still stank hours later.

Of birds Lolores knew less. *Pericos* (parrots, in this case White-fronted Parrots), *guacamayas* (Military Macaws), *urracas* (Magpie Jays), and *coas* (Elegant Trogons) were the most exotic. Urracas are startling in their appearance. They seem to drag a foot-long tail behind them, not at all gracefully. They are communal birds, flying in families. When strange movement sparks their curiosity, they set up a racket, a variety of raucous whistles, squawks, caws, and chucks. They will often follow people for some distance, reporting loudly on the progress of their subject.

Guacamayas are equally obvious in the monte. They nest in cavities of high trees or on cliffs. Their noisy shrieks and laughs can be heard for great distances, often more than a mile. When a flock is foraging (I've seen more than twenty in a group) their collective crowd noise can be deafening. They are an iridescent green from afar, revealing brilliant blue up close. International parrot smuggling and habitat loss have decimated their numbers throughout the sierras, but in Guarijío country they seem to be holding their own.

We also heard and Lolores identified the lengthy delicate song of the *gilguero* (Brown-backed Solitaire). It is a nondescript busy little brown dicky bird. I've heard them in a hundred canyons in the region, but so well does the bird conceal itself in thick underbrush, that only once or twice have I caught sight of it. Lolores was able to describe its appearance well. The males seem to think they will attract more and better females by prolonging their song, so the arias may go on for twenty or thirty seconds. The song of the gilguero is like none other, reminiscent of the prolonged stirring of fragments of broken fine crystal.

Lolores had warmed to the subject. He told us as well of the many feats of chuparrosas (hummingbirds), of which at least five species inhabit the canyons. He spoke of owls, of hawks, of quail, and of chachalacas. He lamented the scarcity

constrictor, *Constrictor constrictor)* and the *huarolúe (babatuco,* indigo snake, *Drymarchon corais).* Lolores exhibited little fear of snakes, unlike many of the people in the lower lands who have elaborated vast and sensational stories about the power and danger of reptiles.[6] I can only surmise that as people of the forest the Guarijíos who often walk through the night have developed a far more accurate body of knowledge of the ways of reptiles than their valley compatriots who live somewhat more removed from the monte or bush.

I was once on the trail when a Guarijío pointed out a babatuco swimming his coily way through a water hole below the trail. For a while I watched it—the jet-black creature was a good six feet long—gracefully moving back and forth as though trolling for food—through the water that was nearly as dark as it. I decided to get a closer look and tried to creep down the bank and approach the water hole. Alas, the snake detected me before I had moved ten feet. It bolted from the pool and disappeared into the pile of deer. He mused on the marauding jaguars, the elusive (and perhaps mythical) onza, a large cat midway between a mountain lion and a jaguar. Lolores was a nature interpreter.

Even at this remote location the steep canyon sides of the Arroyo Bavícora were dotted with mahuechis, from terraces of the canyon bottom to the highest slopes. Lolores pointed out several in various states of succession, including his own, soaring far above us on a steep mountainside. Both upstream and downstream the steep, heavily forested hillsides, already turning brownish gray from the prolonged drought, were dotted with clearings ranging from an acre to many acres, most of them in fallow. Downstream it appeared that an area of more than two hundred acres had been cleared—for buffelgrass, it turned out. Lolores's field wasn't so far away, he said, hardly more than an hour's walk. It seemed to me to be a thousand feet and ten miles above us, but it was not distant in his conception. Knowing that with the first rains he would plant the field and visit it daily to weed and thin the corn, I sweated just thinking about the physical conditions he would have to endure to tend that field: the temperature would be nearly one hundred, humidity over fifty percent, three or four species of gnats swarming and biting him and chiggers waiting to burrow into his skin when he moved through brush. These are but minor inconveniences for him, however. He was already clearing for next year's crop and preparing to burn in May when the slash has dried enough to ignite. Other Guarijíos had demonstrated to me that the forest will not burn, even in the dry season, so it is necessary to hack the trees and shrubs down, gather them into piles, and incinerate the piles. The ashes thus produced also help fertilize the soil. They have been living at Bavícora and working mahuechis for many generations, he said, including his grandfather, great-grandfather and great-great-grandfather. This was an ancient Guarijío site.[7]

I don't know how old the site of Bavícora is, however, nor did Lolores. The old Guarijío homes were thoroughly biodegradable. If abandoned, they would return to nature in a few years, leaving behind only a pile of rocks. The palm would disintegrate and the adobe mud would melt. I have never located any references to Bavícora (or other Guarijío del río places except for Caramechi) in the Río Mayo. Here in the lowlands the Guarijíos did not stay long in one location, for the soils could not support permanent crops. There is no reason to believe they had permanent habitations that survived for more than a couple of generations.

We returned to the village and Lolores vanished, not to be seen again by us. He had cows and other more mysterious business to attend to. It was five years before I saw him again. This time he had become an hermano, a brother of the evangelical faith.

Doug and I roamed through the village. I chatted with people, using a search for palm hats as an excuse. It appears that there are seven or eight discrete clusters of dwellings, each set apart from the others, containing more or less a clan (the Guarijíos of Bavícora are patrilocal). Each compound, for they are, indeed, compounds, contain two to six separate huts, a total of twenty-two or twenty-three families in all. In the case of the Rodríguez compound, two of the jacales were unoccupied, manifesting padlocked doors and unswept porches. One was occupied by a widower who remained puttering about his ramada much of the time. The padlocks were a surprise, especially when I recalled that Cipriano's house at Jánaco didn't even sport a door. But these houses had been built with assistance from the Mexican government, so they would contain mestizo features. The dwellings were pretty much new, apparently built in the early 1980s when the government began in earnest to assist the Guarijíos to atone for their previous persecution. Each tiny house has a poured cement porch, smoothly finished into sections some fifteen inches wide. Too well finished, it seems, for the smooth concrete surface is crumbling in most homes, indicating excessive tooling of the freshly poured cement. The cement was hauled in from Mesa Colorada, one sack to a burro. The real work lay in constructing the trincheras, the terraces. The village is now as terraced as an Andean or Java hillside.

On the far (north) side of the arroyo is the albergue, the boarding school, an attractive palm-thatched building. Children come from nearby ranches and stay at the school during the week. I spoke with a lad who couldn't have been more than seven or eight. He was from El Saúz, a ranch of one house that we passed by en route to Bavícora. He walked in on Monday and returned home on Friday. The walk took about two hours and traversed rugged country. In my country sending a child off alone on a journey to school would be scandalous. In that part of Mexico it is commonplace. Two other lads had visited Mesa Colorada several times. They owned that they were tired when they got there, however.

Several boys and men, including Lolores, collected papaches during my visit as we hiked up the Arroyo Bavícora. They are apparently a mainstay in the diet of the Guarijíos in the fall, an odd looking fruit the size of a tennis ball with enormous irregular dull thorns projecting. When immature they are green, resembling huge parasites growing on the shrub, but turn a yellow-orange when ripe. The pulp is black and full of seeds yielding a bittersweet flavor in which the bitter element wins hands down. Guaríjios and Mayos alike extol papaches for their flavor and for their ability to rid the body of intestinal parasites, surely a virtue in that tropical region. Children especially love them, learning at an early age to scoop the contents from the soft shell without making a mess. I had eaten papaches before and could say little that was commendatory. Doug took a small bite of the fruit and decided against proceeding. Perhaps with more familiarity we would both develop a great appreciation of the fruit. As a consolation, however, we both ate great numbers of the sweet orange, cranberry-sized fruit of the *cumbro (Celtis iguanaea)*. The Guaríjios refused to join us as we stuffed the sweet fruits into our mouths. They later confessed that they didn't eat them because they believed the fruits would harm or even cripple the consumer.

While Doug and I were touring Bavícora, Miguel was filling a plastic feed bag with guaris of different shapes and textures. He said they would be sold in Hermosillo, which I interpreted to mean that he would sell them to someone who sells them in Hermosillo. The women are prolific weavers, sitting for hours engaged in conversation, the sweet, quiet flow of the Guaríjio language nearly uninterrupted. They use *tajcú (Brahea aculeata)*, an attractive palm which grows in abundance on the canyon sides. The guaris are usually the natural color of the palm, but some women dye the material in a solution boiled from brasil wood to produce a most agreeable red color. They also weave petates (mats) from the palms, on which most of the Guaríjios sleep. These give surprising cushion but not enough for my bony body. I would also be apprehensive about scorpions if I were to sleep on a mat. The thatch of the Guaríjio homes is excellent habitat for the tiny *Centroides* scorpions, which pack a sublethal but painful sting. These do not appear to be an item of great concern. I noticed, however, that two older folks slept on *catres,* folding cots with a mattress of burlap, which they must have had hauled in by burro at great expense of labor. Elevating one's body from the ground affords a modest amount of protection from scorpions on the ground but not from those that may drop from above.

The women weave hats from the palm *sa'ó (Sabal uresana),* which also occurs in the region but not as commonly as tajcú. Women say the only reliable source is near Los Bajíos, a long day and a half walk away. Bavícora is known elsewhere as a hat-weaving center, but I found none except for the three at the Rodríguez compound. The hats are double-woven and far cooler than the commercial hats the men have come to prefer.

I asked Lolores what other uses they make of the palm. They eat the fruits regularly, he reported. They are not as tasty as papaches, guamúchiles, or igualamas, but have food value and can assuage hunger. He spoke with others on the subject, and they agreed that the hearts of the palms are also edible, but they showed no inclination to eat any and appeared to evade any discussion of the gourmet virtues of the tree. Harvesting the heart kills or maims the palm, so Guaríjios may refrain from consuming the plant that provides raw material for the women's principal industry.

As the afternoon waned Doug and I watched from above as some little boys at the canyon bottom chased piglets for recreation, trying to lasso them. These lads had become deadly accurate with the *reatas,* roping goats and chickens, fruit hanging in trees, and even each other as practice. Some of the little fellows were also herding burros into the finely built rock corral just above the arroyo bottom. I descended and chatted with two lads who had earlier roped a calf and lashed it closely to the corral, where it bawled incessantly. After several hours they allowed its mother into the corral to nurse and nurture her offspring. I asked one of the boys why they did that. To make the calf tame, was the response. Cows are currently the only commodity produced by Guaríjio men, so boys begin developing knowledge of husbandry early in life.

Some other young lads were bringing long trunks of firewood to their homes, others were tending goats. We saw no young men between the ages of fifteen and thirty. As is the case in countless other villages in the Sierra Madre, they had left, had gone "abajo"—down to the Mayo Valley south of Navojoa or Ciudad Obregón in the Yaqui Valley looking for work. The mountainous rocky terrain simply could not sustain the increasing population.

The Guaríjios of Bavícora view themselves as subsistence farmers and producers, even though they spend a good part of their time punching cows for the ejido. The mahuechi is their most important asset. Its welfare and the relative abundance of rains are their most important economic considerations. As plentiful as land is around Bavícora, Mesa Colorada, and Los Bajíos, I suspect there is not adequate land to support an increased number of mahuechis. As more land is cleared, less is left in forest, a resource without which subsistence farming cannot continue. I believe the Guaríjios are clearing land faster than it is being regenerated by lying fallow. The increasing population cannot but lead to disputes among those who use the communal lands, for, as Lolores says, anyone may put a mahuechi anywhere he pleases, as long as someone else has not claimed the land first. Mahuechi subsistence, no matter how quaint and romantic, will inevitably reach the same limits as any other extensive use of land. Someday soon, the Guarijíos will run out of land for mahuechis.

Mahuechi subsistence is being undermined from a different direction as well. The Mexican government has exerted strong pressure on the Guarijíos to expand beef production as a source of income. In more abstract terms, the government encourages the Guarijíos to sell off the biomass of their lands by converting it into beef which they can market by tapping into the international beef production system, of which Mexico is an important player (Camou Healy 1991). Cows, however, will wreck a mahuechi in only a few minutes by devouring and trampling the crops. One got into the plot of Tiburcio Charramoneta of Loreto while I was visiting with him and destroyed half the corn inside. Furthermore, cows decrease the biomass of fallow plots, leading to decreased soil fertility and diminished corn and bean harvests in the future. So fencing is essential to protect the mahuechis. Fences are a nuisance and lead to disputes. Maintenance of fences is labor intensive, and the fencing itself is expensive.[8]

In its quest to increase production of beef, both for export and internal consumption, the Mexican government has also encouraged the Guarijíos to incorporate more sophisticated range management practices, especially rotation of pastures so that some pastures can be rested while others are being grazed.[9] Such a rotation requires extensive fencing and the herding necessary to move cows from one pasture to another on a regular basis almost certainly requires that the Guarijíos become horsemen. Although older Guarijíos are adamant that they are not horsemen, managing cattle requires horses or mules, both of which require large acreages of pasture. Horses require expensive supplemental feed and veterinary medicines as well. Riding horses and mules requires the purchase of tack—saddles, bridles, and reins, all of which are expensive.

Even more important, however, is the psychological change instilled by the ideology of cattle raising. The mounted cowboy is a powerful Mexican image, a symbol of machismo and independence, one that the younger Guarijío men find appealing. Because they must purchase

Basket with lid. Drawing by Paul Mirocha.

all the accouterments of being a cowboy, they are irresistibly drawn out of their traditional subsistence psychology and hooked into a market mentality. A burro's *fuste* or pack-saddle can be produced by a local craftsman working with native materials such as guásima wood, rope woven from *ixtle,* the agave fiber, or even the plastic thread from discarded nylon feed sacks. Woolen fuste pads and packsaddle blankets were formerly woven by women using locally gathered wool. Tack items, especially saddles and bits, however, must be purchased from mestizo artisans in Alamos or Navojoa. Where the horse appears, subsistence ends, however slowly the change may take place.

The people of Bavícora still raise their own corn and beans. In general, though, crops have been poor since 1990, when summer rains failed, following a series of summers in which rains were inadequate. The increased dryness of summers is of great concern to the men who tend the mahuechis. Although one should not base climatic predictions on anecdotal memories of weather, it is clear that the spring drought has been extended into July for the last eight years, a dire portent for *mahuecheros* and vaqueros alike. One of them remarked to me that it just never seems to rain much any more in the Guarijío country.

Traditionally, men clear the brush and turn over the dirt on their plots in May, then wait for the first rains to plant seed. Some lowland Guarijíos lack their own varieties of corn, probably because they were forced to eat their seed corn. Instead, they purchase hybrid corn and bean seeds from the Yaqui Valley and haul it in by burro. Since most hybrid seeds are not apomictic (producing viable seed) the seed must be newly purchased each year. Once a farmer begins using bought hybrid corn, he is hooked into the cash market. Unlike many corn-growing areas in the region, these hybrid seeds are not selected for drought tolerance or the peculiar growing season of the Guarijío region. They are adapted to the growing season requirements of agribusiness in the Valley Deltas and have never evolved genetic adaptation to the Guarijío climate.

Some traditional planters such as Ignacio Ciriaco in Guajaray, Manuel Rodríguez in Jogüegüe, and Alfredo Ruelas in Bavícora have preserved their old varieties of seed. They have no idea how old it is, just that they and their ancestors before them have always managed to save some seed, even if only a little. The same is true with the Guarijíos de la sierra, where corn is passed from generation to generation as an inheritance. Even with these locally adapted varieties, however, the harvests are nearly always of marginal bounty. In many years no one has any extra corn seed to swap. Those who must buy seed need cash and more plentiful rain.

The harvest is usually gathered in by November. Where frost is not a problem, a delay in the onset of rains can be accommodate by a delay in planting, and intermittent rains do not necessarily result in crop failure if a general heavy rain occurs during the growing season. If sufficient rains do not occur in July, August, and September, however, the crops will fail partially or fully. This year, at least, they had harvested a crop, not a bumper crop, but better than the last two years. Had the hurricane not dumped torrential rains on the area, general famine would have resulted.

The Guarijíos depend on mahuechi harvest not merely for themselves but for their livestock as well. They feed some of their less desirable ears of corn to the cows to fatten them. They save the supplemental cattle feed in elevated huts where the ears are more or less safe from mice and other vermin, then use it as emergency food in the spring drought. Here it was December and the landscape was already drought-starved. Had the storm not arrived in September, I shudder to think of the fate of the Guarijíos, for help from the Mexican government, near bankruptcy due to the recent massive devaluation of the peso, was pretty much out of the question.

I brooded over these dark thoughts as I wandered along the myriad trails that crisscross the canyon. As it grew dark Doug decided to build a fire at our campsite, which was a terrace backed by a rocky hillside. He gathered wood from far away and stacked it up. A couple of young boys watched impassively. Knowing the significance of fires for cooking and warmth among the Guarijíos and the increasing scarcity of firewood, I asked them if they thought it would

be all right to build a campfire there. They looked at each other for a moment.

"No," said one, "I don't think so. The *viejita* (old woman, meaning Doña Nechi) will get mad."

"No, she won't," argued the other one.

"Yes, she will. I know she will." The first stated emphatically. These boys were cagey observers, and I decided then and there to err on the side of conservatism.

I cautioned Doug immediately and went to find Doña Nechi, the blanket weaver. She was returning from far up the rocky hillside as darkness set in, leaning on a staff and slowly working her way down through the brushy outcrops. When she came nearby I approached her and asked, "Doña Nechi, my nephew would like to build a fire. Might we build one here?"

She looked around silently, staring first at him, then at me. The boys had vanished. "Not there," she said, pointing to Doug's pile of firewood. She pointed in the other direction. "In the fireplace under that ramada. That will be all right." Having exerted her authority she walked stiffly away, leaning on her staff, intent on organizing her own household. Doug hastily moved the faggots to the small fireplace and in a few minutes had a cheery fire burning.

So, the old woman had immense authority, at least in this household. Nobody was going to cross her and get away with it. This was hardly a strongly patriarchal culture.

Miguel joined us as we stared at the fire, waiting for Sebastián to announce that dinner was ready. After a long wait I finally said to Miguel, do you know when they will serve dinner? Breakfast?

"You'll need to pay," he said.

I was taken aback. After all, I had brought fifty pounds of food as a gift, but I was in no position to argue. How much? I wanted to know. And when?

"I'll find out," he said and walked over to the hut. A few minutes later he was back. He said nothing.

"How much?" I asked.

"Thirty pesos," he said. "Six o'clock in the morning."

I felt a bit piqued, as though I was being taken but couldn't do anything about it. So I seethed for a few minutes, then gave up my little snit as foolish. We waited around the little fire for the evening meal. I bombarded Miguel with questions. He reported that he had been born at a ranch northwest of Bavícora, but his parents now live in Mesa Colorada. He has five brothers and one sister. All the rest of his brothers and sisters live in Los Jacales, he said, the Guarijío barrio of San Bernardo. Some of them were hermanos de la fe, evangelical Protestants. That probably meant that he was alienated from them, for the traditional Guarijíos and the Protestant converts do not mix well. I knew from others that Miguel imbibed a drop or two of alcohol, a sore point between traditional Guarijíos and Protestants (see chapter 11).

I could get little more information from Miguel. Whether he didn't want to speak or whether he simply had no more to say, I could not determine. I later found that he is known as a taciturn fellow but still do not know whether still waters run deep in his case or if the light is on and no one is home.

We waited around the fire. After another hour of chitchat, mostly between Doug and me, my stomach was gurgling. I asked Miguel, "Will they serve dinner tonight?"

"No," he said. "Only breakfast."

I muttered a few imprecations in my exasperation, wondering why the hell he hadn't told us. Doug and I hurriedly cooked dinner from our meager stash of packaged backpack food, cleaned up, and went to bed. This was not a helpful guide.

I was packed by six-thirty. Doug and I waited around as Miguel showed up with the burros. He had borrowed my headlamp to locate them with. We waited and waited. Finally at 7:30 I walked over to Sebastián's house. They were just stirring there, and I could see that breakfast would be a while. We waited some more. Finally Sebastián indicated that our meal was ready. Before I reached the table, he dragged out the sacks of food I had brought. "Here you are," he said. "We only used the flour and some sugar."

"But I brought the food for you," I protested. "This was in exchange for our meals!" He was chagrined, and he and I immediately understood that Miguel had not communicated anything to him. All this time the Guarijíos had wondered just how presumptuous gringos could be who would bring their own food and demand that someone cook for them.

The beans and tortillas were fresh and tasty, the coffee once again superb. Sonoran Indians prefer coffee made from green coffee beans, which the women toast in a skillet with burned sugar. It is aromatic and rich. Sebastián apologized that our beans could not be fried, but they had no oil, he said. I assured him that I preferred them simply boiled. It was true, sort of. The jar of oil was in the bag.

We left Bavícora on a higher note, now that the misunderstanding about the food had been cleared up. I kept shaking my head in disbelief that Miguel could have nearly jeopardized our community relations by his failure

or inability to communicate what I thought he understood clearly. I worried, and still do, that my poor communication had left that Guarijío family with a bad impression of gringos.

But now, at least for the time being, all was made well. I reflected that I should never have assumed that Miguel would relay things the way I wanted them relayed. I should never assume anything when dealing with people who considered me an outsider. I should have told Sebastián myself. I had been a careless ethnographer. I had neglected one of my own cardinal rules: never assume. My list of rules was long: Always ask. Always err on the side of caution. Don't be afraid of appearing slow or repetitive. Make yourself look dim-witted rather than risk a misunderstanding. Be generous, but not profligate. Treat everyone as if they were highly respected leaders. Be gentle. Don't look anyone in the eye for more than a couple of seconds. Be extra careful about looking at women. If you must speak with a woman less than about fifty, look at the ground or downward when you speak. Never assume. Back down in potential confrontations over masculinity. Remember that submissive behavior relaxes other people. Compliment men on their livestock and on their homes. Try new foods. Learn to read people's expressions. Never assume. If you are going to ask questions, warn others that you are nosey (metichi in Spanish). Show them you are interested in them. Explain why you are taking notes—blame it on your poor memory, attribute it to your fascination with them and their place. Don't get too nosey. Learn to spot jerks and stay away from them. Never assume. Respect others' property. Find out whose property is where. Never, never assume.[10]

Miguel resumed his place on the trail, barking and ordering Alonso the burro up the mountainside, as we began to ascend the long succession of canyons that mark the return trip to Mesa Colorada. Miguel may not have been a stimulating conversationalist or an effective negotiator, but he handled the burros well. And he could walk in the dark.

As we descended the precipitous declivity below Matapaco, leaving behind the grassy mesa and towering over the glittering waters of the Mayo far below us, a Guarijío on horseback passed us herding three burros with empty packsaddles, the second fellow we met that day. He stopped to chat with us and with Miguel, whom he knew. He was on his way to Navojoa, where he would arrive in two days, he said. He was coming from a ranch far to the north of Bavícora. I wanted dearly to inquire what he would be buying in Navojoa and what the burros would be carrying back to the ranch that he could not just as easily buy in San

Bernardo, but I dared not. It would be too snoopy, too metichi of me. The vaquero passed us and for a long while we heard the jingle of his spurs and the clop and thud of his little pack train as they pounded down that steep trail, finally vanishing in the long series of switchbacks cut from the cliffs and forest.

It was about 3:30 when we arrived at Mesa Colorada. Miguel admitted that he was tired after the frenetic pace we had set coming back. He was unloading our trappings when I ran into Juan Enríquez, the yori from Burapaco. He was on horseback where he looked as though he had been born, dusty and sweaty from punching cows somewhere in the nearby hills. Juan, the renowned curandero, remembered me from our previous meeting and asked where we had been. Even though he is a mestizo Juan is quite popular among the Guarijíos, because he is poor, speaks Guarijío, can cure many diseases and infirmities, and always treats the Indians with respect, never patronizing them. When I told him we had just walked to Bavícora and back he told me I was crazy, that it was more then thirty kilometers distant and that I should have gone by horseback. I explained that I didn't ride horses in Guarijío country because they don't and because I get sore as the dickens when I ride for long. He nodded but advised me in the future to take along a horse anyway. "Look David," he told me quite seriously, "if you have a horse, you can ride until you get sore and then walk until you get tired. You have the advantage of both worlds." I suspect he is right. Maybe next time I would try that. But then probably I won't. Why? Because the Guarijíos I like the most don't ride horses. I don't need any more barriers between us when there are enough already.

7
Guarijío Lands

Guarijíos once populated the Sierra Madre well into the watershed of the Río Fuerte. Now, except for two small communities on the Río Oteros (Río Fuerte drainage) they live entirely within the basin of the Río Mayo. Numerous small settlements on the upper Río Batopilillas and other southeastern tributaries of the Mayo are now (or were until recently) Tarahumara. At Cuesta Blanca, a hamlet two mountain ranges east of Loreto, the residents pronounce themselves to be Rarámuri (Tarahumara) and profess themselves unable to understand the Guarijío language, even though some are related to Guarijíos. These, and other natives of the Sierra Madre assert that Loreto is the "last" (easternmost) place where Guarijíos live.

It seems convenient, then, to mark the eastern boundary of Guarijío lands as a line north of Loreto to where it intersects with the Río Mayo.[1] East and north of this short axis is Tarahumara country. South of Loreto the eastern boundary becomes the Oteros/Chínipas drainage. The northernmost Guarijío settlement is apparently at Chiltepín, on Arroyo Chiltepín, a minor tributary of the Río Mayo. The southernmost settlement of Guarijíos is San Bernardo. Los Jacales, a barrio of the town, is largely Guarijío and includes perhaps two hundred Guarijíos. Basicorepa, on the Arroyo Guajaray upstream from Los Bajíos, appears to be the westernmost Guarijío settlement.

Climate

Settlements of Guarijíos del río are concentrated below six hundred meters elevation in the mountainous portion of the Sierra Madre. Only small numbers live higher in a couple of tiny settlements. The climate in this region is generally warm-to-hot to hot-and-sultry. From mid-November through March, temperatures are mild. Although winter mornings can become chilly, even frosty, freezing is practically absent, occurring roughly once every twenty years and in spotty locations even then. Frosts occur more often at some higher locations (at El Saúz at near seven hundred meters, for example), and children and older people are said to suffer from cold during the winter.

The rest of the year is hot. Between early April and mid-October, daily temperatures may exceed 35° C (95° F). From late May through the onset of *las aguas,* usually in early July, high temperatures often exceed 40° C (104° F) in the lower elevations. On occasions temperatures in San Bernardo rise even higher.

The weather is significantly cooler in the domain of the Guarijíos de la sierra. At Loreto, summer temperatures seldom rise above 32° C (90° F). The terrain here lies mostly above fifteen hundred meters. When I stayed for several days at Canelichi in May, I awoke each morning to find my tent covered with frost. The ambient temperature on my thermometer was 2° C (36° F). In winter, temperatures commonly fall well below freezing. Snow, while not common, falls every few years in the town and more often in the Sierra Chuchupate above the valley to the east and the Sierra Canelo to the west. While two generations ago Guarijíos del río commonly went naked (Buitimea and Valdivia 1994; Gentry 1963), this condition would produce inordinate suffering at the higher elevations.

Rainfall averages 660 millimeters at San Bernardo (García 1973) at the extreme southern boundary of Guarijío country and roughly the same at Mesa Colorada. Amounts are probably somewhat higher on the mesas and slopes where most Guarijíos del río live. Rain in these lowlands falls primarily in July, August, and September—more than 70 percent of the annual rainfall. The arrival of las aguas after months of searing, dusty days is greeted with joy in the villages.

In the lowlands, las aguas usually arrive in early July in the form of nearly daily afternoon thunderstorms. These often violent events occur when moist, unstable tropical air originating in the Gulf of Mexico, the Pacific Ocean, and (to a tiny extent) the Gulf of California circulates northward or northeastward into the region. When this warm, wet mass meets the steep mountains they force it abruptly upwards. The mass cools as it rises, forming great thunderheads as it gains altitude, boiling cauldrons of dense clouds visible from up to a hundred miles away.

As the clouds mature and reach the cold air high in the atmosphere, the crowns spread like an anvil. Lightning strikes begin and soon zap the vicinity of the storm by the thousands. Powerful swirling winds stir up the dust, filling every home and all uncovered heads with fine grit. Torrential rains and hail often follow, but they are usually of brief duration. By evening the storms have usually passed, and the nights are refreshingly cool. The night after the first rain is one of excitement and delight, for the air is cleansed of dust and the pounding rain usually brings to the surface long-dormant toads along with a host of new critters that sing and carry on deep into the night.

Modest amounts of rain (locally called equipatas) also fall in December through February in the lowlands. These general and gentle rains may last for several days, forcing the outdoor-oriented Guarijíos to remain in their palm-thatched huts a good deal more than they would like. Late autumn tropical storms strike the area in a hit-or-miss fashion. While these hurricanes are an important source of moisture, they are unreliable. In recent years las aguas, primarily afternoon thunderstorms, on which the Guarijío peasants depend, have generally failed or have produced disappointing amounts of rain. Without las aguas, the Guarijíos' subsistence base is precarious. The capricious equipatas have tended to be scant, withholding the winter moisture necessary to improve forage on ejido lands and jeopardizing the fledgling Guarijío cattle industry that relies on constant forage.

The region around Loreto and associated highland settlements receive considerably more rain than the lowlands along the Río Mayo. Las aguas begin somewhat earlier in the sierras, usually in late June, and continue longer, usually until mid-September. While weather data for Loreto is lacking, the station at Yécora, Sonora, at nearly the same elevation and with similar vegetation, reports roughly a thousand millimeters (forty inches) of rainfall annually (Calderón Valdés 1985, I:171; Hastings and Humphrey 1969:38). Other slightly higher stations in the region report even greater precipitation. Most of it falls during the same cycles as in the lowlands, although a higher percentage falls during the summer months. The equipatas at Loreto and San Bernardo constitute an average of 20 percent of the annual rainfall, but the percentage is highly variable.

Within a few days of the onset of las aguas, the moisture transforms the lowland countryside from a dull gray-brown to a hundred shades of green. Vines grow extraordinarily fast, leaping from shrub to shrub, tree to tree, occasionally embracing the entirety of an etcho cactus. The trees leaf out exuberantly. In the highlands, the rains wash the dust from the pines, oaks, herbs, and grasses. Two hundred varieties of herbs and shrubs send up shoots and buds from a bewildering variety of roots—corms, bulbs, tubers, swollen roots, roots with nodules. Open spaces erupt with color as a huge variety of summer flowers—desmodiums, lilies, native peas, orchids and, above all, composites—illuminates the landscape.

The improved growing weather exacts a toll, however. Insect populations also revel in the moisture and exhibit a newfound exuberance of growth. Their populations explode, and hordes of stinging, biting, and sucking ectoparasites descend on the land. Chiggers, black flies, mosquitoes, and no-see-ums plague the natives but reserve their most aggressive attacks for strangers whose new blood seems especially appealing. In the highlands, black flies are a plague by day (people spend a good deal of their time fanning the pests away) and mosquitoes by night.

As if the bugs were not enough, weeds in staggering numbers appear and grow as if fertilized by magic. For the farmer, the next couple of months become a full-time battle against the encroachment of weeds. Mestizo farmers curse the armies of unwanted plants—*chicurilla, malva, ruina* (in the highlands) and dozens of others including many ensnaring vines—as they fight an often-losing battle against them. Guarijíos accept summer weeds as part of the annual cycle. Although the heat will become sultry and the bug populations explode, the rain brings growth and cleanses the countryside. Guarijíos rejoice with the rains.

The lower temperatures in the highlands lead to different planting strategies for the mountain Guarijíos. They commonly sow their corn in May or June at the height of the spring drought and harvest in October, while the Guarijíos del río delay their planting until the onset of las aguas, usually in early July and hope to harvest in November. The rains at Loreto are more reliable than those at Mesa Colorada but so are the frosts and freezes. River Guarijíos, unlike their mountain counterparts, plant most of their subsistence crops and the only cash crop, ajonjolí, immediately upon the arrival of the first rains. They are unwilling to plant earlier. They fear the precious seed would be lost if the rains were to fail, as they often do.

The dry seasons are of strategic importance in the Guarijío year. Since the weather cycles are usually predictable, the Guarijíos from both the highlands and lowlands have adopted an annual planting cycle. During the spring drought, usually beginning in March and ending with the onset of las aguas in early July, the river Guarijíos clear their mahuechis and prepare the soil for planting. Work on the cornfields is grueling. The steep hillside sites are often laid with more rocks than soil. But that is where the farmers must plant, for flood-free bottomlands are nearly non-existent in Guarijío country, and where they exist they are usually appropriated by yoris. The hillside vegetation is spiny, resilient, and persistent. The farmers battle against it, hack at it with machetes, and pry stubborn roots with steel bars. They stack the slash in piles. When it has dried, they burn it. Often the plot is too rocky for efficient planting, so with great effort the peasant over the months, sometimes years, lugs rocks to the mahuechi's edge and stacks them carefully into trincheras. The mountainsides of the Guarijío region are lined with many ancient trincheras, as carefully crafted as New England rock walls. In the dry season, hillsides appear laced with miniature Great Walls. Once las aguas arrive, the walls disappear beneath a frenzy of weeds and climbing vines. In the fall they reappear as the summer growth browns, withers, and disappears.

In spite of the grueling work (all planting, cultivating, and harvesting is accomplished by hand), the legions of biting, stinging insects, and the muggy heat, many Guarijíos revel in the arrival of las aguas. It is the time of rapid growth of their corn and beans, a time when they can see the sustenance for their families through the following year as it emerges from the ground. Battling the armies of weeds is part of their triumph over hunger and, as several Guarijíos have mentioned, watching that battle, fighting it, and winning it, provides the farmers with immense satisfaction.

In the highlands, the clearing is less arduous, due to less rapid growth of biomass, especially among winter and spring bloomers. By late May or early June, farmers hope to have planted corn, which will lie dormant in the plowed earth until the first rains. By October the harvest will be complete and losses due to frost will be avoided.[2]

Among the mountain Guarijíos, the traditional days of planting and of harvest—June 13, St. Anthony's Day and September 29, St. Michael's Day—are marked by important fiestas. These are the two occasions when a priest from Chínipas arrives at Loreto to bless the planting or the harvest, to say mass, and to baptize and confirm. On those days the Guarijíos claim the old mission of Loreto as their own. They enter the chapel first and yoris follow them. This order of entry is a matter of considerable pride for the Guarijíos, for it establishes the Loreto mission as theirs, as it has been for nearly four hundred years. Oddly, the fiesta, while of great significance to the Guarijíos of Loreto, is not a tuburada.

Soils and vegetation of the highland Guarijío region vary considerably from those below. The highlands have known eons of freezing temperatures and relatively more rain. Hence, the emplaced volcanic rocks are more weathered and soils are more developed. The slopes of the pine and oak forests are often gentler, and more flats suitable for planting are available.[3] Most corn planting takes place in the valleys of the region, where soils are comparatively deep and fertile. Mahuechis are fewer (though widespread), and unlike the river Guarijío region, they do not yet form checkerboard patterns on the hillsides. Clearing requires felling and cutting tall old growth trees—pines and oaks, and plant succession is slower (as is revegetation). Guarijíos from Loreto believe the fertility of their mahuechis last longer than those of the river Guarijíos. This is fortunate, for the proliferation of mahuechis in the great oak and pine forests would be laborious and ecological consequences lamentable.[4] The forests are already under attack by lumberjacks.

The planting in the highlands is often easier, for a plow pulled by oxen or mules opens the earth, and two men working together can plow a couple of hectares in a day. The higher elevation fields, which have the benefit of frost, do not face the same invasion of weedy plants, vines, and shrubs, as below, so their preparations are less difficult. The high mountain soil also yields abundant harvests of potatoes and squashes, and orchards of apples thrive in the region as well.

In the fall drought, usually from mid-September through November, men, boys, dogs, and scarecrows guard the maturing corn harvests. While the weather is warm and delightful, the corn attracts pests and predators and occasional human thieves. Raccoons, coatimundis, deer, opossums, and rodents await the ripening masorcas (ears) as do a myriad of insect pests. The warm, dry days mark a time of great activity for Guarijíos in both regions, for the corn they harvest must last through the year and provide seed for the following year as well.

Once the corn of mahuechis has been harvested, farmers gather the cornstalks and tasol (husks) as well, storing them in outdoor attics for winter and spring livestock fodder. During the harvest of stalks, what appears to be a moving sheaf of cornstalks turns out to be a burro so laden down with the stubble that only its eyes and tail are visible.

Once the corn, stalks, and husks are gathered from the mahuechis of the Guarijíos del río—usually late November—and the bean and squash plants have been reduced to a shriveled, dry mass, the weeds and shrubs slowly reestablish themselves in the mahuechi, as if they had waited months for the farmer to turn his back. By spring, if equipatas have fallen, they have taken over the mahuechi and must be chased and cut once again. Mestizo farmers curse the everlasting onslaught of invading shrubs and persistent weeds. The Guarijíos placidly accept these guests as part of maintaining

Mahuechis on hillside, trail to Bavícora.

a mahuechi and without complaining remove them as an inevitable phase of the rhythm of life.

Topography

Geologists viewing satellite images of the basin of the upper Río Mayo see former highlands in a state of magnificent degradation. The immense rifts and escarpments produced by calderas and basin and range tearing and splitting dominate the landscape. The most prominent active feature is the Río Mayo and its erosive effects. The Mayo originates in the high sierras of Chihuahua at more than twenty-seven hundred meters at Mesa de la Papa. It has cut profound canyons (or taken opportunistic advantage of the depressions produced by calderas) as it flows southwest, then gradually turns and flows due south for a hundred kilometers until it reaches Mocúzari Dam thirty kilometers north of Navojoa, and is diverted for agriculture.

The Mayo and its tributaries flow in the shadows of a series of mountain ranges, generally higher to the northeast. From northeast to southwest, they are the Sierra Chuchupate, the Sierra Canelo, and the Sierra Charuco to the east of the Río Mayo. Crossing the Mayo, the ranges continue from roughly north to south: the Sierra Oscura, the Sierra de la Ventana, the Sierra García, the Sierra Dos Cuates, and the Sierra Sutucame. These (mostly) northwest-southeast trending mountains range in maximum elevation from well over twenty-three hundred meters for the Chihuahuan ranges, to fifteen hundred meters, for the Sonoran ranges. (Please refer to the gazetteer for more information about each range.)

The region is crisscrossed with pack trails that switchback up and down the mountains, sometimes straightening over a rolling mesa or down a gradual drainage. Even in the canyon bottoms the trails crisscross the watercourses, inevitably ascending and descending steep slopes as the nearly vertical walls of the canyon converge and compress the arroyo, squeezing traffic up and out of the bottom to above the cliffs. During exceptionally low river flows, pack trains take advantage of easy passage and remain in the bottom. Floods soon drive them out and rearrange the river bottom, always rolling more boulders downstream.

Burros are the main source of shipment of goods in the region. The traveler often meets pack trains of ten or more burros empty or loaded. They can often be heard well before they are seen; the jingling, clanking, and bumping of their tack, packsaddles, and burdens, and the clopping of their hooves, along with the shouts and curses of the drovers, proceed them. The trails constantly ascend and descend, usually sharply, thus guaranteeing that the frequent traveler will soon sport well-developed calf muscles.

For traversing these slopes, on which loose rocks abound, Guarijíos wear simple huaraches consisting of a sole cut from a tire, a thin pad of leather, and a thong passed through three holes binds the soles to the foot. This universal footwear is known as huaraches de tres puntas. Travelers usually remove them when crossing streams. They balance on a staff as they skillfully work their way barefoot across boulders slick with moss and algae.

Vehicle roadways are few in this region of successive convoluted ranges. The cost of laying out a system of modern roadways would be prohibitive, and the government has never felt the region merited the heavy investment roads would require. A rough dirt track leads from San Bernardo to Guajaray, while another, more passable, reaches Mesa Colorada from San Bernardo.[5] A motor road, portions of which are dreadful, also leads north from San Bernardo to Loreto, Chihuahua, and continues north to Baseaéchic. In Chihuahua, small lumber and ranch roads (hours away from the nearest pavement) lead to most Guarijío settlements. Some villages, such as Guasisaco and Tojíachi, are accessible only by footpaths.

There is hardly a single flat place big enough to call a "place" in all of the Guarijío country. Even mesas are hilly or rolling. Other than a few riverbank terraces where flooding occurs annually, there are almost no usable flats near water. Where rolling mesas lie adjacent to water, humans have invariably founded settlements, permanent or temporary. On steep hillside or canyon settings such as Bavícora, Rancho Nuevo, and Los Aguaros, the Guarijíos have built their homes on carefully constructed terraces suitably close to water to keep ollas full but far enough away that floods will never reach their doorsteps, and strangers following the watercourse will not happen upon their settlements. Los Bajíos, Guajaray, Mesa Colorada, and Todos Santos are all situated on rolling uplands well above the river bottoms. Most residents of the villages must haul water, two buckets on a *palanca* (yoke) for men, a bucket carried on the head for women.

The government has installed pumps and public taps in some villages, but these seldom operate. Only Guajaray and Bavícora have reliable gravity-fed water systems.

The mountains of the Sonoran Guarijío region do not exceed two thousand meters elevation, but their low height is deceptive. They originate near sea level, so the montane mass is equivalent to taller mountains with a correspondingly higher base. The entire region is incised with steep canyons and narrow valleys circumscribed by steep, rugged ranges. Several streams are permanent, especially the Arroyo Batopillillas, Arroyo Limón and its tributaries, the Río Mayo, and the entirety of the Arroyo Guajaray. Apart from these dependable sources, few streams flow the year round. In the late spring the land is dry and most of the watercourses are devoid of water except for isolated aguajes. Guarijíos treasure these often hidden springs and know them well, though they may be concealed under cliffs in deep forest. It is as though they had the water holes mapped in their collective unconscious.

Chihuahua Guarijío country is equally mountainous, but with a higher base. Loreto, at fifteen hundred meters, is surrounded by hills that reach well over twenty-three hundred meters elevation. These slopes are somewhat gentler and easier to traverse than those of the hot country below, due in no small measure to the comparative ease of passage through glades of oak and pine compared with the thorny and dense thickets of the tropical deciduous forest. While the highlands are lacking in rivers, they are better watered by small streams than are the lowlands. Where open valleys occur, most of the trees have long since been cut and cleared and replaced with relatively flat fields of corn, beans, potatoes, and squash. The fields are often separated by trincheras, which make for picturesque viewing when seen from mountain panoramas. Nowadays wire fencing is more common, and some of the trincheras are tumbling down from disuse.

Vegetation

Where lands are undisturbed in the Sonoran Guarijío country—the upper Río Mayo—they are covered with tropical deciduous forest (Yetman et al. 1995). The Mayo region marks the northernmost extension of well-developed tropical deciduous forest on the North American continent. While pockets of tropical deciduous forest can be found farther northwest in the Río Yaqui drainage, species diversity drops dramatically north of the Río Mayo.

Just as tropical deciduous forest thins and vanishes to

The Río Mayo from Mesa Matapaco, view to the southwest.

Sierra García from Rancho el Saúz. Photo by Doug Yetman.

the northwest, so it merges into thornscrub to the west and southwest. Below Mocúzari Dam tropical deciduous forest slowly merges into thornscrub as the vegetation becomes smaller, the canopy more open, and the composition more desert-like, with a greater predominance of cacti and thorny small trees and shrubs.

Ecologist Forrest Shreve (Shreve and Wiggins 1964) suggested the Arroyo Cocoraque between Navojoa and Ciudad Obregón as the dividing point between tropical thornscrub and vegetation of the Sonoran Desert scrub, provoking heated discussion. The dividing line between thornscrub and tropical deciduous forest is equally the subject of much discussion but is generally agreed to be found in the foothills of higher mountains (Yetman et al. 1995). Southeast of the Mayo region, thornscrub is the dominant vegetation type along the coast as far south as Culiacán, Sinaloa. Tropical deciduous forest continues south on the lower western slopes of mountains along the Pacific Coast as far south as Costa Rica. This 2,000-mile-long belt was uninterrupted until the twentieth century when pastoralists discovered that clearing tropical forests enabled them to increase their numbers of livestock, commercial producers discovered the fertility and manageability of soils on gentle slopes, and governments used the clearing as a safety valve for land-hungry peasants. Now more than 90 percent of tropical deciduous forest is gone (Janzen 1988) and with it a habitat of nearly unimaginable diversity. The largest remaining contiguous tracts are found in Guarijío country of southern Sonora and western Chihuahua.

While composition, stature, and density of the Guarijío tropical deciduous forest vegetation vary, trees in excess of twelve meters high tend to dominate the forest. I mention examples of trees to illustrate the variety found in tropical deciduous forest. Species include palo mulato (Bursera grandifolia), torote copal (Bursera penicillata), pochote (kapok, Ceiba acuminata), mauto (Lysiloma divaricatum), tepeguaje (L. watsonii), palo zorillo (Senna atomaria), tempisque (Sideroxylon tepicense), and amapa (Tabebuia impetiginosa). Medium-sized trees (eight to twelve meters high) include huinolo (Acacia cochliacantha), teso (Acacia occidentalis), palo colorado (Caesalpinia platyloba), palo de asta (Cordia sonorae), jaboncillo (Fouquieria macdougalii), copalquín (Hintonia latiflora), nesco (Lonchocarpus hermannii), and the arborescent cacti etcho (Pachycereus pecten-aboriginum) and pitahaya (Stenocereus thurberi). Small trees (six to eight meters tall) and shrubs include cumbro (Celtis iguanaea), palo fierro (Chloroleucon mangense), vara blanca (Croton fantzianus), palo amarillo (Esenbeckia hartmanii), mamoa (Erythroxylon mexicanum), brasil (Haematoxylum brasiletto), sangrengado (Jatropha malacophylla), cacachila (Karwinskia humboldtiana), granadilla (Malpighia emarginata), chopo (Mimosa palmeri), garumbullo (Pisonia capitata), and papache (Randia echinocarpa). The tree-like cacti sibiri (Opuntia thurberi) and nopal (O. cf. wilcoxii) are also common in drier reaches of the forest. The largest trees grow along watercourses, reaching heights in excess of twenty-five meters. Among these are nacapuli (Ficus cotinifolia), tucuchí (F. pertusa), guamúchil (Pithecellobium dulce), igualama (Vitex mollis), and, in cajones, guasimilla (Aphananthe monoica), palo verde (Drypetes gentryi), and bebelama (Sideroxylon persimile). At roughly nine hundred meters (as low as six hundred meters under certain favorable conditions), three species of oaks appear, cusi (Quercus albocincta), encino (Q. chihuahuensis), and encino roble (Q. tuberculata). These oaks play only a minor role among plants used by Guarijíos. At higher elevations these oaks join others to become the dominant trees of the oak woodland.

Guarijíos and other dwellers within the tropical deciduous forest have found its diversity of tree species (more than 150 in the region) much to their liking. They have incorporated a multitude of plant species and plant parts into their lives. It is a rare tree that is not used in one way or another, whether it be the root, wood, bark, sap, leaf, flower, or fruit—or (most significantly) shade. In the entire region I have discovered only a few trees that were unknown to the Guarijíos, and those grew in inaccessible habitats or were sufficiently uncommon that absence of human uses comes as no surprise. One distinctly tropical tree, Bursera simaruba which I found growing in a remote box canyon of the upper Arroyo San Pedro was unfamiliar to Guarijíos living not far away. They associated it with palo mulato (Bursera grandifolia), which it resembles and were surprised and intrigued to discover it was a distinct species. The stately joso de la sierra (Conzattia multiflora), a well-known leguminous tree with a silvery, straight trunk growing up to twenty-five meters tall, has no identified uses among either Guarijíos or Mayos, even though the tree is used for lumber elsewhere in Mexico. My lack of data on these trees may reflect my own incompetence as an ethnobotanist.

On the other hand, Guarijíos identify and use a far smaller percentage of herbs than either shrubs or trees. Furthermore, they often group genera of similar species together under one name (this is especially true of spurges and spiderlings). Herbs are less noticeable and are often more difficult to differentiate from one another. For example, there are a good thirty species of yellow composites in the region, but Guarijíos recognize and name only a few of them as useful plants. It is hard to fault them for this. Even the best botanists see the dycs (damned yellow composites), as they are considered, utter a disparaging oath, and refer them to a specialist. After las aguas begin, a field may harbor thirty species of summer annuals competing for space, including a dozen vines that intertwine with everything else. It is easy to overlook subtle differences in a display of such exuberance, so the Guarijíos' botanical lapse with regard to herbs is understandable.

The tropical deciduous forest undergoes a series of transformations throughout the year. These continuing metamorphoses add to the mystique and beauty of the forest, and are a pivotal factor in the cycle of the Guarijío year. If we look at a tropical deciduous forest landscape in May, for example, it will not evoke poetry of joy. Most trees stand parched and leafless under the searing heat. Flies buzz, gnats whine, and urracas scold occasionally. On a certain day each year, cicadas emerge from the ground, heard before they are seen, and for a few hours they whoosh up their feelings.

A local grasshopper gives off a twangy mating call that sounds like feedback noise from a loudspeaker. Apart from these sporadic sounds, the landscape is silent, save for the mournful plaint of the Red-billed Pigeon.[6] One can almost <u>hear</u> the drought, the heated, ascending air currents, the hot blasts reflected from the ground. Dust puffs up with each step. The unprotected skin burns, the lips blister, and the throat is parched. It is a difficult time even for the hardy Guarijíos. Even so, the nights and mornings are cool and the spirit is refreshed with the dawn. It is Cipriano Buitimea's favorite time of year. He can prepare his *milpa* with no competition from weeds.

During these oven-like days of spring, the forest has no apparent understory, few shrubs, and almost no herbs. The hillsides resemble legions of dead sticks stuck in bare ground. Most herbs have gone dormant or have been gnawed to stubble or torn up by the roots by livestock. In clearings, a few unpalatable weedy shrubs or shrubby weeds survive, but even they take on a listless gray-brown hue except for the nearly black hue of highly toxic *toloache* (Jimson weed, *Datura*). Often the very ground lies barren, and the reddish or yellow volcanic soil stands out among the seemingly lifeless trees. Solitary cows wander forlornly, apathetically along the thousands of cowpaths made visible by the disappearance of chlorophyll, hoping to find an edible leaf, blade of grass, or even the pad of a prickly pear or cholla cactus. This is no jungle. It resembles a bombed out wasteland more than tropical forest. It is so drab that a Guarijío can be detected at a great distance, identified by the brilliant straw-colored hat standing out in the dead landscape.

Two exceptions to this dreary picture are the etcho and pitahaya cacti. These retain their colors bravely. The light-green pitahaya arms turn somewhat yellowish in the heat, their upper branches bearing colonies of white flowers. The etchos endure with their dark green trunk and arms, their bristly ripening fruits burgeoning on the upper arms like straw-colored sea anemones. On some hillsides the yellow-gold newly sprouted leaves of the tepeguaje may lend a hint of color and are harbingers of the approaching transformation, but for some reason theirs is not a refreshing green. It seems to underscore the hopelessness of the landscape.

Even in this time of the hot winds some of the trees flower. Here and there the coral-bean tree or chilicote (*Erythrina flabelliformis*) sends out spears of brilliant red flowers. On the gentler slopes the *guayacán (Guaiacum coulteri)* becomes an umbrella of bright blue-purple. In the deeper forest, leafless branches of nesco fill with lacy, lily-purple

Etcho cacti. In the distance is the Sierra de la Ventana.

blooms. On selected hillsides, hundreds of *palo piojo* trees *(Brongniartia alamosana),* otherwise of little interest, burgeon with blood-red flowers that last for only a couple of days. Branches of the symmetrical palo zorillo are festooned with pale yellow. In a few blessed localities, the amapa amarilla may continue to produce golden flowers well into May. All these trees and more seize their own niche of time, demonstrate their own trickery for luring pollinators, and thus prevent the hillsides from totally capitulating to the drab color Mexicans call mojino. Colorful as these con artists may be, however, they only slightly alleviate the overwhelming gray-brown drabness of the monte mojino.

I have decided that true botanical sophistication in the tropical deciduous forest lies in the ability to identify trees when they are leafless. I've struggled with the nomenclature for years. At first I was bewildered by the dozens of different species, most of which resembled each other—gray, brown, maculate, or black legions of apparently lifeless trunks. I had good teachers, though, men of enduring patience. Several Guarijíos and Mayos revealed to me the mysteries of identification and the secrets to individual species. Even so, I bungled my way through an ersatz apprenticeship. Gradually I began to note lenticels, invaginations, exfoliations, fissures, chlorophylous bark, persistent pods, maculations, presence or absence of thorns, sap color and consistency, aroma, and, most important overall shape and texture, which some call gestalt, others simply Zen.[7] Also important was habit and location—north or south slope, steep or gentle slope, arroyo bottom, mountaintop, acid soil, sweet soil, rocky hill, sandy mound, near trails, or far from trails, bearing machete scars, free from machete scars.[8] When the trees leaf out, identification is far easier, and with a little practice, even the beginner can enjoy the smug satisfaction of correct identifications. Real men don't rely on leaves.

In late June the overall transformation of the landscape begins. Although rains usually do not arrive for a couple of weeks, several species, especially mauto and palo piojo begin to leaf out, and the still desiccated hillsides take on a few brush strokes of tentative light green. When the rains commence, usually in the form of a few brief, abrupt showers, they signal the remaining plants to gear up for growth. If the rain is a real one, the plants seem to know that it is time to put on their new clothes. Within a few days all the trees leaf out and herbs, shrubs, and climbers seem to explode from the ground. The atmosphere within the monte is that of a sauna. Only a few trees present gaudy flowers during the rainy season. The most spectacular is the white *cascalosúchil* (frangipani, *Plumeria rubra*). It is a small tree with blunt branches, each tipped with dense white blossoms in a surrounding of deep green elongated leaves. Most remarkable, however, are the green hues of summer, a hundred shades, at first undifferentiated. Then, with familiarity, each hue becomes identified with a discernible plant signature of idiosyncratic green. Experienced Guarijíos identify trees from a distance by their color the way ewes single out their lambs from the flock by their individual smell. I'm not that sophisticated yet.

In the sauna-like heat of las aguas, insect populations soar almost as rapidly as the number of new leaves. Why? Because herbivorous insects must produce new legions in a hurry to devour the fast-growing leaf canopy, while predators have to be poised to fatten on the huge numbers of herbivores. Most of this must be accomplished within the ten weeks. After that, leaves begin to wilt and fall, so it is a homestead rush to procreate, eat, grow, and reproduce some more. One can perhaps hear beetles munching and gnawing on fruits, stems, and trunks. Chiggers in particular celebrate a coming out. Hordes of them creep up tall weeds and grasses and jump to a passerby. They seek out waist bands and socks. Although they are nearly invisible (just tiny red dots), they seem to lever themselves against tight clothing and burrow into the skin, biting all the while. Guarijíos endure the rashes raised by dozens of bites stoically, as a part of summer. I complain bitterly.

Birds also are revived by this frenzy of growth, and the burgeoning insect population is a cornucopia for the newly hatched chicks as well as older birds. The monte, lately so still, so silent, so shimmering with heat and vastly colorless, now comes alive with the wiggles and flits of hosts of

Up arroyo from Bavícora, December.

feeding birds (oddly silent) and humming insects and a score of newly green hues. The only view I've ever had of a Russet-crowned Motmot came during las aguas. The creature made not a sound. It sat on a low branch, merely looked at me, its small racquet-shaped tail feathers twitching. In five seconds it was gone. The squirrel cuckoo, red against the green backdrop, is equally silent, flitting through the underbrush like a spy. Elegant Trogons, noisy and territorial in May and June, slack off in their calls, pausing to eat, I guess. The parrots and macaws, normally vociferous, are absent or abstain from squawking. Feeding and gorging seem to be more important than vocalizing. The fluorescent green of parrots is well camouflaged in the color mix of the monte.

For six to eight weeks in a good summer the rains come nearly every day. Usually, though, the rains end by the beginning of September in the lowlands, a couple of weeks later in the highlands, and only occasional, spotty storms occur thereafter. As las aguas end, another period, usually dry, begins, lasting until well into December. In September or October an erratic tropical hurricane may blow inland from the eastern Pacific and drench the land with many inches of rain in a short space of time. Heavy rains fell in the lowlands in 1995 and 1996 from such storms. Other storms never make it inland. No storm appeared in 1997. In early September 1998 Hurricane Isis drenched Alamos with a foot of rain in a day. At San Bernardo, thirty miles north, it merely drizzled.

The next transformation of the countryside, more subtle, now begins. At first only a few trees signal the onset of the fall drought. Leaves of *torote papelío (Jatropha cordata)* and sangrengado *(J. malacophylla)* turn bright yellow. The huge, lacy leaves of joso *(Conzattia)* turn golden yellow at the top of the canopy. Soon the Burseras follow, especially torote puntagruesa *(B. penicillata),* whose leaves turn orange yellow in senescence. Those of torote *(B. fagaroides)* also lend an autumnal lilt. The kapok leaves are not far behind, turning a shade of gold tinged with red. The small but numerous *Croton* trees, *fantzianus* and *flavescens,* add a touch of red and gold to the many yellows. If no rains occur, the yellows on the hillsides overtake the greens. Little by little, as October slips into November and the winter begins, the forest loses its jungle-like appearance. Half, two-thirds, then three-quarters of the leaves are gone. The dull ground once again appears among the trees, and the mojino color slowly reasserts itself.

Autumn is my favorite time for hiking. The bugs are mostly gone, the aggressive growth of weeds and vines is over, and impediments to clear trails are wilting and dying. The air is usually still, the silence broken only by the occasional pop of a dehiscing palo piojo pod, a scurry of leaves disturbed by a brief puff of autistic wind, or the rustle of a retreating lizard. The forest is also full of fresh smells—not only the frankincense of the burseras, but also the senescent shrubs and herbs each of which seem to exude a signature aroma. There is usually ample water in creeks and aguajes. The nights are cool, the days warm, but not overpowering. The Guarijíos are relaxed. With help from the rain, their corn is harvested and stored, and their mahuechis lie fallow for six months. It is the time for long conversations and leisurely explorations. Even more important, by late October the marijuana harvest is complete—bagged and shipped—and the trigger-happy owners of illicit fields seem to have eased off on their twitching fingers and are willing to allow unfamiliar faces to pass by unaccosted.

As pleasant as the autumn is, winter and early spring bring the finest flowers of the tropical deciduous forest. By then more than half the leaves of the forest have dropped, but the amapa *(Tabebuia impetiginosa)* and two months later the yellow amapa *(T. chrysantha)* burst into their full glory. Amapa trees turn intensely pink, even more deeply hued if equipatas have been benevolent. The yellow amapas follow in March and April, illuminating the drab landscape with a brilliance that resembles a torch, as Gentry so accurately observed. In March a thousand points of white, the gauzy brilliance of palo de asta *(Cordia sonorae),* punctuate the deepening mojino color. Groves of *batayaqui (Montanoa rosei)* put out clusters of yellow-white blossoms staggeringly perfumed. Bees gather nectar and swell their local enjambres.

Tropical deciduous forest in a wet winter, 1997. Flowering trees are *amapas and batayaquis.* In foreground are *etchos.*

These flowers fade as well under the heat of spring. By April the summer temperatures return, and the skies remain cloudless for weeks on end. The last leaves begin to drop. Deep cracks appear in the hard soil, and the landscape assumes once again an aspect of death or benevolent dormancy. The country once again lies nearly silent, hoping against reality for las aguas to arrive early.

At each stage of the year, the appearance of the forest is ephemeral, far more so than the green of the broad-leaved forests of the eastern United States. The full green lasts for a maximum of ten weeks. The remainder of the year represents a fading of the greens and a slow return of the mojino. Rather than the traditional four seasons of the temperate north, we can discern twice as many distinct seasonal sequences in the tropical deciduous forest. But only people like the Guarijíos, who are attune to the subtle changes in the monte, can adequately sense them. For them each season presents its own tasks and makes available new products of the monte.

In contrast, the mountain Guarijíos live in oak woodland and pine-oak forest where the seasonal change is not as dramatic—or exciting. The exception is April and May, when the oaks slough off their old leaves to make way for the new ones that usually bud out immediately. The leaves of each oak species take on a different shade of brown, from russet to beige. At times during this short period, the oak-covered hills appear devastated by blight, fire, or insect depredations, an intimation of ecological catastrophe. As the spring drought continues, however, the new oak leaves unfurl, and in the space of a few weeks, the hillsides are slowly layered with a fresh wave of greens as varied as the browns they replaced.

Pines, on the other hand, change little in appearance throughout the year. They replace their needles or leaves gradually, never in a dramatic display of deciduous pomp. This is true as well of other less common trees of the higher mountains such as *lolesí (Berberis longipes)* and *juripusi (madroño, Arbutus arizonicus)*.

These higher-elevation forests, in their unlumbered conditions, are more open than the tropical deciduous forests below, and, in spite of the dramatic proliferation of oak and pine species, contain fewer tree species overall. On hillsides the brilliant reddish-pink bark of madroño *(Arbutus xalapensis)* may be visible for miles through the open glades. On the other hand, herbs are noticeably more diverse in the mountains, and shrubs play a more important role on exposed, sunny hillsides. When deciduous trees other than the oaks drop their leaves here, it is in response to cold, not to drought, as in the lower country. The *fresno* (ash, *Fraxinus*), *alamillo* (alder, *Alnus*), *jeco (Prunus)* and maple *(Acer)* drop their leaves in November and remain leafless until early May when the danger of freezing is past. Summer annuals sprout in response to rain, not temperature alone. With the arrival of las aguas, the lower story of hillsides and mountain slopes of the oak and pine forest explode with a variety of flowering plants that challenges the most seasoned botanist. While the number and aggressiveness of climbers is smaller, fast-growing perennials with flowers of every conceivable color, including several orchids, emerge in enormous numbers, often reaching more than a meter in height.

The oaks of the oak woodland include cusi, *encino blanco (Q. arizonica),* encino *(Q. coccolobifolia),* encino prieto *(Q. hypoleucoides),* güeja *(Q. tarahumara),* and *saucillo (Q. viminea).*

Another five species and several hybrids are found nearby in the region (Martin et al. 1998). Some of the specimens grow tall and spreading—commonly in excess of twenty-five meters tall—and nearly as wide, providing abundant shade and bushels of acorns. The oaks are as central to the lives of Guarijíos de la sierra as mezquite and mauto are to the lives of the Guarijíos del río.

As elevation increases above the tropical deciduous forest, the diversity of oaks increases as well, but it is pines that dominate the vegetation. Pines of the pine-oak forest near Loreto are primarily *pino chino (Pinus chihuahuensis), pino llorón (P. lumholtzii), pino (P. engelmanii),* and pino *(P. yecorensis).* While ancient specimens exceed forty meters in height, most of these have been cut down for lumber. Only where private ownership or topographic isolation has precluded timber harvesting can such large specimens still be found. Numerous other species of oak and pine are found in the region, and the species mix alters with elevation change. At the highest elevations of the Mayo region, at roughly twenty-seven hundred meters (at Mesa de la Papa, north of Guarijío country), a forest of mixed conifer grows that resembles high-elevation forests of the southwestern United States. The resemblance ends quickly, though, when one notices the orchids and bromeliads, both terrestrial and arboreal, that frequent the forest, reminding us that this is still a semi-tropical climate.

Other trees of the montane Guarijío region in addition to oaks and pines are structurally important as well. The white-trunked madroño *(Arbutus arizonicus)* and the red-trunked madroño *(A. xalapensis)* grow among the oaks and pines. Trees growing along watercourses include the alamillo (alder, *Alnus oblongifolia*), which grows in nearly impenetrable thickets; *táscate* (Arizona cypress, *Cupressus lusitanica*), host for extensive colonies of poison ivy; *capulín* (jeco, chokecherry, *Prunus serotina*); and, occasionally, *pinabete* (Durango fir, *Abies durangensis*). The pine-oak forest supports a wide variety of herbs and grasses. Common shrubs include manzanita *(Arctostaphylos pungens)* and *chaparita,* the buckbrush *(Ceanothus depressus).* On cutover hillsides these form chaparral so thick they impede passage and inspire audible oaths.

The Madrean oak and pine-oak forests are botanical wonderlands, as fair a landscape as a wanderer could wish for. Meadows burgeon with a vast spread of myriad flowers. Where the countryside has been spared from overgrazing by cows, grasses grow thickly among the spreading oaks and towering pines. The glades are interspersed with several different agaves, cacti, sotols, and yuccas. Terrestrial orchids rise unexpectedly from damp litter, while more densely flowering arboreal varieties grace the branches of oaks and pines. In sheltered and moist locations palm trees mix with the pines and raspberries mingle with begonias.[9] At the height of las aguas the landscape is crisscrossed with rivulets and streams. The mornings are misty, and even at noon the sun appears softened with a romantic filter. Even chiggers and (perhaps) midges seem tolerable in the lush, dreamlike greenery of summer.

The oak woodland often begins abruptly and dramatically above the tropical deciduous forest. Where soils become indurated or hydrothermally altered, the change from one vegetation type to another may take place within a few meters. Often the line of demarcation at a ridgeline or at the turn of a slope is clearly visible from afar. The edge of a mesa may find the two regimes in contact, one giving way to the other within ten meters. Plants of the two communities interact only briefly—a few oaks descend into the tropical deciduous forest, and a few tropical deciduous forest trees such as *algarrobo (Acacia pennatula), palo santo (Ipomoea arborescens),* tepeguaje *(Lysiloma watsonii),* and torote *(Bursera fagaroides)* make forays into the oaks. Gentry spoke quite accurately when he described stepping out of the tropical deciduous forest into the "pleasant land of the oaks." The reverse is equally true, for one can step down from the open glades of oaks into the dense vastness of the tropical deciduous forest.

Where oaks become dominant, pines, beginning with *Pinus oocarpa* are seldom far above. As elevation increases, so does the species diversity of oaks. Soon pine species also proliferate, especially *P. yecorensis,* until the oak forest gives way to a forest dominated by pines but home to numerous oaks as well. Rancho Canelichi and its Guarijío settlement at fifteen hundred meters near Loreto is such a forest. It has never been systematically lumbered, and the mixed-age forest supports a rich diversity of both pine and oak species, each growing to great size and beauty. Tiburcio Charramoneta led me through these woods, dazzling both for their diversity and for the size of the pine and oak trees.

Geology

The western slope of the midsection of the Sierra Madre Occidental, where Guarijíos live, has a sensational geological history, as anyone who has seen or traveled through the country can attest. I relate here, with impossible brevity, and with a lot of help from others, the story of the Guarijíos' geological patrimony.[10]

I shall begin roughly 100 million years ago (Ma). At that time what continental mass of northwest Mexico existed was probably a rolling, flat plateau with little relief. There were none of the mountains we know today, and whatever hills were there were probably low-lying. Mountains had been there before, but over unthinkably long stretches of geological time they had been eroded away until hardly any of the original mountain mass remained.

This unexciting landscape was already in a state of change, however, for the Pacific Ocean floor (the Pacific Plate) had already crashed into the more buoyant continental plate (North American Plate) and in a process called subduction was plunging underneath, while the continent rode on top. This gargantuan collision slowly produced uneasiness in the terrain above, and what would become the Sierra Madre began to rise. This period of mountain building known as the Laramide Orogeny, the period of tectonic compression or collision, lasted from 40 to about 15 Ma and produced the Sierra Madre uplift.

How did the mountain building work? Part of the answer is relatively simple: drive an upside down spatula underneath a sticking underdone pancake on a griddle and push it forward (not upward). The cake will fold and wrinkle in the middle. That's the compression. Colliding plates have the same effect.

The other part is less obvious. The Pacific Plate, with nowhere else to go, and since it is heavier than the North American Plate that rode over it, plunged far down into the earth's crust and even below—the path of least resistance. The friction produced by the colliding plates' grinding and grating created enormous heat, and the buckling effect of the lowering plate thinned the crust above, while the rock of the leading edge melted. The combination of new heat and the new access to the surface caused by the underlying plate's downward motion allowed magma from the earth's mantle to flow towards the surface. For a length of more than a thousand miles colossal volumes of magma—molten rock from the earth's mantle—welled up like subcutaneous tumors and raised the surface. The magma would cool over millions of years into the basement granite or batholith that anchors the Sierra Madre. In places, though, the magma broke through to the surface as volcanoes. These eruptions— beginning in the Eocene perhaps around 40 Ma, produced andesite flows of immense proportions, and they covered the already rising surface with volcanic rock a kilometer thick. Thus was born the Sierra Madre, a very long, narrow highland capped with volcanic rock.

The andesite flows continued well into the Oligocene epoch of the Tertiary period, ending around perhaps around 30 Ma. At that time, the direction of the subducting Pacific Plate changed. The plate no longer moved east. It may have simply lingered in place, while still plunging downward at its leading edge, or it or parts of attached plates may have shifted to the northwest. Or it may have been consumed.

Whatever the dynamics, plate activity switched direction and produced a new wave of volcanism beginning in the late Oligocene through the mid-Miocene (roughly 35–20 Ma). This shift of the underlying plates produced an extensional regime (stretching as opposed to colliding) known as the mid-Tertiary Orogeny. Instead of being compressed into folds, the crust and surface now stretched and tore much like tearing off a poorly cut piece of pizza. As the crust was pulled apart, it thinned, and magma worked its way closer to the surface at the resulting weak points. As the stretched crust thinned, all hell broke loose in the Sierra Madre. A host of cataclysmic explosions blew out several hundred calderas, one as large as forty kilometers in diameter, as wild a period of volcanism as the Earth had known for hundreds of millions of years. These blasts released catastrophic pyroclastic flows, puffing clouds, avalanches of gigantic proportions made up of superheated bits of rock and mud. The flows laid down layers of welded rhyolitic tuff so extensive that by the end of the mid-Tertiary Orogeny, the rhyolites had added another kilometer in depth to the Sierras, thus further raising them. The resulting formations constitute the dominant landscapes visible today. When these tuffs have been exposed by faults or arroyo cutting, they reveal layers chronicling different explosive volcanic events in the same way that scraping old paint off an ancient wall reveals underlying coats and recapitulates its painting history.

As the calderas were blowing their tops off, part of the landscape was altered to show stretch marks. The Madrean pluton that formed during the Laramide Orogeny, the granitic batholith that underlies the Madrean volcanic icing of andesites and rhyolites, appears to be long and skinny, but is deeply and solidly emplaced. To the west of the main mass of the Sierra Madre, the deep foundation is not so secure, and the mid-Tertiary stretching broke off blocks of terrain that subsequently tilted as they sought their center of gravity.

The mid-Tertiary Orogeny grumbled to a close, and the land rested uneasily for a few million years. Around 15 Ma another period of stretching (the Basin and Range era, roughly 15–5 Ma) beset a huge region—nearly all of Nevada, western Utah, western and southern Arizona, and Sonora west of the main bulge of the Sierra Madre were included. Mountains to the west of the main spine were once again mercilessly stretched and huge fault blocks resulted from the tearing, some of them simply dropping out of sight, creating colossal cliffs on the broken edge of the mass left behind. Occasionally basaltic flows from the late Tertiary, perhaps resulting from thinning of the crust produced by Basin and Range stretching—spurted through thin spots in the crust. Their remnants can be seen poking through the vegetation, as on Mesa Matapaco.

While weathering, and erosion, and the generally unharmonious bubblings of Laramide masses of magma have combined to produce an extraordinarily irregular mountainous region in the Sierras, the pluton managed to resist this stretching, tearing, and thrust faulting. Thus the highlands as around Loreto, tend to be less torn and tilted, less tortured than the mountains to the west, while the foothills demonstrate block faulting and tilting. Atop the sierras there are more gentle slopes, more rolling valleys, and proportionally fewer punishing grades. This is a matter of degree, of course, for many steep mountains rise from the rolling plateaus. And in the great Barranca Candameña, from which the Río Mayo issues, (and which may represent a breached caldera) sheer cliffs more than a thousand feet high rise from the bottom.

And so the landscape the Guarijíos know well came to be. It is not by any means finished. Now it is being eroded, as rain, dew, frost, lichens, wind, and chemical processes break down the once proud peaks into smaller and smaller particles, winding up as soil in mahuechis, silts in the river bottoms, or sediments deposited in Mocúzari Lake and elsewhere. Earthquakes in the Guarijío region have not been recorded in modern history. Even so, as Baja California continues to pull away from Sonora, tearing toward the northwest, earthquakes are not out of the question. Something has to settle when great slabs of Earth disconnect.

The scenery of Guarijío country is spectacular thanks to this cantankerous past. Differential erosion of the young volcanic rock plus extensive block faulting of the mid-Tertiary or Basin and Range stretching and the intrusion of dikes into older rock resulted in an often spectacular variety of rock outcroppings, cliffs, and gorges. Calderas usually left sheer walls with globs of older rock embedded here and there as they were blasted into the air. Soft tuffs are usually overlain or underlain with more durable rhyolites, or occasionally basalts. In a few places the colorful tuffs have succumbed to differential erosion. The result is caves of a scooped-out appearance ranging from pea-sized pock marks to grottos a hundred meters wide, ten meters tall, and twenty meters deep. In places water seeps through at contact zones. The amount of water may be rather small, but the seeps are usually surrounded by pockets of dense green vegetation that stand out in the mojino of May and June as clearly as oases in the sand. The caves also provided more or less permanent shelter for many generations of Guarijíos.

The lower foothills (that are often steeper than the higher mountains!) may be covered with dense tropical deciduous forest vegetation, but the soils of the steep slopes that predominate in the lowlands retain water poorly. These hills are checkerboarded with outcroppings of cracked and broken volcanic rock through which rainwater vanishes. Consequently springs and seeps are uncommon. Few perennial streams issue from the porous volcanics. When they do, it is usually in profound canyons where the water cannot be diverted to irrigate fields. In the lowlands, rain is insufficient to assure a good crop, and water is unavailable for irrigation. It seems never to be where it is needed most.

The soils that result from this once-seething den of brimstone are for the most part young and, though fertile, are for the most part poorly formed. There is a marked difference in the soils of the highlands (soils tend to be acidic) and those of the lowlands (soils tend to be alkaline as a result of low rainfall and resultant caliche formation). On the slopes soil horizons are only marginally defined. While hydrothermally altered soils are well known in the Mayo region (Martin et al. 1998), these are scarce in the Guarijío portion of the region. Outcroppings of indurated ash with corresponding white soils are more common. These are acidic and of low fertility. When they can be planted at all, the nutrients they hold are quickly exhausted. The broad hillside behind the settlement of Todos Santos on the Arroyo Guajaray contains such soils. The slopes have a history of mahuechis but have not recovered and are overgrown with hectare after hectare of nearly pure stands of *Dodonaea viscosa,* a coarse shrub that flourishes on soils of indurated ash.

The swidden agriculture practiced by the Guarijíos del río consists of clearing followed by two or three years of cultivation and seven to ten years (or more) of fallow. Corn production after the second or third year drops as the growing corn depletes the soil and renders additional planting not worth the effort. This shifting cultivation forces the Guarijíos to shift their homes as well (a practice the government now discourages for logistical reasons). The poverty of the soil and the steepness of the mahuechis, however, leave the farmers with little choice. Still, the Guarijíos seem to look forward to the hard work of clearing the ground for a new mahuechi. It is as though they are still chuckling about having their own land to clear and rejoicing in the luxury of it all.

Highland fields remain in more or less permanent production. They undulate on gentler slopes amenable to the plow, which is unknown to the Guarijíos del río. Teams of oxen and mules still ply the soil in the highland valleys. At Loreto, most Guarijíos have hillside mahuechis and valley plots as well. The substrate there supports deeper, better-formed soils that can be fertilized when necessary. On the other hand they are not immune from the vagaries of nature, for the crops are subject to freezing and drought.

8
Jacqchí

UP THE RIVER

By now I had been visiting Guarijío lands for nearly three years. I was familiar with most of the villages and caminos, but not with the upper Río Mayo itself. It was time for me to go up the river where I had never ventured. It was time to see the deep canyons and gorges I had heard about before I became too old to do it. It was time to pack my way north from Mesa Colorada, upstream from Huataturi, up where the river is swifter and the buffelgrass is less common, where the Guarijíos have had less opportunity to take on the trappings of mestizo culture, up to where no village has more than three or four homes in a row and the people switch residences depending on hillsides available for mahuechis.

Jacqchí is what the Guarijíos call what *we* call the Río Mayo. Translated, it means simply "river," which is not surprising, since there is only one true river in the region. Guarijíos have long adjusted to hearing the river referred to as the river of their neighbors, the Mayos, but for the Guarijíos, it is still the Jacqchí. Every Guarijío del río old enough to walk has seen it, waded in it, crossed it, and drunk its waters. Jacqchí is the focal point of the Guarijío lands.

Outside of the Amazon basin, the frozen north, and some spots in the Andes, few truly wild places remain in our hemisphere. Although the upper Mayo region is dotted with ranches and Guarijío settlements, it is as wild and unexplored by outsiders as any area in subarctic North America. To get to anywhere at all, one must walk, walk far, walk up and down mountains, wade across rivers and streams, get one's feet wet, get tired, hot, and dusty, pass long periods on the trail without seeing another soul. That in itself is good for the soul.

I love the wildness of Guarijío country. I covet the feeling of solitude in a wild setting. I crave the sight of virgin forests. Still, I find the Guarijío presence in the monte more than a comfort. It is an affirmation of the human spirit. Maybe it's because I know how lightly the Guarijíos tread on the land, at least up to now. If I were to see a modern suburban house set deep in the canyons, I would be resentful. Seeing a roof of palm and a tiny terrace bounded

by a trinchera seems utterly natural, even an improvement on nature.

Guarijío lands are not wilderness in the sense in which most North Americans construe it. There is nowhere in the region where human presence is officially and merely temporary (a defining characteristic of designated wilderness in the United States). Guarijíos (and Mexicans in general) view land as a resource to support them. The idea of a land of human impermanence seems obtuse or even unintelligible. Lands may be pristine, but human presence is everywhere. Where springs issue from the earth, human signs are never far away, whether a hut, a ramada, or a livestock corral. The springs are maintained scrupulously, though they be far from any permanent dwelling.

Yet because the Guarijío way of life requires movable mahuechis, disdains the joining of clans into towns, and cherishes concealment from outsiders, the land has a wildness and naturalness to it that gives it a more primordial feel than many trampled official wildernesses in the United States. Guarijíos tread lightly on the land in more ways than one. And wildness means more than the mere absence of men and women.

Caramechi had a certain aura of mystery that made it a primordial goal for me, like Machu Picchu was until I made it there, and as Chínipas, Chihuahua continues to be. I know Caramechi to be a nearly inaccessible river settlement, surrounded by steep, high, heavily forested mountains. The canyon bottom widens enough there to permit a little agriculture. In 1942 Gentry wrote that a few Guarijío families lived there in the 1930s.

> Caramechi. Indian locality of four or five families, with a Mexican family in residence during the winter, tending a herd of milk cows. It is bordered on the west by the high ramparts of the Sierra de la Ventana, from which three short tributaries discharge into the Mayo at Caramechi. (Gentry 1942:21)

Someone had told me that a few Guarijíos still lived there. I pored over the map and judged that it would be a walk of twenty-five miles each way. Two burros. Two days. Each way. Good distance. Up steep mountains and across valleys and streams. Great country for new plants.

I had to make arrangements in advance or risk losing a day or two trying to round up a guide and pack animals. How was I going to work everything out from Tucson? Leobardo Quiroz was dead and I was still grieving his death.

He was my principal mestizo contact in San Bernardo, where he served as director of the INI that provided assistance to the Guarijíos. Leobardo was a dentist from Huatabampo in the Río Mayo delta. As repayment for his dentistry schooling, he had been required by the government to spend a year in a rural community. He chose San Bernardo. He grew to love the town and elected to remain there when he had completed his year of service. He married a local woman and began a family. He expanded the small house in which he lived, gradually making it into one of the nicest dwellings in San Bernardo. He came to know everyone in the town, even the Guarijíos who live on the mesa on the other side of the arroyo in the barrio called Los Jacales. He became so taken with the Guarijíos that he began to work with them. At some point he was hired by INI, who recognized a natural liaison when they saw one.

Over the nine years he lived in San Bernardo, Leobardo came to know almost all the Guarijíos del río and many Guarijíos de la sierra as well. He developed the boarding schools for Guarijío children, arranged for food shipments, helped provide provisions for tuburadas, maintained a place in San Bernardo where Guarijíos could obtain meals and could sleep, saw to it that they had some medical attention, and helped them with the Mexican justice system. In short, he knew more about the Guarijíos than any other non-Guarijío except maybe Juan Enríquez, the curandero from Burapaco.

Leobardo was no more than thirty-five, a short, cheerful fellow with a perpetual five o'clock shadow and piercing, friendly eyes. His countenance gave off wisdom and a humility that inspired confidence. I contacted him whenever I made a trip into the Sierra near San Bernardo. He helped me obtain guides and told me where it was safe to go and not safe to go. His father-in-law, whose acquaintance I also made, owned a small ranch in Gochico, fifteen kilometers up the Arroyo Gochico from where it empties into the Arroyo Taymuco at San Bernardo. Leobardo helped truck in supplies to Guajaray and to Loreto, sixty-five miles and fourteen hours distant in Chihuahua, gradually gaining the acquaintances of all the ranches and ranchers along the way. Through his relatives and myriad contacts, he learned where dope was being grown and harvested and where the military was carrying out search-and-destroy-and-grab-a-little-for-yourself operations. He knew who in San Bernardo was reliable and who wasn't, knew their family problems and their strengths and weaknesses. He had few axes to grind. People sought him out for advice—dental, medical, and personal. If San Bernardo had one leading citizen, it was Leobardo.

No one will ever know why on a stormy day in September 1996 Leobardo chose to cross the swollen streambed of Arroyo Techobampo on the Alamos road in his pickup truck. He had just crossed it a few minutes earlier, people say, but found that the next arroyo was running so high that he couldn't get across, so he turned back and tried to recross the first. In the few moments since his first crossing the waters had risen and were still rising. In mid-crossing the flood lifted up the pickup like a bath toy and swept it over the concrete spillway that served as a roadway, and the torrent carried the truck down the swollen arroyo bobbing as though it were a cork. Leobardo's wife managed to pull herself out through a window, but his young son and a young schoolteacher also in the pickup's cab never got out. Their bodies were found a short time later. Leobardo's body was never found. Two hundred people, including a contingent of stunned Guarijíos, formed a search party, the greatest manhunt the region had ever witnessed. Nothing. Not a trace. Leobardo met a watery grave somewhere in the muds of Lake Mocúzari.

So now Leobardo was not there to help. I wrote letters to other folks but without much hope of making contact. I was resigned to driving to Mesa Colorada and simply asking around for a guide and burros, knowing full well I would lose a day or two in a frustrating search. I hoped for better results than on the previous trip. Quite frankly, I did not want Miguel the Mumbler for a guide a second time.

The phone rang one night, a few days before I was to leave Tucson. It was a Chicano friend. "David," he said. "I'm calling from the Tucson Community Center. There are some Guarijíos here who wish to talk to you." Good heavens! Never before had such a group of Guarijíos been put up in high fashion in the United States! Cipriano's voice came on the line.

"*Bueno,*" (Hello) he said. I answered.

"*Bueno,*" he said once again. I replied in Spanish. "Hello, Cipriano, how are you and how long will you be here?

"*Si.*" He said. "*Bueno*" (Good).

I repeated a question. Would he dance a pascola?

"*Si,*" he replied. "*Bueno.*"

Click. Dead phone.

I began to laugh. My friend had handed the phone to Cipriano, who had no idea how to use the thing. He hadn't developed phone manners because he wasn't familiar with phones. He probably hadn't heard a sound I had made. I've lived with phones all my life, as has just about everyone I know. Yet I'm intimidated by phones in foreign lands. Now, suppose I had not seen one before and suppose I had no real idea about their use. What would I have done?

The next day I found Cipriano and six other Guarijíos at a meeting of southwestern Indians in Tucson. After exchanging formalities, pleasantries, and introductions, I explained to them that I wanted to hike to Caramechi. Could one of them guide me? One of their number, a diminutive pascola dancer named Manuel Rodríguez, said he could guide me. He was going to Gocojaqui, far up the Mayo. It was only an hour and a half walk to Caramechi from there. Of course he would guide me. Yes, he could arrange for burros and maybe even a mule. Of course. He would wait for me in Mesa Colorada. He would not set out for Gocojaqui until Friday. I would be with him. We shook hands. I was most enthusiastic.

But in the meantime the Guarijíos were overwhelmed with the sights and sounds and pleasures of the big American city and the lavishly furnished hotel room. Manuel explained in a voice of incredulity that the room had faucets with hot water as well, he explained. In wonderment, he showed me his room key—an entry card. Someone had thoughtfully written the room number on a marking tape so that if he could not find the number someone could help him. As is the case with most adult Guarijío men, Manuel did not read, and so he might have a hard time telling someone his room number. He showed me how he used the card. Just slip it into a slot in the door and ¡Zas! The door would open! Imagine! Hot water coming out of a faucet into a sink! A shower! A miraculous toilet. Push a button and whoosh! All clean. All working perfectly. Huge beds with sheets and pillows. Little bottles of shampoo and cute little bars of soap. A television you worked from your hand with a tiny machine. An elevator that made your stomach drop when it went up and fly up when you went down!

I wanted to phone the Guarijíos later but gave up on that idea. Of their number only Cipriano had ever before slept in a hotel, and his experience was in flea-bitten cheap Mexican hotels, not the Holiday Inn in Tucson. They had no interest in going elsewhere. They virtually had to be lured from their rooms to see the sights of the American city. Those Guarijíos were living it up in Tucson. It was probably the one junket in their lifetime. It would be a shame for me to spoil it by talking about Guarijío country to them.

Cornelia Ruelas weaving, Mesa Colorada.

Manuel was in Mesa Colorada when I arrived four days later with Tucson botanist Richard Felger. It was late in the afternoon, hardly time remaining to pitch camp for the night. I searched for Manuel for a while in the village, inquiring from hut to hut. Finally, someone directed me to a ramada where I found him sitting with two friends, all uncontrollably drunk. They were celebrating Manuel's return. As he took another pull of clear liquid from a soda pop bottle, I greeted him, reminded him as gently as I could that he was going to guide me on the morrow to Gocojaqui with two burros and a mule.

"Si. Gocojaqui. Dos burros." He repeated with great effort. "I don't have a burro. I don't have a mule."

Dealing with someone who is drunk is not something I recommend, but in rural Mexico, where nearly all men drink and where getting drunk is perfectly respectable, I couldn't avoid it. I tried to carry on a conversation. It was pointless. Manuel was going to drink more. My companion Richard looked on despairingly. "We're not going to get out of here tomorrow, David," he lamented. I told him not to give up hope.

In a tiny adobe house nearby lived Manuel's sister, Cornelia. She was a cheerful Guarijío woman, married to Ramón Rodríguez (no relation, even though Guarijíos accept marriage to a first cousin), a knowledgeable fellow who had nearly guided me once before but, to my dismay, was unable to. I wanted to talk with Ramón and get his counsel, but Cornelia sadly informed me that he, too, was drunk, or, as she said diplomatically, *"está malo"* (he is sick). He was currently sleeping it off, she said, smiling.

I learned much later that Cornelia is a curandera, apparently the only such healer generally recognized in the region. While *curanderismo* is a Spanish institution, Cornelia seemed to incorporate enough Guarijío elements into her practice that she was called on to administer to Guarijío and non-Guarijío alike. Here is how I found out about her healing power.

One day I sat in the front room of the adobe-walled, mud-roofed house in Mesa Colorada that Ramón and Cornelia had recently built. We chatted over a range of subjects, and they responded rather warmly, I thought, to my endless, often repetitive questioning. Their twelve-year old daughter Berta played with her pet choluga (coatimundi, *Nasua narica*). I noticed after a couple of hours that a young woman was sitting outside holding a swaddled infant. Cornelia had just left, so I asked Ramón if this was another of their children. No, he explained. This was a young woman (she could not have been more than eighteen years old) who had walked up from Mochibampo, a good four kilometers distant, to have Cornelia heal her baby.

I was quite surprised. "Is Cornelia a *curandera?*" I asked.

"Yes," he answered matter-of-factly. "She cures many people here and all around here."

"The baby is suffering from *susto*. Cornelia will heal it with a massage." Susto is a folk diagnosis of an ailment that usually involves an emotional shock followed by fever and, in this case, intense bloating.

Just then Cornelia returned. "May I watch you while you cure the baby," I asked.

"Well, yes." She answered, rather surprised.

I turned to Ramón. "Do you think it would be all right if I were to photograph the healing?"

Ramón hesitated. "Well, perhaps . . ." His voice trailed off. He meant to say "no" but couldn't figure how to do it. Very well, no cameras.

Cornelia brought a small bench from the house and sat down beside the youthful mother who remained on the ground holding her sick infant. The child was clearly ill, listless and dull-eyed. Beside her on the bench Cornelia had placed a jar of ointment similar to Vicks Vapo-Rub and a ceramic teacup with a liquid in it. With supreme confidence and equal gentleness, she lifted the baby from the mother and cradled it in her arms. She poured two spoonfuls of liquid into the baby's mouth. The infant made no objection. "This is chamomile tea with herbs in it," she explained. She then rubbed her free hand with the pomade and uncovered the baby. With practiced hands she massaged the baby's stomach, then its face and forehead. She then applied a technique I had never seen before. She inserted her index finger into the infant's mouth and exerted pressure on the roof of the mouth for about ten seconds. Then she removed her finger. She proceeded to massage the baby's back and bottom, and finally, the back of her head. Then she confidently wrapped the blanket around the child once again and returned it to its mother. The whole treatment had taken no more than three minutes. The child was unmistakably improved. It was more alert, happy, and energetic. The mother smiled weakly, sensing, I thought, the improvement in the baby.

"She brought the child in yesterday," Cornelia explained. "Her little belly was terribly swollen from gas and she had a high fever. I will treat her again tomorrow and the day after. Then she will be fine." The mother walked away in the direction of her home downriver.

I asked her where she had learned to cure. "Well, my mother cured people, but she died when I was very young, so I had to learn it myself. When I moved here to Mesa Colorada, there were no children. All the children died as babies. Now there are children everywhere. I travel to Bavícora, to Guajaray, even to San Bernardino. People ask me everywhere to come to their homes. I do. It is what a *curandera* must do."

Did they pay her? "No, they sometimes give me a little money, but most people don't have any money. They will give me some tortillas or some beans. Sometimes they even give me a *chiva* (goat), but I don't charge anything."

All this I learned much later, but it perhaps explains why I had such confidence in her that day when I needed someone to round up burros for us.

I explained the situation to her. No, she said, her brother Manuel had no burro. But her husband Ramón did, and a neighbor, Lalo, a violinist who had also gone to Tucson, had one as well that he would be happy to loan to us. She would take Manuel in hand and see that we had our burros. I gave her a bag of groceries in return for her help and the

Confluence of Río Mayo and Arroyo Guajaray, near Mesa Colorada.

promise of a breakfast of beans and tortillas in the morning.

Once again Richard was skeptical. There was no way we would have our burros. Manuel could not possibly function the next morning with the amount of alcohol he was putting away, he fretted.

We camped on a gravel bank next to the Río Mayo with the huts of the mesa looking down over us, the dogs barking all night and the roosters crowing a sardonic cheer. The November night was chilly, but not cold. The few mosquitoes lost interest in the crisp air. It was perfect Río Mayo weather.

At dawn we were up and packing. As the sun came up we drove to Cornelia's house. Outside, two tethered burros waited with burronian patience, fustes in place. A perfectly sober and friendly, if subdued Manuel sat waiting for us. Cornelia served us breakfast of tortillas and beans. We piled our trappings into a great mound and Manuel lashed them to the patient burros, cinched Richard's bulky and thick plant press on top, and we were off. Up the Jacqchí.

The Río Mayo originates in high mountains of southwest Chihuahua. One of its tributaries flows over Mexico's highest waterfall, the 832 foot high Cascada de Basaseáchic. In the rainy season the falls are a dreamy paradise of misted brown rock and emerald-green vegetation. In the spring drought the flow is so sparse it usually evaporates before reaching the bottom.

Below the falls the Mayo (at that point the Río Candameña) flows through deep canyons, forging its way south until it meets the Río Moris flowing from the east. The two then form the Río Mayo, some fifty kilometers northeast of the Sonora-Chihuahua state line. By that time the river has a sizeable flow and even in the dry season it can scarcely be forded without getting thoroughly wet. At times the river flows for miles between cliffs many hundreds of meters high, so deep that sunlight reaches the river for only a few hours each day. The portion we traversed consists of steep mountains and cliffs at each side. The river flows over modest rapids, formed by side canyons that deposit their rocky debris in the river. The rapids are followed by quiet stretches with clear, deep pools as much as thirty feet in depth.

Until the river reaches San Bernardo south of the Guarijíos' lands, there is little bottomland suitable for agriculture. Consequently, settlements along the upper Río Mayo have been limited to a few families.

The Mayo was first dammed in 1951 when Mocúzari Dam (technically called Presa Adolfo Ruíz Cortines after the Mexican president) was completed. With the immense reserve of water provided by the impoundment, the lower Río Mayo was opened up for agricultural development. Today nearly 220,000 acres of delta flatlands are irrigated with Río Mayo waters.

Dam builders are seldom pacified by the construction of just one dam. They and their constituent lobbies—irrigators, power companies, contractors, and construction material suppliers, as well as developers, marina suppliers, and promoters of tourism—find profit and fulfillment in the construction of new dams. They are ever vigilant, scanning land and river valleys on foot, from the air, and from satellite images for new sites for dams. No river in the world is safe from their probes, which are more sophisticated and intrusive each day. They view flowing water as an untapped, wasted resource, one that will increase their power, their influence, and their personal fortunes, and hence they carry on their ceaseless campaign to bring nature into their clutches. A friend of mine refers to them as the Dam Mafia.

In 1995 they found a likely dam site, or at least they began to promote a site which they had long hoped to dam. It is near San Bernardo on the Río Mayo. When built, it will back the river up for a good thirty miles. In the process of filling, it will inundate the Mayo village of Chorijoa and the Guarijío villages of Mochibampo and Mesa Colorada. It will bury under many meters of water the fertile little delta of the Arroyo Guajaray and the few Guarijío homes that have been built there. It will smother a series of splendid groves of *sabinos (Taxodium distichum)* that grace the lower Guajaray, and force relocation of the many Guarijío trails that have crisscrossed the region for centuries. It will create a permanent, elongated barrier to the crossing of the river, forcing the Guarijíos to make long detours to follow their accustomed routes. Finally, it will cause immense amounts of precious water to be lost by evaporation as the reservoir slowly fills up with silt. But for a half dozen decades or so it will bring power and profits to a few.

The displacement of native peoples is of little moment to the Dam Mafia. The construction of Huites Dam at the Río Fuerte in Sinaloa, finished in 1995, displaced two Mayo towns and an undetermined number of fields and small ranches. The inhabitants there were pacified with promises of government largesse and mitigation that never materialized. Dam builders' promises and those of whores are of similar reliability. To this day the silvery promises remain unfulfilled.

Manuel had little to say about the proposed dam. He was all business, issuing orders to the devious-looking burros as we plodded north. His commands were three: A low "Hooooe" which meant something like "That's all right now, my little friend," said with a trace of affection used to reassure. A loud "Hoachs" translated roughly as "move it, get going, move your shaggy ass," or thereabouts and was repeated every thirty seconds or so. A third command was an almost untranslatable "Hrul," shouted in anger when a burro left the path or wandered off in an undesirable direction. At times he simply belted out *"¡Burró!"* (Guarijíos tend to switch accents on words borrowed from other languages to the final syllable). When one of the burros with apparent deliberation set off away from the path Manuel exploded into Spanish profanity uttered with a strong Guarijío accent. He relied entirely on his voice to control the burros, spurning any switch or whip (except on very steep slopes where the burros' intransigence would sometimes halt progress altogether).

As I have noticed before, Guarijíos don't provide their burros with names. I do. So I baptized the burros as Alfonso and Germán, much to Manuel's delight. He adopted the silly

nomenclature and for the remainder of the trip remembered from time to time to address the animals with my names and refer to them as such, always with a hearty laugh. He treated the burros with great consideration and restraint, making sure they had ample opportunity to drink at the river crossings and were enclosed at night with food at hand to sustain them. His was a prudent policy. One should treat with consideration the ass that bears one.

The Río Mayo in its lower stretches, like the Guajaray, is a young river, probably no more than 5.5 million years of age, and the boulders in its channel have had insufficient time to flatten and break down.[1] They are large and smooth, covered by moss, which makes them a slippery as if they had been coated with oil. The two crossings before Huataturi slowed us down, as Richard and I removed our boots and donned sandals to wade through treacherous footing. Manuel was the epitome of patience, never urging us to pick up the pace even though he knew we couldn't possibly reach Gocojaqui that day at the rate we were traveling. Before we reached Huataturi we followed a trail inland up a steep hill, then climbed a gradual ascent for the next three miles. We saw Huataturi far below us, got a decent view of fields of corn and buffelgrass along the river's edge. The ridgeline behind us, we walked for another mile on a northern exposure, passing through the finest stand of tropical deciduous forest I have ever seen. Richard and I were close to spellbound by the size of the trees, their health, their variety, and their abundance. Trees such as amapa, copalquín, nesco, and torote copal grew here far larger than any we had seen before. It was the forest that Gentry knew sixty years earlier before machines and commerce made the forest a marketable commodity, before the urge to abolish forests in favor of grasslands for cows became fashionable, and before too many people tried to harvest posts, vigas, beams, and firewood from the forests. Here, hours by foot from the nearest vehicle, those pressures were still mostly absent and the still, damp forest showed little sign of human intervention.

Autumn in the dry tropical forest is a time of silence and transition toward dormancy, as if nature were thinking about things while shifting position every once in a while. Even the birds that linger after the fall migrations hush their singing and calling. Only the fleeting mournful sound of ground doves breaks the stillness. Dead leaves filter from trees to the ground, their fall hardly disturbed by a breeze. The wind had been blowing in the morning, but here in the cathedral-like stillness of the north slope nothing moved.

Only the clop of the burros' feet, the frequent urgings as Manuel cajoled the burros, and the pounding of our boots penetrated the hush. Frequently we plodded through a passage of fragrance, an incense that overpowered the burroy smell of the beasts of burden. I knew it at once as the brisk, aromatic cathedral incense of torote copal *(Bursera penicillata),* a large, spreading tree that frequents the dry tropical forests of Mexico. I mentioned the sweet smell to Manuel who was devoting his attention to the burros. He brightened. "Ah, yes, it is *topocá.* You can smell it before you ever see it. How sweet is the smell!" He hurried off to a tree and stripped a few leaves from the nearly leafless branches. Crushing them, he held them up for us to smell. "And it is good, very good, for sore throat as well." I scribbled in my notebook as Manuel rushed off to open a gate and keep the burros from heading in the wrong direction.

Our trail continued upward at a slow but tiring grade. At times it followed a wide cleared patch of curious history, passed through a breached trinchera, then abruptly disappeared into deep forest. Every half hour or so we halted to rest. The burros always stood quietly. The silence was nearly total. From far off we heard occasional human voices. "Cowboys," responded Manuel to my raised eyebrows. They were chasing maverick cows. A dove mourned. An occasional hawk shrieked to a mate circling far above. Then the silence returned. The light was golden, softening the harsh volcanic ridges and the half-leafless branches of a few dozen different kinds of trees.

The idyll came to an abrupt end. We emerged from the shaded, silent forest into brilliant sunlight on a ridge where we had an unobstructed view of the Río Mayo a thousand feet below. There was no obstruction because the forest had been felled and cleared and the hills, steep, rocky slopes, were covered with buffelgrass. A thousand, two thousand acres of stark yellow grass with only an occasional intrusion of green where a few trees had been spared or cows could not penetrate. I heard the rush of a small rapid at a bend in the river a half mile away. No trees intercepted the sound. Manuel took the opportunity to adjust the burros' loads for the steep descent. "The grass produces more cattle," he said. "I helped to clear the land. The owner, a yori, paid me. There's his house, down below." Far below, a mile away, next to the river were the roofs of a few dwellings. I resented the powerful sun and felt a deep sadness at the loss of the forests, the sacrifice of trees before the golden calf.

The descent was slow and difficult. Unlike the great trees whose leaves intercept raindrops of the heavy summer rains and soften their impact on the soil, the grass provides little protection. The pelting thunderstorms wash away the unprotected earth. The soil is poorer now on the hillsides and the treacherous rocks more exposed at the surface, though hidden by the tufts of grass which grows deeply on the soil made fertile by the recently felled forest. We staggered down the switchbacks through waist-high grass, struggling to keep from slipping on unseen rocks, arriving after a half hour, laden with sweat, thirsty, and hobbling from sore knees at the cool river's edge. Buffelgrass is not a friend to the hiker.

The rancher at Chinatopo, which was the ranch's name, was racing to clear all the forest as soon as he could. Pity. What kind of wanton management could lead him to do that? He stood on his front porch staring, others in his family standing at his side as we walked by on the trail below. I waved, trying to be friendly, all the while harboring dark thoughts about the buffelgrass I had just fought my way through. They waved back, perplexed at the strange looking fellows walking by. I had to look again and again at the ranch house. Though modest and unpretentious, it was well maintained and immaculate. I coveted the place.

The Río Mayo north of Chinatopo appears to dissect a rifted valley northward to where it turns eastward into the deep canyons of Chihuahua. There are bends in the river as it circles impeding hills, but mostly it flows straight down a canyon with sides many hundreds of feet high. At times the gorge is so narrow that in deep flood (as happened in the late 1940s, again in the 1970s, and in 1995) the entire canyon bottom is in flood and for miles there are no beaches. The Guarijíos have alternate trails for just these rare events, but they take far longer and lack the convenient watering holes for the beasts of burden.

There is something magical about these long stretches of canyon, for the forest is moist and deep and the canyon trails are often steep and narrow. Forest covers all but the sheerest cliffs. At one point we met a pack train going the opposite direction, which presented an impasse. The trail that clung to the west cliff above the river was too steep and narrow for us to pass, and there was nowhere to step off the trail and allow the others to pass by us. We solved the problem by retreating, perhaps twenty yards back down the trail and chasing our burros straight up the hill, sliding and causing miniature landslides all the while. The beasts resisted, finding the steep, cramped slope not at all to their liking, but responding to Manuel's imprecations they reluctantly pulled themselves upslope while we held on to trees and let the others pass. It was a rancher and his family from far up

Riding through buffelgrass above Río Mayo near Chinatopo.

the river at San José de Pinal, a good six hours horseback ride to the north, he said. He was riding a horse and leading two others at the front of a train of burros carrying provisions. Behind the convoy walked a little boy and a little girl neither more than six years old, both dressed in clean new clothes. They stared at Richard and me as they walked by, but their politeness made them refrain from asking rude questions. I spoke to them and they answered with respectful politeness staring all the while at my alien features. Once this narrow stretch was done, they would be back on horseback following their daddy northward along the maze of caminos of the Río Mayo.

We waded across the river, recrossed, then crossed and recrossed again, scampered up the nearly vertical wall, clinging to the cliff face. The river flowed deep a hundred, two hundred feet below us. Manuel and the burros patiently remained in the bottom, unable to negotiate the slippery slopes. We stuck to the narrow, rocky trail while they crossed at the rapids, wading across in water nearly to their bellies.

Dusk approached. Wondering about river crossings and rocky slopes after dark, I asked Manuel how far to Gocojaqui.

Oh, three hours or so. He wasn't going to Gocojaqui, he mentioned casually.

I started. "You're not going to Gocojaqui?" I asked, perplexed.

"No, I live at Jogüegüe. That's where I'm going. To my house. Gocojaqui is another hour and a half."

"And Caramechi?"

"Oh, Caramechi! Well, no one lives there anymore. They all moved away."

I was instantly disappointed, but not surprised. Guarijíos are mobile because there is almost nowhere in their lands where they can plant permanently. The young volcanic soils wear out rapidly and must lie fallow for several years— seven to ten—before they regain their fertility. Gentry noted in the 1930s the same phenomenon:

> The Warihío are still given to short local migrations, as was evidenced by groups in the great stony land of the Arroyo Guajaray. Families visited in 1934 at Conejos [Los Bajíos] and another group at Ranchería in 1933 were reported to have left those localities

(the Conejos fishing group going over to the Río Mayo) 3 or 4 years later. The exact reasons for their movements were not ascertained, but it might well have been because of depleted wild food supplies. (Gentry 1963:74)

I swallowed my disappointment. "Ah." I answered, "So we're not going to Gocojaqui or Caramechi?"

"Well, we can, if you wish. We can go there tomorrow or the next day. Tonight we must camp at Charajaqui. It will be too dark to go farther. My wife was born there. There it is, just past that white spot." He pointed far up the darkening gorge to a white sand bar at the river's edge. Between it and us the river passed through a narrow box canyon. We were forced steeply upward following switchbacks.

Manuel had decided and I had no desire to argue. Richard and I were tired and willing to stop anywhere. But Manuel had no blanket. He hadn't counted on two gringos dawdling along the trail. But he had decided we would stay at Charajaqui. I found the place on the topographical map.

"Where will you stay? Do you have relatives there?" I questioned him.

"No," he answered pleasantly. "No one lives there, either. The people who lived there moved away. I'll stay in one of the old houses."

"Won't you get cold?"

He shrugged indifferently.

It took us two more crossings and nearly another hour to reach the bend in the river and the sandbar that was marked as Charajaqui on the map. Richard and I calculated. We had an extra tent and a couple of extra tarps, plus a jacket or two he could use for covers. I explained to Manuel. He seemed delighted.

We pitched camp on a high sandbank at a bend in the river, an idyllic site in the shade of a guamúchil with the river gurgling below, the sheer face of a mountain directly across the Mayo from us and dense forest away from the river. I set up the tent for Manuel and showed him how to work the zipper. He watched intently, unfamiliar with the device. I laid out the tarps and the jackets. He nodded while closing the tent, moving the zipper back and forth.

We ate supper and talked for a while. Manuel waited politely in the background, as though he assumed he didn't belong in our immediate company. I called questions to him. He approached our cooking area, answered, then retreated to his space. We were too tired to carry on for long, and

Berta Rodríguez with her pet *choluga,* Mesa Colorada.

shortly we took to our tents. I waited to make sure he was securely in the tent. The sand was soft, so he wouldn't be uncomfortable. I called through the door to him. He assured me he was fine. Indeed, he was quite taken by the tent and the luxurious protection it provided. I slipped into my own tent and turned off my brain.

We were up well before dawn. Manuel was more energetic than he had been on the previous morning. He owned that he had slept warm and well inside the tent. He liked being in the little house, he said. He went off to round up the burros while Richard and I cooked the breakfast and packed. We shared our gringo food with Manuel who was ever willing to experience international cuisine. He reminded me that he had eaten (undifferentiated) American food in Tucson and had liked it. I walked down to the river and hunkered down to pump and purify Mayo river water when I heard different voices. A couple of young mestizos were conversing with Manuel. Soon they were joined by more, then more yet. A total of ten men in their late teens and early twenties, one on a horse, the rest on foot, passed and presently crossed the river.

In 1993 while I was camping in a remote mountain area with some friends, we were assaulted by two bandits brandishing pistols, who tied up and robbed us. A woman with our group was raped by one of the bandits. Since that time I have been a trifle apprehensive about strangers who appear unannounced in strange lands. Manuel seemed unconcerned, however, which was reassuring to me. I spoke with one of the lads. They were from a "farm" to the north in Chihuahua, working in a place called San Miguel. I always prided myself on my familiarity with Río Mayo geography,

Rock corral made by Guarijíos at Jogüegüe.

but I had never heard of it. They had decided to take a few days off and hike to Navojoa, Sonora, the nearest city, a good sixty miles to the south. They had already been on the trail for a day and a half and had a couple of days still to hike. They had no food, only little hand tote bags with jackets. One of their number carried a juvenile cholugo (a raccoon-like mammal with a long, erect tail and a tapered nose like an anteater) that moved from inside his jacket to his shoulder and stuck out its long, tapered snout. The animal lessened my anxiety. Thieves don't carry pet coatimundis on raids.

After the young men had all crossed the river, one waded back and asked me if I would sell him our tortillas. I pointed to Manuel saying they were his. Manuel was pleased to sell them at a greatly inflated price. The fellows gobbled down the kilo or so of tortillas and vanished down the trail that led to the fast lights, booze, and women of Navojoa. They were surely agricultural workers of the sierra, employed at raising dope. We packed up and left the campsite immediately, plodding up the steep trail toward Manuel's home.

Jogüegüe startled me when we looked down on it from high on the trail. The apparently large house was covered with galvanized metal roofing. It was decidedly mestizo, not Guarijío construction. It had been built thirty or so years ago, Manual explained. He liked it. From the time we fist caught a glimpse of the place it took us a half hour to reach the house. Arriving at the homestead, we passed by a huge, perfectly laid stone wall corral shaded by some acacias and guamúchiles. The house sat on a small knoll some two hundred yards above us. We walked up to near the porch and Manual unloaded the burros. No one came out to see him.

Manuel had told me he had seven children, ranging from infancy to eighteen years of age. His wife had been born at Charajaqui, where we had camped the previous night. Where were they all? I saw a face peer from behind a corner of the open door of the house, then another. When I looked again the faces vanished. I pretended to be busy unloading our trappings. Manuel appeared unexcited, but I knew better because he was returning from a trip to Tucson and had been farther from home than any Guarijío for many miles around. No one from this part of the world had ever been to the United States before, not even illegally. He was returning from a luxury trip where he had been wined and dined courtesy of receipts of U.S. Indian casinos. He had to be brimming with news and his family had to be overwhelmed with curiosity. Their international jet-setting father was home with tales from the unimaginably rich, fabled colossus of the north.

Presently a young woman appeared at the doorway holding an infant in her arms. Gradually other children materialized from the house, a whole line of them. The retinue filtered out, waiting wordlessly to see their cosmopolitan father. The girls were wearing cotton dresses, the boys ragtag T-shirts and battered pants. All except the oldest boy went barefoot. Manuel busied himself with loading our packs onto the porch out of the sunlight and securing the burros. Then he disappeared inside the house. We heard only low voices, but they were happy ones. The family had to assume that he had brought back a couple of gringos from the United States with him. Odd, they must have thought, no one had explained that part of the trip meant bringing some of the natives back with him.

Let me review briefly from chapter 3 the history of the creation of the Guarijío ejidos. It happened only because mestizo ranchers were squatting on Mexican national lands without bothering to claim them, which they could have done with little difficulty before Ted Faubert and Teresa Valdivia began raising hell in the 1970s. When the Guarijíos, with the help of some savvy mestizos (including Teresa) made application for the lands, the ranchers banded together and fought the formation tooth and nail. But they lost. Lands occupied by the ranchers without documented ownership reverted to Guarijíos, who moved in with gusto. In some cases the mestizo ranchers stayed on in the region, living on diminished estates, and have made their peace with the Guarijíos. Others emigrated, not wishing to endure the presence of the Indians on what they had regarded as their private lands. At least one rancher died shortly after the expropriation.

The house and land at Jogüegüe were expropriated during the creation of the ejido Mesa Colorada. Manuel was living in Bavícora at the time and was a virtual peon of the landowner named Sainz. He admits he could hardly believe his good fortune when the house was awarded to him, the house of the very man who had exploited him as a peon.

And so the house and some attachments, including a massive wooden cheese trough, was turned over to Manuel Rodríguez and Margarita Anamea, his wife. While the structure is not of Guarijío design, lacking the neat, sloped palm roof, it is well laid out, large, and clearly to their liking. Too hot in the summer, chilly in the winter, nevertheless it is solidly built. The porch faces west, exposing it to the searing afternoon sun. No Guarijío would ever have endured this design, but Manuel nailed a few stray pieces of galvanized roofing on the outside of one end of the porch to shade them in the afternoon and planned to enjoy the shady porch in the morning.

Even with its shortcomings Manuel and Margarita accept the mestizo trappings and peculiar design of the house in return for the security from the elements it provides. It has two rooms, one of which they use as a storeroom for corn and other grains, the other as a refuge to huddle out of the cold and rain. Unless it is raining hard or unusually cold they sleep on the porch.

Jogüegüe otherwise fits in well with their Guarijío expectations. Below the house, where the valley begins to close like a funnel, Manuel, assisted by other ejidatarios, built the splendid rock corral with sides five feet high and as neat and regular as if they had been of dressed stone. The corral gleams in the sun and will last for generations, a tribute to the ancient genius for rockwork that Guarijíos have shown throughout their lands. It is a great enclosure, nearly a hundred meters long and thirty wide, with two paddocks capable of holding more than a hundred cows if need be.

The arroyo drops precipitously below the house, exposing bedrock and bringing to the surface a small faithful trickle of water. Below the corral it gathers into aguajes and flows over a ten-meter waterfall. Here in a large aguaje the family members bathe and Margarita and her daughters launder the family clothing, all the while looking down the narrow canyon to the towering crags of the Sierra de la Ventana far in the distance. Guarijíos of both sexes love vast, open spaces, the forest hard by, the mountains clear in the distance, cliffs behind and in front. Gentry long ago noted that they love walking up hills and down and become bored with flatlands. Even where their views are limited by the deep canyons in which they live, they catch glimpses of rocky canyon walls and forested hillsides up and down the river or stream.

Washing clothing by hand is fiendishly hard work, but the laundry aguaje is a pleasant place. A fig tree provides dense shade on the southwest side and rock smoothed by eons of flowing water affords a comfortable place to sit on the other. The children romp in and out of the water while their mother and older sister pound and slap the clothing on the hard, scoured rocks. Just downstream is an even larger aguaje, eight feet deep, usually full of clear water. Above the home about three hundred yards is the spring. Margarita and her eldest daughter, and her stepdaughter carry water in jugs or five-gallon buckets on their heads from the spring the long haul to the kitchen. Moving the water is women's work. They transport it without questioning the age-old custom.

Manuel is still giddy over his fortune in taking over that piece of real estate, his parcel of the ejido Mesa Colorada. Another Guarijío family shares the Jogüegüe valley with him and his family, but during our visit they had gone up into the hills to harvest corn and sorghum and wouldn't be back for a while. Manuel was surprised at the interest Richard and I showed in his crops, the amaranth, squash, sorghum, corn, and beans. The valley soil is good, even on the gentle hillside slopes. This year he had gotten a crop, even though las aguas, the summer rains, had come late and were inadequate, as they had been now for the last six years. Some mornings the sons, ages eighteen, ten, and eight, would take a quick run over to Gocojaqui (three miles to the northeast)—the eldest on an ejido horse, the younger lads on foot—and fish for a couple of hours. The talapia they catch are a good addition to the family's otherwise unvaried diet.

The household shares its space with a sizable herd of goats, two piglets, and the normal number of chickens, probably eight hens and a rooster plus a few chicks. In these households there is always a culeca who lays a clutch of eggs then promptly quits laying and hatches the eggs. Savvy women slip eggs from other chickens under her and hatch a larger brood. One Mayo family I know robs chachalaca nests and slips the eggs under a broody hen and winds up with a few pet chachalacas, a pheasant-like bird that most agree is superior to chicken in flavor.

We arrived when nearly all the chivas had kids roughly six weeks old, a good fifteen of them. They were a frolicsome bunch indeed, prancing everywhere they could get without being hooshed away. The household had a *chivero* (goatherd dog) who early in the morning split off the does from the kids and drove the does off to the hills to forage while the kids, still too young to do more than nibble destructively, waited in a pack for their mothers' return. A couple of hours later the does would return. One of the kids would spy them across the valley sauntering back on their return and set up a furious bleating followed by a swirling stampede of kicking and cavorting young goats demanding the immediate return of their mothers.

Manuel also raises a few cows, some of which belong to the ejido, some to him; I couldn't determine which. Below the rock corral he has cleared a hectare or two to plant buffelgrass. The area was a forest of huge etcho cacti and various trees, but in keeping with the Mexican government's desire to make the raising of calves the Guarijíos' economic lifeblood, Manuel had chopped most of them down. Soon, he said, he would plant buffelgrass and fence the area with barbed wire provided by the government. He liked the idea, he said, for it meant more cows to sell to the buyers who venture up the Mayo buying livestock here and there—cows, goats, pigs, and burros—and running the mixed herd downriver when they have gathered as many animals as possible. I tried to imagine the small field with the etchos and trees in place and deplored the loss to no one in particular. I wondered just how much that small section of great cacti and forest had provided in the way of food, medicine, and wood compared with the extra third or fourth of a cow each year it would now provide. The etchos alone—there were perhaps thirty big cacti eight meters tall or more—provide food (fruits), sweets (syrup), protein (seeds), lumber, and medicine every year. I don't know how much beef the buffelgrass will yield, probably no more than one-fourth an additional calf, but I'm willing to wager that the transaction works out to the Guarijíos' detriment. On the other hand, there are lots of etchos around, and the beef means cash. It is easy for me to judge Manuel's calculation. I don't live in his shoes.

After Manuel had spent an appropriate time with his family, he set out a rickety pine table that had been left behind by the mestizo rancher. Margarita served up two bowls of thick yellowish soup, which she pronounced to be *pipián*—a mash of pumpkin seeds. It tasted nourishing, especially when accompanied by corn tortillas. I felt a little guilty about eating the tortillas. They are labor intensive indeed, but the heaviest work, grinding the parched corn in a hand mill, was assigned to the daughter-in-law, María Luz, who had married Manuel's eighteen-year-old son, Inocente. Manuel said María Luz was sixteen, but I doubt she was more than fourteen, if that. She is a painfully shy Guarijío woman who looks away when a non-Guarijío male looks at her. She stood stoically at a hand mill and ground the corn for all eleven of us and for a couple of visitors from Bavícora who happened by on their way to Gocojaqui. The corn was ground again in a metate. Irma, sixteen, the eldest daughter, then shaped the tortillas under Margarita's supervision and cooked them on the comal, a discarded

The kitchen at Jogüegüe.

tractor disk. I wondered about the labor of shelling those hundreds of pumpkin seeds. Who had time to do that? Only women, whose lives are totally dedicated to feeding and nurturing the family. My God, the labor!

I asked Manuel about school for his seven children. He is quite proud that his children get schooling, which was never available to him. Two have finished school. Two more attend the primary school in Bavícora that Doug and I so admired. They leave each Tuesday morning and walk the three and one-half miles to the school, over two drainages, staying with relatives in Bavícora and returning on Friday afternoon. The three youngest children, girls (the youngest was barely a month old) will attend when they reach six years. The schoolteacher, a Mayo from Navojoa, commutes weekends by mule from Mesa Colorada. He enjoys the tranquility in Bavícora, he says. I've been to Bavícora several times and have never seen the school in session.

Manuel and I sat on the porch and watched the sun set over the Sierra de la Ventana ten miles to the west. At one point a ray pierced the natural bridge near the summit that gives the range its name. I asked him if he has many visitors.

"Yes, we do," he replied. "Each September we have a tuburada here. People come from all over, from Bavícora, from El Saúz, from Rancho Nuevo, from Gocojaqui, even from Mesa Colorada and Guajaray. The festival lasts two days. I dance the pascola." He looked at me with understated pride. Not only that, but his father from Bavícora is a *huicantánturi,* a cantador, the singer who supplies the background for the tuburi, the women's dance without which there cannot be a tuburada. "At the tuburada there are people everywhere. Maybe a hundred people. Everyone comes. Even some yoris. All the women, even little girls, dance the tuburi."

And his son Inocente, was he a pascola? Not yet, Manuel said, but he would be. Maybe even a huicantánturi.

As I have observed before, the Guarijíos' preference for family isolation is more than compensated for by their fondness for chitchat. The family laid out their palm petates before dark and retired early, then spent two to three hours talking and laughing before their voices faded off into sleep. And thus it is every night. All family members chime in, not merely the parents. Even the babbling toddlers pitch in their comments, often accompanied by gales of laughter

Rancho Nuevo.

from adults. This intercommunity loquaciousness is startling, for the Guarijíos are taciturn in the company of outsiders or away from their families, comrades, and villages. The Guarijíos' garrulous nature when they talk among themselves strongly reinforces the retention of their language. Their language and their awareness of their language and its expressiveness are what cements them together. The tuburada, with its uninterrupted flow of sones and cantos, the old vocalized music, helps in its own way to maintain the Guarijíos' linguistic identity.

The Rodríguez-Anamea family also spends a good part of the day gathered near the cooking area chatting away while food is prepared. Manuel's house has two kitchens, both outdoors—one on the north side under a ramada for shade in the summers and one in the open on the south side for sun in the winter. The stove is vintage Guarijío, an adobe structure perhaps four feet high with adobe supports to hold a comal and another to hold a grill. On chilly mornings and evenings someone will build a small bonfire away from the stove for family members to warm themselves around. Margarita and Irma are up early every morning to

grind and pat out the tortillas and to prepare *pinole* (toasted and ground seeds) for a breakfast cereal, usually from huehué after which the place is named. As with everywhere else in rural Mexico, the women work all the time. Margarita was nursing her infant who cried a bit more than a healthy baby will cry. Manuel said it suffered from *empacho,* a broad term for digestive distress. He intended to venture down the canyon to Rancho Nuevo, another Guarijío settlement, to gather some *sávila* (aloe) to rub on the baby's umbilical cord and alleviate its pains. He wondered if Richard and I would accompany him, and of course we would, with enthusiasm.

At Manuel's suggestion Richard and I pitched our tents in the front yard six feet from the porch and the rest of the slumbering family. We slept fine, in spite of the goats, one of whose number must have found the tents to be a curious lot and grunted and muffed throughout the night immediately outside. The goats, as devious as cats, sneak onto the porch when they can, to gnaw on anything that might afford nutrition. At night they are mostly enclosed and usually—usually—don't make a fuss. Our visit was an exception.

Rancho Nuevo lies on the Río Mayo a couple of miles down the canyon from Jogüegüe, where the canyon meets the river. It, too, lies on lands confiscated from illegal tenure by mestizo ranchers. Here, however, the Guarijíos built there own houses, Guarijío style, and handsome huts they are, with palm thatch roofs and wattle-and-daub siding. They sit on a narrow terrace perhaps a hundred feet above the river. Immediately adjacent is a small canyon with a reliable spring for irrigating their extensive garden. From the river below one would scarcely notice the huts unless they were pointed out. That is the way Guarijíos like it to be. Live apart, live simply, live discreetly. You may have to move frequently, so there is no sense in using expensive or labor-intensive materials in building a home. Outsiders are always a threat, whether they will harm or will simply lie, cheat, and steal.

On the edge of a terrace an old Guarijío woman sat weaving tranquilly in the shade of a large pitahaya, appearing utterly indifferent to the arrival of a couple of gringos, probably the first she had ever seen. Her fingers deftly knotted strands of palm fiber. The rope grew as we watched. It was a simple *mecate* (rope), she said, intended only as a tether for a couple of young goats who wandered too far away and did damage to their garden. She tied the short cord around a rear leg of the kid and lashed the other end to a ramada pole, thus severely restricting the little goat's mobility and its capacity to inflict terrestrial damage.

Not far from the old woman, whose name was Tranquilina, the skin of a freshly killed coatimundi hung from a cactus. On a nearby stove a pot of the meat stewed on a bed of coals. Coatimundis are voracious omnivores. We had just seen one carried as a pet by the group of young men we had met at the Río Mayo crossing. Doña Tranquilina said the Guarijíos kill only *solitarios,* solitary males who wander apart from the herd of females and juveniles. Guarijíos like the meat, but it is tough, she said. Her husband arrived while we were poking around the house nosily. He led a pack train of burros returning from his distant milpa bearing sacks of dried corn—this season's harvest. The corn was still on the cob. He showed me a few ears, yellow, white, purple, blue, a variety of colors, all considered *maíz blanco* (white corn). He had never bought seed, he claimed. Each year he saved the seed, even in bad years such as the last few seasons, he saved seed to plant the next year. His father, from Bavícora, had given him the seed. He gave me a few ears to bring back. He then proceeded to unload the corn into his hut's one interior room. So the one "room" they had was used to store corn. They lived their entire lives outdoors in

Doña Tranquilina Cautivo weaving palm cord, Rancho Nuevo.

the ample shade of the great palm roof.

The three families of Rancho Nuevo share a fenced garden irrigated by plastic tubing leading from a spring up the canyon. They have several citrus trees—a gift from the previous occupant of the land. In addition they raise sorghum, which does dual purpose—people suck and chew sugary pulp from the thick stalks and feed the seed heads to livestock—pigs and beasts of burden. The garden also produced beans, sweet potatoes, and sweet corn, as well as banana, guava, and mango trees. The garden could hardly sustain three families, but would prove a valuable supplement to the corn and beans raised on the family mahuechis on the distant mountain slopes and the occasional fish from the river below.

José Rogelio Rascón (that was the older man's name) liked his life at Rancho Nuevo he said, only mildly curious about his gringo visitors. The people there usually had enough, fish from the river and vegetables from their gardens and a little *chivito* (kid) every now and then. There was monte everywhere for wood of every sort. They planned to desmontar a few hectares and plant buffelgrass so there would be more cows to sell to the buyers but that would be done next year. Don José felt there was plenty of land. Plenty of land. He remembered well that not even two decades earlier Guarijíos had no land, no place to make their mahuechis and plant their corn. They were virtual slaves of mestizo ranchers who paid them a pittance to plant and harvest corn and beans while the Guarijíos themselves often faced starvation.

We lingered for only a short while at Rancho Nuevo. Richard and I wanted to talk to Manuel about plants along the trail before darkness set in. He had also promised to show us how to roast *jichicones (Hechtia montana),* a plant use neither of us had heard of. As we plodded back to Jogüegüe, Manuel demonstrated how they use several plants, resources we found surprising. They eat the root of *zanzaro* (*Pouzolzia* sp.), a slimy mess, and the seeds of the *guacapí* (pochote), with a nut-like flavor. They like the seeds of the tacapache (bird-of-paradise, *Caesalpinia pulcherrima*) when they are green, and nibble on the tiny fruits of *chiqui pusi* (lantana, *Lantana camara*). If a person has body odor, he or she is prescribed a tea made of the bark from *te'sá* (teso, *Acacia occidentalis*). They make tamales from the seeds of the *sahuí* cactus (*Stenocereus montanus*), treat cramps by rubbing the muscles with the singed fruits of *goy susu (Martynia annua)* mixed with grease. The women give themselves permanents with a mash from the heads of *sí tepa* (sedge, *Cyperus* sp.). And so we spent the rest of the day, Manuel explaining, reexplaining, and repeating, Richard and I writing furiously.

At Jogüegüe, Margarita and Irma, the eldest daughter were washing clothes at the aguaje while the younger children romped up and down the rocks. Manuel climbed up the steep hillside and with a *bacote* (a sharpened agave pole) pried a few spiny-leaved jichicones, each weighing less than a pound, from the shallow soil, and lobbed them down the slope. We watched as he carried the yucca-like plants to his yard and turned over the roasting job to Inocente, his son. The young man built a fire of casually gathered sticks over the octopus-like heads, and in a few minutes a bonfire produced a large handful of hot, onion-like hearts of *Hechtia*. "You can always eat these if there is nothing else. Guarijíos don't need to be very hungry up here in the *monte,*" he said quietly when I asked him about the food. He was a lad of few words.

The roasted heads were reminiscent of a bland baked onion, hardly a culinary delight, but with a nutritious feel to them. Inocente called them *na jichichiconi,* roasted jichicones. He informed us that they were eaten in emergencies only. This was with good reason, for the plants occur in a few places in numerous small clusters but could easily be exterminated if they were regularly harvested for food. Jichicones will never provide the Guarijíos with a dietary staple. I'm not sad about that.

I could not but notice that Manuel's house was quite exposed for a Guarijío dwelling. It was visible for miles, especially from the air. It had cleared land and gentle slopes in three directions, a reflection of its mestizo heritage. Did the soldiers of the army ever land here? I asked him as we ate bowls of beans and munched on tortillas.

"Oh, yes," he answered matter-of-factly. "They come in helicopters every few months looking for drugs—marijuana or poppies. They land right out there." He pointed to a cleared area near the corral.

"Do they harass you?"

He thought for a moment.

"Not too badly. They go into the house and make us stand outside. No, they never ask permission. Then they rifle through all our belongings to see if we are hiding any contraband, things like drugs or firearms—we're not permitted to own any guns, you know. They ask as a few more questions. Then they leave. The helicopters take off, fooom." He spread his arms toward the sky.

It was just a normal search carried out by soldiers trained to carry out the demands of my government. What would be an outrage in my native land was commonplace in a country that jumps to carry out the bidding of the senior trading partner. How was it, I wondered, that my government demanded that other nations do things to their people that would never be tolerated domestically?

On our return trip, after we had trudged over the first high ridge, passed through an intimate valley, climbed another ridge and descended steeply to the Río Mayo, Richard and I decided to explore a box canyon we had glimpsed on our way in. It was just across the Mayo from Charajaqui, no more than a five-minute walk to the entrance. When we had crossed the river I mentioned the canyon to Manuel. He looked around uneasily. "Fine. You should explore it but I should stay with the burros and make sure our things are not stolen. You never know when someone might come along." That was all right, of course, but since we had seen only the party of young men and the rancher and his children in four days of trail hounding, I thought it unlikely. Perhaps Manuel was tired or had had enough of telling gringos about plants. Perhaps he just wished to relax by himself for a while.

Plant hunters love box canyons. These profound crevasses in the thick volcanic rock are the seductive natural wonders of the Guarijío land. The bottoms usually receive little sunlight and tend to be cool and moist even in the hot months, providing a comfortable habitat for plants that find the hillsides too dry or bright. Trees grow much larger in such cajones, as they are called, than outside them, and often trees are found well out of their normal range. Thus had been my experience with Cipriano in the cajón near San Pedro, and, I hoped, such would be the case now.

This fissure appeared as a narrow black void in the distance. I once stared at a similar cajón for the better part of a day, watching the shadows alter its physiognomy as the sun's angle shifted. For a while I saw a flock of chattering White-fronted Parrots appear and a family of raucous urracas disappear inside. They appeared to be attracted by the upper branches of a chalate (*Ficus trigonata*) which must have been in fruit at the time. They had an easy time exploring the cajón, but it was inaccessible to me: the edge was a sheer dropoff of a hundred feet. Without rope I could never make it to the bottom, so I was stuck, gawking into the defile. I'll never know what secrets it held. But this time I was not going to be denied. I was going to discover just what lay within that dark chasm.

As we approached the cajón swallows and butterflies disappeared into the darkness only to reappear as daytime fireworks, for the sun caught their florescent colors as they flitted in and out of the chasm. We climbed into the muddy mouth of the narrow box sinking deep into gummy ooze, for it was only slightly above the river current. In the last flood deep silt had been deposited high above the river's current placid course. We had gone no more than fifty yards when we discovered ascent was nearly impossible, as I had feared. We had arrived at the solid perpendicular rock of a thirty-foot waterfall.

Not to be deterred, we retreated a bit and scampered up the steep side, angled up the hillside, managed to pull ourselves over a rock face and half slid, half walked down into the next tier. Once again at the canyon bottom, but now above the falls, I found that the cajón was a succession of small, dry waterfalls, all in the dense shade of huge figs and other trees fifteen, twenty meters tall, and a jungle of vines and shrubs, but nothing unusual, nothing we couldn't negotiate. The stillness was unearthly. Not a bird sound, not an insect's buzz, hardly a falling leaf. Far above I saw swallows

and a butterfly, but they did not descend to the bottom.

I boulder-hopped up the canyon bottom, reached another tier, then another. The cool air should have been refreshing and invigorating, but I felt clammy. After a few more minutes of scampering over the rocks, I felt a powerful urge to leave the place. I can only describe my feeling as spooky or strange vibes. I didn't experience panic, but something like a deep unpleasantness, most odd in such a lush, cool, vibrantly green place. To my irritation, something was telling me to leave at once. Richard clambered up to where I was lingering. He was equally enchanted by the luxurious vegetation but was uncharacteristically willing to leave as well. He needed no convincing when I suggested we get out of the canyon. We slid and jumped down level after level and climbed rapidly out of that dark, but now less than romantic chasm, and emerged with some relief into the brilliant sunlight of the hillside. Then we plunged downward, hardly cognizant of the thorny trees and shrubs. I had nearly arrived at the riverbank when I tripped and almost fell to the ground. I had staggered into an ancient graveyard. A dozen or so mounds of piled stones were crowned with small, rotting wooden crosses. At the base of each lay a couple of enameled tin cups. This was the Charajaqui cemetery. I felt an eerie premonition of darkness and sorrow. A generation of dead Guarijíos was entombed in this tiny plot. I doubted that any of them had fulfilled their allotted threescore years and ten. Could my instinctive reaction in the canyon have been connected with this graveyard? Could my unconscious have picked up some subliminal warning? Impossible, of course. But, then why did Richard have the same sensations?

Manuel was resting next to the sleepy burros. I told him we had found the cemetery. He nodded knowingly. That was the cemetery, all right, he said. That's where they put dead people. He said nothing more, but seemed quite happy to move on.

We retraced our steps on the narrow trail on the cliff above the river, up and down, slipping and hopping for five kilometers. I had made the crossings faster for us by commandeering an ejido mule for Richard to ride on, while at the river crossings I vaulted up on the haunches of the burro I had named Alfonso. Thus I hitchhiked across the fords, to the dismay of the poor burro who seemed puzzled but resigned to the strange ways of gringos. We arrived in a couple of hours at Chinatopo and rested in a grove of huge guamúchiles on a fine sand bar above the river. It was nearly four o'clock. Four hours of hard hiking lay ahead of us. I was inclined to push on and camp near Huataturi and

Manuel was willing to accommodate.

We had hardly proceeded a hundred yards when we were met by the owner of the ranch, Rosario Rosas, who had heard us coming and walked up the canyon to greet us. He welcomed us generously, inviting us to his house for a cup of coffee. I declined as politely as possible, telling him we had to push on to make it to Huataturi before it was pitch black. He look at me with concern, his kindly face all sincerity.

"You really shouldn't try to make it to Huataturi tonight. It's two and a half, three hours to there. It will be dark and you could get hurt on the trail. Stay here where there is a nice place to camp. You can bathe in the river. The beasts can stay in the corral. It is clean here and you are most welcome."

I looked around at Richard who nodded eagerly to me that the fellow was right. Richard was tired and had many plants to press. He didn't look forward to three more hours in the saddle, especially in the dark. Just thinking about sitting in that saddle made me sore and stiff.

So we stayed. Don Rosario, who was about sixty years old, invited us to come by for coffee at our convenience. "Anything we have is yours," he said. "You can camp here in this little park under the guamúchiles but be careful because sometimes branches break off and fall and you might be hurt. If you would like you can camp nearer my house." There was a hopeful note in his voice.

This was the monster who had mowed down the forest to sow buffelgrass, and he was making it powerfully difficult for me to dislike him. His clothes showed his poverty. Shirt and pants patched, repatched, and patches patched. Sandals, not boots, an old careworn hat, not the new sort that fatcat ranchers wear. He was a humble fellow who craved our company if only for a while, wanted conversation, wanted to learn of the outside world beyond his own ranch, wanted to learn about the United States.

I also knew that the Rosas family had been one of those "exposed" twenty years previously by Ted Faubert as holding Guarijíos in virtual peonage. A good part of the "family" ranch had been expropriated from them when the Guarijío ejidos had been established, including the ranch of El Saúz which, just like Jogüegüe, had formerly been occupied by mestizos. I had visited El Saúz en route to Bavícora and understood why a family would be loath to surrender it to anyone, much less some upstart Indians. The Rosas were said to have opposed the Guarijío takeover bitterly, had been part of the pequeños propietarios who

had united to take all possible steps to prevent the Guarijíos from getting their land.[2] Now I would get to find out just what sort of fellow would fight against Guarijíos getting their land and would wantonly cut down the forest to boot.

When we had set up our camp, I urged Manuel to join Richard and me at the ranch house for coffee. Don Rosario greeted us from a distance and pointed the path to his patio, a great expanse with a dense palm thatch cover, the entirety swept fastidiously.[3] Looking outwards we were presented with a sweeping view of the Río Mayo below as it bent to the west, and the great Sierra de la Ventana that separates the Arroyo Guajaray from the Mayo. I would pay a lot for a place like Rosario owned. He proudly presented one of his sons, perhaps eighteen, a daughter in her early twenties, who confidently held out her hand to shake ours, and a daughter-in-law with a toddler in her arms who shyly acknowledged our presence with the hint of a smile. She was decidedly Guarijío in appearance, contrasting markedly from the light skin and Caucasian features of the mestizo ranch family. "She's from Cuchugüeri, just around the bend in the river," Rosario mentioned, nodding his head toward the young woman. It was a settlement of mestizos and Guarijíos, with a school for all children within a radius of fifteen kilometers. "She is married to my middle son. This is my grandson. His skin is very dark. It's not as pretty as white skin, don't you agree?"

I smiled and said, "No, I don't agree." I explained that I had spent many years, as had Richard, living among the Seris and had grown so accustomed to the rich healthy color of Seri babies that white babies seemed, well, downright pale and unhealthy! "How could any baby be prettier than his grandson? Didn't he agree?"

Don Rosario looked back and forth at us, seemingly confused by all this but agreed that his own grandson was indeed a handsome lad, and he loved him dearly.

We gathered around the table on the handsome porch. I invited Manuel to sit among us and he eagerly joined. The daughter served us cups of boiling hot water and set down a jar of instant coffee to which we helped ourselves.

"Well, don Rosario," I said. "I must warn you that I am a most nosy fellow and am terribly interested in how you live here. I love your place. In fact, I think it is one of the prettiest I have ever seen. You must be fortunate to own it, right?" Thus I began my normal barrage of questions, and he responded with an engaging smile.

"Well, it is beautiful. We've seen the river come up almost to the porch, and that gave us a scare. I love to look at the river every day. I used to have a lot more land, but not now. It has been very hard, though. You see, I'm a widower."

He went on to describe how his wife had died in 1979 leaving him with seven children, the youngest less than a year old. Could she have died from complications of childbirth? I marveled at his ability to raise such a fine family alone. Indeed, the four children we met (the eldest was twenty-five; two daughters lived with a relative in far-off Navojoa) were handsome and respectful, showing signs of a decent upbringing. Yes, it had been terribly hard, raising the children, but they had made out all right. Five children still lived there, and he hoped they would stay. Yet he was sure not all would be able to make a living on the ranch. He was clearing off his land to provide more grass so that he could raise more cows and make a little more money so that his children could stay with him.

Don Rosario spoke slowly but clearly, and, I thought, was enjoying a chance to chat about his personal history. But the afternoon was fleeting and dusk came early to the deep canyon, so I suggested we needed to return to our camp. He nodded but humbly asked if we wouldn't join him for breakfast in the morning. "We don't have much here, just a few beans and tortillas, but . . ."

I assured him we would love to join him. And indeed, it was just what I had hoped for.

The night was superb. The river rippled in the background, and three different owl species hooted at us. I experienced a feeling of deep contentment in that grove of tall guamúchiles, on that sandbar, next to that babbling river, in the company of that Guarijío friend, that fine gringo companion, and on the ranch of that good mestizo man.

Manuel was up well before dawn and rounded up the pack train, which he had corralled downstream in one of Rosario's enclosures. By the time it was light, we were packed up and walking to the ranch house for breakfast. Rosario was waiting for us. We shook hands once again and exchanged morning greetings. Once again I invited Manuel to sit at the table with us. The daughter served us first a bowl of rich venison stew. Rosario apologized for it. "I hope you don't mind eating *venadito*," he said. "It's all the meat we have." I assured him that it was a special treat. The daughter-in-law took our plates and the daughter then served us beans, tortillas, and coffee. We talked all the while. Don Rosario had been born at El Saúz but had lived at Chinatopo for more than forty years. His lands extended quite a way up the river, up past Charajaqui, as a matter of fact. It was tough country for cows, steep, not

much grass. They piped water in from a spring nearly a kilometer away with plastic tubing they bought in Navojoa and lugged in on burroback. The mosquitoes made life difficult in the hot weather, but he had gotten some netting so that they could sleep. Yes, he missed his wife but had his children. That was important.

I asked him about the Guarijíos. He said he knew little, hadn't learned any of the language, but felt he got along fine with them. He saw them regularly as they passed by the ranch, for the principal camino up and down the river was right in front of his house. And they worked for him at times. He made no mention of the struggles of a couple of decades earlier. He wondered where Richard and I were from. Was it far away? Was it near Hermosillo, where he had once visited? (I knew about that visit—the private rancher opponents of the Guarijío ejidos met in Hermosillo attempting to influence the judge against awarding the Indians their ancestral lands.) Did it get cold where we lived? Were there forests?

I thought about the army soldiers harassing Manuel and Cipriano. Did the soldiers ever harass him? No, Rosario said. Every once in a while a platoon would come by, working their way up the river searching for whatever it was they were after. They even would camp right where we had camped, under the guamúchiles, but they showed little interest in the Rosas family, left them alone. By the way, he wondered, if I ever came back, could I bring him a few bullets, just a little box of .22 caliber short shells? I told him no, I couldn't. If I were to be caught with any sort of firearms I would be thrown into jail and left to rot, as other North Americans had been discovering to their dismay. I described how one American was still in jail a year after authorities found a box of .22 bullets in the trunk of his car just inside the Mexican border.

Rosario shook his head. "Imagine that. They won't let us buy any bullets at all. Not even .22 shorts, little bullets to defend ourselves and our livestock from animals and other dangerous things. What good is it to have a rifle if you have no bullets?" I was sympathetic with his position and found myself oozing anti gun-control sentiments. What possible threat to national security would lie in .22 caliber short bullets?

I found myself becoming fond of this man and admiring his tenacity and humility. My mind was still trying to reconcile the contradictions between what I had seen and the history I knew. I looked at Manuel happily finishing his meal and realized the great strides the Guarijíos had made, through their persistence and courage, and the remarkable concessions the mestizos such as Rosario had made. The private ranchers had been forced to accept defeat. Had they all simply recognized that they needed each other to survive in this rugged, tough, wild, beautiful land, and that energy wasted on hatred would detract from the struggle to keep bread on the table and the roof overhead patched? I doubt if all the ranchers did, but I figured that at least Rosario had arrived at that conclusion.

We bade the family goodbye. One of the sons thoughtfully filled up our bottles with boiled water that would be safe to drink. All stood at the edge of the porch as we plodded by, the daughter-in-law holding Rosario's grandson in her arms. A hundred yards downstream I looked back and saw them still standing, watching us fade into the distance and into their memories. Richard had been thinking the same thoughts as I had. "Do you think he would have invited Manuel to sit at the table if we hadn't been there?" he wondered.

I looked at him and smiled. "We do think alike, Richard." I wondered also if the loss of Rosario's wife had in any way been connected with the stressful battle over control of the Guarijío lands.

Struggling up the steep slope of buffelgrass I reacted somewhat differently to the alien pasture than I had a few days earlier. I couldn't begrudge Rosario's desire to have a few more cows so that his children could live a bit better. I despised the effects of the clearing, the loss of the magnificent forest and all the wildlife, the birds, the mammals, the reptiles, the insects that vanished when it vanished. But I could understand better that Rosario was no monster. I reflected on his and other rancher's battle against the Guarijíos and against poverty and wondered what I would have done had I been in his shoes. And I came to no conclusion at all.

Once out of the buffelgrass we reentered the primeval forest, that silent ancient world that penetrated my being with its brooding stillness, reducing me to little more than a simple moving point. The contrast between this paleo-ecological landscape and its natural power with the human-produced buffelgrassland and its overwhelming sense of manipulation could not be greater. This forest defied the reality of human dominance of the planet. The Guarijíos like to move through the forest without a sound, leaving no trace, living where they are not likely to be seen. They were and are, as Gentry said, people of the tropical deciduous forest. This was their world, their place, as much a home to Manuel as the roof of his house. The buffelgrass

pasture was the mestizo world. The Guarijíos would become Mexicanized, as the Mexican government desires them to be, insofar as the forest disappears, for with the forest will go the Guarijíos' way of life. Dams, clearing of pasture, roads, all of them violate the world of the Guarijíos and each in their own way are proving to be a terrible and destructive device, a juggernaut assimilating the gently resistant Guarijíos into the endless uniformity of things.

Such were my pretentious thoughts when I reached the ridge, climbing a hundred yards ahead of Manuel and the burros, with Richard following. The trail led sharply down the other side, another up steeply to the right. I had no inkling of which trail we had taken before. I stopped and looked questioningly back to Manuel.

"*Por 'riba,*'" he called out. (Up.)

I turned left and began to climb upwards toward the east.

"No," he cried. "Up the other way. That trail goes to Bavícora!"

Laughing at myself, I did a one hundred-eighty-degree turn and went up the trail to the right, towards the west. I had no idea that we had arrived at a major crossroads of the Guarijío transportation network. "You need to have a road sign installed, Manuel," I joked. He thought the whole episode was quite funny, wondering how in the world I could have taken such a wrong turn. Without Manuel I would have wound up in five hours at Bavícora sixteen miles from Mesa Colorada. Richard, sitting in the saddle of the mule, got quite a kick out of that crossroads as well, teasing me for leading all astray. And, indeed, I would have.

At Mesa Colorada Manuel unloaded our bundles. I paid him and he looked at the money happily. "I'll buy food and things for my family." He said. "I'll be going back tomorrow morning." He had brought the two extra burros, he said, to carry back provisions he would buy. His sister Cornelia served us some coffee and wondered how we had found Jogüegüe, pleased to hear our accolades for the place. "So you like the Guarijío lands?" she asked, offering tortillas.

More than she could understand, I thought. And I hadn't made it to Caramechi. It would take another trip, then another, then yet another.

9
The Old Man of the Mountains

I was searching for old Guarijío men. It was they who knew the most about plants. Not that old women didn't know their share. They worked magic in their huts, brewing teas, applying poultices, steaming healing roots, grinding bark, straining fruits, boiling, steeping, scalding, decocting. They were the weavers, the sewers, the cooks, and the chemists/pharmacists of the monte as well. They never stopped working. But the old men, those who have spent their many days roaming through the monte; climbing cliffs and great trees in search of honeycomb; chasing terrified white-tailed deer up and down the steep, rocky slopes; running down maverick cows and wayward burros; sleeping where they stopped, covered only with leaves or brush, they were the ones who knew the plants and where they grew. They traveled only by foot, within easy intimacy of the plants, never removed by a horse's or mule's height from the ground or by the horse's speed from the details. While the women were tending their hearths, as men would have them, men were combing the monte in ever widening circles. These were the fellows who had the lore I sought.

But today, deep in Guarijío country, José, the old man, was not with us, as I shall explain, even though this chapter is about him. Lorenzo, a strong, honest, sincere fellow was far younger. Good Lorenzo. Even he had much to teach us as he guided us up the trail from Jogüegüe to Bavícora.

This was truly virgin forest, dazzling in its richness, too isolated to be lumbered, too rough for more than a few occasional cows, too little used to be tarnished by human depredations. It is not the dark forest of spruce and fir of the north nor the immense dripping canopy of the rain forest to the south. The trees of this low forest are but ten to twenty meters tall. They are short and angular in comparison to the tall and erect conifers of temperate forests or the buttressed giants of rainy jungles, but lofty compared with the thornscrub of the coasts and massive compared with the shrubs and low trees of the desert not far away to the west and northwest. The trees of this forest are palo mulato, *algodoncillo,* torote copal, mauto, tepeguaje,

guásima, and a myriad others—more than a hundred kinds, as it turns out.

We trudged up one of two trails joining the two settlements. The other route was longer, but somewhat easier. It was the trail the children of Jogüegüe take to school in Bavícora. This one was more precipitous and steeper, too dangerous for tender children, but with better views. It was as though we were the first men in the world, Richard, Lorenzo, and I, and the three burros and a mule that bore our trappings seemed the primordial beasts.

Lorenzo was an ideal guide: strong, intelligent, well traveled in the monte, a good conversationalist. In his early forties, he was born in Bavícora and traveled there frequently from his home in Mesa Colorada. He was tall for a Guarijío, perhaps five feet eight inches, with a long face and large white teeth that stood out in the dark. He knew how to handle pack animals, when to yell "hrosh" and "yuip" and when to get serious with the malevolent, scheming beasts. Lorenzo was also a teetotaler, which meant that he would probably be reliable. He didn't drink because he was an evangelista, and the strongest precept in the evangelistas' religious platform is that the brethren be teetotalers: no booze. The evangelistas pay a high price for their abstinence: Guarijíos who abstain from the devil's brew are thereby cut off from traditional Guarijío society that virtually *requires* men to drink as part of the tuburada. The altered state of consciousness brought about by imbibing alcohol is as much a part of the fiesta as the rituals themselves. Traditional Guarijíos view the evangelistas as anti-Guarijíos. I don't think the traditionalists ostracize the converts. I think they simply write them off.

For our purposes, though, Lorenzo's abstention meant that he would be ever attentive to us and our journey. We could count on him as a guide, as a conversationalist, and as an advisor. He would show up when he promised. He would make sense when he spoke. He led Richard and me back up the river to Jogüegüe and now up a new trail (for us) to Bavícora.

José Ruelas had nearly been our guide. Here is what happened. For some time I had wanted to go to Gocojaqui, far to the north of Mesa Colorada. The previous year Guarijíos reported that two Guarijío families were living there. Upstream from Gocojaqui is a profound and moist canyon—El Arroyo Limón, the lower drainage of Arroyo Loreto—which I knew would be full of unusual plants to show to Guarijíos and find out what they had to say about them. I have no records of anyone having done biological

José Ruelas.

studies inside the lengthy canyon. Ramón Rodríguez had agreed to lead us there.

I spent a disquieting hour in Mesa Colorada discussing the trip with Ramón. Several people in San Bernardo had said he was the most knowledgeable guide around. Once before, I had tried to retain him and failed. This time I hoped for success. I had found him seated under his ramada in Mesa Colorada with several other Guarijíos drinking home-brewed tepachi from a huge old plastic jug that they passed around as drinking buddies will. When I walked up he looked at me with a tipsy-friendly expression. I asked him if he could guide us to Gocojaqui and Caramechi, and told him I would pay him well. I explained I needed burros and a mule. I said it would be all right if he wanted to take someone else along. He repeated all I had said. Yes, he thought, he could do it. But it might be difficult getting all the burros. He had only two. We wanted three. I would pay someone for the burros, I assured him. Ah, he said, I would pay? His patient, practical wife Cornelia looked on from the background. She urged him to say yes. He could earn more guiding us in a day than working for a rancher in a week. They could surely use the money. At that time they were lucky to be earning three dollars a day. She would help get him going, I thought, the way she had gotten her brother Manuel going a year ago. Maybe.

So as the sun set in Mesa Colorada, I left it at that, uneasy, knowing that Ramón was going to get more drunk and might have a hard time of it the next day. Promises made under the siren song of tepachi are easily forgotten and more easily overlooked.

In the morning I approached Ramón's house with a sinking feeling. Outside I hoped to see burros tethered, with packsaddles in place, the way it had been with Cornelia's brother Manuel a year before. There were no patient beasts standing as statues. Cornelia was gone, Ramon's young children nowhere to be seen. Around the side of the house, one of his teenage sons was leaning against the building absorbing sunlight. He stared at the ground when I asked him. Yes, he said in a barely audible voice, his father was around. He was still in bed. Go in and see him, he said.

The door was open. I peered into the darkness. I barely made out Ramón on the floor huddled among a mass of blankets, covered up to his chin against the November chill. He opened his bloodshot eyes heavily and peered past me. "You'll need to get someone else to guide you," he said, simply. That was that.

Oh, well, I needed to get permission from Lino Leyba, the Guarijío governor anyway. Lino had been away the night before, but now he was there. Lino is a large, rather efficient man accustomed to giving orders. He and his wife operate the only store in Mesa Colorada, hardly an extravagant one, but with a few provisions—sodas, Maseca, a few canned goods. Lino was seated at a small table, totaling up a series of columns with another fellow, an apparent debtor. I waited, then explained my need for burros and a guide. He nodded noncommittally. I would pay well, I assured him. I could even take two guides, but I needed a good guide and burros and a mule. Could he help? He thought he might be able to but not until tomorrow. He dismissed me with a friendly nod.

That was when I ran into the old man, José Ruelas. He was wobbling toward Lino's house. I greeted him warmly, for I had met him several times before. He seemed to remember me from a chat we had had in San Bernardo years ago. I knew of him even then, for he gained a certain prominence for his role in the formation of the Guarijío ejidos. Indeed, Cipriano relates that José was the real leader from Bavícora in the fight to obtain Guarijío lands. You would never have known it to look at him, for each time I had seen him he looked as though he could not possibly survive for long. He had long claimed a certain notoriety for his habit of wandering all over the Guarijío lands, often in an inebriated state. He had been known to accompany Ted Faubert in his travels through the region twenty years earlier.

He also supported a huge shock of salt-and-pepper hair atop a dense black undercoat.

José nodded at me with a slightly intoxicated smile.

I didn't hesitate. "José," I asked him. "Do you think you could guide me to Gocojaqui and Caramechi?"

He straightened up to his full height of five feet. "Of course, I can guide you anywhere you want. I grew up in Gocojaqui! But now there is no one there. Not in Caramechi, either. Only in Tecoripa and Rancho Nuevo."

So we spent an hour talking about a trip. Of course, he couldn't do it until the following day, which was fine with me because he was semi-drunk, not drooling, staggering drunk, just woozy, happy, phrase-repeating, smiley drunk. He would need to find burros and a mule. He didn't have any, he said. He described in detail some of the routes we could follow. All sounded like music to my ears. But, I reminded myself and Richard, who was with me, these were the solemn mutterings of a man influenced by strong drink. He might have promised to climb Mt. Everest.

Richard and I decided to give José a test. Not that I doubted his ability, but I feared that his many years (he claimed to be between seventy and eighty) combined with his fondness for distilled spirits might have dimmed his concentration. We drove him to a canyon not far from Mesa Colorada and put him to work telling us about every plant we saw.

He easily passed the test. He couldn't have lost much over the years. He cited a litany of plant names and uses. He pointed in all directions, enumerating the names of herbs, shrubs, and trees, reciting what they were good for and what he used them for alone, in mixtures, root, stem, trunk, bark, leaf, flower, sap. He chronicled the gradual disappearance of some important plants in the Guarijíos' diet. He lamented the lack of discipline in the children, their unwillingness to work to gather plant foods and make good medicine. José's sight was not good, but he still possessed the vision he was famous for. He told trees by their shapes.

From time to time he produced a pint bottle of clear liquid that he concealed beneath his shirt. He drank it because it gave him energy, he informed us soberly. His regular nips seemed not to affect his cognitive abilities, however. I decided that as a naturalist José with modest blood alcohol was better than many other men stone sober.

And so it was agreed. He would guide us. He promised he would not get drunk that night. I explained to him that our guide had to be sober because he would be our teacher as well. Richard and I set up camp near the river. José brought a nephew down for us to meet. The energetic young man would be accompanying us, José said, because he could handle the bestias (burros and mule). José was a remnant of the old days when the Guarijíos owned nothing, not even a burro, sometimes not even a shirt. He relied on these, he asserted, pointing at his feet. They were broadly splayed from countless leagues of walking. His huaraches were a good inch wider and longer than his feet, making it look as though he walked on small paddles. He didn't like to deal with pack animals, he said.

That was putting it mildly. After all, José is no more than five feet tall, probably weighing in at little more than a hundred pounds. I had no proof, but I'm willing to venture that he had never ridden any beast of burden in his life. He could no more handle a mule or a burro than I could. In fact, I'd take my chances with me as a roustabout rather than leave José to load, unload, goad, hobble, saddle, unsaddle, chase, rope, drive, or lead a single burro. That wasn't why I wanted him to go. I wanted him along for his vast knowledge of the Guarijío country and the plants that grow within it.

He left us in our camp, an abandoned mahuechi overlooking the river, situated a couple of hundred yards from two Guarijío houses. He would have the burros saddled and ready to go at 8:00 A.M. in the morning, he announced, straightening. Richard and I looked at each other and smiled wryly. "Oh, José," I added, almost as an afterthought. "Be sure to tell the Governor Lino that you will be leading us.

He is trying to find someone else to do it."

At 7:00 o'clock in the morning, true to his word, José was at our camp. He had two burros ready, he said, and was looking for a third. Soon he would return, and we would pack up to go.

The dew had been dense that night, and our tents were sopping wet. They had to dry in the sun before we could pack them. Otherwise they would mildew when packed in their tight nylon bags under the hot sun. To dry the tents we lifted them, turned them on their sides, then upside down, then upright once again. A small crowd of children gathered to stare at us and our machinations. It was nearly 9:00 A.M. by the time everything was dry and our things were packed in duffel bags that would withstand the endless bounces, abrasions, and scratches of burro transportation. Mules, an old Guarijío had told me, will avoid brambles. Burros seek them out. Psychopathic beasts of burden, they are.

We waited as the sun heated up the day. No José. Ten o'clock came and went. The audience of children grew bored and drifted away. No sign of the old man. I got to feeling cranky and made petty comments to Richard. Finally I sighed and walked up the road a few hundred yards to where I thought José lived. There he was, standing with a group of Guarijíos drinking tepachi. He saw me and staggered over toward me. *"Un burro."* He said in a thick voice. "I still have to find *un burro.*"

I returned and told Richard the bad news. Well, so much for José. We drove to Lino's house. He was waiting for us. "No," he said, "José can't lead you. He is too drunk. But Lorenzo will guide you, and there," and he motioned with his hand, "are your burros."

And so there they were. Three patient beasts all packsaddled and tethered, waiting under the shade of a mezquite tree. At his home half a kilometer away Lorenzo Sujaguareña was awaiting us. He had a mule saddled and his little bundle of trappings neatly tied and knotted. I discussed arrangements and pay with him briefly. He was in complete agreement. Within an hour we plodded off up the Jacqchí.

We camped once again under the giant guamúchiles of Chinatopo, ate dinner with Rosario Rosas while his daughter and daughter-in-law hovered over us, slept as the wind picked up and swirled river sand around our tents. We trudged on the steep narrow trail on the canyon side, ate lunch at Charajaqui, tramped up the interminable slope, and camped once again at Jogüegüe.

I had hoped to find Manuel Rodríguez at Jogüegüe. He had proven an excellent guide and knew the canyons and many of the plants we hoped to find. I imagined a happy reunion and a supper of fresh tortillas and beans from the large supply of food I brought along. I envisioned a warm welcome from the family I had briefly come to know.

Manuel was not there. He was working somewhere *arriba*—up above in the sierras, his son Inocente reported. Manuel's wife had an embarrassed smile as she nursed a toddler in her lap. I nodded with understanding and asked and received permission to pitch our tents inside the corral where they would be safe from marauding burros and cows.

Lorenzo explained what we suspected. Manuel had gotten a chance to work in marijuana fields far upstream. The pay is good and the *patrones* (bosses) pay cash. Lorenzo, stiffened by his stern Protestantism, did not approve, it seemed but had known enough poverty and humiliation to understood that chamba is hard to come by in the sierra, especially for a Guarijío. All the ejido could pay for a day's work was a few kilos of Maseca, and you could hardly feed a huge family like Manuel's on a pittance like that, he reasoned. The harvest of corn, amaranth, and sorghum hadn't been great that year, so Manuel needed the extra money to buy food. The *narcotraficantes* were a lifesaver. America's anti-drug efforts were maintaining the high price of marijuana and providing work for my Guarijío friends. God bless the Drug Enforcement Agency, I thought. Irony of ironies that the policies of the most wasteful and anti-humanitarian of civilian United States agencies would benefit my friends.

Even now, with their lands apparently secure, the Guarijíos' life is not easy. Their incomes are miserably low. A working man can hardly hope to earn more than $1,500 a year, and few earn even half of that. The cows they guard and chase through the torturously rough country then sell to the buyers bring precious little, especially by the time they have been driven on foot over many miles of mountain trails to the *compradores* (buyers) at San Bernardo. The Guarijíos take the buyers' price or leave it. There is no competition. And there is no regularly delivered medical care for the vast majority of the Guarijíos. Except for the evangelistas, few adult men escape alcoholism. Almost no Guarijíos have anything resembling a real job with decent pay.

So they accept employment offered by the narcos. It is not ideal work. The rate of violence is rapidly increasing. While the narcos provide work, they also have created a culture of murderous violence that has cheapened human life and destabilized the social fabric of the sierras. The Guarijíos acknowledge this grim reality. So does every other serrano native.

Even though the Guarijíos know full well the risks they run by involving themselves with the narcotraficantes—violence, death, repression by the police and the military, leaving their families in peril—they gladly take the work. The alternatives are even worse. From their standpoint, they see no earthly reason why they should not work at raising a crop, especially when the pay is good. For them, raising marijuana is no different for them than raising sesame or garbanzos. Such crops are for export. They put in a full day; they pick up their money. They are unmoved by reported laws governing controlled substances, regulations they cannot fathom. International politics means nothing to them. Food means everything.

A doctor who operated an intermittent clinic among the Guarijíos once asked me why my country was so willing to spend billions and create a police state to keep people from smoking pot. I had no answer, of course, and none of my compatriots do, either. Authorities in my country concoct lies about the marijuana's supposed pernicious effects, fabrications they hardly believe themselves (although they try mighty hard to believe), and young people certainly don't believe them, as the statistics concerning marijuana consumption demonstrate. Marijuana use has traditionally been widespread among rural folk in northern Mexico. If we were to believe the anti-marijuana lobby in the United States, we should predict widespread social chaos, family breakdown, and the undermining of authority in the rural areas. Nothing of the sort happened, of course. But since the advent of the United States' so-called "War on Drugs," the profitability of raising drugs has become so enormous that the sierras have been taken over by highly organized drug lords, the narcotraficantes, the mafiosos. Under their insidious influence, social chaos, family breakdown, and the undermining of authority have indeed occurred.

That social decay has been accompanied by a sensational increase in the availability of Tecate beer, expensive but socially prestigious, and promoted by fabulously successful mass marketing strategies. Beer consumption has destroyed the economy of huge numbers of Mexican families, infinitely more than marijuana. But as far as the Drug Lobby is concerned, beer is fine. Marijuana is an assassin that must be eradicated. And freedom is slavery. War is peace.

So Manuel was off earning wages kept high by my government's policies. I figured he probably would not be back soon, not until the last leaf was baled and transported, probably a couple of weeks later. It would be bad manners for us to camp any longer near Manuel's house in his absence.

It would be disrespectful toward his wife and family. I chose to go to Bavícora instead, putting off once again my ancient hope of visiting Gocojaqui and Caramechi.

It wasn't a bad decision. The trail was steep but through rich forest, and the views were breathtaking. We set off and Lorenzo told us about Jogüegüe. It actually has two houses, one recently built in traditional Guarijío style, the other the old mestizo ranch house where Manuel lives. Lorenzo had mixed feelings about the place, he said. Prior to the Guarijíos' successful fight for their lands, Jogüegüe was in the hands of a mestizo rancher named Sainz. He had been, according to Lorenzo, a wealthy man.[1] He was among those who kept Guarijíos in virtual peonage. "We would work all day for him. What would he give us? A liter of corn and a handful of salt. That is all. Some days he would give a little more, but that was all. If we protested, he would threaten us with the police. Sometimes the police did come and beat Guarijíos who weren't obedient. This Sainz was a bad man. Now he is dead. We have the land." There was no note of triumph in Lorenzo's face. Guarijíos are not given to gloating over victories. The older ones have too many bitter memories of starvation, of brutality, of pain and loss. Gloating is for schemers.

Lorenzo pointed out the different mountain ranges that came into view as we plodded up the slopes: the Sierra Charuco to the southeast, the Sierra Petaquito and Sierra Puerto Amole[2] to the east; the Sierra Rancho Viejo, Sierra de la Ventana, and Sierra García to the west. Far off to the northwest he made out the dim outline of the Sierra Oscura. He had never been there, he said. Something I would rectify, I thought.

Bavícora from above is something out of a travel brochure. A year earlier Doug and I had arrived at night and were deprived of the view from afar. The thatched huts perched precariously above the canyon on tiny flats could easily have been from a different century in a remote island in the South Pacific. The stream flowed noisily now, nothing like the stagnant pools and bare trickles of a year earlier. The hills echoed with the ding-dong of cowbells and the occasional human voice that rose from the canyon sides.

I recalled the difficulty I had had finding a flat place to put my tent on my first visit and told Lorenzo of my concern. He assured me he would find a place. Indeed he did. A small hut next to his sister's house had a wide thatched porch. Richard and I could place our tents there. The owner, Loreto was his name, wouldn't mind. He was off in Mesa Colorada and wouldn't be needing to get into his house for

Lorenzo Sujaguareña loading burro, Mesa Matapaco.

a few days. Loreto had installed a large padlock on the door, which we found reassuring in a perverse way.

From time to time I hear people from somewhere or other bragging that they never lock their doors. The implication is that where they live is crime free. Unlocked doors seem to hint at innocence, refer back to a golden age when neighbors were honest and high moral values ruled the land. Why would a Guarijío want to padlock his house? What would he have that someone would want to steal? I could only conclude that for the owner Loreto it was a symbol. He was marking his house the way a wolf would mark his territory. He could be gone for a few weeks, and the lock would remind everyone that they need not think about taking over his house or helping themselves to the contents.

We set up our tents with a fine view of the rushing stream below and a couple of Guarijío huts on the other side of the canyon. Not twenty feet away Lorenzo's sister, María Antonia lived with her husband, Juan Ruelas and her several children. We were in the midst of Guarijío life and it was very much to my liking. We fell asleep to the sounds of a

village—roosters, burros, cows, pigs, horses, rushing water— and somewhere, a strain of *norteña* music played on a tape player. The music went on nearly all night. No matter how poor rural folk are, someone seems to come up with the wherewithal to buy a cassette player and the batteries to run it. Guarijíos enjoy radio music no less than other folk.

Guarijíos awaken before dawn in the late fall months. It is harvest time. The men have their mahuechis to check and guard, to make sure the ripe masorcas are harvested when ready and are not stolen by marauding beasts or strangers. Raccoons, javelinas, coatimundis, and opossums love corn. People love it too. He who would feed his family must beat the animals to the corn and guard against theft. There are cows to mind as well—sometimes they break into mahuechis and undo many months' work and a year's worth of corn. Often the Guarijíos take all-day trips to Mesa Colorada to buy and sell, or to Rancho Nuevo to exchange. There is no time to waste. In Mesa Colorada, where there is a store (and a larger one in Burapaco only a couple of miles away), men spend a lot of time sitting around. Not so in Bavícora.

kilometers of very rough trail with nearly four thousand feet total elevation gain. Its steepness is compounded by the tendency of the stones that cover the trail to be round and bedevil the placement of the human foot. Climbing up a trail covered with these stones is something akin to running uphill on a surface of ball bearings. At seventy years of age José had done it alone, leaning on his walking stick, with no more thought than if he had been walking to a store.

I thought long and hard about José's small stature. Many Guarijío men are short and thin. I can't recall any that reach six feet in height. The reasons are probably partly genetic, partly nutritional. In a 1992 study of children attending Guarijío boarding schools (Palacios E. et al. 1996), researchers from El Colegio de Sonora found two-thirds of the children studied to be below normal weight for their age. The authors attribute this to poor nutrition in early years, even though most of the children were born after the establishment of the Guarijío ejidos. The small stature of many Guarijío men may be a reflection of the poverty in which Guarijíos have lived for many decades, perhaps even centuries. Even if their stature also contains a strong genetic component, it may reflect a selection favoring small body types in an environment where food is chronically scarce and the terrain punishes excessive weight. As Guarijío nutrition improves, perhaps Guarijío size will increase as well. In the meantime, their diminutive size is probably an advantage.

For all his eccentricity, José is highly respected by Guarijíos. He is widely regarded as the most knowledgeable concerning plants. Cipriano credits José with being the first Guarijío to sound the note of rebellion when they had no land of their own, when they were being held as virtual slaves by ranchers:

The real fight was begun by Mr. José Ruelas, a comrade from the zone of Bavícora. He has always been a chanter for the tuburi, and that's how he came to be acquainted with Edmundo [Edmond "Ted" Faubert], a fellow who came here asking us about our customs and what sorts of things we did. This Edmundo took Mr. Ruelas with him to many places to sing for a tuburi. Then he told him how he might go about organizing the Guarijíos, so that we could have could begin the struggle for our land. It was José who sought everybody out to urge us to fight. He went to Mochibampo and explained the importance of struggle to [the late] José Zazueta. He came up here to my village of Los Conejos to

José Ruelas eating *chichihuó*, Bavícora.

We were up with the first light. I boiled coffee on a tiny gas stove much to the amazement of some onlooking village lads. Before long we were ready, and Lorenzo, as he had promised, was prepared to lead us up the canyon. Then up walked none other than José Ruelas, staggering along leaning on his walking stick. He greeted us nonchalantly. "José," I asked incredulously, thinking of the arduous hike, "How on earth did you manage to make it here?"

"Oh, I got in this morning," he said casually. "I left yesterday morning. I would have made it last night, but there wasn't any moon, and I lost the path. I wound up in a mahuechi."

"So where did you spend the night?" I asked him.

"Right there. I just put my blanket down and went to sleep. I didn't have any water, but I had a few tortillas left. In the morning I saw where I was and walked in. Are you ready to go up the canyon?"

I agreed, of course. And I would be delighted to pay the old guy. From Mesa Colorada to Bavícora is at least thirty inform us that Edmundo wanted to help us. And help us he did. He informed the President that here we were, the Guarijío people. He even took us to Mexico City, to the President's home, but he wouldn't let us in. (Buitimea Romero and Valdivia Dounce 1994:32, translation mine)

Edmond Faubert was the Canadian who found his way into Guarijío country in 1975 to study Guarijío art and wound up working with the Guarijíos to gain control over their lands (see chapter 3). Cipriano credits José with being the first Guarijío to urge his fellows to unite and take up the fight for land. This tiny fellow who at times appeared no more than a caricature of a leader, persevered. He urged, prodded, goaded, and shamed his Guarijío brothers and sisters into a determined struggle.

His fame did not go to his head. José has been a true Guarijío, never wanting to remain long in one place, always living at the brink of economic destitution. I've seen him in San Bernardo, at San Pedro, and here at Bavícora. He travels leaning on a staff and toting a tiny bag containing a water flask, a small supply of tortillas, and a thin cotton blanket. As a result of his nomadic activity, he is known throughout the Guarijío country. His unannounced arrival in one settlement or another evokes no cries of surprise, for everyone knows that he is likely to show up at any time. He is usually provided with food and a roof under which he lays out his blanket. I saw him once arrive at a settlement and without a word of greeting, approach the family's water olla, take a long drink, and sit down. Then he began talking with the family.

In 1998 a small Catholic church was built in Mesa Colorada under the leadership of a North American priest stationed in Yécora in the Sonoran Sierra Madre. In 1999 the priest appointed José Ruelas as guardian and custodian of the church. José is proud of the modest new building with block walls and a galvanized metal roof. Without any sign of self-importance, he showed me the sanctuary, first unlocking the swinging steel doors that were chained together. He knelt at the open doorway and made the sign of the cross. He did this not by rapidly tapping himself on forehead, shoulders, and chest as done traditionally, but with an open palm facing away towards the altar. He made a slow, sweeping outline of the cross. Without a word he proceeded to the front of the church, knelt and repeated his idiosyncratic self-crossing. Then he stepped to the many icons and statues surrounding the altar and made the cross

Niece and nephew of José Ruelas, Bavícora.

for each of these. From a small box on the altar he produced a large glob of incense (resin) he had gathered from *jecahuí (Bursera stenophylla)* plus a small pouch of shavings from topocá *(B. penicillata)*. These incenses were valuable, he said. People from down below had asked him for some, for there is none available there. But he wouldn't take them much. He lit some of each sample. The fragrance was exquisite, the aroma powerful.

We exited the church. José repeated his crossings and knelt once again at the front doors before clanging the doors shut and locking the chain. José was a most conscientious custodian. I suspect, however, that his Catholicism would not meet the doctrinal requirements of most of the hierarchy of the Catholic Church. He has no idea how often a priest will visit, knowing full well that the Guarijíos must share a priest with a host of other indigenous towns in the region, including Maicoba, a Mountain Pima town a ten-hour drive away.

José Ruelas has enough friends or relatives that he can stay in any Guarijío settlement. Juan Ruelas, whose hut was next door to the porch where we tented, was a nephew. José didn't stay with Juan. He slept in two different huts while we were visiting Bavícora. His large family (his current wife is many years younger than he, and he is somewhat confused about how many children he has) seems now permanently located in Mesa Colorada. Two daughters, perhaps seven and nine years old, hug him when he sits down and follow him through the village.

José decries this sedentary life. He laments that it breeds dependence on merchandise and stores. The young people don't want to walk any more, he complains. They ride horses or mules. Or ride in trucks to Alamos or the cities. Bad. They lack respect. They listen to music on radios. They sit around.

He sports a shock of salt-and-pepper hair, a thick mass that would be the envy of most men his age. He wears his years well, complaining only that he cannot see things at a distance to his liking. He has a sharp chin that he juts forward when he is thinking or peering at someone. This bestows a look of dignity upon him. He wears huaraches way too big for his feet. They make him walk sort of like a duck. I couldn't be so gross as to ask him why, but it afforded his feet a good deal more protection than the normal huaraches that end at the margin of the feet. At the end of a day of seeming endless climbs and descents, his feet are fine and mine, clad in high-tech boots, are sore and sweaty.

José told me that when he was about forty years old he had a severe fall and fractured the tibia of his right leg. He was alone in the monte at the time, and no help was available. He bound his leg tightly, using a wild vine, and somehow hobbled to his home, many miles away. The break healed poorly, and to this day the bone juts out of his shin as he willingly demonstrates. He walks with a decided limp, which is not noticeable when he is drunk, for his stagger conceals the limp, or when he is sober, for there is so little flat land in Guarijío country that one is nearly always ascending or descending, which conceals limps. He complains that the injury hurts when he goes on long walks. I can't imagine anyone walking with such a ghastly injury.

He is one of the more well traveled Guarijíos. He has visited Hermosillo several times, as well as Mexico City and Guadalajara. He expresses little interest in returning, however. He would prefer, he says, to remain in the lands where he grew up and roam around, seeing the people he knows, and living as much as possible off the land. He takes much pleasure in gathering foods as he meanders— chalates, chichihuós, chocolás, etchos, guayparines, igualamas, *negritos* (small tree with edible fruit), papaches, *tunas* (prickly pear fruits), and so on. Some require frantic digging, others need cooking. The best kind are those that can be eaten right off the tree.

In spite of his responsibility as custodian of the church, José shows little interest in religion. Although he is nominally Catholic (as are all Guarijíos who have not converted to the Apostolic Church of Faith in Jesus Christ), he pays little attention to dogmas and liturgy. His signs of the cross are rituals he enjoys, but, I think, primarily because he considers rituals important. He has been a cantador for the tuburada and says he will always be one again when the right time comes, when someone asks him "José, we need you for the tuburada."

Lorenzo, on the other hand, is an avowed evangelista. His conversion was a quiet one. Did he feel that the evangelistas were treated fairly by other non-hermanos? No, he rued. His friend Ramón Hurtado, a pastor in the church, was not allowed to preach or build a church in Mesa Colorada. Why? I asked. It was Lino, the governor, he said. Lino didn't like what Ramón preached. Lino liked to drink *vino* (bootlegged mezcal) and brew tepachi. He didn't want anyone interfering with that, so he wouldn't allow Ramón to preach. In Mesa Colorada Lino's word was law. Democracy hasn't quite made it to the Guarijío ejidos, at least when it comes to rules and regulations.

Being an evangelista means being a different kind of Guarijío. While abstaining from alcohol is the most important requirement, the converts also take on the beliefs of fundamentalist Protestant Christianity. They warn of the sneaky presence of the devil, the imminence of the end of the world, and the harshness of the final judgment. Their code includes the behavioral austerity of a Puritan: worldly pleasures are to be eschewed, including smoking, gambling, adultery, fornication, dancing, and participation in pagan festivals like the tuburi. They are fierce capitalists, anti-Communists, and endorsers of patriarchy. I knew the ideology well, for I was raised in Methodist piety and felt curiously sympathetic with the virtues the evangelistas espoused.

Lorenzo might buy into evangelismo, but José wasn't going to, or anything else that might crowd into his options and limit his wanderings. He is too free a spirit, too much his own man to be anything but a Guarijío. For José that includes spending a goodly amount of time brewing or drinking tepachi, or drinking any kind of alcohol-based liquid he can get his hands on. When Richard and I took him for our "test" in a canyon near Mesa Colorada, he carried a hip-contoured pint bottle containing a few inches of clear liquid. He kept the bottle well guarded, stuck

José Ruelas observing corn harvest, Bavícora.

into his belt and tucked under his shirt. Every half hour or so he took a pull from the bottle. To our inquiring looks he offered the explanation that the vino helped him to keep from getting sleepy. It will be a cold day in Hell before José converts to evangelism, I suspect.

So here was José at our doorstep in Bavícora, unannounced and unassuming, hoping, we thought, to be retained as a guide by us once again. We had no choice, but he was welcome at any rate. Indeed, I was ecstatic about his arrival. He had shown that he knew a good deal about plants and was an encyclopedia of Guarijío lore to boot. He was entertaining as well. José (when he is sober) is the sort of fellow you want to have around. In short, José is a kick in the pants to have along on a trip.

Just above Bavícora the canyon of Arroyo Bavícora splits. The north fork, called El Potrerito, cuts back deep into the Sierra Charuco. We worked our way up the south fork, a canyon called Los Plátanos on Mexican topographical maps. It was necessary first to climb far up the south hillside for about a mile before descending into the deep canyon. The canyon bottom was a mass of huge boulders, sheer dropoffs, and a succession of impassable outcrops. We had to bypass all of those.

We pottered up the trail, inviting José to give us lectures on the plants, which he was more than willing to do. Lorenzo listened as though he was part of the audience, adding comments only occasionally. At one point José pointed to a vine and traced it to where it disappeared in the earth. At that point I lent him a trowel. He dug frantically and unearthed a tuber remarkably similar to a sweet potato. "This is a very good food, this *chichihuó*" he assured us. "On the way back I'll dig you some more."

As we descended into the dark canyon, a Guarijío came hurrying down the trail behind us. He smiled as he approached. I stared at him. It was Ramón Rodríguez, the very Guarijío who had been too drunk to guide us on this trip a few days before. Here he was again, having walked more than thirty kilometers from his home, heading up the very trail I had hoped he would have guided me on. What in the world were these Guarijíos up to?

Ramón and our guides exchanged pleasantries. Then he was off. He smiled what appeared to me to be a sheepish grin, bid a hasty and pleasant goodbye. Then he hurried on and disappeared into the canyon and on up into the great mountains above. I asked Lorenzo what Ramón would be doing up there. He mumbled something about a mahuechi. The real answer, though, was that he was probably going to work on an illegal harvest that paid far better than any work he could get in Mesa Colorada. So: Ramón was willing to walk the nearly seventeen miles plus whatever the distance up into the mountains to find work. He would be a knowledgeable fellow, indeed. Damn, if only he hadn't been drunk.

The canyon bottom was dark and moist, obscured by the towering rock walls and mountain peaks above and the shade of the huge trees below. Richard and I wandered among the giants, noting what grew, asking our guides what the Guarijíos had to say about them. There were *arbolillos*, bebelamas, chalates, chunas, guasimillas, *joyarís, laurelones,* and torotes. We wandered inexorably upward, stumbling on every other step as we craned our necks to make out the crowns of the trees. Gradually I realized that our guides showed a reluctance to go farther. I asked them, was there some reason not to venture farther up? "Well," Lorenzo said, "We're not from here, and we don't know what it is like up there."

José added, "There's nothing different up there. Everything you will see you will find here."

Obviously I wasn't going to buy that. If he didn't know the place, how did he know everything upstream would be the same?

"Is there something unsafe? Are there bad people up there?" I asked. They mumbled some vague answer.

Richard and I wandered up the canyon anyway. The trees were bigger and different the farther we went. Among colossal boulders and waterfalls grew gigantic *camuchines,* jecos, tepeguajes, and strange palms, and a host of tropical vines and shrubs. We were in a botanical paradise.

I looked back from where we had come. Lorenzo had re-mained behind, ostensibly to guard our daypacks, which we had left alongside the trail. José followed dutifully, but at a distance. His job was to guide, and he took it seriously. He was guarding me as though I were his personal charge. He continued to glance around nervously. I asked him again. "José, do you think it is dangerous up there?" He looked around, uncertain of what to say. I called to Richard, who was photographing a rare laurel tree. "I think our friends are scared and want to go back," I said in English. "It looks as though we could venture into poppies or mota any minute." Richard agreed, reluctantly, for he was engrossed in the

exotic plant life but was perhaps moved to beat a retreat by his discovery of some cut up sections of bright orange irrigation hose lying in the stream bed. Fragments, they were, of a military attack on someone's marijuana or poppy field.

José and Lorenzo agreed heartily when I suggested that we turn back. They appeared much relieved and became more animated when we emerged from the deep canyon back into the sunshine on the steep canyonside. José dug up more edible roots for us, excavated some for himself and stuffed them in his pocket for roasting back at the village. He gathered berries and picked fruits. He talked about the cultivation of mahuechis as we passed through one cornfield after another. He decried the dependence of the new generation of Guarijíos on the grocery stores of Mesa Colorada and San Bernardo.

That night as we were about to eat our freeze-dried supper on Loreto's *portal* (porch), he suddenly materialized. So he had come back early or hadn't gone to Mesa Colorada as the others had promised. Our tents filled his entire porch and left hardly a few inches for him to pass to the door of his hut. We had our trappings strewed all over, blocking his doorway. Without a word of objection or greeting, he smiled, pulled from his pocket a large key, unlocked the padlock, and disappeared inside the hut. Two minutes later he reappeared, locked the door behind him, nodded with embarrassment, and set off down the steep trail that led away from his hut, *his* hut. Even though we had never been introduced, I ran down the trail after him. "Look, don Loreto," I said. "I hope it was all right for us to use your portal. They said it would be fine, that you were at La Mesa. So here . . ." and I gave him some money. "This is for the use of your *portón*. Please forgive our rude behavior."

He stared at the bill, then looked at me uncertainly.

"Grácias," he said, and walked on down the trail.

When it was time to hike back to Mesa Colorada from Bavícora, José showed up early. He waited with us while Lorenzo searched for the burros and mule. It turned out that the beasts had wandered far, indeed. We had hoped to leave by 8:00 A.M. Lorenzo finally had them corralled and loaded by noon. He had chased the mule through the thorny forest for a couple of miles before roping it and leading it back to the village. Even with the great expenditure of energy tracking down the ornery pack animals, Lorenzo showed no sign of irritation.

As we climbed the steep trail out of the canyon, Richard noticed that José was not with us. "He'll be along," I told him. We kept looking back, as the thatched huts of the village grew tiny below us. Still no sign. Finally, as we neared the pass three kilometers away I heard a clacking sound. José was working his way steadily up the trail, banging his walking stick as he found a secure place to rest his weight with every step. Soon he had caught up with us. As we walked I noted that José took his job as a guide seriously. He never let me out of his sight. If I lollygagged, he lollygagged. If I rushed off looking at some plant, tree, or bird, he went with me. If I stopped, he stopped. If I peered up at a tree, wondering at its identity, he identified it for me without my asking. At one pass I rested to take in the view of the seemingly infinite cascade of mountain ranges in all directions. "There is where I was born," José said, pointing to the northwest. "Rancho Viejo is where I grew up. Now there are bad people there." Drug traffickers, he meant. Then he named all the ranges for me, describing them, telling me who lived there, where there was water, and where there were mahuechis. "Someday you come back, and I'll take you to all of them." I didn't protest.

We walked till well after dark, pausing for only a few minutes at the Guarijío settlement of El Saúz. There two mothers and their children were shucking corn into a large tub. Several children stared at Richard and me wonderingly. The women, proper as they should be, lowered their eyes and pretended to concentrate on their work. Once, though, I caught one catching a sneak glimpse of us, those strange outsiders. The ears of corn were mostly small, hardly more than seven or eight inches long, and were not the full-kerneled, even-rowed specimens we are accustomed to seeing; rather, they are often irregular in shape. The kernels lie in uneven rows and are of greatly varying sizes. Still, they are Guarijío corn, known to them for many decades, unlike the hybrid corns used by "los de abajo" (people from the lower country). That they had managed a crop at all in this year of very late rain, was a tribute to the hardiness of their ancestral seed and the persistence of the Guarijíos.

Behind the house a hundred or so squashes were piled into a mound. I asked the women if I might photograph the pile, and they sheepishly smiled that of course I could, wondering, I'm sure, why gringos would be interested in a pile of squash. José and Lorenzo spoke in the Guarijío tongue with the women, for the men were out working their mahuechis. After only a few pleasantries we sped off, not wanting to make the treacherous descent to Matapaco after dark.

Prior to the formation of the Guarijío ejidos, El Saúz had been claimed by one Andrés Rosas, a mestizo, who exercised his dominion over some seventy-five hundred acres of land (Faubert ca. 1977). When the lands he occupied were adjudicated to have been national, not private lands, Rosas fled and, it is reported, died soon after. Two Guarijío families took over the ranch house (with backing from other members of the ejido) and live there still.

El Saúz is a tough place to eke out a living. While an arroyo flows modestly during periods of rain, it usually dries up for a good part of the year. The permanent water source is a dug-out spring, meticulously maintained, a half kilometer from the ranch house, plus an ephemeral well and a large tank that stagnates during the dry season. The elevation of El Saúz at nearly two thousand feet leaves it subject to frost in the winter. The soil of the small valley to the northeast is thin and stubborn. Even so, the Guarijíos appear happy to battle with the land to produce corn, beans, amaranth, and squashes. Poor though they may be, the Guarijíos of El Saúz appear to be immeasurably better off than when they were peons of Andrés Rosas.

The sun set just as we managed the steep climb to the pass called Puerto Saucito, dropped over the southern side, and left the pines and oaks behind. Darkness set in and an hour later we were still descending, Richard riding the mule now, Lorenzo in front driving the burros. I feared for the old man's safety, but he maintained his steady pace, his walking stick ever tap-tap-tapping on rocks. He walked serenely, unhurried, apparently unfazed by the enveloping dark. I staggered on.

We made camp in a corral, the only flat place for miles and the only place the pack animals could be enclosed. Richard and I stamped down the stiff stumps of dried-out weeds, laid down tarps, set up our tents, mattresses, sleeping bags, table, and chairs. I lit stoves, boiled water, cooked supper, and organized my things. Richard did the same. José nibbled on some tortillas. Then he laid out some gunnysacks, stretched out on them, covered himself with his blanket and was asleep hardly before Richard and I had our tents put up. Lorenzo followed suit and the two were snoring before I had the dishes washed.

For remote camping, I try always to carry a folding table and chair (for note-taking and eating), a camping stove, gasoline, pots, dishes, flatware, lantern, tent, pad, pillow, sleeping bag, rainwear, global positioning system locator, binoculars, two knives, plant press, headlamp, spare batteries, first aid kit, shaving kit, notebooks, maps, water purifying pump, bottles, books, spare boots, plus ridiculous amounts of clothing and food. Guarijíos carry a blanket, gunnysacks, tortillas, and water. They sleep better than I.

José slept late in the morning. I was already up, boiling coffee for everyone. When he awoke, he rose shakily, folded his blanket and the burlap on which he slept, and ate some tortillas. Soon he was snooping about the corral, studying the grasses and dead weeds that survived in the trampled enclosure. Presently he brought a nearly seedless, withered stem of a tall grass to me. "This one used to be important for us," he said in a pedagogical fashion. "We call it *masayá*. Up here everyone used to eat the seeds made into tortillas. But you had to eat the tortillas hot; when they cooled off they would taste bitter."

He explained how the seed heads of the grass ripened before corn, how the Guarijíos would gather the seed in the field, winnow it, and carry it home in *morrales* (hand bags). It was a useful, good food, he said. Then he grew indignant. Nowadays, people are too lazy, too spoiled to gather the masayá. The young people, especially, don't want to expend the effort to gather seeds. They only want to listen to music and buy things in the store. I admired José's conservatism. He was right about the youths of Mesa Colorada and Guajaray. They didn't work as hard as those of the Sierras. Maybe it is because there isn't the opportunity, but his criticisms are well taken.

Richard was energized by José's revelation about the masayá. He considered it to be a wild progenitor of a domesticated grass *(Panicum hirticaule),* which once formed an important source of grain for Guarijíos (Nabhan 1985).

The steep descent to the river—two thousand feet in three miles—was tiring for José. For the first time, he complained of being weary. His leg hurt where he had broken it decades ago. In the climb over Masopaco he rested frequently. At one point I looked back and failed to see him. I waited: still no José. I walked back up the trail to a pass, hoping to spot him. Still no sign. I was about to return to the river when I turned and looked ahead. Far in the distance I saw Richard, Lorenzo, and the burros halting at a gate. Opening a gate for them was José. Somehow, he had taken a shortcut and slipped by me. I shook my head, marveling at his endurance.

At Mesa Colorada, nearly all the men were drunk. Whenever a new shipment of Maseca (corn meal for tortillas, a gift of the government) comes in, a good portion of it winds up being mixed with sugar and fermented into a foul-looking, cloudy corn beer. It is intoxicating, but only if substantial amounts are drunk, which often makes for a terrible mess. That was evident at Lino's place. To the governor I made a

Grassland and José Ruelas, Mesa Matapaco. Trees are primarily *negrito, Vitex pyramidata.*

contribution for the use of the ejido's burros. He was sufficiently intoxicated that he did not respond, but his wife, who stood behind him watching over the store's books, did. She accepted the money eagerly. Lino refused to let me leave until I had signed the guest registry. I moved to leave, but he called to me. "David," he said, motioning to me trying to sound imperious. "Come back."

I went back to him with a touch of exasperation.

"You forgot to write down your telephone number."

José Rodríguez, a friend and former guide, had been drinking with Lino. He staggered over and embraced me, offering me a pull on the plastic jug full of the cloudy *tepachi.* I humored him and detached myself as diplomatically as I could. José Ruelas was at my side, waiting patiently. I paid him. He looked puzzled, stretched the bills out one by one and stared at them. His face slowly phased into a smile of pleasure as he calculated the sum. I could hardly bear to watch as he walked past Lino and José who were quite drunk and stepped gingerly over another fellow who had passed out on the ground. José passed up the jug of tepachi. He ordered a Coke instead from Lino's wife and walked off with it, to my great relief.

I walked with Lorenzo to his home and met his wife and children. They were a friendly lot, happy to see their husband and father home again. I paid him. He also looked at the bills. "One thing, David," he said in his quiet voice.

"What is that?" I answered.

"When you return will you bring me a headlamp, like the one you have?"

How could I not?

10
The Mahuechi

Ignacio "Nacho" Ciriaco, Guajaray.

Nacho is so short that natives in the area refer to him as "Chapo"—"Shorty." I had known Nacho for several years before he let on that he was a pascola dancer. But then Guarijíos are not given to self-promotion. I didn't realize he was a dancer because I had never asked him, and he would never volunteer that information or anything else. He lives in Guajaray, has lived there ever since he was a small child, probably since about 1935. At that time there was no road. I should say there were many caminos –footpaths and pack trails that led in all directions. Then and now an extraordinary network of public and private pathways links all *ranchos,* rancherías, and pueblos of the sierras. But there was no *carretera,* what we would call a road for vehicles. The nearest motor route ended in San Bernardo, a hard day's walk away, and even today a four-hour drive.

Nacho grew up as a peon on a ranch, a virtual slave. The land he worked rightfully belonged to Guarijíos, but the rancher claimed it and used the police to keep the Guarijíos in line. In 1976 Nacho became an ejidatario of Ejido Guajaray, which includes mestizos. He still marvels that he now has his own land.

Nacho had guided me several years earlier as one of several men from Guajaray I retained to show a group of gringos the Arroyo Guajaray. We had ventured into the area to study plants and geology. Two other guides on that trip were more assertive than Nacho. I concluded that he contributed little, so I casually dismissed him as a guide because of his silence. That was my mistake, my presumptive arrogance. A couple of years later I tried to hire him as a guide again, but this time he was busy putting a new palm thatch on his hut and couldn't leave. I asked him then where the palm leaves for the thatch on his house came from. He pointed to the distant mountains— "There," he said, "it's a two-day trip with burros." Then I knew I had to talk with him some more.

For some reason I thought of Nacho one night while I was camped along the Río Mayo, far from Guajaray. I imagined his shy smile, his compelling face with its grim, determined jaw accenting his expression, always with a few days' growth of white beard. I thought of his humble demeanor. As I thought back on that previous trip it dawned on me

that he had contributed a lot more than I had initially recalled. I had mistaken his taciturn behavior for lack of knowledge. Stupid of me. Dumb, and arrogant. A couple of times Nacho had recalled information about plants that the others had forgotten or had never known in the first place. A rule for ethnologists: never take silence as a sign of ignorance. Never assume. Change your ways, get humble, persevere.

The following morning I asked Manuel Rodríguez, who was my guide at the time on the upper Río Mayo, if Nacho would make a good guide. He nodded emphatically. *Sí, sí.* Nacho "Chapo" Ciriaco knows very much. And he knows many of the old Guarijíos. Everybody respects him. *Muy buena gente* (He's a good fellow).

Getting to Guajaray hasn't gotten easier over the years. The channel of the Arroyo Guajaray itself is carved from the volcanic material roughly two kilometers thick— andesites, rhyolites, rhyolitic tuffs, and ignimbrites—that cover the Sierra Madre Occidental. Huge hills and mountains, primarily of rhyolite and of volcanic tuff—rock formed by heavy falls of moist ash—cover the region. None of these regions are high by Rocky Mountain standards (the highest point in the region is barely eight thousand feet in elevation), but they are based at near sea level. They are also torn, dissected, and convoluted. Rock outcrops protrude on all sides—cliffs, sheer walls, spires, monoliths, and ramparts. Where there is no naked rock, the hills are covered with dense tropical deciduous forest.

Any road traversing the Guarijío country must negotiate these rocky slopes and the forest that grows out of them. Since the area contains little if any economically valuable resources, the government has seen no reason to invest the large sums of money necessary to blast roads through the sheer rock. The few roadways that penetrate the region are little more than tracks up the hillsides. Only occasionally have bulldozers or explosives been used and only when the terrain absolutely required them. To make the rough places in the road passable, the government of the Municipio of Alamos pays natives a few dollars a day to fill the holes, shoveling with dirt borrowed from he roadsides. Immediately after this work is accomplished, the roads are comparatively smooth. The superficial tranquility soon erodes away, however. Gravity and the work of truck wheels grabbing for traction tear the loosely tossed soil from the steep roads. Any soil particles left behind are dissolved and rivuleted away by the first rain that comes along. Following the heavy winter rains of 1990, Guajaray was isolated for nearly a month when the torrents made the road impassable—in many places yawning, eroded gaps in the rock and in others mud bogs the consistency of cream cheese.

The track from San Pedro to Guajaray covers only eight kilometers but takes more than an hour to drive and includes seven barbed wire gates that must be opened and closed. I think it is nearly as quick to walk there from San Pedro using shortcut trails, than it is to ride there. Cipriano lives not far away, as I came to know, and he walks to Guajaray in little more than an hour. On the other hand, the road builds a certain suspense as it approaches Guajaray. It caps out over a ridge and the tiny village comes into view far in the distance, a few minute buildings on a treeless plain created over the years as pasture for Guarijío livestock.

Nacho was not at home when I stopped by his place. His open palm-thatched dwelling is easy to find. It is the most attractive home in the village, built with palms burroed in from a canyon more than a day's walk from the village. His daughter, who spoke remarkably good Spanish, nodded toward the monte and said he was out there collecting firewood. She would tell him we wanted him to guide us and would send him down the arroyo to our camp.

Guajaray—perhaps thirty rustic houses plus a school spread over a large area—sits on a "hanging" valley, a mesa of sorts that tilts to the north, then drops rapidly to the canyon bottom. The camp I have used several times is on a sand and gravel bar next to the river, a good mile away and a couple of hundred meters below Nacho's house. A half hour after Richard and I had pitched our tents, he showed up, walking the familiar high stepping, smooth as silk gait of the Guarijíos. He's shorter than many Guarijío men, no more than five feet two inches tall and wiry, probably weighing no more than 120 pounds. He greeted me with the gentle Guarijío handshake. He would lead us anywhere we wished. We talked of canyons, mountainsides, mahuechis, and mesas. I suggested the first visit be to his mahuechi. He was pleased with that. He pointed it out, far up on the huge mountainside on the far side of the river. Only a tiny portion was visible from our camp, but from Guajaray, where the view is more open, it is clearly visible as a yellow blotch in the immensity of vegetation—green in the summer and fall, gray-brown in late winter and spring.

Early the following morning Nacho was there. He arrived noiselessly and waited until I noticed him to say a word. We left his twenty-year-old son Wenceslao to watch over our camp, not so much from fear of thieves, I explained, as from marauding cows and burros, any of which could trample our tents and trappings in a jiffy. I recalled camping in the Sierra Madre with a group of gringos when a cow wandered into the camp while we were gone and showed no respect for a guy line holding up one woman's tent. It snapped like a thread and the tent was badly damaged. Nacho agreed with my assessment, adding that young lads might happen by and throw rocks at our carryall. There were yoris about, he reminded us.

Nacho, Richard, and I wandered for a while along the shoals of the river. Nacho described at length the plants we saw. He told us how to construct a weir for catching fish and what plants to use. He demonstrated how he had once peeled strips from the outriggers of a great fig tree to bind a broken bone. He slashed a piece of bark from another small tree and collected the sap that poured from the wound like so much blood, demonstrating how to apply it to cataracts in the eyes.

Nacho clearly enjoyed telling us what we were seeing. He would warm to the subject, not at all the quiet, retiring fellow I had remembered. He was as curious about us as we were about him. Why were we there? What was the United States like? Most of all, he was eager to show us his mahuechi, his greatest pride, the product of his hands, the source of sustenance of his family. It was close by, he assured us, no more than a half-hour walk up the trail. We would find different plants there from what we found along the river—tubers, roots, weird fruits, and the like.

We waded across the stream, removing our boots to keep them dry. It hurt my feet something awful. I'm a pretty good hiker, I always tell myself. I can follow the Guarijíos for the most part, and keep up with them, even though I tire before they do. But I am a woeful tenderfoot when it comes to wading. The bed of the Guajaray is a clue to the region's youthful origin, as Gentry long ago noted. The

Nacho Ciriaco demonstrates use of fig bark for alleviating sprains.

the steep slopes, often with heavy burdens. They would surely make excellent bicycle racers, for those are the very muscles that make for good climbers among cyclists. Their descending muscles are equally developed; for every steep ascent an equally steep descent remains. And there are many in Guarijío country, which make for powerful legs on the folk who go up and down for a living.

This constant exertion keeps them remarkably physically fit. Nacho and I were wandering through the bush one day when we came upon an enormous fig tree he called *nacapulín*. I wanted some leaves to preserve as specimens, but the lower ones were a good twenty-five feet off the ground. "Nacho," I said to him. "Do you see any way we can get some of those leaves." I thought of something like a bola, or many balls connected by string. When whirled and thrown, they gyrate wildly and will loosen some leaves when they strike a tree. The trouble was, we had no string and no appropriate spheres. Nacho looked at me with a grin. "You want leaves from the *nacapulín*? I'll get you some." With his machete he lopped off a ten-foot bacote of batayaqui, sheared off the branches, leaving only a six-inch hook at the apex. Then, shedding his huaraches, he chose a leafless berraco tree underneath the great fig. He grabbed the eight-inch thick trunk with his free hand and placed a foot flat against the smooth bark. Like a South Sea Islander climbing a coconut palm, he scampered more than ten feet up the tree, his powerful semi-prehensile toes gripping the bark. When he was within grabbing distance, he raised the bacote and snagged a couple of branches. With a vigorous jerk he snapped them off and they fell to the ground. He shinnied back down and handed me the leaf specimens. The entire operation had taken less than two minutes. Nacho was sixty-seven.

Watching us as we waded clumsily across the stream, Nacho gave no hint that he was aware of the physical edge he had over us, though he knew we were a decade younger. It was as though he expected us not to be able to keep up because we were blancos, outsiders who didn't know the Guarijío way. When we had replaced our boots, he led us up the slope. He was right about the distance to his mahuechi. It was but a half-hour brisk walk from the river. An elevation gain of perhaps five hundred feet. We ate lunch below the ancient trinchera that demarks the lower portion of the field. He has no idea how old that rock wall is, only that some old timers made it long before wire was available for fencing. All of the wild Guarijío country is lined with these ancient, anonymous bulwarks that snake up and down hillsides like dark brown miniature Great Walls of China.

riverbed harbors no sand to pad the feet, and precious little gravel, either. The bottom seems nearly everywhere lined with cobbles and even larger rocks, all of which are covered with moss. Some are smooth, which makes them all the more slippery and treacherous, as if they had been lubricated with axle grease. Others are jagged, which makes them dangerous. One of my friends once slipped on a rock while crossing the Guajaray and gashed his head badly on a rock. To this day he bears a mean scar on his temple. I wanted none of that, either, so I moved with excruciating caution. Every step hurt. I was forced to pause each time I moved a foot forward to make sure I would not slip or something would bruise my wimpy feet. It took me more than five minutes to traverse the thirty yards of the ford. Nacho, his pants rolled up above the knees and his huaraches thrown over his shoulder, covered the same distance in a minute. He waited patiently on the other side while Richard and I staggered across.

Nacho's rolled-up trousers revealed a characteristic I have noticed on many Guarijío men: they have bulging calf muscles, over-developed due to their constant climbing up

The trincheras are impossible to date, but the stability of the walls and their uniform dark color hint that they must be more than a century old. I find these old walls as satisfying as fine old churches. Enormous effort and skill went into them so that they would withstand the relentless heating and cooling, the fierce rain and wind of las aguas, and the remorseless penetration of creepers and lichens. Did Guarijíos of old build them to protect their mahuechis? Or were they some other sort of marker?

Richard and I munched on stale bagels while Nacho chewed tortillas. I asked him what he would eat if they had no food at home. Were there things around where we sat that would keep him alive?

He nodded and finished his tortilla. Grabbing a steel bar he had brought, he went to a moist bank adjacent to the arroyo where he began to dig. Shortly he produced a chichihuó the size of a parsnip. In the same way he located a chocolá root and a *raiz de pochote*. He chewed on all three. These were foods they could always rely on. The zanzaro root that Manuel had dug up for us near Jogüegüe was not for us, he stated solemnly. It was a favorite food of javelinas and could be fed to pigs, but wasn't much for people. Richard and I exchanged glances, recalling the slimy texture and weird flavor. Had Manuel been playing a joke on us when he touted zanzaro as a food?

I wondered if a man could survive on these roots and other wild foods. Nacho nodded. "Well, we do, you know. But we still have families to feed, and it is very hard to gather enough food to feed all the little ones. And the women must cook; they can't spend their days wondering in the *monte* for roots and greens."

Nacho's mahuechi is perhaps five acres in size. The slopes approach 100 percent grade, so steep that we were panting by the time we reached the upper portion. Did he ever fall off? I asked. He laughed heartily at this. No, he never had. I wasn't altogether joking, for one could roll a good ways down that hillside and get badly scratched up, I thought. The top of the field was a good two hundred feet higher than the lowest point. It was overrun with a couple of dozen different weeds and small trees, most of which would have to be eliminated before Nacho could plant. Some of them would be eaten by an ejido cow or a goat he would bring up some day to graze the weeds down. What the livestock wouldn't chew up would require more decisions. Some of the most stubborn weeds he would burn. Some he would simply leave, figuring they would not interfere. The field was far too steep to plow, and he has no desire to make it resemble a carefully crafted English garden. The important thing for him is the successful germination of the seed and a productive harvest.

I saw one distinct advantage of the slope: Nacho will never need to stoop in order to work the soil, to weed, thin, or harvest. For cultivating, he could face upslope and hoe straight out in front of him. For harvesting he could face downslope and easily pick the tallest ears of corn.

We wandered through the mahuechi and talked about his crops. He planted corn, beans, and squash, sometimes watermelon. Corn was the most important. He saved enough seed each year for the next year's planting.[1] Every few years he would alter his seed, exchanging corn with another Guarijío, both perhaps benefiting from the resulting broadened genetic pool. This last year had been a bad one. He and his family had eaten all the corn from the mahuechi by early January. Now he had only his seed left for the next summer. Would he ever have to eat his seed? Nacho didn't like this thought, but it was clear that that had happened to him in the past.

From what Nacho was telling me about his mahuechi, I began to see a great difference between him and José Ruelas, who he knows well. José is a traditional gathering Guarijío. He has no mahuechi, or, rather, he does not seem bound by his mahuechi, but prefers to move from one village to another, always willing to assist other Guarijíos in their cultivation in return for some of their food. José is tied to Guarijío lands. He considers them his domain. But he is not tied to any one place exclusively. One is just as likely to find him in Guajaray or San Bernardo as in Mesa Colorada where his wife lives. Nacho, in contrast, is tied to his mahuechi. It forms the center of his universe as it has for decades. The boundaries of the mahuechi may change, as the soil in one plot wears out and must lie fallow for seven years. But there will always be another plot nearby waiting to be cleared and planted. Guarijíos of José's inclinations are few. They are of the old type. Most are like Nacho, dedicating the bulk of their lives to the prosperity of their mahuechis. Yet both are Guarijíos through and through. One doesn't see many young Guarijíos like either one of them.

I asked Nacho why it was that the young people of Guajaray don't speak the Guarijío language. Several of them had come to our camp—both Guarijíos and mestizos—to gape at us. I asked them to tell me some names of animals in Guarijío. None of them knew them. "Don't you speak Guarijío?," I asked them. They looked at each other sheepishly. No, they said none of the young people in the village speak Guarijío. Only Spanish. That is what they learn in their school. They don't seem to care to learn to speak their native language.

Nacho considered my question. The young people don't speak good Spanish, either, he answered. Maybe they don't want to learn the language because they think speaking the language is backward, he thought. Some of his own children cannot understand the language. They cannot understand the tuburada, either.

"How about the tuburada. Are there cantadores?"

"Well, yes. The one in Los Bajíos is very old. When he dies there will be no more tuburadas there. And then there is José . . ."

"José?" I asked.

"José Ruelas. He is the cantador for the tuburada here in Guajaray."

I was amazed. I had known José for some time and hiked with him for many miles. He had never mentioned that he was a cantador.

"But José is old. What will happen when he dies?"

Nacho thought for a moment. "There are still two cantadores in Mesa Colorada," he said, but then added, "They are old, too. I guess in a few years there will be no more tuburadas." He smiled stoically as if this loss had to be accepted tranquilly as had so many other losses in his life.

"Then what will make the Guarijíos different from other people?" I pursued the idea.

"Nothing, I guess." He said, without sadness but, I thought, with a certain resignation.

But then he added. "There are two fellows from Mesa Colorada who might become cantadores. They know *cantos.*" That was hopeful indeed. A cantador has to know enough old folk songs to sing for two nights without repetition. If Nacho thought replacements for José were ready to take up the sonajo, it was good news indeed.

In general, though, the conversation was too sad, especially given the joy in Nacho's face at showing us his mahuechi. We plodded on through it, a hodgepodge of dried out cornstalks, bean plants, squash vines, and a huge variety of weeds, including a colorful array of wildflowers. It seemed impossible that this steep hill could sustain a family, but Nacho firmly believed it could. His was the perpetual optimism of people who have been down and come back. We sat once again and looked out at the distant mountains, the long snake of the Arroyo Guajaray disappearing among the endless curving canyons to the northwest.

"Tell me, Nacho," I said. "What time of year do you like best?"

"I like *las aguas* best," he answered without hesitation.

"Isn't it awfully hot and humid and buggy then?" I asked. I thought of the plagues of chiggers and biting flies and mosquitoes.

"Oh yes, it is hot and the bugs are bad. But it is so beautiful then. I get up before the sun and hike up here to my *mahuechi.* All day long I cut down weeds and plant and watch over the young corn shoots. I make sure that the beans and squash and watermelon are growing right. Sometimes my boys come up to help me. Oh, yes, there are *baiburines.* They make a rash around the waist and in other parts that itches terribly. Then there are *moscos* (biting flies), too. But everything is green. It is a good time. I stay up here until the sun is setting. When the corn is ripe I stay all night. This is where I like to be, here in my mahuechi. It is my land. I have to watch my corn growing."

Nacho knows full well, though, that his survival and that of all the Guarijíos is at the mercy of the rains. I asked him about the recent spate of dry summers.

"Well, many years we had no rain in July and not much in August. Las aguas never came. Those were bad years, like last year. I've already run out of corn. I don't know what we will do now." Probably have to rely on the government, on INI, I thought.

Hardships were nothing new to Nacho. Countless times he had relied on the land for food, for there had been no corn, few fish in the river, and only a few rags for clothing. I could not conceive of the poverty these people endured just twenty-five years earlier when the landlords kept them perpetually on the brink of starvation. Maybe that was why many of them are so small; maybe it is really nothing genetic, just a protective reaction to constant lack of calories in the diet. A diet chronically low in protein will affect body size, but one low in calories can result in severe disruption of development. Nacho showed no signs of the latter. He was as lithe as a deer and smart.

When we returned to our camp, Nacho wondered if we would like to visit the spring where the village water originates. He sweetened the pot by noting that there were large trees there, many sabinos and joyarí, the great Euphorbiaceous tree that flourishes in moist box canyons. Wherever the joyarí grow, there are bound to be other unusual tropical plants.

In the morning he arrived early and we set off. Richard wrenched his back and stayed behind, much to his disgust. Nacho led me across the river and back. We followed ancient and modern trails; we picked up the main camino to Mesa Colorada, ten kilometers away, then just as quickly turned off on a more indistinct route. It led us to an abandoned mestizo ranch they called El Guayabo (the guava). The owners were long gone, Nacho said without explanation. A few planted trees still grew on the ranch, but the buildings were dusty and showed the absence of people. Not far away we picked up an old roadway, a rough track where once a vehicle had driven in from way below. It was public health workers, Nacho said, come to spray insecticide to control malaria. Some people contracted the disease from time to time, but no one had recently.

We plodded on, across abandoned mahuechis once given over to raising sesame seeds for cash, but now only a jungle of short chírahui and vinorama trees with their potent thorns. Nacho led me to a large *jaiboli,* a rare agave species known for producing excellent mezcal. It was one of the few specimens left near the village, he said. Once there had been many, but too many people cut them down for food and beverage. Now one had to climb far up into the Sierra de la Ventana to find enough plants to collect. Would I like to climb up there? Would a priest like to pray? I answered silently.

At an arroyo Nacho explained where the Guarijíos gathered honey and papaches. He showed me great fig trees—one of them a nacapulín, a different kind of fig from others he had pointed out—whose fruit is superior to others. We stood under its spreading canopy of dense green. Did the tree produce a lot of fruit, I asked. "Oh, you should see all the fruits here. And the animals that come. Foxes and skunks, cholugos and raccoons, bats and parrots, and so many birds you can't even count them. We have to climb up to get the fruits. If we don't the animals will get them first. Any that fall to the ground are immediately attacked by all kinds of *animalitos*—insects, ants, bees, and other creatures. It's like a little village of animals here."

A solitary sabino, perhaps twenty meters high grew nearby. Farther up there would be many more, he assured me, many more. And there were. Many. They grew thickly, stately scions of the arroyo. A hundred yards above the last sabino, the arroyo ended abruptly in a toweringly deep cajón. The moist cliffs rose slanted over vertical. Water seeped from a variety of places. It was deliciously cool, shaded by towering joyarí and bebelamas above, a profusion of lower trees and shrubs below. A black plastic tube snaked from one of the seeps that had been cemented in and capped. This was Guajaray's water supply, carried via PVC tubing a good three kilometers to the village. It never ever went dry here, Nacho said proudly. He had been visiting this spring for sixty years. He should know.

We sat listening to the unending drip and trickle of the pure water that seeped from the many tiny springs. Urracas began scolding us. I paid them little heed until it dawned on me that they were not scolding us at all, but they were acting as watchbirds: they were warning us that someone else was nearby. Nacho was already looking around, alerted automatically by the harsh clucks of the jays.

I probably should have been alarmed by the figure that emerged from the thick brush within the cajón, for he was wearing a rifle over his shoulder. Nacho saw him before I did and nodded almost imperceptibly. On closer view I recognized the fellow as a young man from Guajaray out hunting for a venadito or *javelín.* He stopped by the spring for a drink and to enjoy the cool shade.

I had reason to be nervous, as I was about to find out. On the following trip, Richard and I were camped on the Guajaray after having arrived in the village a few hours earlier. I stopped and greeted Nacho and checked in with Eliazar Valenzuela, just to let them know we were around. Nacho would guide us the next day up the Sierra de la Ventana. We unloaded the Toyota and set up our camp at dusk beside the stream. We ate dinner in the dark, our table illuminated by a brave little gas lantern. We washed the dishes and packed things away. I was just preparing my bed in my tent, hoping for an hour or two of reading and notes when I heard heavy, rapid footsteps outside. A light shone in the tent and a youthful voice ordered *"¡Fuera!"* (Get out!) Still dressed, I unzipped the tent and put on my boots. As I stepped outside, I felt a cold steel barrel slammed against my forehead. *"Muévate tu pinche culo por allí"* (Move your fucking ass over there), the voice ordered in Spanish. Another held Richard at gunpoint. My assailant tore my headlamp from my head and shoved me to the ground. *"¿Dónde está el dinero?"* (Where is your money?), he demanded. I told him it was in my tent in my backpack.

"Get me your fucking money," he ordered. I rose slowly. He shoved the gun to my head and pushed me toward the tent. He wore a headlamp and illuminated the interior of my pack over my shoulder as I rummaged through it for my billfold. I showed it to him. Inside was about $100 in dollars and pesos. He snatched it and ordered me back to where the other was guarding Richard. Once again he shoved me to the ground. He then yelled at Richard, "Where is your money." Richard, flat on the ground, did not understand. "Where is your fucking money," he shouted again. I told him Richard did not understand his Spanish. I would find Richard's money, I said. I asked Richard in English. It was in his daypack, he said. I told the bandit.

Once again he pulled me to my feet and jammed the pistol to the back of my head. "Get the money," he ordered in Spanish. I did as he said. It took a while to find Richard's billfold, but finally I located it, the thief looking over my shoulder as he held the barrel of the pistol to my head. He snatched a wad of dollars, about $300 we later ascertained.

He ordered me to my feet. "Now, empty out your pockets." I did so. I gave him a small amount of U.S. change and a handful of pesos. I also handed over my prized Swiss Army knife.

"Where is your fucking watch?" He demanded to know.

"I don't have one." I told him truthfully. This is why I don't bring one, I thought.

He handed the knife back to me. "Put it away," he ordered.

He pushed me to the tent again and began to tell me what they planned to do. His breath stank of stale tequila and his voice was a bit slurred. He became impressed with his eloquence. I was crouched, he was immediately behind me, talking so much that I could see the barrel of his pistol pointed away. Oh, how I wanted to disarm him! I was sure I could overpower him easily. But heroism was not in order. I remained passive. He was not from around there, he lied. He bragged that he would go up to this village of Guarajay or Guajaray whatever it was and rob the store. I told him there was no store. "Well, then we'll rob the fucking Indians who just kill anyway. By the way, where are you from?"

I told him.

"Oh, I didn't know you were a gringo. Please excuse this. When I've got money from the fucking Indians I'm going to come back and give you your money back." I nodded and agreed with everything he said. I would have agreed that the earth was flat and Benito Juárez was the King of England.

Finally they decided to leave. The other assailant had said almost nothing. I had a sudden inspiration. *"Miren ustedes"* (Look), I said. "Here you are, leaving with all our money. You are leaving us with nothing for expenses. How can you do that? You should at least leave us something." I could feel Richard saying to himself, "For God's sake, Yetman, just shut up and let them go." But I was indignant. "How can you leave us with nothing?" I asked. The main assailant acted confused. "Well, how much do you want?"

"Leave us forty dollars," I asked.

The assailant looked at the roll of bills in his hand. He peeled off two and threw them on the ground. A twenty and a ten, it turned out. Then he returned, putting the pistol to my head once more. "Get in the little house," he said. I did.

"Now, lie down."

I did.

"Stay lying down. Go to sleep. We will be back early in the morning."

I agreed. They ran off. I heard heavy footbeats. It might even have been a horse or a mule. They were gone.

The night was miserable and long. In the morning I reported to Eliazar and to Nacho what had happened. They were dismayed. Thereafter I made reports to the police in Alamos. I could never again camp freely anywhere in Mexico's sierras.

But the robbery was more an unpleasant notice than a real deterrent to me. I wasn't about to let a couple of scoundrels keep me from the Guarijíos. Nearly all of Mexico is increasingly plagued by highwaymen. The road into Guajaray offers a dozen gates and countless ruts where a vehicle must come to a stop, places ideal for robbers to lie in wait, then strong-arm a vehicle when it stops or when someone leaves the vehicle to open a gate. I simply had to accept the danger and hope to survive. The Guarijíos and their lands were by now deeply in my blood and I had too much unfinished work to be deterred by young punks and their pistols.

Nacho was shocked by the robbery, even though he knows full well of the violence of which narcos are capable and the culture of violence that spins off the drug traffic. He also knows hardship beyond anything I can conceive. He told me of times when there was nothing to eat. The corn was gone. No beans, no squash. All gone. Even the roots they ordinarily relied on, pochote, *chichihuó, masasari,* for example, would not suffice. There were times of drought when the soil was hard as a rock, impossible to dig. They even went without clothes. "We worked all day for yoris, the *pequeños propietarios,* for a couple of liters of corn. That's what they called working *a medias,*"—sharecropping. Who can feed a family on a couple of liters of corn?"

Now, he says, things are better. Even so, when their corn runs out, they may have nothing to eat. Then they have to eat whatever they can scrape from the land. Children still get sick from not having enough to eat.

But Nacho accepts these facts and remains optimistic. No matter how bad things are, the Guarijíos are better off than they were twenty years ago. He now has his land. His sons can have land, if they choose. The Guarijíos can walk freely on their own land and not be assaulted on the whims of the landlords. Life is still a struggle. But the struggle is now with the land to make it produce, not with people who stand between them and the land.

140

Loreto, Chihuahua. Jesuits built a mission here in the early seventeenth century. Guaríjios live on the periphery.

11
The Highlands

The forests of the Río Mayo Basin—tropical deciduous forest (what natives refer to as *monte mojino*) in the lowlands, oak woodland and pine forests above them in the highlands—teem with plant varieties. More than three thousand plant species are to be found in the fifteen thousand square miles of the greater Mayo region, five times the number of plant species found in all of Great Britain, nearly as many as in the hundred thousand-plus square miles of Arizona.[1] For the Guarijíos (and for the many mestizos who live in the region as well) the knowledge of which plants can be used as food, which for making artifacts, dyes, medicines, fibers, lumber, livestock food, and such things is vital. The river Guarijíos live in Sonora in the monte mojino. The mountain Guarijíos, on the other hand, live in the oak and pine forests of Chihuahua. If I were to find out what plants these mountain people used and what they thought of them, I would have to spend some time among them.

At the time of my first trips to Guarijío country, I had not planned to visit Guarijíos in Chihuahua. The river people of Sonora knew them only vaguely. They had a hard time understanding the highlanders' language, they claimed. Those folk lived in the land of oaks and pines, not in the monte mojino. They never attended the tuburadas of the river people, so the Sonorans had no cultural reciprocity with the Chihuahuans. Other researches have even written that the mountain people called themselves by a different name.[2]

Lorenzo told me, though, that he had met Chihuahuan Guarijíos. He had walked once to Guasaremos two decades ago when there were still Guarijíos living there. He had visited two small villages a day's walk from Bavícora where the Guarijíos knew both the highland and the river dialects. They weren't so very different from the people of Bavícora, he said (remembering Bavicorans themselves spoke with a slightly different accent than those of Mesa Colorada, only eighteen miles away). That settled it for me. If Lorenzo had gone there, I had to go there.

There was another reason for me to venture into the highlands. In 1997, with Richard Felger's help, I received a grant from the National Geographic Society to study the plants used by Guarijíos. Part of our proposal included a

study of the Mountain Guarijíos and what they could teach us about plants. I had a second reason to venture into the Sierra Madre in search of Guarijíos.

Shortly before he died, Leobardo Quiroz had provided me with a detailed description of families in Loreto, high in a valley in Chihuahua. In those days, before he was swept away by a flood, truckloads of supplies would depart weekly from San Bernardo and make the grueling, fourteen-hour journey to Loreto where Guarijío children are schooled in an albergue. Hurricane Ismael washed out the road in September 1995. It was repaired, barely. Then Hurricane Fausto washed it out again in September 1996. And by then Leobardo was dead, and no one else had any reliable information. My notebooks were stolen by thieves who broke into my vehicle one night in Caborca. All my notes from Leobardo vanished with the theft of that precious book. I had to reconstruct what he told me from memory fragments.

The unending washouts on the Loreto road meant that San Bernardo was no longer the shipping point for goods for the albergue in Loreto. The best I could determine was that it was now necessary to reach Loreto from above, from the highlands of Chihuahua, an additional day's drive but at least much of it by paved road. The route leads over Mexico Highway 16 east of Hermosillo, climbs up into the Sierra Madre at Yécora, and winds through the wooded mountains and canyons into Chihuahua. This time I was accompanied by tree-ring specialist Mark Kaib. We turned south from the heavily forested mountains at Basaseáchic, Chihuahua, site of Mexico's highest waterfall at 235 meters, and ventured south along lumber roads. The route passes through lofty, pine-clad valleys and near Tarahumara villages where winter temperatures are freezing and summer rains bountiful. The valleys have fertile volcanic soils that yield corn, beans, potatoes, squash, and orchards of apples, pears, and peaches. And, of course, marijuana. We followed old trails outlined in dotted lines on Mexican topographical maps. I verified our locations with a satellite-controlled global positioning system (GPS), a hand-held device that has eliminated the possibility of being lost for those who combine maps and a GPS.

Exploring is not what it once was. One day soon satellite images will be available in resolutions so fine that they will virtually duplicate the landscapes taken in by the naked eye. The images will be projected from a portable computer screen. Exploration in that day will consist of verification and comparisons of landscapes. Future explorers will also have satellite-relay cellular telephones with built-in global positioning systems. They will be able to talk to anyone within the reach of a phone. At the summit of the Sierra Charuco they will follow up-to-the-minute Dow Jones stock quotes. Our imaginations, which make exploration into a quest, a novel comparison of the envisioned with the actual, will atrophy.

The fancy tools didn't make the trip any easier or smooth the road. They served only to tell us we were on the right trail. Loreto still lay more than a hundred kilometers and eight pounding hours southwest of Basaseáchic. The road dropped into semiarid valleys, then up once again into the heavy pine-oak forests of the Sierra Madre. Down and up, curving, switchback-heavy trails cracked with washouts and unforgiving rock. We met but a handful of vehicles the entire day. Once we departed from the main track, three hours from Loreto, we met exactly one vehicle, a truck from the INI on its way out from Loreto.

Loreto is an ejido of Guarijíos and yoris. It covers some fifteen thousand acres. The village lies in a rolling valley at the base of the Sierra Chuchupate, named for a small plant with legendary curative properties. The prosperous settlement consists of perhaps fifty houses spread over an expansive grassy, rolling clearing dotted with fields and pastures, a most bucolic scene. At its lower end, the valley constricts quickly into a steep canyon and opens up only intermittently below. The Guarijíos prefer to live inside the forest, away from the open meadow, while yoris live closer together in the open areas.

When we arrived, workers were swarming over a new sawmill they were in the process of installing. Someone, apparently a disgruntled former employee, had set the old one on fire. It had burned to the ground. For five years the Loreto Ejido had no sawmill, and the trees of the sierras were spared. Now a new onslaught against trees would begin. The ejidatarios' income is dependent on cutting trees. Each tree left behind represents a loss of cash. Since government regulations on cutting are *never* enforced, there are only romantic and idealistic sanctions against cutting all marketable trees. These amount to feeble quibbles in the light of practical daily needs. Tomorrow's concerns are relegated to the trash bin of sentimentality. Each felled tree represents fifty dollars or so. Each standing tree has no monetary value.

I have walked through Madrean ejidos of open, treeless valleys where thirty years ago no view was possible thanks to the density of the forest. Then logging began. The forest was not clear-cut. Only a few trees at a time were felled.

Each year a few more were taken. Only gradually did the landscape acquire an open aspect. Eventually, however, only crooked trees useless for lumber were left behind. No plan for reforestation existed. The ejidatarios did not know what they would do next. The result was time-release clear-cutting.

I found a young Loretan who understood what we were looking for: older Guarijíos who had a good knowledge of the area and of the plants. Such searches for good guides were never easy. Mestizos invariably respond to my question, "Who around here is the best person to tell me about plants that you use here?" by saying *"Mi papá"* (my father). It took a while for me to make it clear that I wanted to find older Guarijíos. At first people acted as though I was a bit daft, wanting to talk to Guarijíos, who weren't very social and didn't speak good Spanish, they thought. One fellow warned me that all Guarijíos wanted to do was get drunk. I persisted, though, and finally, made my point. I offered to pay Ismael, a yori lad, to lead us to *guarijíos viejos,* and the search was on.

Even with his help, it was discouraging. The first subject was Guillermo, who lived on the edge of town. He was a rugged old fellow perhaps in his late sixties. He looked at me blankly, then suspiciously, when I explained that I hoped he would guide us into the monte to gather plants and tell us about them. Although the pay I offered was well above what he could possibly earn, he begged off. "I don't know anything," he said. Then, as if in afterthought he mumbled *"Tengo chamba"* (I have work.).

"Look," I told him. "We are not police, we are not going to harm you. We are gringos from way off in the United States. We want you to teach us about the plants around here. Tell us what you know. We will be students, you will be the teacher."

He was not impressed. Nope. He had work to do. Try Arcadio, he suggested. "He knows more than I do and he doesn't have to work."

But Arcadio was even less interested. He eyed us with suspicion verging on hostility. He dismissed us immediately. He also had work. He had to be a watchman at the new sawmill. He couldn't possibly go with us. Try Martín, he said. Martín knew more than anyone else. We should have gone there in the first place, he intimated.

Our youthful mestizo guide shrugged his shoulders as

Mountain Guarijío country near Loreto.

we drove toward Martín's part of town. The Guarijíos were afraid, he said. They were sure we were up to no good. They never trusted outsiders, he said. Maybe they thought we were prospectors lying about what we were doing, which was really to find gold. They didn't even trust people in the town.

Getting to Martín's place was an adventure. It was nearly dark when we parked on the top of a grassy hill and started hiking from there—down into a small valley, across a wash, then up a hundred foot cliff using handholds. Ismael knew the route up the rocky face, but we didn't, and it was dusk. Nevertheless we kept up and followed right behind him, much to his surprise, I thought. After about fifteen minutes, we topped out on the cliff and panting, entered a courtyard at each side of which were shake-roofed Guarijío homes, tidy, clean, and well maintained. From the cleanly swept courtyard, we could see the entire Loreto valley and the Sierra Chuchupate towering over it. We asked for Martín and as luck would have it, he was just returning from rounding up his cows and goats for the night. I explained our quest, adopting the most submissive posture I could manage.

He eyed me up and down, looking at my white skin, hearing my proper, accented Spanish, seeing my unfamiliar but clearly upper class clothing. "No," he said. "I can't. I have *chamba*." I pleaded with him. All we needed was one day of his time. The pay was very good. He would decide where we would go and what we would talk about. He would be paid just to walk and talk with us.

It didn't work. He would not be convinced. "Try Guillermo," he suggest, "or Arcadio. They will help you." I explained that they had recommended him. He was not moved. "No," he said with finality. "I have too much work."

So we descended the cliff with heavy hearts and not a little trepidation—it was nearly dark. It had begun to appear that our arduous trip was going to be in vain.

When we reached our vehicle Ismael made a final suggestion. "Maybe we can talk to Nicolás. He lives not far away. Maybe he will go with you."

As if by divine intervention Nicolás came down the trail at that very moment, nearly hidden underneath a huge sheaf of fodder he was lugging home for his horses and cows. We followed him to his house, which was in the oaks and pines at the edge of the village, overlooking the valley. Once again I went through the elaborate explanation, trying to appear even more submissive, hoping to impress upon him that we were virtually begging for his services.

"No," he said. "I can't possibly help you. I have *chamba*. I have cows. I have a *mahuechi* to attend to. There is no time."

I pleaded with him. He wavered. "Look, don Nicolás," I argued with my most earnest diplomacy. "How about this? We'll come here early in the morning. You go with us for an hour. If you don't like the work, you tell me and we'll quit. I'll pay you and that will be all. Just give us a try. All you do is point to plants, trees, shrubs, herbs, and tell us what they are called in your language and what you use them for. That's all. You are a teacher. I am the student. I will write down what you say."

He thought for a moment. Clearly this was a good opportunity to make some easy money and, from the look of him, he could use it. *"Muy bien,"* he responded. "I'll go with you for an hour. Early in the morning."

And we were at Nicolás's place early after a fitful night of little sleep in the boys' dormitory of the boarding school where locals had urged us to say for safety's sake. Ismael had not been encouraging. "All he really wants to do is drink. That's what he does with his money." He had said. I had said nothing.

We found Nicolás waiting. He opened and closed an improvised gate on a trail. We stepped over a rock wall and set off across a small valley and into the hills. My notebook and a plant press were at the ready. I had barely met Nicolás, so this conversation was our first. He was a homely fellow in his mid-sixties, energetic, nervous, and wiry. He had a large scar on his cheek. I'd have to know him better before I could ask him about its history. He appeared anxious to get this ordeal over with. We hadn't gone a hundred yards before I stopped him under a small tree growing in a ravine. "What is this called, don Nicolás?" I asked.

He looked at it briefly. "That sonofabitch is a *guasiqui*. Sonabitch it has a fruit you can eat, sonofabitch."

"And is the wood good for anything?"

"Sonofabitch wood is for handles. We use it a lot."

Another shrub was flowering nearby. "How about this one?" I pointed to it.

He looked at and broke off a small branch, handing it to me. "This sonofabitch is *chaparita*, that's what the yoris say. We, the Guarijíos, call it sonofabitch *teguachá*.

"And what is it good for?"

"Well, sonofabitch, if a child has *pujos* [bloody stools], we take the leaves and these little berries," and he showed me green fruits the size of tiny peas, "and we grind them up. Then we make a tea from the sonofabitch and give it to children to drink. Sonofabitch works for older people, too."

Every time he used the word *cabrón,* I had to suppress a laugh. I explained to Mark just what Nicolás was saying and Mark appreciated the earthy Guarijío language as well. We moved into oak woodland, and Nicolás gave us names and uses for the myriad oaks—around twenty species grow in the region. He described the special qualities each one had, insulting each with a *sonofabitch* or two, noting which had edible acorns, which were best for firewood, for medicine, for fence posts, for building houses. Yes he had heard that lumber companies were beginning to cut down the great oak forests of the sierras, but no, they hadn't arrived yet at Loreto. Here they only cut down pines. Sonofabitch. He didn't work cutting sonofabitch trees.

And he led us on and on. For five hours we wandered down the valley, following the narrowing canyon. He showed us how he cut the bark of the Durango fir, never removing more than half the circumference of the tree so as not to harm it. That bark was his special remedy for pneumonia, fevers, and colds. All the trees in the grove bore scars where he had harvested the bark. "This sonofabitch place is where I cut. No one else. No one bothers me here. Sonofabitch." Nearby was his mahuechi. He pointed to another field he had abandoned twenty years earlier. Pines and junipers had begun to grow in the former clearing. He talked about agaves, about sarsaparilla, about maples, about alders.

Nicolás lived alone. His son and his son's wife lived in a hut adjacent to his, he said. His wife was gone, whether she was dead or had departed for greener pastures he did not say, and I was not in a position quite yet to be nosy. He was also a member of the Ejido Loreto, with full ejido rights. That meant that he was entitled to a milpa and to cut wood, gather firewood, and graze livestock as he wished. But, as I found out later, neither he nor any of the other Guarijíos in the ejido are active in ejido politics. They are marginalized both by their retiring dispositions and by the fact that the real power in the ejido lies with non-Guarijíos, the yoris. They understand laws better, they have better connections and know how to use political power. They control the new sawmill and that will be where the best jobs lie and where the most valuable trees will be sawed into lumber. The Guarijíos will probably profit very little from this or any ejido enterprise, Nicolás thought. Though their land is more fertile than the lands of the river Guarijíos, though their nutrition appears to be better, and their living conditions an improvement over those who live below, their marginalization from mestizo society is the same.

The hours with Nicolás flew by. We crossed and recrossed the stream that tumbled on its way to the Río Mayo, forty miles to the southwest. He became quite talkative after a

while. He warned us against drinking from the stream. "They throw all sorts of sonofabitch wastes into it," he complained. He told us about the old Guarijío customs, about their tuburadas, pascolas, and Easter ceremonies. There were no longer tuburadas in Loreto, he explained ruefully. There were no pascolas. Now they had to visit Tojíachi, a two-hour walk from Loreto, to participate in a tuburada. In another few years, maybe twenty, maybe fifty, there would be no more tuburadas. The young people aren't interested. Some of the children spoke the Guarijíos language, he granted, but in the schools the teachers were yoris and didn't want the kids speaking a language they and the yori children could not understand, so the children weren't allowed to speak Guarijío in the schools.

Nicolás said he had never spoken with the Guarijíos de abajo. He knew people who had, though. They reported the river Guarijíos spoke differently, but they were able to understand each other all right. Did he know any Tarahumaras? No. He never went far enough away to see Rarámuris (there is a Tarahumara settlement about four hours northwest of Loreto). He knew they had a reputation for being runners. They could run for whole days, he had heard. He himself had never run that long, only for a few hours at a time and that was when he was a younger man. Now he just walked all the sonofabitch time. All day. Every day. That's what life was for the Guarijíos.

Just after noon we returned with Nicolás to his hut (I refer to it as a hut, not to demean it, for it is nicely constructed, handsome, and well maintained, but to convey the impression of its size and its intent. Most activity takes place outside, not inside, in spite of the cold winters and chilly mornings of spring and fall). As we drew near, he became more nervous, saying he needed to check on his cow to make sure she didn't run too far away. I understood, I said, and paid him. I asked him what other older Guarijíos would be good to talk to. He suggested a fellow named Canelichi. He lived *sonofabitch* far away, though, but he was good. Nicolás was in a hurry to leave. I asked him, could I come back another time and talk with him again? He looked at the hundred-peso note I had given him and nodded with the closest he had come to a smile. "Yes," he said. "You can." And he hurried off.

As it turned out Canelichi was not a person, it was a ranch some eight kilometers south of Loreto. Other people informed us as we asked our way through Loreto, that the fellow we should look for there was an old Guarijío named Juan de Diós Zapata. He spoke the language and knew many

Tiburcio Charramoneta and the author, Canelichi.

things, Loretans assured us.

We found Canelichi. It consisted of two of the prettiest Guarijío huts I have seen in one of the fairest small valleys I have seen in all of Mexico. It was part of a private ranch owned by don Pablo Enríquez, whose house lay a kilometer down the valley. He was a distant relative, he said, of the Enríquez of Burapaco and thereabouts.

Don Pablo, an older, talkative mestizo was in his early seventies. He lived on the ranch with two sons, one of them married with a family. The ranch occupied nearly six thousand acres, much of it in heavy pine and oak timber. He had never allowed the ranch to be lumbered, he said. He allowed just enough trees to be cut to suffice for the buildings on the ranch. Other than that he enjoyed the ranch the way it was. He loved the craggy cliffs and the high slopes and the pure water of the stream. He was also proud of a couple of large trucks he had, and I figured he must have been generating a pretty decent income to be able to afford them. Guarijíos had been living on the ranch when his father bought it more than fifty years ago, he said. They were tenants, but he charged them no rent and allowed them to select plots for their mahuechis—exacting only half the crop as payment. He spoke to the Guarijíos as one speaks to children, but when I saw children come up and put their arms around him and he responding as if they were his own, I knew his relationship with them was hardly a highly patronizing one.

Don Juan de Diós was sitting on a stump when I drove up. I could see at once that he was too old to do much fieldwork, probably in his eighties. No, he couldn't help me, he said, and he was not just being shy or modest. He didn't

hear or see well. He didn't really know the names, it had been so long since he had used them. Don Pedro urged him to help us, but he shook his head sleepily. Finally a younger man convinced him, and he agreed to go into the bush with us, but mostly because the fellow was his nephew Tiburcio Charramoneta, and he volunteered to go as well.

Tiburcio turned out to be a fine fellow in his mid-sixties, serious, hard working, Guarijío thin, of medium height with soft, gentle eyes and a dark round scar on his right cheek. He reeked intelligence. He lived with his family in a well-maintained shake-roofed house with walls of freshly plastered adobe and only a stone's throw from a sparkling clean rivulet that originated in the nearby slopes of the Sierra Chuchupate. Tiburcio had children and grandchildren living with him and in another hut next door where one of his sons lived with his Guarijío wife. The children were impeccably well mannered, and appeared to be well nourished and well clothed as well. Two young girls of unsurpassed beauty carried buckets of water from the stream to their garden. Three boys rounded up livestock and chased around playing the games that boys play. They and two little girls—a parade of seven Guarijío children—hiked each week to school in Loreto, eight kilometers away, leaving early Monday morning and returning on Friday afternoon. I saw them return that first afternoon, parading down the trail lugging their books in little backpacks, their clothes neat and clean. They all smiled shyly but politely. When they had set down their packs and greeted their parents, the older girls approached Mark and me and melted our hearts as they offered their hands in the gentle Guarijío handshake. The lads came by as well, hiding their curiosity about us well. It was only when I invited them to look inside our tents that they relaxed their guard and exclaimed how strange and wonderful all our trappings were. And, of course, they were right.

I spent a couple of days at Canelichi. Tiburcio showed me how he makes soap from yucca roots. He excavated a tuber called *savalique* they roast like a potato. He cut a section of salsaparilla vine for tea. He led me on a long passage up a steep hill through virgin oak-pine forest to a glade where a few dozen bushy *sotol* plants grew. Here he harvested a sheaf of the thin, long, stiff leaves from the bushy bases. These he would take to his wife, Nicolasa to weave into a basket. He showed me a flowering sotol stalk. "Yoris call these *sotoles,* but these are different from the others. We call them *huiricos.* Do you see the seeds, David? I collect them and plant them so that we will always have enough

Tiburcio's home, Canelichi.

plants. When they get older we roast the *cabeza* [heart]. We will always have food here." We walked back slowly through the nearly silent forest, pines towering over a hundred feet above us. Giant oaks seventy-five feet tall burgeoned in open spaces where pines didn't grow. Tiburcio stopped often to explain to me the hidden lives of many plants. He grabbed handfuls of manzanita berries and munched on them. I did so as well and was surprise at their refreshing, sour-sweet taste.

Nicolasa, Tiburcio's wife, agreed to weave a basket with the sotol leaves. She is a frail, gentle Guarijío woman, born at a village named Majoy a few hours and several valleys to the east. She was orphaned early in life and was raised by a sister. In her home only Guarijío was spoken. The family lived entirely on what they raised. Their clothing was mostly rags sewn together. All the men worked as sharecroppers or day laborers for yori ranchers. But, she said, they had enough to eat and were happy. She had known Tiburcio most of

her life, and he married her when she was very young. He is sixteen years older than she.

Nicolasa was pleased with her life in the verdant, forested valley, even though she worked from dawn to dusk almost nonstop caring for her family. She sat on a straight-backed chair under the shade of a spreading willow tree and began weaving the sotol leaves. She warned me of the need to be careful when handling the leaves. She showed me the leaf blades that bear thousands of tiny serrations capable of cutting through skin like a razor. Nicolasa had woven guaris for years, an art she had taught herself since her mother had died when she was five. She was now teaching her daughters to make the baskets, lest the art be lost. As she spoke her fingers flew, and within ten minutes she had formed the base of the basket, perhaps six inches square. An hour later the product was finished, a handsome, strong rectangular container of bright green ideal for stowing pine nuts, chiles, corn, or pennies. I photographed the basket to her immense pleasure. (see p. 214)

Tiburcio raised corn and beans in his mahuechi, high on the steep slope, five hundred feet above the valley floor. It took him nearly a half hour to reach it, but the soil was good, he said. There was no room in the narrow valley for mahuechis. His would last three or four years, then he would abandon it and clear another, he said. There was ample land on the other side of the ridge, on the slopes of the next valley over, but he liked to be able to see his corn from his home. That was a good idea, I agreed. If Guarijíos were not inclined to complain, Tiburcio was even less so. He had enough food and clothing and a good roof over his head to protect him from the snow and cold of winter. His children went to school, his son had a fine wife and they had land. There was little more that one could ask for, he thought.

But he also acknowledged that he sharecropped the land. The owner, who treated the Guarijíos with respect, Tiburcio thought, received half the harvest as a "fee" for use of the land. Tiburcio's father had worked a similar arrangement with the rancher's father. Due to the land's fertility and the general reliability of the rains, he could usually count on sufficient harvest to produce a surplus even after he had provided Don Pablo with his half share. Even during the prolonged drought of 1998–1999 he had managed to produce a good crop, thanks to the fertility of the mountain soils and the soil's ability to retain moisture at that altitude.

Tiburcio's children do not speak Guarijío. I asked him about that. He was sorry they did not, he said, and hoped they could learn the language. He had wanted the children to speak Spanish so they would do well in school. (I interpreted this to mean that he feared they would be ridiculed as indios if they were known to speak Guarijío.) But now he wished the schools would teach Guarijío. He hoped his children would marry Guarijíos, not yoris. Yoris are weaker, morally and physically, he thought. "Our Guarijío blood is stronger. We have better resistance to disease and corruption. We don't fight among ourselves. Yoris are jealous of other peoples' work. They work apart from each other. They fight each other. They try to steal each other's jobs. They try to steal our jobs." I wondered how true that was and needed much more time to find out.

The Guarijíos of the sierra unite under the leadership of a traditional elder called a selyeme, what the mestizos call a gobernador or governor. Gentry had noted the authority of selyemes in the 1930s, but the term is not familiar to Guarijíos del río. I asked Tiburcio about the selyeme. He explained that the traditional authority among them is vested

in the selyeme's office. The current selyeme was named Mingo Gilaremo. He no longer lived in Loreto, but his influence extended from the nearby hamlet where he made his home. His biggest responsibility is to see that the church is well maintained. He requires all able-bodied Guarijíos to assist in work projects involving the church (or other community functions, if necessary). If those summoned by the selyeme don't show up, he arranges for them to come another day. His authority has only social sanctions, but, Tiburcio says, all the Guarijíos show up when Mingo Gilaremo asks them to. The yoris consider this system strange, but even they recognize the authority of the selyeme over the Guarijíos.

Formerly, Tiburcio said, the selyeme was in charge of tuburadas as well. But now there are no tuburadas in Loreto, so the selyeme of Tojíachi, where there are tuburadas, extends his authority even to Loreto. When Mingo dies, his authority will pass to an appointed successor.

Mingo was nearly seventy, I learned. I hoped to visit him, but he had moved (temporarily, people said) to the village of San Fernando near Santa Ana. Even so, his authority reigned in Loreto. Tiburcio was vague about succession if Mingo should die suddenly.

The office of the selyeme was still potent. It gave me hope that Guarijíos of the sierra were still serious about being Guarijíos.

I returned to Canelichi in September of 1999. The summer rains had been abundant, almost excessive. The roads were muddy and eroded from the nearly incessant rains. During the precipitous descent from the mountain pass above the village, I found that the erosion produced by logging had forced abandonment of the original steep road. A "new" road had been bulldozed across the steep hillside. It was deeply eroded and slippery. I marveled how the heavily laden lumber trucks could ascend that morass of volcanic clay.

In the valley the new sawmill exhaled a thick cloud of smoke that lingered heavily in the humid air. The slopes were crisscrossed with drag marks and freshly cut stumps protruded mutely from the torn and washed soil. It took an hour to descend into the valley. The new sawmill swarmed with workers—nearly all the ejidatarios including the Guarijíos—are employed there. Nicolás Tadeo, who had sworn (literally) that he would never work there, was stacking freshly sawed boards. Each earned 50 pesos a day (about $6).

The road to Canelichi, steep in both directions, was being heavily used by lumber trucks. The four-wheel drive Chevy I was driving spun through fresh mud up to the pass that separates the Mayo drainage from that of the Fuerte. Part of the old road had been bermed over and a new track led downward through fresh mush the texture of modeling clay. I worked the steering wheel furiously, churning though the mud and muttering that I could never ascend that oily ooze of a climb. Once I passed through the gate and onto don Pablo's land the road assumed its rough but passable texture of the previous year.

I asked Tiburcio about the lumber operation. He, after all, is an ejidatario, even though he lives on a private ranch and does not work at the sawmill. He thought the Guarijíos in general approved of the operation. They would cut down all the pines on the more than fourteen thousand acres of the ejido. After that the mill would close down. There would be no more pines, because no one was planting new ones, and there would be no seeds to guarantee a new generation of pines. The valley would suffer, but for now there was work. Guarijíos had none of the important jobs. Their work was stacking the lumber as it came off the conveyor, loading it on trucks, and helping burn the rapidly accumulating piles of sawdust.

Tiburcio thought the other ejidatarios treated the Guarijíos rather badly. They insulted them, called them disparaging names, and refused to include them in the important business of the ejido. The Guarijíos' role in the ejido business was as marginal as their habitation in the valley of Loreto.

The Loreto Guarijíos taught me enough to enlarge greatly the information I was compiling. The plants they used were mountain plants, some dipping south from the Rocky Mountains, some thrusting north from the tropics, others endemic or native to the Sierra Madre. Most of the plants they showed me are unknown to the Guarijíos del río who lived thousands of feet lower. The mountain Guarijíos live a different kind of life. They have not gone through the struggles to obtain land, have not been held in similar peonage by latifundistas, do not appear to have experienced the physical suffering so familiar to people like Cipriano Buitimea, Nacho Ciriaco, and José Ruelas.

Yet they, too, lived at the margins. The Ejido Loreto was not formed until the mid-1970s under the Echeverría administration. Most of the ejidatarios are non-Guarijíos, men whose roots are elsewhere but who were permitted to become ejidatarios in conformity with national policy at that time. Prior to that, Guarijíos worked as sharecroppers for local ranchers. Life was difficult then, Tiburcio acknowledged. They were poorer, with ragged clothing and

Pine-oak forest near Loreto.

no medical care. But they usually had enough to eat and had their homes, because they settled on national lands and where left alone by the ranchers. They had no knowledge of the political developments that shook the Guarijíos below during the seventies and early eighties.

Guarijíos also suffer exclusion from the social options open more easily to Mexicans of lighter skin, of unaccented Spanish, and of approved customs. Mestizos have more *roce social*—political and social pull. They know how to talk to politicians and bureaucrats. They have connections in other villages and know their way around, hayseeds though they may be. They know how to get government subsidies for their crops.[3] The Guarijíos are shy, averse to assertiveness. All the while they face the same cultural pressures to conform, to abandon their language and their tuburada, to act like mestizos so that their children will not be viewed as backwards and oafs. Furthermore, Anglo missionaries are active at Arechuybo, a few hours' walk from Loreto. They bring the austerity of evangelical Christianity and its mixed blessing of liberation from alcoholism and destruction of native cultures. Evangelism is a temptation that all Guarijíos must weigh.

The sawmill operation highlights the economic desperation of the Guarijíos. They seem to realize the long-term ecological catastrophe the operation will have on their ejido. They and other mountain folk are not naïve about the consequences. Don Pablo Enríquez, owner of the Canelichi Ranch spoke with me about the effects of the logging. Two months earlier, members of the ejido had commenced logging on his lands, without his permission. They bulldozed a new road and tore up a hillside.

"When I found out about it I was upset, of course," he told me sadly, but without anger. "But I was in Navojoa for a month at the time with my ailing wife, who was visiting a doctor. When I arrived and found what they had done, I put a fence across their road. But what else could I do? They are my neighbors and I have to live with them."

While I was visiting that July, the fine stream that runs through don Pablo's property flowed muddy for the first time ever. Neither Tiburcio, nor his wife Nicolasa, nor don Pablo had ever seen it run muddy before. Cloudy, yes. Muddy, no. Nicolasa wondered how she would wash clothing. I asked don Pablo about the muddy water. "It's from the logging," he said. "When they cut down the trees, nothing is left to hold the water. It is so foolish. Without the forest there is no water. Everything washes away, and then nothing holds in the rain. Then the rains don't come. Without water we die. The ejido is killing the forest and is killing all of us." He was sad, perhaps despondent, but felt powerless to do anything. He blamed the wealthy buyer from Cuauhtémoc who had provided the sawmill for the ejido. The ejidatarios *had* to cut down all the forest just to pay for the infernal machine.

Tiburcio also knew all this. He chose to keep his mouth shut. The Loreto Guarijíos were employed at the sawmill, making good money.

I have much to learn about the mountain Guarijíos. I will accept Tiburcio's invitation to return once again. I will hike to Tojíachi and Arechuybo to find old men who know plants. But such explorations will have to wait for another time. I have more to tell about the Guarijíos of the river.

12
The Preacher and the Heathen

It was hard to think of Ramón as a preacher. After his death from a stroke, I still thought of him as a friend and Guarijío. I think he wanted to be thought of as a preacher.

I had never thought of Guarijíos as evangelizers, surely as fire-and-brimstone prophets of the end of the world. They were no Jeremiahs, I thought, for they are for the most part quiet, retiring, individualistic, and unassertive. Indeed, apart from the tuburada, which all traditional Guarijíos hold as sacred, they seem to be little influenced by organized religion. They are nominal Catholics, a reflection of historical influence of Jesuits and other clerics. Traditional Guarijíos, however, do not attend mass, church, or temple. If a priest appears in the vicinity, they respect him. They might even attend mass or request a baptism, but once he is gone, they retain little outward sign of being Catholics. Even with the new church in Mesa Colorada, their religion is well concealed. José Ruelas showed a newfound enthusiasm for genuflecting and crossing himself, but these appeared to be more a fondness for ritual than a deep emotional commitment to Catholicism.

Still, there are signs of persistent Catholicism. I saw a twelve-inch cross hanging on a post in one family's ramada. When I asked about it the owner told me it protected the house by helping keep out evil spirits and bad people. It also marked the house as *cristiano,* he said. And what did that mean? Mostly it meant that the family attended the tuburadas and respected the old traditions, which meant that they respected and exalted the tuburada. I gathered it also suggested all those human qualities Guarijíos endorse—hard work, loyalty, modesty, and acceptance of Guarijío traditions.

I did discover more significance to the term *cristiano.* To be a cristiano also meant that when a family member dies, someone would make a potion from the bark of the *brea,* a common palo verde. Each Guarijío, young and old alike, would dip a cornhusk into the potion and sprinkle a few drops of the sanctified water on the deceased before burying the body. The cemetery Richard and I stumbled into near Charajaqui vaguely resembled a Christian holy ground: ersatz coffins, a mound of stones over the graves to protect the corpses from the depredations of coyotes and other vermin, a small wooden cross staked into the stones over each grave, and, usually, some modern utensil such as a tin cup or even an old tin can as a tribute to civilization.

Hermangildo Zaila, the council president of Los Jacales, the Guarijío barrio of San Bernardo, summed up well the traditional Guarijío religion: "We have our own brand of Catholicism. We don't need a church. We do our ceremonies in our own way. We sing songs, we do the *tuburada.* That is our religion. That is what makes us Christians." Priests might disagree. Guarijíos do not mention doctrines, dogmas, or creeds. They probably have no position on the issue of apostolic succession or the doctrine of the Immaculate Conception.

Ramón Hurtado, however, was a San Bernardo Guarijío and an evangelist. He was a member and pillar of the Church of Faith in Jesus Christ of San Bernardo. He was one of a small but growing group of Guarijíos (perhaps sixty Guarijíos del río) who consider themselves to be *de la religión* (of the religion). They also refer to themselves as hermanos. They use these terms to set themselves apart from Catholics. In spite of Mexico's violently anti-Catholic period of the 1920s and its (recently softened) anticleric stance, one usually assumes that any given Mexican is Catholic, even if only nominally. Hermanos wish to make their dissociation publicly known.

Mayo friends of mine find it curious that my background is Protestant (or Christian non-Catholic). They associate Protestantism (or Christian non-Catholicism—members of one fundamentalist church deny that they are Protestants) with charismatic evangelical fundamentalism. They are intrigued that the United States is more Protestant than Catholic and imagine that if this is so our society must rock with the sounds of tent revivals. I think Ramón has the same conception. I explained to him that my father was a Methodist minister. He viewed that with skepticism, especially on learning that I did not attend services and did not count myself among the saved, or worry about Armageddon. I needed saving, he figured.

He's right. But I've sat through countless prayer meetings, hymn sings, revivals, and camp meetings. So my religious background, however, remote from the practices of charismatic evangelicals it may be, does provide me with insights into workings of the local evangelical churches, the zeal for conversions, and the anticipation of grave and noteworthy events to come.

San Bernardo's Catholic church is a small, white building fronting on the village's wide and bleak plaza. It has no

Ramón Hurtado, 1995, San Bernardo. Photo by David Burckhalter.

resident priest but is a visita of the cabecera in Alamos. The priest visits only occasionally to say mass and conduct rites of passage. At masses, Guarijíos are not numbered among the congregation. They would probably not be welcomed by the yori parishioners. Or at least that is the perception of the Guarijíos. Most of the time the evangelical church, a small, plain adobe house with a spacious ramada where most services are held, is the only religious influence in town. In contrast to the Catholic church, the congregation is made up of Guarijíos and a few other poor people.

When I knew Ramón well, he was a small white-haired man in his mid-sixties, portly, if such a term can be applied to Guarijíos who are nearly all gaunt and short. He greeted people with a shy smile and an air of hard work and determination about him. He spoke softly, betraying a Guarijío timidity and reluctance to be involved with non-Guarijíos. His message was decidedly non-Guarijío. He warned that the world is full of evil and vice, the work of Satan himself, who seeks to deceive good people and lead them into sinful ways. I couldn't imagine Ramón raging from a pulpit, his

face covered with beads of sweat alternating with tears, haranguing the Devil and the sinful alike, calling down the fires of hell as he stirred the congregation to march to the altar and proclaim themselves born again and repentant of their past life of sin (and contribute to the offering plates). But that was not his style, anyway. His was a ministry of quiet charisma. He moved gently among Guarijíos and non-Guarijíos alike prodding them to cast off their sinful lives and join the ranks of the saved, for saved they will be when the day of judgment arrives if they will only repent, he assured them. And that fearful day is imminent, he insisted.

Ramón reflected that before he was converted to evangelism, he lived as other worldly people around him, dissipating his life in general carousing, ignoring the needs of his family, and not providing guidance to his wife (now deceased) and children. He attended tuburadas, he said, and joined in the vices, the drinking, and other things (I assume he meant sexual license). Somewhere in the mid-1980s Ramón experienced conversion from the traditional nominal Guarijío Catholicism to evangelical Christianity. "That was when I began reading the Bible," he said, smiling as if in confession. "Before that I had many vices. I got drunk, didn't take care of my family. I threw away the money my family needed." His Guarijío-influenced Spanish was carefully formed and his delivery was deliberate, contrasting sharply with the rapid-fire delivery of more practiced revivalists. (Mayo Indians are especially given to becoming evangelical preachers and often take up the ways of evangelical oratory.)

Ramón gave up his worldly ways, he said, and the Devil with them. He focused instead on hard work and caring for his children, who were left motherless when they were young. He explained to me how the Devil works his way through vice. He gently denounced the vices as he enumerated them: drinking (the vice always mentioned first), smoking, dancing, gambling, and *mujeres* (women). He now steadfastly avoided the tuburada and the ways of the Guarijíos. They are the way of sin, he said. The Bible preaches against the tuburada, he assured me. I didn't ask for book, chapter, and verse. I thought of Cipriano's relating of the origin of the tuburi from God and His Wife. Wouldn't the psalmist approve of the tuburada?, the Devil said in my head. But I shut up.

"Look around you, David," Ramón warned me. "Everywhere are signs of the end of the world. Jesús is coming back, just as the Bible predicted." I asked him when he had taken up preaching. He smiled his humble, boyish smile. "I'm not a preacher," he said. "I can read and write, but I've never gone to the school where they train you to preach. I guess I preach, but I'm not a preacher! I go wherever God wants me to go. I go to the Guarijío pueblos, to the ranches, and I preach the word of God. I go to Huataturi, to Guajaray, to Chorijoa, even to Bavícora. I just preach about the Bible and what it says about sin and vices and warn that the dancing in the tuburada is a sin. The *hermanos de la fe* help me. They give me courage to continue. I guess that is why other people call us *hermanos*."

Ramón didn't go to Mesa Colorada to preach, however. Lino Leyba, the traditional governor there at the time, didn't like the aleluyas' message and refused to permit preaching in the village. Ramón thought it was because almost everyone in Mesa Colorada likes to brew tepachi, a mildly alcoholic drink. They didn't like Ramón or anyone else preaching against it. Guajaray was fair game, even though the converts there were few. There was no governor there to order him around. The governor over Guajaray was Rafael Méndez who lives in Los Bajíos, four hours by foot up the valley.

Ramón could frequently be seen riding seated in the bed of a pickup or standing crammed into the back of cattle trucks with many other Guarijíos as they journeyed to Alamos or Navojoa. Often he was heading to the cities to meet with other hermanos in prayer meetings, revivals, and gospel events. They preached the brotherhood of man [*sic*.] In their congregations there are no rich or poor, Indian or mestizo, light or dark skinned. All men are equal and all women are equal (though men and women are not apparently equal). They refer to each other as "brother" and "sister." The pastor of the San Bernardo church is a Mayo (as are the schoolteachers throughout the Guarijío pueblos.)

There was no language problem, however, since the services are conducted in Spanish, as are all gospel services in the region. Giving up the life of sin means giving up the native language that is so closely associated with the pagan customs of indigenous life. The evangelical churches are great simplifiers of diverse cultures. Their message is at once one of egalitarianism (a repudiation of Mexico's deeply stratified class system) and patriarchy—women and men are one under Christ. But women must still obey their husbands. The culture promoted is mestizo. The ideology is capitalism.

I first met Ramón in the early 1990s. I was leading a group of plant collectors returning from a foray into the Sierra to the north of San Bernardo. We had stopped at the town's general store for a soda. I asked the proprietor, an amiable mestiza, if anyone in the town made masks. She assured me that a man named Ramón did and dispatched a young boy to fetch him. Fifteen minutes later Ramón appeared toting a large bag full of masks. My companions eagerly snatched them up. I made Ramón's acquaintance then and over the next few months we became friends.

Ramón lived in a barrio of San Bernardo (population 1,200) called El Coyotero. He chose not to build his hut in Los Jacales where most of the other San Bernardo Guarijíos live. Ramón and the other Guarijíos lived at opposite ends of town and had little to do with each other socially. Ramón's plot of land was more or less at the bottom of San Bernardo. To get there it was necessary to park a block off the plaza and walk a couple hundred yards down the hill along a footpath, cross a wash, and enter his land through a gate, watching all the while for protective dogs. His place exemplified the Guarijío preference for living apart from the presence of other families. Ramón's lot had a more prosperous appearance by far than anything in Los Jacales, in spite of the need to walk a good distance to get there. His property was low lying, adjacent to a heavily vegetated small arroyo that after good rains runs intermittently. During heavy rains the wash was impossible to cross.

No one bothered him at his home. His lot had large shade trees and was planted with citrus, guava, and bananas. Until latifundistas began to clear-cut their lands for buffelgrass in the 1980s and early 1990s, thick tropical deciduous forest grew on the hillside behind his lot. It had flourished there for eons, a bountiful reservoir of firewood, lumber, herbs, and wild foods that continued unbroken to the north and west for many miles. Now the hills adjacent to his lot have been clear cut and are covered with an seemingly unending sea of the grass that for much of the year is a dull yellow. Firewood is now much harder to come by.

Ramón's small adobe house was shaded by giant guamúchil trees. The property by necessity had been entirely fenced with barbed wire or high impenetrable piles of sharp-spined chírahui or vinorama to keep out roving livestock that would quickly have decimated his orchards and garden. A path led downward from the house, through a swale and into the shade of his small arbor-like orchard. It emerged, then climbed a hundred yards up the hillside, through a gate to his workshop where he sometimes slept. There, in the shade of a ramada or outside under a guamúchil, he carved palo mulato into pascola masks, guásima and goathide into drums, and *palo chino* into trays and troughs.

Ramón's tools were basic, a hand saw, a power drill with a few largely dull drills, rusted chisels, a couple of ancient hammers, rasps, and hacksaws, pieces of sandpaper, and tempera paints. He kept a supply of horsehair, clipped from the tails and manes of local horses, to add a touch of mystery to the masks. Working with a son-in-law he turned out several masks each working day. The principal themes of the masks were vampire bats; grotesque humans bearing ears of corn in their mouths; jaguars; owls; and surrealistic, grimacing semihuman faces, often with mouths wide open, painted in a variety of colors—pagan themes, monsters, corn gods, snakes, and spirits, miscellaneous demons from Satan's realm. These he sold to the occasional outsider who climbed the hill to visit his workshop. If no one ventured by, once a week or so he would gather his merchandise into a bag and take it with him on the bus to Alamos, thirty miles away, where he sold it to tourists or to a shop that marketed his wares. He commented very little on the symbolism of the masks, saying only that they are old Guarijío themes, as though the Devil might slip into the story if he were not careful.

Ramón also made mellow-throated drums. He stretched pigskin over a circle of steamed guásima, pulled it taut, and let it dry. Music runs in his blood, for with modest persuasion he would extract a violin from its shelf in his tiny hut and play a pascola song or two. When he finished playing, he would often denounce the music as pagan or prohibited by the Bible. Others who knew him swear that when he was a *músico* for the tuburada, before he became an *aleluya,* he could play for twenty-four hours almost nonstop without repeating a son. Even when I knew him he kept a cassette tape of pascola music in his hut. He enjoyed listening to it from time to time, sinful or not.

The violin Ramón plays was a gift from Valente Hurtado, another San Bernardo Guarijío and Ramón's cousin. Valente lives in a different barrio, not Los Jacales. He is also an hermano de la fe, a further irony. I got to know him one day when the old Suburban I was driving through San Bernardo overheated. I found the town's one mechanic, a mestizo, working in his shop—it consisted of a ramada projecting from his little house. He raised the hood looked at the engine. It took only a few seconds for him to tell me the clutch on my radiator fan had ceased to operate.

"Clutch on a fan?" I exclaimed, immediately convinced that this was a backwoods mechanic who knew nothing of modern vehicles.

"Yep," he said. "Look." Then he traced a diagram in the dirt. He showed me that a small heating element in the fan expanded with increased temperature causing a clutch to engage. "That way," he said with great importance. "On cold mornings the water in the radiator will heat up faster and your heater will work more quickly because the fan is not cooling the radiator."

I admit I was fascinated. "So, what do I do to fix it?"

"You just weld some bolts across the clutch. It won't work any more, but who needs quick heat here in San Bernardo?"

I was skeptical. You don't mess around with a high-speed fan. It could tear apart at high rpms and shear a hole in the radiator, taking a few hoses with it. "How do you know this?" I asked him.

"Look," he answered confidently. "I'll show you." He went to his old Chevy truck and opened the hood. He fumbled and clanked around for a few minutes, then emerged, holding the radiator fan. "Here," he said triumphantly. "Look at mine. I've been driving with it this way for five years."

Sure enough, around the center of the fan four bolts had been welded, fixing the gap that the high-tech clutch was meant to bridge when it got hot enough. I was convinced.

"Terrific. But where do I get it welded. Alamos? Navojoa?"

"No, no." He said, laughing. "Go over to Barrio San Bernardo and look for Valente. Here. I'll go with you." And he did. And Valente had a welder. He found an old bolt, cut off four lengths of an inch and a half and with perfect ease welded them on the hub of the fan, disarming the clutch. We returned to the mechanic's place. He replaced the repaired fan and the belts. For a grand total of $8 I had a smooth-running vehicle once again.

Reflecting on this later, I found it odd that the mechanic hadn't referred to Valente as a Guarijío. Yoris usually identify race right off. I didn't know until I met his family that Valente was Guarijío and spoke the language. He was the only Guarijío welder, probably one of the very few Guarijíos who practiced a commercial craft. He had become a welder after he had converted to the evangelical church. He had given up most of his Guarijío ways. But he still makes violins and his wife still speaks Guarijío. His several children don't know a word of the language. Valente is a stalwart of the evangelical congregation in San Bernardo.

For several years I visited Ramón, always buying a few masks or drums. I must have purchased fifty masks over the years. I brought various friends and acquaintances to San Bernardo to see his work. How much did he charge for the masks? *"Barata"* (cheap), he would always say, and he was right. Usually he would have ten or so in various states of readiness. His shop was always a pleasant pile of fragrant wood shavings derived from torote prieto or palo mulato. Then he would go on to tell me of his certainty that we were seeing the last days of the world before Jesus would return in his kingdom. He told me of visiting the United States, for many years the only Guarijío who had done so. He performed at Indian powwows throughout the Southwest. He had visited Santa Fe, Phoenix, Los Angeles, had flown in large and small planes. None of this had changed his life, but the word of God had, he said. Was I a Christian? he asked. I hedged, pointing out once again that my father, whom I viewed as a saint, was a Methodist minister. He noted my weak equivocation. He decided I would be a hard sell, but he would never give up.

One day I brought some Mayo friends of mine down the long bumpy dirt road from Alamos to meet him. They had heard my descriptions of Ramón's artistry and had long expressed a curiosity in his masks and drums. They plodded with me down the hill and over the wash, through the shady arbor, then up the long path to his shop. He welcomed them quietly and watched in silence as they looked over his masks. When they struck up a conversation he began to advise them of the need to give up their worldly ways, to recognize the advent of the final days, to repent, and to accept Jesus Christ. My Mayo friends, one of whom had been a pascola dancer, were not accustomed to this talk and discreetly retreated with their masks, expressing wonder at what they thought was the insanity of the fellow, a pity since he made such nice masks, pagan masks at that. These masks produced no conflict with their brand of Catholicism. They rather enjoyed images of the Devil and the diabolical. Pascola masks usually have a playful air about them. But for evangelicals there is nothing playful about the Devil.

The evangelical Protestant movement among indigenous Mexicans brings with it an ideological undercurrent of capitalism. The fundamentalist creed stresses hard work, savings, self-denial, patriarchy, individual responsibility, and good works. There is little to distinguish the evangelical's creed from hardcore New England Puritanism. Anthropologist Mary O'Connor, studying the rise of the evangelical movement among Mayos, found them strongly sympathetic with U.S. capitalism, not inclined to take up broad social issues beyond those of individual purity and self-denial. Guarijío traditions do not easily mesh with this model, for the tuburada is pagan, communitarian, and festive. When Guarijíos are converted, they give up much more than their fondness for alcohol and the tuburada. They come to adopt a wholly different range of cultural beliefs.

Still, I found Ramón a great source of knowledge, a reliable craftsman, and an honest observer. When he was not speaking of his conversion or of his preaching mission, he was a good field guide. We drove to some canyons near San Bernardo to look at plants so that he could tell me what they were called and describe what they were good for. He had forgotten many Guarijío names, he said, but he remembered well what they were called in Spanish. He knew that women could take a tea brewed from a mixture of the sap of batayaqui and the leaves of palo colorado if they didn't want to have children. He taught me that chicura boiled and drunk as a tea would cleanse a woman after childbirth and that the bark of copalquín brewed into a fine tonic to strengthen weak blood.

We talked for hours about his life and work. I was surprised to learn that Cipriano Buitimea, the most traditional of Guarijíos, was a close relative of Ramón's. When I mentioned this to Cipriano, he would from time to time talk to me about Ramón. Ramón never mentioned Cipriano unless I brought the subject up. It was as if he were practicing denying his Guaríjío relatives, his Guaríjío language, and his Guaríjío upbringing. His mother was part Mayo, he said, and he was raised speaking Guaríjío, Mayo, and Spanish. Now he speaks only Spanish, the language of the Bible, he says. He thought Spanish was the more important language. In his home, only he now was conversant in Guaríjío. I surmised that he would be content never again to speak in his native tongue. It would be useful only to communicate the word of God to Guaríjíos who spoke no Spanish. And few of those were left. Before long, Ramón would forget how to preach in Guaríjío.

Ramón worried about the increasing violence in San Bernardo. It was spawned, he thought, by drug traffic. Most young men were involved in one way or another with the narcotraficantes, he fretted. He interpreted these dreadful developments as another sign of the end of the world. Signs of the violence were everywhere. The old formula for the breakdown of morality—that people young and old lacked *respeto* (respect) would no longer suffice. The fact was undeniable: life in the region was downright dangerous. Ramón was reluctant to venture into the monte that surrounds San Bernardo. There he and I could easily be robbed, he warned. He told of the recent death of a young man, a friend of his family, in a drug-related murder. "He was just sitting in his house when they came up to the door and shot him! They will kill anybody."

Still he went with me to the monte. I parked the utility vehicle I was driving next to the winding mountain road as we climbed up Cañon el Papachal a few miles north of the town. From the road we were still able to view Los Pilares, three red rocky formations that resemble fifty-foot high goblins. They are landmarks for all who venture up and down the Río Mayo in the vicinity of San Bernardo. Though we had them in sight, Ramón was uneasy leaving the vehicle there, but we had no choice. Later he reluctantly led me down a path to a hot spring on the Río Mayo where I bathed in the tepidly warm water. When we later returned to the village, he was much relieved. "The *mafiosos* rob and kill anybody. They would rob me, even though I have nothing."

Over the years the violence in San Bernardo has shown no sign of letting up. A murder occurs at the least every couple of months, a dramatically high rate for a village of twelve hundred. Ramón hoped that the conversion of more people to his church would help but still feared for his (and everyone's) safety. San Bernardo has acquired the reputation as one of Sonora's most violent villages. Police and the military constantly patrol the roads and the soldiers comb the countryside in a futile attempt to suppress the insanity. Most people view them as part of the problem, as part of the narcotics trade themselves.

Ramón said nothing of the social and political intrigue that swirled around him. His new religion preached detachment from the world of politics. He protested some of the injustices in San Bernardo, the bad treatment of poor people and Indians by the police and by the rich, the exploitation of Guaríjío lands, and the change in climate he believed the planting of buffelgrass has brought about, but had little to say of events beyond. His religion required him to concentrate his sights on the next world, not on this one. He had no comment on the spectacular events in Chiapas in 1994 and the aftermath of massacres and intrigue. His job was to preach the word of God and attend the nightly services at his church where the pastor is a Mayo. These proceedings were often noisy and usually several hours long. The neighbors must have prayed for tranquility. When outside pastors, church officials, or brothers came from other places, Ramón's home became a temporary boarding house.

Ramón's mission began to take him beyond San Bernardo. I frequently stopped by to visit and purchase masks and found him away, his shop door locked, the ramada and its chairs empty, an eerie silence about the place. He was away preaching or teaching the Bible. He explained that he preached in other places, carrying his simple and humble message of alternating carrot and stick, salvation and damnation, redemption and castigation. He always traveled light, stowing his meager belongings in a shopping bag and a small gym case.

His neighbors up the hill on the other side of the creek always acted surprised that he was gone. "Why, don Ramón is usually there," they would say. "We saw him just yesterday, or was it the day before?" He told them very little. They are mestizos. Ramón preferred to exit San Bernardo by a hidden pathway that winds through the wash. Here he could not be seen as he plodded along his route through the dense bushes and scrubby trees. He could catch the bus at the end of town or slip unseen into the church. Guaríjíos like to move quietly, unobtrusively, as if being seen might subject them to danger. It probably has in the past. In this Ramón was still Guaríjío through and through.

I invited him to drive with me one day from San Bernardo to the nearby Mayo village of Vado Cuate. I waited for him at the edge of town in the government *casita* (cabin) the director of INI allowed me to use. Ramón wanted it that way, no ceremonious picking him up where everyone in town might see. I watched him materialize from the bushes via a path from the wash. It concealed him until he was nearly at my car.

Before we arrived at Vado Cuate he warned me that everyone in the village would be drunk. "They are always drunk here during the day, David. That's why they are so poor. They need the word of God." To be sure, I couldn't find a grownup soul to talk to who was sober. Even an old mestiza woman was tipsy. She had an ultra-high thin voice and spoke as though she had been inhaling helium. It seemed to me that Ramón was thinking of preaching to her of the evils of drink but thought better of it.

Alcoholism claims a ghastly number of lives among Mayos and wrecks a lot of life among Guarijíos as well. Ramón was painfully aware of its consequences. The evangelical proscription from drinking is an eminently practical solution to an overpowering social problem. Quite simply, the first requirement for people to get their lives in order is to end drunkenness and debauchery. The social roots of these human curses are not a matter of great interest to evangelistas, only their elimination. And, indeed, the converts, if they stay that way, seem in fact to stay on the wagon, to give up the dissolute life and devote more time to their families. The ideological trappings accompanying the abandonment of alcohol are another story.

Ramón lived worlds apart from Los Jacales, located a half mile away on the north side of the Arroyo Taymuco, the permanent stream that separates the poverty-stricken barrio from the rest of San Bernardo. There fifty or so Guarijío families eke and scrape a living from the soil and from others, an existence as marginal as that of any indigenous people in northwest Mexico. They are viewed as semioutcasts among their own people, they say, because they have steadfastly rejected the intervention of the governmental INI. INI (the Mexican equivalent of the Bureau of Indian Affairs) oversees numerous programs for Guarijíos of the ejidos to the north. It provides emergency food assistance, fencing for livestock, veterinary supplies to the ejidos, simple medical care, boarding schools, and even clothing. None of these services are available to the Guarijíos of Los Jacales because they stubbornly refuse to accept INI's jurisdiction. Even so, Hermangildo Zaila, their elected councilman told me they are proud of their independence.[1] They wish to do things on their own such as founding their own school, joining other independent indigenous groups—56 of them—from Mexico and beyond in a pan-indigenous organization, and maintaining their own rituals.

Violinist José María "Chémali" Yocuivo, Los Jacales, San Bernardo.

I asked Ramón about Los Jacales. He said little, preferring, I thought, not to say negative things about people. He had tried preaching there and had some success, but it was evident that Los Jacales had not proved fertile ground for his proselytizing. He was somewhat apprehensive about being accepted there.

Los Jacales (The Shacks) sits atop a mesa above the Arroyo Taymuco, across the broad watercourse from the rest of San Bernardo. Pigs and dogs scavenge among the garbage that is strewn over the steep slopes that drop from the mesa to the arroyo. The houses and the intricate network of slatted fences and gates that separate them (the lack of adequate land has forced the Guarijíos into crowded housing) are situated on borrowed land. The Ejido San Bernardo, a mestizo ejido, has agreed to allow the Guarijíos the use of part of their common lands. Indeed, the barrio has been there for decades, but permission to use the lands could be revoked at any time. Guarijíos have petitioned the government to give them title, so far to no avail. The government's attitude is that if Los Jacales doesn't recognize them, they will not recognize Los Jacales. The ejido can hardly be enthusiastic about losing part of its acreage. Until the day arrives when the Los Jacales Guarijíos have their own land, they will occupy the land at the pleasure of the ejidatarios of San Bernardo.

Hermangildo is a short man in his early forties, heavy set for a Guarijío. He wore a bright flowery shirt that could have helped him pass for a Hawaiian. When I met him and asked if I we could talk about life in the barrio, he led me into his yard. He sat down at a table under a large ramada where the barrio meetings are held, as if prepared for a press conference, and peered across the table at Richard Felger and me. He seemed fiercely proud of the independence of Los Jacales. The government provided no services to Los Jacales, he said, but at the same time the residents were not beholden to anyone except the ejido that had loaned them the use of the land. The men work clearing lands for local ranchers for twenty pesos a day, well under the minimum wage of twenty-eight pesos ($3.50 US). They also were constantly looking for work, sometimes selling a load or two of firewood, pitahaya fruits, or papaches. Almost certainly they work from time to time for mafiosos in some aspect of drug commerce.

Because they were so poor, they had constantly to comb the monte for things to eat. Hermangildo took Richard and me for a tour, demonstrating thirty different plants within a quarter mile of the barrio that could be eaten or made into medicine. Some of them are scorned by other native peoples and mestizos. Hermangildo was undefensive about that. "When you are as poor as we are, you use everything you can." As examples of their self-sufficiency, he pointed out that the barrio maintains its own pump to lift water from the arroyo a hundred feet below to taps in the village. They staffed their own school, which had been built by the government, but was never provided with a teacher.

The teacher in the school was Norma Parra, an energetic and bright Guarijía in her late twenties. She had not yet been paid by the government for teaching the school because she was not licensed. She had four years of schooling to go before she could be certified, but in the meantime she vowed she would teach the children to read and write and speak Guarijío so that they would not lose their culture. "The INI came to the Guarijíos twenty-two years ago. Even then they didn't want children to learn in their own language. We want our children to learn in Guarijío. The INI wants our children to be good yoris. We want them to be Guarijíos." Indeed, many of the children of the barrio appear to be fluent in the language, certainly more so

than in more remote centers like Guajaray and Mesa Colorada where the children are instructed in Spanish by government-sponsored Mayo teachers. "We want our children to grow up understanding that they are Guarijíos. If they lose their culture they will be just like anyone else. We don't want INI running our school. That is why we are independent of INI. We have our own tuburada here on December 24 and 25 to celebrate Christmas. People come from all over. The children learn about the tuburada. José Ruelas comes from Mesa Colorada. He is the cantador. He sings of animals, plants, about rain and beehives, about insects and thunderstorms. The children love the songs. We want to remain Guarijíos.

"We are training new cantadores here in Los Jacales. In the other Guarijío pueblos there may be no new cantadores, but here in Los Jacales we will have them. We don't want our culture to die out."

Hermangildo agreed. "Some people are born to be cantadores. I have an uncle up the Río Mayo in Mesa Colorada. He will be a cantador. He was born singing, and I hope he will sing all his life. Maybe they won't have cantadores in Los Bajíos or in Bavícora, but we will have a cantador here."

Many of the Los Jacales Guarijíos have relatives in Colonia Sonora, a poverty-stricken agricultural settlement of tarpaper and plywood shacks south of Ciudad Obregón in the vast agribusiness complex of the Río Yaqui Delta. Guarijíos often migrate there to work for a season as day laborers and earn some cash, hoping to return to their lands and plant corn and beans when the summer rains arrive. The Colonia serves as an ersatz reception center for Guarijíos, who would otherwise be lost in the vast, fast world of the mestizos. There they constitute a decided underclass, abused and exploited by mestizos, but find comfort in the community in exile. Some Guarijíos live most of their lives there, but they all hope to return to live and die among the Guarijíos of the Río Mayo.

I never got the feeling from Ramón that he was infected with the overwhelming attraction to the land that I felt among other Guarijíos, including those from Los Jacales. I didn't see him in 1997 except for a brief encounter when our vehicles passed on the road near San Bernardo. He was seated with a dozen other Guarijíos in the back of a pickup truck. I got out and shook his hand, and he responded in the gentle Guarijío way. He told me he would be returning soon to make masks. The next four times I visited his home he was away. I wondered if something had gone wrong in his life.

In February 1998, I learned that Ramón had suffered a debilitating stroke. The blood clot in his brain left him without the ability to talk clearly or to coordinate his movements. A year later I visited him. He no longer could carve masks and trays as he once did. He apologized for not being able to play the violin. He had given his away. He lived nearly alone, tended only by a young son and the few church members who stopped by occasionally to check on him. He had almost no income. The once prosperous homestead showed signs of the relentless onslaught of the tropical deciduous forest. Yet Ramón still looked for the Day of Judgment, hoping to see it before death clouded his vision. He attended evangelizing missions and listened to others do the preaching.

The loss of Ramón as an evangelist represents a severe setback to the proselytizing efforts of the evangelicals. Ramón was the most important Guarijío witness for the aleluyas, a peripatetic Habakkuk. For the preservation of the Guarijío way, the loss of his influence may be a bonus. For me, the blood clot that stole Ramón's voice and his wry smile was a mean thief that stole a friend.

In 1998 and 1999 the murders continued in San Bernardo. One night in July a series of gunshots echoed through the village. Police were summoned to the scene of the shots. Inside a house only a hundred meters from the police station, which had recently been reinforced with extra personnel to combat the high rate of homicides, they found the body of a young man who had long been sought for the murders of at least four people. Early police reports listed the cause of death as a gunshot to the head. The death was pronounced a suicide.

The killings occurred in 1999 as well. In one shootout two young men killed each other. A month later another youth was found murdered. The local police invariably label these homicides as *adjuste de cuentas* (adjusting of accounts), something to do with vengeance for duplicity in dealing drugs.

The appalling increase in crime in Mexico's sierras (and cities) seems to know no upper limit. It is part of what locals call a general *caida*—the deterioration of Mexican society, particularly, in the Guarijío country, of the old ties that bound mountain and hill people together[2]. The breakdown of traditional rural Mexican society as I knew it began in the late 1960s and has escalated in the 1990s. It coincides remarkably with the internationalization of marijuana production, both industrial and agricultural (which are often hardly distinguishable) and the ascension of marijuana into the global economy.

For nonevangelical Guarijíos, the rise of the drug Mafia is another chapter in their unending confrontation with outside forces. Their struggle to protect their lands was probably ongoing at the time of contact with the conquering Spaniards. The battles with the Spaniards were but a continuation of territorial protection. The struggle continued with the infiltration of miners and settlers, then *hacendados,* then ranchers, and now the mafiosos. The end of the brief period of euphoria for the Guarijíos at owning their own lands may well occur within the next couple of decades. For the Guarijío way, the end of the world may be almost as nigh at hand as Ramón Hurtado foretold.

Ramón died in early 2000. A second stroke finished him off. A younger fellow from Chorijoa is said to be carving masks, now that Ramón is gone.

13
Guarijíos and the Global Economy

SOME OBSERVATIONS AND STRONG OPINIONS

Back in 1995 in Saucitos, Cipriano and I ran into Juan Enríquez, the yori curandero. He broke the bad news to us about the outbreak of a rabies-like disease among cows. His words underscored a dilemma the Guarijíos del río must now face. If they become cattle ranchers (as the government wishes) they will have to abandon their traditional subsistence economy. If they abandon their traditional economy, they will risk their economic future, and probably their ethnicity as well. Whichever path they choose portends grim prospects.

As I see it, their newly acquired lands and livestock amount to a two-edged sword. The lands are now securely theirs. They boast a herd of cows provided by the government and periodic welfare benefits as well. But even with adequate rainfall for their mahuechis, the Guarijíos cannot create a subsistence economy, no matter how much they or I want it to be otherwise. Their cows may be their downfall.

Can cows be bad for a rural economy and mahuechis? The Guarijíos have surprised me many times and may surprise me again, but all the historic and present realities of their land, the underdeveloped Mexican economy, and the structural inequalities of globalization appear to be working against them. Cows and mahuechis are symbols of this systemic underdevelopment.

The Guarijíos are socially and economically marginalized, relegated to the extreme periphery of Mexican society. Their economic situation seems to me to saddle them with guaranteed pauperhood. How have I arrived at such a pessimistic conclusion? I find three causes or roots of the situation.

First, through its development policies, the Mexican government has already determined that Guarijíos will be assimilated into a cash economy. Mexican policy for dealing with indigenous people is that all will be assimilated into Mexican society and assume Mexican identity. The best way to accomplish this is with an economic hook.

Why is assimilation of such moment to Mexico? Pri-marily because Mexicans fear (with good reason) independent nationalistic movements (such as the rebellion in Chiapas in late 1994) that may spring up and divide the nation. They also fear that the colossus to the north might just support an insurgency. Mexico has a long, tormented history of centrifugal tendencies and the constant fear of loss of central control.[1]

The second reason for my pessimism is that the material goods that Guarijíos need and have come to expect are products of an industrial society that must be purchased with cash. Guarijíos cannot produce them, so they have to sell something to come up with cash. The need for cash is placing impossible demands on the Guarijíos and their lands.

Third, without basic land use changes and drastically altered development policies involving massive capital investment, the land cannot fully support the more than a thousand people who live on the two ejidos of the Guarijíos del río. The ability of ejido Loreto to sustain a population of six hundred people is equally dubious.

Cows and their needs lie at the heart of these three points. I will discuss them one by one.

The government has promoted cattle raising as a source of income for the Guarijíos, in fact the only one.[2] It grubstaked the initial herd of cows and still makes low-cost loans and grants available to the ejidos for purchasing additional cows and fencing. In especially dry times, the government also provides free or low-cost feed supplements. The government's largesse, however, is not calculated to promote self-sufficiency but to ensure the Guarijíos a slot in the international beef market. Their role (along with thousands of other small-time rural ranchers) is to produce feeder calves that will be mature on their mothers' milk, then be sold, fattened, marketed, butchered, packaged, and consumed elsewhere. Whether the end consumer lives in nearby Navojoa or in Tokyo makes no difference. The demand for Guarijío beef and the price that will be paid for it are independent of the Guarijíos, or even of Mexico. The beef industry is like a far-flung, international assembly plant, with the feeder calves at the lowest-paid end of the assembly line. To the extent that Guarijíos are enmeshed in the global currency of beef, they can never control their economic destiny. Viewed from a simplistic neoliberal standpoint, the Guarijíos are entirely expendable from the Mexican economy, even as the Mexican economy is largely expendable from the standpoint of the United States' economy. The doctrine of comparative advantage allocates to the Guarijíos the advantage of abundant pastures and

1995 desmonte for buffelgrass near Chorijoa. Trees and shrubs were felled, mounded, and burned. Most of the remaining etchos died by the year 2000. Photo by David Burckhalter.

nonexistent infrastructure costs. What it ignores is the systematic underdevelopment of their economy that results.

It is easy to gloss over the ongoing marginalization of Guarijíos and other groups of rural poor in Mexico as part of the growing pains of a "developing" country. If we look at poverty indices, however, at the vast gap between Mexico's tiny wealthy class and its huge impoverished class, Mexico is as underdeveloped as it ever was. There are recent reports of an improved economy, lower unemployment, and better incomes, but these are scattered. The poor of Mexico partake of a smaller and smaller portion of the country's wealth. Their marginalization and that of the Guarijíos is not a temporary state. The Guarijíos will not gradually migrate upwards in the economy. Their poverty is structural, as is that of Mexico in general.[3] Lest we doubt this, we have but to consider the daily increasing tide of Mexican economic refugees attempting illegally to cross into the United States.

But more of cows. The Guarijíos have considerable experience with cattle raising. For several hundred years they have tended cows, first for Jesuits, then for hacendados, later for local ranchers, and now, for themselves. I spoke with several men who hoped that by raising their own cows they could make *panela* (cottage cheese) for themselves and their families. But the government plans permit no such local intervention. To develop their cattle industry, Guarijíos must view cows' milk as a marketable item, not as food for their families. To gain weight for the market, calves must suckle the milk from their mothers, milk that otherwise could be (and long has been) drunk by humans or made into cheese for their own consumption. Thus cows' milk is every bit as much a commodity as commercial feed intended for producing commercial beef. If it is consumed by a Guarijío, whether as milk or as cheese, it is an element of self-subsistence. If it is consumed by a feeder calf instead, it is a commodity.

The government encourages the Guarijíos to produce more cows, to squeeze more and more kilos of beef from the pastures. The resultant bovine pressure works against the land's natural productivity. Uses of the monte now enjoyed for free by Guarijíos, such as mahuechis, firewood, posts, home construction, medicinal herbs, wild foods— and shade (!)—cannot compete with cattle. Where market cows graze, all other potential uses of the land are subordinated or sacrificed. I noted earlier the change in the Bavícora landscape from lush to arid once cow production gained ascendancy. Similarly, once a mahuechi has been converted into a buffelgrass pasture, it cannot, except over geological time, return to mahuechi.

Let me clarify this critically important point. The tropical deciduous forest includes an abundance of plants that are of no use to cows. Leaves growing high in trees out of cows' reach or succulent plants rendered inaccessible by thickets are an inconvenience for cows. The ubiquitous thorns pierce cows' mouths or feet. Cows may refuse to nurse calves with parts of cacti embedded in their heads or mouths. Many plants have leaves, roots, and flowers that are toxic or repugnant to the cows' taste. All these are waste plants for the pastoralist. Consider the great bulk of plant metabolism and growth expended ("wasted" from a cattle raiser's viewpoint) in tree trunks and inedible plants that cannot be put to use by cows. The government pronounces these to be "waste," an economic obstacle to development.[4] So government agents promote *desmonte* (clearing) of forest lands. Once the forest is felled and burned, they recommend planting exotic African buffelgrass. Why? Because the grass can support at least three times as many cows and because cows that graze on buffelgrass usually get fat more quickly than those that forage in the forests.

For a while, that is, a decade or so, most of the biomass in the cleared pasture is convertible into beef instead of unexploited plant material, even though the total biomass, the sum of all the plant materials growing on a piece of land, is drastically reduced (see, for example, Búrquez et al. 1999). Unless the pasture is intensely managed, however, the grass gradually atrophies, and the soil's fertility drops. Fewer cows can find enough food to eat. If a rancher is wealthy, he may renew the grass by burning, he may grub the soil with a bulldozer to bring new nutrients to the surface, or he may even apply chemicals to enrich the soil. These renewing operations are expensive, as out of reach to Guarijíos as mink stoles. When their pastures become exhausted, when the buffelgrass languishes from lack of nutrients, chírahui and vinorama are usually the only large plants that succeed. They are scrubby, thorny, species that choke out other, more useful trees and are of little use themselves. Southern Sonora is dotted with pastures that were cleared, sowed with buffelgrass, declined in production, and today are eroded, rocky plots with few desirable plants and little soil remaining.[5]

Raising cows as commodities represents a slow mining of the soil, an assault on the biomass of the Guarijío lands. The cows consume the plant material and the trace elements derived from the soil. Their hooves compact the soil, decreasing absorption and increasing runoff. The clearing for pastures depletes the capacity of watersheds to retain water and release it slowly. So each pound of beef produced contains within it a trace of the ejido land from which it comes and a tiny fraction of the watershed. The traces and fractions accumulate. With the sale of calves, part of the land goes with them, and what each calf leaves behind is a slightly worsened commons. It also represents a drain of Guarijíos' currency, for care of cows requires cash—for veterinarians, for vitamin supplements, for commercial feeds in time of drought, for fence, for water improvement, and for shipping.

Some mahuechis near Guajaray that were being planted with buffelgrass seed in 1998 are an instructive example. They were cleared, and the seed was broadcast after the third year of corn harvest. Those pastures are now hooked permanently into buffelgrass, for it ends the natural succession and revegetation of the plant-fallow-plant cycle that lasts about a decade. That much monte is now permanently ceded to single use of the land that once had multiple uses in ongoing cycles.

The loss of a few hectares of monte will have no effect on the Guarijíos, but the loss of several hundred or a thousand hectares will indeed. Without plenty of monte—thousands of hectares—the Guarijíos cannot survive as a people. Every hectare of desmonte means a hectare less of firewood, building material, medicinal herbs, food, and the other myriad of things Guarijíos do with plants. Gathering firewood is in itself a major activity and requires prolific monte. All the villages show heavy harvesting around the village limits, and every day Guarijíos must venture farther into the monte to gather wood. When the monte is deliberately stripped of all wood, the daily journeys become farther yet. When I tramped into the monte with Ignacio Ciriaco, he lugged a stout trunk of firewood a couple of kilometers to his home. Nothing of that size was available closer, for all had been harvested.

Ironically, in the last decade, drug lords have begun laundering money by buying large ranches in Guarijío country. Every month new sales occur. The mafiosos clear away the forest, hiring Guarijíos to do the clearing, as if they were soldiers forcing prisoners to dig their own graves. At Mochibampo, mafiosos have cleared the hills of the east bank and sowed buffelgrass. The same is true near Burapaco, near Chorijoa, near San Pedro, near Sejaqui, and near Chinogüira. Since the massive desmontes have been completed, erosion of the hills has increased, and, the natives claim, it is hotter than it used to be.

More cows, then, mean fewer forest products. The cattle economy also hooks Guarijíos inexorably into a cash economy, my second reason for pessimism. Milk from the Guarijíos' cows could go into making panela, a valuable source of protein for a protein-poor people. Instead, the milk goes to fattening calves for sale. The Guarijíos are shipping away protein they need for themselves. So the Guarijíos must *buy* the little cheese they can afford, cheese from factories in distant places like Chihuahua. Commercial cheese purchased with cash on a Guarijío table is a symbol of failed nutritional potential. The same can be said for milk-fattened calves. Slowly, insidiously (I think), the need for cash to buy cheese and a hundred other items is locking the Guarijíos into the Mexican economy and, as Mexico's economy becomes fully neoliberalized, into the global economy. And because the Guarijíos now have no other product to sell (except for their labor), the dominant culture will ultimately absorb them and strip them of their

Guarijío house in the *monte,* Bavícora.

land-related traditions. The sale of calves is the hook of assimilation. Economic desperation combined with a desire for material goods available only from the dominant culture is the prod. Each year many, if not most Guarijío men and some women venture to the Mayo and Yaqui Deltas for a few months to work as agricultural day laborers in the hope of accruing some cash so they can afford to live the rest of the year in the monte they love.[6]

This second point is hardly original. The transition from subsistence to a cash economy has meant the end of hundreds of local cultures worldwide. As regrettable as this may seem, Guarijíos are no different from all other people in the world: they need better clothing, medicine, tools, and merchandise. To get these they need cash. To get cash they must sell their labor or sell a product. Cattle is the only product they currently have.[7] The ravages of cattle are undermining the Guarijío way of life.

The third reason for my pessimism about the future viability of Guarijío ejidos is that in the long run their land as it is now used cannot support their current population.

The Los Bajíos and Mesa Colorada ejidos are large—about twelve thousand acres. They both provide adequate land for mahuechis if only the rains will come. The little plots, the mahuechis of five to ten hectares, can feed a family, even perhaps generate a small amount of surplus of corn and beans. But many more Guarijío children now survive infancy, so families are larger. In a generation or so land per capita will be far less abundant. The amount of wood harvested for firewood, posts for fence, and timbers for construction, all necessary for the subsistence way of life, cannot continue to increase. The threshold of sustained yield of woods has been reached and surpassed around the villages, and any increase in harvest portends a decrease in the forest. With good rain the ejidos can produce corn to feed their current population indefinitely. But for any substantial increase in population, or with a continued dry cycle, food self-sufficiency will be difficult, if not impossible.[8]

At the present rate of clearing, in only a couple of decades, the proliferation of mahuechis will have exhausted the supply of readily usable plots.[9] More and more forest will

Guarijío home scene, Mesa Colorada.

Boys carrying bucket of water on *palanca,* Mesa Colorada.

be cut down as pastures proliferate, and the monte, the source of Guarijío subsistence, will slowly disappear. Part of this transition will be due to the government's urging to increase cattle production. Part will be due to simple population pressure.

The Guarijíos depend on others for industrial products, clothing, food, and medicine. It is doubtful that their marginal livestock operations can provide for their cash needs and their mahuechis produce self-subsistence in food as well. A ranch of six thousand hectares (the size of Los Bajíos ejido) might provide an affluent lifestyle for one or two or even five families, but cannot provide for the basic needs of seventy.[10]

Mahuechi subsistence farming is an excellent strategy in areas of relatively abundant, hilly land with low human population densities and adequate rainfall. Seventy families, however, cannot hope consistently to produce a significant surplus in grains. The production per person on hillside mahuechis (which are farmed by hand-held hoes) is necessarily less than that on flatter plowed *temporales* (rainfall-watered fields) and far below the yield on commercial irrigated acreage. In terms of another index, the yield of corn per hour of human labor on a mahuechi production is astronomically lower than that of irrigated agriculture.[11] Chemical fertilizers that might increase production are generally out of the question. They cost money, and Guarijíos are the poorest of the poor. A sack of fertilizer costs nearly half the market value of the corn produced. Any purchases for farming inputs undermine the subsistence economy.

As the Guarijíos know well, mahuechi-based subsistence is also unreliable. During the summer droughts of 1989–2000,

most crops in most years produced stunted yields, or even nothing at all. In spite of the Guarijíos' amazing ability to extract crops out of parched soil, many would have perished had the government not provided free food supplements. The mahuechi's significance is far more economically symbolic than economically real.

And so when Juan Enríquez brought the news of pseudorabies that day long ago in Saucitos, it awoke me to the perverse local effects of the global economy: the Guarijíos are raising cows because the Mexican government wants them to sell the cows into the international market as a means of regional economic development. The loss of even small numbers of livestock to pseudorabies or other diseases, or to predators, will have grave economic effects on the Guarijíos, dependent as they have become on cows as their cash "crop." Moderate droughts severely compromise the caloric consumption of both cows and Guarijíos. These consequences will only hasten the Guarijíos' absorption into the uniformity of mestizo culture. The Guarijíos' economy is a third-world economy within a third-world nation. The Guarijíos' dependence on the Mexican economy parallels the Mexican economy's dependence on developed economies.

As I noted in chapter 11, the reliance of mountain Guarijíos of the pine-oak forest on the sale of lumber, while perhaps less tenuous than complete dependence on cattle, is no more capable of sustaining the Guarijíos for the long term than is the reliance of the Guarijíos of the tropical deciduous forest on cows and mahuechis. Possibly the ejido Loreto could become a tree "farm," but the present practice of clear-cutting without seedling replacement will eliminate its forests within a decade.

Lorenzo's son rides a homemade scooter downhill, Mesa Colorada.

The precariousness of this commodity-based economy leads to ironic consequences. My travels though Guarijío lands have convinced me that the biggest single source of revenue for the Guarijíos is probably not the sale of *becerros* (calves), as the government had hoped, but payments from the mafiosos who hire Guarijíos to transport marijuana and, quite possibly, to raise it as well. No published data have assayed the influence of drug traffic on the Guarijío economy, but by all anecdotes it is considerable. Mafiosos reportedly pay three times the minimum wage. They pay with cash. No receipts are involved. The elusive Guarijío can evade any government attempts at enforcement or confiscation, even if such should exist, by hiding in the rugged mountains and deep canyons in a hundred nearly inaccessible locations. (That is one reason the mafiosos like the Guarijíos.) Guarijíos would far prefer to climb up into the convoluted mountains and be paid a hundred pesos a day to cultivate and harvest marijuana, than descend into the monotonous flats of the river deltas and work for forty pesos a day busting their backs cultivating cotton. So would I.

Whatever the extent of its cultivation in Guarijío lands, the value of mota is determined by the international price of marijuana, just as is the world price of any other commodity. As a pot-proletariat, the Guarijíos are further incorporated into the global market. Through the perverse morality of that same market, the narcos have come to be the only Mexicans investing in rural Mexico, and the Guarijíos are to that extent beneficiaries of the drug policies of the United States, who keep marijuana prices high. The drug traffic is ultimately destructive, however, for narco-related violence surrounds the Guarijíos. But even beyond the bullets and blackmail of the narcos, the drug trade produces lasting dependency in those whose labor is spent moving the contraband crops and who have come to rely on that income. Drug lords leave nothing of lasting value in the wake of their operations. Instead, they bequeath a heritage of easy money that denigrates productive work. Many young Guarijío men appear little interested in traditional work, either in cultivating a mahuechi, or as conventional day laborers. They want the quick rewards dished out by the mafiosos. It is difficult to denounce their decision as irrational.

Cipriano and others are unequivocal on the Guarijíos' need for continuing governmental assistance. INI now provides the Guarijíos free transportation from Mesa Colorada and San Bernardo to Alamos, with a small fleet of trucks at their disposal. INI also provides food supplement programs and very limited medical services. Stock-raising supplies are also made available in limited quantities, and the government maintains roads, after a fashion, boarding schools for children in several towns, and limited technical assistance in agricultural programs. It is difficult to determine the actual per capita value of these services, but their absence would have an immediate and deleterious effect. People would suffer without them, and Cipriano is clear on this point. The INI director informed me in late spring of 2000 that the severe and persistent drought had brought near starvation conditions to many Guarijío families. At that time government assistance programs were inadequate and could not reach the largely isolated population. The Guarijíos' reliance on the government is guaranteed to perpetuate a paternalistic relationship.

The Guarijíos survive on the extreme margins of international commerce. The gross domestic product of all Guarijíos combined is probably little more than a half million dollars. Their lives are determined far more by the natural cycles of the cosmos, earth, and humans than by the artifices of computer-driven financial markets. It seems inevitable, though, that they will be drawn closer and closer into the endless uniformity of things until there are no longer Guarijíos, just undifferentiated humans separated into a small economic elite and an enormous mass of the desperately poor.

For the time being, however, they persist in their chosen, quaint way of life, a model for the anthropologist and the agrarianist, a fundamentally (and only recently) happy people in a land capable of producing much bounty. As the exhilaration of owning land fades into the reality of the struggle for personal and group survival, they will be learning a great deal. Cipriano believes that they will be prepared to deal with the new challenges. I seem to join him in harboring a naïve faith that they will endure.

The tuburadas renew the annual cycles of community and corn, of human fertility and plant fecundity. The Guarijíos I have known and dozens like them continue to plod happily along their endless trails. Their legs remain sinewy, their eyes ever alert for panales and venaditos. There is also an enormous amount they can teach us, and some of us must continue to learn from them. Theirs is a vibrant, intact community, though it appears to be little more than a collection of huts scattered over a vast and tortured land. I hope their grandchildren can walk the same trails in the same spirit.

14
Why All This about Plants?

In this volume I emphasize the plants of the Guarijío region and how the Guarijíos use them. For some readers this constant mention of plants may seem burdensome or obtuse. I have dual rationales for my preoccupation with plant life, however. First, I am curious about plants and have for years been taken with the diversity of plant life in the region. Second, and more important, my interest has a remarkable congruency with the Guarijíos' knowledge and their interest. With the help of Richard Felger, I have been able to log more than three hundred plant species that they use or know, and that suggests a massive bank of knowledge on a subject they deem important. In short, I used a study of plants as a hook to get to know the Guarijíos. I found that questions about this or that plant, what it was called, what it was good for, what sort of flower it had, what kind of fruits, acted as a natural icebreaker and led to conversations that never ended. The Guarijíos are (for good reasons) a retiring people. Once they became convinced that I was truly interested in plants, we had plenty to talk about forever. Plants gave me an entry into the Guarijíos' way of life.

There are undoubtedly many plant species that escaped my notice. There are even more plant uses that I have not recorded, often because I failed to ask the proper question or because I overlooked a plant as we wandered through the region. This is all the better, for it leaves further research for those who will follow and who will have a better eye than I for the plants and a better ear for the Guarijío answers.

Only those with focused botanical interest will want to wade through the plant list in chapter 15. Yet even the layperson can appreciate the critical role that plants play in the Guarijíos' lives. Anthropologists who fail to incorporate the wide variety of plants used by a people are bound to omit vital ethnographic details. Ethnobotanists who fail to see beyond the empirical details of the routings of plant parts will miss out on the larger cultural roles that plants play.

In this section I present a Guarijío plant primer, descriptions of nine plants as examples of how deeply plants penetrate the Guarijíos' everyday life. These plants are of sufficient interest, I think, that most readers will find their uses extraordinary. I hope this introduction will whet a curiosity that will lead to a further perusal of the List of Plants.

While most ethnobotanists seem to be preoccupied with medicinal uses of plants, I have stressed other uses as well. Pharmaceutical companies have paid representatives combing the earth for plants whose naturally produced chemicals may hide secret molecules for curing disease and elixirs for prolonging life. I find the native peoples' uses in their own lives to be far more interesting. Furthermore, the clues we gather from plants as to what people are up to have been neglected by traditional ethnologists. I find Cipriano's dedication to using whatever he can find to alleviate suffering among the Guarijíos to be a fabulous anthropological fact, much more important than any pharmacological secrets he may have enshrined in his work. The remarkable ability of José Ruelas to gather wild foods holds my interest far more than any spliceable gene those foods may contain. Ignacio Ciriaco's litany of lumber and household uses of plants gives me a valuable map of what this land is about, much more so than the potential adaptability of amapa to a commercial market.

I have outlined various uses of plants and reduced them to a few categories: food, medicine, lumber, and occasional others, including dyes, livestock, industrial or chemical uses, and what we might consider cultural, religious, or peculiarly Guarijío uses.

Here are some prominent representatives. The Guarijío name is listed first, followed by the Spanish name in parentheses.

Capiyá (chocolá)

Jarilla chocola (Papaya family)

Capiyá is a remarkable endemic plant well known to the Guarijíos. The nondescript leafage grows during las aguas to nearly a meter in height. With the end of the rains, the leaves and stem quickly wither and expire. The green fruits mature in the fall, ripening to resemble pink unshelled pecans. They fall to the ground and remain there untouched by animals, the only fruit I know that remains unscathed amid the profusion of scavenging animal species.

Food: While foraging animals eschew the fruits, people readily collect and eat them. They have a slightly tart flavor, not at all unpleasant. Guarijíos enjoy the fruits, green or ripe, on a tortilla with salt and chiltepin. The starchy roots, which form a basal support for the stem, are roasted in a fire and are an important source of dietary starch. Gentry

Chocolás and lime, Bavícora.

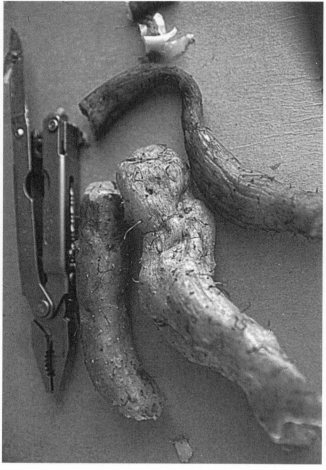

Chichihuó, Bavícora.

(1942:187) had the roots analyzed and found their starch to be potato-like in quality and nutritional value. In Bavícora, José Ruelas dug up some roots and took them back to Bavícora where he roasted them. He then ate them with enthusiasm while we were hiking.

Because the leaves and stem of the plant are ephemeral, one must be prepared to photograph it during the humid and buggy month of August, when it reaches maximum growth. I have never managed to catch the plant on film.

Chichihuó
Dioscorea remotiflora (Sweet potato family)
Chichihuó is a long, robust, many-stemmed vine that leafs out profusely in las aguas. The leaves soon wither and turn reddish brown. In some areas it is quite common. Guarijíos can spot the vines from a considerable distance. They keep track of areas where the vines abound.

Food: The carrot-shaped, tuberous root is relished. It is boiled in water and eaten alone or with a lime and salt, which are said to mask the slightly bitter flavor. Several Guarijíos were eating them during one of my trips to Bavícora. José Ruelas readily identifies the thin, dried vine and traces it to the tuber, then excavates it, following the vine to the thickened root as though he were a badger. José maintains that chichihuó is not eaten "below," that is, in Mesa Colorada or Guajaray, where people can purchase foods from stores. He feels people there are too soft and

lacking in enterprise to dig up wild food. He asserts that chichihuó can satisfy hunger as well as any other food. It is quite common in some areas, but around remote villages it seems to have been eradicated or rendered scarce due to over harvesting. It is surely a candidate for domestication.

Chiquí (etcho)
Pachycereus pecten-aboriginum (Cactus family)
A common, large columnar cactus reaching heights of more than twelve meters, the etcho is the dominant cactus of the Sonoran tropical deciduous forest and of incalculable importance to the Guarijíos. It is distinguishable from the pitahaya *(Stenocereus thurberi)* by the tendency of its arms to emerge from the trunk well above the ground, while the pitahaya is usually (though not always) without a significant trunk. The arms also tend to grow parallel to the (visible) main trunk axis, while those of pitahaya tend to grow at various angles to the vertical.

Etcho door, Sejaqui.

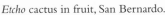

Etcho cactus in fruit, San Bernardo.

Etcho fruits are distinct from those of other cacti in the region. They are covered with spines so dense that the rind or skin cannot be seen. Thus, from a distance the mature fruits appear golden brown from the thousands of four to five centimeter-long spines. This protective apparatus is intimidating indeed, yet the spines are rather weak, and the fruits can be handled gingerly without fear of the spines penetrating the skin. The species name of the cactus refers to an anthropological oddity: the fruits were formerly made into combs. The spines were strong enough to give the hair a good brush but weak enough to present little hazard to the comber. Such brushes were in use during the lifetimes of older Guarijíos, and all agree that in a pinch they would use them still. With the help of a Mayo friend, I once tried combing my hair with one. With a few years' practice, I might succeed.

Hermangildo Zaila states unequivocally that for the Guarijíos of Los Jacales the etcho is the most important plant, especially for food and drink. Its importance is hardly less elsewhere. All the river Guarijíos I asked named chiquí as their most important plant.

Construction: Lumber from the etcho is to be found in the household of every Guarijío del río. Guarijíos use the sturdy wood from the *tarelas* (arms) of the cactus to make tables and doors. The house of doña Isabel Ruelas of Sejaqui was protected by a stout etcho door. The thick trunks may be used for ceiling beams and upright posts, or for making other furniture as well. Wood from the trunk is especially popular for producing *tarimes* (bed frames) often crisscrossed with rawhide strips for a mattress. It is not unusual also to see tarimes made several decades ago still in use, sometimes covered with bamboo canes of otate. Thin panels of etcho wood are also used in constructing Guarijío harps for ceremonial purposes. The wood makes passable firewood.

When fields are cleared for mahuechis, it is customary to leave the etchos standing. This practice leaves a valuable source of shade for the panting cultivator, for the shade of the etcho is valued above that of any other hillside plant. The fruits are also a source of snacks for the hot months when clearing must be carried on. Some of these orphaned, solitary sentinels die of sunburn and dehydration when deprived of the accompanying forest, but most survive as the soil is gradually spent, and the mahuechi reverts to forest. When pastures are converted into buffelgrass, however, the etchos often die within a couple of years, and new ones seldom sprout up.

Food: The tennis ball-sized fruits, the pulp of which is eaten in great quantities, constitute an important component of the Guarijío diet. They first appear in late May, then in large numbers in early June, and continue to mature through late June and early July. Nearly all adult Guarijíos have become expert harvesters. The fruits are ripe when the rind splits open and a bit of iridescent purple or dark red shows through the forest of spines, indicating it is time to harvest. They are carefully pried from the cactus with a specially designed bacote. They are pulled open (it takes practice) and the fruity pulp is scooped out.

In addition to eating the fruits, Guarijíos remove and store the seeds *(machihuí),* about half the size of BBs. To do this they boil the fruit until the pulp separates from the seeds. They then strain the pulp from the fruit in a colander or a length of coarse muslin, and then wash the black mass of seeds. They spread these on a petate in the sunlight, and when they are thoroughly dry they store them in a *morral* (woven handbag). When the time comes, they grind the seeds in a hand mill or on a metate and mix them with *nixtamal* (moistened corn flour) to make tortillas, or they grind the seeds alone to make *jípoca (atol de semilla de etcho)* a gruel rather like cream of wheat. The *atol* (gruel) is made and eaten in many households. It is still widely drunk in dilute form as a refreshing and fortifying beverage.

Once the seeds are removed, the pulp is boiled until it thickens into *miel* (syrup). The syrup stores well and may be the only sweetener available for many months. Nacho Ciriaco reports that some Guarijíos still make wine from the syrup. Hermangildo Zaila reports that although few people still make it, the wine that is made is very strong. Mestizo moonshiners in the region produce ample *lechuguilla* (agave liquor) and Guarijíos produce a mild corn beer from commercial Maseca (corn meal) to complement the etcho wine.

In Bavícora it was customary to celebrate the ripening of etcho fruits with a tuburada. It lasted two nights and featured both the traditional tuburi and pascolas.

Medicine: A wedge of the living flesh is directly applied to scorpion stings, which are common in the region. An alternative procedure for counteracting a sting is to cut a piece of flesh from the cactus and squeeze it like a lime into a glass. The resulting drops are drunk. Alternately, the flesh is stewed and the liquid drunk. Nacho Ciriaco claims you can even chew on a piece of the flesh and benefit from the remedy. Sometimes curers carry out all the preceding procedures. Cornelia Ruelas applies the moist flesh to sores and all manner of insect bites and stings. For "bad" stomach, she cooks the flesh and administers the tea to the patient. For scabies, she recommends a wash made from the cactus flesh.

Saparí, temuchí (mezcal)
Agave bovicornuta (Agave family)

This most attractive agave is fairly common in the Guarijío mountain country beginning in upper tropical deciduous forest and extending well into pine-oak forest. It is uncommon outside of Guarijío country. It has wide yellow-green leaves armed with cowhorn-like spines along the leaf margins, hence the species name *bovicornuta.* While saparí is neither the commonest nor the most widely used agave in the Guarijío region (that honor rests with *Agave vivipara*), it is surely the most attractive. Large specimens reach more than a meter in diameter and nearly as tall.

Food: Guarijíos roast and eat the head with the pencas (leaves) cut off below the bright green pigmented portion. Cipriano reports that the flowers are also edible.

To prepare an agave for roasting, the Guarijíos lop off the flowering stalk *(quiote)* as it emerges from the rosette. A year or so later, when the leaves begin to wilt, they excavate the starchy remnant and with a machete hack off all the pencas, preserving only the starchy center called the cabeza. They dig a pit *(maya),* build a fire, and when the coals die down, bury the head, and leave it for about thirty-six hours. They then excavate the pit and use their teeth to scrape off the sweet meaty tissue where the leaf remainder joins the head, as if eating a huge artichoke leaf remnant.

Saparí is also the agave of choice in the region for making mezcal, perhaps because *A. vivipara* and *A. jaiboli,* both preferred for eating and brewing, have been excessively harvested over the decades. Gentry (1982) noted that *A. bovicornuta* contains high levels of saponins and exudes caustic juices. For this reason, he believed it was considered inferior for mezcal and basically inedible.

Implements: The stalks of the agave are frequently harvested to make bacotes for collecting cactus fruits, both etchos and pitahayas.

Saya plant showing edible root.

Ramón Rodríguez making angarilla, Mesa Colorada.

Sayú (saya)

Amoreuxia cf. *palmatifida* (Cochlosperm family)

This remarkable little plant is widely recognized when its showy, large yellow to orange flower appears, usually following summer rains. Its bright green, dissected leaves also reveal its presence. The thickened roots are eagerly consumed, excavated from the ground with enthusiasm. Since the greenery and flowers appear only at the height of las aguas, when heavy humidity, high temperatures, and throngs of nasty ectoparasites visit the land and ethnobotanists work elsewhere, herbarium collections of the plant in the Guarijío region are few.

Saya flourishes in dense, clay soils of bottomlands and would seem to be a logical candidate for domestication. I have assigned it tentatively to species *palmatifida*. Final identification requires measurement of fruits and seeds.

Although sayas are harvested in considerable numbers and cannot escape detection with their showy flowers, their numbers seem to be holding, a happy development for all consumers and especially for the Guarijíos.

Artifacts: These black seeds, which bounce like superballs when they strike the ground upon being dropped, are also sealed inside bulis and used as sonajos.

Food: Some natives eat the pods and the flowers uncooked. The raw tuberous root, reminiscent of a radish, has an agreeable, slightly sweet flavor and is highly endorsed by natives. It is roasted as well and used as a starch. The seeds are ground and made into a refreshing drink or a coffee substitute.

Tajcú (palma)

Brahea aculeata (Palm family)

B. aculeata is a small palm, reaching a maximum of eight meters in height. The petiole is toothed, unlike that of *Sabal uresana,* the other palm well known in the region. Guarijíos have a precise knowledge of the location of the trees in the region. Tajcús are numerous at Bavícora, less so at Jogüegüe, where the trunk of a specimen had been notched to facilitate climbing for harvesting the fruits. Palms in the Guarijío country appear in general to be overharvested. They also appear to grow in habitats where water is available and homes can be built, sad news for the palms. Still, Guarijíos value the trees and are loath to endanger their vigor or life.

Construction: The roofs of more isolated Guarijío homes in the lowlands are usually thatched with the *pencas* (fronds) *(tajcuupa oala).* These are most agreeable in appearance. When correctly laid down, the sloped roofs are watertight and quiet during a rain. They are said to last ten years. The palm keeps the interior cool in the summer and warm in the winter.

Food: Guarijíos eat the fruits *(tajcú tajcara),* and formerly ate the hearts of the trees. Manuel Rodríguez reports that they no longer eat the hearts because it involves killing the increasingly scarce trees.

Twine: Men and women alike weave rope by twisting the fibers into long strands and weaving them together. Ramón Rodríguez of Mesa Colorada produces fine angarillas from such a rope, making first a stiff frame from guásima branches, when weaving a taut web of the rope.

Weaving: Women weave a variety of guaris and petates from the cogollos. (The best guaris are made from pencas of *Sabal uresana,* however.) Since a dozen or so women weave for the retail market, the Guarijíos are inclined to travel considerable distances to gather the cogollos.

Talacáo (batayaqui)

Montanoa rosei (Sunflower family)

Batayaqui is a small tree or multistem large shrub with a straight, narrow trunk or stems. It colonizes in moist areas in tropical deciduous forest, where it may become abundant. Although it is common in tropical deciduous forest of the lowlands near San Bernardo, it seems to reach its northern limit only a few miles north of Mesa Colorada. In February, batayaqui flowers prolifically, the whitish-yellow dense blooms exuding a powerful perfume most attractive to bees. Indeed, the sweet aroma can become overpowering as one passes through groves of the plants. The trunks or stems are easily felled with a machete, but the plants revive and soon send up a replacement stalk.

Construction: Straight young stems were reportedly used many decades ago for arrows. The springy older poles, up to five centimeters in diameter, are woven into walls and fencing for homes and often are covered with daubed mud. Shorter lengths are used to build cages for small livestock and captured animals. The poles may serve as cross-hatching for flat roofs. When covered with a thick cushion of grass, they are sufficiently resilient to hold the thick layer of dirt that serves as the outer roof.

Medicine: The bark or root is mashed and placed on a bad molar to alleviate the pain. When a woman's menstrual blood will not stop flowing, the root is boiled into a tea and administered until the bleeding stops, according to Lorenzo Sujaguareña. Ramón Hurtado reported that the leaves boiled together with leaves of *Caesalpinia platyloba* produce a tea than can prevent conception.

Tochiyó, tochiguó (palo santo, morning glory tree)

Ipomoea arborescens (Morning glory family)

One of the most remarkable trees of the tropical deciduous forest, tochiyó is common in the region, extending into oak woodland as well. The smooth, gray-barked trunk grows rather elephantine at the base, but loses its diameter rapidly to decurving branches that depart every which way. Thus, although the trunk may measure nearly a meter in diameter at the base, it tapers quickly and seldom exceeds twelve meters in height. The tree flowers when leafless in the winter and early spring. The showy white flowers grow at the tips of the branches and are visible from a distance as so many white points of light on the graying winter landscape. With the summer rains, the large (twelve-centimeter) leaves appear in abundance, and branch tips extend into tendrils, even winding around stems and branches of adjacent trees. José Rodríguez mentioned tochiyó first when he was asked which plants were most important for the Guarijíos.

A handsome yellow-trunked variety, sometimes considered var. *pachylutea* is found in higher regions of the tropical deciduous forest. Many individuals of this cast are found just north of San Pedro and on the road between San Bernardo and Loreto. They appear to be larger than the gray-barked variety and tend to flower throughout the spring into May.

Insect Repellent: The wood is burned for the smoke that is said to drive away mosquitoes.

Livestock Food: The tree's wood is fine emergency fodder for cows, being soft and pulpy. It is chopped into small chunks and fed to them. At Matapaco, a *guacasí carocara*—a club-like tool about thirty centimeters long and eight centimeters thick—had been carved from tochiyó. This was attached to a cord and suspended from the neck of a wandering cow to keep her (or him) from bolting from the herd. The heavy and dangling weight slows and confuses the cow.

Medicine: Nacho Ciriaco observes that the *choquín* (sap) is useful. He recommends cutting off a piece of bark and sucking and chewing on it if you are bitten by a scorpion or for snakebite. He says that it takes away the pain. Nacho's brother-in-law was bitten on the ankle by a coral snake *(Micrurus diastema),* he recalls. He used this remedy and it helped him. If he survived, he is fortunate, for the coral snake is highly venomous.

Several Guarijíos recommended the sap as a pain reliever for aching molars. A drop of it applied to the infected tooth will alleviate the pain. However, it will also cause the tooth to fall out, so it should be used judiciously, they warned. José Rodríguez mentioned that a tea made from the bark should be administered to those suffering from *soleados* (sunstroke) to reduce the overheating and discomfort.

Wild Animal Food: The flower corollas fall softly to the ground in late winter. Deer are quite fond of them, and Guarijíos recognize the flowers as an important source of food for their favorite game target.

Topocá (torote, torote puntagruesa)
Bursera penicillata (Frankincense family)

The tallest of the common burseras of the tropical deciduous forest (up to fifteen meters tall), topocá is also the most aromatic. In the fall the dense crown of serrate leaves more than five centimeters long turns bright yellow, sometimes even reddish, evoking intimations of New England October. Even with only a modest familiarity with the tree, one can usually detect its presence by aroma alone. In late fall, when the region is often without wind, the fresh incense scent of topocá accentuates the clean beauty of the silent forest. Its bark is smooth and gray, without exfoliations. The relatively blunt branch ends (hence the Spanish common name puntagruesa—thick tip) help distinguish topocá from other burseras when it is leafless. Simply sniffing the tree can dispel any further doubt.

Ceremonial use: Although the tree does not produce as much sap as *B. stenophylla,* a mixture of bark and sap smells sweet when burned and is used in local churches as incense. José Ruelas, who was designated as sacristan of the newly constructed (1998) Mesa Colorado Catholic Church, collects pouches of the incense and stores them near the altar for censers.

Implements: The wood is carved into feeding and watering troughs, trays, and other utensils.

Medicine: Nacho Ciriaco recommends a tea from the bark for coughs. I tried it and found it fragrant and pungent. It didn't do any harm. Several Guarijíos note that it is also effective on colds and *gripa* (influenza) as well. Manuel Rodríguez keeps a supply of it in his home as a remedy during the winter months.

15
Ethnoflora of the Guarijíos

David Yetman and Richard Felger

Methods

All the plants listed below were documented in connection with this study except where otherwise noted. Vouchers of each plant are to be found in the Herbarium of the University of Arizona (ARIZ), herbaria in Mexico (USON, MEXU), and others in the southwestern U.S. Vouchers were made of plants below either in connection with this study or with prior related collections in the region, some by Howard Scott Gentry, others by colleagues of ours who accompanied us or who were involved in the publication of *Gentry's Río Mayo Plants: The Tropical Deciduous Forest and Environs of Northwest Mexico* (Martin et al. 1998). Further vouchers are noted in *Trees of Sonora, Mexico* (Felger et al. 2001). In the case of cacti and orchids, all recent vouchers are housed in Mexican herbaria, particularly that of the University of Sonora (USON).

Unless otherwise noted, all the species listed were identified by Guarijío consultants who were present when the plants were documented. They were asked to identify the plants, provide the name in Guarijío and in Spanish, describe the uses (current and historical) of the plant, describe its habitat, and add any other pertinent information. When possible they were requested to demonstrate the use. As much as possible, information garnered from one consultant was corroborated by another. In some cases, idiosyncratic names are included in the list, but the overwhelming majority are widely used common names. All consultants were compensated for their assistance.

Many of the plants were similarly identified by Howard Scott Gentry during his studies of the 1930s and included in *Río Mayo Plants* (Gentry 1942). We have noted many of these, especially where our consultants reported uses identical with those Gentry recorded nearly seventy years earlier.

A Note on the List

We gratefully acknowledge funding from the National Geographic Society and the Wallace Research Foundation, which underwrote much of the work from which this ethnoflora was derived. The plants are listed alphabetically by family. Entries list scientific name and author followed by Guarijío name, followed by Spanish and/or English common names in parentheses. Genera are listed in the index, along with Spanish common names. In most cases the plant's habitat is indicated. In this list of flora the term "tropical deciduous forest" is abbreviated TDF.

A Note on Pronunciation
David Yetman

I transcribed Guarijío names using the Spanish alphabet. Thus I use *gu* or *hu* instead of *w*, *c* instead of *k*. I have found significant variance in plant names from the list described by Miller (1996), who obtained much of his plant nomenclature from secondary sources. In many cases I found it impossible to distinguish between the Guarijío *r* and the *l*, since the two are interchanged subtly. I often encountered variations on the name for a plant. I usually chose the most commonly used form. Field research may find local variations in pronunciation.

Guarijío (Spanish)
Terminology for Plant Anatomy

Bark, inner—sapara	(cáscara de adentro)
Bark, outer—japera	(cáscara)
Branch (of a shrub)—joguara	(rama, mata de arbusto)
Branch (of a tree)—cujura	(rama, mata de arbol)
Fruit (of a plant)—cajpórame	(fruta, bola)
Leaf (of corn)—pacasagua	(hoja de máis)
Leaf (of a palm)—pahuara	(penca)
Leaf (of tree)—saguara	(hoja de arbol)
Palm strips—lajtátiami	(pencas)
Root—nahuara	(raíz)
Sap—cho'í, choquín	(goma, jugo)
Sap, runny—nerora	(jugo)
Seed—ahori	(semilla)
Tree—cusi, cujú	(arbol)
Vine—panira	(enrededera, huirote)

Guarijío Flora

Acanthaceae—Acanthus Family

Elytraria imbricata (Vahl) Pers.
machilí guasira, nachachíchicoli
(cordoncillo, cola de alacrán)

A common herbaceous perennial in TDF, flourishing in the shade of the forest canopy. A slim inflorescence emerges from a cluster of leaves, hence one of the common Spanish names, which means "scorpion tail."

Medicine: The root is brewed into a tea for fever and grippe and is taken to relieve toothache. It is also excellent livestock fodder.

Tetramerium nervosum Nees
saya huehuásira (cola de víbora)

This is one of several herbaceous perennials that grow quickly in response to winter or summer rains in TDF. They constitute basic forage for livestock, given the scarcity of native grasses, perhaps due to many decades of heavy grazing.

Tetramerium sp.
(pichiacaida, rama de toro)

Medicine: Hermangildo Zaila reports that he uses this as a general medicine, especially for lower back or kidney pain, malaria, and susto. He gathers three roots and brews it into a tea, which he then administers to the patient.

Agavaceae—Agave Family

Agave bovicornuta Gentry
temuchí, saparí (mezcal)

This most attractive agave is fairly common in the Guarijío mountain country beginning in upper TDF and extending well into pine-oak forest. It is now used for producing mezcal, even though Gentry believed it was not amenable to liquor production. See discussion in chapter 14, p. 170.

Guarijíos do not use a general term for agaves. Mestizos refer to agaves in general as *mezcales,* though the term *lechuguilla* is used as well.

Agave jaiboli Gentry
temechí, jaiboli (mezcal)

Jaiboli is a very large agave with leaves over 1 m in length, wider than those of *A. vivipara,* but narrower and lacking the spatulate shape and yellow-green color of *A. bovicornuta.*

Agave jaiboli, near El Saúz.

It appears to be endemic to the Guarijío country, having been found only in the region. Guarijíos say that it is uncommon, perhaps because its habitat tends to be isolated in the region, or perhaps due to overharvesting, as was the case during Gentry's studies in the area. A healthy population grows along the trail between Puerto Matapaco and El Saúz. Yetman found a diminutive agave with similar overall appearance on Cerro Sibiricahui near Masiaca, Sonora. There it is also called *jaiboli,* but the inflorescence has not been studied to establish identification. Gentry believed that "jaiboli" was a Mexicanization of "highball," since the jaiboli was made into liquor. The name is apparently a very old one, however.

Food: The head is roasted as with other agaves. Guarijíos report that mestizos also use it to produce mezcal.

Agave polianthiflora Gentry
chahuí (mezcal)

A diminutive agave, each rosette seldom more than 20 cm wide, it frequents rocky slopes in pine-oak forest. The leaves are usually less than 15 cm long with white stripes along the margins and curly white filaments issuing from them.

Food: Although these agaves are small, they are rather common and are roasted and eaten as other agaves. Tiburcio Charramonate demonstrated by cutting off the leaves with a pocketknife, leaving the *cabeza,* about the size of a tangerine, ready to roast. Tiburcio noted that the *chahuís* cook much more quickly than the heads of the vastly larger *A. bovicornuta* and *A. shrevei.*

Agave shrevei **Gentry subsp.** *shrevei*
morao (mezcal blanco)

The plants common in the vicinity of Loreto are tentatively referred to this species. *Morao* is a small to medium-sized agave with gray leaves and recurved spines on the margins. It grows in oak and pine-oak forest. The plants are few-leaved and handsome. Nicolás Tadeo warned that the terminal spines harbor venom that hurts mightily when one is pricked by it.

Artifacts: The tips are often used to prise foreign objects such as splinters from the skin.

Food: Nicolás pronounced them to be very good eating when roasted.

Agave vilmoriniana **A. Berger**
jagüé (amole, octopus agave)

This strange plant often occurs in large numbers on the vertical surfaces of volcanic cliffs, giving the dark old basalts the appearance of being covered with enormous green spiders. The leaves tend to curve downward limply, the margins are entire, and the tips are only weakly spined.

In cultivation the plants are more robust than in the wild, often more than 1.5 m wide and equally high. The leaves of cultivated plants grow more upright, but still are downward flexed toward the tips.

Soap: The leaf is pounded and the mash swished around in water produces soap for washing clothing or as a shampoo from live or dead, dry leaves. José Ruelas affirmed the report of other Guarijíos that if you use the shampoo you will not get gray hairs. He has a shock of salt and pepper hair.

Agave vivipara **L. var.** *vivipara*
[= A. angustifolia **Haw. var.** *angustifolia*]
magí (lechuguilla)

Magí is a medium-sized agave with narrow, dagger-shaped leaves. It is the most common agave in the lowland areas of the region. The leaves grow to more than 1 m long.

Food: The principal method of preparing and eating this agave is as follows: when the plant begins to send up a *quiote* (flowering stalk), Guarijíos lop it off near the base. The plant is then left for up to a year while, they say, the cabeza becomes ripe. When the harvester observes senescence in the plant, he chops off the leaves near their bases with a machete and excavates the cabeza (the "head" from which most of the leaves have been cut off), lopping off the root mat. He transports the head by burro to be roasted as a sweet. The Guarijíos roast the heads in a *maya* (excavated pit) for about thirty-six hours. The bottom of the pit is lined with hot coals, and stones are placed directly on the coals. The cabeza is placed directly on the hot stones, and a light blanket of palm *cogollos* (central unfolded leaves) is placed on top. This protective layer serves to keep dirt off the roasting cabeza. Then the cogollos are covered with soil, and the cabeza slow-roasts. After the cabeza is exhumed, people surround it, waiting eagerly until it is cool enough to eat. The short stem and leaf bases (pencas) become molasses-like in flavor and are a prized source of sweet. The roasted penca is placed, basal end forward, into the mouth and pulled out as the teeth scrape off the sweet starch as in eating an artichoke "leaf." In this way thousands of agaves are harvested. Because the stalk is not able to mature and produce seed, numbers of all agaves in the region except for *A. vilmoriniana* have tended to decrease, according to Guarijíos. Still, they manage to find sufficient numbers to continue the harvesting. On occasion Guarijíos engage in the manufacturing of mezcal (liquor) as well, but mostly this is done by mestizos.

José Ruelas reports that the flowers are also eaten.

Agave wocomahi **Gentry**
totosá, wacomahi (mezcal cenizo)

A handsome, uncommon agave with broad, gray-green leaves. It grows to more than a meter tall and wide in upper TDF. It is perhaps over-harvested and hence found flourishing only at a distance from settlements. Howard Scott Gentry described this species, and many others.

Beverage: Totosá is not used in making mezcal, according to Lorenzo Sujaguareña, who first pointed it out. Lorenzo is a teetotaler, hence his knowledge of mezcal-making is probably limited. Others have suggested that it makes superior hooch (Gentry 1982).

Food: The head is roasted and eaten. Gentry (1982) reported that the flowers were cooked and eaten like squash.

Yucca grandiflora Gentry
sahuiliqui (yuca)

This attractive yucca may gain tree-like stature. It is a higher-elevation plant, found in oak woodland where it is conspicuous, and on drier hillsides of pine-oak forest. Nevertheless, it was known to José Ruelas and Nacho Ciriaco, who live in TDF.

Food: The banana-shaped fruits are eaten raw or preferably roasted.

Yucca madrensis Gentry
soco (sonogua)

A bushy yucca growing on drier slopes in the pine-oak forest.

Cordage: The tough leaves are spliced together and used to bind loads on burros and as an all-purpose binding material.

Soap: *Soco* is still used to make soap in remote Guarijío settlements. Tiburcio Charramoneta of Canelichi demonstrated the technique for producing the soap. He digs up the fleshy roots. With a machete he removes the bark covering of the root mass, leaving the white, inner flesh exposed. Placing the mass on a solid surface, he beats it repeatedly with the blunt side of an axe. The spongy material is laden with lather-producing liquid and provides enough soap to wash several tubs of clothing and several people as well. Some Guarijíos plant seeds to perpetuate the plant, useful as it is as a free source of soap.

Aloeaceae—Aloe Family

Aloe vera (L.) Burm. f. [= *A. barbadensis* Mill.]
(sávila)

This succulent-leaved perennial forms large clonal colonies near settlements and persists long after settlements are abandoned. Manuel Rodríguez pointed out a large patch of aloes growing near Rancho Nuevo.

Medicine: This plant, native to the Old World, is routinely cultivated throughout the region for its healing powers. The leaves are scorched until they split. The liquid that runs out is applied to cuts. For a condition called *ardullo,* a tea is brewed from the leaves and drunk. According to Cipriano Buitimea, with ardullo, you feel a heat inside, like an internal pimple. He reports that people regularly use the leaves for various ailments. Elsewhere the gelatinous flesh is used for a variety of skin ailments.

Amaranthaceae—Amaranth Family

Amaranthus cf. *leucocarpus* S. Watson
huehué (bledo)

Huehué is a summer annual growing to about 1 m tall.

Food: The tiny blackish seeds are ground and eaten toasted or in tortillas. The seeds begin to mature in August. The seed heads of the mature plants and the remainder of the plants are often crimson. *Huehué* is reported formerly to have been widely planted in mahuechis but is now seldom planted or eaten. José Ruelas attributes this demise to the general lassitude of people who live "down below, where they have stores and don't want to plant their food." He reports that at a tuburada, when it hasn't rained, they eat huehué to bring on the rain.

Medicine: Cipriano Buitimea touts huehué flour as the only available remedy for the rash from poison ivy. It is rubbed on the affected area.

Amaranthus palmeri S. Watson
huehué (bledo, careless weed)

Populations of this common summer annual vary enormously from year to year, depending on the extent and timing of las aguas. Those plants that are not harvested when young grow to be troublesome weeds laden with dense, spiny inflorescences. The tiny spines (actually the small bracts on female plants) cause a rash or even worse allergic reaction in many people.

Food: Guarijíos harvest the young wild plants in great numbers and cook them as greens shortly after they spring from the ground following the onset of summer rains.

Amaranthus (cultivar)
guasorí

This cultivated variety of amaranth yields more seed than huehué. White seeds were gathered from a garden at Rancho Nuevo.

Food: Guasorí is eaten in the same way as *Amaranthus* cf. *leucocarpus.*

Amaryllidaceae—Amaryllis Family

Hymenocallis sonorensis Standley
cojcosagua (cebollín de arroyo)

This spider lily, which grows along moist watercourses, has showy white flowers.

Livestock Food: The plant is apparently not eaten by people but is an important food for livestock, especially during the frequent droughts that plague the region.

Anacardiaceae—Cashew Family

Rhus aromatica Aiton
chocopa'ari (aigritas)

A common shrub in pine-oak forest.

Food: The reddish fruits are sometimes eaten but lack the piquant taste of those of *R. terebinthifolia*.

Rhus terebinthifolia Schltdl. & Cham.
chocopa'ari (aigritas)

A larger shrub than *R. aromatica*, its leaves turn bright red before falling to the ground. It sometimes nearly reaches the size of a small tree, but its weak branches retain its shrubby character.

Beverage: The red, currant-sized fruits are gathered and brewed into a refreshing tea with a lemony taste.

Toxicodendron radicans (L.) Kuntze
que cáguare (hiedra)

Poison ivy is viewed as a potent plant, as it is indeed. In the cajón of Arroyo San Pedro it grows in great sheets, covering large portions of the lower cliff faces, spreading out onto trees and the ground in the canyon bottom, forming a venomous blanket of bright green. In the pine-oak forests near Loreto it is equally common. Guarijíos avoid the plant, cautioning that contact with it produces a rash that moves up the arms and legs. They warn that even being near it can bring on the terrible skin affliction. If one sleeps under a tree infested with the vines, he or she runs the danger of being infected by tiny drops of liquid from the vine. This is especially true in April when the vine is in flower. The only remedy known to river Guarijíos is to grind amaranth (huehué, *Amaranthus* cf. *leucocarpus*) into a powder and rub the powder on the affected parts. Nicolás Tadeo of Loreto in the mountains assured us that an effective remedy for the rash consisted in rubbing the affected area with crushed grape leaves (See *Vitis arizonica*, below). In the 1930s natives likewise warned Gentry of the plants' bad properties.

Apiaceae—Parsley Family

Coriandrum sativum L.
(cilantro, coriander)

Cilantro is a well-known aromatic winter-spring annual grown in gardens. Guarijíos grow it in pots or small gardens, using it as a spice or medicine.

Medicine: They sometimes combine cilantro with other medicinal plants (e.g., *Abutilon incanum*, *Tournefortia hartwegiana*, and *Vitex mollis*) to remedy a variety of ills.

Ligusticum porteri J. M. Coult. & Rose
guase mochi (chuchupate)

The thick root of this perennial herb with white flowers in umbels is widely used medicinally by indigenous people and mestizos alike. It is found only in the higher pine-oak forest, usually above 2,000 m, where it is gathered commercially and sold in the lowlands. In spite of heavy harvesting, the plant is rather common in relatively undisturbed forests above Loreto. The Sierra Chuchupate, which forms Loreto's eastern flank, is named for the plant.

Medicine: Most natives of the region keep a supply of dried chuchupate on hand to be brewed into a tea as a remedy for aches and pains, digestive problems, and respiratory ailments. It is probably the best-known medicinal herb in the region and, along with copalquín, is one of the best-known herbs in all of northwest Mexico.

Prionosciadium townsendii Rose
salapí (saravique)

This interesting perennial herb is found intermittently in moist soils along relatively undisturbed watercourses in the pine-oak forests. It has huge, deeply lobed leaves (30 by 30 cm), a cluster of yellow flowers in July and long leaf stalks similar to those of rhubarb.

Food: The carrot-shaped root is a popular starchy food. It is roasted and eaten like a potato. Tiburcio Charramoneta dug up a plant and assured us that it was tasty indeed.

Apocynaceae—Dogbane Family

Plumeria rubra L.
turoco, tosánami (cascalosúchil)

A small tree seldom more than 4 m high, it is identifiable when leafless by its milky sap, thick and the blunt tipped stems, and rough appearance of the bark. It grows on cliffs and rock faces from thornscrub through TDF well into oak woodland. The plants bloom with attractive white flowers in summer.

Medicine: For settling a stomachache, the stem and roots are sliced, chopped, and mixed with the bark of *guásima* (*Guazuma ulmifolia*), and the mash is brewed into a tea. The plant is also said to be effective for a condition called *juguásari*, in which the whole body aches and the sufferer does not want to eat. José Ruelas warned that this remedy is effective for some sufferers but not for all. Hermangildo Zaila treats patients with earache by dripping the milky sap directly into the ear.

Stemmadenia tomentosa **Greenm.**

pei'chí (berraco, huevos de toro)

A tree to 7 m tall with prominent leaves about 10 cm by 5 cm that ooze milky sap when picked. The twin fruits, resembling testicles, as Gentry also noted, when ripe split open to reveal seeds embedded in bright red-orange arils.

Medicine: The milky sap that oozes from a leaf picked from the tree is rubbed on sores to heal them. Nacho Ciriaco recommends the milky sap to heal a boil or abscess. He collects the sap, drips a few drops on a leaf, and places the leaf on the infected skin. He promises that within a day the growth will come to a head and will not get infected. Cipriano Buitimea pronounces the sap also to be effective on rashes and cuts. Guarijíos use milky sap of various plants (*Ficus petiolaris, Euphorbia* spp.) to heal similar infirmities. Gentry was told of similar virtues of *berraco*.

Utensils: Lorenzo Sujaguareña reports that some Guarijíos carve spoons from the wood.

Vallesia glabra **(Cav.) Link**

sitavaro (sitavaro)

This shrub is extremely common near Alamos and is used by Mayos in a variety of ways. It seems odd, then, that it is known only casually to the Guarijíos. This is perhaps because regionally it does not occur north of the environs of San Bernardo and hence is not to be found in most of the Guarijío region. José Ruelas believes that only near Tepara, on the upper Río Mayo well north of Mesa Colorada, does the plant grow in Guarijío lands. The name is probably of Cáhita (Mayo) origin.

Medicine: José Ruelas recalls that the root was roasted and ground and a poultice was applied to skin outbreaks from measles. He believes this treatment is no longer necessary, due to modern vaccines. Hermangildo Zaila still uses it for outbreaks of pimples, however.

Aquifoliaceae—Holly Family

Ilex tolucana **Hemsley**

cusi seyóname (palo verde)

This attractive 10-m tall spreading tree of the pine-oak forest is rather common along the streambed at Canelichi.

Construction: The wood is widely used for firewood and for fencing.

Wild Animal Food: Birds flock to the blue fruits the size of currants, which turn red in the fall.

Araliaceae—Ginseng Family

Aralia humilis **Cav.**

tanipari (palo santo, tepatete)

A small tree to 6 m tall on hillsides in pine-oak forest. It has attractive small white flowers in umbels.

Artifacts: Tanipari has gray bark and wood tough enough to be shaped into axe handles, gun stocks, and the neck of violins.

Medicine: The bark is gathered and dried and made into a tea said to be good for the kidneys and for diarrhea. Nicolasa Escruz of Canelichi maintains a stock of bark strips among her pharmacopoeia. The tree is also well known to river Guarijíos.

Arecaceae—Palm Family

Brahea aculeata **(Brandegee) H. E. Moore**

tajcú (palma)

This is a rather small palm, often not reaching more than 8 m in height. It is an important plant for basket construction, weaving, and food. For a discussion, see chapter 14, p. 171.

Brahea nitida **Andre**

metajcú (palma)

A palm somewhat similar to *B. aculeata,* but with smooth (unarmed) petioles, more strongly bicolored leaves, and smaller fruits. We found it in riparian habitat of a deep canyon in the Guarijío country, and it is probably rather widespread in remote canyons and on cliffs.

Basketry: Metajcú is reported to be not as good for weaving *guaris* (baskets) as *B. aculeata,* because the pencas are thicker, but it is still used.

Cordage: Children in Bavícora wove strong rope from castoff pencas, stripping off long leaf tips and twisting the fibers together deftly. From these they wove the rope.

Food: Manuel Rodríguez reports that people eat the cogollos of the trees (as palm hearts).

Sabal uresana **Trel.**

sa'ó, tajcú (palma real)

A robust palm growing to more than 10 m high. It bears huge leaves. *S. uresana* is more restricted in distribution in Guarijío country than is *B. aculeata.* A population is found near Machimbampo to the southeast of Guajaray. Mestizo cowboys journey there and to other sites in the

Tonchi *(Marsdenia edulis)*. At this stage, these pods are readily eaten.

surrounding mountains and cut pencas for sale to Guarijío basket and hat weavers.

Basketry and Weaving: The best baskets are woven from this palm, as are fine, double-woven hats. The lack of trees within easy access has limited Guarijío production of hats in recent years. They appear to be woven only at Los Bajíos and Bavícora. Although Guarijíos extol the virtues of the hats, most of them are sold to outsiders. The boys and men prefer the commercially manufactured variety available at Burapaco and San Bernardo.

In spite of the shortage of pencas of this palm, women journey to Mesa Colorada to attend workshops on weaving sponsored by the Instituto Nacional Indigenista (INI) and seem to find an adequate supply of the weaving material.

Aristolochiaceae—Birthwort Family

Aristolochia quercetorum Standley
(hierba del indio)
This is a trailing perennial found near arroyos throughout the lower elevations of the region. We have been unable to ascertain a Guarijío name.

Medicine: José Rodríguez recommends a tea brewed from the root for curing *empacho*.

Asclepiadaceae—Milkweed Family

Asclepias lineria Cav.
(hierba de la víbora)
A small bush with herbage resembling small pine branches. It is common in the pine-oak forest, sometimes occurring in large thickets.

Medicine: Tiburcio Charramoneta reports that the leafy branches are boiled and applied hot directly to a snakebite. He could not recall a Guarijío name for the plant.

Marsdenia edulis S. Watson
sohueri (tonchi)
A large, often corky, thick-stemmed vine with fruits the size of small mangos that dangle from the vine as it curls through trees. In a dry autumn when most trees have dropped their leaves, the pod-like fruits become most visible and attractive. The plants and green fruit ooze milky sap when subjected to the slightest disturbance. When the fruits mature, they burst to expose cottony fluff that wafts away with the wind. The pod "shells" drop to the ground where they may persist for months, resembling small coconut husks.

Food: The tasty fruits are eaten roasted (or occasionally eaten raw) when young and tender, as they were in Gentry's day. The bark is stripped from the thick vines and the milky stem beneath is chewed and sucked on.

Matelea tristiflora (Standley) Woodson
mahoí pihualá (teta de venado)
A common summer-growing woody vine around San Pedro.

Food: The fruits, which resemble green Christmas-tree ornaments, are eaten when green, usually roasted.

Asteraceae—Sunflower Family

Acourtia sp.
(tosacora)
We were unable to document a use for this rigid-leaved herb of the pine-oak forest, but Tiburcio believed there formerly was one.

Acourtia thurberi (A. Gray) Reveal & R. M. King
pipichohua
A lavender-flowered herbaceous perennial about 1 m tall growing in upper TDF.

Medicine: *Pipichohua* is eagerly sought for its wiry roots, which are purported to have broad medicinal powers. Cornelia

Rodríguez maintains a supply of them, which she cleans off scrupulously and twists into hanks much like thick yarn. She prepares an infusion by boiling the roots into a tea. Cornelia pronounces the medicine to be a good remedy for colds, urinary problems, and "bad stomach." The tea is intensely purple.

Ambrosia ambrosioides (Cav.) W. W. Payne
chicurá (chicura, canyon ragweed)

A common perennial growing in bottomlands; it is one of the best-known plants of the region. It becomes shrubby, often growing in dense thickets to about 2 m high. The triangular-shaped leaves, often exceeding 20 cm in length, are rough and sticky.

Livestock Food: Mules and burros savor the leaves, often stopping along the trail to steal a mouthful. Horses refuse even to nibble at them.

Medicine: The roots are made into a tea that is drunk to "cleanse" a woman after childbirth, according to José Ruelas and several others. The drink is widely used to ease labor pains as well. To enhance its curative power it is sometimes combined with several other medicinal plants (e.g., *Abutilon incanum* and *Vitex mollis*). This common remedy is administered to women pre- and postpartum.

Ambrosia confertiflora DC.
chipué (estafiate)

This rank perennial herb is locally abundant in overgrazed pastures. Cows refuse to eat it, so it prospers when its competitors are gnawed away. In the vicinity of stock tanks or watering holes entire pastures may be covered with *chipué* and *toloache* (*Datura* sp.), an equally unpalatable herb.

Medicine: For bloating (gas), a tea is made from the leaves and drunk, says Manuel Rodríguez. Cipriano Buitimea recommends a tea as a remedy for *dolor de corazón* (heartache). He explains that you know you have dolor de corazón when your heart hurts. He notes that tea brewed from the root is as effective as one decocted from the leaves, but lacks the bitterness. He recommends that the tea be administered three times a day until the pain goes away. This remedy is said to be especially effective for children.

José Ruelas acknowledged that the plant has other uses, but could not recall them.

Ambrosia cordifolia (A. Gray) W. W. Payne
chipué (chicurilla)

An extremely common small shrub made more common

by overgrazing. It survives on wasted pastures even after much soil has been lost to erosion.

Livestock Food: Cattle refuse to eat *chipué,* but mules and burros relish it in times of drought or when grasses and other more succulent fodder have been grazed away.

Baccharis salicifolia (Ruiz & Pav.) Pers.
guachomó, guagualuasi (mountain Guarijío)
(batamote, seepwillow)

A shrub with willow-like leaves extremely common in arroyo bottoms, *guachomó* sometimes grows in dense thickets over 2 m tall with strong stems. These thickets probably play an important role in controlling floods by stabilizing the channel and decreasing the velocity of run-off. The plants cast a characteristic and agreeable aroma over bottomlands when the air is moist. When one descends from the hot uplands into a valley hosting a live stream (especially at dusk) the scent can be quite strong and brings memories of fresh water to quench the parched throat.

Construction: At Los Jacales the community ramada at Hermangildo Zaila's house sported a layer of guachomó above the *latas* (ceiling cross-hatching) to provide a cooling effect.

Fishing: Guarijíos at Los Aguaros and at Guajaray weave the stems into a weir for trapping fish in the river.

Medicine: Guachomó has a multitude of uses among the Guarijíos. Nacho Ciriaco and Cipriano Buitimea agree that the root is a good remedy for *mal de orín* (i.e., when you need to urinate, but cannot). They mash up the root, put it in water, and recommend it be drunk in place of drinking water. As a remedy for a headache, they pluck some young leaves, wrap them in a cloth so that the leaves are exposed, and bind them to the head so that the leaves are touching the skin. This procedure is widely used for a feverish head as well.

Bebbia juncea (Benth.) Greene
(hierba de pasmo)

This sparsely leaved small shrub is common in disturbed soils in the southern extremes of Guarijío country.

Medicine: This is one of several plants called *hierba de pasmo* for its virtue in healing sores, infections, and toothaches. Eliseo Armenta of Los Bajíos said his family uses it frequently for such purposes. He could not provide a Guarijío name, lamenting that he no longer speaks Guarijío.

Centaurea cyanus L.
jíhiohue

Jíhiohue, a wild relative of bachelor buttons, is a low composite with showy lavender ray flowers, blooming in May in pine-oak forest.

Medicine: Nicolás Tadeo maintains that the sap that flows from the leaves is an effective cure for body sores. He recommends that it be directly applied to the sore.

Eupatorium quadrangulare DC.
juhuecori, guaysi yenira (lengua de buey)

Lengua de buey (ox's tongue) is a robust large-leaved perennial to 4 m tall found in moist soils along shady arroyos, usually in deep canyons of TDF. Mature stalks are square in cross section, hence the species name.

Medicine: For headache, José Ruelas recommends pressing a large leaf to the head or placing several in a hat. Others mash the leaves, mix them with oil, and apply the mixture to boils. Cipriano reports that a tea made from the roots (which are said to be "hot") will help induce and facilitate labor in women. The leaves are also reported to be useful for sunstroke, a malady seen during the cloudless, burning days of late spring. Fresh leaves are rubbed on the forehead to help cool the victim.

Gnaphalium leucocephalum A. Gray
cusiteri (gordolobo, pearly everlasting)

Cusiteri is a perennial herb to 60 cm tall with white woolly flower heads resembling large pearls. It is one of a number of species sometimes assigned to the genus *Pseudognaphalium* called *gordolobo. G. leucocephalum* along with *G. canescens, G. stramineum,* and *G. viscosum* likely are the aromatic gordolobos used medicinally. The commercial gordolobo widely distributed in Mexico likely represents several species of *Pseudognaphalium* (Thomas R. Van Devender, personal communication 2000).

Medicine: The inflorescences ("flowers") are widely brewed into a tea taken as a remedy for fever and aches and to promote good digestion. Cipriano prescribed it one day when Yetman developed an asthmatic cough, and Dolores Ruelas, his wife, prepared the medicine. Yetman drank it and got no worse.

Guardiola platyphylla A. Gray
(matagusano)

A bushy herbaceous perennial 1–2 m tall.

Veterinary Medicine: Nacho Ciriaco reports that ranchers used to boil the leafy stems and bathe cattle infections with the resultant tea to kill screw worms. They poured the liquid down the hole left by the maggots. It is not used much any more, because the screw worms have been largely eliminated in a national campaign.

Hymenoclea monogyra Torr. & A. Gray
jejeco (jeco, jécota)

Jeco is a shrub reaching 3 m in height, with narrow leaf segments or leaves. It is common in arroyos where it withstands heavy floods and helps stabilize the channel.

Construction: Guarijíos weave the straight, small-leaved branches into ramada roofing.

Livestock Food: Nacho Ciriaco pronounces it to be a good food for burros.

Medicine: For scabies, a condition common in children and characterized by body sores and a rash, Nacho reports that the leaves are boiled in a pot and the resulting liquid used to wash the body. The ailment is especially common in June when the weather is very hot. This remedy is still commonly used, he says.

Lasianthaea podocephala (A. Gray) K. M. Becker
mayomecha (peonilla)

Mayomecha is the local name for this yellow-flowered small perennial herb that is widespread in the pine-oak forest. The name may not be of Guarijío origin. At any rate, the uses of this aromatic plant are widely known.

Medicine: For empacho and stomachache, the root is crushed, made into a tea, and drunk. Both Nicolás Tadeo and Tiburcio Charramoneta pronounced it to be an effective remedy.

Matricaria chamomilla L.
(manzanilla, chamomile)

This non-native cultivated household herb is planted from seed passed from household to household. It is a popular medicinal plant among Guarijíos.

Medicine: The flower heads are brewed into a tea said to be effective in relaxing victims of susto. Cornelia Rodríguez administered two teaspoonfuls to an infant suffering considerable distress from a distended stomach. At the same time she massaged the baby for a few minutes. The cure appeared to be remarkably effective.

Montanoa rosei B. L. Rob. & Greenm.
talacáo (batayaqui)

Batayaqui is a large multistemmed shrub or small tree with straight, slender stems or trunks. In some TDF habitats it becomes common indeed. See discussion in chapter 14, p. 172.

Parthenium tomentosum DC. var. *stramonium* (Greene) Rollins
guasaraco

A large shrub or small tree growing in isolated populations throughout Guarijío country, sometimes exceeding 7 m in height. It has ascending branches, large deltate leaves, dark green above and white beneath, and dense clusters of tiny white flowers.

Beliefs: Children wear crosses made from the small branches or twigs so that they will not be easily frightened and as protection against harm. When Guarijíos used to cross the Río Mayo on rafts made from chilicote, they would stick a cross made from *guasaraco* into the wood to insure that they would cross safely.

Nacho notes that people respect the guasaraco and do not cut it down or harm it. If they do, evil will befall their families; perhaps they may all die prematurely. Hermangildo Zaila reports that many years ago his ancestors made crosses from it. If it rained too much, they would make a cross from it and the rain would go away.

Medicine: Lorenzo Sujaguareña recommends rubbing oneself with the leaves to alleviate cold symptoms, especially aches. Nacho Ciriaco recommends the powder from the scraped bark instead. He finds it more effective if mixed with cooking oil and placed on a rag.

Senecio salignus DC.
(ruina)

We were unable to ascertain a Guarijío name for this common shrub with bright yellow flowers and resilient, gripping roots and springy branches. Perhaps this is because it is commonly viewed as a nuisance for its proclivity for springing up in pastures and mahuechis in riparian and semiriparian areas as well as in other disturbed soils in oak woodland and pine-oak forest. It is unpalatable, perhaps toxic, to cattle, according to mestizo cowboys in the region. Guarijíos are not given to complain about it, noting only that yoris refer to it as *ruina* (ruination). It shows up in Guarijío mahuechis as well, but, because their plots are located on high, rocky hillsides, the plant is far less a problem for them.

Tagetes jaliscana Rydb.
sempóari (sampoal, marigold)

Sampoal is one of numerous yellow composites blooming in summer in the pine-oak forests. It is aromatic, as are all members of the marigold genus. The Guarijío name is derived from the Spanish.

Medicine: Tiburcio Charramoneta reports that the leaves and root are brewed into a tea effective for stomach problems.

Tagetes lucida Cav.
jurí (yerbanís)

The leaves of this 1-m tall summer herb with yellow flowers exude a strong pleasant smell of licorice when crushed between the fingers.

Beverage: In the sierras, the leaves and stems of *jurí* are widely brewed into a refreshing tea. Children at Canelichi recommended it highly, as did their parents.

Tithonia calva Sch. Bip. var. *calva*
nacasora (mirasol)

A shrubby, tree-like sunflower erratically common in upper TDF and lower oak woodland. The rangy branches are nearly bare. The large leaves are few in number in the dry season, but more numerous during las aguas. The showy yellow flower heads often exceed 15 cm in diameter. According to José Ruelas, the Guarijíos like the pretty flowers, but do not use the plant. Lorenzo Sujaguareña believed it had a use, but could not recall one.

Verbesina synotis S. F. Blake (batayaqui)

This shrubby upright composite is said to have orange flowers that turn black with age. The leaves when crushed have a strong, perfume-like aroma. It is common on hillsides in pine-oak forest, growing to nearly 2 m high.

Construction: The stiff stems are used for roof slats, poles, and the matrix for walls.

Begoniaceae—Begonia Family

Begonia gracilis Kunth
chocopa'ari (aigritas)

Begonias are common in the pine-oak forest, especially in moist soils near watercourses. The flowers are usually a delicate pink.

Food: Guarijíos suck on the stems, which have a slightly piquant but refreshing flavor. The Guarijío and Mexican name (translated "sour taste") reflects this property.

Medicine: The stems are thought to be an aid to digestion.

Berberidaceae—Barberry Family

Berberis longipes (Standley) Marroq. & Laferrière
lolesí, yoresí (palo amarillo)

A handsome small tree reaching 10 m in height, with dense leafage, it is common on hillsides in pine-oak forest. The margins of the longish leaflets are entire or sometimes with a few teeth. Like other members of this worldwide genus, the inner bark is bright yellow.

Dye: The women of Bavícora use a dye made from the heartwood to produce a mustard color in their palm baskets. The bright yellow wood is chopped into small pieces and boiled. The long strands of palm are steeped for a day in the liquid. Guarijíos venture to distant mountains for branches of the tree and bring them down on burros, for Bavícora lies in TDF, well below the pine-oak forest.

Food: Guarijíos relish the blue/black fruits, reporting them to be sweet and tasty. They must compete with birds for the fruits.

Fuel: The wood is sometimes used as firewood but is generally inferior for this purpose to the more common oaks and pines of the region.

Betulaceae—Birch Family

Alnus oblongifolia Torr.
topocá (alamillo, alder)

The trees reach more than 30 m in height and are common in riparian situations in pine-oak forest, and sometimes occur at lower elevations. They often grow in dense thickets bordering watercourses making access to water difficult. The larger individuals provide admirable shade.

Artifacts: Guarijíos have little use for the tree, but Nicolás Tadeo reports that its wood makes decent trays.

Bignoniaceae—Catalpa Family

Tabebuia chrysantha (Jacq.) G. Nicholson
tabuí yoresí (amapa amarilla)

The most spectacularly flowering tree in the region, the *amapa amarilla* brings a touch of brilliant gold to the somewhat dreary spring landscape. The blooms can be seen from great distances. The flowers are best appreciated by standing directly beneath them and seeing the sun's rays filter through the golden mass. With the flowers refracting the sun, the whole earth takes on a golden aspect.

Usually somewhat smaller than *T. impetiginosa,* these

Amapa. This very large tree grows in Arroyo Jogüegüe where there is little danger of its being cut down.

hardwood trees seldom exceed 12 m in height. They flower in late March through mid-May and are rather less common than *T. impetiginosa*. A tree 13-m tall near Guajaray is well known in the region. It can be seen from the town when it is in flower. Our Guarijío consultants informed us that amapa amarilla leaflets are rounder than those of amapa rosa. The bark is also rougher, they say.

Construction: The wood is used for lumber to make vigas and *horcones* (porch posts) in houses, just as that of *T. impetiginosa*. Yellow amapa wood is said to be harder than that of pink amapa, but trees of the former are scarcer than pink ones.

Tabebuia impetiginosa (DC.) Standley
tabuió (amapa)

A rather straight-boled tree, it reaches 15 m in height, and infrequently more. A well protected tree in Arroyo Jogüegüe is more than 25 m tall. Amapas flower in December-March, producing a profusion of pink flowers that contrast most satisfyingly with the gray-green monte of winter. White-flowered amapas are occasionally found.

Construction: The wood is the preferred lumber for building houses, since it resists rot and termite infestation. Most older mestizo houses in the region boast vigas and horcones of amapa. Guarijíos (who were in the past precluded by landowners from harvesting the lumber) now use the beams occasionally. Ramón Hurtado of San Bernardo scavenged old vigas from a collapsed house and stacked them in his yard to build a house for his son.

Medicine: Cipriano Buitimea described how to excise the inner bark by carefully removing the whitish "cover" or outer bark and collecting the inner bark, then brewing the substance into a tea for treating *mal de orín,* a condition common in men in which they experience difficulty in urinating. Hermangildo Zaila recommends chewing the bark to strengthen the teeth and gums.

Bombacaceae—Kapok Family

Ceiba acuminata (S. Watson) Rose
guacapí (pochote, kapok)

This species of kapok tree often reaches 15 m in height. The trunk is set with varying numbers of large, often blunt but occasionally sharp thorns. The large branches often extend a considerable distance from the bole, giving the tree a rather sudden, broad crown. In October the large leaves turn yellow and brown, presenting a most agreeable addition to the mosaic of fall colors in the TDF. In the dry season the leafless branchlets, which grow at right angles to branches, assume a zigzag aspect. The pendant mango-sized fruits explode into cottony softballs in winter.

In Gentry's studies during the 1930s, *pochote* was used in a variety of ways. We found this situation unchanged.

Beverage: José Ruelas says the bark is brewed into a tea drunk as a substitute for coffee.

Construction: The young shoots and trunks are often straight. These are suitable for use as gate posts. The soft wood is used to make troughs for feeding animals and for light roofing beams.

Food: The Guarijíos used to eat the root, and some still do, according to Nacho Ciriaco. He reports that it has a sweet flavor. Manuel Rodríguez demonstrated the edibility of the seeds by harvesting some and presenting them to us. They have a rich, nutlike flavor. One would need to exert considerable effort to gather sufficient fruits to provide seeds for a meal, however.

Medicine: A tea from the bark is widely reputed to be a good remedy for a "bad" stomach or malaise.

Boraginaceae—Borage Family

Cordia sonorae Rose
camahuí (palo de asta)

A common tree reaching 10 m tall with a straight bole. *Camahuí* grows well on drier hillsides and valleys. When cut or coppiced, it can sprout and survive, even in remarkably dry conditions. The leafless tree flowers a dazzling white in late March and April.

Artifacts: The hard, tight-grained wood is the best for making handles for implements. It is also used for the guide poles for plows.

Tournefortia hartwegiana Steud.
tatachinole ("hot permanent hairdo" in Mayo) (tatachinole)

A perennial herb or subshrub growing 1 m tall, with scorpion-tail-like flowering branches. The currant-sized fruits gradually turn from white to black.

Food: Hermangildo Zaila of San Bernardo eats the berries and offered some to children, who eagerly accepted them. The Mayo name for the plant has been incorporated by the river Guarijíos.

Medicine: For a woman to cleanse *(sanar)* herself or for menstrual cramps, the root is boiled into a tea drunk three or four times a day for several days, according to several Guarijíos. According to some, cilantro enhances the effects of the tea.

Brassicaceae—Mustard Family

Descurainia pinnata (Walter) Britton
jasá (pamita)

This delicate annual tansy mustard grows with cool season rains. It is not known in the higher elevations of the region.

Food: Nacho Ciriaco reports that Guarijíos eat the uncooked leaves raw as greens. Hermangildo Zaila refers to *jasá* as *"quelite de los indios"* (Indian greens) and adds that at times very poor Guarijíos "must eat the greens to survive."

Medicine: Hermangildo maintains a supply of dried leaves. He boils these into a tea and administers it to people complaining of *dolores* (generalized pain). Nacho Ciriaco reports that this use of jasá is popular with mestizos.

Dryopetalon runcinatum A. Gray
guacharay (mostaza, mustard)

A white-flowered annual wild mustard.

Food: The young plants are eagerly sought after during the equipatas when they shoot up in numbers proportional to the abundance of rains. They are eaten fresh as greens, chopped up in beans, rolled into tortillas, etc. They have a clean, crisp taste with a slight mustard-like bite.

Medicine: José Ruelas reported that the seeds were once used as a remedy but could not recall what it was.

Bromeliaceae—Pineapple Family

Hechtia montana Brandegee
hichiconi (mescalito)

This terrestrial bromeliad often grows in large numbers on exposed rocks on canyon walls. The plants form colonies of rosettes like small agaves. The silvery, succulent leaves are armed with sharp, recurved spines. On certain arid slopes littered with volcanic rock, the plants occur in great numbers, making passage difficult unless the lower legs and ankles are well protected. While sizes vary, the largest seldom exceed 30 cm in diameter and height, excluding the flowering stalks.

Food: José Ruelas informed us that hichiconis once were a popular source of food but had fallen out of favor. "They don't eat them much any more. We used to roast them, burning off all the leaves. We would eat all that was left." Manuel Rodríguez, however, still eats the hearts from time to time. He demonstrated how the hearts are prepared. He loosened several of the plants with a bacote of *pitahaya*. With a machete he removed as many of the older dry leaves as possible, leaving only the bases. He then built a fire over the remaining "heads" roasting them for about twenty minutes. When they were well charred, he scraped off the outside, revealing the succulent, white, onion-like hearts. They tasted remarkably like a bland onion. (See Felger and Yetman 2000).

Tillandsia elizabethiae Rauh
guala jichiconi (mescalito del monte)

An epiphytic bromeliad with pretty purple flowers found in moist TDF canyons. While it is well known, it has no apparent use, except as cattle fodder in dry cycles. The Guarijíos admire the beauty of the flowers.

Tillandsia recurvata L.
uchapoli (mescalito, ballmoss)

A small epiphyte of TDF and pine-oak forest, it has no apparent local human use.

Livestock Food: It is relished by cattle and goats and is valuable in the dry season when it falls from the tree and is soon gobbled up by the livestock.

Buddlejaceae—Butterfly-bush Family

Buddleja cordata Kunth
(tepozana)

This spreading 8-m tall tree provides cool shade along roadsides in the pine-oak forest. In early fall the small yellow flowers appear in large numbers, attracting many bees and other insects. Although it is rather common in the drier parts of the Guarijío sierras, we have been unable to obtain a Guarijío name.

Medicine: The leaves are brewed into a tea said to be a good remedy for coughs and colds. The reputation of *tepozana* as an effective source of medicine is widespread in the region.

Buddleja sessiliflora Kunth
huatohué (tepozana)

A shrub to 4 m tall, with dense foliage of leaves to 20 cm or more in length, it is found in open canyon bottoms, as along the Arroyo Guajaray.

Medicine: The roots are brewed into a tea that is drunk by women to cleanse themselves if their blood will not stop flowing during menstruation or after childbirth. Nicolás Tadeo of Loreto reports in addition that Guarijíos of the region wrap the leaves in a rag and bind a sprain or break. The poultice will reduce swelling, he says. Gentry noted the same remedy.

Burseraceae—Frankincense Family

Bursera fagaroides (H. B. K.) Engler
nopoto'oro, yoquito'oro (torote, de agua)

These common burseras have exfoliating greenish to yellowish bark and persistent fruits. The bark exfoliations are usually a nearly transparent yellow-brown. The trees grow to 10 m tall. The most ubiquitous of burseras in the TDF, they alone have no distinguishable use. Nacho Ciriaco says the trees make passable firewood when dry.

Palo mulato (Bursera grandifolia). The bark is widely used to brew a refreshing and invigorating tea. Photo by T. R. Van Devender.

Bursera grandifolia (Schltdl.) Engler
mulato (palo mulato)

A handsome tree to 13 m tall with bark ranging from green to red with large, russet-colored papery exfoliations that help identify the tree. The inner bark is bright red and lacks fragrance. The heartwood is white and also lacks the incense of certain other members of the genus. *Palo mulato* is an extremely well-known tree.

Beverage: Cipriano reports that it makes a tea that refreshes and is drunk routinely when coffee is not available. The tea turns one's urine red, as we can testify.

Masks: The late Ramón Hurtado preferred the whitish wood of palo mulato for carving into Guarijío ceremonial masks to that of other local burseras.

Medicine: The bark is brewed into a tea for pneumonia and to strengthen the blood. It is nearly as popular as *copalquín (Hintonia latiflora).* Many palo mulato trees near

human habitation bear scars that bear witness to frequent harvesting of the bark. Nacho says that for cuts, the dried and ground bark is applied and rubbed in. He reports that with such treatment the cut heals in a short time without infection.

Bursera lancifolia (Schltdl.) Engler
to'oro (torote copal)

When leafless, this tree can easily be confused with *B. fagaroides.* Their bark exfoliations are similar, but fruits of *B. lancifolia* tend to remain on the tree for a shorter length of time and in the dry season the branches are grayish, rather than yellow-green in color, as in *B. fagaroides.* The leaves are much larger than those of *B. fagaroides,* and the leaflets are fewer, larger, and lance-shaped. The wood and branches are fragrant, while *B. fagaroides* is largely without aroma.

Aromatics: The sap is collected and burned for the pleasant scent. It is not as aromatic as that of *B. stenophylla,* however.

Masks: The wood is sometimes used for carving ritual masks worn by pascolas during the tuburada.

Bursera laxiflora S. Watson
to'oro ochóname (torote prieto)

A large bursera with smooth gray bark and a meandering, thick bole. The bark does not exfoliate. Individuals grow as tall as 13 m and often appear readily climbable, spreading about as wide as they are tall. *B. laxiflora* is the only bursera in the Guarijío region that leafs out at any season in response to rains. The sap is somewhat fragrant. The extremities of the branches become purplish in color, an aid during the dry season in distinguishing the tree from *B. penicillata* and *B. stenophylla,* in which the branches remain gray.

Artifacts: People carve the dried wood into bowls and plates, which, according to Nacho Ciriaco, adds flavor to the food.

Masks: Ramón Hurtado carved the wood into pascola masks.

Medicine: The bark and the small branches are brewed into a tea taken as a remedy for cough, a use practiced among mestizos as well.

Bursera penicillata (DC.) Engler
topocá (torote, torote puntagruesa)

The tallest of the common burseras of the TDF, it is also the most aromatic. See discussion in chapter 14, p. 173.

Cipriano Buitimea with *Bursera simaruba,* San Pedro.

Bursera simaruba (L.) Sarg.
(torote colorado)

The largest of the burseras of northwest Mexico, *B. simaruba,* the gumbo limbo of the Caribbean, reaches heights in excess of 25 m. In Sonora *B. simaruba* is known only from a few deep, moist canyons with permanent water. The trees we recorded in Arroyo San Pedro probably represent the northernmost and westernmost population in North America, and the only known population west of the Río Mayo. We have not documented a Guarijío name. Cipriano Buitimea had seen the trees before and initially considered them merely large individuals of *B. grandifolia.* We demonstrated some differences, and he began to note others: the bark and resins smell different; the sap is less gummy; the leaves are differently shaped; the bark is coppery or even blood-bronze; the trees are bigger and the trunks taller and straighter. As he examined the first large tree, Cipriano cut a few notches in the large trunk and pocketed the chips that fell out. When we returned to the tree an hour later, considerable sap had oozed into the fresh cut and had dripped

onto the ground. We lent Cipriano a bag and he collected a couple of teaspoons of the fresh gum. "This might be a good remedy," he said. "I will try it." He called the tree "torote colorado." A year later he reported a lack of encouraging results but thought there would be other uses for it.

The tree's heartwood is reddish pink, which helps distinguish the tree from *B. grandifolia,* which it most resembles. *B. simaruba* tends to have dark green bark when young, nearly blood red when older. The bark has only small exfoliations, while *B. grandifolia* exfoliates in sheets. *B. simaruba* is also more nearly upright than that of any of the other burseras of the region, all of which tend to be spreading trees with meandering trunks.

Bursera stenophylla Sprague & Riley
jecapí, jecahuí, tecahuí (torote copal)

This large, spreading tree is less common than other hillside burseras. It has smooth gray bark without exfoliations, which distinguishes it from *B. fagaroides, B. lancifolia,* and *B. grandifolia.* The leaves are large and the leaflets tiny, bestowing a lacy aspect. Leafless, the tree can be distinguished from *B. penicillata* by the slender rather than thick, blunt branch tips. The terminal branches of *B. laxiflora* tend to be reddish in color, while those of *B. stenophylla* are gray.

Aromatics: The sap (*copal*) also the most fragrant of incenses. José Ruelas gathered several fist-size lumps to burn as incense in the newly constructed Catholic church in Mesa Colorada. Guarijíos use it to sweeten the air inside their houses.

Artifacts: The wood is carved into feeding and watering troughs for animals.

Medicine: The aromatic sap is sometimes collected and used in teas as a remedy for colds and cough.

Cactaceae—Cactus Family

Carnegiea gigantea (Engelm.) Britton & Rose
(sahuaro)

We have not verified the existence of sahuaros in Guarijío lands, but José Rodríguez, a reliable consultant, assures us that they grow on an arid hillside southwest of Mochibampo. His description matches that of the sahuaro. It is known from arid, south-facing slopes and basaltic hillsides east and south of Navojoa (see Martin et al. 1998:274).

Food: José reports that the fruits are gathered and eaten. Though not as popular as those of pitahaya or etcho, they are relished nonetheless.

Echinocereus scheeri (Salm-Dyck) Scheer var. obscuriensis A. B. Lau.
hue tchurí (biznaguita)

This cactus growing on cliff faces has long, slender, dangling arms and red to purple flowers. No uses have been documented, but Cipriano thought there might be something for which it was good.

Echinocereus stoloniferus W. T. Marshall var. *tayopensis* (*W. T. Marshall*) *N. P. Taylor.*
hue tchurí (biznaguita)

A multiple-stemmed cactus seldom more than 15 cm tall, slender, short, spines and large, bright yellow flowers. It is often common on drier hillsides and on rock outcrops.

Medicine: For earache or for pimples or boils inside the ear, the stem is roasted to remove the spines. A drop of the flesh is squeezed into the ear for earache. The same use is noted by Mayos of the coastal plains for several species of *Mammillaria*.

Ferocactus pottsii (Salm-Dyck) Backeb.
hue tchurí (biznaguita, barrel cactus)

A stout barrel cactus, often more than 40 cm wide. It has stout, rigid hooked spines.

Food: The flesh cooked with *panocha* (brown sugar) is considered a delicacy throughout the region. Gentry (1963:92) reported that the seeds were removed from the fruits, dried, and ground into flour or atol. No Guarijíos have mentioned this use of seeds to us.

Livestock Food: Cattle eat the fruits during the dry months when other forage is scarce.

Mammillaria spp. including *M. grahamii* Engelm. and *M. standleyi* (Britton & Rose) Orcutt
hue tchurí (biznaguita, fishhook cactus)

Small, densely spined cacti commonly found in protected places such as rock slopes and cliffs and under trees in dry habitats.

Food: The small red fruits resemble miniature chile peppers. Children carefully pluck them from between the quill-like and hooked spines and eat them like candy. We like them, too, especially as snacks along the trail. One must eat many in order to have snacked sufficiently.

Mammillaria sp.
tchurí (biznaguito)

Small, globose cacti densely covered with spines. Perhaps more than one species.

Biznaga (Ferocactus pottsii), near El Trigo de Russo, Chihuahua.

Medicine: Cipriano Buitimea gave specific instruction for medicinal use of the plant. For cramps, he said, one should peel the "heads" (stems), then cover the cactus flesh with a cloth and mash it with the feet. Next one should rub the liquid that oozes through the rag onto the areas that are cramping. He reports that this is a remedy he and his wife often use to alleviate cramps in their patients.

Opuntia aff. *pubescens* Pfeiff.
huitchiposi (cholla)

The Guarijío name for this cholla is apparently adapted from Mayo terminology.

Medicine: According to Nacho Ciriaco, for treating a broken finger the spines are burned off a chunk of cactus, and the moist "flesh" is bound on top of the injured digit to promote healing and repair of the fracture. He earnestly endorses this practice, citing personal experience.

Opuntia robusta Pfeiff.
jilú (tuna tapón, prickly pear)

This remarkable prickly pear has very large pads, exceeding 40 cm in width, and red fruits. The pads are so large they sometimes give the plant a grotesque appearance noted even by those with little interest in plants. In the pine-oak forests of southern Sonora and southwestern Chihuahua, between 1,300 and 1,700 m, *jilú* is rather common and important to the natives.

Food: The fruits are harvested and eagerly eaten in September. They are carefully beaten with brushy branches or rolled vigorously on the ground to remove the *aguates* (glochids), then peeled and eaten. The newly green pencas (pads, *hilá nacala*) are also sliced, roasted, and eaten with tortillas.

Opuntia thurberi Engelm. [= *Cylindropuntia thurberi* (Engelm.) F. M. Knuth]
sevelí, sehueri (sibiri)

This is a rambling cholla of the TDF to 5 m tall, its skinny branches growing every which way. The trunk sometimes assumes tree form. One may absent-mindedly grasp the tree-like trunk while walking and find a hand filled with spines. The new growth bears tubular, fleshy, green leaves about 3 cm long. The fruits are fleshy, green and persistent.

Food: Old timers ate the tender leaves that are present on the new growth. In some areas they are still eaten, often nibbled on as a snack along the myriad Guarijío caminos. We ate them and found them delicately salty and tasty. Guarijíos warn that they must be eaten before they age, for they are said to dry out and stiffen into spines. Guarijíos also eat the fruits. They are quite tart, but we found them tasty, especially when eaten with tortillas and tempered with lime juice.

Medicine: The fruits are boiled and the resultant tea is drunk as a remedy for stomachache and diarrhea. Nacho Ciriaco described the treatment: when you have diarrhea you cut the fruits in half and boil three of them in half a liter of water. He prescribes drinking this liquid until the diarrhea is gone.

Opuntia wilcoxii Britton & Rose
nopá (nopal)

A shrubby to arborescent prickly pear, sometimes growing as tall as 4 m or rarely 5 m with a recognizable trunk.

Food: Guarijíos eat the tender pads (pencas or *lajtátiami*) and the fruits. The young pads, bright green in color, are lopped off with a machete. They are then chopped up and sautéed or boiled and eaten with tortillas. The flavor is somewhat reminiscent of okra.

Medicine: Isabel Ruelas of Sejaqui recommends a tea made from the roasted root as a remedy for bloating of the stomach.

Opuntia cf. *wilcoxii*
tosanapo (tuna blanca)

An arborescent prickly pear growing on the hillside near Guajaray. The flowers are said to be white.

Food: Nacho Ciriaco informed us that the fruits of *tosanapo* are sweet, with a peach-like flavor. The pencas are also eaten as *nopales*.

Tarime—bed of etcho wood and hide strips, Mesa Colorada.

Opuntia cf. *wilcoxii*
setanapo (tuna colorada)

In contrast with the above, which it closely resembles, the fruits of this prickly pear, which grows only a few yards from a *tosanapo*, are sour, while the flowers are said to be yellow-white. The Guarijío names of these two cacti refer to the different colors of the flowers.

Pachycereus pecten-aboriginum (Engelm.) Britton & Rose
chiquí (etcho)

A common, large columnar cactus reaching heights of more than 12 m. The etcho is the dominant cactus of the Sonoran TDF and of incalculable importance to the Guarijíos for food, lumber, and medicine. See discussion in chapter 14, pp. 168-170.

Pitahaya barbona near San Pedro. Fruits are without spines, hence easy to eat.

Pilosocereus alensis (Vaupel) Byles & Rowley
matácachi (pitahaya barbon)

This handsome columnar cactus reaches 5 m or more in height. It is distinguishable by the dense eruptions of cottony strands near the tops of the upright arms. It is surprisingly common in parts of the Guarijío country.

Food: Guarijíos are especially fond of the sweet fruits, which are rendered even more attractive by the absence of *espinas* (spines).

Stenocereus montanus (Britton & Rose) Buxb.
sahuí (sahuira)

A large columnar cactus similar in stature, habit, and appearance to the etcho. It is found only in mid-elevations of the TDF and is uncommon in the Guarijío region. We have no record of it north of Arroyo Gochico east of San Bernardo, yet river Guarijíos are familiar with it. It is common in the Sierra Sahuaribo to the southeast of Mesa Colorada and in Sinaloa.

Food: The fruits are said to be the tastiest of all cactus fruits.

Stenocereus thurberi (Engelm.) Buxb.
mehueli (pitahaya, organ pipe cactus)

This prominent columnar cactus is especially common on drier slopes and outcrops. Most organ pipes are less then 6 m tall, but taller ones are not unusual. Near San Bernardo some grow in excess of 12 m with over 100 arms.

Construction and Other Uses: The arms of the cactus, dead or living, shed of their covering, are used for just about everything imaginable, including, as Nacho reported, torches. Fencing and house construction in the region would be unthinkable without pitahayas, which are used universally for cross-hatching in roofs. The wood of the trunk makes excellent beams, and the split wood of the arms can be woven into walls, or placed side to side to make a goat- and dog-proof fence.

Food: Guarijíos relish the pitahaya fruits. In July and August these are gathered in great numbers wherever the cacti abound. Eaten fresh they are delectable and satisfying. Children consume great numbers of them, their mouths painted red from the strong juice. The pulp is sometimes boiled into *miel* (syrup). The fruits are sometimes dried and stored.

Harvesting the fruits is accomplished by means of a *bacote* with a wooden point lashed onto it. The ripe fruits are skewered and wiggled from the arms of the cactus. The fruit spines are extremely sharp, unlike the relatively harmless ones of the etchos, so exposing the fruit requires practice and patience. The spine clusters on the fruits tend to fall away as the fruits ripen.

Caprifoliaceae—Honeysuckle Family

Sambucus nigra L. subsp. *cerulea* (Raf.) R. Bolli [= *S. mexicana* DC. of authors]
(sauco, elderberry)

The elderberry is a common spreading tree or large shrub to 10 m tall, though usually shorter, in oak and pine-oak forest. It is found close to human habitations, even though some natives swear it is a native plant. The lack of a Guarijío name suggests that its arrival is recent. A large tree grew on a hillside near Guarijío homes at Canelichi. It was May and the tree was flowering prolifically in large white clusters, attracting many bees with its powerful aroma.

Beverage: Guarijíos report that they often brewed a refreshing tea from the flowers.

Medicine: The tea was also reportedly effective at reducing fevers, aches, and headaches.

Caricaceae—Papaya Family

Jarilla chocola Standley
capiyá (chocolá)

Capiyá is a remarkable endemic plant important to the Guarijíos' diet. See discussion, chapter 14, pp. 167–168.

Celastraceae—Stafftree Family

Wimmeria mexicana (DC.) Lundell
machicari (algodoncillo)

This is a sturdy, muscular tree that reaches 10 m in height. The maculate bark is notable for its natural artistry, showing swirls of brown, gray, purple, red, and white plus all intervening shades. With age small vertical sections of bark curl and exfoliate in seemingly random patterns. When these sections are removed and broken horizontally, the pieces seem to be held together by tiny cottony fibers, hence the Spanish name *algodón* (cotton). When the tree flowers in spring, bees find the prolific white blossoms much to their liking.

Pitahaya near San Bernardo.

Construction: The wood is used for fence posts and vigas. It is very strong but does not endure as long as *mauto* or *cacachila*.

Medicine: The bark is brewed into a tea drunk as a remedy for colds. The beverage is drunk hot or cold in place of water until the condition improves. Lorenzo Sujaguareña notes that only the flaking pieces of bark are used.

Chenopodiaceae—Goosefoot Family

Chenopodium ambrosiodes L.
pazote (epazote)

This aromatic annual abounds after rains. The Guarijío name is of doubtful origin, but the plant is so widely used that ancient derivation from the Nahuatl *epazote* is entirely possible.

Food: The leaves are added to stews and meats as a flavor enhancer.

Medicine: A tea brewed from the leaves is widely viewed as effective in eliminating intestinal parasites.

Clethraceae—Clethra Family

Clethra mexicana DC.
mecoquí (carnillo)

A 10-m tall handsome evergreen tree fairly common in canyons in the lower pine-oak forest. When growing alone it is often upright and rather pyramidal in shape. In competition with other trees it may take on an oak-like shape. The undersides of the large, oak-like leaves are densely haired and prominently veined.

Artifacts: The wood is carved into durable trays and utensils. *Mecoquí* is the favored wood for such artifacts.

Beverage: The leaves are brewed into a refreshing tea.

Cochlospermaceae—Cochlospermum Family

Amoreuxia palmatifida DC. and . . .
sayú (saya)
and *A. gonzalezii* Sprague & Riley

This remarkable plant is widely recognized when its showy, large yellow-orange flower appears, usually following summer rains. It is an important food plant. See discussion, chapter 14, p. 171. Most or all of the sayú population of the Guarijío region are *A. palmatifida,* but some may be *A. gonzalezii,* which can be distinguished by its larger fruits and different seeds.

Convolvulaceae—Morning Glory Family

Ipomoea arborescens (Willd.) G. Don
tochiyó, tochiguó (palo santo, morning glory tree)

One of the most remarkable trees of the TDF, it is common in the region, extending into oak woodland as well. It is used in a variety of ways, including as a remedy for snake-bite or toothache, and as cattle feed. See chapter 14, p. 172 for discussion.

Ipomoea bracteata Cav.
[= *Exogonium bracteatum* (Cav.) Choisy]
ca'morí (jícama)

A strong perennial vine that grows on shrubs and trees of TDF. *Ca'morí* flowers are surrounded by showy pink bracts that are visible for some distance. The actual flowers are inconspicuous. In late winter or early spring, the colorful bracts appear high up in seasonally denuded trees, often fooling the botanist into thinking he or she has seen a new kind of flower.

Cordage: Nacho Ciriaco adds that the vine is widely used to secure bundles, an inexpensive twine.

Food: The root, reportedly sweet, is widely eaten. Excavation of the root is usually difficult but worth it, according to José Ruelas.

Ipomoea sp.
si'toli (trompillo, morning glory)

This morning glory is a vine with lavender flowers, possibly *I. pedicellaris.* So far identification of the species has eluded us, for we have seen only the bare vine.

Medicine: Nacho Ciriaco reports that if a woman does not wish to have a child, she will sometimes eat the seed of *trompillo,* grinding up the seeds, mixing the gruel into water, and drinking it.

Cucurbitaceae—Melon Family

Cucurbita argyrosperma C. Huber
var. *palmeri* (L. H. Bailey) Merrick & D. M. Bates
[= *C. palmeri* L. H. Bailey]
jaragu chijpuame; jarabe chipurí

This is a robust vine climbing into trees and bearing heavy, globose gourds.

Medicine: For "bad" stomach and for parasites, the gourd is cooked on top of ashes. When it is cooked, a hole is made into the top of the gourd, and the liquid from inside taken as a medicine—not a lot, since it is bad tasting. Lorenzo Sujaguareña suggested that it is a reliable remedy for these ailments.

Cucumis melo L.
(chichicoyote, coyote gourd)

The coyote melons form on vines that climb over shrubs and into trees. This weedy species is native to Asia.

Food: Hermangildo Zaila maintains that the seeds of the melon can be eaten if they are carefully washed and all the pulp and other matter is discarded.

Medicine: Hermangildo also reports that a tiny bit of the melon chewed or drunk as a tea is "good for what ails you." One cannot stand much more, he acknowledges. Specifically he prescribes it for aching bones, fever, and toothache.

Ibervillea fusiformis (E. J. Lott) Kearns
gua'leí (sandía de venado)

Gua'leí is a perennial vine climbing into trees so that the gourds ripen while hanging well off the ground. One of these nearly struck Richard Felger in the head as he rode by on a mule. He was delighted with this accidental discovery of the gourd.

Medicine: Several men have reported using the tough vine is as a partial cast for sprains and breaks. They wrap the green stems around the sprain, bruise, or break. It helps heal and protects. José Ruelas relates that he broke his tibia more than forty years ago. He recalls that wrapping with the vine helped heal and protect the break (although it healed poorly). In his early seventies he still wandered throughout the convoluted canyons and mountains of the Guarijío land, so the treatment had at least some virtue.

Cupressaceae—Cypress Family

Cupressus lusitanica Mill. var. *lusitanica*
haguoli (táscate)

This stately, symmetrical conifer with dark green foliage reaches 30 m in height in moist canyons in pine-oak forest.

Construction: The wood is widely used for lumber for constructing houses. It is said to be more durable than pine and is especially valued for building cabin floors. Young trees are often harvested for vigas, for the larger trees are far too bulky for that purpose. The tree appears to be conserved by natives, for many old and tall individuals line the Arroyo Loreto and other mountain watercourses. Tiburcio Charramoneta reports that he plants *haguoli* seeds from time to time to assure a perpetual supply of the valuable trees.

Juniperus scopulorum Sarg.
haguoli (táscate, juniper)

This juniper of the pine-oak forest is uncommon in the region.

Ceremonial Use: For tuburadas, Guarijíos burn the branches for their fragrant smoke. When the tuburada is drawing to an end, the participants place a blanket over their heads and trap the smoke under the blankets, filling it like a tent, breathing in the aromatic smoke.

Taxodium distichum (L.) Rich. var. *mexicanum* (Carrière) Gordon [= *T. mucronatum* Ten.]
jaguori (sabino, bald cypress)

These stately trees reach 25 m in height or more in a few favorable locations. They are found along watercourses with permanent water. In late winter the leafage turns rust colored as the great trees shed their needles, replacing them with bright green foliage. A large flourishing population grows along the lower Arroyo Guajaray, where they withstand the onslaught of considerable flooding and the pounding by transported cobbles and flotsam. Another population at El Sabinal, the spring that is Guajaray's water source, is much less exposed to severe floods but appears to be lacking in vigor and contains diseased individuals.

The trees are important nesting sites for a variety of birds, including Military Macaws, as Gentry (Martin et al. 1998:192) noted: "and with raucous cries and brilliant plumage enhance the somber atmosphere of the groves."

Construction: The wood is used for lumber, furniture, and trays. It is very good wood, José Ruelas reports. It is seldom harvested, however, both because of government protection, already initiated at the time of Gentry's explorations and because of the impracticability of cutting through the stout trunks of rather hard wood.

Cyperaceae—Sedge Family

Cyperus cf. *canus* J. Presl & C. Presl
sí tepa (baquillo)

This is a common tufted sedge growing in clusters at the water's edge. The heads flower prolifically. We found it below a waterfall in Arroyo Jogüegüe.

Soap: The "seed heads" are mashed and made into a hair conditioner that leaves a permanent wave. Manuel Rodríguez related this use with a broad smile.

Dioscoreaceae—Yam Family

Dioscorea remotiflora Kunth
chichihuó

Chichihuó is a long, robust, many-stemmed vine that leafs out profusely in las aguas. As Gentry noted, the root is an important food source. For discussion, see chapter 14, p. 168.

Ericaceae—Heath Family

Arbutus arizonica (A. Gray) Sarg.

juripusi (madroño, madrone)

The madrone is a common tree in oak-pine forest of the Río Mayo, reaching more than 12 m in height, but usually shorter. *A. arizonica* characteristically has checkered bark and often lacks the bright red or white trunk of *A. xalapensis.*

Artifacts: The hard wood is used as fence posts and is popular for making rifle butts and pistol grips. It is sometimes carved into figures. It polishes to a rich, smooth finish.

Beverage: A refreshing tea is made from the bark.

Food: The fruits are eaten, though they are reported to be not as tasty as those of the other juripusi *(A. xalapensis).*

Arbutus xalapensis Kunth

juripusi (madroño, madrone)

The bark of this handsome tree often peels away in papery sheets to reveal a bright red, sometimes stark white, surface. The brilliant color of the trunks of some trees stands out from a distance.

Food: The fruits of this madrone are considered superior to those of *A. arizonica.*

Construction: The wood is used as is that of *A. arizonica* but is considered superior to that species.

Arctostaphylos pungens Kunth

juí (manzanilla, manzanita)

This evergreen manzanita bush has red bark, brittle hardwood branches, and berries that are green when young, turning orange with age. It is abundant in portions of the pine-oak forest and seems to flourish in areas where fires have not occurred for many years or where overgrazing has destroyed native forage.

Food and Beverage: Guarijíos eat the berries off the bushes as they ripen in May and also brew them into a refreshing tea. Berries are also an important trail or snack food that travelers munch on.

Wild Animal Food: Guarijíos note that the berries are most popular with wild animals such as coatimundis. The black bears that feast on the berries in the United States have been exterminated in Guarijío country and in most of the Sierra Madre.

Erythroxylaceae—Coca Family

Erythroxylon mexicanum Kunth

momoa (mamoa)

Momoa is a large, full shrub or small, many-trunked tree of TDF with dense leafage and hard wood. It seems to prefer hydrothermally altered soils but grows elsewhere as well.

Construction: The trunks are used for fence posts.

Euphorbiaceae—Spurge Family

Croton ciliatoglandulifer Ortega

tatarí, tajtari, tasiporo

This small shrub is common in overgrazed bottomlands. It has glandular-sticky herbage and blooms opportunistically at any season. The star-like white flowers are curiously attractive. Nacho Ciriaco reports that if you rub a leaf on the skin anywhere, it will heat up the skin. The Guarijío name translates roughly as "It is hot."

Dye: Gentry (1942) reported that the Guarijíos formerly mashed and boiled the leaves to make a black dye for their wool blankets and other woven articles. No Guarijíos weave now, so that use is no more.

Fish Poison: Nacho demonstrated that a twig is cut up and pounded. Then it is thrown into the river and will kill fish that can then be eaten without harm.

Croton fantzianus F. Seymour

sejcó (vara blanca)

A large shrub or small tree to 7 m tall with mottled gray and white bark. The stems are slender and resilient and tend to grow straight. The plants occur in great numbers in the southern parts of Guarijío country but appear to be absent or scarce farther north at the same elevation with similar soils in Guarijío lands.

Construction: The *palos* (slender trunks) are used for broom handles, for latas on which brush, then soil are laid, and for vigas as well. Where the plant abounds, especially in Sonoran TDF to the south of Guarijío country, it is heavily harvested. Two-meter lengths of the trunks are sold to buyers for use as tomato and grape stakes in commercial agriculture, primarily in Baja California (Lindquist 2000).

Medicine: For empacho, both José Ruelas and Nacho Ciriaco emphatically recommend cutting up the roots and soaking them raw or boiling them. They suggest that the resultant tea should be drunk until the situation is improved.

Croton flavescens Greenm.
jusairó, sejcó (vara prieta)

This species resembles a smaller and bushier version of *C. fantzianus,* and seldom grows to tree size. It is common in Guarijío country. In the dry season, especially after the summer rains, leaves turn red, pink, and yellow, adding a most agreeable appearance to the landscape.

Construction: Jusairó can be used for stakes and roof latas, but lengths long enough are seldom found around settlements due to overharvesting.

Medicine: As a remedy for empacho, the root is sliced and steeped in water, and the liquid is drunk, just as with *C. fantzianus.* According to Hermangildo Zaila, for a skin cut, the bark is scraped and the scrapings are applied to the cut.

Drypetes gentryi Monach.
joyarí (palo verde)

Joyarí is a tree sometimes growing in excess of 25 m tall with a spreading crown in deep moist canyons of the lowlands, where it is routinely found. It typically grows along with *Aphananthe, Sideroxylon persimile,* and *Trophis,* with which it may form a continuous canopy. In the cajón of Arroyo San Pedro it is also found with *Bursera simaruba.* Joyarí provides profound shade.

Construction: José Ruelas believes the lumber used to be used for building. The trees are so large as to be not useful for most other purposes. Even if the wood were shown to be of commercial significance, joyarí grows only in isolated deep canyons where commercial exploitation would be impractical.

Euphorbia colletioides Benth.
jumete (candelilla)

This is a spindly shrub 2 to 3 m–plus tall with weak, thin branches that ooze milky sap with the slightest breakage. Its small flowering clusters appear when the plant is virtually leafless.

No one could recall a use for the plant, but it appears to afford good nourishment to burros. They seem immune to the rumored toxic properties of the plant's prolific latex. José Rodríguez warns that the latex is strong enough to kill anyone who comes into contact with too much of it. It will destroy the eyes and burn the skin, causing blisters, he says.

Euphorbia colorata Engelm.
jiyoque, sehuáchari

An attractive perennial herb resembling a miniature poinsettia. It is abundant from TDF through pine-oak forest. The bases of the elongated horizontal bracts are bright red, making it unmistakable. It is often one of only a few herbs thriving through the periods of searing heat and drought.

Medicine: It exudes a milky sap said to be effective at healing sores and cuts. Tiburcio Charramoneta pronounces a tea brewed from the root to be an effective remedy for pains, especially those of the back and the joints.

Euphorbia spp., including *E. heterophylla* L.
(golondrina, spurge)

Several annual and herbaceous perennial spurges in the subgenus *Chamaesyce* are common in the Guarijío region, and the Guarijíos apparently do not distinguish among them.

Livestock Food: Goats relish the plants.

Medicine: Guarijíos boil the herb and put drops of the liquid in the ear for earache.

Jatropha cordata (Ortega) Müll. Arg.
guajpé (papelío)

This common TDF tree reaches 8 m in height. It has a truncated crown, succulent wood, exfoliating bark, and bright shiny green leaves that are present only during the summer rainy season. If the tree is cut down, it usually sends out shoots and new multiple trunks develop. The wood is odorless, which distinguishes it from most burseras. It also produces large quantities of runny sap when it is injured, unlike the burseras, which produce thicker sap that flows much more slowly. *Guajpé* sap is a powerful staining agent and has left its mark on many thousands of shirts and trousers.

Medicine: The "inner bark" is boiled with cinnamon, and the tea is drunk for cough.

Jatropha malacophylla Standley
jeyó (sangrengado)

Jeyó is a rather strange large shrub or small tree, seldom exceeding 5 m in height with a short trunk or (more commonly) no trunk at all. It is not climbable but seems to be a tree all the same. Its blunt-tipped branches tend to grow outward and upward from multiple trunks, sometimes curling inward. The large leaves, which are present only during the summer rainy season, are similar to leaves of *aliso* (sycamore), growing from the tips of the branches. When the bark is cut, clear to reddish sap flows profusely, hence the common Spanish name, derived from *sangre* (blood).

Medicine: The sap is applied to sores, especially on the head. Nacho Ciriaco recommends cutting a piece of stem and immediately applying the end of the cut piece to the head sore. He also reports that *la llorida* (the sap) cleanses the eyes and is especially good for cataracts. He laments that hardly anyone uses it nowadays except elders and traditional people. The treatment makes the eyes run and the sap burns, so the treatment is not pleasant and may be intimidating to the uninitiated. His grandfather prescribed applying the sap at least once a day but not more than two or three times, and, Nacho says, the prognosis from this treatment is quite good. He had never tried it. The wood isn't good for anything else, he laments.

Ricinus communis L.
yorimaqui, jupa'ará (higuerilla, castor bean)

The castor bean is a rather attractive introduced shrub or small tree found in great numbers in areas where soil has been disturbed. The Guarijío name refers to mestizos (yoris), an indication that it is a recent arrival in Guarijío country. The plant and seeds are known to be highly poisonous.

Medicine: The pounded seeds or leaves are applied directly to the forehead to alleviate headache. A tea is made from the leaves for fever, according to José Ruelas. We are skeptical of the latter, since the leaves are highly poisonous.

Sebastiania cornuta McVaugh
jahué (hierba la flecha)

This verdant, nearly evergreen shrub or small tree has copious and caustic milky sap. It is common around Mesa Colorada. The populations of the plant are localized, entirely absent from some areas while frequent in other similar habitats. When the leaves are removed, milky sap flows from the point of detachment. The Spanish name refers to the arrow poison for which it is widely reported to have been used (but not by Guarijíos).

Medicine: To clean and promote healing of a cut, Lorenzo Sujaguareña recommended breaking off a leaf and allowing a point of milky sap to collect on the tip. One should then carefully apply the point to the cut, taking care not to get the sap on anything else. He warns that the leaves will burn if care is not taken to avoid touching the adjacent healthy skin. Lorenzo's caution reflects the reputed toxic nature of the milky sap.

Sebastiania pavoniana (Müll. Arg.) Müll. Arg.
johué, guarajuí (brincador, jumping bean tree)

Guarajuí is a slender and compact tree. Its narrow trunk grows straight; the branches tend to droop. In the late fall the leaves turn bright red and can be seen for some distance. The fruits develop in spring and fall. From each fruit three "beans" fall out. Each may be infested with a moth larva whose movements (especially when moderately warmed) cause the "beans" to move around or "jump."

The milky sap is toxic, causing vomiting, according to Manuel Rodríguez.

Play: The seeds—jumping beans—are used as playthings.

Tragia nepetifolia Cav. var. *dissecta* Müll. Arg.
taiguali, tejéhuari (rama quemadora)

This trailing, semivining perennial herb has stinging hairs. It is rather common in pine-oak forest but is seldom found in TDF. The botanical identification is tentative.

Medicine: Nicolás Tadeo claims that for severe cases of stomachache the leaves are applied to the stomach and held in place by a knotted rag. He says that this remedy invariably alleviates the condition.

Fabaceae—Legume Family

Acacia cochliacantha Willd.
sinalá (chírahui, boat-thorned acacia)

Sinalá is a widespread shrub or small tree growing in huge numbers in the TDF, with boat-shaped spines. In areas with disturbed soil, sinalá occurs in pure stands of thousands of individuals. It is often considered a nuisance. It and *vinorama (A. farnesiana)* are the first trees to re-establish in cut over areas. Natives of the region say that the life of the sinalá in abandoned mahuechis seldom exceeds 25 or 30 years. With practice, one can judge the chronology of human use of a tract of land by the relative size and shape of the sinalá. Few other tree species in the region manage to become established in such extensive pure stands. Natives believe the *chírahuis* affect the soil, preventing other trees from becoming established.

The reddish thorns tend to grow wide and turn gray with age, providing the tree with a most distinct appearance and the basis for the English language name. In death, the branches bend over in a characteristic shape. Seeing an entire field of dead trees all curved over in the same direction is a weird experience, as Gentry noted many decades ago.

Construction and Fuel: The wood is used for firewood and can be used in making ramadas and roofs.

Food: Feliciano Armenta reports that the seeds in tender green pods are edible and often are eaten right off the tree by travelers. Gentry (1963:93) found that Guarijíos ground the seeds into powder for making atol or tortillas.

Livestock Food: The *péchitas* (pods) are good livestock fodder. In times of drought burros tear off and consume long strips of bark. Their depredations may even kill most of the aboveground part of the trees, although new shoots will usually appear from the base.

Medicine: For mal de orín, Nacho Ciriaco recommends taking spines from three different trees, boiling them, and drinking the tea.

Acacia constricta A. Gray
cucahuecha (garabato, whitethorn acacia)

This shrubby acacia is often found growing on waste places and in overgrazed pastures in the highlands near Loreto (oak woodland and pine-oak forest), where it is the counterpart to the more tropical *A. farnesiana*. This identification is tentative.

Medicine: A tea is made from the bark and the root and taken as a remedy for stomachache.

Veterinary Medicine: Guarijíos also report that cattlemen brew the same tea and pour it down a cow's throat after she gives birth to prevent infection and assure a good supply of milk.

Acacia farnesiana (L.) Willd.
cu'cá, huejchaca (mountain Guarijío) (vinorama)

This is an extremely common shrub or small tree, occasionally growing as tall as 10 m. At lower elevations vinorama is aggressive, quickly colonizing disturbed soils or abandoned mahuechis, where it becomes difficult to eradicate. *Cu'cá* blooms prolifically in the spring with yellow, marble-sized flower heads. They are most fragrant, attracting many bees.

Medicine and Belief: The root is put into water after being chopped up. The resulting liquid can be drunk or rubbed into the scalp to relieve nightmares and to help one forget anger. It is regarded as a general tranquilizer, according to José Ruelas and Cipriano Buitimea, who note the plant's calming effect. The sweet fragrance of the flowers and the root as well are said to produce a calming aroma. (Ironically, the plant causes tension and hostility in ranchers and farmers for its tendency to take over cropland and pastures.)

Acacia occidentalis Rose
te'sá (teso)

A medium-sized to large tree with a thick trunk, *teso* is common in bottomlands throughout the region. It often grows in open woodlands rather than in dense *bosques* (woods). The larger trees may exceed 13 m in height. The whitish flowers produce a powerful perfume. Blooming in March, the flowers soon fade to brown, giving the tree a somewhat dirty appearance. It is regarded by Guarijíos as a most useful tree.

Construction: Straight trunks are used for house building and other construction. Sections of the trunk are carved into utensils.

Medicine: The bark is brewed into a tea recommended for people with bad body odor. If they drink the tea they will not stink any more, according to Manuel Rodríguez.

Acacia pennatula (Cham. & Schltdl.) Benth.
yepohuecha (algarobo)

Usually a small tree, hardly larger than a good-sized shrub, it occasionally grows into a spreading tree. One such tree near San Pedro is in excess of 10 m tall and nearly as wide. *A. pennatula* flourishes in open habitats and rocky soils near the oak zone, especially on indurated ash. Its large spines turn white with age and taper quickly from a broad base to a sharp point. Flowers are yellow and in dense, rounded clusters.

Food: The *chuuca* (sap) is scraped off the bark and eaten as a sweet. José Ruelas says he ate it a lot when he was young.

Livestock Food: Nacho Ciriaco notes that burros gobble up the péchitas.

Tanning: The bark is used to cure leather, producing a dark brown color.

Acacia russelliana (Britton & Rose) Lundell [= *A. coulteri* Benth., missoplied]
mahuó (guayavillo)

This small- to medium-sized tree with hard wood superficially resembles mauto. Its bark is more silvery, however, and the wood lacks the reddish tinge of the heartwood characteristic of mauto.

Construction: The trunks make fine vigas and posts. It is one of the most sought-after woods for construction of homes and outbuildings.

*Hourijata—*ironwood *(Chloroleucon mangense),* San Pedro.

Brongniartia alamosana **Rydb.**
huitapochi (palo piojo, vara prieta)

A rather common small tree reaching about 8 m in height. It remains leafless during the long dry season. Its bark is covered with whitish lenticels that are said to resemble lice, hence the name, *palo piojo* (lice-tree). In the late spring it produces sparse, maroon to blood-red flowers that wilt almost immediately on being picked. The pods may dehisce explosively during the quiet of the fall, the sudden *pop* causing momentary elevation of the blood pressure of those souls wandering nearby.

Fuel: The wood makes for passable firewood for cooking, but that is about the extent of its use.

Caesalpinia caladenia **Standley**
huitapochi (palo piojo)

This small tree has gray-white bark and whitish lenticels. It is locally common in TDF but absent over large tracts. Its uses are the same as those of *Brongniartia alamosana.*

Caesalpinia platyloba **S. Watson**
hueraquí (palo colorado)

This important small tree is renowned throughout the region, though its height seldom exceeds 8 m and its trunks 15 cm in diameter. It produces racemes of brilliant yellow flowers in the late spring. The pods turn reddish orange when they ripen. They remain on the branches well into the summer. The leaves also persist well after they have withered and turned reddish brown. Together the old pods and dry leaves impart a reddish color to the tree's branches during the dry season, hence the probable origin of the Spanish common name palo colorado (red tree). The bark exfoliates in small pieces, leaving a reddish scar beneath. The wood is strong and hard.

Construction: Trunks are used for vigas and horcones in houses and general construction purposes. The wood is said to be resistant to rotting and infestation by termites, and the trunk grows to just the right thickness for fence posts. Hence many thousands of trees in the region are cut for fencing. With this heavy harvesting, larger trees are rare near human habitation and roads. Fortunately, the tree proliferates readily, and young trees are common throughout the more arid slopes of the region, while new shoots spring from cut stumps.

Caesalpinia pulcherrima **(L.) Sw.**
tacapache (tavachín, bird-of-paradise)

This slender-stemmed shrub is common along *caminos* of the region. *Tacapache* produces voluptuous flowers. The banner is yellow and the remainder of the flower is brilliant red-orange. It is native to South America and though common and naturalized in the region, it appears to be confined to areas frequented by humans.

Food: Manuel Rodríguez introduced us to the green and tender developing seeds, which many Guarijíos eat right off the branches while on the trail.

Medicine: Nacho Ciriaco recommends mashing the root and placing the mass directly onto a sore to heal it.

Chloroleucon mangense **(Jacq.) Britton & Rose var. leucosperum (Brandegee) Barnaby & Grimes [= ** Pithecellobium undulatum **(Britton & Rose) Gentry]**
huorijata (palo fierro)

Huorijata is a striking, spreading, multitrunked tree to 8 m tall. The bark on the muscled trunks is as maculate as a giraffe, with interplaying patterns of white, gray, black, and sometimes green. The branches often spread out farther than the tree is tall, arching nearly to the ground. Livestock seek out the shade and cover, resting under the tree as if in a small barn. The trunks are often hollow and are believed to be good habitat for lizards, especially the spiny iguana *(Ctenosaurus hemilopha)*.

Construction and Fuel: The wood, though brittle, is good for posts and also for firewood. If straight sections of trunk are available, they can be used for vigas and horcones, but these are uncommon.

Food: Gentry reported that the seeds were ground and eaten as flour or atol. We found no Guarijíos who continue this practice.

Medicine: Ramón Rodríguez reports that pieces of the trunk boiled "for a while" are good for healing bruises. The liquid is drunk, not applied to the skin, he notes.

Conzattia multiflora (B. L. Rob.) Standley
sejhuahuí (joso)

This stately tree has silvery bark and a smooth, straight bole. It grows at mid- to higher elevations in TDF, especially preferring more moist hillsides. It is said by Guarijíos to be the tallest tree in the forest, reaching over 25 m in height. It is one of the last trees to leaf out with the summer rains and one of the first to lose its leaves. The pods persist, providing an orange-brown contrast with the silvery smooth bark.

The wood is said to be of no use, however. Cipriano complains that if you cut the tree down, the wood quickly disintegrates.

Coursetia glandulosa A. Gray
cahosamo, samó (samo, samo prieto)

A large shrub or small tree with multiple trunks and yellow-white flowers. The springy branches often curve in semi-arches.

Food: José Ruelas reports that Guarijíos used to eat the buds. He laments that nobody eats them now.

Medicine: A lac that insects produce on the branches of occasional plants or populations is gathered and marketed throughout Mexico as a remedy for digestive problems in children. Guarijíos are aware of this use and agree that it may be effective, but do not often use it.

Crotalaria pumila Ortega
jojlino (buli de Diós)

A nondescript thinly leaved annual herb growing on disturbed soil and in waste places. The plant produces pods with loose seeds that produce a whooshing sound when shaken.

Food: Some Guarijíos pronounce the seeds to be edible, but they are not commonly eaten.

Play: Children formerly (and to a small extent currently) use branches with pods adherent as a toy in playing pretend tuburada. The swishing sound is said to be close to the sound of the *bulis* shaken by the cantador of the tuburi, and the children thus pretend to be dancing the tuburi.

Desmanthus virgatus (L.) Willd.
(popote)

A slender-stemmed, small herb leafy during the summer rains.

Artifacts: The long, springy branches are harvested to make brooms.

Diphysa occidentalis Rose
jusiro (huiloche)

Jusiro is a large shrub or small tree with multiple straight trunks and very hard wood, well known in the region. The bark is smooth and slightly ridged with lenticels. The tree flowers yellow in the winter months when largely leafless. The dry pods are inflated. Many plants show signs of harvesting, indicating the popularity of the slender, tough trunks and branches.

Artifacts and Construction: The resilient wood is widely used for latas in roofs and is often split for making sturdy stools, where the pieces form the stiff cross members that hold up the seat, usually formed from goat skin. From time to time it is also harvested for canes and for walking staffs. Many older Guarijíos carry their *bastones* (staffs) around with them. Thick pieces can become formidable clubs.

Diphysa racemosa Rose
quiquisohua, jiparique (flor de iguana)

This tall, spindly shrub of many branches has sticky leaves. It seems to abound near trails and on disturbed soil in certain localities, and it is uncommon over much of its range.

Medicine: Feliciano Armenta reports that both the leaves and the root are brewed into a tea deemed effective on scorpion stings. He recommends washing the sting with the liquid.

Diphysa suberosa S. Watson
juyépori (corcho)

This is a strange, small tree with thick, pine-like, fissured bark with a corky texture. The branches seldom extend more than a meter or so from the main trunk, causing the tree to appear malformed. The puffy, thin-walled pods, characteristic of the genus, help identify it. A tree much photographed by gringo botanists near Mesa Colorada is about 8 m tall.

General: The bark can be used for corks, hence the Spanish common name, *corcho* (cork).

Medicine: The dark hard wood of the tree is made into a tea and drunk for *catarro* (head colds). A tea brewed from the heartwood is thought to strengthen the heart.

Erythrina flabelliformis **Kearney**
guaposi (chilicote, coral bean)

A single or multitrunked tree with soft but enduring wood. It tapers quickly from the base and seldom grows more than 10 m high, although the base may exceed 50 cm in diameter. The light brown bark is veined with white. The trunks often bear broad, rather harmless thorns. When still leafless in May the tree flowers with brilliant red spears sometimes visible from afar. The persistent pods partially dehisce, but retain the large bright red seeds for months. The seeds can often be found on the ground near the base of the tree untouched, hence the belief among gringos that coral beans are poisonous.

Construction: Logs of the thick, light wood are lashed together to make *caquera* (rafts) for crossing the Río Mayo and may be harvested for this purpose on the spot if flooding conditions persist on the river.

Furniture: Comfortable stools of solid wood and benches are fashioned from the easily worked wood. Though the wood seems as soft as balsa, such furniture lasts for many years.

Medicine: The seed is crushed and mixed with water. The liquid is poured into the ear to kill an insect that has lodged inside.

Utensils: Guarijíos carve corks for their *bulis* (gourd canteens) from the soft, resilient wood.

Eysenhardtia orthocarpa **(A. Gray) S. Watson**
pahuió, tenipari (mountain Guarijío)
(palo dulce, kidneywood)

Palo dulce is a small, nondescript tree with very hard wood and rough bark, nowhere common, but not at all rare. It bears racemes of small, delicate white flowers in spring. In Cañon Papachal near San Bernardo an individual tree grows to nearly 9 m high. Most plants in the TDF are much shorter. In the pine-oak forest *tenipari* regularly reaches 10 m in height.

Fuel and General: The fine wood is used for firewood (which seems a shame) and to make tool handles. Lorenzo

Brasil tree *(Haemoxylum brasiletto)* near Chinatopo.

Sujaguareña reports that fence posts made from the wood are said never to rot. Gentry reported that the wood could be used to make wheel bearings.

Livestock Food: The herbage and pods are said to be excellent fodder for cattle, goats, and deer, hence the Spanish common name *palo dulce* (sweetwood).

Haematoxylum brasiletto **H. Karst.**
huichilaco, juchachago (brasil)

Brasil is a common small tree in TDF, seldom growing more than 7 m tall. It is a striking plant, for the trunk is convoluted and deeply indented or fissured, and color variations in the bark give it a most agreeable mottling. It produces small but showy yellow flowers in warm and hot weather. Because of its manifold uses, it is heavily persecuted and large trees are seldom found within a few kilometers of human habitations. The general utility of the wood is similar to that of *cacachila*, Nacho Ciriaco says.

Construction: The fissured trunks make beautiful and long-lasting fences and corrals.

Dye: Many Guarijío women use the red heartwood to produce a dye that tints palm *cogollos* for weaving into *petates,* baskets, etc.

Fuel: Brasil makes the best firewood in the region, burning with a greenish flame. Hundreds of Guarijío households burn brasil wood every day.

Haematoxylum sp.
machicari (brasil chino)

This is an undescribed shrub to 3 m tall superficially resembling *H. brasiletto,* but smaller in stature and with noticeably smaller leaves and orange-yellow rather than bright yellow flowers. The trunks do not develop the indentations or fissures characteristic of *H. brasiletto,* and the Guarijíos universally view it as different from the latter.

Medicine: For women whose menstrual blood does not stop flowing, a tea is brewed from chunks of the reddish heartwood. When this deep red beverage is drunk it will stop the flow, according to Hermangildo Zaila.

Havardia mexicana (Rose) Britton & Rose
[= *Pithecellobium mexicanum* Rose]
huahuichó (palo chino)

This is a large, mesquite-like tree often common in bottomlands. Its bark is similar to that of *Acacia occidentalis* and *Prosopis glandulosa,* but the tree is larger and more elegant than *A. occidentalis,* and its wood is a deeper red. Its leafage is more lacy and airy and its leaflets far smaller than those of mesquite. *Palo chino* produces a profusion of round white flower clusters in late March, somewhat later than the flowering of *A. occidentalis.* The trees may grow to 15 m tall. North of Mesa Colorada it is less common than *A. occidentalis.*

Artifacts: The wood is not good for much, says Lorenzo Sujaguareña, but Ramón Hurtado used it to make both musical instruments and furniture, with agreeable results. On occasion he also carved pascola masks from the red wood.

Dye: The bark and wood are used for dyeing leather and other objects. In the canyon wall of the cajón of Arroyo San Pedro the sides of a natural *aguaje* or waterhole have been diked into a tub used to cure entire hides. Leather dyed with chino bark is reportedly softer than that dyed with bark of mauto *(Lysiloma divaricatum).*

Indigofera suffruticosa Mill.
chijju (añil, indigo)

The indigo plant is a robust, erect shrub to 2 m tall growing prolifically in scattered moist waste places. When the fruits mature they adhere to the drying brown stalks and branches like clusters of tiny black sickles or miniature bananas.

Dye: The women used it to dye wool a deep blue-purple when they wove *fajas* (sashes) and *cobijas* (blankets). Now no Guarijío women weave and the art of producing the dye may soon be lost.

Leucaena lanceolata S. Watson
guasigua

This tree to 6 m tall is scattered in moist canyon bottoms. It has soft, brittle wood. Guarijíos have not ascribed any use to the plant but note that burros eat the *péchitas.*

Lonchocarpus hermannii M. Sousa
[= *Willardia mexicana* (S. Watson) Rose]
japiró (nesco, Venus tree)

A common but solitary hardwood tree growing to 10 m tall. In TDF its trunk is mostly straight. The gray, smooth bark is invaginated in a most sensuous fashion. The leafy crown though dense is narrow and appears somewhat truncated. In April and May the tree produces a profusion of bright purple blooms that illuminate the desiccated landscape. The wood quickly rots, so it is not good for much.

Fish Poison: A decoction made by boiling the bark is used to stun fish. Guarijíos also report that they used to mix the mashed root with dirt and make a *tamal,* then throw it in the water. It would kill fish, they said.

Medicine: The same infusion is applied to animals for mange and to people for scabies and dry skin. The root is also used to make a bath to get rid of lice. Although Guarijíos endorse the antimange properties of the bark, their dogs are often mangy. When we mentioned this, Lorenzo Sujaguareña commented that it was too much work to bathe a dog.

Lysiloma divaricatum (Jacq.) J. F. Macbr.
ma'a (mauto)

Mauto is the dominant tree of the Sonoran TDF. Untold numbers of these trees grow into an anvil shape to about 10 m high, sometimes in nearly pure-stand canopies. In areas remote from human habitation and the need for fences, individual trees grow as tall as 25 m. With age the bark peels into concave strips 10–20 cm long, which give the trunk a characteristic appearance. The wood is reddish, becoming more so when exposed to air. Mauto produces small white flowers in the summer when fully leafed out. During the late spring the tree loses most or nearly all of its tiny leaflets, but the wispy flat pods may persist on the branches, gradually breaking apart and falling away in pieces, thus providing a handsome backdrop to the clear sky of the dry season.

The tree often leafs out a brilliant green in June just in advance of the rains, which it seems to closely anticipate. The bright, fresh leafy foliage sways mightily in the winds of summer *chubascos* (thunderstorms). Mauto is perhaps the most versatile wood in the region, faster-growing than brasil and with straighter trunks than mezquite.

Construction: The wood is widely used for horcones, fence posts, and general construction. No wood is better for these purposes, according to José Ruelas.

Food: The *péchitas* (green pods) are edible raw as a last resort, says Feliciano Armenta. Older Guarijíos would dry and grind them, he said, but he wouldn't want to eat the atol thus prepared.

Medicine: The bark is widely reported to be good for alleviating diarrhea when brewed into a tea.

Tanning: Nacho Ciriaco says the bark is also used to cure hides. He believes those cured with mauto are tougher and rougher than those cured with palo chino (*Havardia mexicana*).

Lysiloma watsonii Rose
machahuí (tepeguaje)

A solitary, often imposing, handsome tree or sometimes a shrub. It is readily identified by natives throughout the upper TDF well into the oak forest. In favorable conditions it may grow to about 20 m tall, but mature trees often reach less than one-third that height. The dark, rough bark resembles mezquite, but the open, angular habit and lacy leaves that wave easily in the wind distinguish it from the latter. *Tepeguaje* leafs out in April and May, the new leafage green-yellow, but quickly darkening to a brilliant green. The shade welcomes the traveler in the heat of May and June when hardly any other tree retains its leaves. It is one of the few trees in the TDF that invites climbing.

Construction: Tepeguaje wood, though not especially hard, is quite dense and will endure for many years. The strongest gate posts for slide-pole gates are made from the wood. The posts are carved into beams, then a series of holes 8 to 12 cm wide are drilled or chiseled. The beams are set upright into the ground, and round poles passed

Tepeguaje (Lysiloma watsonii) in a corral at El Saúz.

through the holes, thus preventing the unwanted passage of livestock while permitting humans and pack trains to pass through by removing the horizontal poles.

Food: The seeds from the new freshly green and immature pods are edible raw. Gentry reported that the seeds were ground and mixed with water and drunk as an atol.

Medicine: Many people drink a tea brewed from the bark for illnesses, especially gastritis, says José Ruelas. We found several homes with a supply of the bark tucked away in the roofing. The tea is also poured onto sores to promote healing.

Utensils: The wood is used to make *bateas* (trays).

Macroptilium sp. or perhaps *Galactia* sp.
(cola del diablo)

A viney perennial growing in a moist cajón near Guajaray. We were unable to collect flowers or fruits.

Medicine: Nacho Ciriaco reports that for snakebite the root is mashed and applied directly to the bite.

Mimosa distachya Cav. var. laxiflora (Benth.) Barneby
(gatuña, catclaw)

Gatuña is a large shrub or small tree of disturbed soils and waste places. It is armed with vicious claw-like spines that often detain the passerby or claim pieces of skin. The purplish to pink to white flowers are visited by hordes of bees. We have not ascertained a Guarijío name.

General: Hermangildo Zaila reports that the branches are stripped of spines and bound to make brooms. We take his word for this, for we saw no example and would shrink from working with the branches of such a thorny shrub.

Mimosa palmeri Rose
cho'opó (chopo)

Chopo is a large shrub or small tree with a straight trunk and often skimpy leafage, the branches armed with small but vicious spines. The bark is fissured with rough and peeling strips. Chopo seldom exceeds 7 m in height. It grows primarily in upper TDF but is also found sporadically at lower elevations. In the fall the leaflets turn slightly yellow-orange, making the tree readily identifiable. Near El Saúz the fall landscape becomes dotted with yellow-orange spots, revealing the proliferation of chopos in that area. The trunks are usually straight, but resist close examination due to the spines. It is a tree of considerable virtue, in spite of its nasty spines.

Construction: Chopo is an excellent wood for posts.

Fuel: Charcoal made from chopo is popular in towns and cities in the region, a threat to most large chopos.

Medicine: Hermangildo Zaila reports that for cough, swollen tonsils, and diarrhea, a tea is made from the bark and helps in all cases. Others mention that the bark is chewed to strengthen gums.

Tanning: The bark is stripped from the trunks and used to cure hides. This use is not common, since mauto is more readily available and equally effective.

Parkinsonia aculeata L.
guacapora (guacaporo, Mexican palo verde)

This spreading palo verde tree may grow to 10 m tall and is common in thornscrub near human habitation. It is less common in the TDF, usually found only in places with disturbed soils. The leaves have long and slender stringy segments and the flowers are bright yellow. The spines along the branches can be most intimidating.

Medicine: According to Nacho Ciriaco, a wad of the leaves is tied together and boiled in water. The resultant tea is then drunk for coughs. He demonstrated this technique and recommended that we remember it for use the next time we have a cough.

Parkinsonia praecox (Ruiz & Pav.) Hawkins [= Cercidium praecox (Ruiz & Pav.) Harms]
hupués (brea, palo brea)

Brea is a small tree with long, scraggly branches. It proliferates on disturbed soil and waste places in the lowlands such as those near San Bernardo. The yellow flowers with reddish anthers and stigmas appear in March, often covering the plant. The pods persist to a dark red-brown, providing an agreeable contrast with the green of the bark.

Beliefs: Hermangildo Zaila reports as follows: "When a Christian dies, we strip bark from a limb and throw it into a basket. We mash or chop it up and then soak it in water. Each person takes an ear of corn and dips it into the liquid, which is now a holy water. They sprinkle a few drops of the blessed water over the dead person."

Food: Many Guarijíos eat the oozing gum or sap as a sweet.

Medicine: The pliable gum or sap is rubbed vigorously on the chest as a remedy for chest colds, according to Hermangildo.

Piscidia mollis Rose
jopoé, cu'u tusánami (palo blanco)

This is a common 10-m tall tree with a thick trunk growing in the more arid parts of the region. It resembles an oak more than a legume. The trunk is gray and the leaflets large, silvery and crinkled. It flowers in summer, producing white and pink flowers and large four-winged fruits. An attractive tree, it grows well spaced in deep bottomland soils, often in combination with *Acacia occidentalis, Havardia mexicana,* and *Ipomoea arborescens.* When lands are cleared for buffelgrass or for mahuechis, the trees are often left standing.

Construction: The heavy wood is used throughout the region as a base for porch horcones made from amapa (*Tabebuia* spp.) on mestizo houses. The village of Sejaqui, near Guajaray, still has several such buildings. Nacho Ciriaco recalled building one such house when he was young.

Fish Poison: When they have no means of catching fish, Guarijíos use the root to do the trick. They mash it well, then place a handful in the water near where there are fish. "Just like that" the fish will float to the surface, for it paralyzes them. Norma Parra remarked that "It is our fishhook."

Pithecellobium dulce (Roxb.) Benth.

maicochini, maicochún (guamúchil)

The *guamúchil* is a large, scraggly tree very common in canyon bottoms and near human habitations. The tree is a prolific colonizer. Given its ubiquity near human settlements and its absence elsewhere, it appears probable that it is naturalized in Guarijío country. Its local origins are shrouded in mystery, but it is probably native farther south in Mexico. The pods are flat and curved or loosely coiled, alluded to in the generic name, which means "monkey's earring." They contain a sweet, spongy filling. Guamúchil produces dense shade, but also sheds branches in the wind in a most disquieting fashion, making camping beneath its canopy a dubious proposition. In deep soils trees grow rapidly to more than 20 m tall. Several individuals in a large grove on the banks of the Río Mayo at Chinatopo were at least that height in the mid-1990s. According to a local rancher, they were planted in the mid-1960s. The bark at first is smooth and gray, with large horizontal spine scars that superficially resemble rings. With age the bark exfoliates in thick pieces on the trunk and lower limbs. The tree blooms in late winter and into spring with many small, white flowers, attracting swarms of bees. The trees are valued for shade and food. Manuel Rodríguez showed us a pill container in which he carries guamúchil seeds. He likes to plant them in suitable places wherever he goes. Both Guarijíos and mestizos view a tree growing in their yard as an economic and esthetic asset.

Construction: The wood is used for benches and for roofing beams, though considered inferior to amapa, mauto, and palo colorado for such purposes.

Food: The young pods are eaten raw or toasted on a *comal,* often in great quantities. Detractors report that eating them results in much gas and tends to give the consumer halitosis.

Medicine: Although the bark gives off a vomit-like smell when freshly peeled from the tree, a tea brewed from it is reportedly a good remedy for "bad" stomach.

Prosopis glandulosa Torr. var. *torreyana* (L. D. Benson) M. C. Johnst.

jupa'ará (mezquite, mesquite)

A spreading tree with a thick and often meandering trunk that may reach 1 m in diameter, mezquite is of major importance to Guarijíos. The trees grow in great numbers in loamy soils of bottomlands primarily around human settlements and livestock corrals in TDF. On dry or overgrazed hillsides the plant may grow as a spiny shrub. Under optimum conditions, trees may exceed 15 m in height but usually are considerably shorter. They usually (but not always) shed their leaves in early spring. In April they produce small yellowish flowers and later produce varying quantities of pods called *péchitas.*

Construction: Mezquite is an important source of lumber for construction of houses and general industrial use. The thick, strong trunks make excellent horcones and vigas. The wood is widely used for building corrals.

Food: Some péchitas are considered edible, but they are not widely eaten in the region or by Guarijíos.

Fuel: The wood is second only to brasil for cooking fires, producing a hot flame with little smoke. Guarijíos use all parts of the trees, even dry twigs, which make fine kindling.

Livestock Food: The péchitas constitute an important source of animal fodder in summer and fall if the rains fail.

Medicine: The bark and gum are brewed into a tea and the liquid applied to the eyes for *mal de ojo* (probably conjunctivitis, but also the mestizo term for the "evil eye"). The whitish gum, chewed or steeped into tea, is said also to be good for fever, as is the root. Cipriano Buitimea maintains that for measles, the kind that affects people internally and produces *pujos* (bloody stools), he steeps mezquite leaves in cold water and prescribes the resultant tea.

Rhynchosia precatoria (Willd.) DC.

(chanate pusi)

This is a vine common in the lower reaches of Guarijío country. It is curious for the currant-sized seeds, that ripen hard and shiny, half red and half black.

Beliefs: Guarijíos and other natives of the region regard the seeds as bringing good luck and enjoy carrying them in their pockets. So do we.

Senna atomaria (L.) H. S. Irwin & Barneby

juracosi (palo zorillo)

Juracosi is a spreading drought-deciduous tree to 10 m tall, common in TDF. The leaves are bright green above, lighter green beneath, often 20 cm long with leaflets each 5–12 cm long. They have a faint but distinctly pungent odor when crushed. The loose, dark bark is often maculated with gray designs. Older trees exhibit occasional invaginations on the trunk. The tree flowers yellow in May when mostly leafless. Cipriano Buitimea maintains one in his yard at Jánaco. It provides fine shade after it leafs out in mid-June but is not much help during the driving heat of May. The fruits are long, pendulous pods to 30 cm long that may persist for many months, sometimes making the tree appear alive with small green snakes.

Construction: The wood can be used in constructing houses and ramadas, even if it isn't the best.

Food: Bees flock to the flowers, producing honey valued by the Guarijíos.

Medicine: The leaves are bound to the head in a rag to cure headaches, according to José Ruelas and Nacho Ciriaco.

Senna pallida (Vahl) **H. S. Irwin & Barneby**
quichi suva, quichisohuira (flor de iguana)

This is a common shrub that produces bright yellow flowers throughout the year. At times it is nearly the only plant in flower. Guarijíos mentioned no use for it but noted that spiny-tailed iguanas *(Ctenosaura hemilopha),* large native lizards, eat the flowers, hence the name that both in Guarijío and Spanish translates as "iguana flower."

Zornia reticulata **Sm.**
machilí (contraveneno)

This low perennial herb has showy yellow flowers.

Medicine: Machilí is well known in the pine-oak forest as a remedy for scorpion stings. Scorpions find roof latas and shakes much to their liking and are a constant presence throughout Guarijío country. The leaves and inflorescence of *machilí* are steeped into a tea that is drunk to alleviate the pain of the sting. The liquid may also be applied directly to the area of the sting.

Fagaceae—Beech Family

Quercus albocincta **Trel.**
aguacume, cusi (cusi)

The *cusi* is a small oak tree at the lower limit of its range, about 600 m, in Guarijío country. At higher elevations, it becomes a fine, spreading tree renowned for shade, acorns, and firewood. Trees may grow as tall as 15 m in Guarijío country and spread over a similar expanse. The bark is dark and fissured. The leaves—to 20 cm long—are shiny light green with distinctive bristle-tipped lobes. Cusi is one of three lowland species of oak (along with *Q. chihuahuensis* and *Q. tuberculata)* found in the lower foothills and as such is more familiar to river Guarijíos than to mountain Guarijíos. The name cusi is used widely in the Sierra Madre of Sonora and Chihuahua to refer to *Q. albocincta*

and various other black-barked oaks. The name appears to be of Guarijío or Tarahumara origin.

Construction and Fuel: The wood is good for building and makes excellent firewood.

Food: The mountain Guarijíos, in whose lands *Q. albocincta* is uncommon, acknowledge the superiority of its acorns for human consumption. Lorenzo Sujaguareña of Mesa Colorada pronounced them to be highly edible, in contrast with others, which he scorned.

Medicine: Guarijíos scorch the bark, chop it up finely, and place the ashes on a sore to help it heal. Nacho Ciriaco has also used the unscorched bark as a remedy for empacho, boiling it and administering it as a tea to be drunk.

Quercus arizonica **Sarg.**
tojá, mabacú (encino blanco, Arizona oak)

A medium- to large-sized oak in the pine-oak forest.

Fuel and Construction: *Tojá* is used as firewood and for stakes. The wood is not as strong as others and deteriorates soon after being cut, so it tends to be scorned as a source of construction lumber. For fence posts it is recommended and widely used.

Livestock Food: The acorns are said to be excellent for pigs, but for humans the cusi is better, most agree.

Quercus chihuahuensis **Trel.**
tojá (encino, Chihuahua oak)

A common white oak at lower elevations, it is found along with *Q. albocincta* and *Q. tuberculata,* sometimes appearing on soils of indurated ash at elevations below 700 m. The spreading trees, usually smaller than *Q. albocincta,* often grow to 10 m tall. The bark is light grayish and checkered. The leaves are shallowly lobed, fuzzy, and dull-colored. The acorns are considered inedible.

Fuel: The wood is burned for fuel.

Medicine: Ramón Rodríguez maintains that the ashes from incinerated bark will alleviate the pain of burns when sprinkled on the affected area.

Soap: For making soap, a large pile of wood is gathered and burned. The ashes are placed on a cloth and water is poured over them. The liquid is collected and heated with pig fat and a utilitarian soap congeals from the mess. Both José Ruelas and Nacho Ciriaco report that such soap was made in their homes when they were young. We have no record of other oaks used for this purpose.

Leaf of *güeja* oak *(Quercus tarahumara),* Canelichi.

Güeja oak *(Quercus tarahumara),* Canelichi.

Quercus coccolobifolia **Trel.**
chayó (encino prieto, encino manzana)

A medium-sized oak, taller than 10 m, of the pine-oak forest. The tough, roundish leaves are somewhat yellow-pubescent below.

Dye: Nicolás Tadeo mentioned that the bark is commonly harvested for dyeing hides. The bark is shredded and soaked. Hides are added to the solution and soaked for up to twenty days. They emerge from the soaking a reddish color.

Fuel: The wood is considered to be inferior to that of other oaks as firewood.

Quercus durifolia **Seemann**
cibulá, guachichili (encino prieto)

A medium to large-size, dark-barked oak to 25 m tall, with smallish, ovate leaves green above and whitish below.

Fuel and Construction: *Cibulá* is used indifferently for firewood and lumber.

Quercus hypoleucoides **A. Camus**
pahoutó (encino, silverleaf oak)

A common oak in the lower to middle pine-oak forest. Its slender oblong leaves are dark green above, fuzzy white beneath and often have a few teeth on the margins. Under good soil and moisture conditions it becomes a large tree, sometimes reaching a height of 25 m.

Fuel and Construction: *Pahoutó* is one of the better firewoods, and due to its often long, straight trunks, is vulnerable to extensive commercial lumbering. It is widely used by Guarijíos as a lumber tree as well.

Quercus perpallida **Trel.**
(encino cacachila)

A large, rather narrow-trunked oak. It is common near Canelichi. We have been unable to ascertain a Guarijío name for the tree.

Fuel and Construction: The wood makes acceptable firewood and lumber.

Quercus tarahumara Spellenb., J. R. Bacon & Breedlove

togohué (encino roble, güeja, hand-basin oak)
This strange oak frequents acidic and indurated ash soils. In the Guarijío region it is a small tree, reaching 10 m, but usually much smaller. It produces enormous concave, leathery leaves that seem to overwhelm the branches. On the boughs they rattle against each other in the wind, while the dead leaves crack loudly when trampled upon. On the tree they appear like so many dark green umbrellas. Tiburcio Charramoneta observes that the leaves remain the same color throughout the year, hardly changing even when new.

Fuel: Guarijíos use the wood for firewood but for little else.

Quercus tuberculata Liebm.

saga'ó, sajahué, sajahuó (encino roble)
A spreading oak to 10 m tall, it grows in upper TDF, the oak zone, and on acidic soils well below the oak zone. The bark is a flaky gray, the leaves shiny above, duller below, with shallowly lobed margins.

Construction and Fuel: The wood is widely used for firewood and horcones.

Food: The acorns can be eaten raw or cooked, according to Lorenzo Sujaguareña, though they are not a great food. He has spent many days on foot, following Guarijío caminos, and has eaten them to survive.

Wild Animal Food: Nacho Ciriaco scorns the acorns as human food, saying they are better left to javelinas. Cipriano Buitimea says they are good food for deer.

Quercus viminia Trel.

guachichiri (saucillo, willow-leaf oak)
The well-named willow-leaved oak attains a height of 15 m in the pine-oak forest, becoming a great, spreading tree providing abundant shade and protection from sudden rain showers.

Construction and Fuel: Its wood is widely used for fence posts, house beams, and firewood.

Fouquieriaceae—Ocotillo Family

Fouquieria macdougalii Nash

chonolí (jaboncillo, palo pitillo, tree ocotillo)
Chonolí is a strange tree growing to 10 m tall with a trunk to 30 cm in diameter or more. It is most common on xeric slopes where it may be reduced to shrub size. The bark is yellow-green, sometimes with diamond-shaped patterns. At

Javier Zazueta and *chonolí (Fouquieria macdougalii)* near Huataturi.

times it exfoliates in sheets. The branches are skinny, curling arms that extend in every which way. This drought-deciduous tree leafs out any time of year in response to moisture. The bright red tubular flowers appear after rains and at other times as well.

Medicine: Lorenzo Sujaguareña reports that the bark is an effective remedy for aching molars. Members of his family chop up a piece of bark and apply it to the afflicted tooth. Nacho Ciriaco's family does the same.

Soap: The bark, pounded and moistened, has been used for soap, as Nacho Ciriaco points out, but he has never used it himself. Other natives still use it, however, and the Spanish name *jaboncillo* refers to the bark's soapy properties.

Hydrangeaceae
—Hydrangea Family

Hydrangea seemannii L. Riley
joyapí (salsaparilla)

A large, scandent shrub or spreading vine in pine-oak forest near watercourses, *joyapí* often produces a stem as thick as a man's arm. It may virtually cover smaller trees and often grows across cliff faces. It flowers heavily and fragrantly in May.

Medicine: The leaves are brewed to make a tea taken to cure pneumonia, aches, and pains. Such a tea is said to be "good" for the blood, a general tonic. Nicolasa Escruz recommends regular use of the tea to strengthen the heart.

Hydrophyllaceae—Waterleaf Family

Nama hispidum A. Gray
tejposi teroquira (talón de topo)

While this low annual was given a name, no one could recall a use for it.

Nama jamaicense L.
(quelipa)

A low-lying, inconspicuous annual with small lavender flowers.

Food: Several Guarijíos note that when the greens are young and tender they are eaten boiled or fried with tortillas and salt.

Phacelia gentryi Constance
tuchiquí ta'ara (pata de pájero)

A winter-spring annual with irritating herbage and pale lavender flowers.

Food: According to Hermangildo Zaila, the very young plants are eaten when they are green and tender, before flowering, and are much relished at Los Jacales. Given the plant's highly irritating and bad-smelling qualities, we are surprised and somewhat skeptical of this report. We await a year when equipatas make the plant available for taste testing.

Iridaceae—Iris Family

Tigridia pavonia (L. f.) DC.
palásehua

This spectacular tiger lily grows on moist soils along streamsides in the pine-oak forest, where it is well known to Guarijíos. It has three large petal blades of bright reddish orange surrounding a yellow spotted cup.

The Guarijío name means simply "beautiful flower."

Food: Gentry (1942) reported that Guarijíos roasted and ate the bulbs. We have been unable to replicate his findings. Perhaps this knowledge has been lost to the Guarijíos.

Krameriaceae—Ratany Family

Krameria erecta Schultes
(tahué, ratany)

A small, densely branched shrub with stubby branches and small grayish leaves.

The uses are the same as for *K. sonorae,* below. This is probably the "other" *tahué* to which Lorenzo referred.

Krameria sonorae Britton
(tahué, ratany)

A scrubby shrub with sparse foliage, it is relatively uncommon in the Guarijío region. We have not ascertained a Guarijío name for the plant.

Medicine: *Tahué* root is widely used among native peoples south of the Guarijío region as a remedy for healing sores and as a tea for aching kidneys. Among the Guarijíos, Lorenzo Sujaguareña reported that it and another tahué was used for some remedy, but he could not recall what. This suggests that some knowledge of the plant has been lost. Hermangildo Zaila, however, recommends a tea decocted from the root as a remedy for tonsillitis and diarrhea.

Lamiaceae (Labiateae)—Mint Family

Hedeoma floribundum Standley
mapá (orégano)

A low annual with lavender flowers in the pine-oak forest.

Food and Beverage: Several Guarijíos report that it is widely used as a seasoning and to brew a refreshing tea.

Hyptis albida Kunth
bibinó, huibinó (salvia, desert lavender)

A common, straight-stemmed shrub to 3 m tall found in great numbers in bottomlands and less frequently on hillsides. The shrub has a gray appearance, even when in full bloom with tiny purple flowers. The leaves and twigs are densely gray-pubescent, which probably adds to their ability to burn. The herbage and flowers are highly fragrant.

Fumigant: The branches are gathered into bunches and torched to fumigate a room or a house. The fragrant smoke is said to have a cleansing and calming effect.

Medicine: The leaves or roots are made into a tea for "cleansing" women during labor and after birth. The tea is rendered more effective when mixed with the bark of *Callaeum macropterum* and *Vitex mollis,* according to José Ruelas. He believes the same tea is also effective for colic of the stomach. Nacho Ciriaco claims that the leaves placed on the forehead are a good remedy for headaches. Hermangildo Zaila says the flower branch is brewed into a tea for the same purpose.

Hyptis suaveolens (L.) Poit.
comba'ari (chani)

This coarse but fragrant annual is greatly esteemed. Large bunches are gathered and stored in the home to keep them handy for food and medicine. The seeds are highly hygroscopic—swelling when wet.

Food: The atol of *comba'ari* is considered a food as well as a medicine.

Medicine: The fruits of *H. suaveolens* are often used in the field to remove foreign objects from the eye. A seed is put directly into the eye. It quickly absorbs moisture and apparently sucks the foreign body into it, swelling to become large enough to be easily removed with the foreign body attached. José María Yocuivo of Los Jacales in San Bernardo recommends the seeds drunk in an atol to cure empacho, usually considered to be something lodged in the digestive tract, or simply constipation. He considers this an especially good medicine for children. The mixture acts as a mucilage agent similar to psyllium seed, and relieves the problem.

Mentha arvensis L. var. *villosa* (Benth.) S. R. Stewart
(poléo)

We have not verified this perennial herb, but it is well known among the mountain Guarijíos. Gentry (1942, 1963) collected it among mountain Guarijío near Memelíchic and reported that it was made into a refreshing tea and was also used for sore kidneys and as a calmative.

Lauraceae—Laurel or Avocado Family

Cinnamomum hartmannii (I. M. Johnst.) Kostermans
chihuana cara (laurelón, oreja de chiva)

A large evergreen tree to 12 m tall densely covered with thickish, elongated leaves. In Guarijío country it is restricted to a few deep moist canyons in TDF. Although the fruits are edible, Guarijíos made no mention of them.

Medicine: For numbness, José Ruelas grinds the leaf and rubs the affected area with it.

Litsea glaucescens H. B. K. var. *subsolitaria* (Meissner) Hemsl.
ahuírali (laurel, bay leaf)

A large shrub, becoming a small tree with age. It is known to the Guarijíos of Bavícora, who journey to the pine-oak forest to collect the leaves.

Beverage and Food: The long leaves are routinely harvested by Guarijíos who brew them into a tea acclaimed for its flavor and use them as a spice when cooking wild meat such as javelina and venison.

Medicine: The leaves are brewed into a tea acclaimed for its ability to alleviate aches and pains.

Persea podadenia Blake
chihuana cara (laurelón)

This wild avocado is a large shrub to medium-sized tree found in moist canyons in TDF. Its fruits are not eaten, however, and it appears to have little use, but Cipriano Buitimea says Guarijíos view the trees as a valuable source of shade.

Loranthaceae—Mistletoe Family

Struthanthus palmeri Kuijt
(toji, mistletoe)

This mistletoe is commonly parasitic on oaks and mezquite. Its slender leaves reach 10 cm in length.

Medicine: Cipriano Buitimea thought it was a remedy but could not recall what it was. Hermangildo Zaila recommends a tea made from the flower or stem of plants growing on tepeguaje as a remedy for mal de orín. Mistletoe from other trees is not as effective, he says.

Malpighiaceae—Malpighia Family

Bunchosia sonorensis Rose
mi'isi ca'ochara (pardo)

The translation of the Guarijío name for this spreading shrub means "cat testicles," and the fuzzy, two-lobed fruits match its name. It was noted growing in a side canyon of the Arroyo Guajaray. Although the fruits are eaten elsewhere in the region (Yetman and Van Devender 2001), Nacho Ciriaco could not recall eating them. This plant may be a different species from *B. sonorensis* growing farther south.

Callaeum macropterum (DC.) D. M. Johnson [= *Mascagnia macroptera* (DC.) Nied.]
cochisónoma, cojchisísora (mataneni)

Mataneni is a common low shrub that opportunistically becomes a robust vine and invades most trees and shrubs with reckless abandon. Its yellow, prolific blooms cover many fences and hedgerows in springtime. It blooms sporadically throughout the year. The papery-winged fruits are conspicuous in May.

Cordage: The vines are used to tie or lash any old thing, for example, vigas or horcones for ramadas.

Fishing: Hermangildo Zaila tells of using the vines to string shrimp caught in the Río Mayo. Stringing them enabled the gatherer to carry the shrimp without a basket. They would have a *ristra* (string) of shrimp.

Medicine: The leaves are brewed into a tea to "cleanse" a woman during labor and after parturition. José Ruelas reports that the tea is more effective if it includes leaves of *Hyptis albida* and *Vitex mollis* as well.

Malpighia emarginata DC.
siré (granadilla)

A large shrub or a small, multi-trunked, twisting tree to 3 m tall, with maculate bark. In the dry spring it may be completely leafless and appear indistinguishable from several other species.

Food: In years of good rain the pink flowers of summer mature into bright red fruits the size of blueberries that are sweet and succulent and can be plucked and eaten from the branch. In drier years the fruits can be dry and tasteless.

Fuel: The wood can be used for firewood.

Malvaceae—Mallow Family

Abutilon incanum (Link) Sweet
tosaporo (pintapán)

An erect shrub common in open or disturbed habitats that grows rapidly with the summer rains. With good rain the straight stems reach nearly 2–2.5 m in height.

Artifacts: When the stems are mature (but not dry), they are harvested in large bunches. These are then allowed to dry somewhat, then bound snugly roughly one-third the distance from the base to the growth tip. Thus they serve well as brooms.

Medicine: Hermangildo Zaila reported a procedure by which a woman who cannot conceive can be rendered fertile: He makes a knot of the root of four different tosaporo plants and boils them into a tea. The woman who desires to become pregnant should drink this tea four times a day. He notes that the potion will be rendered more effective by steeping it with chicura *(Ambrosia ambrosioides),* cilantro *(Coriandrum sativum),* and manzanilla *(Matricaria chamomilla).*

Martyniaceae—Devil's Claw Family

Martynia annua L.
consusu, tan cócochi, (aguaro, uña de gato)

A robust, erect annual prospering on disturbed soils and waste places, reaching 1.5 m in height. The showy pink and white flowers mature into grotesque rigid black woody capsules the size and appearance of large beetles, with a pair of sharp hooks that grab onto clothing or socks. It is impossible not to be intrigued by these strange growths, for they are like no other fruits.

Beliefs: Nacho Ciriaco claims that people make a small string of the fruits and hang it in the doorway of their house to keep out the Devil. He claims that the sharp claws scratch him.

Medicine: The entire fruit is toasted, ground, and rubbed on the body for aches and cramps. José Ruelas reports that he used to plant the seeds in appropriate places wherever he went. On the trail one day we met another Guarijío, Jesús Corpo of Huataturi, who had gathered a large bag of the fruits that he was taking to the market in Navojoa, some 80 miles distant. He claimed that *consusu* is an effective remedy for diabetes.

Proboscidea parviflora (Wooton) Wooton & Standley subsp. *parviflora*
aguaro (aguaro, devil's claw)

A robust annual to 1 m tall growing rapidly following summer rains. It produces attractive flowers of varying purples. The fruits—about 15 cm long and 5 cm wide—have a long beak that splits longitudinally into two long, curving claws. These dry capsules lie in wait for innocent passersby who experience momentary terror when the springy claws grab onto clothing or feet.

Food: The claws are pulled apart and the black seeds contained therein are chewed. The seed coats are usually spat out.

Medicine: Hermangildo Zaila reports that for high blood pressure, the green fruits are scorched and mashed. The pulp is mixed with cooking oil and rubbed all over the body.

Moraceae—Mulberry Family

Dorstenia drakena L.
nacachíchicore (baiburilla, flor de oreja)

A common low perennial herb with a small underground caudex and one to few large, drought-deciduous leaves. It is widespread in TDF, especially in moist canyon bottoms. The thumb-size caudex with many small, protruding roots is found just below the soil surface. The distinctive fruiting bodies are rather like dollar-sized discs mounted on a long stalk. Cipriano Buitimea observes that the fruiting body resembles a human ear, hence the common name he gives it, *flor de oreja* (ear flower).

Medicine: The thick "root" (caudex), widely used in the region, is gathered and prescribed by native healers. For fever and fright the Guarijíos make a tea and rub the liquid on the body and also drink the tea, taking advantage of the plant's reputation for soothing. Nacho Ciriaco prescribes the plant for earache. He cooks and mashes the root, steeps the mash, and puts a few drops of the liquid in the ear several times a day. "It is a good remedy," he says. "I've used it."

Cipriano Buitimea pronounces the root (caudex) to be an effective treatment for toothache. The root is chopped and a piece is placed directly on the tooth.

Ficus cotinifolia H. B. K.
guaourócochi (nacapuli)

Nacapuli is a large fig tree with aerial roots and roundish leaves. Some trees grow in excess of 25 m tall and equally wide. They are commonly found in moist places where they utterly dominate arroyo banks or moist places on rocky slopes. The aboveground root systems often form intricate and agreeable patterns, seeming to flow down rock slopes.

Nacho Ciriaco notes that the nacapuli's shade is valuable, for it often retains its leaves through the hot dry season.

Livestock Food: In times of food scarcity, Guarijíos cut down small branches as forage for cattle and for goats.

Food: The small figs are eaten fresh, but they are regarded as less tasty than those of *chalate (F. trigonata)*.

Medicine: Nacho demonstrated how Guarijíos pull off a narrow strip of bark and tie it around a sprain or bruise like a bandage. He reports that more than thirty years ago he dislocated his knee while alone in the monte. He wore a wrap of nacapuli bark for months, and the injury healed completely. For breaks, Nacho recommends using a piece of *carrizo (Arundo donax)* as a splint and binding it with nacapuli bark.

Utensils: The Guarijíos make trays from the wood of nacapuli. The wood is soft enough to work with simple tools but hard enough to endure household use.

Ficus insipida Willd.
huilocochi, tchuná (tchuna)

The *tchuna* is a huge fig, often exceeding 20 m in height, with acute leaves to 15 cm long. Tchunas are rather more common than *F. cotinifolia* in Guarijío country and during our study we saw a large number of young trees in moist watercourses throughout the warmer parts of the region. When the limbs become so massive as to be in danger of breaking off, the tree appears to form buttresses, which invite climbing up and shinnying down. In hot weather tchunas' and nacapulis' ample crowns give off a relentless fine mist that comes as a surprise, then as a relief, to those seated below, who are then dismayed to learn that it consists of the excretions of millions of tiny insects. The trees must lose enormous quantities of water this way, but the phenomenon also alters its microclimate significantly.

Livestock Food: Cows and burros eat the leaves in times of scarce forage.

Food: The fruits are eaten but are pronounced to be not as good as those of *chalate (F. trigonata)*.

Utensils: The wood is carved into dishes and various arts and crafts.

Ficus pertusa L. f.
tucuchí (nacapulín)

The only small-leaved fig in the region, its leaves are typically less than 10 cm long. *F. pertusa* is less common than either *F. cotinifolia* or *F. insipida*. It also grows to great size, reaching in excess of 20 m in height. The tree has an odd habit whereby new shoots entwine the existing trunk, sometimes adding layers upon layers, as though the trunk were covered with a mat of uniformly gray snakes.

The shade provided by *tucuchí* is especially cool, according to Guarijíos.

Food: Nacho Ciriaco pronounced the dark reddish-brown fruits to be sweeter than those of *nacapuli*. He noted when the fruits are ripe, the trees entertain a wide diversity of fauna. Birds, bats, skunks, coatis, plus a myriad of insects, all come for the fruits, so for twenty-four hours a day the trees are a hubbub of animal activity. A large tree must yield at least a ton of fruit, so there is enough for all, he says.

Two species of parrots (Lilac Crowned and White-fronted)

especially *urracas* (Blue-throated Magpie Jays) who noisily keep watch over their territories from the branches.

Food: Guarijíos are in unanimous agreement that the fruits eaten fresh are very good.

Medicine: The bark or a leaf placed on the wrist or arm of a child afflicted with susto seems to have a calmative effect. Nacho Ciriaco recommends placing a few drops of the milky sap on a leaf and wrapping the leaf around a sprained finger or other part. Always put the leaf on top of the sap, he advises. Cipriano Buitimea heartily recommended strips of the root bark tightly wrapped around a sprain or break. The sap and bark are also used among Mayos to heal sprains and breaks (Yetman and Van Devender 2002).

Ficus trigonata **L.**
guagüurí (chalate)

Chalates grow into enormous trees, spreading out more than 25 m, dominating entire sections of arroyos and providing food and shelter for untold numbers of organisms. Some huge trees might well be thought of as ecosystems in themselves. The trunks, often multiple, can exceed 1 m in diameter. An individual tree in a side canyon of Arroyo Bavícora is nearly 30 m tall. The large (up to 20 cm long) leaves are blunt, as opposed to the acute leaves of *tchuna (F. insipida)*.

Food: Chalates yield the best fruits for eating. It is easy to fill up on the fruits if one does not mind competition with and consumption of the miscellaneous wasp larvae that inhabit all wild figs.

Utensils: Benjamín Valenzuela of San Pedro makes wooden trays and bowls from the wood.

Trophis racemosa **(L.) Urb.**
pu'sí, u'sí

Trees reaching 12 m in height are fairly common in deep, moist canyons in association with *Aphananthe, Drypetes,* and *Sideroxylon persimile.* The lobed leaves taper abruptly to a drip point. The red fruits ripen in May and June.

Food: The fruits are eaten but must be prepared. Cipriano Buitimea reports that the fruits are the size of coffee beans. An older fellow he knows cooks the fruits and removes the skins by squeezing the cooked fruits. The resulting mass has the texture and taste of beans. An alternative preparation is to grind them whole. The fruits that mature after arrival of las aguas are said to be easier to prepare and eat because they are more tender.

Tescalama (Ficus petiolaris) near Chorijoa.

and flocks of the Mexican Parrotlet frequent the trees (especially when they are in fruit) and provide a shower of color.

Ficus petiolaris **H. B. K.**
guajtori (tescalama, rock fig)

The rock fig is a small- to medium-sized and sometimes large tree. It seldom reaches the large proportions of other figs in Guarijío country but merits special description due to its fantastic diversity of shape. The bark is yellow-white, in contrast with the gray bark of other local figs. The trees tend to grow on rocky slopes above water sources, sometimes on the sheer sides of cliffs many dozens of meters above a watercourse. The roots then cascade down the slopes groping for water, sometimes growing so prolifically as to resemble a white waterfall. The large and thickish leaves are dark green above, heart-shaped with prominent pink venation. It is hard to retain one's dignity and refrain from climbing around on tescalama roots in the way that young lads do. Many creatures seek out the fruits,

Myrtaceae—Guava Family

Psidium guajava L.
guayaguasi (guayabo, guava)

The guava tree has become naturalized in some remote canyons of Guarijío country, where it flourishes. Cipriano Buitimea's brother planted some trees a kilometer above San Pedro. Nacho Ciriaco says that two trees at El Sabinal, some 3 km from any habitation, are native. He notes, however, there is a ranch on the mountain well upstream from the two trees.

The trees grow to some 8 m tall, perhaps taller under ideal conditions. They have handsome mottled-brown trunks with smooth bark. The large leaves are heavily veined.

Food: The fruits are relished fresh by humans and animals. Guarijíos and others work the fruit pulp into a paste, which they dry and preserve.

Medicine: The leaves are boiled into a tea and taken for hangover.

Psidium sartorianum (O. Berg) Nied.
choqué'i (arrellán)

This is a slender tree of the well-developed TDF, growing to 10 m tall. The bark is a mottled brown. It is nowhere common but appears here and there in canyons and moist hillsides. Three trees grew at El Sabinal near Guajaray, in the company of guavas. Another well-known tree is located in a steep declivity in Arroyo San Pedro less than 1 km from San Pedro. The fruits are small and fleshy.

Food: The fruits are quite good for eating, according to Nacho Ciriaco. Gentry as well found them to be popular. Nacho reports that higher up in the mountains above Guajaray trees grow larger and yield larger fruits that are a bit sour but have an appealing taste.

Nolinaceae—Beargrass Family

Dasylirion wheeleri Rothr.
selé (sotol)

This sotol is found at mid elevations in the Mayo region, near El Saúz at 700 m and Loreto at 1,500 m.

Baskets and Adornment: Women weave utilitarian, durable baskets from the tough fiber. During Holy Week mountain Guarijíos report that they adorn the Virgin Mary with flowers from the stalk or perhaps from leaves woven to resemble flowers.

Food: The heart is roasted and eaten like that of an agave.

Nolina aff. *affinis* Trel.
huirico

An uncommon, low-lying, nearly stemless plant, with long slender and tough leaves with razor-sharp minutely serrated edges.

Basketry: *Huirico* is the plant fiber preferred by Guarijío women in the Loreto area for weaving baskets. Two small populations grow in an area of little more than a hectare each on the lower slopes of the Sierra Chuchupate. These plants are maintained by Tiburcio Charramoneta of Canelichi and are harvested by him to supply his wife Nicolasa Escruz with weaving material. Tiburcio collects seeds from the flowering stalks and plants them to perpetuate a good supply of the pencas.

Tiburcio gathered a sheath of huirico for Nicolasa so that she could demonstrate for us the art of making baskets. The source of the leaves was a two kilometer walk from her home at Canelichi. When Tiburcio delivered the leaves, Nicolasa sat in a chair and immediately began to weave. The pencas were woven as they were presented, without soaking or splitting. The basket, about 15 cm square and equally deep, took roughly and hour and a half to weave.

Ceremonial use: Guarijíos in the pine-oak forest harvest the seeds and sew them into cocoons for ténaborim, the leg rattles worn by pascola dancers in the tuburi. The hard seeds produce an agreeable soft swish when shaken inside the cocoons.

Nyctaginaceae—Four-o'clock Family

Boerhavia coccinea L.
B. erecta L.
mochiná (mochi, spiderling)

Sprawling perennial herbs *(B. coccinea)* or summer annuals (e.g., *B. erecta*) with sticky leaves and stems. Boerhavias are common on disturbed and undisturbed soils in the TDF and elsewhere in the region.

Medicine: For measles, the roots are boiled and the liquid drunk as a tea. Nacho Ciriaco reports that he took the medicine when he was young—for a month as *agua de uso* (in place of drinking water). Nowadays the remedy is not used due to the availability of measles vaccine.

Nicolasa Escruz weaving *guari* from blades of *huirico,* Canelichi, Chihuahua.

Boerhavia sp.
taimúchil (guananupila)

This is an unidentified species of summer annual, perhaps *B. erecta.*

Medicine: For measles the root is cooked and the liquid applied to the skin eruptions. It apparently has somewhat different healing properties from *B. coccinea,* which is a perennial. Nacho thought it might be a general remedy for sores.

Pisonia capitata (S. Watson) Standley
susutí (vainoro, garabato)

Susutí is a widespread shrub, vine, and messy tree that receives mixed reviews from the human community. As a shrub it grows into gnarly, viney arms that develop into nearly impenetrable thickets guarded by vicious thorns to 15 cm long that can inflict painful punctures. As a tree it sometimes produces a dense, tent-like canopy providing excellent shade and even a hiding place. As a vine it may overpower other shrubs and trees, competing with *Celtis iguanaea* for dominance along watercourses. Cattlemen curse the plant like none other, for cows learn to retreat to thickets of *vainoro* during roundup and cannot be rousted from their fortress-like hiding place without damage being inflicted on horse and horseman.

In general it is viewed as being good for nothing except that the leaves suffice as emergency cow feed. Nacho reports that a small bee visits the flower and takes the nectar to its hive to make a clear kind of honey. The bees do sting, he warns.

Salpianthus macrodontus Standley
cotamó (guayavilla)

A common bush up to 2 m tall with thickened, deep roots, it is abundant on disturbed soils and waste places. Farmers and ranchers often denounce it as a bothersome weed. Its flowers are dirty brownish white and assume a characteristic appearance. When they are crushed they smell strongly like a guava, hence the common Spanish name, which means "little guava."

Food: The old-time Guarijíos would eat the root before there was maize, according to Lino Leyva of Mesa Colorada and Hermangildo Zaila of Los Jacales. Gentry (1963) reports that an old Guarijío maintained that before they had corn, they ate the *cotamó* root. In the mountains, however, Guarijíos believe they have cultivated corn from time immemorial, and cotamó is absent. It would seem odd if the highland Guarijíos had corn while the lowlanders had no recollection of it.

Medicine: Nacho Ciriaco recommends cotamó for an aching molar. It is administered by pounding the root, making a needle of the fibrous material, then forcing it into the cavity. Others make a decoction of the leaves and take it to relieve fever.

Oleaceae—Olive Family

Fraxinus velutina Torr.
(fresno, velvet ash)

Fresno is a small, straight-boled tree reaching 10 m in height in oak woodland and pine-oak forest. The Guarijíos of the Loreto region did not have an indigenous name for it. The tree was possibly imported into the region and has since colonized.

Tools: Fresno's hard wood is used for handles for axes and tools.

Opiliaceae—Opilia Family

Agonandra racemosa (DC.) Standley
murió (palo verde)

A thin, solitary tree with dark bark reaching 10 m in height. The twigs with simple leaves tend to droop, a characteristic useful in identifying the tree. It manages to retain its leaves after most other trees have dropped theirs in the dry season. It occupies a wide variety of habitats in the lowlands but is nowhere common.

Construction: The wood is used sporadically for beams and posts in houses.

Medicine: Nacho says that for lowering a fever, people thoroughly mash a handful of leaves, boil them, add salt, and drink the resultant tea.

José Ruelas related and translated for us the following song, which he and other cantores sing for the tuburi:

Ya huirachi suhuera	*Song of the Palo Verde*
Ya huirachi suhuera	At the edge of the patio
Suhuerachi hueri	At the edge of the patio
Hueri mulió	The palo verde stands tall
Mulió, mulió	The palo verde
E cahuira	Its shade is cool and soothing
E cahuira	Cooling shade

Orchidaceae—Orchid Family

Bletia roezlii Rchb. f.
quiquí

Quiquí is a name commonly given by Guarijíos to orchids with pseudobulbs that exude a mucilaginous substance when crushed. *Bletia roezlii* is one of several such orchids in the region. It is a terrestrial orchid, sending up a slender stalk up to 50 cm tall. The flower is a delicate yellow with purple

accents around the margin and a reddish lip.

Adhesive: Guarijíos use the sticky liquid from the crushed pseudobulbs as glue. When it has been heated and dried it can be worked, even sanded. They dry it to produce resin for their violin bows. They also melt bits of the resin on a hot knife to glue various artifacts together.

Laelia eyermanniana Rchb. f.
quiquí

This *quiquí* forms colonies on oak trees above San Pedro and other oak woodlands. The showy flowers are lavender. Gentry (1942) reported that Guarijíos of the 1930s maintained that the presence of quiquí was a warning against planting corn. Since the oaks of the middle Río Mayo tend to grow on indurated ash or hydrothermally altered soils, both of which are acidic, the observation makes sense.

Adhesive: The pseudobulbs are used like those of *Bletia roezlii,* above.

Oncidium cebolleta (Jacq.) Sw.
chiguajáguara (cuerno de chiva)

A common orchid with handsome yellow and brown flowers colonizing on rocks and trees in the region. The clustered thick leaves are up to 20 cm long.

Medicine: As a remedy for malaria, a leaf is cut off and chopped into pieces, then boiled in water. *Copalquín* (*Hintonia latiflora*) wood (not the bark; the bark is too bitter for children) is added to enhance the effectiveness of the remedy. The resulting liquid is drunk, a glassful three times a day until the symptoms recede. This recipe was taught to Cipriano Buitimea by Juan Enríquez of Burapaco, a mestizo known to be knowledgeable in remedies.

Orobanchaceae—Broom-rape Family

Conopholis alpina Liebm. var. *mexicana* (S. Watson) Haynes
hipachí (flor de tierra)

A root parasite of the pine-oak forest that sends up clusters of shoots about 20 cm high resembling a forest of miniature chlorophyll-free conifer trees. It is abundant in May near Loreto and at Canelichi in pine-oak forest.

Wild Animal Food: Although Guarijíos do not eat the plants, they observed that the seeds ("nuts") of the plants are an important food source for *guijolos* (wild turkeys) and *ardillas* (squirrels), both of which they hunt and eat.

Papaveraceae—Poppy Family

Argemone ochroleuca Sweet sub*sp. ochroleuca*
tajíchuri (cardo)

This common prickly poppy with yellow flowers is found in large numbers in dry washes and pastures where soil has been disturbed. It is spiny and unappetizing to livestock.

Medicine: Nacho Ciriaco recommends the plant for curing pinkeye (*mal de ojo,* conjunctivitis). He says that a drop of the sap (*el caldo*) in the corner of the affected eye will heal the condition. Cipriano Buitimea adds that the sap is also effective for other eye afflictions (e.g., itching, cloudiness). The seeds are also ground and taken in water to purge the stomach and digestive tract. They reportedly work quickly as a purgative.

Passifloraceae—Passionvine Family

Passiflora suberosa L.
semojari (ojo de venado)

This vine is found entangled in shrubbery of the pine-oak forest towards the end of las aguas.

Food: The fruits are relished raw when they are young.

Pinaceae—Pine Family

Abies durangensis Martinez
mateguó (pinabete, Durango fir)

A stately, symmetrical conifer growing in moist canyons and north-facing slopes in the vicinity of Loreto. All the trees we observed there were less than 10 m in height, but they grow much taller at higher elevations.

Medicine: Nicolás Tadeo regularly harvests the bark, collecting it in bags from what he refers to as "his grove" of trees, some 2 km south of Loreto. He boils the bark into a tea and administers it to himself and relatives for pneumonia, aches, and fevers. His grove along Arroyo Loreto all bore large scars from years of bark harvesting. Nicolás assured us, however, that the bark collectors are careful not to girdle the trees.

Pinus chihuahuana Engelm.
guoj'có (pino chino, Chihuahua pine)

A rather small pine with dark bark, *pino chino* in the Guarijío area seldom exceeds 13 m in height. It has sparse clusters of needles about 10 cm long and cones that persist on dead or living trees for several years.

Adhesive: Pino chino is reputed to produce more sap than other local pines. This sap is widely used an adhesive, especially to help provide a waterproofing for roof shakes. The sap also holds the shakes in place while they are being installed.

Grooming: Nicolás Tadeo reports that in former times Guarijíos would use the cones to comb their hair to get rid of lice.

Pinus engelmannii Carrière
guoj'có (pino, Apache pine)

This large tree reaches 40 m tall at the highest elevations of Guarijío country. Individuals of this size grow on Rancho Canelichi, which, according to its mestizo owner, has never been lumbered. The tree has very long (30 cm) needles in large clusters.

Construction: This *guoj'có* produces excellent lumber and, alas, is widely cut for commercial purposes. It also produces fine roof shakes.

Fuel and Torches: Guarijíos also gather *chojpí* (fatwood, small pitch-filled sticks) from trunks of dead trees (and from very old living ones) to use as kindling or as a torch.

Horticulture: Tiburcio Charramoneta mixes the pitch with beeswax and covers grafting scars on the fruit trees he plants. This protects them from infection and attack by insect borers, he believes. Juan de Diós Zapata reported that people also burn the pitch as a room fragrance.

Medicine: The *cogollos,* or shoots of young trees are often gathered to brew a refreshing tea that also has restorative powers, according to Tiburcio. Nicolás Tadeo reports that the sap (*jupánaloim*) is used by some as a remedy but could not recall what it is good for. Tiburcio also collects sap or pitch (*choi guojcó*) from a small tree growing not far from his home. He uses this as an all-purpose remedy. He rubs a rag in the pitch and binds it over a bruise or break, or over a muscle spasm. Tiburcio maintains that this practice is the best remedy for bodily injuries.

Pinus lumholtzii B. L. Rob. & Fernald
guoj'có (pino llorón)

A small pine (to 13 m tall in the Guarijío region) with small cones. The needles droop uniformly, giving the tree a "sad" appearance. It is often called *pino triste,* or sad pine. *Pino llorón* means "crybaby pine."

Its uses are the same as for other pines in the pine-oak forest.

Pinus oocarpa Schltdl.
guoj'có (pino, eggcone pine)

The eggcone pine is the most common pine of Guarijío country. The trees reach about 20 m under favorable conditions but seldom exceed half that in river Guarijío country. The hard, unopened cones in fact are egg-shaped. The needles are long, in excess of 25 cm. A small population well known to river Guarijíos grows on the north side of the Sierra Matapaco between Bavícora and Mesa Colorada.

Construction: The lumber is made into roofing shakes, boards, and beams. Since it grows rather far from most river Guarijío settlements, it is not widely used by them. In Gentry's time (Gentry 1942), lumberers would cut trees in the high mountains and drag them by mule to the low country where they would sell them. Now most of the large trees accessible to mule-driving lumberers have disappeared.

Fuel and Torches: The wood is burned for heating and cooking. Boughs thick with pitch are collected and used as torches.

Pinus yecorensis Debreczy & I. Rácz
guoj'có (pino)

This pine has bushy clusters of very long needles. Perhaps the most common pine in the montane Guarijío region, it attains heights of more than 30 m under favorable conditions.

Construction and Fuel: It is widely used for firewood, lumber, and for making roof shakes.

Piperaceae—Pepper Family

Piper jaliscanum S. Watson
(rodilla, cocolmeca)

A bushy plant to 3 m tall with broad leaves tapering to a point. In the region it is confined to deep, moist canyons such as the Cajón or Arroyo San Pedro. Cipriano says the common name (*rodilla* = knee) reflects the appearance of the swellings botanists call leaf nodes. The name *cocolmeca* is of indigenous origin but is probably not Guarijío.

Medicine: Feliciano Armenta reports that the leaves are boiled, and the resulting decoction is applied to stiff joints and sore muscles. He applies the liquid to his arms when he must work hard all day.

Plumbaginaceae—Plumbago Family

Plumbago scandens L.
hupechura (plumbago)

A semi-herbaceous bushy perennial common in TDF.

Veterinary Medicine: Nacho Ciriaco recalls that the root was formerly mashed and ground into a powder. A few particles of this powder were sprinkled over screw-worms *(gusano barrenador)* or over the burrowing holes they would leave in a calf or a cow after she gave birth. This treatment would kill the screwworms. The release of countless millions of sterilized male screwworms has made the infestations much less of a problem than they used to be, and Guarijíos no longer apply the cure.

Poaceae (Graminae)—Grass Family

Aristida ternipes Cav. var. *ternipes*
guatoco (otatillo, spider grass)

This is a robust, tufted perennial grass. When not subject to heavy grazing, it may reach more than 1 m in height. Thick patches may be found on rocky hillsides where cattle cannot venture.

Construction: Strands of the grass are used in strengthening adobe and mud walls.

Medicine: *Guatoco* is brewed into a tea and drunk as a cure for spider *(turusi)* bites.

Arundo donax L.
pa'aqué (carrizo, cane)

A bamboo-like grass apparently introduced to the New World by Spaniards and now found widely scattered alongside permanent water throughout the region. It grows into dense, nearly impenetrable groves 3 to 4 m tall.

Construction: Guarijíos are aware that Mayos in the lower Río Mayo Delta use the *carrizo* for building walls, but they prefer *batayaqui (Montanoa rosei)* and other springy poles to the less solid carrizo.

Furniture: At Mochibampo, Guarijíos laid the canes side by side with the ends resting on beams or suitable straight surfaces. This then formed the summer bed, comfortable because the reeds are springy and cool since air can pass through the spaces between the canes. The bed is abandoned in cold weather, since the cold seeps through the canes and chills the sleeper.

Heteropogon contortus (L.)
Roem. & Schult.
ujchú (carrizo)

Ujchú is a harsh perennial grass that grows in thick colonies. It grows on hillsides in TDF well into oak woodland.

Construction: This grass is widely used in roof construction in areas where palm leaves are unavailable. The grass is placed in thick mats on top of roof *latas*. Dirt is then placed on top of the grass. A roof so constructed is remarkably cool and will last for many years. It is heavy, though, and must rest on sturdy vigas and horcones. Guarijíos will stuff *angarillas* (woven rigid saddlebags) full of the grass and transport it to their homes.

Lasiacis ruscifolia (H. B. K.) Hitchc.
(carricito)

A reedlike grass that does not grow in excess of 4 m tall or 3 cm thick at the base.

Livestock Food: In times of drought, the Guarijíos will gather burro loads of carricito and take them to pastures for their cows.

Muhlenbergia dumosa Vasey
pu'a caa (bambú, bamboo muhly)

This is a tufted perennial grass, growing to 1.5 m height. It is usually found in moist places in TDF.

Medicine: The roots are brewed into a medicinal tea taken for headache and administered for influenza in children, according to Manuel Rodríguez.

Muhlenbergia elongata Beal
pa'a ypíchera (guayquillo, escoba)

Brooms: A tall, stiff perennial grass, it is gathered, bound tightly, and shaped into brooms, according to José Ruelas.

Muhlenbergia scoparia Vasey
pa'a (zacate aparejo)

A tufted perennial grass.

Packsaddles: Tufts of the grass are gathered and stuffed into packsaddles and angarillas (open packsaddles woven of palm or *ixtle* [agave fiber] of Guarijío design) to protect objects during transport along Guarijío trails.

Otatea acuminata (Munro)
C. E. Calderon & Soderstr.
otate (otate)

Otate is the bamboo of the Río Mayo, growing in foothills and higher portions of TDF. While most useful, it grows only spottily throughout the sierras. The name appears to be of Aztec origin but may be aboriginally Guarijío as well.

Construction: The stalks are widely incorporated into construction of walls and roofs. The long poles are frequently used as racks and are built into *zarzos,* drying racks suspended from the ceiling as protection from marauding domestic pets and rodents. In parts of the sierras otate is harvested and taken to the lowlands where it is sold.

Furniture: Otate stalks are widely used for beds. The canes are laid side by side parallel to the sleeper and provide a springy yet resilient mattress.

Panicum hirticaule J. Presl
var. *miliaceum* (Vasey) Beetle [= *P. sonorum*]
sahuí

Food: This panic grass formerly constituted an important part of the Guarijío diet. According to José Ruelas, it was widely sown, planted in June and harvested in October and November. When the grain turned the color of coffee, he recalled, the Guarijíos would harvest it. It reaches knee high. José believes it is now planted only in Bavícora, and Lorenzo Sujaguareña agrees. Other Guarijíos have quit planting it because they have lost the seed or they are not interested in planting it any more. Nabhan (1985) describes finding the grass near Guasaremos and showing it to Howard Scott Gentry who had collected and written about it in the 1930s.

Juan Ruelas of Bavícora, the only present-day planter we found, presented us with a small bag of the tiny seeds. In that village is it made into an atol, and the seeds are ground into flour and made into pinole (a thick beverage). Juan assured us that *sahuí* is nutritious, but its harvest requires considerable labor.

Panicum hirticaule, var. herticaule silvestre wild variety
masayá

José Ruelas collected dried samples of this grass near where we were camping in a grassland below Mesa Matapaco at about 600-m elevation. He pronounced it to be a wild form similar to *sahuí.*

Food: José recalls that Guarijíos formerly ate the grain frequently because the seed heads ripened earlier than those of either *sahuí* or corn. They would gather the stalks and rub the seed heads on a *metate* (grinding stone) to loosen the grain. They would then gather the grain and take it to their homes, where it would be cooked into tortillas. José warned that these tortillas should be eaten hot, because when they cool the grain becomes bitter. *Masayá* ripens in August, he says. José reports that the grains can be distinguished by their colors: the seed head of sahuí is often reddish, while that of masayá is more chocolate colored. José lamented the fact that people nowadays do not gather masayá.

Phragmites australis (Cav.) Steud.
jaqui puca (carrizo)
A tall, bamboo-like grass reaching 3 m or more in height. It is common in a few moist areas of still or standing water. Its range may be much restricted due to the arrival centuries ago of its competitor, *Arundo donax,* from across the sea.

Construction: The tall stalks are woven into walls and roofs.

Setaria grisebachii E. Fourn.
tecoribasi (cola de ardilla)
S. liebmannii E. Fourn.
(cola de ardilla)
Very common summer annuals.

Livestock Food: Guarijíos identified these two grasses as desirable food for livestock but gave no further uses.

Sorghum bicolor (L.) Moench
tashuí (caña)

Food: *Tashuí* is a 2-m tall sugar cane raised locally for that purpose. Natives eagerly chew on the ripe stalks. We were offered some at Rancho Nuevo and found the center sweet but somewhat dry.

Polygonaceae—Buckwheat Family

Antigonon leptopus Hook. & Arn.
ca'mori, masasari (sanmiguelito, queen's wreath)
A very common vine with triangular leaves. With the coming of las aguas, the vine explodes with growth and bright pink bracts and flowers. As the rains continue, the vine creeps aggressively into adjacent vegetation, often covering shrubs and trees and blooming with exuberance. It is believed by many to be a breeding place for *baiburines,* the chiggers that abound in the region in summer. The Mayo name for the plant is *nasasari.* Guarijíos believe Mayos influenced their language. The dual nomenclature is a good example of Mayo cultural hegemony over Guarijío culture.

Food: The root is excavated and eaten like a *jícama.* It is pronounced to be sweet.

Polygonum aff. *persicaria* L.
(quelite)
A perennial herb growing sometimes abundantly scattered among moist cobbles in watercourses. We found it in Arroyo Guajaray near Guajaray.

Food: The leaves are boiled and eaten as a green.

Rhamnaceae—Coffeeberry Family

Ceanothus depressus Benth.
teguachá (chaparita, buckbrush)
A large, thorny shrub growing in pine-oak forest. On cutover hillsides it may form extensive chaparral-type thickets.

Medicine: Leaves and small branches are gathered and ground into a pulp. The entire mass is boiled and administered especially to children as a tea to cure *pujos* (bloody stools) and alleviate diarrhea. Nicolas Tadeo and Tiburcio Charramoneta both recommend it as an effective remedy for this affliction.

Gouania rosei Wiggins
gua'leí (güirote de violín)
A common vine in TDF. Its Spanish name is derived from the tendency of the tendrils to curl as in the neck of a violin.

Cordage: Lorenzo Sujaguareña uses the vine from time to time to lash loads onto burros.

Karwinskia humboldtiana (Roem. & Schult.) Zucc.
jimuari, imora (cacachila)
A rather delicate shrub or small- to medium-sized tree common throughout TDF and into oak woodland. The smooth leaves are dotted and streaked with black glands, mostly noticeable on the underside, leading to the common name "dot-dash plant." The fruits mature from red to black. The seeds are highly poisonous.

Construction: The wood is very good for fence posts and house posts (horcones).

Food: Children eat the fruits and spit out the seeds, José says, but in general people don't eat them because they make you *tullido*—dizzy or disoriented. Gentry was told the same in the 1930s.

Medicine: The black root is chopped and boiled into a tea for healing a "bad" liver, says José Ruelas. This remedy is appropriate when one has a sore liver. Nacho Ciriaco says the leaves are brewed into a tea to cure mal de orín. Put a handful of leaves into two liters of cold water, allow it to steep, then drink it, he suggests. Hermangildo Zaila claims that ashes from the burned trunk mixed in water makes for a good cure for gastritis.

Rosaceae—Rose Family

Potentilla thurberi **A. Gray var. *thurberi***
setánami nagual (hierba colorada)

A small perennial herb common in moist soils of the pine-oak forest. It resembles a strawberry plant, but has a much-thickened root.

Medicine: The flesh of the root is red and is widely used medicinally, reported throughout the region as being imbued with remarkable curative powers. Guarijíos in the Loreto area steep the root into a tea that they drink for toothache. Although they recommended it highly, they did not prescribe it for a mestizo lad from Canelichi who suffered greatly from a diseased molar.

Prunus gentryi **Standley**
P. zinggii **Standley**
guasiqui, jej'có, teguachá (mountain Guarijío)
(jeco)

These are coarse-barked trees with shiny green leaves like the common cherry tree. They grow to 10 m tall in moist soils of canyons of the pine-oak forest. Guarijíos do not distinguish between the two species.

Food: The yellow fruits are eaten in June and July when tender. They are said to be ready to eat when they turn *siyóname* (yellow), according to José Ruelas.

Tools: Among the mountain Guarijíos the wood is used to make handles for implements.

Prunus serotina **Ehrh. subsp. virens (Woot. & Standley) McVaugh**
(capulín, chokecherry)

A small tree with shiny, bright green leaves. It grows along arroyos in the pine-oak forest. Guarijíos with whom we spoke had no Guarijío name for it.

Food: The tree produces red fruits that taste sweet at first but are often followed by a bitter sensation. Still, the fruits are eagerly consumed by natives.

Fuel: The wood is used for a variety of purposes, especially as firewood since it outlasts pine and is easily ignited.

Rubus strigosus **Michx. var. *arizonicus* (Greene) Kearney & Peebles**
colalaí (mora, raspberry)

Vines growing in shady places in higher mountains, especially along streams. The fruits ripen in summer. We tentatively assign the plant to this variety.

Food: Raspberries are relished by Guarijíos of the pine-oak forest as by people everywhere.

Rubiaceae—Madder Family

Cephalanthus salicifolius **Humb. & Bonpl.**
guatájori (nimbre)

A short, thick-trunked tree with heavy, willow-like leaves. It generally grows at the edge of permanent flowing water in the TDF. The gnarled trunk may approach a meter in diameter at the base, but in boulder-strewn riverbanks it may grow like a misshapen cylinder. It appears to be effectively anchored in streambeds where it helps to control erosion. The flowers are aromatic.

Medicine: Pieces of the root are chewed to relieve toothache.

Hintonia latiflora **(DC.) Bullock**
jutetió (copalquín)

An important and widely known small tree with a straight trunk. While trees in excess of 8 m tall are seldom seen, one more than 15 m tall grows not far from Chinatopo. The gray bark is usually smooth, though dotted with lenticels. On larger trees one side (frequently the south side) is often corky, checkered, and brownish white. Leaves are usually confined to the crown. The large, pendant, extremely fragrant funnel-shaped flowers appear from early through late summer and dangle from the branch tips. The brownish fruits persist for several months.

Medicine: Guarijíos recommend tea brewed from the bitter bark as a remedy for lack of appetite or energy. They attribute this malady to excessively thin blood, a condition which the bark is said to rectify. About one liter of the decoction is made by boiling the bark, sometimes flavored with cinnamon to ameliorate the bitterness. The tea is usually drunk on an empty stomach. This liquid is also variously recommended for parasites and diabetes. Cipriano Buitimea recommends using the wood rather than the bark as a remedy for malaria because it is not as bitter and is more palatable to children.

Many trees near trails and roads show scars where bark has been harvested. In southern Mexico intact trees are rare, so great is the reputation of the bark's healing propensities. The bark is ground and marketed commercially throughout Mexico.

Construction: The wood is used for posts and beams because it produces straight timbers.

Randia echinocarpa DC.
josocura (papache)

Papache is a strange shrub or small tree with even stranger fruits. The trunks of fruit-bearing trees and shrubs and their branches tend to arch rather than grow straight and develop opposite thorns to 10 cm long. The rounded bodies of the fruits are usually 5–8 cm in diameter with a hard rind and irregular, blunt, decurved tubercles or spines often 2–3 cm long. Green when maturing, the fruits turn yellow on ripening and blackish in senescence. They often persist on the branches long after drying and turning black. The pulp, a rather ugly black mass containing numerous seeds, has a strange sweet and bitter flavor.

Food: Virtually all Guarijíos, but especially little boys, relish the fruits, a fact noticed by Gentry. The flavor is like coffee, according to some. They determine the ripeness of the fruits by shaking them. If they feel the mass shaking inside, it is ripe. With some little practice one can make a hole and suck out the pulp, experts claim.

Medicine: Many people attribute medicinal qualities to papaches, but Guarijíos attribute those claims to mestizos. Some Guarijíos, including Nacho Ciriaco, use the fruit (eaten on an empty stomach) to expel stomach parasites.

The root is reportedly a good remedy for toothaches. Mashed and applied to the ailing tooth, the root purportedly makes the tooth fall out. Cipriano Buitimea reports that placing a piece of bark in the mouth and chewing it will cure a bleeding sore in the mouth.

Randia laevigata Standley
guacabé, guacahué (sapuchi)

A scrubby, spindly, sometimes spreading tree to 6 m tall, it sends out brittle-looking branches that are tipped with broad leaves 15–30 cm long. The leaves are bright green when fresh but quickly take on a yellowish tinge. The brilliant yellow flowers are not often noted by botanists, probably because they bloom in June at the height of the scorching spring drought and turn black when dry. The avocado-sized fruits are green, turning reddish, then dark with maturity, generally in October. *Sapuchis* seem to grow best on soils of indurated ash (hydrothermally altered) soils, often in association with *Quercus albocincta, Q. tuberculata,*

Papache fruit *(Randia echinocarpa)*. The strange fruits mature in the fall.

and *Vitex pyramidata.* They are most common at the transition from TDF to oak woodland.

Food: The fruits ripen in October, and the gooey pulp is eaten fresh. Nacho Ciriaco reports that the pulp is chocolate-colored.

Randia obcordata S. Watson
cabijósocura (papache borracho)

A shrub about 2 m tall, with straight branches and opposite thorns. It is common in lower elevations of TDF. The fruits are the size of large cherries, mottled green when immature and yellow when mature. The fruits are especially popular with woodpeckers, which break through the tough husk to extract larvae that infest the fruits.

Food: The fruits are often eaten, but according to Guarijíos, if one eats more than four or five, one will stagger as though drunk. The Spanish common name means "drunken papache."

Randia sonorensis Wiggins
josocora quehuechi, cahui júgauri
(papache del zorro, papache borracho)

A spindly but generally symmetrical shrub or small tree similar in habit to *R. obcordata.* It is common in upper TDF into oak woodland and pine-oak forest.

Food: According to José Ruelas, old-timers ate the fruits regularly. Cipriano Buitimea and Tiburcio Charramoneta report that people still eat them, but they are hardly worth the effort because they are so full of seeds. Feliciano Armenta recommends eating no more than four or five, the point at which some people are made dizzy. At Canelichi in pine-oak forest, however, the natives report that they eat them with no ill effects.

Nacho Ciriaco holding peeled *papache,* Guajaray.

Rutaceae—Citrus Family

Casimiroa edulis La Llave & Lex.
ajpé, jijira (chapote)

A spreading tree sometimes reaching 15 m in height with large, bright green leaves. The trees are cultivated, sometimes along canyon bottoms, for their delicious fruit. Under favorable conditions, they may persist and become naturalized. The rounded fruit are well known in American tropics. When in flower the trees attract large numbers of bees. Cipriano Buitimea reports that his mother planted the trees found in Arroyo San Pedro. At Burapaco one had been planted in the yard of a home occupied by a mestizo. It was well known to Guarijíos of Mesa Colorada. Ramón Rodríguez reports that *jijiras* are quite common in the midstretches of Arroyo Limón, a major northern tributary of the Río Mayo, and grow wild there.

Food: The sweet fruits are eaten fresh. Gentry (1942) reported that lads would venture many kilometers in search of them.

Medicine: The bark is steeped into a tea and regularly administered to diabetics to relieve the symptoms associated with that disease.

Esenbeckia hartmanii Robinson & Fernald
toshcura (palo amarillo)

This is a large shrub or small tree with multiple rough-barked trunks and dark green leafage following rains. The bark is varied shades of brown with small flaking pieces. The plants seldom rise more than 6 m and are especially common on the hillsides south of Chinatopo. When the limber branches break, the wood is revealed to be yellow, hence the common Spanish name.

Fuel: The plant is not widely used. The branches can be used as kindling wood when superior woods are not available.

Salicaceae—Willow Family

Salix bonplandiana H. B. K.
huatosí (saúz, sauce, Bonpland willow)

This willow may grow to more than 15 m in height along the Arroyo Guajaray, where it is an important source of shade. The trees with their strong roots also play a role in stabilizing the banks along the youthful arroyo. It is also found elsewhere in the region along watercourses.

Religion: The young leafy branches are woven into house crosses, crucifixes that are hung in Catholic homes. Many Guarijíos observe this practice on May 3, *el día de la cruz* (the Day of the Cross). Others simply leave them posted as a sign that they are *cristianos.*

Utensils: Some people make trays and spoons from the wood.

Sapindaceae—Soapberry Family

Cardiospermum corindum L.
sinohui ujoara (bombillo, balloon vine)

A common perennial vine with delicate white flowers. The fruits mature into ping-pong-ball-sized balloons that dry on the vine and resemble small paper lanterns. When buffeted by breezes, dried seeds inside the pods may produce a rustling that is unnervingly reminiscent of the first microseconds of a rattlesnake's rattling.

Medicine: A tea is made from the root to alleviate and heal snakebite, according to Hermangildo Zaila.

Dodonaea viscosa (L.) Jacq.
caguachamó, tarachiqui (jarilla, hopbush)

An almost evergreen shrub, occasionally a small tree, sometimes locally common on indurated ash or altered soils and in waste places toward the upper margins of TDF and into oak and pine-oak forest. The fruits are papery winged like those of hops. Near Todos Santos the shrub dominates an entire hillside.

Construction: The leafy branches are used to construct walls and ceilings. In the lowlands where palm *(Brahea aculeata)* is not available, grass is often placed on top of interwoven branches of *jarilla* and that in turn is covered with wetted clay dirt to form a roof.

Sapindus saponaria L.
jutuhuí (abolillo, jaboncillo, soapberry)

A large, nearly evergreen tree with dense foliage to 15 m tall growing along watercourses. The bark is usually dark or mottled brown. The leaf stalk is winged between the large leaflets, a help in identifying the tree. It produces a profusion of small white flowers. The flowers quickly fall and litter the ground below. The marble-sized fruits, which are reportedly high in saponins, are amber-colored when ripe and may turn blackish.

Medicine: If a baby is doing poorly on mother's milk (i.e., if mother's milk gives a baby diarrhea or "bad stomach"), Guarijíos administer "green" water made by pounding a *jutuhuí* leaf and dissolving the mash in water. Nacho maintains that the infusion cleanses the baby's stomach. His family has used this remedy for generations, he says.

Soap: Guarijíos mash the ripe fruits to produce soap for washing clothing or even a baby. Nacho Ciriaco, who still uses this soap, pronounces it to be better than commercial soap.

Serjania mexicana (L.) Willd.
huhuqío, guaquiquió (güirote espinoso)

A common, tough vine found throughout moist areas of TDF, often growing far into the tallest trees. The stems become more than 5 cm thick, tend to be square in cross section, and are covered with hard, small prickles or serrations that can cut flesh like a knife. The vine often grows close to the ground, crossing paths to gain access to nearby trees, and has thus tripped many travelers.

Medicine: The leaves or stems are a good remedy for a painful heart, according to José Ruelas. The fresh leaves may be bound to the chest or boiled into a tea, which is drunk. José explains that the symptoms of a painful heart are "that one's heart hurts." For cough, Nacho Ciriaco recommends cutting off a piece or section of the vine including the leaves. This section is doubled over and over and wrapped around itself, forming a knotted coil. The whole thing is submerged in boiling water. The resultant liquid is drunk to alleviate the cough.

Cipriano Buitimea claims the vine and leaves, prepared per Nacho's instructions, are also a cure for *viruela loca* (smallpox or, more likely, chicken pox, since the former has been eradicated). The preparation is made as above, but instead of being drunk, the resulting decoction is used as a bath or wash.

Sapotaceae—Sapote Family

Sideroxylon persimile subsp. *subsessiliflorum* (Hemsl.) T. D. Pennington
jachojcá, jichucá (bebelama)

A large, tall-crowned and spreading tree of the deep, moist barrancas, sometimes reaching nearly 25 m in height. It often grows along with *Aphananthe, Drypetes,* and *Trophis.* It is found exclusively along watercourses, whereas *S. tepicense* may be found on hillsides and ridge tops.

Food: The fruits are generally viewed as tasty, but may burn the mouth if eaten fresh in excess. Some people eat them with milk to keep them from stinging the mouth. Cipriano Buitimea reports that if they are cooked they will not burn the mouth.

Mayos use the names *júchica* (Mayo) and *bebelama* (Spanish) for members of this genus.

Sideroxylon tepicense (Standley) T.D. Pennington
cajé (tempisque)

A tall, slender, often spreading tree, the *tempisque* grows in Sonoran TDF. Nowhere abundant, it is nevertheless found throughout the region in a variety of habitats. Most trees are less than 15 m tall but may reach 25 m under favorable conditions.

Food: Gentry (1942:205) noted as follows: "Tree 10–15 m. high, with spreading branches. Widely, but rather infrequently scattered throughout the barrancas where it is nearly confined to the arroyo margins. It bears a small, yellow, edible, stemmed fruit, about the size of a large cherry when ripe in [March through] June, which is eagerly sought by the natives. It has a sweet flavor with a granular texture, but the skin is rough and will cauterize the mouth if many are eaten. The natives eat them raw or cook them up into jam, and during their season, many are sold in the market of Alamos." We have not found them in markets, but they remain popular in rural, mountainous parts of the Sonoran TDF.

Saxifragaceae—Saxifrage Family

Heuchera rubescens Torr. var. *versicolor* (Greene) Stewart
seguá (jardín)

This herbaceous perennial of the pine-oak forest produces branches of pretty pink and white flowers. The Guarijíos are so taken with the blooms that they gather the seeds and sow them in their gardens. Some people even transplant

Chiltepines drying, Mochibampo.

the plants to their homes, reports Tiburcio Charramoneta. The Guarijío name means simply "flower" while the Spanish name means "garden."

Scrophulariaceae—Snapdragon Family

Mabrya geniculata (Rob. & Fernald) Elisens subsp. *geniculata*
corarí

A tender perennial herb growing on rock faces in canyons. The flowers are lemon yellow.

Medicine: For skin spots that lose pigment (probably psoriasis), a leaf is applied directly to the bleached spot and rubbed. The leaf will often adhere to the skin, according to Cipriano Buitimea. It may restore the skin's color, he says.

Penstemon wislizenii (A. Gray) Straw
chaéhuori

A perennial of pine-oak forest, this penstemon flowers bright red in late summer. The Guarijío name means "handsome." Guarijíos ascribe no particular use to the plant but are widely familiar with it and enjoy its beauty.

Selaginaceae—Spike-moss Family

Selaginella pallescens (C. Presl) Spring var. *pallescens*
cocherá (flor de piedra, resurrection plant)

This resurrection plant grows on rock faces in isolated canyon locations.

Medicine: For liver pain, Guarijíos immerse a plant in cool water for a few hours and drink the liquid. The tea is also said to be a good remedy for the kidneys and associated back pain. The plant is believed capable of dissolving rock and thus the tea is believed equally efficacious at dissolving kidney stones.

Selaginella spp.
cocherá (flor de piedra, resurrection plant)

Several species of spike moss are found in the Guarijío region. As is the case with *S. pallescens,* the plants are soaked in water (not cooked) and steeped for a few hours. The liquid is then drunk as a remedy for liver or kidney pain, according to José Ruelas.

Simaroubaceae—Quassia Family

Alvaradoa amorphoides Liebm.
ma'ácita ("little mauto") (palo torsal)

An uncommon large shrub sometimes growing into a tree to 7 m tall in TDF. The long, pinnate leaf pattern can easily cause it to be confused with a legume. The flowers and fruits are in racemes.

Fuel: The wood provides kindling and firewood for emergencies, according to Lorenzo Sujaguareña, who identified the tree.

Solanaceae—Nightshade Family

Capsicum annuum L. var. *aviculare* (Dierbach) D'Arcy & Eshbaugh
co'cor'í (chiltepín)

Chiltepín is an erect shrub with spindly branches growing to nearly 2 m tall with small white flowers. The fruits mature into pea-sized chiles beginning green and turning bright red in maturity. The plants are often found adjacent to ancient and modern trails, suggesting that humans are involved in their dissemination. Gentry expressed concern for the future of the chiltepín due to the rough methods of harvesting, but populations appear to be doing well.

Food: These small chiles, everywhere relished, add a fiery touch to food. They are eaten green (fresh) or red (dried). They dry well and are stored by most families. The degree of hotness is variable. Those of the mountains are believed by some to be hotter than those of the valleys and plains.

Nearly every Guarijío household keeps a saucer or small bowl of dried chiltepines on the table. The tiny firecrackers are crumbled into beans or tortillas.

Datura discolor **Bernh.**

tecuyabi (toloache, Jimson weed)

A robust, spreading low annual with large leaves and showy, large white to (rarely) light pink funnel-form flowers. The plants flourish on disturbed soil and waste places, especially around corrals and in fields where growing conditions may be ideal. The fruits are covered with many intimidating spines. Livestock avoid the plants, and during dry spells *toloaches* may be the only plants to be found over a large area where cattle traffic is heavy. The leaves, stems, and roots of plant are generally believed to be toxic if eaten, and the Guarijíos warn about the plant's dangers.

Medicine: For *pasmo* (infections and general localized malaise) and for swellings, the leaves are heated and pressed onto the affected place (external use only).

Nicotiana glauca **Graham**

toripipa (tabaco cimarrón, tree tobacco)

Guarijíos consider the plant, which often reaches the size of a small tree, interesting, but attribute no use to it. Widely naturalized, it is native to South America.

Nicotiana tabacum **L.**

papante, huipá (macuchi, tabaco rústico, tobacco)

A locally grown annual tobacco to 2 m tall.

Medicine: A tea brewed from the leaves is believed to be a good remedy for *gripa* (influenza).

Smoking: The dried, crumbled leaves are rolled into a cornhusk and smoked. At fiestas the air is often fragrant with the smoke. At that time use by women is socially acceptable, and many can be seen puffing on rather large cigarettes. In January 1999, several Guarijíos sowed *huipá* seed in a plot of moist river soil 10 by 30 m on the gently sloping bank of the Río Mayo at Mesa Colorada. If the crop was not washed out, the planters believed it would be sufficient for the village for a year.

Physalis **sp.**

tulumisi (tomatillo)

This *tomatillo*, a rather common weed, produces green fruits covered by a membranous shield. These plants are said by Guarijíos to be wild plants of the cultivated variety popular in Mexico. If this is so, the plant is *P. philadelphica* Lam.

Food: Some people (mestizos) eat the fruits of one species, according to José Ruelas, but traditional Guarijíos do not. Cipriano Buitimea, on the other hand, finds them edible. They are the basis for popular green salsas in Mexico.

Plot sown with *huipá*—native tobacco, Río Mayo at Mesa Colorado.

Solanum americanum **Mill.**

maneyoqui, manilochi (chichiquelite)

A fast-growing annual often appearing in great numbers following sustained rains, especially equipatas. The small white flowers produce round fleshy pea-sized fruits that turn blackish at maturity.

Food: The leaves are steamed or boiled and eaten with tortillas. They constitute a favorite green of the Guarijíos. As such they constitute a most important source of vitamins in the Guarijío diet, which is often lacking in fresh vegetables. Cipriano Buitimea also reports that children pick the black fruits of the older plants and eat them.

Solanum erianthum **D. Don**

huatauhuí (cornetón del monte)

A shrub or small tree, sometimes exceeding 5 m in height with an expansive crown. It flowers opportunistically and produces black round fruits. Guarijíos are universally familiar with it but have not to our knowledge ascribed uses to it.

Solanum tridynamum **Dunal**

palohusi pusira (sacamanteca, ojo de liebre)

A bushy perennial to nearly 1 m high common along trails, roads, and other disturbed places. The flowers are bright violet with yellow anthers. It often flowers during the dry season when nearly all other plants are dormant. The Guarijío and Spanish names translate as "jackrabbit's eye."

Food: Nacho Ciriaco notes that the fruits are mashed and sprinkled into milk to coagulate it for cheese.

Medicine: Cipriano reports that the flowers are gently pressed into the ear to restore hearing to the deaf.

Hand-rolled cigarette of *huipá* and cornhusk, Guajaray.

Sterculiaceae—Chocolate Family

Guazuma ulmifolia Lam.
agiyá (guásima)

A common spreading tree in bottomland soils and along watercourses, growing to over 10 m in height. It is generally absent within the upland TDF. It grows rapidly and cut limbs regenerate quickly. The hard, prickly fruits are the size of small pecans.

Food and Livestock Food: The green fruits are edible and may be an important food source in times of scarcity. José Ruelas reports that the seeds are removed from the fruits and pulp is pounded to make a thick mash. This gruel is toasted, then ground further and boiled with water to make an atol. José laments that people no longer eat it as much. He recalls that Guarijíos used to carry it in a morral with roasted agave—for lunch. Others have mentioned the use of the ground dried seeds brewed into a coffee substitute. Burros eat the fallen fruits.

Furniture: The tough, resilient wood is widely used for making furniture, stools, musical instruments, and other artifacts. Most *guásimas* near settlements show signs of limbs having been harvested and trees pollarded.

Medicine: According to José Ruelas, a tea brewed from the bark calms the stomach when the stomach feels hot and the patient feels like throwing up. Nacho Ciriaco reports that the bark is boiled into a tea and drunk for scorpion stings. He has been stung many times, and he has used it often. The remedy always seems to work. The same tea is drunk to alleviate fevers. Nacho recalls that his mother administered it to him when he was a child—to be drunk in the afternoon and in the morning as well.

Theophrastaceae—Joe-wood Family

Jacquinia macrocarpa Cav. subsp. *pungens* (A. Gray) B. Ståhl
(sanjuanico)

Sanjuanico is a small tree with dense, compact leafage. Its leaf tips are needle-sharp, and its fruits are cherry-sized hard round balls, green when fresh and turning mustard color. It is widespread in thornscrub and TDF. It is nearly absent in Guarijío country, however, perhaps due to the heavier vegetation cover that makes competition more difficult for the tree whose optimum habitat appears to be in arid thornscrub.

Medicine: Most Guarijíos in the southern villages (Los Jacales, Mesa Colorada, Mochibampo) are familiar with it and recommend toasting, grinding, and steeping the leaves into a tea for fever. They also boil the flowers into a tea to alleviate diarrhea. Several consultants believed the round fruits were useful for something or other, but could not recall what it was. And strangely, they could not recall a Guarijío name for the tree.

Tiliaceae—Linden Family

Heliocarpus attenuatus S. Watson
sanalí (samo, samo baboso)

A small, slender tree reaching 6 m in height, with gray bark and delicate leaves. The branches spread out considerably. The tree grows sporadically through the TDF and extends below into more moist sectors of thornscrub. The persistent dried fruits, no more than 2 cm in diameter, turn wispy brown with age. They resemble miniature sun images, hence the generic name meaning "sun fruit."

Adhesive: Strips of bark are steeped in buckets of water or sometimes boiled. When the aqueous solution is mixed with sand and lime, it makes the *mezcla* (mixture) adhere better. There is no need to add cement, according to Nacho Ciriaco. The mixture froths when it boils, hence the common name *baboso* (foaming).

Cordage: Guarijíos use long strips of the bark to bind roofing shakes, latas, and various bundles. The bark is said to shrink as it dries, ever tightening the binding.

Medicine: The bark is brewed into a tea taken to cure bloody stools, especially in children. Nacho believes the remedy is more effective if the bark is soaked in cold water and is not boiled. A concentrated elixir of the brewed bark reportedly can also induce vomiting.

Heliocarpus palmeri S. Watson
samo ochóname (samo prieto)

A shrub or slender tree similar in aspect to *H. attenuatus* and with larger leaves. The bark is speckled and shiny brown. None of the Guarijíos we worked with could recall a use, though several had heard of uses for it.

Turneraceae—Turnera Family

Turnera diffusa Schult.
(damiana)

A diminutive perennial subshrub with small yellow flowers, it is often found growing from cracks in bedrock. We have been unable to ascertain a Guarijío name.

Medicine: The whole plant is brewed into a tea to alleviate *pasmo,* a condition women are said to be prone to get: their limbs feel cold, their bones ache, and they may be unable to conceive. The tea is said to make them feel warmer and to be invigorating for anyone. The plants are often gathered and stored in the house for future use. An elixir of *damiana* is widely marketed in Mexico as an aphrodisiac.

Ulmaceae—Elm Family

Aphananthe monoica (Hemsl.) Leroy
mohuarí (alamillo, guasimilla)

One of the largest trees in the region, it is confined to deep, moist canyons where it grows to more than 30 m in height, providing luxuriant and abundant shade. The leaves have a serrated edge and a characteristic elm-leaf appearance. *Mohuarí* is invariably found growing with *Drypetes, Sideroxylon persimile,* and *Trophis.* Trees growing in the deep box canyon called El Rincón de las Ardillas, 1 km north of Todos Santos, are the northernmost known.

Construction: Mohuarí is said to be good for lumber. Populations of the trees are usually remote from settlements, and the size of the trees precludes easy harvesting.

Celtis iguanaea (Jacq.) Sarg.
carocá'a (cumbro, garabato)

A shrub, vine, or small tree that grows into massive, impenetrable thickets. The emerging branches produce twin spines and thorns up to 15 cm in length that can inflict terrible puncture wounds. Cattlemen curse the plant for its inclination to cover pathways and provide refuge for errant cows. Vines sometimes grow into the tops of tall riparian trees and produce a crown of leaves that compete with the host's own leafage. In the fall the plants produce tasty orange fruits the size of blueberries. These can be easily collected, even on horseback.

Food: Guarijío consultants seemed reluctant to talk about the plant. They said the fruits are edible, but that they do not eat them. Finally Lorenzo Sujaguareña confessed that when he was a child he ate so many of them he grew tired of eating them. Nacho Ciriaco says people don't eat the fruits because "le hace tullido" (they make you lame). Children do eat them, but they are not good for them, he notes. We have eaten many and have suffered no apparent ill effects. Yet.

Celtis reticulata Torr.
machaquí (cumbro, netleaf hackberry)

A solid-trunked tree with gray bark and dense foliage, seldom more than 8 m tall. It is rather common growing on low-lying valley benches. It is seldom found in close association with other trees of the TDF.

Guarijíos appear universally familiar with the tree, but none has ascribed a use to it.

Urticaceae—Nettle Family

Parietaria hespera D. B. Hinton
tomaari

This is a widely distributed small winter annual. We found it growing in bottomland along the Arroyo Guajaray.

Food: The herb is eaten when it is young. It is said to be especially tasty when sautéed in fat and mixed with cornmeal to form an atol.

Pouzolzia cf. *palmeri* S. Watson
zanzaro (huevo de cochi)

This is a straight-stalked shrub growing pole-like to 2 m high. It produces many tuberous roots somewhat like small potatoes. The reddish-brown bark exfoliates in russet sheets and is covered with white lenticels. The many white flowers grow close to the stalk. We found it on steep, semimoist slopes in TDF. The Spanish name means "pig testicles."

Food: Manuel Rodríguez demonstrated the edibility of the tuberous roots. We found them to be edible, but coated with prolific slime that is a deterrent to culinary enjoyment. José Ruelas remarked, "We used to eat it, but no more. The root is all right to eat, not tasty, but edible. It is good for pigs." Nacho Ciriaco notes that people can eat the root, and that javelinas love them.

Verbenaceae—Verbena Family

Lantana camara L.
chiqui pusi (confiturilla, lantana)
A many-stemmed bushy shrub with clusters of many yellow and orange flowers. The fruits are fleshy and blackish when ripe.

Food: Guarijíos eat the small globose fruits.

Verbena gooddingii Briquet
chiqui pusi (quelite)
A small annual or short-lived perennial growing in moist places with showy clusters of pinkish flowers.

Food: According to Hermangildo Zaila, the greens are eaten as *quelite* when the plant is very tender. When it matures the leaves become harsh.

Vitex mollis H. B. K.
juguari, cajúguari (igualama)
A spreading tree to 15 m or more, common along watercourses in TDF. The bark is brown flecked with white. The violet and white flowers (April and May), 1.5–2 cm in diameter, are highly fragrant and attract many bees and other pollinators. The cherry-sized fleshy fruits are black when ripe.

Food: The fruits are stewed and eaten, a favorite of native peoples throughout the region. When consumed raw, the fruits may be tasteless and bitter but are reminiscent of plums when stewed with sugar.

Medicine: The bark and root are mixed with leaves of *Callaeum* and *Senna atomaria,* and/or the roots of *Ambrosia ambrosioides* and cilantro to make a tonic to "cleanse" a woman during and after childbirth.

Vitex pyramidata B. L. Rob.
cajuari (negrito)
A small, bushy tree with dense foliage, it is especially prevalent on Mesa Matapaco and in upper TDF. The flowers are more nearly blue than those of *V. mollis*. The fruits are black, appearing in autumn. The tree grows in xeric conditions, often on hydrothermally altered soils and at the margin between TDF and oak woodland.

Food: The black fruits are eaten, even after they dry on the tree. José Ruelas ate them raw one day as we hiked, though they were dry and tough. Most people stew them, he said, with some disdain.

Vitaceae—Grape Family

Vitis arizonica Engelm.
jeyulí, uirí (uva cimarrón, wild grape)
Wild grapevines are common in oak woodland and pine-oak forest.

Food: The wild grapes are widely eaten, even though they are tiny and require a large number to constitute a mouthful. One must get them early, before birds and small mammals get them.

Horticulture: Some Guarijíos report that the seeds are dried and planted near houses to provide shade.

Medicine: Nicolás Tadeo and others report that the only cure for a poison ivy rash is to rub it with the crushed leaves of *jeyulí.*

Zamiaceae—Cycad Family

Dioon edule Lindl. var. *sonorense* (DeLuca et al.) McVaugh & Pérez de la Rosa
(palma de la virgen, palmilla)
Cycads are uncommon in the region but are well known to many Guarijío men. They grow in restricted mountain canyons where trails tend not to go. Several or more plants are usually found growing together, while for miles around there may be no others. Guarijíos note certain locations where they are to be found. One of these is in the high mountains near Los Bajíos. The other is in the Sierra de la Ventana above Caramechi. We have not seen them in Guarijío country.

José Ruelas believes the leaves were once used in making guaris. He is perhaps mistaken in this.

Zygophyllaceae—Caltrop Family

Guaiacum coulteri A. Gray
(guayacán)
A compact, often symmetrical tree to 8 m tall with a sturdy, stout trunk. The dark green pinnate leaves are 2–6 cm long. The prolific, deep blue flowers appear in late April and May where they stand out, for few colors illuminate the countryside in those sere months. The wood is extremely hard. The tree is nowhere common but occurs over a broad range of habitats, ranging from coastal thornscrub through TDF. We have been unsuccessful in finding a Guarijío name.

Medicine: The bark is brewed into a tea believed to be effective for asthma.

Religion: Nacho Ciriaco reports that Guarijíos do not cut down the tree or harm it because evil will come to the family. All family members may die prematurely if you harm a tree, he warns. For this reason, he says, people respect it. He doesn't know anybody who has had harm from the tree, but everybody knows you shouldn't hurt it. He believes that if you burn it and breathe the smoke, your hair will fall out, so they do not use the tree for firewood. According to Hermangildo Zaila, *guayacán* gives the best shade in the lowlands, so the Guarijíos guard the trees.

Unidentified plants

cusí picaeme (rama lechosa)

Tiburcio Charramoneta described this plant from a distant mountain. A bee sting treated with its milky sap is instantly better, he said. We cannot provide a more comprehensive description of the plant.

tomaari (quelite)

Nacho Ciriaco described this, a leafy plant whose greens are gathered for food. They are said to be tastiest when sautéed in fat. They appear only when rains are abundant, he said, so we were unable to find it. Several plants are called tomaari.

tapalancate (helecho, fern)

José Ruelas brought us a withered and broken sample of this small fern. He reports that the "branch" and leaves are cooked and the tea drunk for "bad kidneys." The symptoms of bad kidneys are lower back pain. Cipriano Buitimea agrees that this and other ferns are good for alleviating body aches.

APPENDIX A

Gazetteer of the Guarijío Region

All locations are in Sonora unless otherwise noted. Nearly all population figures are courtesy of INEGI, the Mexican government census office.

Arechuybo, Chihuahua. Former Guarijío village now mostly mestizo atop a mesa. The Guarijíos have moved away from the village to its outskirts. 27° 52.5′N 108° 33′W. Pop. 600 (1980). Elevation 1,500 m.

Arroyo Bavícora. Drainage originating in the Sierra Charuco, entering the Río Mayo 2 km south of Charajaqui. It is formed at Bavícora from the intersection of two deep canyons with rich vegetation. The section downstream from Bavícora flows through a deeply incised canyon and becomes difficult to follow until it reaches the Río Mayo.

Arroyo El Tuburi. Drainage between El Saúz and Bavícora with stretches of permanent water and moist canyon vegetation. The point at which the trail between the two settlements crosses the stream is a popular rest stop. El Tuburi empties into the Arroyo Bavícora roughly 2 km downstream (southwest) of Bavícora.

Arroyo Guajaray. Major tributary of the Río Mayo entering from the northwest near Mesa Colorada. Its generous flow seldom varies except in times of high rainfall. It flows through Guarijío ejidos and is familiar to the people of the region. Its side canyons support low elevation semi-deciduous forest and northern extensions of several gallery forest trees such as *Aphananthe monoica, Drypetes gentryi,* and *Sideroxylon persimile.* Canyon walls at times exceed 300 m in height.

Arroyo Limón. A major stream of the middle stretch of the Río Mayo, draining the Sierra Canelo and the Sierra Chuchupate, both in Chihuahua. Loreto, Chihuahua lies on an upper tributary. Over its 100-km length, the drainage harbors long stretches of deep, dark canyons. Perhaps 2 km from its conjunction with the Río Mayo lies Gocojaqui, an intermittently occupied Guarijío settlement.

Arroyo San Pedro. Drainage originating in the rough volcanics of Sierra Dos Cuates. It passes through deep *cajones.* Only at Rancho San Pedro are there flats capable of supporting more than a single dwelling and some fields. It empties into

the Río Mayo from the west 2 km south of Mochibampo. *Bursera simaruba* is found in moist upper canyons.

Basicorepa. Guarijío settlement of two to six families in a small valley, a kilometer north of the Arroyo Guajaray upstream from Los Bajíos. 27° 42.2′N 109° 1′W. Pop. 6 (1990). Elevation 500 m.

Bavícora. Guarijío village of fifteen–twenty families 20 km by air north of Mesa Colorada on the Río Mayo. It is situated in an arroyo of the same name, which drains the Sierra Charuco into the Río Mayo. The palm-thatched homes and school are built on carefully constructed terraces well above the arroyo. Several of the women weave attractive guaris. When pencas of *Sabal uresana* are available, they also weave fine hats. 27° 40.5′N 108° 47.5′W. Pop. 89 (1990). Elevation 600 m.

Burapaco. Guarijío and mestizo settlement north of San Bernardo and west of the Río Mayo, situated on a broad, rolling mesa adjacent to the Arroyo San Pablo. It is now a somnolent hamlet occupied by several mestizo and about ten Guarijío families and is a meeting point for many Guarijíos. A tuburada is held in early December. A store owned by the Enríquez family is the best stocked in the region. It is the source of most of the hats worn by Guarijío men. The name in Mayo means "deer out there." Formerly an oasis of sorts set amidst a vast, forested upland, it is now surrounded by an ever-expanding sea of buffelgrass. 27° 33′ 30"N 108° 53′W. Pop. 53 (1990). Elevation 220 m.

Cañada el Rincón de las Ardillas. A deep, moist side canyon of the Arroyo Guajaray, emptying from the east some 3 km north of Los Aguaros. It originates in the Sierra García and forms part of a convoluted canyonlands where volcanic rock has been deeply incised by the action of water and, perhaps, block cracking. The canyon can only be traversed on foot for half a kilometer, where a tall cliff, a waterfall during the rainy season, arrests forward progress. Enters Arroyo Guajaray at 27° 39′N 108° 59′W. Elevation 370 m.

Canelichi, Chihuahua. A private ranch with three Guarijío families in residence. The ranch, about 8 km south of Loreto, has never been lumbered commercially and hosts a fine example of Madrean pine-oak forest. The Guarijíos plant corn on mahuechis and care for cattle for the ranch owner. Downstream the canyon deepens rapidly and becomes a major tributary of the Río Oteros, ultimately the Río Chínipas and the Río Fuerte. 27° 44.3′N 108° 31.5′W. Pop. approx. 20 (1998). Elevation 1,420 m.

Cañon Cajonchi. The western branch of the Arroyo San Pedro that splits half a kilometer west of Rancho San Pedro.

The deep cajón has walls nearly a thousand feet high. The upper drainage has been used for many years by Guarijíos who have constructed huts on small ledges and have planted fruit trees and prickly pear cacti. The cajón harbors rich vegetation including *Cinnamomum* and *Bursera simaruba*.

Caramechi. Gentry in 1942 described it as follows: "Indian locality of four or five families, with a mestizo family in residence during the winter, tending a herd of milk cows. It is bordered on the west by the high ramparts of Sierra de la Ventana, from which three short tributaries discharge into the Mayo at Caramechi" (Gentry 1942:22). The settlement was abandoned in 1995, perhaps only temporarily. As of 1998 it was still uninhabited. 27° 48´N 108° 52´W. Pop. 26 (1990). Elevation 320 m.

Charajaqui. Intermittently occupied settlement on a well-concealed terrace above a broad bend in the Río Mayo. It is sometimes occupied by up to two families. The trail from Mesa Colorada to Jogüegüe and parts beyond crosses the Río Mayo here and passes close to the settlement, though one could easily walk by it unaware of its existence. In 1996–98 it was uninhabited. 27° 42´N 108° 51.5´W. Elevation 300 m.

Chinatopo. Mestizo-owned ranch of the Rosas family who operate a mostly self-supporting ranch. The handsome though rustic ranch house is situated picturesquely above the Río Mayo at the southern terminus of a long uninhabited stretch. Rosario Rosas and his sons have carried out considerable clearing and seeding with buffelgrass in the area. Just north, along a broad sandbar on the eastern riverbank, is a fine grove of guamúchil trees more then 30 m tall that germinated in 1965 or thereabouts. 27° 39.2´N 108° 52´W. Elevation 280 m.

Chorijoa. Gentry in 1942 noted: "Old Indian pueblo of Guarijíos or Macoyahuis, now in decay. Eight or ten families of mixed blood remain in residence" (Gentry 1942:22). The Macoyahuis spoke Cáhita and may have been merely an isolated Mayo group identified by their village, Macoyahui, to the south of San Bernardo. The name "Chorijoa" probably means "damaged house" in Mayo. Some speakers insist it means "place of the quail;" *choli* = quail in Cáhita; *Cholijoa* = place of the quail. Now a mestizo/Mayo settlement on Río Mayo 8 km NNW of San Bernardo, it is surrounded by patches of tropical deciduous forest. In 1998 one Guarijío family was in residence. 27° 28´N 108° 52´W. Pop. 65 (1990). Elevation 200 m.

El Saucito. Settlement of five Guarijío families on Arroyo Los Estrao about 5 km west of Burapaco. The inhabitants are given over to raising cows in addition to their traditional mahuechi farming. 27° 33.5´N 108° 55´W. Pop. approx. 25. Elevation 300 m.

El Saúz. Ranch formerly owned by the Rosas family, now part of Mesa Colorada ejido. It is situated in a broad, rocky valley along an intermittent watercourse where large figs and tepeguajes grow. Several mahuechis nearby produce corn, beans, and squash. Chopó *(Mimosa palmeri)* is especially abundant near the ranch. Its higher elevation makes it cooler in hot weather than the sweltering Mesa Colorada. 27° 28´N 108° 48´W. Pop. approx. 8. Elevation 760 m.

El Trigo (de Russo), Chihuahua. Mestizo town in oaks and pines on a small *llano* (flat) on the eastern slopes of the Sierra Charuco. Three Guarijío families inhabit a separate "neighborhood" and live much to themselves. Some 6 km to the west, in a forested canyon, lies Rancho Quemado, which was built by the Russo family in the 1930s. The family purchased lands in the region, apparently from Guarijíos. See Guasaremos. 27° 34.2´N 108° 40´W. Pop. 120 (1990). Elevation 1,500 m.

Gocojaqui. Settlement on the Arroyo Limón, with Guarijíos intermittently in residence. The flow is permanent, and the stream is home to native fish and introduced talapia. Guarijíos from other settlements visit the stream to fish and enjoy the water. 27° 42.5´N 108° 50´W. Pop. 27 (1990). Elevation 340 m.

Guajaray. Primarily a Guarijío village, with a few mestizos in residence. The village has a school and a small store and an elected commissar. With the encouragement of the Mexican government, the village has grown since the formation of the Guarijío ejidos. Guajaray is now home to some twenty Guarijío families, one of whom maintains a cellular phone from which calls can be placed to anywhere in the world. The village sits at the end of a wide valley from which the forest has been cleared, making it hotter than the surrounding forested countryside. The valley constricts to the northeast. A trail passable by motor vehicles descends about a kilometer to the arroyo and several deep pools. 27° 35´45"N 108° 55´W. Pop. 154 (1990). Elevation 330 m.

Guamúchil. An uninhabited settlement located 2 km south of Los Bajíos at the intersections of two large washes with the Arroyo Guajaray. Many abandoned mahuechis are visible on the hillsides from the site. 27° 39.5´N 108° 58.5´W. Elevation 360 m.

Guasaremos, Chihuahua. In 1942 Gentry wrote the following: "Rancho situated in a picturesque valley on the western slope of Sierra Canelo. Bought from the Guarijíos for a 'song' about sixty years ago, it was later taken over by the Italian Russo, and a fortlike house was constructed. The vicinity is under intensive cultivation. It lies at the upper limits of the Short-tree Forest and is bordered by oak hills" (Gentry 1942:22). Gentry's collections indicate a diverse flora including many rare species. Barney Burns, Gary Nabhan, and Tom Sheridan made a memorable visit to the area for Native Seed Search in search for fresh seed of the potential cultigen *Panicum sonorum* (Nabhan 1985), now referred to as *Panicum hirticaule*. No Guarijío families remain at the lush, productive settlement, what might be viewed as the Guarijíos' Manhattan. They have settled instead on tiny *ranchos* not far away. 27° 39.5´N 108° 42.5´W. Pop. 20 (1990). Elevation 800 m.

Guasisaco, Chihuahua. Village of nine Guarijío families on Arroyo Limón approximately 8 km north of El Trigo de Russo. I have not visited the village, but it is said to be traditional in its orientation.

Huataturi. Guarijío settlement of four families on the east bank of the Río Mayo 6 km north of Mesa Colorada. It is surrounded by private ranches. The residents harvest fish from the river and corn from their mahuechis. Some women weave baskets. The name means "good willow" in Mayo. 27° 36.5´N 108° 51.5´W. Pop. approx. 25 (1998). Elevation 240 m.

Jánaco. Hilltop settlement of one Guarijío family. At one time a mestizo shack occupied the site. Now a handsome Guarijío *jacal* sits atop the hill. An unfailing aguaje below the site provides fresh water. The site presents spectacular views of the Sierra Charuco and the Sierra de la Ventana. 27° 33.5´N 108° 56´W. Pop. 7. Elevation 480 m.

Jogüegüe. Settlement of two families on former mestizo ranch owned by the Saenz family. Manuel Rodríguez works his mahuechis nearby. A large corral is so well constructed that it appears to be of dressed stone. Immediately to the west the arroyo forms a series of cascades and large pools. A trail leads northeast to Bavícora. The name means "place of amaranth" in Guarijío. 27° 42.5´N 108° 49´W. Pop. 15. Elevation 440 m.

La Junta. Guarijío settlement of two families at the confluence of the Río Mayo and the Arroyo Guajaray, near the village of Mesa Colorada. Groves of tall sabinos grow on the Guajaray just upstream. 27° 35´30"N 108° 53´30"W. Elevation 250 m.

Loreto, Chihuahua. Gentry wrote: "Settlement of Mexicans and Guarijíos; population about 500. In rolling, parklike country of the Sierran top, and well watered. Self-supporting with cattle, mountain maize, beans, potatoes, and some garden truck. On the main trail from the upper Mayo country to the Chínipas basin" (Gentry 1942:23). Loreto is called Ignacio Valenzuela on maps, but universally referred to by its older name. A new lumber mill has been installed by the ejido that employs fifty members. The settlement is spread over a large area with large clearings and pastures. In the green of summer, it presents a most bucolic portrait when viewed from above. A boarding school for Guarijío children is located in the town. Supplies were trucked in from San Bernardo, fourteen hours away, until 1996. Now they come in through Chihuahua. The Arroyo Loreto, polluted by village drainage, flows south of the village into increasingly deep canyons, eventually becoming the Arroyo Limón, a major tributary of the Río Mayo. 27° 45´N 108° 33.5´W. Pop. 309 (1990). Elevation 1,500 m.

Los Aguaros. Well-concealed Guarijío settlement of two families situated on a cliff shelf overlooking the Arroyo Guajaray. They have constructed a fishing weir in the arroyo, which flows a hundred feet below their aerie. Unless the settlement is pointed out, the visitor will not be aware of its existence. 27° 39´20"N 108° 57´55"W. Pop. 16 (1990). Elevation 350 m.

Los Bajíos. Also known locally as Conejos, a Guarijío village on the Arroyo Guajaray. In 1942 Gentry wrote: "Locality of Guarijío Indians, who are reported to have moved out recently. In 1934 there were five families in residence, living principally on maize and fish from the Guajaray. A league southward is the Mexican rancho of Guamúchil" (Gentry 1942:22). It is now home to 25 families and is the site of an *albergue* (boarding school) for Guarijío children. The government built a tall *tinaco* (water tower) painted brilliant white, which has never held water but which makes a convenient landmark. Water must be hauled instead up a cliff face from the Arroyo Guajaray a kilometer away. The surrounding mountainsides are checkerboarded with mahuechis in various stages of succession. Maize crops have generally failed in recent years. Fish are less numerous now but still harvested as a dietary staple. Nearby are incised, moist side canyons of considerable botanical interest. Overflights of the environs reveal little disturbance of the tropical deciduous forest. A few women in the village still weave hats of palm *(Sabal uresana)* and guaris. 27° 40.5´N 108° 59.5´W. Pop. 139 (1990). Elevation 400 m.

Los Estrao. A settlement of six families on Arroyo Estrao near the roadway that reaches Guajaray. 27° 33.5´N 108°

57′W. Pop. approx. 36. Elevation 560 m.

Los Jacales. A Guarijío *colonia* or neighborhood of perhaps thirty Guarijío families, a part of San Bernardo. It lies on the northeast side of the Arroyo Taymuco, which splits the community. The homes, built close together and entirely of native materials, lie on a bluff overlooking the arroyo, one hundred feet below, from which the residents often must fetch water. 27°24′N 108°50.5′W. Elevation 220 m.

Mesa Colorada. Guarijío administrative village on a bluff overlooking the Río Mayo some ten leagues (40 km) north of San Bernardo. The road ends as the Río Mayo disappears into deep canyons upstream, and the mountains converge. From here all traffic north must proceed on foot. Mesa Colorada was not inhabited until the Guarijío ejidos were created in the early 1980s, so it lacks the united sense of a village. An *albergue* or boarding school for Guarijío children is located in the heart of the populated area. A modest cultural center has been dedicated to José Zazueta, hero of the struggle for Guarijío liberation in the 1970s. The nearby mouth of the Arroyo Guajaray dumps its warm waters into the colder Mayo, and the resulting bottomlands produce modest crops. Some villagers plant *ajonjolí* (sesame seed) in the flatter portions of the valley to the north. 27° 34′N 108° 52′W. Pop. 215 (1990). Elevation 250 m.

Mesa Matapaco. A broad, slightly tilted plain 500 ha in area, elevated above the surrounding countryside and 500 m. above the Río Mayo. It appears to be an ancient flow of basaltic lava that filled a valley. The durable rock withstood the erosion that removed the surrounding softer ash, leaving the mesa standing alone. The heavy tropical deciduous forest on its flanks obscures its geological history. The trail to Bavícora crosses it. It supports perhaps the best-preserved grassland in Sonora, hosting a wide variety of native grasses, as well as fine specimens of *Vitex pyramidata*. 27° 37′N 108° 50.5′W. Elevation 700 m.

Mochibampo. Hamlet of Guarijío families on both sides of the Río Mayo some 2 km south of Mesa Colorada along the river. The road that used to lead to the village was washed out in 1996 and has not been repaired, so access is by beast or by foot. Some villagers plant sesame seed as a cash crop. A mestizo rancher on the east side of the river has cleared most of the adjacent hillsides and planted buffelgrass, detracting greatly from the forested appearance of the hills. Guarijíos have recently begun to imitate him. 27° 33′N 108° 51′W. Pop. approx. 100. Elevation 200 m.

Rancho Nuevo. Settlement of two Guarijío families on a small ridge above the Río Mayo, well hidden from sight of those journeying up and down the river. The palm-roofed huts, less than a decade old, are superbly built. A spring nearby provides water for an ample garden and mahuechi. 27° 42.5′N 108° 51′W. Pop. approx. 12. Elevation 300 m.

San Bernardo. In 1942 Gentry wrote: "Pueblo of about 300 people with some outlying agricultural lands. It is the end of the automobile road and thus a junction between wheel and foot travel on the route to Chínipas in Chihuahua. It has two or three very meager shops, and good meals may be obtained at the house of Señora Matán. There are a few families of Guarijíos" (Gentry 1942:25). It is now a town of about thirteen hundred, down from more than three thousand at the height of a mining boom in the 1980s. It is rumored to be a node for marijuana distribution and is notorious for its high rate of homicide. At the southeast end of town, the government has established a center for assistance to the Guarijíos. Truckloads of Guarijíos, stacked in the bed like upright poles, depart and arrive regularly from Alamos and Navojoa. On the north side of the Arroyo Taymuco, atop a mesa, sits the barrio of Los Jacales where more than a hundred Guarijíos live. Roads now lead off in all directions, including Chínipas, and trails provide access to the precipitous and floristically rich canyons draining the western Sierra Sahuaribo. Los Pilares are spectacular stone pillars, a landmark on the western side of the Río Mayo. Since Gentry's day much of the surrounding forest has been cleared and planted with buffelgrass or crops. A dam on the Río Mayo is planned to the south. 27° 23′30″N 108° 50′45″W. Elevation 210 m.

San Pedro. Former mestizo ranch, now a part of the Ejido Los Bajíos. One Guarijío family is in residence nearby, and a mestizo-Mayo couple also resides here. Volcanic cliffs and rich tropical deciduous forest surround the small group of adobe buildings. Slightly to the north are oak forests growing on soils of indurated ash. Less than a kilometer to the west are moist incised canyons with rich semi-deciduous tropical forest. 27° 33′N 108° 57′W. Elevation 580 m.

Santo Niño. Former mestizo settlement, now abandoned, on the Arroyo Guajaray. 27° 36′N 108° 53′W. Elevation 240 m.

Sejaqui. Primarily mestizo village on the road to Guajaray from San Bernardo, with two Guarijío families in residence. It is surrounded by mountains covered with dense tropical deciduous forest. Much of the land is in private ranches whose owners have begun clearing the forest and seeding with buffelgrass. 27° 30′N 108° 55.5′W. Pop. 216. Elevation 480 m.

Sierra Canelo, Chihuahua. A rolling collection of mountains southwest of Loreto. The highest point is just over 2,300 m. Its name is apparently derived from the cinnamon (canela) colored volcanic rock outcroppings. The Canelo (Canelas) ranch is at 27° 43´N 108° 36.3´W. Elevation 1,500 m.

Sierra Charuco, Sonora-Chihuahua. A massive escarpment on Sonora-Chihuahua border. 27° 33´N 108° 43´W. Highest point ca. 2,000 m.

Sierra Chuchupate, Chihuahua. In 1942 Gentry wrote: "High mountain just east [northeast] of Loreto in the Sierra Cajurichi-Canelo axis. So called from the fabulous herb of that name [*Ligusticum porteri*], reputed to have undoubted medicinal values for injuries, sores, 'dolores,' etc. The higher elevations of this mountain are clothed with High Pine Forest" (Gentry 1942:25). The summit is nearly 2,300 m high. It is home to magnificent oak forests as well as the pines mentioned by Gentry. Rancho Canelichi lies near the southeastern edge of the range. The slopes not in private hands have been heavily lumbered for pine and fir. It is rumored that oaks will soon follow as fodder for pulp mills in Chihuahua. There is a different Sierra Chuchupate to the north. Elevation 2,300 m.

Sierra de la Ventana, Sonora-Chihuahua. Knife-like range rising abruptly west of the Río Mayo north of Mesa Colorado. It separates the Arroyo Guajaray from the Río Mayo and extends northward west of the Mayo. 27° 41´N 108° 55´W. Elevation 1,380 m at the summit.

Sierra Dos Cuates. Twin rhyolitic peaks visible from Guajaray and rising sharply from the village. The Guarijíos of the region have roamed and gathered in the rough terrain for as long as they can remember. 27° 34´N 108° 59´W. Elevation 1,100 m at the summit.

Sierra Oscura, Chihuahua. Large range north and west of Guarijío country. The Arroyo Guajaray drains a large portion of the sierras. From its highest points the Río Mayo appears as the Colorado River from the Grand Canyon. Highest point approx. 2,100 m.

Sierra Sutucame. A common name given to the large range of mountains northwest of San Bernardo with maximum elevation of less than 1,500 m. Sejaqui is nestled among the foothills of the range. Their highest slopes have oak woodlands, but the predominant vegetation is tropical deciduous forest.

Talayote. Tiny rancho of two Guarijío families in the wild hill country between the Río Mayo and El Saúz. The surrounding forest is rich in natural vegetation and is little affected by humans, although numbers of cattle have increased in recent years. The inhabitants have cleared small mahuechis and fetch water from a dependable aguaje fed by plastic tube leading from a spring half a kilometer east of the settlement. Chalillo Ruelas, a Guarijío with reportedly great spiritual powers, lives here. 27° 39´N 108° 50´W. Elevation 500 m.

Tecoripa (Boca Arroyo del Carrizo). Village of three Guarijío families upstream on the Río Mayo from Rancho Nuevo, some 2 km south of Caramechi. 27° 46.3´N 108° 52´W. Pop. 16 (1990). Elevation 320 m.

Todos Santos. Guarijío settlement of four families on a modest cleared terrace overlooking the Arroyo Guajaray. A large sector of the steep hillside to the west was once cleared for milpas and now is home to vast stands of *Dodonaea angustifolia*. Natives raise traditional crops including native cotton. 27° 37´50"N 108° 57´25"W. Pop. 29 (1990). Elevation 300 m.

Tojíachi, Chihuahua. Major Guarijío settlement north of Loreto on the Arroyo Tojíachi. There are two hamlets, Tojíachi de Abajo, and Tojíachi de Arriba, which sits some 50 m above the latter, 2 km to the east. 27° 50.1´N 108° 30.2´W. Pop. 80 (1990) in both villages. Elevation 1,120 m.

Notes

Chapter 2

1. A league is roughly four kilometers, two and a half miles.

2. Usually, though, there would be a slight spelling difference and the Guarijío pronunciation would place the stress on the ultimate syllable, while the Mayo would be on the penultimate. Thus the Mayo word for *Sideroxylon tepicense* is ca'ja while in Guarijío it is ca'jé; for *Acacia occidentalis* the Mayo is teso while the Guarijío is tesá. There are many such similarities in nomenclature of natural entities.

3. Eber and Rosenbaum (1993) note of highland Maya of Chiapas that "Married couples often behave like best friends in the privacy of their homes. They help each other with child care and chores and spend long, animated evenings around the fire discussing the smallest details of their own and others' lives" (p. 162).

4. I learned in 1998 that many children from Oaxacan families (Mixtecos and Triques) working as migrant laborers near Hermosillo were denied entrance to elementary school because their parents cannot document their children's registration.

5. I brought beans with me. Most Guarijíos cannot afford to buy them, and in drought years their mahuechis yield few.

6. Apologists for early colonists and missionaries in northwest Mexico point to the Spanish introduction of beef as an important dietary contribution of the Spaniards. Reff (1991) argues that beef and wheat, the two supposedly most important contributions were not used by indigenous Sonorans until well into the twentieth century. My experience corroborates his findings. Most Mayos and Guarijíos prefer wild game to domesticated flesh and corn tortillas to flour ones.

7. Zazueta died of pneumonia in the early 1980s before the Guarijío ejidos were officially created. It was Zazueta, Cipriano believes, who instilled the spirit of unity and sense of purpose among the Guarijíos that ultimately enabled them to acquire the ejidos. He was repeatedly threatened, beaten, and jailed for his efforts.

Chapter 3

1. The ejido is a parcel of land owned in common by shareholders called ejidatarios. The Mexican government retains the commonly owned lands in trust for the ejidatarios. Until 1992, parcels on ejido lands were granted to members in usufruct but could not be sold, leased, or rented. Changes to the Mexican Constitution at that time permitted privatization of parcels under certain conditions. See Yetman and Búrquez (1998).

2. See p. 15 and p. 115 for descriptions of military maneuvers.

3. Gentry (1963:72) found the use of the name Macurahui limited to those who identified themselves as Macoyahuis, an ancient people identified with a village of the same name on the middle Río Mayo some twenty kilometers south of San Bernardo.

4. The Río Mayo bears the name of the Guarijíos' more numerous neighbors to the south. The word "Mayo" in the language of the Mayos refers to the mauto tree *(Lysiloma divaricatum)*. The Mayos refer to themselves as *yoreme*. The Guarijío word for the Río Mayo is Jacqchí.

5. Sauer's map (1934) shows the range of Varojíos (Guarijíos) extending well east of the Río Chínipas at the time of conquest. Their eastern limit is now well west of the Chínipas and has been so for some centuries.

6. For estimating the population Sauer (1935:23) assumed a mean family size of six. He also relied on missionary records of the number of baptisms and number of children under indoctrination. He also noted a population of the Chínipas of 4,000 and for the Guazapares/Témoris of 3,000 (1935:4).

7. This figure is derived from various sources but primarily from the late Leobardo Quiroz, who was for many years the director of the National Indigenous Institute operation in San Bernardo, Sonora. The Guarijío population compares with roughly 60,000 Mayos, 60,000 Tarahumaras, and 30,000 Yaquis.

8. A useful summary of the earliest archival materials on the Guarijíos can be found in Haro and Valdivia Dounce (1996) and Aguilar Zeleny (1996).

9. Sauer dates the founding of the Chínipas mission as 1626 (1934:33). Apparently it foundered and was refounded in 1676.

10. For the full text of this story see Alegre (1888:193). The Spanish viewed the killings of the Jesuits as murders and viewed the dead clerics as martyrs. However, seen from the Guarijío viewpoint, it may have been a desperate and justified action to rid their country of the source of pestilence that was decimating indigenous people throughout Mexico. The priests had undoubtedly been repeatedly asked to leave. Most indigenous people (not all) resented the intrusions of the Spaniards and the clerics, viewing them as unwanted freeloaders and intruders maintained by the force of arms. If we consider that most native peoples' populations had decreased by more than half as a result of imported diseases, we can better understand their desire to see the invaders expelled from their lands. For a detailed analysis of the role of disease in the region, see Reff 1991.

11. Ocaranza (1942:22–23) describes the next several decades as follows: "Las varohíos apóstatas volvieron a su 'antigua gentilidad' a pesar de que volvió un misionero, con escolte de soldados, intentando el reducirlos a la fe cristiana nuevamenta. En tal ocasión huyeron hacia 'las entrañas de la Sierra derramadas por ella en varios y distintes estalages . . . esto mismo sirvió

para que los varohíos, los guazapares y otras naciones quedaran dueñas de la sierra y estorbaran el paso a otras naciones no reducas todavía, pero que deseaban serlo, a la vez que convertían aquellos abruptos lugares en madriguera de 'malos cristianos' que pertenecían a la nación maquiahui muy principalmente. La situación de los varohíos cada día fué más lamentable, y, por último, no tuvieron otro remedio que penetrar al seno de la Tarahumara, confundirse con la nación del mismo nombre, perder su idioma y adoptar el que hablaban los tarahumares." (The apostate Guarijíos returned to their "ancient paganism" in spite of the return of a missionary escorted by soldiers, who sought to reduce them again to the Christian faith. In response, they fled to the depths of the Sierra, scattering throughout it at various points and [obscure] . . . and thus the Guarijíos, the Guazapares, and other nations remained in control of the sierra and prevented access to other peoples who had not been reduced but who wished to be, at the same time forcing them into their havens of "bad Christians," primarily Maquiahuis (Makurawi, Guarijíos). The situation facing the Guarijíos grew worse each day and finally they were forced to migrate into the heart of Tarahumara country, mix with those people, lose their language, and adopt the Tarahumara tongue.) Ocaranza jumped too quickly to his conclusion. These is no independent evidence that the Guarijíos were absorbed by Tarahumaras, or adopted the Tarahumara language.

12. I have cited several standard sources, including Alegre (1888), and Pérez de Ribas (1645). Other sources include Decorme (1941), and Dunne (1948). The latter rely on the same archival sources cited by Almada, but he cites material unavailable to them, hence I rely heavily on Almada.

13. That a town as remote and insignificant as Chínipas would prove such an important source of archival documents is ironic considering its topographical situation. It is situated on the Río Chínipas at an elevation of 440 m. The steep Sierra Milpillas and Sierra Sahuaribo (referred to locally as the Cordillera Santa Gertrudis), tower 1,500 m above it to the west and south. Downstream to the southeast is a profound gorge that to this day denies access to and from the Río Fuerte. To the east rises a seemingly unending series of mountain ranges that gradually peak at the ramparts of the Barranca del Cobre. To the north the mountains are even more formidable, increasing in height to more than 2,800 m in the upper Río Mayo.

In 1676, at the time of establishment of the mission of Chínipas (named for the indigenous people who lived there) the principal point of access was from the south and west, near what would become Alamos. Then, as now, the roadway northwest from El Fuerte de Montesclaros traversed the undulating and heavily forested foothills to the Sierra Milpillas and dropped dramatically more than 600 m to the river. After the founding of Alamos, a road led north, then abruptly east, ascending through the narrow valley of the Arroyo Taymuco,

which ultimately empties into the Río Mayo near San Bernardo, Sonora. The old road (and the current road) reached the top ridge of the Sierra Milpillas, wound among the pines and oaks along the undulating mountaintop for a few miles, climbed abruptly to a ridge, then dropped precipitously through a seemingly unending series of hairpin turns, to reach the Río Chínipas. From there, when the river was high, one had to be (and still has to be) ferried across. Access from Chihuahua was (and still is) even more difficult. A northeastern route from El Fuerte, Sinaloa, followed ancient trails crisscrossing a seemingly unending series of ragged mountains. Some time in the nineteenth century a route was established between San Bernardo, on the Río Taymuco, north across the Sierra Charuco to Babarocos (not to be confused with San Luis Babarocos on the Río Mayo), and down the Arroyo Babarocos to the Río Chínipas. Both these routes through Sonora are in use today. The roughly 100-km drive from Alamos to Chínipas via Arroyo Taymuco takes eight hours when the road is in good conditions.

Other routes led from Moris, Chihuahua and from Batopilas via La Bufa, an impossibly difficult trail. When the Chihuahua-Los Mochis Railroad was completed in the 1950s, Chínipas was made more accessible, but the nearest point, Témoris, is still a good two hours from the railroad by poor dirt road. Vehicles must be shipped by train to Témoris, which is not accessible by motor vehicle.

In the seventeenth century, however, Chínipas was no more isolated than many other settlements of mountainous northwest Mexico. Nearly all transportation at the time was on foot, horseback, or pack animal. From its founding as a mission in 1676 through the early nineteenth century, Chínipas was a thriving and important administrative and mining center, ideally suited for development of a small city. It has abundant water, and it is situated at a broad bend of the Río Chínipas where the mountains to the east form a bowl emptying to the west, a geological coincidence that produced a bountiful supply of fertile flats ideal for agriculture. Mines upstream and in nearby drainages, especially in places like Batopilas and Tepago on the Río Urique, depended on Chínipas as an administrative and commercial center.

With the development of modern transportation in the nineteenth century, Chínipas was left behind and with good reason: the costs of providing improved vehicular access would be astronomical. Chínipas remains cut off from the main flow of current events. Almada's work is a remarkable achievement under any standards, is made the more remarkable by the thoroughness with which he combed through the ancient documents of Chínipas, which was even more isolated in the 1930s than it is now. He was a tough historian.

14. Almada's book is out of print. Unfortunately, he provided no citations for the sources of his information.

15. Sauer, however, remarks that "Their speech is still fairly distinct from both Cáhita and Tarahumara" (1934:36).

16. Here the padre is confused or his narrative ambiguous. The natives of Chínipas spoke their own language, distinct from that of the Guarijíos.

17. It is important to recall that the highest estimates of Guarijío population, 7,000 (Sauer), still put Guarijío numbers well below the estimated Tarahumara population of over 60,000.

18. Moris, Maycoba, and Yécora were Lower Pima towns. The Moris (Morichi) were widely regarded as brave and fierce fighters.

19. Usually, indigenous people rebelled against Jesuit prohibition on polygamy, drinking of alcohol, performing pre-Columbian ("pagan") rituals, and hunting. It is also clear from early accounts that a good proportion of hunters and gatherers refused to accept reduction, preferring to retain their nomadic ways.

20. Arbelaez (1991) notes Jesuit requirements: "A strict sedentary life and Catholic chastity, indoctrination, and social norms were introduced. Autochthonous religious practices were prohibited and hunting and gathering banned unless directed and supervised by the priest. Monogamy, strict control of sexual relations, and discipline were harshly implemented."

21. See Reff (1991) for a sustained discussion of the role of disease among the indigenous people of the region and implications for administrative policy of generalized depopulation.

22. Of the eleven Jesuits expelled from the Chínipas region, only one was a Spaniard (Almada 1937:203–4). The remainder were German, French, Italian, Bohemian, and Arabian. It is understandable that the Crown might have questioned the loyalty to the Spanish Crown of such a preponderance of alien clerics. And it is legitimate to wonder whether such priests could view their religious obligations to the heathen and their political obligations to Spain as being congruent.

23. The priest is being optimistic. The journey is arduous, over relentless steep hills and rocky, treacherous trails.

24. Batopilas, an important mining town on the Río Batopilas in the profound barrancas of the Río Fuerte system should not be confused with Batopilillas on the Arroyo Batopilillas in the Río Mayo basin.

25. Beginning in the mid-1820s, Yaquis and Mayos were in nearly continuous rebellion for a century. Opatas rebelled as well, though their numbers dwindled through assimilation and disease until they were no longer an important social factor in Sonora by the 1870s. Yaquis, and to a lesser extent, Mayos, came to constitute the principal work force in Sonora, working as miners, cowboys, and agricultural laborers far beyond their traditional lands. Spicer (1962) provides an excellent account of their activities in the nineteenth century.

26. For an account of the Banderas rebellion see Spicer (1962:60–64).

27. I am assuming that Yaquis and Mayos had not settled among the Guarijíos of Babarocos. In the 1930s Gentry found Guarijíos at Babarocos (H. Gentry, personal communication, 1992).

28. This was an early manifestation of the capitalist transformation of Mexico, ultimately expressed in the Laws of the Reform of 1857. Missions were thereby converted to simple churches. Each was independent, though subject to the authority of the church hierarchy. The Franciscan Order no longer owned missions and had no particular authority. Lands outside the church buildings became private property (or, in rare cases, property of indigenous communities).

29. Notes for Gentry's monograph were derived from his travels in the 1930s. Richard Felger reports that Gentry complained that the material in the monograph was included in the original Río Mayo Plants but was excised by the editors as being insufficiently botanical (see Hadley and Gentry 1995).

30. Caramechi is in the municipio of Alamos in Sonora.

31. Edward Spicer, for example, has but one brief reference to them in his influential Cycles of Conquest (1962).

32. Anthropologist A. L. Kroeber, also at the University of California, also suspected that Guarijíos were still to be found in the region. Gentry mentioned to me that Kroeber passed over Gentry in favor of students more highly trained in anthropology.

Gentry's account is as follows:

> I went to the UC library, one of the biggest and best libraries in the West and I couldn't find anything on the Río Mayo. There was [Paul] Standley's Trees and Shrubs of Mexico, which of course included the Río Mayo country. I read Carl Lumholtz, and I also went back to Schrimper's classic on world vegetation.... I was struck by the lack of information about the Río Mayo. I thought, here's a place that's almost unknown. Maybe there's an opportunity here for me to go back, have a program, and write up the biology of the Río Mayo. I was well trained. I'd had a very full eight years of undergraduate study. Kroeber said, "I can't pass on that. Why don't you go over and talk to Dr. Carl Sauer, head of Geography, he has an interest in that stuff down there, I'm sure." So I walked over and got acquainted with Sauer.
>
> Sauer was entirely different. He was not a withdrawn personality, as Kroeber was. Sauer was very open and interested in my proposal. "Oh," he said, "Yes, Dr. Gentry." He flattered the hell out of me, called me a doctor, and I was only a B.A., so I must have been talking reasonably well for him to mistake me for a Ph.D. man when I wasn't. I was old enough to be. I was thirty. Sauer told me that he and Dr. Kroeber had both been through the Río Mayo independently of each other, the year before. They had both been in the little town of San Bernardo at the end of the road to

the Río Mayo, but at different times, and they had both recognized people there as Guarijío Indians. There had been no record of those Indians since they had been described by Guzman, Cortez's lieutenant who had gone up the West Coast, pacified the Indians and collected slaves along his route. Guzman was the worst of them all, I think. Sauer said that the chronicler with Guzman had talked about the Guarijío Indians in the *barranca* of the Río Mayo. Kroeber had identified them by their language, but there had been nothing written since Guzman's time. Kroeber and Sauer had thought they were extinct. Sauer told me that if I was going to work in that country to take all the notes I could on the Guarijíos. Sauer said, "You could go up there and live with them. You could get a lot of first-hand material and be very welcome" (Hadley and Gentry 1995:186–87).

33. The substance of this history of the guerrilla movement is derived from the Historia General de Sonora, volume 5, from the writing of Teresa Valdivia Dounce and from discussions with her, and from recollections of various Guarijíos.

34. For a well-written account of the episode see Valdivia Dounce (1994).

35. President Luis Echeverría (1970–1976) was no more opposed to massacres than was his predecessor, Gustavo Díaz Ordaz, the Butcher of Tlatelolco. Echeverría apparently planned the massacre of Corpus Christi in 1971 in which an unspecified number of students marching in a peaceful demonstration were attacked by paramilitary goons organized through Echeverría orders. Many were murdered, but the numbers of dead were never established. Echeverría apparently ordered the bodies burned (see Krauze 1997:744–52). The massacre of kidnappers, no matter what their principles, would hardly have raised his eyebrows. Since Mexico has no capital punishment, just retribution could never be achieved through normal channels of justice.

36. In spite of judicial findings that the mestizos were illegally occupying national lands, they were compensated for the lands they lost when the Guarijío ejidos were formed.

37. Sonoran indigenous folk refer to mestizos as *blancos*, regardless of their skin color. In Mexico skin color is a powerful determinant of class status and all classes agree that dark Indians occupy the lowest position in Mexican society while white skinned descendants of Spaniards occupy the highest positions. Mexican commercial advertisements exalt light-colored skin, conveying the impression that glamorous, intelligent, successful people have light skin and hair.

38. A *pequeño propietario* (small landholder) is simply an owner of private land, as opposed to an *ejidatario,* a member of an *ejido* or communally owned land. The Mexican constitution prohibits anyone from owning more land than that required to run 500 cows, the defining limit of *pequeña propiedad.* In

reality, few, if any, of the small landholders who fought the Guarijíos cause tooth and nail were wealthy by western standards, and none even approached owning 500 cows. Most lived modestly, usually without electricity and without substantial money to purchase commodities. They were wealthy compared with the Guarijíos, however, which demonstrates the degree of the Guarijíos' poverty at the time.

39. At that time, i.e., prior to the late 1970s, no Guarijíos owned land; all worked in virtual peonage for pequeños propietarios.

40. Dr. Leobardo Quiroz, a dentist in San Bernardo who became director of the INI Guarijío programs, a fellow much loved and respected by the Guarijíos. He was killed in a flash flood in September 1996, an incalculable loss for the Guarijíos and for San Bernardo.

41. Alejandro Aguilar notes the following: "in reality Guarijíos are not known as being good with their fists. When they go to drink in San Bernardo, Alamos or Navojoa, it is not unusual for them to return badly beaten because they are very naïve and enter bars with their hands down and their chests puffed out. . . . As a result of this type of situation some have been killed" (Aguilar Zeleny 1996:155).

42. Not, however, in Guajaray. That ejido includes a majority of mestizos, who had no inclination to join the Guarijío cause and who were probably aligned with some of the landlords.

43. But only to study. Tere ran into obstacles and threats when she began doing something to change the Guarijíos' plight.

44. Valdivia Dounce mistakenly attributed to Gentry an authoritative treatise on prickly pear cacti. Gentry's monumental work on agaves (1985) remains the definitive work on the subject. Tere rather endearingly refers to Gentry following her conversation with him as Dr. Scott, a reflection of the Latin tradition of carrying the father's and mother's last names and shortening the surname to the patronymic. Howard Scott Gentry thus became Dr. Scott.

45. It would be difficult for mestizos to establish occupancy prior to the 1880s, when the Enríquez family, now of Burapaco, moved into the region and acquired some lands.

46. The article, "Los guarijíos de Sonora: resumen etnográfico" was printed in *México Indígena* 16 (1979:1–8). It is evident that Tere tried scrupulously to avoid inflammatory language. The article also sorely lacks the censored section.

Chapter 4

1. The huicastame is commonly referred to as a *cantador,* sometimes as *cantaturi. Cantador* is of Spanish derivation. *Cantaturi* is a mixture of Spanish (cantador) and Mayo (*turi* = good).

2. Later, however, to add to my confusion, a delegation from Guajaray arrived at Los Bajíos to attend the fiesta.

3. This loss was perhaps not as calamitous as it would be for Tarahumaras or Mayos. Gentry (1963) reports that Guarijíos

told him they did not plant corn until recent years (well prior to 1934, the time of his note taking). Instead they used the starchy root of a common weed called *guayavilla (Salpianthus macrodontus)*. This suggests that corn in the lowlands does not have an ancient history of selection for the peculiar growing conditions and could be more easily replaced than the corn of peoples whose centuries of selection have produced the corn ideal for their habitat. My findings, while they do not contradict Gentry, suggest that corn was probably present for longer than Gentry's informants believed.

4. The new church in Mesa Colorada was constructed under the auspices of priests from Yécora who are assigned to indigenous people of the region. Yécora is a ten-hour trip from Mesa Colorada, and the priest visits a maximum of four times a year.

5. Renewed interest in the Guarijíos among the Catholic clergy is probably derived from the increasing success of evangelical Protestant groups in converting Guarijíos.

6. I am reminded of the trenchant comment by Clifford Geertz (1973:453): "Societies, like lives, contain their own interpretations. One has only to learn how to gain access to them."

Chapter 5

1. Passin (1944) estimated the 1940 Guarijío population of Chihuahua at between thirteen and fifteen hundred.

2. This is not to fault Mexican census takers. I believe that many Sonoran Guarijíos are living permanently or temporarily in *colonias* near Ciudad Obregón where they are employed intermittently as day laborers for commercial agricultural enterprises. Others in Chihuahua have migrated to cities like Ciudad Cuauhtémoc or Chihuahua for the same reason. These displaced Guarijíos may or may not have been included in the census data.

Jesús Armando Haro, a medical doctor who worked extensively to bring medical services to Guarijíos, estimated a 1992 Sonoran Guarijío population of 1055 (Haro et al. ca. 1994).

3. This is in sharp contrast with mestizo towns and villages, where houses are generally close together or even share common walls.

4. Guacavaqui is a Cáhita (Mayo) word.

5. While the more traditional tuburadas have been free of distilled alcohol, this has changed in recent years. Guarijíos attribute this to mestizos who bring liquor to the fiestas. However, the practice of brewing a mild beer called tepachi from corn flour has also been increasing. The brew is made by Guarijíos.

6. The term *pajacola (pascola)* is derived from the Cáhita *pajcola* or old man of the fiesta. Mayo, Opata (now extinct but with contemporary traditions), Seri, Tarahumara, and Yaqui festivals also include pascola dancers.

7. Tuburadas at La Junta, with but a couple of huts, and Jogüegüe with three, may forgo this bit of ritual.

8. At the tuburada of Los Bajíos on May 15, 1995, the harpist was a heavy blind fellow who was transported by mule along the rough ten-kilometer trail from Guajaray.

9. Various authors spell the dance *tuguri* and *tuwuri*.

10. The dance has close associations with the *tutuguri* of the Tarahumaras. This name appears to be simply the plural of *tuguri*, hence is linguistically nearly identical with the Guarijío. The tutuguri includes both men and women, however, and is thus distinct from the Guarijío tuburi (Merrill 1983).

11. I owe this characterization to Cipriano Buitimea Romero.

12. A detailed assessment of medical needs and rates of mortality and morbidity among Guarijíos as of the early 1990s can also be found in Haro et al. (ca. 1994).

13. Ann Fadiman in her remarkable book on the Hmong of Laos, *The Spirit Catches You and You Fall Down* (1997), cites an authority on the Hmong, a people of the high mountains who noted a similar phenomenon in the gait of the Hmong. "When a Hmong was obliged to descend to the lowlands . . . he could easily be identified by his peculiar gait. . . . Accustomed to frequenting steep, rocky paths . . . he would forget he was walking on a smooth, flat road, and he would raise his foot too high with each step, as if he were climbing a staircase or feared he were going to trip. On the plain a Miao [Hmong] was as much out of his element as a sailor on dry land" (p. 120). In contrast, after spending several years among the Mayo of the coastal plains, I became used to seeing their gait, which, though smooth, does not float like that of the Guarijío. The Mayos of Sonora need not concern themselves with potential boulders and steep slopes, for most of their lands are unvaryingly flat.

14. Miller conducted most of his research among the Guarijíos de la sierra. His prime locations were in two small villages northwest of Arechuybo (Miller 1996). Barreras studied the language spoken by Guarijíos del río (1996).

15. The Ejido Guajaray was formally created in 1976. It contains 5,024 hectares and includes a mestizo majority. Ejidos Los Bajíos and Mesa Colorada were created in 1982. Their membership is exclusively Guarijío.

16. The active role of the government in promoting cattle grazing was by no means confined to Guarijíos. It represents a general policy of the government with respect to rural lands and smallholders. For a detailed account of the history and mechanics of the policy, see Camou Healy (1991).

17. They are not alone in this, of course. Teachers everywhere resent their pupils' speaking an alien tongue. Teachers assume that children are saying bad things about them, are saying dirty things, or are hatching antisocial plots. Teachers often like to see native languages banned in their classrooms. It was no different in my country. Hispanic children were forbidden to speak Spanish in the schools of the small Arizona town where I was raised. Black children have historically been forced to speak the "King's English" rather than their own dialect, for which they were and are continually corrected by their teachers.

Chapter 6

1. Linguist Wick Miller distinguished between Guarijíos del río (river Guarijíos), who live in Sonora on the Río Mayo and nearby, and Guarijíos de la sierra (mountain Guarijíos), who live in the mountains in Chihuahua. Miller spent several years studying the Guarijío language. His life was tragically cut short by an accident before he could publish his principal works.

2. Guarijíos, like the Seri Indians of northwest Sonora, are traditionally organized along clan, rather than village or tribal lines. Preferring isolated rather than community living, until the last decade they had no general organization capable of representing them as a people, nor did they readily conceive of such an organization. This proved difficult for the Mexican government, which demanded someone who could be signatory to documents and act as a legal representative for the Guarijíos. The gobernador at Mesa Colorada (his actual home is in Chinogüira, a few miles away) satisfies the Mexican requirement, but the legitimacy of his office among Guarijíos remains uncertain.

3. Hurricane Ismael on September 15, 1995 dumped more than ten inches of rain on the Río Mayo region, causing intense flooding everywhere. The Río Mayo in the Guarijío region reached its highest level in a quarter of a century, perhaps the highest level ever recorded. It produced dramatic scouring of arroyos and river bottoms and caused great erosion on the ubiquitously overgrazed pastures. It temporarily relieved the dreadful drought of the mid-1990s, however, producing sufficient soil moisture to provide for a modestly successful harvest of corn and beans among the Guarijíos.

4. Guarijíos are most attentive to cleanliness. At one point my nephew and I had seven Guarijío men riding with us in the carryall. We detected no body odor from them. On the other hand, I fear they detected body odor from us. The lack of running water at the "new" (government-sponsored) communities (Guajaray, Los Bajíos, and Mesa Colorada) has made their lives difficult, for until recently in all three pueblos water was be hauled from distant rivers. All three have government-installed water storage and delivery systems, but none of them work consistently. The pump at Mesa Colorada was destroyed by the floods of September 1995. The gravity-feed system at Guajaray often runs out of water, and the pump and storage tank system at Los Bajíos never worked properly and has not worked at all since 1993.

5. The Enríquez family also has a long history of exploitation and contentiousness with the Guarijíos. See chapter 3.

6. A remarkably well-informed Mayo on whose expertise I have repeatedly called for identifying plants, solemnly informed me that a child in a nearby village had been bitten by a gecko and died before reaching the hospital.

7. Gentry (1942) notes, however, that Guarijíos reported to him that formerly their staple food was the fleshy root of guayavilla (*Salpianthus macrodontus,* Nyctaginaceae) which "were beaten up, dried, then ground into a fine powder-like flour. Mixed with a little water, it was made into tortillas." Some Guarijíos still view the plant as a food source, but those few seem never to have eaten it; they prefer corn. The report does suggest that guayavilla may have been a food source three generations ago. For some lowland Guarijíos much of their seed is purchased. Bavícorans, however, save their seed from year to year.

8. As of 1995 the Mexican government had provided barbed wire free to the Guarijíos. In the wake of Mexico's financial troubles, however, state and local governments have been forced to drastically curtail spending, and programs like free fencing are likely to be among the first to be axed.

9. Rotation of pastures may not increase production substantially in the Guarijío region simply because rainfall is not sufficiently distributed to establish different growing seasons. Nearly all precipitation in the region falls between July and September, which is the same time that plants (including grasses) put on most of their growth. Unless substantial equipatas fall, during the remainder of the year, "resting" a pasture will do little good, for there is little growth activity and allowing a pasture to lie fallow gains nothing, thus defeating the purposes of rotating pastures.

10. Over the years I wasted a lot of time searching in Mexico for sophisticated plant consultants among native peoples. I followed the procedure in each new village of asking the first people I met, "Who here in X knows best the plants of the monte?" I always assumed I would receive an objective answer. Wrong. I discovered that the overwhelmingly common response was "My father." Why? Because of the powerful loyalty Mexicans express toward their family and especially toward their fathers. For a rural Mexican to suggest that someone beside the family patriarch might have more knowledge about *anything* native was akin to treason. It was only after spending a lot of time and money on less-than-sophisticated guides that I realized the error of my ways. I then replaced my simple question with more roundabout questioning and have since had more satisfactory results.

Chapter 7

1. This should not be taken too literally. At Guasisaco and Guadalupe Victoria, both on the Río Oteros southeast of Loreto in the municipio of Chínipas, settlements of Guarijíos are to be found. Unverified reports locate a small colony of Guarijíos in Chínipas on the Río Chínipas.

2. Traditionally, they plant on June 13, St. Anthony's day. Usually, however, they plant a few days earlier.

3. Even so, mestizos tend to control the best land. Guarijíos are typically relegated to marginal plots.

4. Even so, I was astonished when Tiburcio Charramoneta

informed me that he sprays his corn and beans with Parathion and fertilizes with urea. Spraying and fertilizing are not universally practiced among Guarijíos, however.

5. This road is passable only with a four-wheel drive or high-clearance vehicle. A dirt road from Quiriego intersects with the San Bernardo road to Guajaray. The San Bernardo route crosses the Río Mayo at Mexiquillo, some ten kilometers south of San Bernardo.

6. An exception to this bleak scenery can be found in cajones (box canyons) where evergreen broadleaf trees are hosts to the nesting of a wide variety to bird species.

7. Many members of the family Burseraceae or boxwood (seven species in the Guarijío region) exude abundant aromatic compounds. One of them *(Bursera penicillata)* produces such an abundance of pleasant terpenes that it can easily be detected by smell alone, even before the tree is seen.

8. As I note in the plant list, several trees, including guayparín *(Diospyros sonorae),* guamúchil *(Pithecellobium dulce),* and *guacaporo (Parkinsonia aculeata),* and shrubs *tavachín (Caesalpinia pulcherrima),* and chiltepín *(Capsicum annuum)* are usually found only near human habitation or trails, suggesting that they have long associations with humans and may have been imported to the region from elsewhere. One can usually rule out these when trying to identify a tree or shrub remote from a settlement or trail.

9. I am indebted to Phil Jenkins of the University of Arizona Herbarium for this observation.

10. Paul Damon, of the University of Arizona, John McPhee (1998), Bob Scarborough and Dave Thayer, both of the Arizona Sonora Desert Museum.

Chapter 8

1. Baja California began to rift away from the mainland about 12.5 million years ago, creating a depression known as the Proto-Gulf. The Gulf of California did not open until roughly 6 million years ago. The rifting apparently created depressions on the new mainland one of which was slowly filled in by the newly arrived Río Mayo. The present location of the delta of the Río Mayo is probably even younger since volcanism during the Pliocene (5–2 Ma) and the early Pleistocene (2 Ma) undoubtedly affected the course of the lower portion of the river. See Lonsdale (1989) for an interpretation of these geological events.

2. Under article 27 of the Mexican constitution the maximum size of a *pequeña propiedad* is defined as the amount of land necessary to raise a maximum of 500 cows. A pequeño propietario is anyone who owns such a holding. Any land larger is considered *latifundia,* which is prohibited by the same article, meaning that it can be taken by the government and distributed. The prohibition is routinely ignored in Mexico. Often it is circumvented by conveying ownership of adjacent parcels to family members, each of whom will own enough land for 500 cows.

3. The term "don" is used as a term of respect for men over fifty or so. For women the equivalent term is "doña."

Chapter 9

1. Wealthy, that is, compared with Guarijíos who had nothing. None of the ranchers who had enslaved Guarijíos would have been considered wealthy by contemporary United States standards. They lived in a tough region under tough conditions and had few luxuries.

2. In my early notes I had written down "Puerto Jamón" (Ham Pass). When later on I was verifying the names I mentioned Puerto Jamón and several Guarijíos got a good laugh at my expense. Puerto Amole is "Agave Pass"! Such are the perils of taking notes. The Guarijíos often have strong accents that mislead the unskilled gringo ear.

Chapter 10

1. Gentry (1962:85) observed rather disparagingly that Guarijíos seldom planted enough corn to last them through the year. Either cultivation practices have changed or alterations in land tenure have enabled the Guarijíos to plant larger plots. Or, perhaps Gentry studied an insufficient sample of Guarijío mahuechis.

Chapter 11

1. The Greater Mayo region is the square defined by 26.5° to 28.5°N, 108° to 110°W. This is the area whose plants (2,865 taxa) are described in *Gentry's Río Mayo Plants: The Tropical Deciduous Forest and Environs of Northwest Mexico* (Martin et al. 1998). Since the 1998 publication, nearly 100 additional taxa have been collected.

2. Teresa Valdivia Dounce (1994) believed that the mountain Guarijíos referred to themselves as Guarojíos. My studies show that some do, some don't.

3. Through a federal program entitled Procampo farmers may receive direct payments for producing most food and certain forage crops. There is a considerable bureaucracy around the program, however, and those with more political influence are more likely to get payments and bigger checks.

Chapter 12

1. His actual title is Consejo Mayor de la Tribu Guarijío de San Bernardo. The group also elects a tribal governor.

2. I must point out, however, that the traditional mestizo society also experienced shockingly high rates of social pathology. Teresa Valdivia notes in *Sierra de Nadie* the report of a rural doctor who found that nearly all serrana mestiza women experienced depression, nearly all men were alcoholics, and there was a high incidence of bestiality.

Chapter 13

1. The constitutional prohibition against foreign ownership of lands within 100 kilometers of the Mexican border is a good example. The rationale for the prohibition is the disastrous history of Texas, when foreigners moved into the border region and slowly became a majority, controlling the land and political allegiances, all to the disadvantage of Mexico.

2. E. Camou Healy (1991) elaborated this point for Sonora as a whole. This isn't quite true, though pretty much so. In 1997 the INI promoted basket weaving as a source of cash for Guarijío women. The major problem with this shortsighted endeavor is the limited supply of palm for fiber. The workshops were held in Mesa Colorada. The nearest palms were hours away, and the supply was probably not capable of meeting the demand. In 1999 Pizza Hut had reportedly signed a contract with the Guarijío Tribe (whatever that is!) for a minimum of a ton of chiltepines (see List of Plants). And so Guarijíos will comb their lands to overharvest chiltepines in order to afford affluent North Americans the opportunity to experience the exquisite burn of the chiltepín. So far as I can determine, the government has done no long-term assessment of the consequences of such a massive harvest of an indigenous plant. (Note: It appears that this rumored business opportunity fell through for unexplained reasons.)

3. For an impassioned elaboration of this point, see Ruiz (1998:217–27).

4. In a conversation with a friend of mine, a prominent Sonoran government agronomist denounced the native ironwood *(Olneya tesota)* as an "invasive" pest. Ironwood is a key species of the Plains of Sonora Subdivision of the Sonoran Desert, a tree of critical ecological significance. It is native to the region but is considered a pest once a pasture has been cleared and sown with buffelgrass.

5. Intact tropical deciduous forest performs an extraordinary service in preventing erosion. Although the forest has only a sparse understory, the vast expanses of new leaves that erupt with the onset of the rainy season (or slightly before) absorb the energy of falling raindrops, slowing the rain's descent, elongating the period of ground wetting, and thus preventing erosion. Buffelgrass pastures have no such built in energy absorbers. Erosion is magnified greatly once the forest is gone. Although the grass appears to give nearly total ground cover, studies by Búrquez and associates indicate vastly increased erosion around the base of the plants (Búrquez et al. 1999).

6. I do not wish to oversimplify this account. A mixed cash-subsistence economy is clearly possible, and examples are available (see, for example, Netting 1993). To achieve a stable relationship, however, the viability of subsistence farming must originally have been demonstrated. In the Guarijíos' case, they apparently never were true subsistence farmers simply because in recent times they had no land to farm and on which to develop a traditional subsistence economy.

7. Ironically, the single biggest factor in destroying subsistence economies in northwest Mexico has been the development of high-yield, input-intensive hybridized varieties of basic grains. The Center for Improvement of Maize and Wheat (CIMMYT) that developed these varieties is located in Ciudad Obregón, not far from the dismal colonia where Guarijíos hope to find work as day laborers. Once the small farmers purchase the hybrid seeds, they are generally hooked into a perpetual cash relationship with the grain dealers, for the seeds do not yield viable seed for the following year. They must be purchased each year. They also yield poorly in the absence of fertilizers—which must be purchased as well.

8. Throughout eastern Sonora fields that once grew corn and beans for family consumption now produce alfalfa and sorghum for feeding cows destined for the market. See Yetman (1996, 95–108) for an elaboration of this point.

It is important, however, not to rest predictions of doom on increased population and the corresponding stress on resource availability. Both Ester Boserup (1981) and Andrew Chayanov (1966) studied the effects of population increase on peasant farming strategies and found that production may well increase as population increases as strategies change and individual attitudes are also altered. My point is that as production is now constituted and organized (and urged on by the Mexican government) the Guarijío lands cannot support any population increase.

9. The steep hillside behind the tiny settlement of Todos Santos on the Arroyo Guajaray is now heavily overgrown with the shrub *Dodonaea viscosa,* a plant with few uses that prospers on overexploited soils high in volcanic ash. Mahuechis worked by the men of Todos Santos are now far removed from the village.

10. Mexican cattle experts estimate that mountain Sonoran ranges require roughly 50 acres per cow (methodology based on calculations from Camou Healy 1991.) This ratio of cows to land would work out to only 120 cows on the 6,000 acres of the Los Bajíos ejido. The average calf brings a maximum of $200 U.S., so in a good year the most the ejido could hope for in cattle sales would be about $24,000. Even if we double this figure by assuming good rainfall and improved range conditions, the total can hardly exceed $50,000. This would be divided among at least fifty families, perhaps more.

11. This comparison must not be applied too literally. The pioneering work of Chayanov (1966) in the 1920s demonstrated that calculating output efficiency by comparing commercial (i.e., wage paying) agriculture with peasant (i.e., nonwage-paying, family labor) agricultural is impossible because the strategies of production are wholly different.

Glossary

Note: Guarijío words are marked with (G).
For common plant names, see chapter 15.

a medias	"for half," sharecropping
abajo	below
abuelito, abuelita	grandfather, grandmother
adjuste de cuentas	adjustment of accounts, usually refers to killings among drug traffickers
agua de uso	drinking water, liquid drunk in place of water
aguaje	spring, natural pool of water
ajonjolí	sesame seed
alaguasi-im (pl)	(Guarijío) the fiestero in charge of arrangements for the tuburada (probably derived from Spanish
alguacil	(constable)
albergue	boarding school
aleluya	hallelujah, derogatory term used to refer to evangelical Protestants
algodón	cotton
aliso	sycamore
angarilla	basket-like container strapped onto beast of burden
ardilla	squirrel
ardullo	a heat inside, like an internal pimple
arriba	up above
atol	gruel
atrasado	backwards, poorly developed
babatuco	indigo snake, *Drymarchon corais*
bacanora	moonshine agave spirits distilled in Sonora
bacote	sharpened pole
bagre	catfish
baiburín	chigger
barata	cheap
barbecho (en)	fallow
bastone	staff
batea	tray
becerro	calf
bestia	beast of burden
bichi	naked (Sonoran term)
blancos	whites; in this context, people of comparatively light skin color

bobito	gnat
borracho	drunk
borrega	ewe
bosques	woods
buli	gourd used to carry drinking water, gourd rattle
cabecera	the central church presiding over remote mission churches or visitas
cabeza	head; heart of an agave or yucca
cabrón	a very common profanity perhaps best translated as "sonofabitch"
cachimba	head lamp
cacique	local tyrant, chieftain
caida	downfall, deterioration
cajón	box, box canyon
camino	road, path, trail
campesino yori	mestizo peasant
cana	gray hair
canario	canary dance
cantador	singer for the tuburi
cantaturi	cantador
canto	chanting ritual song
canto	song
caquera	raft (G)
carga	load, bundle
carretera	highway, improved road
cascabel	rattle, bell
casita	cabin
castellano	Spanish
catarro	head cold
catre	cot
cha'éhuari	see *ténaborim*
chachalaca	a tropical game bird, *Ortalis poliocephala*
chamba	work (often day labor), business
chilango, chilanga	resident of Mexico City
chiva	doe, female goat
chivero	goatherd, usually a dog
chivito	kid
chivo	buck, male goat
choi guojcó	pitch (G)
chojpí	fatwood, small pitch-filled sticks (G)
cholugo	coatimundi, *Nasua narica*
choquín	sap (G)
chubasco	thunderstorm
chuparoso	hummingbird
chuuca	sap (G)
co'ópoli	Mexican moccasin, *Agkistrodon bilineatus* (G)

coa	flamboyantly colored bird, Elegant Trogon, *Trogon elegans*	*gobernadores tradicionales*	traditional governors
cobija	blanket	*gobernador*	governor
cogollo	leaf bud, palm branch shoot	*gobierno*	government
cohete	skyrocket, firecracker	*gripa, gripe*	influenza
colonia	neighborhood, often a slum	*guacamaya*	Military Macaw, *Ara militaris*
comal	griddle	*guacasí carocara*	a club-like tool about thirty centimeters long and eight centimeters thick (G)
comprador	buyer, especially of cows and goats		
conejo	rabbit		
copal	incense, usually from *Bursera stenophylla*	*guacavaqui*	indigenous term for a stew of meat, bone, and vegetables (beans, squash, and potatoes) traditionally served at a tuburada or other fiesta
coralillo	coral snake, *Micrurus diastema, Micruroides euryxanthus*		
corua	boa constrictor, *Constrictor constrictor*	*guajuóy*	mosquitoes (G)
coyol	bell dangling from a belt, worn by pascola dancer	*guari*	indigenous term for handmade basket
		Guarijíos de la sierra	highland or mountain Guarijíos
credencial	identification card		
cristiano	Christian	*Guarijíos del río*	lowland, river Guarijíos
culeca	broody hen	*guíjolo*	wild turkey
curandero	curer, usually using mixture of herbal and spiritual cures	*hacendado*	plantation or ranch owner who lives on his land
desmontar	to clear (land), fell trees	*hermano*	brother
desmonte	land clearing	*hermanos de la fe*	brothers in the faith
dolor de corazón	heartache	*horcón*	post, porch post
dolores	generalized pain	*huaraches de tres puntas*	three holed sandals
ejército	army		
ejidatarios	members of the ejido	*huaraches*	sandals, often with sole made of tire rubber
ejido	communally owned and governed land (Mexico)		
		huarolúe	indigo snake, *Drymarchon corais* (G)
empacho	a generic term for digestive distress	*huicantánturi*	cantador, singer at the tuburi (G)
encino	oak	*huicastame*	cantador (G)
enjambre	wild beehive	*indio*	Indian, usually a pejorative term
equipatas	winter rains, so-named because their gentle drumming is said to resemble the drumming of horse's hooves	*isahuira cuyabi*	a pebble-filled gourd with a handle (G)
		ixtle	agave fiber
		jabalí	javelina, peccary
ermita	hermitage; in the tuburada it is an altar on which the saints are placed	*jacal*	hut, shack
		javelín	javelina, peccary
espina	spine	*jejenes*	no-see-ums, vicious biters
evangelismo	evangelism	*jícara*	gourd sliced in half, used for dipping, etc.
evangelista	evangelical, member of evangelical Protestant church	*jípoca*	porridge of etcho seeds, *atol de semilla de etcho*
fajas	sashes	*jornalero*	day laborer
fanega	unit of measure, 1.58 bushels	*judiciales*	state police
fiestero	fiesta sponsor	*juez*	judge
flor de oreja	ear flower	*la ley fuga*	"law of flight," assassination based on claim that a prisoner attempted to escape
fuste	packsaddle made of wood for burros or mules		
		lana	wool
ganadero	rancher	*las aguas*	local term for the summer rains, commonly daily thunderstorms
gilguero	bird, Brown-backed Solitaire, *Myadestes obscurus*		

lata	thin poles used for ceiling cross-hatching
latifundia	large estate
latifundista	owner of large estate, landlord
laurel	bay leaf
lechuguilla	agave liquor
león	mountain lion
llano	flat
llorida	sap
los de abajo	people from the lower country
lucha	struggle, fight for land
machihuí	chiquí seeds (G)
macuchi	tobacco
macurahue (macurawe)	name often used by Guarijíos to refer to themselves
mafioso	drug dealer, drug raiser
mahuechero	dirt farmer, one who plants a mahuechi
mahuechi	indigenous term for cornfield raised by slash and burn technique
maíz blanco	white corn
mal de ojo	conjunctivitis, pinkeye, evil eye
mal de orín	a condition common in men in which they experience difficulty in urinating.
malva	name given to a variety of Malvaceae, mostly globemallows
mano	hand; grinding stone held in the hands for making corn flour
máscara	mask
Maseca	packaged ground corn flour
masorca	ripe ear of field corn
maya	excavated pit
mecate	rope
mestizo	person of mixed indigenous and European ancestry
metate	grinding stone for producing flour
metichi	snoopy, gossipy
miel	syrup, honey
milpa	cornfield
¡Mira!	Look!
mochomos	leaf-cutter ants
mocúzari	black flies (G)
mojino	gray-brown, the color of dry season landscape in the Guarijío region
monte mojino	tropical deciduous forest
monte verde	vegetation, especially trees, that are green year round
monte	the bush, forest, scrub, natural vegetation
morral	handbag
mosca	fly

mosco	biting gnat or other flying, biting pest
mosquitera	mosquito netting
mota	marijuana
motéquichi	gnat (G)
mugre	grime
mujer	woman
municipio	county
muri	chigger (G)
músico	musician
nacantáturi	see *cantador*
nahuí	boa constrictor, *Constrictor constrictor* (G)
narco	short for narcotraficante
narcotraficante	drug trafficker
negocio	business
nixtamal	moist corn dough
norteña	northern
olla	pot, often ceramic
onza	a large wild cat, reportedly bigger than a bobcat and smaller than a mountain lion, said to be especially fierce
otra banda	the other side (usually of an arroyo or wash)
pajacola	pascolas, ritual dancers (G)
palanca	yoke (for carrying buckets)
palo	slender trunk
panal	honeycomb
panela	regional term for cottage cheese formed into small wheels
panocha	brown sugar
partera	midwife
pascola	masked, ritual dancer
pasmo	infections and general localized malaise
pastilla	pill
patrón	boss
péchita	pod
penca	palm frond, leaf blade, tender pad of cactus
pequeño propietario	private property owner, small landholder
perico	parrot
petate	woven palm mat used for sleeping
pichicuate	Mexican moccasin, *Agkistrodon bilineatus*
pila	storage (water) tank; storage battery
pinole	ground parched grain, a thick beverage
pipián	gruel made of pumpkin seeds
portal	the large porch of most houses in the region, running the entire length of the house
portón	doorway, large door
pujo	bloody stool

quiote	stalk
rabia	rabies
raíz	root
rama	branch, plant, often referring to marijuana
ramada	open, shaded canopy, usually of four or more poles with a dirt or palm roof
ramadón	a large ramada; a ramada for pascola dancers
ranchería	small settlement
rancho	ranch, tiny settlement
rarámuri	Tarahumara
reata	lasso, rope
religión	religion
represo	small dam or diversion structure
respeto	respect, honor, social acceptance, dignity
ristra	string
roce social	political or social influence, pull
roncha	rash
sa'ori	ordinary houseflies (G)
sanar	to cleanse
sandía	watermelon
santa cruz	holy cross
santo	saint; in the case of the tuburada, it may be any decorative item
satanal	Devil's fiesta
savalique	tuber (G)
selyeme	traditional leader of mountain Guarijíos
serrano	pertaining to the mountains, often used to refer to mountain dwellers
sexenio	six-year term of office
siyóname	yellow (G)
soleados	sunstroke
solitario	older male coatimundi
sonajo	a pebble-filled gourd with a handle, rattle
son	folk song
susto	fright
tabaco rústico	native-grown tobacco
tajcú tajcara	fruits of *Brahea aculeata* (G)
tajcuupa oala	pencas of *Brahea aculeata* (G)
talapia	introduced fish
talega	cloth, funnel-like coffee strainer
tamal	tamale
tapeste	bed consisting of a frame with canes or leather strips laid across to support the sleeper
tarela	arm (G)
tarime	see tapeste
tasol	cornstalks and husks gathered as fodder
temporal	rainfall-watered fields
ténaborim	indigenous word for the long strands of pebble-filled cocoons worn by pascola dancers
tepachi	a weak alcoholic drink brewed from corn flour
testimonio	autobiography
tigre	jaguar
tinaco	water tower
tortolita	a small dove
trinchera	rock wall, terrace
tuburada	the ritual festival of the Guarijíos
tuburi	women's dance in the tuburada
tullido	lame, crippled
tuna	prickly pear fruit
turusi	spider (G)
tuwuri	alternate spelling of tuburi
urraca	Magpie Jay, *Calocitta formosa*
vaquero yori	Mexican cowboy
vaquero	cowboy
venado, venadito	deer, usually white-tailed in the Guarijío region
viejo	old
vino	local name for mezcal liquor
visita	local chapel of a centrally located church, the cabecera
yori	term for mestizo used by indigenous people of northwest Mexico
zarzos	drying racks suspended from the ceiling

Bibliography

Aguilar Zeleny, A. 1996. Makurawe, los guarijío. *Estudios Sociales: Revista de Investigación del Noroeste* 6:143–62.

Alegre, F. J. 1888. *La historia de la compañia de Jesús en Nueva España.* Special collections, University of Arizona Library, Tucson.

Almada, F. 1937. *Apuntes históricos de la región de Chínipas.* Chihuahua: Gobierno del Estado.

Arbelaez, M. S. 1991. The Sonoran Missions and Indian Raids of the Eighteenth Century. *Journal of the Southwest* 33:366–77.

Barreras Aguilar, I. 1996. Características de la lengua guarijío de Mesa Colorada, Son. *Estudios Sociales: Revista de Investigación del Noreste* 6:113–42.

Beals, R., R. Redfield, and S. Tax. 1943. Anthropological Research Problems with Reference to the Contemporary Peoples of Mexico and Guatemala. *American Anthropologist* 45:1–21.

Boserup, E. 1981. *Population and Technological Change: A Study of Long-Term Trends.* Chicago: University of Chicago Press.

Buitimea Romero, C., and T. Valdivia Dounce. 1994. *Como una huella pintada.* Hermosillo: El Colegio de Sonora.

Búrquez, A., M. Miller, and A. Martínez-Yrízar. 1999. Mexican Grasslands, Thornscrub, and the Transformation of the Sonoran Desert by Invasive Exotic Buffelgrass. Unpublished manuscript. Hermosillo, Sonora: Universidad Nacional Autónoma de México, Centro de Ecología.

Calderón Valdés, S. (editor). 1985. *Historia general de Sonora.* 5 volumes. Hermosillo: Gobierno del estado de Sonora.

Camou Healy, E. 1991. *Potreros, vegas, y mahuechis.* Publicación no. 35. Hermosillo: Gobierno del estado de Sonora.

Chayanov, A. 1966. *The Theory of Peasant Economy.* Homewood, Illinois: The American Economic Association.

Decorme, G. 1941. *La obra de los jesuitas mexicanos durante la época colonial 1572–1767.* Mexico City: Antigua Librería Robredo de José Porrua e Hijos.

Dunne, P. M. 1948. *Early Jesuit Missions in Tarahumara.* Berkeley: University of California Press.

Eber, C., and B. Rosenbaum. 1993. That We May Serve Beneath Your Hands and Feet: Women Weavers in Highland Chiapas, Mexico. In *Crafts in the World Market,* edited by J. Nash. New York: State University of New York Press.

Fadiman, A. 1997. *The Spirit Catches You and You Fall Down: A Hmong Child, Her Doctors, and the Collision of Two Cultures.* New York: Noonday Press.

Faubert, J. B. E. ca. 1977. Un Caso Extremo de Marginación: Los Indígenas Guarijíos en Sonora. Unpublished manuscript.

Felger, R. S., M. F. Johnson, and M. F. Wilson. 2000. *Trees of Sonora, Mexico.* New York: Oxford University Press.

Felger, R. S., and D. Yetman. 2000. Roasting the Hechtia out of it: Hechtia montana (Bromeliaceae) as a Food Plant in Sonora, Mexico. *Economic Botany* 54:229–33.

Fontana, B., J. B. E. Faubert, and B. Burns. 1977. *The Other Southwest: Indian Arts and Crafts of Northwestern Mexico.* Phoenix: Heard Museum.

García, E. 1973. *Modificaciones al sistema de clasificación climática de Köppen.* Mexico City: Universidad Nacional Autónoma de México, Instituto de Geografía.

Geertz, C. 1973. *The Interpretation of Cultures.* New York: Basic Books.

Gentry, H. S. 1942. *Río Mayo Plants.* Washington, D.C.: Carnegie Institution.

———. 1963. *The Warihío Indians of Sonora-Chihuahua: An Ethnographic Survey.* Anthropological Papers No. 65. Bureau of American Ethnology Bulletin 186. Washington, D.C.: Smithsonian Institution.

———. 1982. *Agaves of Continental North America.* Tucson: University of Arizona Press.

Hadley, D., and H. Gentry. 1995. Listening to My Mind. *Journal of the Southwest* 37:178–245.

Haro, J. A., L. Acosta, J. Cañez, G. Cordero, B. E. Lara, R. Román, M. R. Palacios, S. Tena, V. Salazar, P. Salido, and M. S. Saucedo. ca. 1994. La construcción de un sistema local de salud intercultural: un modelo para los Guarijíos de Sonora. Hermosillo-El Colegio de Sonora: Proyecto Silos-Guarijío. Unpublished manuscript.

Haro, J. A., and T. Valdivia Dounce. 1996. Notas para la reconstrucción histórica de la región Guarijía en Sonora. *Estudios Sociales: Revista de Investigación del Noreste* 6:11–37.

Hastings, J. R., and R. Humphrey. 1969. *Climatological Data and Statistics for Sonora and Northern Sinaloa.* Technical reports on the meteorology and climatology of arid regions No. 19. Tucson: University of Arizona.

Hinton, T. 1983. Southern Periphery: West. In *Southwest,* edited by A. Ortiz, pp. 315–28. Handbook of North American Indians, vol. 10, W. C. Sturtevant, general editor. Washington, D.C.: Smithsonian Institution.

Janzen, D. 1988. Tropical Dry Forests: The Most Endangered Major Ecosystem. In *Biodiversity,* edited by E. O. Wilson, pp. 130–37. Washington, D.C.: National Academy Press.

Kroeber, A. L. 1934. Uto-Aztecan Languages of Mexico. *Ibero-Americana No. 8.*

Krauze, E. 1997 *Mexico: Biography of Power.* New York: Harper Perennial.

Lindquist, C. 2000. Dimensions of Sustainability: The Use of Vara Blanca as a Natural Resource in the Tropical Deciduous Forest of Sonora, Mexico. Ph.D. dissertation, University of Arizona.

Lonsdale, P. 1989. Geology and Tectonic History of the Gulf of California. In *The Eastern Pacific Ocean and Hawaii,* edited by E. Winterer, D. Hussong, and R. Decker, Geological Society of America, Geology of North America Vol. N:499–521.

Martin, P. S., D. Yetman, M. Fishbein, P. Jenkins, T. R. Van Devender, and R. Wilson. 1998. *Gentry's Río Mayo Plants: The Tropical Deciduous Forest and Environs of Northwest Mexico.* Tucson: University of Arizona Press.

McPhee, John. 1998. *Annals of the Former World.* New York: Farrar, Straus, & Giroux.

Merrill, W. 1983. Tarahumara Social Organization. Political Organization, and Religion. In *Southwest,* edited by A. Ortiz, pp. 290–305. Handbook of North American Indians, vol. 10, W. C. Sturtevant, general editor. Washington, D.C.: Smithsonian Institution.

Miller, W. 1983. Guarijío Linguistic Change and Variation in Its Social Context. Unpublished manuscript.

———. 1996. *Guarijío: gramática, textos y vocabulario.* Mexico City: Universidad Nacional Autónoma de México.

Millman, J. 2000. A New Future for Mexico's Workers: Hot Job Market Eases Pressure to Emigrate. *Wall Street Journal,* April 14, 2000.

Nabhan, G. 1985. *Gathering the Desert.* Tucson: University of Arizona Press.

Netting, R. 1993. *Smallholders, Householders: Farm Families and the Ecology of Intensive, Sustainable Agriculture.* Stanford: Stanford University Press.

Ocaranza, F. 1942. *Parva crónica de la Sierra Madre y las Pimerías.* Instituto panamericano de geografía e historia no. 64. México: Editorial Stylo.

Palacios E. M., R. R. Pérez, M. Saucedo T., and M. Benítez S., 1996. La nutrición en algunos albergues indígenas de Sonora. *Estudios Sociales: Revista de Investigación del Noreste* 6:67–84.

Passin, H. 1944. A Note on the Present Indigenous Population of Chihuahua. *American Anthropologist* 46:145–47.

Pérez de Ribas, A. 1645. *Crónicos de los triunfos de nuestra santa fe.* Original copy in Special Collections, University of Arizona Library, Tucson.

Reff, D. 1991. *Disease, Depopulation, and Culture Changes in Northwestern New Spain, 1518–1764.* Salt Lake City: University of Utah Press.

Ruiz, R. 1998. *On the Rim of Mexico. Encounters of the Rich and Poor.* Boulder: Westview Press.

Salazar, V., and P. Salido 1996. El contexto regional Guarijío. Un encuentro con la pobreza extrema. *Estudios Sociales: Revista de Investigación del Noroeste* 6:39–66.

Sauer, Carl. 1934. Distribution of Aboriginal Tribes and Languages in Northwestern Mexico. *Ibero-American* 5:1–94.

———. 1935. Aboriginal Populations of Northwest Mexico. *Ibero-American* 5:10.

Shreve, F., and I. Wiggins. 1964. *Vegetation and Flora of the Sonoran Desert.* Stanford: Stanford University Press.

Singer, M. 1955. The Cultural Patterns of Indian Civilization. *Far Eastern Quarterly* 15:23–26.

Spicer, E. H. 1962. *Cycles of Conquest.* Tucson: University of Arizona Press.

———. 1980. *The Yaquis: A Cultural History.* Tucson: University of Arizona Press.

Valdivia Dounce, M.T. 1979. Los Guarijíos de Sonora: resumen etnográfica. *México Indígena* 16:1–8.

———. 1994. *Sierra de nadie.* Mexico City: Instituto Nacional Indigenista

West, R. 1995. *Sonora: Its Geographical Personality.* Austin: University of Texas Press.

Yetman, D. 1996. *Sonora: An Intimate Geography.* Albuquerque: University of New Mexico Press.

Yetman, D., and A. Búrquez. 1998. Twenty-Seven: A Case Study in Ejido Privatization in Mexico. *Journal of Anthropological Research* 54:73–95.

Yetman, D., and T. R. Van Devender. 2002. *Mayo Ethnobotany: Land, History, and Traditional Knowledge in Northwest Menco.* Berkeley: University of California Press.

Yetman, D., T. R. Van Devender, P. Jenkins, and M. Fishbein. 1995. The Río Mayo: A History of Studies. *Journal of the Southwest* 54:294–335.

Index

Note: Numbers in bold refer
to figures.